TASC Prep

Fourth Edition

Our 80 years' expertise = Your competitive advantage

---

2 Practice Tests + Proven Strategies + Online

ACKNOWLEDGEMENTS

Special thanks to the team that made this book possible:
Arthur Ahn, Laura Aitcheson, Mikhail Alexeeff, Gina Allison, Alexis Ferreri Beardsley, Kim Bowers, Erik Bowman, Julie Choi, Margaret Crane, Alisha Crowley, Lola Dart, Boris Dvorkin, Paula Fleming, Tom Flesher, Joanna Graham, Allison Harm, Jack Hayes, Gar Hong, Kevin Jacobson, Wyatt Kent, Rebecca Knauer, Jennifer Land, Heather Maigur, Terrence McGovern, Terrence McMullen, Eli Meyer, Kathy Osmus, Anthony Parr, Rachel Pearsall, Apollo the puppy, Neha Rao, Rachel Reina, Teresa Rupp, Scott Safir, Katie Sollenberger, Glen Stohr, Alexandra Strelka, Caren Van Slyke, Lee Weiss, and many others who have shaped this book over the years.

TASC Test Assessing Secondary Completion is a trademark of the Data Recognition Corporation, which neither sponsors nor endorses this product.

This publication is designed to provide accurate information in regard to the subject matter covered as of its publication date, with the understanding that knowledge and best practice constantly evolve. The publisher is not engaged in rendering medical, legal, accounting, or other professional service. If medical or legal advice or other expert assistance is required, the services of a competent professional should be sought. This publication is not intended for use in clinical practice or the delivery of medical care. To the fullest extent of the law, neither the Publisher nor the Editors assume any liability for any injury and/or damage to persons or property arising out of or related to any use of the material contained in this book.

10 9 8 7 6 5 4 3 2 1

ISBN: 978-1-5062-2963-8

Kaplan Publishing books are available at special quantity discounts to use for sales promotions, employee premiums, or educational purposes. For more information or to purchase books, please call the Simon & Schuster special sales department at 866-506-1949.

CONTENTS

UNIT 3: MATHEMATICS

KAPLAN'S TASC BOOK AND ONLINE CENTER

WELCOME

Congratulations on your decision to pursue high school equivalency, and thank you for choosing Kaplan for your TASC preparation! This book and the included online resources will be all you need to prepare for the TASC. To help you create a study plan, let's start by walking you through everything you need to know to take advantage of your book and your Online Center.

YOUR BOOK AND ONLINE CENTER

This book contains a complete study program, including:

- Detailed instruction covering the essential concepts of Reading, Writing, Mathematics, Social Studies, and Science
- Effective methods and strategies for every question type
- A pretest featuring questions from all sections of the TASC, designed to help you diagnose your strengths and weaknesses
- Over a thousand practice questions, plus answer explanations for each
- A timed, full-length practice test

Your Online Center also includes two kinds of videos. In your study plan, each chapter of the book has an accompanying "Preview" video. These videos introduce concepts and skills that are fundamental to that chapter. **Watch each Preview video prior to reading and working through that chapter.** Each Preview video is organized around a stated learning objective and includes skills-building exercises. (But if you don't have access to a computer, don't worry—the Preview videos help you prepare for the book's chapter, but the test-taking skills you need are all included in the book.)

Now, suppose you have mastered the concepts that are necessary for passing the TASC and you believe you might be able to score at the higher "Career and College Readiness" scoring level. The Career and College Readiness scoring level is designed to tell colleges and employers that you have mastered higher-difficulty high school content. If you plan to go on to college, it's wise to try to score at this level. (Visit www.tasctest.com or ask your local adult learning center for additional information.)

If you have mastered the fundamental TASC concepts laid out in the book and are working toward the "Career and College Readiness" scoring level, go to your Online Center and click on "Advanced Material for Career and College Readiness." This section of your study plan contains videos that explain low-emphasis, high-difficulty concepts tested on the TASC. That is, the concepts explained in these videos are not worth many points on the TASC test: you will likely see only one or two questions about each one. But they will be important if you are trying to maximize your score.

We **strongly recommend** that you not study the "Advanced Material for Career and College Readiness" until after you have mastered the material in the book. Going straight to this advanced material is not a shortcut to a higher score; the only thing the advanced material can do is help you push an already high score somewhat higher.

Step 1: Register your Online Center.

To take full advantage of your Kaplan study resources, visit kaptest.com/moreonline. Click on the word "TASC" and answer the questions that appear.

After creating your username and password, log in to your syllabus at kaptest.com. There you will be able to access videos that reinforce concepts covered in this book. Each chapter has a preview video you'll want to watch before reading that chapter.

Step 2: Take the pretests.

Begin by learning what strengths you're already bringing to the TASC and what subject areas you need to work on most. To do so, take the diagnostic pretests at the beginning of each unit. These pretests are not designed to simulate the TASC, but rather to assess the essential skills you'll need to pass the TASC.

When you've completed the pretests, check your responses against the answers and explanations that follow them. Be sure to review the explanations for each question; by doing so, you'll learn a great deal about why the right answer was right, and you'll start building your TASC skills.

Step 3: Fill out the study planners.

Once you've compared your answers to the correct answers, use that information to fill out the study planners on pages xvi–xx. These study planners will give you a rough estimate of which subjects are your strongest and which need the most work.

If you can, it is wisest to study and review *all* of the topics tested by the TASC. However, if you are pressed for time, the study planners will help you prioritize those topics that present you with the greatest challenges.

Step 4: Create a study plan.

Before you begin your studies, make a plan—and then stick to it.

To begin with, **make a study schedule**. Make a list of all your commitments: jobs, family, sports, holidays, trips, and anything else that takes chunks of your time. Figure out how you can fit a few hours of TASC study into that schedule each week. The amount of time you have to spend might vary, but try to spend at least six hours a week studying. The amount of time you study in one session can also vary. In the beginning, study for as long as you can hold your focus; if that is only 15 minutes, that's fine. Continue to add time onto each study session until you can build up the stamina to study for two hours straight. You might want to do three study sessions, of two hours each, every week. If you want to take the TASC soon, you might need more time each week.

Be realistic in your planning; if you are overly ambitious in creating your study schedule, you may find it difficult to follow through. Also be sure to take at least one day off from studying each week so that you don't exhaust yourself. Most importantly, once you've made your study schedule, **stick to it.** Treat it like a job and discipline yourself accordingly. Imagine yourself "clocking in" at the beginning of a study session and "clocking out" at the end of it.

Think about how you'll cover all five tests between now and the time you would like to take the TASC. If your state allows you to take the TASC subject tests on different days, you may choose to study (for example) Reading and Writing first, and then take the Reading test and the Writing test, before you move on to Mathematics or another subject. If you plan to take the five subject tests all at once—or if your state requires you to do so—you will have to **allot the months you have to study** among the five subjects.

It's normal to be stressed about taking the TASC. Throughout your studies, **manage your stress** so that it doesn't get in the way of your learning. To do so, keep yourself on a regular sleep schedule, eat right, exercise, and continue to spend time with friends and/or family. If you're studying and find yourself becoming very stressed and anxious, step away for a moment. Take a walk, work out, cook a meal, work on your car, play sports, do breathing exercises, meditate—do something healthy to release your stress and then return to your studies. Don't fuel your studies by loading up on caffeine or sugar: you won't be able to focus well.

Step 5: Learn and review, practice and review, assess and review.

Once you have your study schedule in place, begin work on the concepts presented in this book. You'll do this in three stages:

> **Learn and Review:** Each lesson presents you with information you need to learn to master the TASC. Carefully read and absorb each lesson, paying particular attention to the bolded words and to the "Key Ideas" presented in the left margin of the lesson page. When you are finished, review any concepts that gave you trouble before moving on to the practice questions.

> **Practice and Review:** Each lesson ends with practice questions that will ask you to apply the concepts you just learned. Do the practice questions without worrying about how much time you're taking, but don't stop there! After you do a practice set, review each question's explanation (found in the back of the book). Ask yourself what you did right on that question and what you could have done better. This review will help you learn more about what you need to work on.

> **Assess and Review:** At the end of each chapter, there will be another set of practice problems that test you on all of the concepts presented throughout the chapter. Reviewing your answers and studying the explanations will provide you with a good assessment of which topics you are comfortable with and which topics you should spend more time on.

Another key component of review is periodically revisiting concepts you haven't studied in a while. For example, you might begin by studying reading and then move on to math. If you do, pause every week or so while studying math to review what you learned about reading, so your reading skills don't get rusty.

If you are working on learning math concepts, you may want to cut out the "Math Memory Aids" sheet in the front of this book (pages xi–xii). You can carry it around with you and use it to work on memorizing important math concepts whenever you have a few minutes in your day.

Step 6: Take the practice tests.

Once you have studied all the concepts the TASC assesses, take the practice tests that begin on page 561. These tests are designed to mimic the TASC as much as possible. Time yourself, just as you will be timed on the real TASC.

Score your practice tests using the practice test answers and explanations in the back of the book, and fill out the practice test scoring charts that follow those explanations.

Step 7: Confirm your readiness to take the TASC.

As of the time of this printing, the makers of the TASC exam have not released scoring information. If scoring information becomes available, we will post it in your Online Center.

You may decide that you need to study some subjects more before taking the real TASC. If you are ready to test, contact your state's department of education, or visit that agency's website, to learn how to register for the exam.

As you approach Test Day, do a review of all the concepts in this book in the week or two before you take the real TASC. Then, the day before the test, don't study. You need to be rested to do well.

GOOD LUCK!

All of us at Kaplan wish you the very best of luck on the TASC. If you absorb the concepts presented in this book and do well in your practice, walk into the test feeling confident. As you take the test, be sure to keep breathing deeply and don't let stress get in the way. You can do it!

MATH MEMORY AIDS

You may tear this sheet out of your book to serve as a portable study resource.

Order of operations	**Method for solving word problems**
Simplify a mathematical expression in this order: Parentheses, Exponents, Multiplication, Division, Addition, Subtraction, and work Left to Right. Remember: *Please excuse my dear Aunt Sally, Love Ron*.	Step 1. What is the **question** asking me to find? Step 2. What **information** from the problem do I need? Step 3. Which **operation** do I need to perform—addition, subtraction, multiplication, or division? Step 4. What is my **solution**? Step 5. Does my answer **make sense**?

Order of operations

Simplify a mathematical expression in this order:
Parentheses, Exponents, Multiplication, Division, Addition, Subtraction, and work Left to Right

Remember: *Please excuse my dear Aunt Sally, Love Ron*.

Method for solving word problems

Step 1. What is the **question** asking me to find?
Step 2. What **information** from the problem do I need?
Step 3. Which **operation** do I need to perform—addition, subtraction, multiplication, or division?
Step 4. What is my **solution**?
Step 5. Does my answer **make sense**?

Distance formula

distance = rate × time

Remember this formula by creating a "dirt graph" as follows. ("Dirt" is a word play on "*d = rt*.")

$$\frac{d}{r \times t}$$

Cover the letter of the item you want to solve for, and what remains visible is the formula you need.

Percent, part, and whole

base × rate = part

Use a similar box to remember how to figure out the relationships among percent, part, and whole.

$$\frac{P}{B \times R}$$

Cover the letter of the item you want to solve for, and what remains visible is the formula you need.

English measurement

Length
1 foot (ft) = 12 inches (in)
1 yard (yd) = 3 ft
1 mile (mi) = 5280 ft

Time
1 minute (min) = 60 seconds (sec)
1 hour (hr) = 60 min
1 day = 24 hr
1 week = 7 days
1 month = 28, 30, or 31 days depending on the month
1 year (yr) = 12 months (mo)

Weight
1 pound (lb) = 16 ounces (oz)
1 ton (t) = 2000 lb

Volume
1 cup (c) = 8 fluid ounces (fl oz)
1 pint (pt) = 2 c
1 quart (qt) = 2 pt
1 gallon (gal) = 4 qt

Metric measurement

Length unit: meter (*m*)
Mass or weight unit: gram (*g*)
Volume: liter (*l*)

Prefix	Symbol	Value relative to base unit
mega	M	10^6 or 1,000,000
kilo	k	10^3 or 1,000
hecto	h	10^2 or 100
deka	da	10^1 or 10
base	(no prefix)	1
deci	d	10^{-1} or $\frac{1}{10}$ or 0.1
centi	c	10^{-2} or $\frac{1}{100}$ or 0.01
milli	m	10^{-3} or $\frac{1}{1000}$ or 0.001
micro	μ (the Greek letter mu)	10^{-6} or $\frac{1}{1,000,000}$ or 0.000001

Common fraction-decimal equivalencies

$$\frac{x}{10} = 0.x \qquad\qquad \frac{1}{3} = 0.33\overline{3}$$

$$\frac{1}{9} = 0.11\overline{1} \qquad\qquad \frac{1}{2} = 0.5$$

$$\frac{1}{8} = 0.125 \qquad\qquad \frac{2}{3} = 0.66\overline{6}$$

$$\frac{1}{5} = 0.2 \qquad\qquad \frac{3}{4} = 0.75$$

$$\frac{1}{4} = 0.25$$

Trigonometric identities

Remember *SOH-CAH-TOA* (pronounce it "so-cah-toe-ah") for the following:

$$\sin\theta = \frac{opposite}{hypotenuse}$$

$$\cos\theta = \frac{adjacent}{hypotenuse}$$

$$\tan\theta = \frac{opposite}{adjacent}$$

Statistical values

Mean: $\dfrac{sum\ of\ all\ values\ in\ the\ set}{number\ of\ values\ in\ the\ set}$

Median: the middle number in a set of numbers. If the set has an even number of items, the median is the mean of the two middle numbers.

Mode: the value that occurs the most in a data set. (A data set may have no modes or multiple modes.)

Range: the difference between the highest and lowest values in a data set

Standard deviation: a measure of how spread-out the data set is. (Do not memorize how to calculate standard deviation for the TASC test; simply be familiar with what it means.)

Operations with exponents and radicals

$$a^x \times a^y = a^{(x+y)} \qquad\qquad a^{-x} = \frac{1}{a^x}$$

$$a^x \div a^y = a^{(x-y)} \qquad\qquad a^{\frac{x}{y}} = \sqrt[y]{a^x}$$

$$(a^x)^y = a^{xy} \qquad\qquad (a^x)(b^x) = (ab)^x$$

$$\sqrt{a^2} = |a|$$

$$\sqrt{ab} = \sqrt{a} \times \sqrt{b}$$

$$\sqrt{\frac{a}{b}} = \frac{\sqrt{a}}{\sqrt{b}}$$

$\sqrt{a+b}$ does NOT equal $\sqrt{a} + \sqrt{b}$
(and the same applies to subtraction)

Multiplying binomials

$(x + a)(x + b) = x^2 + bx + ax + ab$

Work in this order: First, Outer, Inner, Last
Remember: *FOIL*

Circumference and area of a circle

$C = \pi d$ Remember: *Cherry pie's delicious.*
$A = \pi r^2$ Remember: *Apple pies are, too.*

Area formulas for polygons

triangle: $A = \frac{1}{2} \times base \times height$
square or rectangle: $A = length \times width$
parallelogram: $A = base \times height$
trapezoid: $A = \frac{1}{2} \times height \times (base_1 + base_2)$

Surface area formulas

Square or rectangular prism: $SA = 2(length \times width) + 2(width \times height) + 2(length \times height)$

Right regular pyramid: $SA = (\frac{1}{2} \times perimeter\ of\ base \times slant\ height) + base\ area$

Cylinder: $SA = 2\pi rh + 2\pi r^2$
Cone: $SA = \pi rs + \pi r^2$ where s is slant height
Sphere: $SA = 4\pi r^2$

MATHEMATICS REFERENCE SHEET

On the next two pages, you will find mathematical formulas that will be provided to you on Test Day.

Volume

Cylinder: $V = \pi r^2 h$

Pyramid: $V = \frac{1}{3} Bh$

Cone: $V = \frac{1}{3} \pi r^2 h$

Sphere: $V = \frac{4}{3} \pi r^3$

Coordinate geometry

Midpoint formula:

$$\left(\frac{x_1 + x_2}{2}, \frac{y_1 + y_2}{2} \right)$$

Distance formula:

$$d = \sqrt{(x_2 - x_1)^2 + (y_2 - y_1)^2}$$

Slope: $m = \frac{y_2 - y_1}{x_2 - x_1}, x_2 \neq x_1$

Special factoring

$a^2 - b^2 = (a - b)(a + b)$

$a^2 + 2ab + b^2 = (a + b)^2$

$a^2 - 2ab + b^2 = (a - b)^2$

$a^3 + b^3 = (a + b)(a^2 - ab + b^2)$

$a^3 - b^3 = (a - b)(a^2 + ab + b^2)$

Quadratic formula

For $ax^2 + bx + c = 0$

$$x = \frac{-b \pm \sqrt{b^2 - 4ac}}{2a}$$

Interest

Simple interest formula:
$I = prt$

Interest formula (compounded n times per year):

$$A = p \left(1 + \frac{r}{n} \right)^{nt}$$

A = Amount after t years

p = principal

r = annual interest rate

t = time in years

I = Interest

Trigonometric identities

Pythagorean theorem: $a^2 + b^2 = c^2$

$\sin \theta = \dfrac{opp}{hyp}$

$\cos \theta = \dfrac{adj}{hyp}$

$\tan \theta = \dfrac{opp}{adj}$

$\sin^2 \theta + \cos^2 \theta = 1$

$Density = \dfrac{Mass}{Volume}$

Central angle

$m\angle AOB = m\overset{\frown}{AB}$

Inscribed angle

$m\angle ABC = \dfrac{1}{2}m\overset{\frown}{AC}$

Intersecting chords theorem

$A \cdot B = C \cdot D$

Probability

Permutations: $\quad {}_nP_r = \dfrac{n!}{(n-r)!}$

Combinations: $\quad {}_nC_r = \dfrac{n!}{(n-r)!\,r!}$

Multiplication rule (independent events): $P(A \text{ and } B) = P(A) \cdot P(B)$

Multiplication rule (general): $P(A \text{ and } B) = P(A) \cdot P(B|A)$

Addition rule: $P(A \text{ or } B) = P(A) + P(B) - P(A \text{ and } B)$

Conditional probability: $P(B|A) = \dfrac{p(A \text{ and } B)}{p(A)}$

Arithmetic sequence: $a_n = a_1 + (n-1)d$ where a_n is the nth term, a_1 is the first term, and d is the common difference.

Geometric sequence: $a_n = a_1 r^{(n-1)}$ where a_n is the nth term, a_1 is the first term, and r is the common ratio.

PRETESTS

The pretests at the beginning of Units 1–5 are intended to help you decide what you need to study in order to pass the actual TASC exam. After you take the pretests, you will check your answers and then use the Pretest Study Planners to determine your course of study.

The pretests are designed to assess fundamental TASC test skills in an efficient manner. Thus, they are shorter than the actual TASC exam. In addition, these pretests do not cover the highest difficulty content. Thus, they will enable you to get a sense of how well you are prepared to demonstrate fundamental TASC skills. Finally, these pretests do not employ some of the technology-enhanced question formats you will see on the real TASC. To see what the actual TASC exam will be like, flip through the *Practice Tests* beginning on page 561.

STEP 1: Take the following pretests that correspond to the five TASC test areas

Language Arts: Reading, pages 2–9

> 20 questions

Language Arts: Writing, pages 80–87

> Part I: Language Skills—18 questions

> Part II: Essay

Mathematics, pages 170–180

> Part I: Quantitative Reasoning—18 Questions

> Part II: Algebraic Reasoning and Geometry—22 Questions

Social Studies, pages 454–465

> Part I: Social Studies Skills—10 Questions

> Part II: Social Studies Content—26 Questions

Science, pages 528–539

> Part I: Science Skills—10 Questions

> Part II: Science Content—25 Questions

> Most of the questions are in multiple-choice format. The essay requires writing an extended response. For the **multiple-choice questions**, you may fill in the circles next to the correct answers in this book, or you can write your answers on a separate piece of paper.

STEP 2: Check your answers with the *Pretest Answers and Explanations* sections that follow the pretests.

STEP 3: Fill in the *Pretest Study Planners*, starting on page xvi. These charts will allow you to target your problem areas so that you can study in the most efficient manner.

STEP 4: Use the study planners on pages xvi–xx to map out your work.

KAPLAN TASC TEST STUDY PLANNERS

If you have not already done so, take the pretests that begin the five units. Then check your answers against the Pretest Answers and Explanations that follow the tests. Use your results to fill in the charts that follow so that you can target the areas that need the most work.

LANGUAGE ARTS: READING, 20 QUESTIONS

Circle the question numbers that you answered correctly in the second column. Write the number correct in the third column. If you do not have time to review all of the Reading sections, target your study to the content areas in which you missed several questions.

Content Area	Question Numbers	Number Correct Out of Total
Interpreting Informational Text Pages 12–37	1, 2, 3, 4, 5, 6, 7, 12, 13	_____ out of 9
Analyzing Informational Text Pages 38–53	8, 9, 10, 11, 14, 15	_____ out of 6
Reading Literature Pages 54–71	16, 17, 18, 19, 20	_____ out of 5

LANGUAGE ARTS: WRITING

Part I: Language Skills, 18 questions

Circle the question numbers that you answered correctly in the second column. Write the number correct in the third column. If you do not have time to review all of the Writing sections, target your study to the content areas in which you missed several questions.

Content Area	Question Numbers	Number Correct Out of Total
Writing Effective Sentences and **Connecting Ideas** Pages 90–119	2, 6, 9, 10, 12, 17	_____ out of 6
Using Grammar Correctly Pages 120–139	1, 3, 8, 14, 15, 18	_____ out of 6
Using Writing Mechanics Pages 140–157	5, 7, 11, 13	_____ out of 4
Polishing Your Writing Online chapter	4, 16	_____ out of 2

LANGUAGE ARTS: WRITING

Part II: Essay

Circle the question numbers that you answered correctly in the second column. Write the number correct in the third column. If you do not have time to review all of the Writing sections, target your study to the content areas in which you missed several questions.

Content Area	Question Numbers	Number Correct Out of Total
Unpack the Writing Prompt Online chapter	1, 2, 3, 4	_____ out of 4
Read the Passage(s) with the Prompt in Mind, **Develop a Thesis Statement**, and **Collect Supporting Evidence** Online chapter	5, 6, 7	_____ out of 3
Draft Your Response Online chapter	9	My score is _____ based on the Drafting Checklist, page 89.
Revise and Edit Your Response Online chapter	10	My score is _____ based on the Revising and Editing Checklist, page 89.

MATHEMATICS

Part I: Quantitative Reasoning, 18 Questions

Circle the question numbers that you answered correctly in the second column. Write the number correct in the third column. If you do not have time to review all of the Mathematics sections, target your study to the content areas in which you missed several questions.

Content Area	Question Numbers	Number Correct Out of Total
Number and Quantity Part I: Problem Solving Pages 184–221	6, 8, 9, 13	_____ out of 4
Number and Quantity Part II: Decimals and Fractions Pages 222–245	3, 7, 14, 15	_____ out of 4
Number and Quantity Part III: Ratio, Proportion, and Percent Pages 246–265	2, 5, 11, 17	_____ out of 4
Statistics and Probability Pages 266–305	1, 4, 10, 12, 16, 18	_____ out of 6

Part II: Algebraic Reasoning and Geometric Measurement, 22 Questions

Circle the question numbers that you answered correctly in the second column. Write the number correct in the third column. If you do not have time to review all of the Mathematics sections, target your study to the content areas in which you missed several questions.

Content Area	Question Numbers	Number Correct Out of Total
Algebraic Expressions Pages 306–327	1, 2, 3, 8, 10, 13	_____ out of 6
Functions Pages 328–373	6, 9, 11, 12, 15, 17, 19, 22	_____ out of 8
Geometry Pages 374–417	4, 5, 7, 14, 16, 18, 20, 21	_____ out of 8

Part I: Social Studies Skills, 10 Questions

Circle the question numbers that you answered correctly in the second column. Write the number correct in the third column. If you do not have time to review all of the Social Studies sections, target your study to the content areas in which you missed several questions.

Content Area	Question Numbers	Number Correct Out of Total
Determine Central Idea and Draw Conclusions and **Interpret Words and Ideas** Pages 468–471	1, 2	_____ out of 2
Analyze and Evaluate Author's Purpose and Evidence Pages 472–475	3, 4, 5, 6	_____ out of 4
Analyze Relationships Between Materials and **Interpret Data and Statistics** Pages 476–481	7, 8, 9, 10	_____ out of 4

Part II: Social Studies Content, 26 Questions

Circle the question numbers that you answered correctly in the second column. Write the number correct in the third column. If you do not have time to review all of the Social Studies sections, target your study to the content areas in which you missed several questions.

Content Area	Question Numbers	Number Correct Out of Total
U.S. History Pages 486–499	1, 2, 10, 17, 18, 19, 20	_____ out of 7
Civics and Government Pages 500–517	4 ,5, 6, 21, 22, 23	_____ out of 6
World History Online chapter	7, 8, 9, 13, 14, 15	_____ out of 6
Economics Online chapter	3, 11, 12, 24, 25	_____ out of 5
Geography Online chapter	13, 16, 25	_____ out of 3

SCIENCE

Part I: Science Skills, 10 Questions

Circle the question numbers that you answered correctly in the second column. Write the number correct in the third column. If you do not have time to review all of the Science sections, target your study to the content areas in which you missed several questions.

Content Area	Question Numbers	Number Correct Out of Total
Comprehend Scientific Presentations Pages 542–543	1, 2	_____ out of 2
Use the Scientific Method Pages 544–545	3, 4	_____ out of 2
Reason with and Apply Scientific Information Pages 546–549	5, 6, 7, 8	_____ out of 4
Use Statistics and Probability Pages 550–551	9, 10	_____ out of 2

Part II: Science Content, 25 Questions

Circle the question numbers that you answered correctly in the second column. Write the number correct in the third column. If you do not have time to review all of the Science sections, target your study to the content areas in which you missed several questions.

Content Area	Question Numbers	Number Correct Out of Total
Life Science Online chapter	1, 4, 5, 6, 9, 10, 16, 22, 24, 25	_____ out of 10
Earth and Space Science Online chapter	2, 8, 12, 13, 14, 15	_____ out of 6
Physical Science Online chapter	3, 7, 11, 17, 18, 19, 20, 21, 23	_____ out of 9

ABOUT THE TEST

Language Arts: Reading

The TASC™ Reading Test assesses your ability to understand and analyze written passages. You will read a passage and then answer several questions about it. You will have 75 minutes to answer 50 questions, which will be based on 7 or 8 passages. Reading Test questions will include multiple-choice and multiple-answer formats. Some will be two-part "evidence-based selected response" questions; the second part will ask you to identify reasons that support your answer to the first question. See pages vi–viii for more information about these questions.

Seventy percent of the Reading Test will cover nonfiction and informational text. Questions in this portion target skills such as:

- Identifying an author's main point
- Describing the structure of a passage
- Analyzing an author's argument
- Restating or applying ideas from the passage
- Understanding words in the context of an informational passage

Pages 12–53 of this unit cover these skills.

Thirty percent of the Reading Test will cover fiction. Questions in this portion target skills such as:

- Understanding plot, character, and theme
- Describing the structure of a story
- Understanding figurative language
- Understanding words in the context of a fictional passage

Pages 54–71 of this unit cover these skills.

See the "TASC Blueprint Alignment: Tables and Notes" section in the online chapter "About the TASC" for more information about how material in this unit aligns to CTB/McGraw-Hill's published TASC test blueprints.

LANGUAGE ARTS: READING PRETEST

Directions: You may fill in the circles next to the correct answers or write your answers on a separate piece of paper.

Questions 1 through 5 refer to the following passage about introverts.

Excerpted from "Don't Call Introverted Children 'Shy'"

1   Imagine a 2-year-old who greets you with a huge smile, offering a toy. Now here's another child who regards you gravely and hides behind his parent's leg. How do you feel about these two children? If you're like most people, you think of the first child as social and the second as reserved or . . . "shy." . . . But this misses what's really going on with standoffish kids. Many were born with a careful, sensitive temperament that predisposes them to look before they leap. And this can pay off handsomely as they grow, in the form of strong academics, enhanced creativity, and even a unique brand of leadership and empathy.

2   One way to see this temperament more clearly is to consider how these children react to stimuli. When these children are at 4 months, if you pop a balloon over their heads, they holler and pump their arms more than other babies do. At age 2, they proceed carefully when they see a . . . toy robot for the first time. When they're school age, they play matching games with more deliberation than their peers. . . . Notice that none of these things—popping balloons, toy robots, matching games—has anything to do with people. In other words, these kids are not antisocial. They're simply sensitive to their environments.

3   But if they're not antisocial, these kids are differently social. [Children with this type of temperament are highly likely to grow up to be introverted, but s]hyness and introversion are not the same thing. Shy people fear negative judgment, while introverts simply prefer less stimulation. . . .

4   Children with an alert, sensitive temperament also pay close attention to social cues and moral principles. By age 6, they cheat and break rules less than other kids do—even when they believe they won't be caught. At 7, they're more likely than their peers to be described by parents and caregivers as empathetic or conscientious. As adults, introverted leaders have even been found to deliver better outcomes than extroverts when managing employees, according to a recent study by management professor Adam Grant of the Wharton School of the University of Pennsylvania, because they encourage others' ideas instead of trying to put their own stamp on things. And they're less likely to take dangerous risks. . . .

5   But we wouldn't want to live in a world composed entirely of cautious introverts. . . . The two types [introverts and extroverts] need each other. Many successful ventures are the result of effective partnerships between introverts and extroverts. The famously charismatic Steve Jobs teamed up with powerhouse introverts at crucial points in his career at Apple, cofounding the company with the shy Steve Wozniak and bequeathing it to its current CEO, the quiet Tim Cook. . . .

6   The ideal scenario is when those two toddlers—the one who hands you the toy with the smile and the other who checks you out so carefully—grow up to run the world together.

Reprinted with permission. Susan Cain, *Time*, January 26, 2012.

1. Which one of the following best expresses the main idea of the passage?

   - ○ A. Companies should include both introverted and extroverted workers on teams.
   - ○ B. There are advantages to being sensitive and introverted.
   - ○ C. Children who are sensitive are more deliberate when playing a game.
   - ○ D. Introverts simply prefer less stimulation than others do.

2. According to the passage, children with sensitive temperaments are more likely to be which of the following?

   - ○ A. empathetic
   - ○ B. risk-taking
   - ○ C. antisocial
   - ○ D. noisy

3. According to the passage, the partnership between Steve Jobs and Steve Wozniak is an example of which of the following?

   - ○ A. the negative consequences of a mixture of different personality types in the workplace
   - ○ B. a successful collaboration between two introverts
   - ○ C. a successful collaboration between an introvert and an extrovert
   - ○ D. a combination of people who should "run the world"

4. Which one of the following is the best summary of the second paragraph?

   - ○ A. Some children respond more dramatically than others to unfamiliar or startling events.
   - ○ B. Observing how children respond to stimuli is the best way to study different kinds of social behavior.
   - ○ C. Children who are perceived as "shy" are actually more sensitive than other children to stimuli in their environments.
   - ○ D. If sensitivity in a child is not corrected by around age 2, that child will grow up to be an oversensitive adult.

5. Based on the passage, which one of the following activities would an introvert most likely prefer?

   - ○ A. enjoying a quiet dinner with a handful of friends
   - ○ B. going alone to a club to enjoy loud dance music
   - ○ C. accompanying one friend to a crowded street festival
   - ○ D. participating solo in a sport called "extreme ice-slope surfing"

Questions 6 through 10 refer to the following information about forklifts and the related diagram.

Excerpt from "Forklift Safety Guide"

1   Driving a forklift differs from driving a car. In a car or truck, the front wheels steer the vehicle. A forklift has the steering wheels in the rear. The rear end of the forklift swings in a circle around the front wheels, which support most of the load. The operator must check that there is room for the rear end to swing when making turns. This clearance can be maintained in your workplace by permanently marking aisles with painted lines or arranging storage racks in a way that creates obvious aisles for travel. However, these marked aisles will only be effective if you keep them clear of stored materials.

2   A forklift is not as responsive as a car when the steering wheel is turned. Rear-wheel steering makes it difficult to stop a forklift quickly or swerve and still maintain control. It is important, then, not to drive a forklift fast or around corners quickly.

3   Driving with the load downhill can result in loss of the load and control of the forklift. If you drive a forklift on an incline, you must keep the load on the uphill side. Otherwise, you may have no weight on the wheels that steer, and you can lose control! The load could also fall off or cause the forklift to tip.

4   Often a large forklift load obstructs the driver's view in one direction. It may be necessary to travel long distances with the load to the rear (in reverse for most forklifts). Use extra caution when traveling in reverse.

Adapted with permission from the State of Washington, Department of Labor and Industries.

6. According to the passage, which one of the following is an effect of rear-wheel steering on a forklift?

   ○ A. The front wheels carry most of the load.
   ○ B. The driver may have some difficulty in controlling the forklift.
   ○ C. There is a danger that the forklift will tip over.
   ○ D. The forklift driver may have little visibility.

7. Which one of the following identifies a pair of things or ideas between which the author draws a contrast?

   ○ A. driving a forklift and driving a car
   ○ B. the turning radius of a forklift and the turning radius of a car
   ○ C. a warehouse with clearly marked aisles and a highway with clearly marked lanes
   ○ D. driving a forklift in reverse and walking backward

8. Together, the passage and the graphic support which one of the following conclusions?

   ○ A. A forklift should never carry a load taller than the forklift itself.
   ○ B. A forklift should travel backward only when traveling downhill.
   ○ C. A forklift cannot drive uphill unless it is carrying a load.
   ○ D. A forklift that is traveling downhill with a heavy load should travel backward.

9. Which of the following best describes the author's purpose?

   ○ A. to inform drivers of cars about the differences between driving a car and driving a forklift
   ○ B. to warn the general public about the dangers of forklifts
   ○ C. to explain safe practices to forklift drivers
   ○ D. to describe the difference between skilled and unskilled forklift drivers

10. Which of the following best describes the organization of the passage?

   ○ A. The author lists potential dangers inherent in forklift driving and explains how to avoid them.
   ○ B. The author states that forklift driving is dangerous and gives examples of forklift accidents to support that idea.
   ○ C. The author lists the features of forklifts and describes their benefits.
   ○ D. The author explains the pros and cons of forklift driving to present a balanced picture of the value of forklifts.

Questions 11 through 15 refer to the following selections about genetically modified organism (GMO) foods.

World Food Prize Goes to Three Biotech Scientists

1   The World Food Prize Foundation took the bold step of awarding this year's prize to three pioneers of plant biotechnology whose work brought the world genetically modified crops.

2   Van Montagu and Chilton independently developed the technology in the 1980s to stably transfer foreign genes into plants, a discovery that set up a race to develop tools to genetically engineer plants. It allowed other scientists to incorporate genetic traits that allow plants to better withstand drought and extreme heat and to fight off pests and disease. Fraley was the first to successfully transfer immunity to specific bacteria into a plant. Fraley genetically engineered the first herbicide-resistant soybean in 1996.

3   Genetically enhanced crops are grown on more than 420 million acres in nearly 30 countries by over 17 million farmers worldwide, the foundation said. More than 90 percent of the users are small, resource-poor farmers in developing countries.

4   Many U.S. farmers credited genetic modifications in corn with saving last year's crop from all but total devastation, as half of the nation endured the worst drought in 60 years. Modern corn plants are more stable and can withstand a wider variety of climate conditions because of genetically improved leaves, roots, and reproductive capability.

5   Fraley said biotechnology will enable the farming industry to meet the needs of a growing global population. "We know we need from a demand perspective to double food production around the world in the next 30 years," he said.

Adapted from David Pitt, "World Food Prize goes to 3 biotech scientists," Associated Press, June 19, 2013

Dangers of GMO Foods

1   The rise in autoimmune diseases, infertility, gastrointestinal problems, and chronic diseases may be associated with the introduction of GMO (genetically modified organism) foods. In a position paper by the American Academy of Environmental Medicine, the authors ask all physicians to consider the role of GMO foods in the nation's health crisis and advise their patients to avoid all GMO foods whenever possible. The Academy also recommends a moratorium on GMO seeds and calls for immediate independent safety testing and the labeling of all food items containing genetically modified products.

2   As the reliance on GMO seeds expands worldwide, concerns about food supply and safety continue to escalate. Genetically engineered seeds are identical in structure, and if a problem affects one particular crop, a major crop failure can result. For example, following the recent failure of three GMO corn crops in three South African provinces, the Africa Centre for Biosecurity has called for an investigation and immediate ban of all GMO food. Corn is a primary source of food for southern African nations.

3   Most GMO seeds are genetically engineered to be herbicide tolerant and resistant to insect infestation and disease. Environmentalists worry that the characteristics of GMO crops may encourage farmers to increase their use of herbicides and pesticides, which will raise human consumption of dangerous toxins. GMO crops also manufacture their own pesticides, which puts further poisons into humans and soil and may cause unforeseen changes in the environment.

Adapted from Susan Brassard, "Dangers of GMO Foods," Livestrong.com, September 2, 2010

11. The author of Passage 1 most likely notes that the majority of GMO crops are cultivated by "small, resource-poor farmers in developing countries" in order to

○ A. highlight how GMO foods can be harmful to struggling farmers.

○ B. suggest that GMO foods can be beneficial to struggling farmers.

○ C. illustrate how GMO foods can be more expensive for consumers.

○ D. explain why GMO crops often fail.

12. Passage 2 is primarily concerned with

○ A. the uses and misuses of GMO foods.

○ B. the origin and development of GMO foods.

○ C. the unexpected benefits of GMO foods.

○ D. the safety and reliability of GMO foods.

13. What can be inferred from the first paragraph of Passage 2?

○ A. American physicians, as a group, are completely unaware of the potential dangers of GMOs.

○ B. The labels of some foods containing GMO ingredients do not indicate that the products contain genetically modified components.

○ C. GMO foods have been proven to cause certain chronic conditions.

○ D. Independent safety testing has been completed for most GMO foods.

14. The two passages primarily disagree about whether or not

○ A. GMO foods can help support a growing world population.

○ B. GMO foods are better able to withstand drought and insect infestation than natural foods.

○ C. GMO foods are largely a positive development for global food production.

○ D. scientists who study GMO foods are worthy of recognition.

15. Passage 2 cites the example of a major crop failure in South Africa to illustrate the dangers of planting GMO seeds. Which paragraph in Passage 1 offers a counterexample that weakens this position?

○ A. paragraph 1

○ B. paragraph 2

○ C. paragraph 4

○ D. paragraph 5

Excerpted from *Black Beauty*

1   The first place that I can well remember was a large, pleasant meadow with a pond of clear water in it. Some shady trees leaned over it, and rushes and water lilies grew at the deep end. Over the hedge on one side we looked into a plowed field, and on the other we looked over a gate at our master's house, which stood by the roadside. . .

2   One day, when there was a good deal of kicking, my mother whinnied to me to come to her, and then she said:

3   "I wish you to pay attention to what I am going to say to you. The colts who live here are very good colts, but they are cart-horse colts, and of course they have not learned manners. You have been well-bred and well-born; your father has a great name in these parts, and your grandfather won the cup two years at the Newmarket races; your grandmother had the sweetest temper of any horse I ever knew, and I think you have never seen me kick or bite. I hope you will grow up gentle and good, and never learn bad ways; do your work with a good will, lift your feet up well when you trot, and never bite or kick even in play."

4   I have never forgotten my mother's advice; I knew she was a wise old horse, and our master thought a great deal of her. Her name was Duchess, but he often called her Pet.

5   Our master was a good, kind man. He gave us good food, good lodging, and kind words; he spoke as kindly to us as he did to his little children. We were all fond of him, and my mother loved him very much. When she saw him at the gate she would neigh with joy, and trot up to him. . . . All the horses would come to him, but I think we were his favorites. My mother always took him to the town on a market day in a light gig.

6   There was a plowboy, Dick, who sometimes came into our field to pluck blackberries from the hedge. When he had eaten all he wanted, he would have what he called fun with the colts, throwing stones and sticks at them to make them gallop. We did not much mind him, for we could gallop off, but sometimes a stone would hit and hurt us.

7   One day he was at this game, and did not know that the master was in the next field, but he was there, watching what was going on; over the hedge he jumped in a snap, and catching Dick by the arm, he gave him such a box on the ear as made him roar with the pain and surprise. As soon as we saw the master, we trotted up nearer to see what went on.

From *Black Beauty*, by Anna Sewell. Used by permission of Random House, Inc.

16. Who is the narrator in this passage?

   ○ A. a servant
   ○ B. a hired plowboy
   ○ C. a young horse
   ○ D. a child

17. What is the setting of the story?

   ○ A. a town
   ○ B. a racetrack
   ○ C. a forest
   ○ D. a farm

18. The narrator's account of his youth can best be described as

   ○ A. melancholy.
   ○ B. contented.
   ○ C. regretful.
   ○ D. humorous.

19. The narrator would most likely describe the master in the story as

   ○ A. affectionate and protective.
   ○ B. arrogant and abusive.
   ○ C. playful and light-hearted.
   ○ D. bold and aggressive.

20. The mother's speech in paragraph 3 most likely serves to

   ○ A. correct the narrator for playing too roughly.
   ○ B. assure the narrator he will grow up to win races like his grandfather.
   ○ C. reprimand the narrator for insulting the master.
   ○ D. accuse the narrator of stealing blackberries.

STOP. Congratulations! You have completed the Reading pretest. Your next step is to check your answers with the Reading Pretest Answers and Explanations that begin on the next page and then fill in the study planner that appears on page xvi.

READING PRETEST ANSWERS AND EXPLANATIONS

1. **B. There are advantages to being sensitive and introverted.** The main idea of a passage is the idea that is most important to the author. The author wrote this passage to convey the idea that being introverted can be beneficial. Choices (C) and (D) both contain ideas the author expresses, but neither of those are the main idea of the entire passage. Choice (A) might be a reasonable inference based on the fifth paragraph but is not the author's main point.

2. **A. empathetic** The fourth paragraph states that children with sensitive temperaments "are more likely than their peers to be described by parents and caregivers as empathetic or conscientious." Choice (B) is contradicted by the author's statements that sensitive children tend to grow up to be introverts, and that introverts are less likely than others "to take dangerous risks." The author says explicitly that sensitive children "are not antisocial," so choice (C) is incorrect. Choice (D) is not supported by the passage.

3. **C. a successful collaboration between an introvert and an extrovert** The author mentions the partnership between Jobs and Wozniak in order to support her point that "[m]any successful ventures are the result of effective partnerships between introverts and extroverts."

4. **C. Children who are perceived as "shy" are actually more sensitive than other children to stimuli in their environments.** The author's purpose in the second paragraph is to help her readers understand the temperaments of the so-called "shy" children introduced in the first paragraph.

5. **A. enjoying a quiet dinner with a handful of friends** The author explains that introverts are not antisocial, so an introvert will not necessarily prefer to be alone. However, introverts are more sensitive to stimuli in their environment, so an introvert would not be likely to prefer loud dance music (B) or a crowded street festival (C). Moreover, the author says that introverts are "less likely to take dangerous risks," and you can infer that "ice slope surfing" (D) is a dangerous sport.

6. **B. The driver may have some difficulty in controlling the forklift.** Paragraphs one and two discuss rear-wheel steering in forklifts. According to the second paragraph, rear-wheel steering is the reason why forklifts are not as responsive as cars and can be difficult to control.

7. **A. driving a forklift and driving a car** The first and second paragraphs discuss the differences between driving a car and driving a forklift.

8. **D. A forklift that is traveling downhill with a heavy load should travel backward.** The third paragraph explains that, when driving a forklift with a load on an incline, "you must keep the load on the uphill side." The graphic reinforces this by showing a forklift with the load on the uphill side. The arrow above the graphic points in two directions, and this suggests that the forklift should keep its load on the uphill side and travel backwards even when going downhill.

9. **C. to explain safe practices to forklift drivers** The author is primarily concerned with helping drivers of forklifts understand and use safe practices. The author's primary focus is on safety, not on convincing people that forklifts are dangerous, as choice (B) suggests, or describing different kinds of forklift drivers, as choice (D) suggests. The differences between driving a car and driving a forklift (A) are discussed in the passage. However, the author's purpose in discussing those differences is to help forklift drivers understand how to operate forklifts safely.

10. **A. The author lists potential dangers inherent in forklift driving and explains how to avoid them.** Each paragraph discusses a different potential danger of forklift driving. 1st paragraph: the forklift's wide swing when turning; 2nd paragraph: the difficulty of controlling a forklift; 3rd paragraph: the dangers of driving on an incline with the load facing downhill; 4th paragraph: large loads that obstruct the driver's view. Each paragraph also discusses how best to deal with those dangers.

11. **B. suggest that GMO foods can be beneficial to struggling farmers.** This detail supports the overall purpose of the passage—to highlight the benefits of GMO foods for world food production. The fact that "small, resource-poor farmers" would choose to produce GMO crops implies that these are more reliable and potentially more lucrative than natural crops.

12. **D. the safety and reliability of GMO foods.** Passage 2 primarily discusses how GMO foods can pose a threat to human health and how GMO crops can be especially susceptible to massive failures.

13. **B. The labels of some foods containing GMO ingredients do not indicate that the products contain genetically-modified components.** The last sentence of the first paragraph states that the American Academy of Environmental Medicine called for "the labeling of all food items containing genetically-modified products." Therefore, at least some GMO foods do not yet have this labeling.

14. **C. GMO foods are largely a positive development for global food production.** The authors of the two passages disagree primarily about whether GMO foods are beneficial or dangerous.

15. **C. Paragraph 4** In Passage 1, Paragraph 4 details how GMO corn crops survived a devastating drought that natural corn crops would not have been able to withstand. This addresses the issue of reliability raised by the example of the South African corn in Passage 2.

16. **C. a young horse** The context clues in the passage indicate that the speaker is actually a horse. In paragraph 2, we learn that the speaker's mother "whinnied," and in paragraph 4, she is specifically referred to as a horse. In paragraph 5, the speaker mentions that he and his mother are the master's favorites among all of the horses.

17. **D. a farm** The description of the setting in paragraph 1 indicates that the story takes place in a rural location. In paragraph 6, the speaker's reference to an event that occurred in his "field" also supports this setting.

18. **B. contented.** The overall tone of the speaker's account is positive. The passage describes the pleasant setting of his childhood, the respect he had for his mother, and the kind treatment he received from his master. Even the one negative memory, the occasional teasing by the plowboy, serves to show how the speaker was cared for by his master.

19. **A. affectionate and protective.** Paragraph 5 describes the master's gentle way of treating his horses. Paragraph 7 recounts how the master punished the young boy who was harming the horses.

20. **A. correct the speaker for playing too roughly.** The mother's speech is introduced in paragraph 2 after the phrase "when there was a good deal of kicking." Toward the end of the speech in paragraph 3, the mother implores the speaker to "grow up gentle and good" and "never to bite or kick even in play."

LESSON 1

Main Ideas and Details

The Main Idea

A writer has a message, or **main idea**, to get across. Sometimes the main idea is stated directly; often you have to figure it out yourself. You can find the main idea by asking, "What is the *most important* point the writer is making?" Most of the information in a passage will point to and explain the main idea.

As you read this passage, ask yourself what *main* point the writer is making. The answer will be the main idea.

> When I am reading a poem, I rarely feel alone in the room. The poet and I are together. It's as if the poet wrote a secret diary years ago. I am unlocking it as I sit alone and read.
>
> At times I don't understand what a poem means. I just like the way it sounds or the strange images that it provokes. The world is so peculiar in a poem. At the same time, it is so enticing. Sometimes I understand exactly, as if the poet is whispering to me, as if we shared the same experience.
>
> I must be fully concentrated on reading, or I cannot enter the world of a poem. There are too many daily tasks to attend to—tasks that are very far removed from the magic and imagination involved in a poem.
>
> On a cold, snowy day, I cuddle up inside my apartment and read and read. Then, I'm free to ride through the imagination of all those who came before me.

▶ Which of the following statements expresses the main idea?
  (1) The writer has a love of poetry.
  (2) The writer cuddles up on cold days to read.

You are correct if you chose **(1)**. While the passage mentions that the writer reads on cold days, the main point of all the information is how much the writer enjoys reading poetry.

Each paragraph has a main idea. To find the main idea of a passage with more than one paragraph, put together the ideas from all the paragraphs.

Supporting Details

A writer explains the main idea of a passage with supporting details. **Supporting details** include facts, examples, descriptions, and specific pieces of information. When you read, you need to identify details that support the main idea.

▶ Which detail helps you understand the writer's main point?
  (1) At times, the writer does not understand a poem.
  (2) The writer feels poetry is filled with magic and imagination.

You are correct if you chose **(2)**. That detail helps you see that the main idea is the writer's love of poetry. The fact that the writer doesn't always understand a poem is true, but it alone does not support the main idea.

PRACTICE 1

Questions 1 through 5 refer to the following passage from a diary.

EXCERPTED FROM *ARIADNE'S THREAD*

1   I feel I have never had a home. All my life moving from place to place. The only thing that remained the same, that was stable, was Oklahoma. Even the landscape never changed. The towns there never grew up into cities. The people were the same each year, wearing the same clothing, saying the same things.

2   The search for a homeland is part of the Chickasaw migration legend. It was ordained by the deities and began in the past when the people lived in the land of the "setting sun." During the days they would walk over the land, searching for their home. The priests carried a pole. They carried it in their hands by day and planted it each night. During the night it moved about and by morning it would be pointing the direction they were to travel. For a while it commanded the people to journey east, toward the morning sun. They crossed the Mississippi River eventually, and on the other side, the pole finally ceased to move during the night. The land was settled, crops were planted. It became known as the Old Fields. But one morning the pole leaned westward. The people gathered together and began the long journey back. They abandoned their village but did not feel sorrow because the pole had commanded it.

3   And I am still moving, looking for a home. I don't know if I will ever escape my tradition, my past. It goes with me everywhere, like a shadow.

By Linda Hogan from *Ariadne's Thread*, edited by Lyn Lifshin, New York: Harper & Row, 1982.

1. How does the author describe herself?

She feels as if she is

A. searching for a place to call home
B. doomed to stay in Oklahoma
C. tired of the sameness in her life
D. being shadowed by failure

2. Who do the Chickasaw believe are responsible for making them move?

A. the priests
B. white people
C. themselves
D. the gods

3. Why did the Chickasaw not feel sad when they left their homes in the east?

A. They knew they were headed to a better place to live.
B. They had been forced to move east to begin with.
C. They were returning to their ancient homeland.
D. It was simply part of their beliefs to follow the pole.

4. Which of the following best summarizes the main idea?

The writer

A. has always lived in Oklahoma and plans to stay there
B. feels trapped by tradition and wants to move far away
C. understands that her tendency to search is part of her Chickasaw heritage
D. believes that people in Oklahoma are all the same

5. How does the statement "I don't know if I will ever escape my tradition" (paragraph 3) support the main idea?

It shows that the writer

A. is trying to escape by moving around
B. lives in a more modern time
C. believes in the power of Indian legends
D. accepts that she is Chickasaw

STUDY ADVICE

Remember that practice has three levels: Learn and Review, Practice and Review, and Assess and Review. For each lesson, absorb the concepts on the left page. Then practice using the page on the right, and carefully review the explanations in the back of the book. Finally, use the question sets at the end of each chapter to assess your progress. Don't forget to review the explanations for those question sets, too.

Rephrasing and Summary

Rephrasing Ideas

Rephrasing an idea means putting it into your own words. For example, a friend may tell you that a movie wasn't worth the eight dollars she spent to see it. You might then tell a co-worker that your friend said the movie was no good.

As you read the passage below, rephrase in your mind what you are reading.

> In Canton, Ohio, we take our desserts seriously. There are two local candy stores that receive over 90 percent of the city's candy business: Heggy's and Baldwin's. Those who prefer Heggy's won't befriend anyone who buys their sweets at Baldwin's.
>
> My family has always patronized Heggy's. At the Heggy's factory, Gerty wraps by hand each large chocolate candy in clear cellophane wrap. She's in the back of the store with her hairnet, seated at a table filled with hundreds of chocolates. My favorite chocolates at Heggy's are the dark chocolate creams, peanut clusters, and caramels.
>
> Heggy's aficionados point out that their candy of choice is a larger size and therefore superior. The rivalry runs deep . . . at Easter, Hanukkah, Christmas, Thanksgiving, and all occasions. Baldwin's loyal followers claim its sweets are sweeter. It's a feud over the best chocolate in town.

▶ How do the people of Canton feel about chocolate candy?
  (1) They consider it a serious health issue.
  (2) They feel it's important enough to take a stand on.

You are correct if you chose **(2)**. The phrase "take our desserts seriously" means that the candy is important to people.

On the Reading Test, the correct answer will not always use the exact words from the passage. You will have to recognize that an idea has been rephrased.

Summarizing Ideas

If you want to tell a friend about a movie you liked, you might **summarize** what happens in the movie. You certainly will not give all the details—that would take too long. A summary includes only the most important facts and ideas.

▶ Which of the following statements best summarizes the difference in opinion over the candy?
  (1) Some people prefer Heggy's candy because it's bigger, while others prefer Baldwin's because it's sweeter.
  (2) People argue whether to buy Heggy's or Baldwin's candy for different holidays.

You are correct if you chose **(1)**. The last paragraph sums up the difference in people's opinions. Statement (2) merely states a detail in the last paragraph.

KEY IDEAS

- To rephrase an idea, put it in your own words.
- To summarize, choose the most important details that explain the main idea of a piece.

TASC TEST TIP

As you read a TASC passage, check your understanding by pausing occasionally to see if you can rephrase and summarize what you are reading.

PRACTICE 2

Questions 1 through 3 refer to the following business letter.

EXCERPTED FROM *THE ENCYCLOPEDIA OF BUSINESS LETTERS*

Dear Richard,

1.   Attached is a copy of my June 8th letter to Customer Service. After having my car serviced on June 30th, the list of problems has grown. These matters need your immediate attention.

2.   Although I did finally receive my copy of the warranty after waiting two months, it is not bumper-to-bumper as Mr. Schecht promised. It also requires service at your facility unless the warranty administrator waives that requirement. I purchased the car from you at a premium price with the expectation that I would have a bumper-to-bumper warranty that I could use at any dealer. I never would have bought this car from you if I knew about these limitations. I expect two things: A written waiver from the warranty administrator that allows me to have warranty service performed at any dealer, and a wrap-around warranty, provided at your cost, that turns this limited warranty into the promised "bumper-to-bumper" warranty.

3.   I expect an itemized list of registration costs, and the exact amount of credit I received from the Department of Motor Vehicles for the canceled plates voucher I gave to Mr. Schecht. If there is a refund due, I expect it within 15 days.

4.   I expect a proper bill of sale that itemizes and describes the payments for the alarm system and the extended warranty, and includes all the items on the original bill of sale.

5.   Your mechanic was unable to locate a cause for the burning smell. The smell persists. I expect your written assurance that if and when the cause for this smell becomes known, you will repair the problem at your cost.

6.   The mechanic did *not* repair the left front marker light, although he promised he would. Enclosed is a copy of your invoice for this repair, which wasn't made, as well as an invoice from another dealer who actually made the repair. I expect reimbursement for $22.90.

cc: Joe Smith, Department of Consumer Affairs

1. The problems that the writer mentions in the first paragraph and outlines in his letter include which of the following?

   A. receiving repairs the writer did not ask for
   B. rude treatment
   C. lack of proper paperwork
   D. the premium price paid for the car

2. What does the customer want done about the burning smell?

   A. the mechanic to find the cause of the smell
   B. the car to be repaired free of charge if the cause of the problem is discovered
   C. a refund of the money that was paid to have the problem fixed
   D. reimbursement for having the problem fixed by another dealer

3. Which of the following statements best summarizes this letter?

   A. A letter to customer service was never responded to and is being attached.
   B. Mechanics have been unable to fix one problem and did not fix a second.
   C. The service and warranty on the customer's car have been unacceptable.
   D. Some dealers and garages are better than others.

Application of Ideas

When you **apply ideas**, you use information you already know in a new but similar situation. For example, suppose you know that a friend loves country music. When you need to buy a gift for that friend, you walk past the jazz and rock sections in the music store and head straight for the country. You're applying what you've learned about your friend to help you choose a gift.

To apply ideas when reading, look for elements in the new situation that are similar to elements in the passage you have read. Read this selection and then see if you can apply some of the ideas in it.

> When the delivery truck pulled up to my house the day before my mother's birthday, I knew her gift had finally arrived. I was excited. Not only had I ordered a beautiful art book for her, but I'd also ordered a mystery novel for myself and a book each for my nephew and niece. I couldn't resist buying them while I was choosing my mother's gift from an online bookstore. The carton looked bigger than I expected, but perhaps it had a lot of filler to keep the books from becoming damaged.
>
> I lugged the huge box into the kitchen so I could open it and begin wrapping my mother's gift. I tugged at the industrial staples and then tore open the carton. To my surprise, it was filled with many copies of the same book. To make matters worse, it was a book I had not ordered. *Who Moved My Cheese?* What kind of book was that? And who would order *one* copy of that book, let alone 11? I certainly didn't want these books. I knew my family wouldn't want them either. They wanted *The Art of Diego Rivera*, *Harry Potter*, and Dr. Seuss. So much for buying online. I'm sticking to in-store buying.

▶ Which of the following situations is most like the situation that happened to the writer?
  (1) buying groceries only to discover you brought someone else's bag home
  (2) buying 11 boxes of the same pasta at the store

Option (1) is correct. It shares the elements of intending to buy something and getting the wrong thing by mistake. The second option is wrong because the writer did not intentionally buy 11 copies of the book. Now try this question.

▶ If the writer attended an auction, she would be most likely to
  (1) decide which item to bid on and how much she would bid
  (2) get involved in the excitement and bid on many things

You are correct if you chose **(2)**. The writer states that she couldn't resist buying additional items when she was shopping online. Therefore, she seems the type to get caught up in buying things. If she had carefully chosen which book to buy her mother and had ordered only that one, then option (1) would be correct.

Questions 1 through 4 refer to the following excerpt.

EXCERPTED FROM *MAKING THE MOST OF YOUR MONEY*

1   Once you stop using credit cards, three things will happen.

2   You will buy less—and whatever you do buy will probably be a less expensive model or make. Studies have found that people spend more when they pay with plastic, because it doesn't feel like real money. When it is real money, you're more sensible.

3   Your total debt will shrink rapidly. You are paying *off* back bills, you are not adding new ones, and you have extra money because you're buying less. That surplus cash will reduce your debt faster than you could imagine.

4   You will grow incredibly smug. You're the first on your block to get out of debt. Others will follow, but you'll be the first.

5   I'm not against credit cards. They're easy to use. They're handy. If your card has a low annual fee and a 25-day, interest-free grace period for paying your bills, you're getting monthly loans for practically nothing. What I'm against is buying more on your credit cards than you can pay for at the end of the month.

6   Once you've fought your way out of debt you can start using credit cards again—but only for the convenience of not carrying cash. Your days of debt are done. A big expense may sometimes drive you over the limit. A stereo. A llama. A hot-air balloon. Whenever you limp home, back in debt, recite your mantra: "From now on, I'm not going to put down a charge card for anything." Stick with it until you're free again.

From *Making the Most of Your Money* by Jane Bryant Quinn, New York: Simon & Schuster, 1991.

1. According to the writer, becoming debt-free is a behavior most similar to

   A. overcoming a bad habit
   B. learning a new trick
   C. forgetting a friend's birthday
   D. setting a good example

2. If you have five credit cards with high interest rates and no grace periods, how can you become debt free?

   A. pay your debt off slowly so that you have extra cash for necessities
   B. never use the credit cards
   C. use them only when it is not convenient to carry cash
   D. cut up four of the credit cards right away

3. Which of the following situations is most like the process of becoming debt free?

   A. driving a car
   B. wearing a patch to give up smoking
   C. losing weight by avoiding all-you-can-eat buffets
   D. running a marathon race

4. Earlier in the book, the author made the statement "It's so simple that I'm almost embarrassed to mention it. Don't borrow any more."

   Based on this information and the information in this passage, with which of the following statements would the author most likely agree?

   A. "Money is the root of all evil."
   B. "You can never have enough money."
   C. "Live within your means."
   D. "You deserve only the best."

STUDY ADVICE

Mastering new skills, such as applying ideas from a Reading passage, takes practice. The more you work on these skills, the stronger they will become.

Cause and Effect

When one event or idea influences another, there is a cause-and-effect relationship. For example, if you forget to fill your car with gas, the car will stall. The lack of gas is the **cause,** or the reason. The stalled car is the **effect**.

As you read this passage, look for cause-and-effect relationships.

> He is deceptively sweet upon waking up, and lets out a large yawn, showing his thin pink puppy tongue, and simultaneously letting out a high-pitched squeaking sound. Not two minutes later, he's eaten my favorite magazine and stuffed his entire head in the kitchen wastebasket to find a leftover turkey bone. The pup searches under the bed, on top of the dresser, and beside the nightstand for anything to chew. He's on a rampage in the morning—it's just his puppy nature.
>
> To calm him down, we head to the park for one hour of exercise with the other neighborhood dogs. Afterwards, he plays with his stuffed animal squeaky toy, sleeps for an hour, then finds his favorite bone. He lies down like an angel, chewing with contentment.

▶ What causes the puppy's owners to take him to the park?
(1) They like to see the other neighborhood dogs.
(2) The puppy is acting too wild and energetic.

You are correct if you chose **(2)**. The first paragraph describes wild behavior, and the second paragraph says, "To calm him down, we head to the park . . ."

▶ Why is the puppy so wild and energetic?
(1) It is just the way a puppy is.
(2) He has a behavioral problem.

You are correct if you chose **(1)**. The writer doesn't indicate that the puppy's behavior is a problem. In fact, she clearly states that it's just the puppy's nature.

▶ What effect does the activity in the park have on the puppy?
(1) It calms him and tires him out.
(2) It teaches him to obey his owner.

You are correct if you chose **(1)**. When they get back from the park, the puppy plays quietly, sleeps for an hour, and then lies down to chew.

▶ Why does a walk in the park have a calming effect on the puppy?
(1) because the puppy enjoys seeing the other dogs
(2) because the puppy gets plenty of exercise

You are correct if you chose **(2)**. The exercise brings on the effect—calm behavior. This cause is not directly stated. You have to apply what you know about exercise and its effects in order to understand the relationship.

KEY IDEAS

- To determine the cause of an event, answer the question "Why did this happen?"
- To determine an effect, ask yourself, "What was the result?"

ON THE TASC TEST

In a Reading Test passage, a writer might discuss one cause and all its effects, one effect and all its causes, or a chain of events in which each effect becomes the cause of another event.

PRACTICE 4

Questions 1 through 5 refer to the following excerpt from an essay.

EXCERPTED FROM "THE DEPRESSION"

1　Some events are so important that their influence cuts across class lines, affects all races and ethnic groups, and leaves no region untouched. The depression of the 1930s was such an event. No one who lived through those years in the United States could ever completely forget the bread lines, the millions of unemployed, or the forlorn and discouraged men and women who saw their mortgages foreclosed, their dreams shattered, their children hungry and afraid.

2　The depression was precipitated by the stock market crash in October 1929, but the actual cause of the collapse was an unhealthy economy. While the ability of the manufacturing industry to produce consumer goods had increased rapidly, mass purchasing power had remained relatively static. Most laborers, farmers, and white-collar workers, therefore, could not afford to buy the automobiles and refrigerators turned out by factories in the 1920s, because their incomes were too low. At the same time, the federal government increased the problem through economic policies that tended to encourage the very rich to over-save.

3　Herbert Hoover, a sensitive and humane engineer, had the misfortune of being President when the depression began. Even though he broke with the past and used the power of the federal government to stem the tide of depression, especially through loans to businesses and banks, his efforts proved to be too little and too late.

From "The Depression" from *Generations: Your Family in Modern American History*, 2nd ed., edited by James Watts and Allen F. Davis, New York: Alfred A. Knopf, 1974, 1978.

1. According to the authors, why was the depression of the 1930s so important?

　A. It could have been prevented.
　B. It was a time of economic hardship.
　C. It affected nearly everyone.
　D. It was unforgettable.

2. According to the passage, which of the following was an effect of the depression?

　A. Many people lost the mortgages on their homes.
　B. The stock market collapsed in October 1929.
　C. Herbert Hoover was elected president.
　D. The rich began to save too much of their money.

3. According to the passage, which of the following was one cause of the depression?

　A. a static stock market
　B. low worker incomes
　C. not enough productivity
　D. laborers refusing to buy products

4. In the early part of the depression, what effect did government policies have on the economy?

　A. Banks and businesses began to need loans.
　B. They had little effect.
　C. Some of the poorer people were helped.
　D. The very rich were helped.

5. One person who lived during the depression stated, "I can remember one time, the only thing in the house to eat was mustard. . . . And we can't stand mustard till today."

This account supports which of the following ideas from the passage?

　A. Workers should have been paid more.
　B. The depression touched everyone.
　C. Herbert Hoover could have done more to help the economy.
　D. The depression left people emotionally scarred.

Comparison and Contrast

You are probably familiar with comparing and contrasting whenever you go shopping. If you are looking at two cars or even two bottles of aspirin, you want to know if the price of the two is the same or different.

Writers **compare** to point out what is similar and **contrast** to point out what is different about ideas or things.

As you read this passage, look for things being compared and contrasted.

> In December, it seems everyone is hurrying to bake holiday treats, decorate, and buy gifts. Some holiday shoppers trek through store after store, while others prefer catalog or online shopping. Just two of the holidays that keep everyone so busy this time of year are Christmas and Hanukkah.
>
> These holidays are, of course, times of celebration. People plan parties and family get-togethers. Both involve gift giving. Both also coincide with the winter solstice in the Northern Hemisphere, a time when many ancient cultures rejoiced.
>
> Christmas is a celebration of the birth of Jesus, though celebrating Christmas on December 25 did not become common until the fourth century.
>
> Hanukkah, the Jewish Festival of Lights, celebrates the belief that a flask of oil sufficient for only one day miraculously burned for eight days in a temple in the second century B.C.E. That's why on Hanukkah an additional candle is lit each evening until, on the eighth night of the holiday, eight candles are burning.

▶ What is the writer comparing and contrasting?
   (1) methods of shopping
   (2) Christmas and Hanukkah

You are correct if you chose **(2)**. The similarities and differences between the two holidays are the focus of the discussion. Two methods of shopping are merely mentioned.

▶ What is one basis on which the writer compares the two?
   (1) time of year celebrated
   (2) kinds of meals served

You are correct if you chose **(1)**. The similarities discussed in this passage include the time of the winter solstice in the Northern Hemisphere, close to when each holiday is celebrated.

▶ What is one basis on which the writer contrasts the two?
   (1) gift giving
   (2) their histories

The correct answer is **(2)**. The two holidays have very different histories. Both holidays involve gift giving, so that is not a point of contrast.

PRACTICE 5

Questions 1 through 5 refer to the following excerpt from a diary.

EXCERPTED FROM *DIARIES OF THE WESTWARD JOURNEY*

1   Mr. West from Peoria, Ill. had another man, his wife, a son Clay about 20 years of age and his daughter, America, eighteen. Unfortunately Mr. West had gone to the extreme of providing himself with such a heavy wagon and load that they were deemed objectionable as fellow argonauts. After disposing of some of their supplies they were allowed to join us. They had four fine oxen. This wagon often got stalled in bad roads much to the annoyance of all, but as he was a wagon maker and his companion a blacksmith by trade and both were accommodating there were always ready hands to "pry the wheel out of mire."

2   A mule team from Washington, D.C. was very insufficiently provisioned . . . [by] Southern gentlemen "unused to work. . . ." They deserted the train at Salt Lake as they could not proceed with their equipment and it was easier to embrace Mormonism than to brave the "American Desert."

3   Much in contrast to these men were four batchelors Messers Wilson, Goodall, Fifield and Martin, who had a wagon drawn by four oxen and two milch cows following behind. The latter gave milk all the way to the sink of the Humboldt where they died, having acted as draught animals for several weeks after the oxen had perished. Many a cup of milk was given to the children of the train and the mothers tried in every way possible to express their gratitude.

By Catherine Haun from *Women's Diaries of the Westward Journey*, edited by Lillian Schlissel, New York: Schocken Books, 1982.

1. What did Mr. West do that allowed his group to join the wagon train?

A. make wagons for the others
B. bring four fine oxen
C. offer milk to the children
D. leave some of his possessions behind

2. What purpose did the cows serve?

A. They led the oxen through rough terrain.
B. They carried children when wagons were full.
C. They provided milk and pulled wagons.
D. They provided food and replaced the mules.

3. Which of the following is contrasted in this excerpt?

A. the provisions of each group of travelers
B. the stability of each of the wagons
C. the number of people in each group
D. the ability of each group to feed the children

4. Suppose the writer were comparing a woman with five children who could sew and cook to one man with an old ox. Which of the following would be her most likely response?

The writer would

A. be happy to have people who could cook and sew
B. prefer to add fewer people to the group of travelers
C. feel sorry for the man and welcome him
D. offer the man one of her own animals

5. Based on the information in this excerpt, how is this trip similar for all the travelers?

A. They must cooperate and work together.
B. They will be rewarded for their efforts.
C. They have similar backgrounds and relate to each other.
D. They have all been forced to go on the journey.

LESSON 6

Conclusions and Generalizations

Conclusions

A detective draws a **conclusion** when he looks at different pieces of evidence and figures out who committed a crime. A doctor draws a conclusion when she looks at different symptoms and figures out what illness a patient has. You, as a reader, can draw a conclusion when you take pieces of information and put them together to figure out something that the writer has not directly stated.

See what conclusions you can draw from this notice sent by an employer.

> Thank you for sending your resume in response to our newspaper advertisement. We consider our company—and especially our employees—to be the best. And we want to keep it that way. For that reason, we carefully review each resume that is sent to us. We want to ensure that our company and the new employee we hire are a perfect match.
>
> This process, of course, takes some time. We want to assure you that your resume is part of this process and will be reviewed. If we feel we have an opening that matches your qualifications, we will contact you. If you have not heard from us within ten business days of the postmark of this notice, be assured that we will keep your resume on file for one year and review it when future openings arise.

▶ If a job applicant has not heard from this company three weeks after reading this notice, what can she conclude?
  (1) The review process is taking longer than expected.
  (2) She did not get the job that she applied for.

Option **(2)** is correct. The notice says that the review process takes some time. It also says that the company will contact the applicant if it feels she matches the opening. Finally, if she doesn't hear from the company within ten business days, her resume will go on file. You can conclude that the review process takes about ten business days, and if she hasn't been contacted in that time, she didn't get the job.

▶ What kind of notice can you conclude this is?
  (1) a personal note sent to this individual applicant
  (2) a form notice sent to all applicants

Again, you're correct if you chose **(2)**. The way the notice is worded, with no personal details, lets you conclude this. You can also use your knowledge of the real world and business form letters to conclude that this, too, is a form letter.

▶ What conclusion can you draw about the company's attitude?
  (1) It cares about its employees and their job satisfaction.
  (2) It cares only about profits and employee productivity.

You are correct if you chose **(1)**. The fact that the company states not only that it considers its employees to be the best but also that it takes the time to communicate sincerely with potential employees lets you conclude that.

PRACTICE 6.1

Questions 1 through 5 refer to the following excerpt from an autobiography.

EXCERPTED FROM *THE STORY OF MY LIFE*

1   Once there were eleven tadpoles in a glass globe set in a window full of plants. I remember the eagerness with which I made discoveries about them. It was great fun to plunge my hand into the bowl and feel the tadpoles frisk about, and to let them slip and slide between my fingers. One day a more ambitious fellow leaped beyond the edge of the bowl and fell on the floor, where I found him to all appearance more dead than alive. The only sign of life was a slight wriggling of his tail. But no sooner had he returned to his element than he darted to the bottom, swimming round and round in joyous activity. He had made his leap, he had seen the great world, and was content to stay in his pretty glass house under the big fuchsia tree until he attained the dignity of froghood. Then he went to live in the leafy pool at the end of the garden, where he made the summer nights musical with his quaint love-song.

2   Thus I learned from life itself. At the beginning I was only a little mass of possibilities. It was my teacher who unfolded and developed them. When she came, everything about me breathed of love and joy and was full of meaning. She has never since let pass an opportunity to point out the beauty that is in everything, nor has she ceased trying in thought and action and example to make my life sweet and useful.

3   It was my teacher's genius, her quick sympathy, her loving tact which made the first years of my education so beautiful.

From *The Story of My Life* by Helen Keller.

1. What can you conclude about the writer's view of learning?

A. It is rewarding and one of life's joys.
B. It is better with a strict teacher.
C. It happens very slowly, if at all.
D. It happens most often when you are alone.

2. What conclusion can you draw about the writer's character?

The writer is

A. self-centered and demanding
B. confused and searching
C. fearful and shy
D. insightful and grateful

3. If Helen's teacher was trying to teach her addition, what method would the teacher most likely use?

A. make Helen stand and recite addition facts for one hour every day
B. assign an abundance of addition homework
C. show Helen how addition is used in everyday life
D. ask a well-known mathematician to teach the subject

4. How are the thoughts in this personal account organized?

A. as a comparison with a frog followed by a contrast
B. as a problem followed by its solution
C. in chronological order, or time sequence
D. as an anecdote followed by a generalization based on the anecdote

5. Later in her story, Helen compares a child's mind to a shallow brook "which ripples and dances merrily over the stony course of its education. . . ." Based on this information and the excerpt above, what is similar about the tadpole and a child?

A. They learn from others.
B. They are eager to grow into adulthood.
C. Youth can make them do dangerous things.
D. Their development is not entirely smooth.

Generalizations

A **generalization** is a broad statement about a group of people, objects, or things, or about a type of event. Usually, it takes something that is true in one specific case and extends it to every possible case. For example, "My hometown celebrated Independence Day with fireworks last summer," is a fact about a specific Fourth of July in a specific town; a generalization could be "Every Independence Day, my hometown celebrates with fireworks."

► Identify one statement with *F* for a fact and the other with *G* for generalization.
   (1) Every clerk in the store focuses on customer service more than any other aspect of the job.
   (2) Tina, the manager of the women's shoe department, helps customers select just the right pair of shoes.

If you identified option **(2)** as being a fact and option **(1)** as being a generalization, you were correct. One hint that **(1)** is the generalization is the word "every." Words like *all, never,* and *always* show up in sentences that make broad, sweeping statements. The sentence about Tina, on the other hand, gives specific information about a specific person and so is not a generalization.

Generalizations can be valid and true when properly made. A writer can support a generalization with an example (like Tina, above) and information that shows why the example represents the whole group. Often, a generalization is too broad to apply to every member of a group, and a good writer will acknowledge that there are exceptions.

"Dogs are typically more attached to their owners than cats are, due in part to their evolution as pack animals. My dog will jump up to meet me as soon as I get home from work, while my cat will continue napping serenely until hunger motivates him to do otherwise."

► What example is given to support the generalization that "Dogs are typically more attached to their owners than cats"?
   (1) Dogs evolved as pack animals.
   (2) The author's dog jumps up to meet her, while her cat ignores her.

The example of the author's dog's attachment to her, **(2)**, illustrates and supports the generalization that most dogs show greater attachment to their owners. The specific example helps to show that the statement is based on experience.

Writers sometimes make the mistake of drawing **faulty generalizations** based on too little information. Imagine a person who bites into an apple, finds a worm, and concludes that all apples have worms in them. Since a generalization is a broad statement, a **valid generalization** requires broad knowledge to justify it. A generalization about American cities is more likely to be faulty if the writer bases it on only one city but is more likely to be valid if the writer supports it with knowledge of 20 cities. With a larger sample, the writer is also better able to know whether to qualify a generalization as something that is true in most, but not all, cases.

► Identify one statement with *FG* for a faulty generalization and the other with *VG* for a valid generalization.
   (1) Every breed of dog has four legs, so almost all dogs have four legs.
   (2) Some dogs bark at kids, so all dogs must dislike or fear children.

You are correct if you chose **(1)** as the valid generalization: the writer shows awareness of many different types of dogs. Option **(2)** is a faulty generalization; dogs may bark at children for reasons other than fear or dislike.

PRACTICE 6.2

Questions 1 through 3 are based on the following newspaper editorial.

OPINION: DOUBTS ABOUT GLOBAL WARMING

1   Shady Hollow was hit yesterday with record cold temperatures. And yet, despite this deep freeze, we'll continue to be subjected to the doctrine of global warming.

2   There is plenty to be said for fuel economy—anyone who lived through the energy crisis of the 1970s learned that lesson the hard way—but it's time we dispense with the terror campaign of doomsday climatology and recognize it for the pseudoscience that it is. Whenever Shady Hollow gets a big hit of winter weather, common sense tells us that the idea of "warming" seems fishy, yet climatologists insist on playing the same tune. More and more, this tune is taken up by policy-makers and government bodies, who steer our administrations accordingly. It must be the case that ivory towers have good weather stripping and excellent heating systems; as for the man on the street, he's finding his street a chilly one these days.

3   The simple fact is that it is logically impossible to reconcile a record cold temperature with the idea that it's getting warmer. A record cold temperature, and this may be worth spelling out, means exactly this: it has never been colder on this date in recorded history. If "warming" means what it sounds like it means—that temperatures are rising, not falling—then there is a real problem here, because that is quite simply not what is happening.

4   It may take years to get out from under the orthodoxy of the accepted opinion on climate change, but the facts themselves will not go away. Sooner or later, we'll be forced to acknowledge that we're still bundling up, and when that happens, we can stop building policy discussions around fictions.

1. What is a generalization that is made in paragraph 3?

  A. Shady Hollow has the coldest temperatures in the region.
  B. Global warming can only be valid if it predicts high temperatures.
  C. On the whole, temperatures are not rising.
  D. If children are taught a simpler theory, then a more complex theory should be set aside.

2. What evidence does the author give to support his generalization about global warming?

  A. Shady Hollow was hit with a record cold temperature yesterday.
  B. Ivory towers have good weather stripping.
  C. It may take years to change opinions on climate change.
  D. There is plenty to be said for fuel economy.

3. Which of the following pieces of information would put the author in a better position to make a generalization about climate change?

  A. an account of the energy crisis of the 1970s
  B. minutes of policy discussions from the 1970s through today
  C. interviews with the "man on the street" from the 1990s through today
  D. worldwide data tables of temperatures from the 1980s through today

Word Choice

Writers make careful decisions to select words that will impact their audience. One choice that writers make is to select words that have a **connotation** associated with a particular image or feeling. Think of the different connotations of *dog*, *mutt*, and *man's best friend*. The word *dog* has a neutral connotation; it just describes the animal. To some, the word *mutt* would have a negative connotation, while the phrase *man's best friend* would have a positive connotation.

▶ Assign a *P* (positive) or an *N* (negative) to the following words to indicate the connotation that might be associated with them:
(1) shack
(2) villa

You are correct if you assigned an *N* to (1) and a *P* to (2). The word *shack* probably brings to mind a small, poorly built or run-down building. On the other hand, the word *villa* might be associated with a house in the country-side or a vacation destination.

Writers use **figurative language** to make their descriptions clearer and more vivid. They use **similes**, which use the words *like* or *as* to compare two things; for example, "Her new coat fit like a glove." This indicates that the coat fit perfectly. Another type of figurative language is a **metaphor**, which implies a comparison between two things. One familiar metaphor is "Life is a journey"; this compares two dissimilar things in order to describe life. A third figure of speech is **personification**, by which a writer assigns human characteristics to something that is not human. For example, a writer may describe a storm as "slashing at the windows and knocking on the door."

> If you look very carefully, you can find the island of Ascension on a map about midway between Angola, in Africa, and Brazil, in South America. This South Atlantic island has a population of about 1,000 people and is home to an important GPS ground antenna and a British air force base. Its volcanic terrain greets visitors with a forbidding aspect; place names like "Comfortless Cove" indicate how rocky and uninviting Ascension Island may appear. Even so, with its dry subtropical weather, excellent sport fishing, and unique wildlife, this barren outpost attracts about 1,000 tourists each year.

▶ What does the personification in the third sentence suggest about Ascension Island?
(1) Tourists are forbidden to visit the island.
(2) The island doesn't look like a good place to visit.

You are correct if you chose (2). The writer refers to the island as if it were a person with an unfriendly appearance. Since the last sentence states that tourists do visit the island, you know that they are not forbidden to do so.

KEY IDEAS

- Writers choose words carefully to make an impact on the reader.
- They deliberately choose words with positive, negative, or neutral connotations.
- Writers also use figurative language such as similes, metaphors, and personification to enhance descriptions.

TASC TEST TIP

Read closely to see how a writer's word choice affects how you picture something or feel about it. You may have to answer questions that require an awareness of the impact of both words' connotations and figurative language.

PRACTICE 7

Questions 1 through 5 refer to the following product description.

A COOL NEW BLANKET

1   Many people rely on electric blankets to keep warm on winter nights without turning on expensive central heating. In summer, though, there's no alternative to noisy fans and energy-hogging air conditioners if you want to stay cool . . . until now. The Starlight company recently introduced its newest product: an electric blanket that keeps you cool even on sweltering summer nights.

2   The CoolForter blanket works like an electric blanket, but it feels like a dream. The blanket contains a full tenth of a mile of flexible hose, fully insulated between layers of soft cotton. A small, quiet compressor refrigerates the safely enclosed cooling chemical and circulates it continuously through the coils. The CoolForter coddles you in refreshing comfort, and you never have to worry about waking up shivering. That's because your sleeping temperature is precisely controlled by the built-in thermostat, which can be adjusted to your exact temperature preference.

3   Your CoolForter blanket also matches your decorating preferences: the replaceable cover comes in a wide variety of bland colors to suit any décor. If you decide to redecorate, choose from a selection of fun and gaudy prints to liven up your room.

4   Best of all, the CoolForter saves you money every time you use it. Consuming an average of just 80 watts, the twin-size blanket is like a regular household lightbulb, costing just pennies per day to run. It's an investment in comfort that will pay for itself many times over the lifetime of its generous ten-year warranty and beyond.

STUDY ADVICE

To practice spotting figurative language, similes, metaphors, and personification, pay particular attention to advertisements. Think about how an ad's wording conveys a strong positive connotation about the product being advertised (or a negative connotation about the competitor's product).

1. In paragraph 2, what is compared to a dream?
   A. an electric blanket
   B. the flexible hose used in the CoolForter blanket
   C. the cotton insulating layers
   D. the CoolForter blanket

2. What could be a reason that the writer used the word "coddles" in paragraph 2?
   A. to show that the blanket keeps its user warm
   B. to show that the blanket is a pleasant indulgence
   C. to show that the blanket keeps its user cool
   D. to show that the user can wrap herself up in the blanket

3. What word could the writer have used instead of "chemical" in paragraph 2 that would have a less negative connotation?
   A. fluid
   B. antifreeze
   C. contaminant
   D. water

4. Which word in paragraph 3 means "neutral" but has a negative connotation?
   A. decorating
   B. replaceable
   C. bland
   D. gaudy

5. Why is "like a regular household lightbulb" from paragraph 4 an effective use of a comparison using figurative language?
   A. It reminds the consumer that, while a lightbulb generates heat, the CoolForter blanket keeps its user cool.
   B. It makes the CoolForter blanket seem ordinary.
   C. It emphasizes the difference in cost between running a regular lightbulb and operating a compact fluorescent lightbulb.
   D. It allows the consumer to compare the CoolForter's energy usage to that of a familiar item.

Defining a Word Using Context

Sometimes the TASC Reading Test will ask you to identify the meaning of a word used in a passage. If you do not already know what the word means, you can use **context clues** to infer the word's meaning. Context clues are hints from the surrounding sentence or sentences.

Sometimes context clues will tell you that the unknown word has a *positive or negative charge*—that is, that most people would view it as good or bad.

Example 1: Jack woke up in a cheerful mood. The sun was shining, and he and his wife were planning to visit the beach. However, when he looked out the window, Jack saw ominous clouds on the horizon.

As used in the passage above, *ominous* most nearly means
  A. causing confusion
  B. concerning the weather
  C. foretelling a bad event
  D. like cotton candy

Choice **(C)** is correct. The word *However* signals a contrast. At first, Jack is happy and planning a nice outing. Thus, what comes after the word *However* is bad, so you can infer that *ominous* has a negative charge. That narrows the choices down to (A) and (C). Confusion (A) does not make sense in this passage.

Sometimes the sentence will have transition words that indicate that the unknown word means something *similar to* some other word or phrase in the sentence.

Example	Transitional word or phrase	Meaning of italicized word
The budget negotiations were difficult; indeed, they were almost a *quagmire*.	The word *indeed* signals that *quagmire* is similar in meaning to *difficult negotiations*.	an awkward or complicated situation
After winning the tournament, the dance team members were *exuberant*. Accordingly, the team threw a wild party!	The word *Accordingly* indicates that a wild party is a logical result of people feeling *exuberant*.	lively, full of excitement

Sometimes the sentence contains clues that the unknown word's meaning *contrasts with or is the opposite of* some other word or phrase in the sentence.

Example	Transitional word or phrase	Meaning of italicized word
Julie found the party *dreary* rather than enjoyable.	The phrase *rather than* signals that *dreary* and *enjoyable* are opposites.	dull or depressing
Farouk peered anxiously at the narrow footbridge. Nevertheless, he *intrepidly* walked onto it.	The word *Nevertheless* is a contrast word. You can infer from it that *anxiously* and *intrepidly* are opposites.	bravely

Sometimes context clues may suggest only that the unknown word has a positive or negative charge. Even if that's all you can infer, you still may be able to eliminate some answer choices, improving your chance of guessing the correct answer.

KEY IDEAS

- The TASC Reading Test will sometimes ask you to define a word that appears in a passage.
- Context clues allow you to infer the meaning of an unknown word.
- Context clues may tell you whether the word has a positive or negative charge and what relationship the unknown word has to the rest of the sentence.

TEST TIP

When you need to determine what an unknown word means, pay particular attention to the nearby transitional words—that is, words like however, moreover, nevertheless, for example, *or* because. *Those words give you hints about how the unknown word relates to the other ideas in the sentence.*

PRACTICE 8

Example	Context clues	Test-taking strategy
On the one hand, Pete's new job was boring. On the other hand, it was *lucrative*.	*On the one hand . . . On the other hand* signals a contrast between *boring* and *lucrative*. Those words might not exactly be opposites, but they probably have opposite charges. Since *boring* is negative, *lucrative* is likely positive.	Eliminate any answer choices that have a negative charge or no charge at all. (In fact, *lucrative* means *providing a large amount of money*.)
The beautiful flowers gave off an *alluring* fragrance.	The sentence tells you that the flowers were *beautiful*, and it describes their odor as a *fragrance*, which is a positive word. Thus, *allure* probably has a positive charge.	Eliminate any answer choices that have a negative charge or no charge at all. (In fact, *alluring* means *appealing*.)

<u>Exercises 1 and 2</u> are designed to help build your context skills.

1. Amelia struggled into her warm coat, found her hat and mittens at the back of the closet, and took one last gulp of hot coffee. Then she stepped out into the cold wind. Hugging her arms around her, she reminded herself that this freak snowstorm was an anomaly. That thought cheered her up a little.

   a. What context clues in the above passage might help you determine the meaning of the word *anomaly*?

   _____

   _____

   b. Based on those context clues, what do you think *anomaly* means?

   _____

2. Gloriana has excellent taste in clothes. _____ she went shopping last Saturday at Jo's Boutique.

   The sentences above could mean very different things depending on which connecting word or phrase goes in the blank. Use checkmarks or Xs to indicate whether each word or phrase, if inserted in the blank, would suggest that Jo's Boutique sells clothes in good taste or clothes in bad taste.

	Suggests Jo's has good clothes	Suggests Jo's has bad clothes
Nevertheless,		
Accordingly,		
Not surprisingly,		
However,		
Therefore,		
Yet		
That's why		

3. Dinner at the MacAllisters' house was delicious, as always, but the mood was tense. The host and hostess were friendly toward us but spoke to each other only rarely. We thought perhaps the MacAllisters had had a tiff before the guests arrived.

   What does the word *tiff* mean in the passage above?

   A. cocktail
   B. small accident
   C. argument
   D. discussion

4. Sneering faintly, the professor handed the corrected essays back to the students. He told the students that their essays had reminded him of kindergarten exercises, except with weaker logic. Jacinta had looked forward to the professor's feedback because his lectures had been educational, so she was disappointed by his hauteur.

   As used in the passage, what does *hauteur* mean?

   A. instruction
   B. arrogance
   C. distance
   D. ignorance

Writer's Tone and Point of View

Tone

A writer usually has a certain attitude toward the subject he or she is writing about. This attitude is the **tone** of the piece. The tone is not directly stated. You have to sense it by the writer's choice of words and manner of expression.

As you read this drama review, ask yourself, "What tone of voice would the author have if she were reading this aloud to me?"

> Watching actor Brian Dennehy as Willy Loman in the stage production of *Death of a Salesman* was transforming. I know intellectually that live theater is better than movies. Movie actors reshoot scenes until they are perfect. An actor on stage has one chance to get it right. It is immediate. The actors are breathing human beings in the same room with you. Theater provides the opportunity for strong emotions to surface, right there, in the moment. Seeing a play often envelops me in energy.
>
> But I've never gone so far as to cry at a theater performance until now. I cried because Dennehy's Loman reminded me of my father, of the brevity of our lives, of how easy it is to waste our lives. This was not an intellectual response. I suddenly heard what this man on stage was saying—his life wasn't worth living, though he had tried hard and had a devoted wife and two sons. It didn't matter that this play was written in the 1940s. Mr. Dennehy stood on stage and roared at us about our lives now. It was hard-hitting, emotional drama.

▶ Which of the following best describes the tone of this piece?
  (1) positive and somewhat awed
  (2) cool and objective

The correct response is **(1)**. The writer states positive opinions. She also chooses short, clipped expressions—"It is immediate" and "right there, in the moment"—that by themselves create a sense of drama and awe. If the tone were cool and objective, you would not sense the writer's emotional attitude toward the play.

Point of View

The **point of view** of a piece is "where the author is coming from"—that is, the writer's background and experiences that may affect her opinions. For example, when you read an editorial in a newspaper, you can usually tell whether the writer has a liberal or a conservative point of view.

▶ What point of view does the writer of the review above have?
  (1) that of a person who prefers sitting at home watching TV
  (2) that of an enthusiastic theatergoer

You are correct if you chose **(2)**. You can conclude that the writer goes to the theater ("Seeing a play often envelops me") and enjoys it ("theater is better than movies"). Knowing this helps you evaluate the merits of the review.

PRACTICE 9

Questions 1 through 5 refer to the following review.

EXCERPTED FROM "TALKING BACK TO THE TUBE"

1   CBS delivered a television low mark called *Big Brother*. Focusing on ten fame-seeking, people-pleasing, hair-teasing losers willing to submit to surveillance by a nation of snoops for three months, it was so bad that it wasn't even good. Forget about camp reversals that transform trash into the perversely fascinating, forget about the Cheese Factor, which allows a pop-cultural product to be moldy and musty and stinky and still taste good. *Big Brother* was so bad that even Jean-Paul Sartre would have yawned, and the dude wrote hundreds of pages about useless passion in *Being and Nothingness*.

2   But something good did come of *Big Brother*, something wicked and warped and witty, something created by people with way too much time on their hands and way too much venom in their bite. While the reality series was channeling banality through the cable cords and over the airwaves six nights a week, a small crew of writers were deconstructing and eviscerating the tedium on the Internet. They were taking hours and hours of prime-time dross and turning it into decadent, amoral, sharp, electronic gold.

3   Internet sass.

4   You gotta love it, if only because it keeps razor-tongued fanatics and uncensored savants off the streets and out of trouble.

5   Not only was there a site devoted entirely to the ridiculing of CBS, *Big Brother*, its ten cast members, their families, host Julie Chen, and the gaseous *Big Brother* house pug, but a number of other general interest sites, notably Salon.com, spent the summer providing wry daily updates on the non-goings-on of the non-people in the non-house. They, too, took the non-pulse of a DOA television series and gave it a semblance of life on the Internet.

Excerpt from "Talking Back to the Tube," by Matthew Gilbert. Reprinted courtesy of the *Boston Globe*.

1. Who are referred to as "razor-tongued fanatics and uncensored savants" (paragraph 4)?

   A. the television writers
   B. the television cast of *Big Brother*
   C. the Internet writers
   D. the Internet audience

2. Which of the following best summarizes the reviewer's point about *Big Brother*?

   A. The Internet reviews were much more interesting than the TV show.
   B. The TV show was so bad that it was funny.
   C. Internet writers are better than TV writers.
   D. The main problem was with the ten people on the TV show.

3. What opinion is supported by the statement "even Jean-Paul Sartre would have yawned, and the dude wrote hundreds of pages about useless passion" (paragraph 1)?

   A. The show was boring.
   B. The show should have been longer.
   C. The show needed more passion.
   D. The show was incomprehensible.

4. Which of the following best describes the tone of this review?

   A. apologetic
   B. nostalgic for earlier shows
   C. informal and hip
   D. objective

5. From whose point of view is this piece likely written?

   A. a television script writer
   B. a person who hates watching TV
   C. someone knowledgeable about the media
   D. a disgruntled fan

Text Structure

Writers make choices about how to organize informational and nonfiction materials based on their purpose. You have already seen two text structures: cause and effect, which shows how one thing made another happen, and comparison and contrast, which illustrates similarities and differences.

There are other **text structures** often used for informational text:

- **Example**—introduces an unfamiliar topic and then follows with common examples to aid understanding.
- **Pros and Cons**—explains a situation by first presenting its benefits and then portraying its deficiencies in order to present both sides.
- **Chronological Order** or **Process**—presents details in the order in which they occur; also referred to as a **sequence of events**.
- **Elaboration**—makes a statement and indicates that additional information or an explanation will follow.

These text structures use different types of **transitions** to guide the reader from one idea to the next. Many of these are familiar to you.

Text Structure	Purpose	Sample Transitions
Example	Organizes illustrations that support a concept	for example, for instance, such as, to illustrate
Pros and Cons	Shows benefits and drawbacks	on the one hand, on the other hand
Chronological Order or Process	Describes events and procedures	before, after, next, following, meanwhile, until
Elaboration	Expands with additional details	additionally, furthermore, moreover

Practice using an understanding of text structure by reading the paragraph and answering the question below.

> Today, there are millions of workers who are not employees in the traditional sense; they are called "contract workers." These are self-employed individuals who have contracts with different businesses. For example, a graphic artist may have several different clients and design a newsletter for one and a website for another. Contract workers pay for their own equipment, supplies, and benefits—such as health insurance.

▶ What is a detail from the passage that explains the concept of "contract workers"?
  (1) They are not employees in the traditional sense.
  (2) They may have contracts with several businesses.

Choice **(2)** illustrates the concept of contract workers by explaining that they have several different clients rather than one employer. Choice (1) does not help to explain contract work; it just explains what contract workers are not.

PRACTICE 10

Questions 1 and 2 refer to this scientific experiment.

COWPOX, SMALLPOX, AND IMMUNITY

In 1796, British physician Edward Jenner conducted an experiment intended to help develop a viable treatment for the deadly smallpox disease. Some time before, he had noticed that dairymaids in his village commonly became infected with cowpox. Cowpox is an illness that is very similar to smallpox, but it is not deadly. The dairymaids who caught cowpox later turned out to be immune to smallpox. This led Jenner to experiment with whether he could make a test subject immune to smallpox by first infecting that person with cowpox. His test subject was a young boy named James. First, Jenner made small cuts on James's skin and inserted liquid from the cowpox sores of a local dairymaid. After being exposed to the disease, James caught cowpox and later recovered. After the boy's recovery from cowpox, Jenner exposed James to smallpox and found that the boy was immune. Today, scientists and medical professionals know that the cowpox and smallpox viruses are so similar that the body's immune system cannot tell them apart.

1. What step in the process came before James's recovery from cowpox?

   A. his immunity to smallpox
   B. exposure to the cowpox disease
   C. scientists' discovery that cowpox and smallpox are similar
   D. Jenner exposing James to smallpox

2. Which of the following phrases from the passage provides information about the order of the steps in the process?

   A. "cannot tell them apart"
   B. "Jenner made small cuts"
   C. "After being exposed to the disease"
   D. "make a test subject immune"

Question 3 refers to this discussion of gardening.

THE UPS AND DOWNS OF GARDENING

Planting and maintaining a backyard garden can have many benefits, but it also brings challenges. On the one hand, successful gardeners often express deep feelings of accomplishment and satisfaction in their gardens. Gardening can involve good exercise and fresh air, and spending time outdoors can be a healthy escape from everyday responsibilities and concerns. A flower garden provides a beautiful view that often attracts delightful visitors, including butterflies and hummingbirds. A vegetable garden provides nutritious food and can add up to significant savings on your grocery bill. An herb garden can supply alternatives to unhealthy ingredients such as salt and oil.

On the other hand, planting and maintaining a garden can be very expensive and time-consuming, and a garden may fail despite your best efforts. Proper soil and fertilizers must be bought, and plants or seeds must be chosen. It is also important to consider the watering and feeding of the garden to ensure proper growth. A number of factors beyond your immediate control may affect the success of your garden. If the season's weather is extreme in any way—too dry, too rainy, too hot, or too cold—it can damage tender plants and undo your hard work, wasting your investment of time and money. Similarly, invasive pests and diseases can be devastating to your home garden and can be difficult and expensive to control.

3. Which of the following is one of the writer's arguments against planting and maintaining a backyard garden?

   A. Time outdoors often alleviates stress.
   B. A number of factors can damage a garden.
   C. Having too many daily chores is stressful.
   D. Rain is bad for a garden.

STUDY ADVICE

Congratulations—you're almost done with the first chapter of this book! The last few pages of each chapter will give you additional practice items to reinforce what you've learned in that chapter. Before you begin the first of these on the next page, you may want to review anything that seemed challenging in the lessons so far.

INTERPRETING INFORMATIONAL TEXT PRACTICE QUESTIONS

Questions 1 through 4 refer to the following excerpt from an autobiography.

EXCERPTED FROM *THE LIAR'S CLUB*

1   That fall my school career didn't go much better. I got suspended from my second-grade class twice, first for biting a kid named Phyllis who wasn't, to my mind, getting her scissors out fast enough to comply with the teacher, then again for breaking my plastic ruler over the head of a boy named Sammy Joe Tyler, whom I adored. A pale blue knot rose through the blond stubble of his crew cut. Both times I got sent to the principal, a handsome ex-football coach named Frank Doleman who let Lecia and me call him Uncle Frank. (Lecia and I had impressed Uncle Frank by both learning to read pretty much without instruction before we were three. Mother took us each down to his office in turn, and we each dutifully read the front page of the day's paper out loud to him, so he could be sure it wasn't just some story we'd memorized.)

2   He let me stay in his office playing chess all afternoon with whoever wandered in. He loved pitting me against particularly lunkheaded fifth- and sixth-grade boys who'd been sent down for paddlings they never got. He'd try to use my whipping them at chess to make them nervous about how dumb they were. "Now this little bitty old second-grader here took you clean in six plays. Don't you reckon you need to be listening to Miss Vilimez instead of cutting up?" When Mrs. Hess led me solemnly down the hall to Frank Doleman's office, I would pretend to cry, but thought instead about Brer Rabbit as he was being thrown into the briar patch where he'd been born and raised, and screaming *Please don't throw me in that briar patch!*

From *The Liar's Club* by Mary Karr, New York: Penguin Books, 1995.

1. If the writer had attended an elementary school dance, which of the following might she have done?

    A. made fun of everyone as they danced
    B. sat and played chess with the boys
    C. been too shy to dance with anyone
    D. hit a boy in the arm to get his attention

2. What is meant by the statement "I . . . thought instead about Brer Rabbit as he was being thrown into the briar patch where he'd been born and raised and screaming *Please don't throw me in that briar patch!*" (paragraph 2)?

    A. She was so upset that she wanted to scream.
    B. She was just pretending she didn't want to go to the principal's office.
    C. She hoped the teacher would let her back in class if she pleaded with her.
    D. She was afraid of what would happen in the principal's office.

3. What type of principal was Frank Doleman?

    A. strict
    B. ineffective
    C. unusual
    D. mean

4. Later in the autobiography, the narrator describes herself as "small-boned and skinny, but more than able to make up for that."

    Based on this description and the excerpt, which of the following best describes the narrator?

    A. confident
    B. serious
    C. friendly
    D. hopeful

Questions 5 through 9 refer to this article about soda.

TURNING BACK A SUGARY TIDE

1   The popular soft drinks known as soda, pop, or both trace their origins all the way back to 1767, when English chemist Joseph Priestley invented a method for carbonating water. Over the last two and a half centuries, soda has risen to prominence primarily as a sweet beverage for social occasions. By the mid-1990s, soda had become the beverage of choice for adolescents. This increase in consumption has not been without negative consequences. Since the early 1980s, obesity rates for young Americans have risen steadily, as has the incidence of juvenile diabetes, heart disease, and myriad other ailments related to poor diet.

2   To counteract the harmful effects of overindulging in soda, federal, state, and local governments have taken steps in recent years. First Lady Michelle Obama promotes healthier diet choices and campaigns against childhood obesity. Several states now require that restaurants post calorie information next to all menu items, including beverages. In a controversial move, New York City mayor Michael Bloomberg proposed banning the sale of sodas over 16 ounces in city eateries. Additionally, many school districts around the country have banned the sale of soda in school vending machines.

3   These efforts appear to be paying off: latest statistics indicate that the percentage of teens who consume soda daily has fallen from 75 percent in the 1990s to 62 percent in 2009. However, most teens who abandon soda as a daily beverage replace it with other high-sugar choices, such as juice or energy and sport drinks. While many of these products have slightly less sugar than soda, the net impact of regular consumption is likely to be just as damaging in the long term. Regulating the sale of soda is a step in the right direction, but more can be done to educate young people about the dangers of a diet overflowing with sugary beverages.

5. Which of the following best describes the tone of this article?

   A. playful but informative
   B. pessimistic and sarcastic
   C. concerned but hopeful
   D. neutral and inquisitive

6. Which of the following best describes the author's point of view on reducing soda consumption?

   A. The sale of soda should be outlawed due to the beverage's negative impact on health.
   B. Consuming diet soda is healthier than consuming regular soda.
   C. A young person's decision to consume soda is a personal choice that must be respected.
   D. Young people will choose healthier beverages if they are better educated about the dangers of consumption of sugared beverages.

7. According to paragraph 3, what will likely be the "net impact" of regularly consuming juice, energy, and sport drinks instead of soda?

   A. Teenagers who consume these beverages instead of soda will avoid the health hazards associated with soda.
   B. Soda manufacturers will likely go out of business since fewer consumers will be purchasing their products.
   C. Young people who drink these beverages regularly will eventually suffer from the same ailments as those who drink soda regularly.
   D. Many of the teenagers who drink juice, energy, and sport drinks will choose healthier food options to supplement their diets.

8. According to the passage, the author most likely regards the steps to curb soda consumption described in paragraph 2 as

   A. disruptive but essential
   B. effective to some extent
   C. invasive and extreme
   D. well-intentioned but unenforceable

9. In the beginning of paragraph 3, the words "These efforts" refer to which of the following?

   A. Creating soda from carbonated water
   B. Recommending energy and sport drinks instead of soda
   C. Reducing excessive consumption of soda
   D. Increasing educational programs about the effects of soda

Questions 10 through 12 refer to the following business document.

EXCERPTED FROM *INDEPENDENT CONSULTANT'S BROCHURE AND LETTER HANDBOOK* BY HERMAN HOLTZ

1   The National Association of Temporary Services (NATS), which represents the nation's temporary help employers, testified today before the House Ways and Means Committee on the employer mandate and related provisions of the President's Health Security Act (H.R. 3600).

2   Edward A. Lenz, NATS senior vice president, legal and government affairs, said that the temporary help industry supports the principle of universal coverage, but has serious concerns that the cost of mandates could weaken the ability of the temporary help industry to act as a "jobs bridge" to regular, full-time employment.

3   According to Lenz, the temporary help industry has recently "assumed a new and vital role—by helping to ease the burden on individuals during the current restructuring of the American work force. Temporary work offers displaced workers a critical safety net of income, benefits, and skills training and often provides a bridge back to regular, full-time employment."

4   In addition, the Association is concerned that the mandates, as currently structured, would "also impose enormous administrative burdens" due to annual temporary employee turnover in the range of 400 to 600 percent. If employer mandates are adopted, Lenz urged Congress to create a mechanism that relates premium payments to hours worked, such as a simple payroll tax.

10. Which of the following states one of the main concerns of NATS?

A. NATS won't be able to offer skills training to temporary employees if the government mandates coverage.
B. There will be an increase in turnover of temporary employees if the government mandates coverage.
C. The cost of mandated coverage will lessen the ability of NATS to hire and supply temporary workers.
D. Restructuring the work force is a burden to all Americans.

11. According to the press release, why have businesses supplying temporary help become even more necessary?

A. Many workers are losing their jobs and need temporary jobs until they find permanent work again.
B. There is not enough work for everyone to have a full-time permanent job.
C. The job turnover rate has gone as high as 400 to 600 percent.
D. More and more workers do not want permanent full-time work.

12. What is the overall purpose of this piece?

A. to stimulate debate over universal health insurance coverage
B. to impress both the Congress and the president
C. to describe various alternatives to mandated coverage
D. to raise awareness of an issue

Questions 13 through 16 refer to the following excerpt from a historical feminist speech.

EXCERPTED FROM *A TREASURY OF THE WORLD'S GREAT SPEECHES*

1   We have met here today to discuss our rights and wrongs, civil and political, and not, as some have supposed, to go into the detail of social life alone. We do not propose to petition the legislature to make our husbands just, generous, and courteous, to seat every man at the head of a cradle, and to clothe every woman in male attire. None of these points, however important they may be considered by leading men, will be touched in this convention. As to their costume, the gentlemen need feel no fear of our imitating that, for we think it in violation of every principle of taste, beauty, and dignity; notwithstanding all the contempt cast upon our loose, flowing garments, we still admire the graceful folds, and consider our costume far more artistic than theirs. Many of the nobler sex seem to agree with us in this opinion, for the bishops, priests, judges, barristers, and lord mayors of the first nation on the globe, and the Pope of Rome, with his cardinals, too, all wear the loose flowing robes, thus tacitly acknowledging that the male attire is neither dignified nor imposing. No, we shall not molest you in your philosophical experiments with stocks, pants, high-heeled boots, and Russian belts. Yours be the glory to discover, by personal experience, how long the kneepan can resist the terrible strapping down which you impose, in how short time the well-developed muscles of the throat can be reduced to mere threads by the constant pressure of the stock, how high the heel of a boot must be to make a short man tall, and how tight the Russian belt may be drawn and yet have wind enough left to sustain life.

2   But we are assembled to protest against a form of government existing without the consent of the governed—to declare our right to be free. . . .

From a speech at a woman's-rights convention by Elizabeth Cady Stanton, as reprinted in *A Treasury of the World's Great Speeches*, edited by Houston Peterson, New York: Simon & Schuster, 1954, 1965.

13. Which of the following best rephrases the lines "Yours be the glory to discover . . . how long the kneepad can resist the terrible strapping down which you impose" (paragraph 1)?

   A. Men do not understand how uncomfortable women's clothes are.
   B. Women will not resort to wearing pants or other restrictive men's clothing.
   C. Men will only understand women when women dress like them.
   D. Men and women will be equal only when they both wear belts and collars.

14. What is a "stock" (paragraph 1)?

   A. a man's jacket
   B. a wooden frame holding a prisoner
   C. a loose shirt
   D. a cloth worn around the neck

15. If the speaker attended a fancy tea party, which of the following would she be most likely to do?

   A. be on her best behavior
   B. speak up about current events
   C. treat the hostess like royalty
   D. comment on everyone's clothing

16. Later in the speech, Stanton states that "over the horns of bigotry and prejudice will be our way." Based on this and the excerpt, you can conclude that Stanton is giving this speech for what reason?

   A. Women are fighting for the right to vote.
   B. Women are tired of being made to wear dresses.
   C. Husbands need to be made just and generous.
   D. Many people mistakenly judge others by their appearance.

STUDY ADVICE

Don't forget to review the answers and explanations, and compare them to your own work. Doing so will give you valuable information about what kinds of mistakes you're prone to. Then you can practice to avoid those mistakes!

Purpose of Text

When you read TASC Reading Test passages, it is important that you comprehend not only what the author is writing about but also the **purpose**—the reason *why* he or she is writing this passage. Authors of nonfiction passages have one or more of the following purposes:

KEY IDEAS

- Writers have different reasons, or purposes, for writing.
- The main purposes for writing are to narrate a story, to inform, to persuade, and to entertain.

- **Narrate**—Narrative passages typically recount events chronologically, that is, in the order in which they happened. Examples include a person's life story and hour-by-hour developments in a news story.

- **Inform**—The author seeks to present facts and data to explain a subject, situation, or idea. Examples include news articles, financial summaries, and scientific findings.

- **Persuade**—The author seeks to change readers' minds, and the passage includes the author's opinions, recommendations, or conclusions. Examples are political speeches, newspaper editorials, and entertainment reviews.

- **Entertain**—Authors writing to entertain are trying to amuse or interest their readers. Examples include a humorous memoir or articles about celebrities.

Read the paragraph and answer questions about the writer's purpose.

> According to market research, video games sales—including digital downloads and apps—in the United States topped $15 billion in 2010. The most popular game genres were Action (21.7% of sales), Sports Games (16.3%), and First-Person Shooter (15.9%). Family Entertainment games accounted for only 9.1 percent of sales.

TASC TEST TIP

As you are reading passages on the test, ask yourself, "Why did the author write this story, article, or speech?" That will help you to understand the purpose.

▶ What is the writer's purpose for this paragraph?
   (1) to present facts about video game sales
   (2) to convince readers that Family Entertainment games' sales should be increased

▶ Imagine there is an additional sentence at the end of the paragraph. "Because popular games in the Action and First-Person Shooter genres may contain extremely graphic violence, parents must be educated about how to monitor their children's purchases and game play." What would be the purpose of the revised paragraph about video games?
   (1) to entertain readers with an amusing fact about video games
   (2) to persuade parents to become more involved in their children's use of video games

In the first question, choice **(1)** is correct because the writer gives facts and not persuasive information. In the second question, once the information about violence has been added, choice **(2)** is correct because the statement offers a recommendation to persuade, not entertain, parents.

APOLLO

After an explosion damaged critical systems on the spacecraft of the Apollo 13 mission, the three astronauts aboard were forced to make the journey back to Earth inside the Lunar Module (LM), the small vessel originally designed to land on the Moon's surface. Using the LM as a "lifeboat" provided the astronauts with enough oxygen and water for the return trip, but it also introduced a new problem: there was no way to recycle used air. To solve the problem, engineers back on Earth cataloged all of the spare parts and detachable pieces inside the Apollo modules. From these, they prototyped various devices the astronauts might use to make filters to use inside the LM. The Earth-based engineers talked the astronauts through the process of constructing and installing the makeshift filters. The engineers' quick thinking and creativity provided the astronauts with a way to maintain breathable air throughout their journey back to Earth.

1. The purpose of the paragraph above is to

   A. explain how the Lunar Module worked
   B. tell how creative engineers saved astronauts
   C. inform about the space program's value
   D. convince that engineers are essential workers

SALES TAX

Our state should cut all sales taxes on the purchase of new automobiles to encourage buying new cars. Older cars do not run as cleanly as new vehicles and, thus, contribute to air pollution. Additionally, older cars are less safe to operate. One study estimates that last year, as many as 500 deaths or serious injuries from accidents in our state could have been prevented by the sorts of safety features that are standard on newer-model cars.

2. The writer most likely includes the fact about preventable deaths or serious injuries in automobile accidents because it

   A. is the conclusion the writer is trying to prove
   B. supports the writer's main recommendation
   C. may shock readers into becoming safer drivers
   D. will encourage legislators to cut sales taxes

Questions 3 and 4 are based on this passage.

SILK: NOW AND THEN

Modern consumers do not appreciate the historical importance of the fabric silk. Silk fabric is valued for its smooth texture and shimmering appearance. It is also highly absorbent, making silk clothing comfortable in both high and low temperatures. Today, silk fabrics remain somewhat more expensive than cotton cloth and synthetic textiles, but many would be surprised to learn that silk was arguably the most important product in Asia and Europe for nearly 1,000 years.

Originally, sericulture—the technology of making silk cloth from silkworm cocoons—was known only in China. Around 2,000 years ago, nomads from Central Asia would travel to China to trade horses and other goods for silk cloth. As these nomads ventured West, silk became known to people in the Middle East and Europe. Over time, traders established routes over 4,000 miles long from China to Europe that became known as the Silk Road. Throughout the ancient and medieval world, silk was the preferred fabric for the robes of royalty and the very wealthy.

3. This purpose of this passage is to

   A. criticize ancient peoples for overvaluing silk
   B. explain how silk fabrics are made
   C. entertain readers who enjoy historical travel
   D. inform about the historical importance of silk

4. How does the information in the second paragraph support the purpose of the passage?

   A. It illustrates why silk remains an expensive product today.
   B. It refutes the notion that silk is a valuable product in the modern world.
   C. It provides examples of silk's historical importance in trade and culture.
   D. It compares the value of silk to that of other products from Asia.

Effectiveness of Argument

You may think of an argument as being a quarrel between people. However, in reading and writing, an **argument** consists of the following:

- A **conclusion** (that is, main point) about something
- The **evidence,** which is support that is given for the conclusion
- The author's **assumptions**, or ideas the author takes for granted, behind the argument

Writers should provide supporting evidence for their argument; otherwise, they are just making an unsupported claim. You may need to read carefully to **infer** their assumptions.

Read the argument below and answer the questions that follow.

> In the past few years, the majority of state governments have passed laws making it illegal to send text messages while driving. These laws are clearly a good decision for which legislators should be praised. Drivers are 23 times more likely to have accidents while texting than they are while driving undistracted. It is common sense that the government has a responsibility to protect its citizens from the recklessness of a careless few.

1. What is the writer's argument about anti-texting laws?
   - (1) Such laws are a good idea because drivers are prone to accidents while texting.
   - (2) The majority of state governments have passed laws making it illegal to text while driving.

2. What evidence is given in support of the author's argument?
   - (1) Drivers are 23 times more prone to accidents while texting.
   - (2) Members of state legislatures should be praised.

3. Which of the following is likely one of the author's unstated assumptions?
   - (1) Drivers must police themselves to avoid dangerous situations.
   - (2) A state government should pass laws to ensure citizens' safety.

The answer to Question 1 is **(1)**. The author's opinion is that anti-texting laws are "good" and "should be praised." The rest of the argument supports that opinion. The answer to Question 2 is **(1)**. A statistic such as "23 times more likely" is typical of the factual evidence you can expect to see on the TASC. The answer to Question 3 is **(2)**. We know that the assumption that governments should protect citizens is a premise of the author because he praises legislators for passing these laws to make roads and highways safer.

KEY IDEAS

- An argument is a statement that takes a position.
- An argument consists of a conclusion about the issue and supporting evidence.
- Critically reading an argument involves understanding the stated or implied assumptions behind the claim.

TASC TEST TIP

On some passages, writers may use terms such as "for these reasons," "it follows that," or "therefore" to indicate their conclusion. In other cases, you may have to carefully analyze the passage to find the argument.

Questions 1 through 4 refer to this passage about the minimum wage.

MAKING MINIMUM WAGE WORK FOR WORKERS

1   The minimum wage is the lowest salary that a company can legally pay its employees. The federal minimum wage is the lowest allowed in the nation, but many states have set minimum wages higher than the national number.

2   Several states have taken the sensible step of automatically raising their minimum wage to adjust for inflation and consumer price increases. This policy ensures that low-paid workers are paid a stable, livable income over the long term. Raising the federal minimum wage, however, requires direct action by lawmakers. As a result, over the past 40 years, the federal minimum wage has not kept pace with the rate of inflation. Nowadays, full-time minimum-wage workers earn so little money that many have fallen below the poverty line. In the case of the minimum wage, the federal government should follow the lead of the states. Congress needs to establish automatic wage increases triggered by increases in inflation and changes to the consumer price index. That is the only way to ensure sustainable earnings for hardworking citizens.

1. Which of the following is the main point of the passage?

   A. States' minimum wages differ from the federal minimum wage.
   B. The federal government should automatically raise the minimum wage to match price increases.
   C. The federal minimum wage ensures a comfortable living for people earning it.
   D. State minimum wages are the result of political games played with people's livelihoods.

2. What is the writer's argument about states that automatically raise their minimum wages?

   A. Those states' wages have not kept pace with the rate of inflation.
   B. People earning more than minimum wage in those states are wealthy.
   C. Those states have many workers in poverty.
   D. Those states have systems superior to the federal system of manual increases.

3. What evidence is given to support the author's argument?

   A. Some states have minimum wages lower than the federal minimum wage.
   B. The federal government should adjust its minimum wage automatically.
   C. Over the past 40 years, the federal minimum wage has not kept pace with inflation.
   D. As a result of inflation, $1 in 1972 was worth more than $5 is worth today.

4. Which of the following is most likely to be one of the author's assumptions?

   A. Employees under the age of 18 might be paid less than the minimum wage.
   B. Ensuring sustainable incomes for hardworking citizens is a responsibility of lawmakers.
   C. Employees earning the federal minimum wage cannot support themselves and their families.
   D. The past 40 years have experienced significantly higher inflation than was expected.

STUDY ADVICE

On page 38, you learned to ask yourself *why* an author wrote a passage, and you learned that sometimes authors want to persuade their readers about something. The questions on this page are about *how* an author goes about persuading her readers.

LESSON 3

Validity of Arguments

Just because a writer makes an argument does not mean you have to accept it as **valid**, or convincing. You need to analyze the supporting evidence. Below are some types of **support for arguments** and ways that you can question their legitimacy.

Type of Support	Description	Questions to Ask
Facts	Objective facts that can be tested or measured	Is the information complete, or is it partial or selectively chosen?
Data or Statistics	Numerical data that have been gathered or sampled	Do the numbers accurately represent the subject? How were they gathered?
Examples or Anecdotes	Stories to demonstrate the "truth"	Are the stories true? Are they relevant?
Authority	Testimonials from a recognized authority	Does the person really know the issue, or is he or she a spokesperson or celebrity?
Causality	Assertions that one thing caused another	Is this really a cause, or is it just a related factor?

In addition to analyzing the evidence, you need to be aware that sometimes writers use **emotional appeals** based on fear, pity, or getting you to "jump on the bandwagon" of the argument's popularity.

Gasoline prices spiked suddenly in the Weston metropolitan area last week when the local oil refinery went offline due to a facility-wide computer malfunction. Shortly thereafter, the average number of miles driven daily by Weston residents fell by a whopping 55 percent. Clearly, the higher gas prices were responsible for the decline in miles driven.

▶ What is the argument in the paragraph?
  (1) Higher gas prices were responsible for the decline in miles driven.
  (2) The spike in gas prices was due to a computer malfunction at the local refinery.

▶ Which of the following undermines the writer's argument?
  (1) Oil refineries have stopped production in the past.
  (2) Last week, a blizzard struck the Weston area, causing a state of emergency that required all nonemergency vehicles to stay off the roads.

For the first question, choice **(1)** is correct. The writer concludes that high gas prices caused the decline in driving and uses the background about the refinery shutdown as support. For the second question, choice **(2)** is correct. The writer's argument is faulty because she assumes that the high price of gasoline was the only cause of the reduction in driving. Choice **(2)** supplies another reasonable explanation for the reduced driving, thereby weakening the argument.

PRACTICE 3

Questions 1 through 4 refer to this passage about voting technology.

DIGITAL VOTING: A BETTER WAY TO COUNT

1   The large-scale adoption in 1996 of direct-recording electronic (DRE) voting marked the beginning of an era of superior voting technology. For as long as elections have been held, voting systems have been flawed in various ways. In mid-18th century America, voters called out their selections publicly. This assured an accurate count but meant voting could not be private. Paper ballots, on the other hand, were anonymous but could be easily forged or miscounted.

2   The next innovation was the mechanical-lever voting machine, introduced in the late 19th century. The use of this voting system peaked in the 1960s. Over the next several decades, the mechanical-lever machines were replaced by two early electronic voting systems: bubble sheets recorded by optical scanner and punch cards processed electronically. All of these systems were prone to glitches, such as the notorious "hanging chads" and unreadable ballots in Florida after the 2000 U.S. presidential election.

3   Now, many jurisdictions use all-electronic DRE systems. Every step of the voting process is electronic: the ballot appears on a screen, the voter indicates his or her selection via buttons or touch-screen technology, and results are stored on a memory card. In DRE voting, there is always a record of a voter's choices, and there is no chance of voters filling in the wrong bubble or of poorly punched cards that cause votes to go uncounted. For all of these reasons, DRE is clearly the most secure and accurate voting system available.

1. The main point of the passage is that

  A. unlike optical-scanning and punch-card voting systems, DRE voting is completely electronic

  B. punch-card voting systems caused a problem in the 2000 presidential election

  C. DRE systems offer more security and accuracy than other voting systems

  D. elections in America have changed greatly over the years

2. Which of the following is evidence to support the writer's argument?

  A. When technology changes, voting systems change along with it.

  B. DRE voting avoids problems associated with other voting systems.

  C. Several voting systems have become obsolete because they violated voters' privacy

  D. No modern-day election would ever be conducted using a public voice vote.

3. What evidence is given to support the writer's argument?

  A. Each voter's choices are recorded in the DRE voting system.

  B. Mechanical-lever voting machines were replaced by other mechanical voting devices.

  C. Punch-card voting involves electronic processing.

  D. In the mid-18th century, public votes were popular.

4. Which of the following is an example of faulty reasoning that weakens the argument?

  A. The writer claims that punch-card systems contributed to problems in the 2000 presidential election without providing any support for the claim.

  B. The writer suggests that DRE voting was responsible for the demise of older voting systems, overlooking the possibility that there might have been another cause.

  C. The writer fails to consider that even if DRE voting addresses all the flaws of previous systems, it may introduce other flaws of its own.

  D. The author fails to provide evidence that voters in 18th-century America were wary of elections.

LESSON 4

Text Related by Theme or Topic

On the TASC Reading Test, you may need to read related **paired passages** and answer questions based on your understanding of both of them. The two texts will be related by **topic** (what the passages address) or **theme** (the writer's message about a topic). You will need to understand each passage on its own and be able to **synthesize** (blend) information to draw a conclusion.

Below are two paragraphs about the same topic. One is a news story, and the other is an opinion piece. Read both selections and answer the questions based on your understanding and analysis of both texts.

News Story

Candy, greasy meals, and high-calorie sodas may be banned in U.S. elementary and high schools. According to news reports, new standards proposed by the Department of Agriculture would replace such items as fried potato chips with baked chips and sugary sodas with lower-calorie sport drinks. These regulations are a result of a child nutrition law, passed by the U.S. Congress to combat childhood obesity.

Response Letter

The paper announced that the government will be mandating "healthier food" in school cafeterias. Doesn't the government have anything better to do than to "babysit" our schools? Shouldn't the schools be focused on improving education, not monitoring behavior? Where is the research to show that school meals account for childhood obesity? This is just one more government intrusion into our personal lives.

▶ What is the topic of both of these selections?
   (1) greasy food in school cafeterias
   (2) new guidelines for healthy school meals

▶ What information is given in the news story?
   (1) The government is "babysitting" our schools.
   (2) Certain unhealthy foods may be banned from public schools.

▶ Which relevant argument is made in the response letter?
   (1) The new regulations are a good way to help combat childhood obesity.
   (2) The new regulations are a poor idea because monitoring student behavior is not a school's responsibility.

The correct choice in the first question is **(2)** because the news story reports on the regulations while the response letter criticizes them. In the second question, choice **(2)** is correct because it summarizes the factual information in the news story. The correct choice in the third question is **(2)** because the writer of the response letter clearly states her opposition to the new regulations.

PRACTICE 4

Questions 1 through 4 refer to the paired passages below.

Passage 1

The online piracy of digital files is a major problem for the music industry. From 2004 to 2009, 30 billion songs were downloaded illegally, representing a loss of billions of dollars of revenue. Recent legislation, along with the shutdown of certain major file-sharing websites, has begun to stem the tide of piracy. The organization representing the music and recording industry, however, reports that the annual harm to the economy from piracy may be as high as $12.5 billion dollars a year. More must be done.

Passage 2

Online piracy is harmful to the music industry, but not only for the reasons the industry claims. The financial harm caused by piracy is often exaggerated. The recording industry's estimates are based on the prices of songs and the number of songs downloaded; in reality, a person who illegally downloaded 10,000 songs would download only a fraction of that number if forced to pay for each file. As a result, the actual loss of revenue caused by piracy is certainly much lower than the industry estimates. However, a fear of piracy has made investors cautious about signing new, experimental artists. That in itself is a cause for concern and a reason more needs to be done to halt illegal downloading.

---

1. The topic of both passages is

   A. ways in which industries can exaggerate financial harm
   B. examples of recent legislation to protect an industry
   C. online piracy of music files
   D. the signing of new, experimental musicians

2. The main argument of Passage 1 is that

   A. new, experimental artists are necessary for the music industry to succeed
   B. additional action to combat online piracy is warranted because piracy causes financial losses to the music industry
   C. the shutdown of major file-sharing websites was a positive development because they contributed to $12.5 billion per year in damages
   D. from 2004 to 2009, 30 billion songs were downloaded illegally

3. Which claim in Passage 2 supports the conclusion drawn in Passage 1?

   A. Fear of piracy makes it difficult for new, experimental acts to get signed.
   B. Recent legislation has begun to reduce the amount of online music piracy.
   C. A person who downloads music illegally would likely download fewer songs if he or she had to pay for them.
   D. Financial harm from illegal music downloads is often exaggerated.

4. With which of the following statements would the writers of both passages agree?

   A. Online piracy of digital files has a harmful effect on the music industry.
   B. Online piracy of digital files causes serious damage to the economy.
   C. The main reason to combat online piracy is to ensure that new, experimental artists can find investors.
   D. Music is important for a healthy society to function properly.

LESSON 5

Texts with Opposing Arguments

You have learned about writers' arguments and have seen how the Reading Test may require you to work with two related texts. In some cases, you may read two selections that have **opposing arguments** about the same topic. Read the selections below and think about the authors' claims, the **assumptions** or the thinking behind their positions, and the supporting evidence for each.

Argument	Opposing Argument
Coal, the source of half the energy in the United States, has been the dirtiest of all fossil fuels because it creates harmful emissions when burned. Help is on the way with the development of new "clean coal" technologies that reduce coal's environmental impact. These new technologies purify exhaust gases as coal burns (wet scrubbers) and prevent the formation of harmful emissions in the first place (low-NOx burners). There is even gasification, which avoids burning coal altogether.	*"Clean coal" amounts to just an advertising slogan. Don't be fooled by claims about new technologies making coal a clean-burning fuel. The hazards to our environment start well before that. Coal mining wastes huge amounts of water—70 to 260 million gallons daily. Today's mining companies now use mountaintop removal, instead of traditional mining, to extract coal. Forty-nine states have issued fish intake advisories due to high mercury concentration in water, much of it due to run-off from coal mining.*

▶ What is the topic of both of these selections?
  (1) preventing air pollution from coal
  (2) the usefulness of "clean coal" technologies

You were right to pick choice **(2)**. The Argument suggests that "clean coal" will reduce coal's environmental impact, while the Opposing Argument contends that coal will continue to harm the environment.

▶ What type of evidence is provided in the Argument?
  (1) statistics demonstrating the effectiveness of "clean coal" technologies
  (2) facts about new "clean coal" technologies

Here, choice **(2)** is correct. The Argument lists and briefly describes the new technologies.

▶ How does the Opposing Argument confront the underlying assumption of the Argument?
  (1) It points out environmental damage caused by coal before it is burned, when "clean coal" technologies are not used.
  (2) It cites studies showing that "clean coal" technologies are less effective than their advocates claim they are.

Choice **(1)** is correct. Impacts from mining, water waste, and mercury run-off are among the other harms cited in the Opposing Argument.

PRACTICE 5

ARGUMENT: Rating Systems for Movies Are Beneficial

In 1968, the Motion Picture Association of America (MPAA) replaced the complicated, morals-based Hays Code with the current, user-friendly MPAA rating system. This system is designed specifically to help parents decide whether a movie is appropriate for their child. Every parent in America knows what G, PG, PG-13, and R mean and can use these ratings to quickly judge suitability. Moreover, ratings now include descriptions that give even more information that parents can use to assess content and make wise movie-viewing decisions for their children. MPAA ratings take the guesswork out of at least one aspect of parenting!

OPPOSING ARGUMENT: Movie Rating Systems Are a Joke

A movie's MPAA rating—G, PG, PG-13, or R—is a familiar tag that parents, in particular, use to make fundamental decisions about family entertainment. Sadly, the rating system is more a marketing tool for the industry than a useful guide for parents. Consider that, in the early 1980s, unknowing parents exposed their children to alarming gore and violence under the PG rating, prompting the creation of the PG-13 rating. The result is that now, a movie that includes violence, drug use, gore, and sexual content can be marketed as a family-friendly PG-13 experience. Parents are better off finding an unbiased source of realistic reviews than trusting the MPAA rating system.

---

1. The topic of both passages is

   A. violence in movies
   B. good and bad parenting decisions
   C. the MPAA movie rating system
   D. motion picture marketing strategies

2. Which of the following is the main point of the Argument?

   A. The MPAA rating system replaced the Hays Code.
   B. The MPAA rating system is a useful tool for parents.
   C. Parents should consult a variety of sources before deciding which movies to allow their children to watch.
   D. The G, PG, PG-13, and R ratings are familiar and easy to understand.

3. The writer of the Opposing Argument would agree with which of the following statements?

   A. Parents overreacted to movie content in the 1980s.
   B. The PG-13 rating introduced a helpful distinction to the system.
   C. Violence and drug use are examples of family-friendly movie content.
   D. The MPAA rating system should not be trusted.

4. Which of the following conclusions could be drawn about the writer of the Argument?

   A. She largely approves of the MPAA rating system as a guideline for parents.
   B. She allows her children to watch movies rated PG but not those rated PG-13.
   C. She is wary of how the MPAA rating system judges violent content in movies.
   D. She believes that the Hays Code was detrimental to the movie industry.

STUDY ADVICE

How long are your study sessions? Start by studying for as long as you can easily focus on the material—which might be 15 minutes or an hour. Gradually train yourself to focus on the material for longer stretches, until your study sessions are two to three hours each. After all, you will need to maintain your focus on Test Day.

LESSON 6

Texts with Related Graphic Information

When you read nonfiction and informational text in a textbook, magazine, or website, it is often accompanied by a **graphic**—an illustration, photograph, or diagram—that helps you to understand the information. On the TASC Reading Test, you may need to combine information from text and graphics to draw conclusions and to make observations about how the graphic supports the information in the text. Practice with the text and graphic below.

"Mayfield" No More? The Changing American Household

Although *Leave It to Beaver* was a fictional television show, many advertisements, politicians, and movies still echo its portrayal of the typical American household of the 1950s: a married couple with children. A closer look at government statistics shows that it might be time to retool that image; today, fewer than half of American households are husband-wife households. In fact, more than a quarter of American households are now occupied by one person living alone—a significant group for marketers to target, as those who live alone are entirely responsible for all household purchases.

Percent Distribution of Households by Type

One person alone 26.7%
Husband-wife family households 48.4%
Two or more nonrelated people 6.8%
Male homeowner/renter with other family 5.0%
Female homeowner/renter with other family 13.1%

Source: U.S. Census Bureau

▶ What is the topic of the story and the graphic?
   (1) the composition of American households
   (2) advertising on *Leave It to Beaver*

If you answered **(1)**, you were correct. The story outlines the current make-up of American households, and the graphic supplies factual detail.

▶ How does the pie chart support the information in the story?
   (1) It provides statistics comparing American households in the 1950s with American households today.
   (2) It confirms the story's point about current household composition and provides additional details not discussed in the story.

Choice **(2)** is correct. The pie chart supplies statistics about husband-wife households (48.4%) and single-resident households (26.7%) that match the article's assertions and show the proportion of Americans living with other family and with roommates to whom they are not related.

KEY IDEAS

- The TASC Reading Test may present some selections with accompanying graphics.
- Read the passage carefully and analyze the graphic.
- Evaluate whether each question is based on the text, the graphic, or a combination of the two.

TASC TEST TIP

When you see that a graphic accompanies a selection, ask yourself, "Is this graphic providing supporting material, or is it providing additional information?" If you understand that, you will be better able to answer the test questions.

PRACTICE 6

<u>Questions 1 through 3</u> refer to the following passage and the two figures below.

Gerrymandering: An Electoral Advantage

1   The term *gerrymander* is used to describe the process by which electoral districts are given curious shapes in order to favor the interests of the party in power of a state legislature. Through this process, the governing political party tailors the electoral map to group unfavorable neighborhoods into a few districts likely to vote for the opposition while configuring the majority of districts to favor the party in power.

2   Figures 2(a) and 2(b) show how a governing political party can benefit from gerrymandering. In both figures, there are 40 gray squares and 60 white squares, and the area is divided into four equal-sized districts. In Figure 2(a), the white-square party will win only two seats out of four, but in Figure 2(b), the white-square party will take three of the four districts, as most of the gray votes are consolidated into one oddly shaped and geographically separated district. In fact, Illinois's 4th Congressional District is similar in shape to the gray district in Figure 2(b).

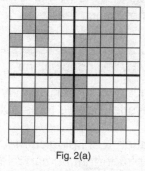

Fig. 2(a)

Geographically Uniform
Districts

Fig. 2(b)

Gerrymandered Districts

1. Which of the following is the main point of the passage and figures?

   A. Illinois's 4th Congressional District has now been in existence for over 200 years.
   B. Curiosity is the most important ingredient in the democratic process.
   C. Gerrymandered congressional districts are a major threat to the democratic system.
   D. Governing parties can use their power to shape electoral districts to their advantage.

2. Which of the following conclusions can be drawn from the passage and the figures?

   A. Gerrymandering is more common in Illinois than in other American states.
   B. Through gerrymandering, a governing party can be elected to a greater number of seats than its voter support might otherwise allow.
   C. Through gerrymandering, impartial committees draw boundaries to keep elections fair.
   D. Gerrymandering convinces citizens who would ordinarily be unfavorable to a party to change their votes.

3. In what way do the figures support the passage?

   A. They illustrate the advantages a party can obtain through gerrymandering.
   B. They predict victory for the gray party in the upcoming election.
   C. They are more relevant to Chicago than to rural Illinois.
   D. They show that voter turnout will continue to decline if governing parties continue to gerrymander districts.

ANALYZING INFORMATIONAL TEXT PRACTICE QUESTIONS

Questions 1 through 4 refer to the following passage about communication technology and the accompanying cartoon.

SOCIAL NETWORKING AT WHAT COST?

1   Sit in any restaurant or coffee shop long enough, and you're bound to witness a familiar scene: a couple, a family, or a group of friends gathered to enjoy a meal, but instead of conversing, each person at the table sits staring at his or her cell phone. In this age of social media, the question arises: does technology enhance or limit our ability to make strong emotional connections with other people?

2   Social networks have broadened with the expansion of communication technology. We connect easily with new acquaintances, old friends, potential clients, and complete strangers. For loved ones who are separated by distance, technology provides an important lifeline. Soldiers, deployed for long tours of duty, meet their newborn children over video chat. Grandparents, limited by ill health, watch their grandchildren grow through pictures and videos posted to social media sites.

3   With all the benefits of social media, however, come considerable costs. Each new connection we make (and old acquaintance we maintain) demands time, energy, and emotional investment. This often comes at the expense of time we could give to the most important people in our lives. Moreover, much of what we share through social media is superficial or entertaining. Only when technology is used to enhance our deepest, most valuable connections can it be considered real progress for humankind.

MUELLER

"A bunch of friends are coming over to stare at their phones."

© 2011 Peter Mueller from Cartoonbank.com. All rights reserved.

1. What is the purpose of the passage and the cartoon?

   A. to discuss different forms of social media
   B. to suggest a new form of communication technology
   C. to examine ways in which modern families use technology to communicate
   D. to discuss whether communication technology helps or hurts relationships

2. What is the topic of the passage and the cartoon?

   A. maintaining long-distance relationships
   B. how technology affects interpersonal connections
   C. the limits of social media
   D. the expense of new technologies

3. Which of the following details in the cartoon supports the author's point of view in the passage?

   A. The caption reveals that the woman is expecting friends to visit.
   B. The woman in the cartoon is speaking on the phone with a computer nearby.
   C. The woman in the cartoon is alone.
   D. The caption reveals that the woman's friends will use their phones during their visit.

4. Together, the cartoon and the passage support which of the following conclusions?

   A. New communication technologies may offer exciting ways for people to establish new friendships.
   B. New communication technologies may adversely impact important human relationships.
   C. New communication technologies may offer positive solutions for friends who are separated by distance.
   D. New communication technologies may help people to complete several tasks at once.

THE GIANT SQUID: MORE THAN COLOSSAL?

1   The giant squid is the world's longest cephalopod. Based on measurements of over 100 full specimens (including adult and adolescent individuals) recovered from the stomachs of sperm whales and other predators, scientists have determined that the giant squid can reach a length of 13 meters.

2   Some have argued that the honor of longest cephalopod should instead go to the colossal squid, a distant relative of the giant squid, but this belief is incorrect. It is true that the colossal squid may outweigh its giant cousin. However, of the few specimens of the colossal squid (all of them juveniles) described in the scientific literature, the longest measured ten meters. Therefore, the giant squid wins the length contest.

3   No other cephalopod is even close in length to either of these animals. For example, the giant Pacific octopus, the world's longest octopus species, has a maximum arm span of only about six meters. The giant squid's status as the world's longest cephalopod remains uncontested.

5.   The main point of the passage is that

A. the colossal squid weighs more than the giant squid
B. the giant squid is the world's longest cephalopod
C. the giant Pacific octopus is the world's longest octopus species
D. the giant squid can reach a length of 13 meters

6.   Which of the following best summarizes the writer's argument in paragraph 2?

A. The colossal squid is the world's longest cephalopod.
B. The colossal squid is a distant relative of the giant squid.
C. The giant Pacific octopus is not as long as the giant squid.
D. The giant squid is longer than the colossal squid.

7.   What evidence is given to support the writer's argument in paragraph 2?

A. The colossal squid can weigh more than the giant squid.
B. The giant squid is the world's longest cephalopod.
C. The length of the longest known colossal squid specimen is ten meters.
D. The giant Pacific octopus has a maximum arm span of only about six meters.

8.   Which of the following is an example of faulty reasoning that weakens the writer's argument?

A. The longest known colossal squid is ten meters long, so there is no colossal squid longer than the longest giant squid.
B. The giant Pacific octopus is the world's longest species of octopus, but it is not as long as the giant squid.
C. Many specimens of the giant squid have been measured.
D. Because sperm whales prey on giant squid, they must also prey on colossal squid.

Passage 1

The use of mercury amalgam for dental fillings has already been banned in several European nations, and it should also be banned in the United States. The mercury contained in amalgam fillings slowly leaches into the mouth and is swallowed. It is then absorbed by the small intestine and accumulates in various body tissues, including the brain, kidney, and liver. In 2001, a study reported that patients with a higher number of amalgam fillings also had higher occurrences of cancer, respiratory disease, and diseases of the nervous system. Therefore, it is clear that this accumulated mercury causes a variety of health problems.

In addition to its health impact, the mercury released from dental amalgam has a number of damaging environmental consequences. Mercury waste produced by dental offices is sometimes directly disposed of into sewage water or landfills. Mercury can leach from landfills into groundwater and get into rivers and lakes. It has been estimated, for example, that dental amalgam is the source of 4 percent of the mercury found in the water of Lake Superior.

Due to the alarming health and environmental consequences of mercury amalgam, dental fillings should be made from resin composites instead. These composites are already becoming popular due to their cosmetic appeal, so banning mercury amalgam will create no consumer backlash. There are demonstrable advantages (and no disadvantages) to banning mercury dental amalgam in the United States.

Passage 2

In recent years, uneducated consumers have expressed a growing fear of the mercury commonly found in dental fillings. The environmental impact of mercury is serious, and the release of mercury into the environment must be better controlled. However, the health risks associated with mercury amalgam fillings are minimal.

It is well-known that people who have mercury amalgam fillings absorb small amounts of mercury. However, most of this mercury is excreted in the urine. To date, no convincing scientific study has demonstrated that mercury absorbed from dental fillings causes any serious health problems. Because mercury amalgam fillings tend to last longer than resin composite fillings, amalgam is preferable for use whenever there is no cosmetic need for a tooth-colored filling.

However, the disposal of mercury amalgam in dental offices absolutely must be regulated. The Environmental Protection Agency estimates that 40 to 50 percent of the mercury in the wastewater processed at public treatment plants comes from dental amalgam. This is inexcusable, especially because devices that remove mercury from wastewater are inexpensive and easy for dental offices to use. While mercury amalgam should remain available because it is more durable than composites, every dental office must have a device to remove mercury from wastewater.

9. The topic of both passages is

   A. groundwater contamination
   B. mercury dental amalgam
   C. resin composite fillings
   D. dental health risks

10. What is the main argument of Passage 1?

    A. Mercury amalgam fillings are not unhealthy, but their disposal should be regulated for environmental reasons.
    B. Resin composite should replace mercury amalgam for dental fillings because it tends to last longer.
    C. Mercury amalgam fillings should be banned because they are unhealthy and bad for the environment.
    D. Mercury dental amalgam leaches mercury into a patient's mouth and can damage the liver.

11. Which statement best describes the supporting evidence in paragraph 3 of Passage 2?

    A. It appears convincing at first glance, but no source is cited.
    B. It is a seemingly convincing statistic, but the source is untrustworthy.
    C. It is an unconvincing statistic from an untrustworthy source.
    D. It is a convincing statistic from a reliable source.

12. In paragraph 3, the author of Passage 1 states that "These composites are already becoming popular due to their cosmetic appeal, so banning mercury amalgam will create no consumer backlash." Which of the following is an assumption the author of Passage 1 makes about consumers?

    A. Consumers have no other reason, such as cost or durability, to prefer mercury amalgam to composite fillings.
    B. Consumers will be happy with whatever material they are offered for dental fillings.
    C. Consumers are not generally vocal about their preferences.
    D. Consumers never discuss the choice of filling material with their dentists.

13. The writer of Passage 2 would be most likely to agree with which of the following statements?

    A. Mercury amalgam fillings should be banned because they are unhealthy.
    B. Resin composite fillings look better than mercury amalgam fillings when each is used on visible tooth surfaces.
    C. Mercury contamination of public wastewater is an unimportant issue.
    D. Resin composite fillings are preferable to mercury amalgam in all cases.

14. Which of the passages has weaker supporting evidence and why?

    A. Passage 1, because it cites no sources for the study or the statistic it cites
    B. Passage 1, because it argues that mercury should be banned in dental fillings
    C. Passage 2, because it cites the Environmental Protection Agency as the source of a statistic it cites
    D. Passage 2, because it argues that mercury used by dental offices should be better regulated

15. The information presented in Passage 2 suggests that Passage 1 includes which of the following examples of faulty reasoning?

    A. Resin composites are already gaining in popularity.
    B. The use of mercury dental amalgam has already been banned in several European nations.
    C. The mercury released from dental amalgam has damaging environmental consequences.
    D. Mercury that accumulates in body tissues causes a variety of health problems.

Plot Elements

Plot refers to the events in a story. Generally, the events are told in order—what happened first, next, and so on. Understanding the order of events, (the sequence) can help you see which events caused or affected others.

A story usually contains at least one **conflict**, or problem. The conflict may be between characters, within a character, or between a character and nature. Conflict creates tension. When it is resolved, the tension ends.

The following excerpt is about a brother and sister whose mother has a tumor. As you read it, look for the order of events and the conflict.

> Robert didn't phone until evening. His voice was fatigued and thin. "I've moved her to the university hospital," he said. "They can't deal with it at home."
>
> Kate waited, saying nothing. She concentrated on the toes of her shoes. They needed shining. *You never take care of anything*, her mother would say.
>
> "She has a tumor in her head." He said it firmly, as though Kate might challenge him.
>
> "I'll take a plane tomorrow morning," Kate answered, "I'll be there by noon."
>
> Robert exhaled. "Look," he said, "don't even come back here unless you can keep your mouth shut and do it my way."
>
> "Get to the point."
>
> "The point is they believe she has a malignancy and we're not going to tell her. I almost didn't tell you." His voice faltered. "They're going to operate but if they find what they're expecting, they don't think they can stop it."
>
> For a moment there was no sound except an oceanic vibration of distance on the wire. Even that sound grew still. Robert breathed. Kate could almost see him, in a booth at the hospital, staring straight ahead at the plastic instructions screwed to the narrow rectangular body of the telephone. It seemed to her that she was hurtling toward him.

From "Souvenir" by Jayne Anne Phillips, from *Black Tickets*, NY: Delacorte Press, 1979. Reprinted with permission of Jayne Anne Phillips.

▶ When did Robert decide not to tell his mother about the tumor?
    (1) before talking to Kate
    (2) after discussing the issue with Kate

(1) is correct. Robert has already decided what to do when he calls Kate.

▶ Which of the following identifies a conflict in this excerpt?
    (1) Kate tells Robert she will fly there tomorrow.
    (2) Robert tells Kate that she must do as he says.

(2) is correct. Robert challenges Kate. That creates tension.

PRACTICE 1

Questions 1 through 4 refer to the following excerpt from a short story.

EXCERPTED FROM "THE PIECE OF STRING"

1   The countryman looked at the Mayor in astonishment, already terrified by this suspicion resting on him without his knowing why.

2   "Me? Me? I picked up the pocket-book?"

3   "Yes, you, yourself."

4   "On my word of honor, I never heard of it."

5   "But you were seen."

6   "I was seen, me? Who says he saw me?"

7   "Monsieur Malandain, the harness-maker."

8   The old man remembered, understood, and flushed with anger.

9   "Ah, he saw me, the clodhopper, he saw me pick up this string, here, Mayor." And rummaging in his pocket he drew out the little piece of string.

10   But the Mayor, incredulous, shook his head.

11   "You will not make me believe, Maître Hauchecorne, that Monsieur Malandain, who is a man we can believe, mistook this cord for a pocket-book."

12   The peasant, furious, lifted his hand, spat at one side to attest his honor, repeating:

13   "It is nevertheless God's own truth, the sacred truth. I repeat it on my soul and my salvation."

14   The Mayor resumed:

15   "After picking up the object, you stood like a stilt, looking a long while in the mud to see if any piece of money had fallen out."

16   The old fellow choked with indignation and fear. . . .

17   He was confronted with Monsieur Malandain, who repeated and maintained his affirmation. They abused each other for an hour. At his own request, Maître Hauchecorne was searched. Nothing was found on him.

18   Finally the Mayor, very much perplexed, discharged him with the warning that he would consult the Public Prosecutor and ask for further orders.

From *Collected Novels and Stories* by Guy de Maupassant, translated by Ernest Boyd, copyright 1922 and renewed 1950 by Alfred A. Knopf, a Division of Random House, Inc. Used by permission of Alfred A. Knopf, a division of Random House, Inc.

1. What was the peasant doing when he "lifted his hand, spat at one side to attest his honor" (paragraph 12)?

   A. thinking of striking the Mayor
   B. swearing that he was telling the truth
   C. pleading to the Mayor for mercy
   D. performing a peasant ritual

2. How did the peasant react when confronted with Malandain, the harness-maker?

   He

   A. became choked with fear and indignation
   B. tried to explain what had actually happened
   C. became respectful and subdued
   D. confronted him and then asked to be searched

3. Which of the following statements best describes the conflict in this excerpt?

   A. A town mayor is abusing his authority.
   B. A peasant leads a harsh life and is often at odds with others.
   C. A peasant is accused of taking a pocketbook.
   D. Someone has lost a pocketbook with a great deal of money in it.

4. What is the most likely reason the harnessmaker is believed?

   A. A string can't be mistaken for a pocketbook.
   B. The peasant was looking in the mud for money.
   C. The harness-maker is higher in social status than the peasant.
   D. Other people saw the peasant pick up a pocketbook.

Inferences

To understand a story, you can't just rely on what is directly stated. You also need to "read between the lines," or make **inferences.** An inference is based on information you are given *plus* what you have learned about the real world—the way things happen and the way people act.

As you read this excerpt from a story, look for suggested meanings behind people's actions and words.

> "Last night?" The old blue eyes looked blank, then brightened. "Ah no, I must have taken one of my Seconals. Otherwise I'd have heard it surely. 'Auntie,' my niece always says—'what if there should be a fire, and you there sleeping away?' Do what she says, I do sometimes, only to hear every pin drop till morning." She shook her head, entering the elevator. "Going up?"
>
> "N-no," said Mrs. Hazlitt. "I—have to wait here for a minute." She sat down on the bench, the token bench that she had never seen anybody sitting on, and watched the car door close on the little figure still shaking its head, borne upward like a fairy godmother, willing but unable to oblige. The car's hum stopped, then its light glowed on again. Someone else was coming down. . . .
>
> The car door opened. "Wssht!" said Miss Finan, scuttling out again. "I've just remembered. Not last night, but two weeks ago. And once before that. A scream, you said?"
>
> Mrs. Hazlitt stood up. Almost unable to speak, for the tears that suddenly wrenched her throat, she described it.

From "The Scream on Fifty-Seventh Street" by Hortense Calisher, from *Tales for the Mirror*, reprinted in *Women and Fiction*, edited by Susan Cahill, New York: New American Library, 1975.

► What happened before the beginning of this excerpt?
   (1) Mrs. Hazlitt heard a scream the night before and asked Miss Finan if she heard it too.
   (2) Mrs. Hazlitt asked Miss Finan about her health and whether she is sleeping well.

The correct answer is **(1).** You can infer it from details such as "Last night?" and "Not last night, but two weeks ago. And once before that. A scream, you said?"

► What is the most likely reason that "tears suddenly wrenched" Mrs. Hazlitt's throat?
   (1) She was upset at Miss Finan's inability to remember.
   (2) She was relieved that Miss Finan had heard a scream too.

You are correct if you chose **(2).** Mrs. Hazlitt is so relieved that someone else heard the scream that she has to fight back tears.

PRACTICE 2

Questions 1 through 4 refer to the following excerpt from a short story.

EXCERPTED FROM "THE STORY OF AN HOUR"

1   [Louise] knew that she would weep again when she saw [her husband's] kind, tender hands folded in death; the face that had never looked save with love upon her, fixed and gray and dead. But she saw beyond that bitter moment a long procession of years to come that would belong to her absolutely. And she opened and spread her arms out to them in welcome.

2   There would be no one to live for during those coming years; she would live for herself. There would be no powerful will bending her in that blind persistence with which men and women believe they have a right to impose a private will upon a fellow creature. A kind intention or a cruel intention made the act seem no less a crime as she looked upon it in that brief moment of illumination.

3   And yet she had loved him—sometimes. Often she had not. What did it matter! What could love, the unsolved mystery, count for in face of this possession of self-assertion, which she suddenly recognized as the strongest impulse of her being!

4   "Free! Body and soul free!" she kept whispering . . .

5   Some one was opening the front door with a latchkey. It was [her husband] Brently Mallard who entered, a little travel-stained, composedly carrying his grip-sack and umbrella. He had been far from the scene of accident, and did not even know there had been one. He stood amazed at [her sister] Josephine's piercing cry; at Richards' quick motion to screen him from the view of his wife.

6   But Richards was too late.

7   When the doctors came they said she had died of heart disease—of joy that kills.

From "The Story of an Hour" by Kate Chopin.

1. How did Brently Mallard generally feel toward his wife?

He

A. had always loved her
B. kept her at arm's length
C. liked to play practical jokes on her
D. had cruel intentions toward her

2. Which detail best expresses Louise's vision of her future?

A. that bitter moment
B. she'd weep again
C. spread her arms out in welcome
D. blind persistence

3. What was the doctors' meaning when they said that Louise died of "joy that kills" (paragraph 7)?

They thought that

A. she was overcome and thrilled to see her husband
B. she was excited about her upcoming life of freedom
C. her heart was worn out from giving so much love
D. her heart was weakened from the strain of living

4. Why did Louise die?

A. She was overcome with relief.
B. She was shocked that she would not be free.
C. She was confused by feelings of love and hate.
D. She thought there would be no one to live for.

STUDY ADVICE

As you're getting settled into your study schedule, remember to build in rewards and breaks. Celebrate a job well done with a fun outing. Commemorate your successes in practice with a study partner or with your cheering section (family or friends). You need these moments to build confidence, which is a necessary component of success.

Character

Characters are the people who inhabit a story. The personalities and motivations of characters are often stated directly by the **narrator**—the person telling the story. Sometimes you can also infer characters' personalities or motivations by what they do, what they think, and what they say.

As you read this excerpt, look for details that describe each character.

> Axel Olsen was going to paint Helga Crane. Not only was he going to paint her, but he was to accompany her and her aunt on their shopping expedition. Aunt Katrina was frankly elated. Uncle Poul was also visibly pleased. Evidently they were not above kowtowing to a lion. Helga's own feelings were mixed; she was amused, grateful, and vexed. It had all been decided and arranged without her, and, also, she was a little afraid of Olsen. His stupendous arrogance awed her.
>
> The day was an exciting, not easily to be forgotten one. Definitely, too, it conveyed to Helga her exact status in her new environment. A decoration. A curio. A peacock. Their progress through the shops was an event; an event for Copenhagen as well as for Helga Crane. Her dark, alien appearance was to most people an astonishment. Some stared surreptitiously, some openly, and some stopped dead in front of her in order more fully to profit by their stares. "*Den Sorte*" dropped freely, audibly, from many lips.
>
> The time came when she grew used to the stares of the population. And the time came when the population of Copenhagen grew used to her outlandish presence and ceased to stare. But at the end of that first day it was with thankfulness that she returned to the sheltering walls of the house on Maria Kirkplads.

From "Quicksand" by Nella Larsen, in *The Norton Anthology of African American Literature*, edited by Henry Louis Gates, Jr., and Nellie Y. McKay, New York: W.W. Norton, 1997.

▶ Which of the following describes Helga?
   (1) attractive, down-to-earth, embarking on a new life
   (2) self-centered, smug, enjoys being watched

Choice **(1)** is correct. An artist is painting her, suggesting she is attractive. Yet she prefers not to be the center of attention (see the end of the last paragraph).

▶ Which of the following would Olsen most likely do at a party?
   (1) snub the hostess if the wine was below his expectations
   (2) offer to drive anyone home who needed a ride

Choice **(1)** is correct. Apply what you know about people with "stupendous arrogance" (see the end of the first paragraph) to answer this question.

KEY IDEAS

- Characters are the people in the story.
- You can understand a character by noting what the narrator tells you directly as well as by inferring from the character's appearance, actions, words, and thoughts.

ON THE TASC TEST

A common kind of question asks you to choose how a character would act in a different situation, based on what you know about the character's personality.

PRACTICE 3

Questions 1 through 3 refer to the following excerpt from a story.

EXCERPTED FROM "HIZAKURIGE"

1   "I shall never forget it," the witch went on. "When you were ill you gave your sickness to me. Our only child, who had to carry on our name, grew weak and thin because there was no rice to fill his empty stomach. Every day the bill collectors were knocking at the door and the rent remained unpaid. Yet I did not complain—not even when I slipped in the dogs' dirt in the lane."

2   "Don't talk of it," said Yaji. "You'll break my heart."

3   "And then, when through my labors I had saved enough money to buy a kimono, I had to pawn it for your sake and never saw it again. Never again did it come back to me from the pawnbroker's."

4   "At the same time you must remember what a pleasant place you are in now," said Yaji, "while I have to worry along down here."

5   "What? What is there pleasant about it? It is true that by the help of your friends you erected a stone over my grave, but you never go near it, and you never contribute to the temple to get the priests to say prayers for my soul. I am nothing to you. The stone over my grave has been taken away and put into the wall, where all the dogs come and make water against it. Not a drop of water is ever placed on my grave. Truly in death we suffer all sorts of troubles."

6   "True, true," said Yaji.

7   "But while you thus treat me with neglect," the witch went on, "lying in my grave I think of nobody but you and long for the time when you will join me in the underworld. Shall I come to meet you?"

8   "No, no, don't do that," said Yaji. "It's really too far for you."

9   "Well then, I have one request to make."

10   "Yes, yes. What is it?"

11   "Give this witch plenty of money."

12   "Of course, of course."

13   "How sad the parting!" cried the witch. "I have yet much to tell you, countless questions to ask you, but the messenger of Hell recalls me!"

14   Then, recovering from her trance, the witch twanged her bow.

From "Hizakurige" by Jippensha Ikku in *The Longwood Introduction to Fiction*, Boston: Allyn and Bacon, 1992.

1. Why does Yaji say, "No, no, don't do that . . . It's really too far for you" (paragraph 8)?

   A. He is trying to be more considerate than he had been in the past.
   B. He is reluctant to see the ghost of his wife.
   C. He has no real interest in seeing his wife again.
   D. His wife can't really travel to him anyway.

2. Which of the following is the best description of the witch?

   A. caring
   B. unconvincing
   C. untrustworthy
   D. thoughtful

3. Earlier in the story the witch, speaking as Yaji's wife, says, "Ah, what agony I went through when I was married to you—time and again suffering the pangs of hunger and shivering with cold in the winter."

Based on this information and the excerpt, what kind of husband did Yaji seem to be?

   A. angry
   B. kind-hearted
   C. responsible
   D. neglectful

Theme

Every story has a subject. The subject might be about fighting a war or growing up in poverty. But there is more to a story than its subject. As a reader, look for what the author is trying to say about the subject. That is the **theme**—the message the author wants the reader to understand. In fiction, the theme is often a statement about life. For example, the theme might be that fighting in a war changes a person's life forever.

The theme may be directly stated. If it is not, you can infer the theme from the characters' thoughts and actions and from the things that happen in the story.

As you read the following excerpt, ask yourself what message about the people and their lives the author is trying to tell you.

> While the boys were getting the Doctor's horse, he went to the window to examine the house plants. "What do you do to your geraniums to keep them blooming all winter, Mary? I never pass this house that from the road I don't see your windows full of flowers."
>
> She snapped off a dark red one, and a ruffled new green leaf, and put them in his buttonhole. "There, that looks better. You look too solemn for a young man, Ed. Why don't you git married? I'm worried about you. . . ."
>
> Sometimes the Doctor heard the gossipers in the drugstore wondering why Rosicky didn't get on faster. He was industrious, and so were his boys, but they were rather free and easy, weren't pushers, and they didn't always show good judgment. They were comfortable, they were out of debt, but they didn't get much ahead. Maybe, Doctor Burleigh reflected, people as generous and warmhearted and affectionate as the Rosickys never got ahead much; maybe you couldn't enjoy your life and put it into the bank, too.

From "Neighbor Rosicky" by Willa Cather, from *Obscure Destinies*.

► Which of the following statements is the theme of the story?
  (1) A good life is measured in terms of love, not money.
  (2) People should not gossip about others.

You are correct if you chose **(1)**. Doctor Burleigh's thoughts at the end of the excerpt help you understand that this is the author's main message.

► Which of the following details supports the theme?
  (1) Mary Rosicky lovingly "worries" about the doctor.
  (2) The Rosickys keep out of debt.

Again, you are correct if you chose **(1)**. The flowers Mary grows, the fact that she snaps off one to give the doctor, and her expressed concern for him all show her warmth and happiness. They help support the theme that the doctor reflects on.

PRACTICE 4

Questions 1 through 5 refer to the following excerpt from a short story.

EXCERPTED FROM *GONE FISHIN'*

1   Early morning is the best time. You're fully rested but not awake enough to remember how hard it all is. Morning is like being a child again, and morning before the sun is out is like those magic times that you hid under the bed and in between the clothes hanging in your mother's closet. Times when any kind of miracle could come about just as normal as a spider making her web.

2   I remember waking up in the dark once when I was very small. I jumped right out of bed and went up next to the screen door on the back porch to see what kind of fantastic thing was going on outside. At first I couldn't see anything but there was a clopping sound, nickering, and a deep voice that made me feel calm and wondering. Slowly, coming out from the darkness, I saw a gray shimmering next to a tall black pillar. The shimmer turned into a big horse and the pillar became my father holding out an apple and cooing in his bass voice, "Ho! Yeah, boy," even though the horse was tame and eating from his hand.

3   I drifted into sleep thinking that we were poor and didn't own a horse. When I woke up it was light and there was no horse to be seen. I asked my father about it but he told me that I was dreaming—where were poor people like us going to find big gray stallions?

4   But there were horse chips behind the barn and hoofprints too.

5   I decided that it was a magic horse and man that I'd seen. From that day on I believed that magic hides in the early morning. If you get up early enough you might find something so beautiful that it would be all right if you just died right then because nothing else in life could ever be better.

From *Gone Fishin'* by Walter Mosley, Baltimore: Black Classic Press, 1997.

1. In the story, the boy _____ after hearing his father's explanation.

    A. feels confused
    B. finds a new explanation
    C. no longer trusts his father
    D. tries to convince his father

2. Which of the following is the best description of the boy?

    A. hard-hearted
    B. imaginative
    C. skeptical
    D. chatty

3. What is the most likely reason the boy decides he saw a magic horse and man?

    A. He wants to reconcile what he saw with what his father told him.
    B. He enjoys magic and likes to make up stories.
    C. He wants to prove his father was mistaken.
    D. This kind of miracle can happen.

4. Which of the following would the father probably enjoy most?

    A. daydreaming about the future
    B. having enough money to pay some bills
    C. keeping his son's hopes up about getting a new bicycle for his birthday
    D. sharing ghost stories around a campfire

5. Which of the following statements fits the theme of this story?

    A. False hopes will not get you anywhere.
    B. Dreams really can come true.
    C. Adults cannot see what children see.
    D. Morning and youth are full of possibility.

STUDY ADVICE

Remember, you'll be able to work on more questions at the end of this chapter. So, if you are struggling with a topic and don't feel you have more time to spend on it right now, flag it for later! Keeping a good list of what you should come back to is important in organizing your study plan.

Style and Point of View

Style

A writer has many choices when deciding how to write a story. A writer may use long, complex sentences; short, clipped sentences; or anything in between. A writer may use flowery or formal language, slang, or spoken dialect. One writer may use vivid images or symbols, while another writes a plain, spare story. The individual characteristics that a writer chooses—sentence structure, choice of words, use of images, and other devices—are all part of the writer's **style.**

As you read this excerpt, look for the characteristics that this particular author chose. Ask yourself what effect they have on your understanding of the writing.

> The only part of the night I recall without feeling anger or sadness is loading the horses. Andy and I hardly had the fencing up before Brett came along with the first ten or twelve. . . . A couple of roans and an Appaloosa stood out in that first bunch in the starlight, and a bay with a roached mane. Then Ed brought up a second bunch, about fifteen mostly dark but a palomino and two paints in there, I remember. Andy and I shooed them up the ramp, which clattered and thundered under their hooves. It was a cool night, still. I could feel the horses on my skin, their body heat swirling around us. I could . . . hear their nostrils fluttering. I felt hard muscle ripple under my hand when I clapped a hip to steer them around. I felt their tails slap my back, and caught a glint in their bared eyes.

From "Stolen Horses" by Barry Lopez, from *Writers Harvest 3*, edited by Tobias Wolff, copyright © 2000 by Share Our Strength. Used by permission of Dell Publishing, a division of Random House, Inc.

▶ What is the effect of the author's description of the horses?
  (1) It creates a depth of feeling for the horses' vitality.
  (2) It provides insight into what the characters are doing.

You are correct if you chose **(1).** The vivid, descriptive details allow you to imagine the horses and sense their vitality and strength.

Point of View

Another choice a writer makes is which **point of view** to write from. Will the narrator be outside the story, watching and revealing the characters' actions and perhaps even their thoughts and feelings? If so, the writer will use *third person* point of view. Or will the narrator be a character in the story, able to report only what he or she thinks? In that case, the writer will use *first person* point of view.

▶ Which of the following indicates that the narrator is a character and so we can know only his thoughts?
  (1) "The only part of the night I recall . . ."
  (2) "Then Ed brought up a second bunch . . ."

(1) is correct. The narrator tells his own thoughts. A clue is the word *I*.

PRACTICE 5

Questions 1 through 4 refer to the following excerpt from a short story called "Coach."

EXCERPTED FROM *AN AMATEUR'S GUIDE TO THE NIGHT*

1   "This apartment your mom found is like an office or something. A studio for her to go to and get away every now and then. . . ."

2   "She wants to get away from us," Daphne said.

3   "Definitely not. She gave me a list, is how this whole thing started. She's got stuff she wants to do, and you with your school problems and me with the team—we're too much for her, see? She could spend her entire day on us, if you think about it, and never have one second for herself. If you think about it fairly, Daphne, you'll agree." . . .

4   She made a sigh and marched over to a trash can to deposit her slumping cone. Then she washed up at the children's drinking fountain and rejoined Coach, who had finished his Brown Cow but had kept the plastic spoon in the mouth.

5   "What was on this list of Mom's?" Daphne asked.

6   "Adult stuff," Coach said.

7   "Just give me an example."

8   Coach removed the plastic spoon and cracked it in half.

9   "Your mother's list is for five years. In that time, she wants to be speaking French regularly. She wants to follow up on her printmaking."

10   "This is adult stuff?" Daphne said.

11   Coach raised a hand to Bobby Stark. Stark had three malt cups in a cardboard carrier and he was moving toward the parking lot.

12   "Hey, those all for you?" Coach called out.

13   "I got a month to get fat, Coach. You'll have five months to beat it off me," the boy called back.

14   The people at some of the tables around Coach's lit up with grins. Bobby Stark's parents were grinning.

15   "Every hit of that junk takes a second off your time in the forty—just remember that!" Coach shouted.

16   Stark wagged his head ruefully, his cheeks blushing. He pretended to hide the malts behind his arm.

From *An Amateur's Guide to the Night* by Mary Robison, copyright © 2001, reprinted with the permission of The Wylie Agency, Inc.

1. What is Bobby Stark's attitude?

   A. He worries about his weight problem.
   B. He takes things in stride.
   C. He is looking forward to the sports season.
   D. He feels unfairly criticized by the coach.

2. Because of the narrator's point of view, what does the reader know?

   A. only Bobby Stark's actions
   B. thoughts and feelings of the characters
   C. the actions and speech of the characters
   D. only Daphne's thoughts and feelings

3. Through their dialogue, what kind of relationship can you conclude the characters have with each other?

   A. informal
   B. tense
   C. suspicious
   D. deteriorating

4. Later in the story, Coach has this discussion with his wife, Sherry: "'It's like my apartment,' Sherry said. 'A place apart.' Coach cut her off. 'Don't go on about how much you love your apartment.'"

Based on this information and the excerpt, which of the following best describes Coach in his discussion with Daphne?

   A. brutally frank
   B. angry and hostile
   C. loving and warm
   D. not entirely honest about his feelings

Figurative Language

Figurative language refers to words that are being used to mean something other than their actual, literal meaning. Writers and poets use figurative language to help paint a mental picture in the reader's mind. Instead of saying, "His voice was soothing and pleasing," for example, a writer might say, "His voice was like velvet."

Figurative language often compares two different things. Sometimes the comparison is signaled by the words *like* or *as*, but not always. A writer might also say, "His voice was velvet." Another favorite technique of writers and poets is to give a human characteristic to something nonhuman, such as, "The wind sighed."

As you read this poem, look for figurative language and what it might mean.

The School Children

The children go forward with their little satchels.
And all morning the mothers have labored
to gather the late apples, red and gold,
like words of another language.

And on the other shore
are those who wait behind great desks
to receive these offerings.

How orderly they are—the nails
on which the children hang
their overcoats of blue or yellow wool.

And the teachers shall instruct them in silence
and the mothers shall scour the orchards for a way out,
drawing to themselves the gray limbs of the fruit trees
bearing so little ammunition.

From "The House on Marshland" from *The First Four Books* by Louise Gluck. Copyright 1968, 1971, 1972, 1973, 1974, 1975, 1976, 1977, 1978, 1980, 1985, 1995.

▶ What is suggested by comparing apples to "words of another language" in the fourth line?
   (1) a sense of strangeness, not a part of one's world
   (2) useless things that have no meaning

You are correct if you chose **(1)**. A language different from your own can seem strange and removed. The mothers feel removed from the world of teachers and schoolchildren.

▶ What does the word *shore* in the fifth line refer to?
   (1) the other side of an ocean
   (2) the world of the classroom

You are correct if you chose **(2)**. The mothers in the poem think of school as far away from them.

PRACTICE 6

Questions 1 through 5 refer to the following poem.

EXCERPTED FROM "DÉJEUNER SUR L'HERBE" ("LUNCH ON THE GRASS")

1   It's pleasant to board the ferry in the sunscape
    As the late light slants into afternoon;
    The faint wind ruffles the river, rimmed with
        foam.
    We move through the aisles of bamboo
    Towards the cool water-lilies.

2   The young dandies drop ice into the drinks,
    While the girls slice the succulent lotus root.
    Above us, a patch of cloud spreads, darkening
    Like a water-stain on silk.

3   *Write this down quickly, before the rain!*

4   Don't sit there! The cushions were soaked by
        the shower.
    Already the girls have drenched their crimson
        skirts.
    Beauties, their powder streaked with mascara,
        lament their ruined faces.

5   The wind batters our boat, the mooring-line
    Has rubbed a wound in the willow bark.
    The edges of the curtains are embroidered by
        the river foam.

6   Like a knife in a melon, Autumn slices
    Summer.

7   *It will be cold, going back.*

Tu Fu, "Déjeuner sur l'herbe," translated by Carolyn Kizer, from *Carrying Over: Poems from the Chinese, Urdu, Macedonian, Yiddish, and French African.* Copyright © 1988 by Carolyn Kizer. Reprinted with the permission of The Permissions Company, Inc., on behalf of Copper Canyon Press, www.coppercanyonpress.org.

1. What is compared to "a water-stain on silk" (Stanza 2)?

   A. foam on the edge of the river
   B. rain clouds approaching
   C. lotus root juice on a tablecloth
   D. ice cubes dropping into cold drinks

2. What is meant by the statement "lament their ruined faces" (Stanza 4)?

   A. They could no longer smile.
   B. They were growing old.
   C. The rain caused their makeup to run.
   D. The wind was chapping their faces.

3. Why is "The edges of the curtains are embroidered by the river foam" (Stanza 5) an effective use of figurative language?

It helps the reader see that

   A. the people forgot to close the windows and curtains
   B. the wind is so strong that it is blowing spray from the river into the boat
   C. the curtains are beautifully edged with lace
   D. the river is rising quickly

4. According to the speaker, how was the change from summer to autumn (Stanza 6)?

   A. quick and easy
   B. halting and uncertain
   C. slow and predictable
   D. pleasant and smooth

5. Which of the following words best describe the tone of this poem?

   A. gentle and calm
   B. humorous and playful
   C. wry and observant
   D. dry and formal

STUDY ADVICE

The TASC Reading Test will include some passages from plays or poems. Use the same skills you've been learning to understand plays and poems: look for the author's point of view, tone, and use of figurative language.

Literary Text with Related Images

The TASC Reading Test may give you a literary text to compare to an image. The topic of both will be the same, and it will be up to you to determine their similarities and differences.

Note the similarities and differences between an excerpt of Washington Irving's 1819 short story "Rip Van Winkle" and James Hamilton's painting depicting a scene from the story:

> "On entering the amphitheatre, new objects of wonder presented themselves. On a level spot in the centre was a company of odd-looking personages playing at nine-pins [that is, bowling].
>
> They were dressed in a quaint outlandish fashion; some wore short doublets, others jerkins, with long knives in their belts, and most of them had enormous breeches, of similar style with that of the guide's . . . The whole group reminded Rip of the figures in an old Flemish painting . . .
>
> By degrees Rip's awe and apprehension subsided. He even ventured, when no eye was fixed upon him, to taste the beverage, which he found had much of the flavor of excellent Hollands [gin]. He was naturally a thirsty soul, and was soon tempted to repeat the draught. [Eventually] he fell into a deep sleep."

Excerpted from Washington Irving's "Rip Van Winkle," 1819.

Detail from James Hamilton's *Scene on the Hudson (Rip Van Winkle)*, 1845.

Example 1: Which of the following is depicted in the excerpt from the story but *not* in the painting?
(1) Rip's fascination with the men playing nine-pins
(2) Rip drinking until he relaxed

Choice **(1)** is correct. In the excerpt, Rip Van Winkle stares with "wonder" at the men. In the painting, Rip is facing away from the men, absorbed in his drinking. Both the excerpt and the painting depict Van Winkle drinking until he relaxed. In the excerpt, the phrases "his eyes swam in his head, his head gradually declined, and he fell into a deep sleep" signal that Rip is relaxing. In the painting, Rip's posture, sprawled on the ground, indicates the same thing.

PRACTICE 7

<u>Question 1</u> is based on the excerpt and image on the previous page.

1. Which of the following important characters mentioned in the excerpt is not noticeable in the painting?

A. Rip's dog
B. the Flemish painter
C. Rip's companion
D. Rip himself

<u>Questions 2 and 3</u> are based on the excerpt below.

Later in "Rip Van Winkle," Rip awakes to find that he has slept through the Revolutionary War. He returns to his village, only to find it greatly changed.

> He now hurried forth, and hastened to his old resort, the village inn—but it too was gone. A large rickety wooden building stood in its place, with great gaping windows . . . and over the door was painted, "the Union Hotel, by Jonathan Doolittle." Instead of the great tree that used to shelter the quiet little Dutch inn of yore, there now was reared a tall naked pole . . . and from it was fluttering a flag, on which was a singular assemblage of stars and stripes—all this was strange and incomprehensible. He recognized on the sign, however, the ruby face of King George, under which he had smoked so many a peaceful pipe; but even this was singularly metamorphosed. The red coat was changed for one of blue and buff, a sword was held in the hand instead of a sceptre, the head was decorated with a cocked hat, and underneath was painted in large characters, General Washington.

Excerpted from Washington Irving's "Rip Van Winkle," 1819.

2. **Part One:** What is Rip's impression of the changes he finds in his village?

A. He thinks the village is more charming than before.
B. He finds the changes unsettling.
C. He likes the fact that the village has been modernized.
D. He is unhappy about the alteration to the sign, but pleased to see the new Union Hotel.

Part Two: Which of the following phrases justifies your response? Select two.

☐ "assemblage of stars and stripes"
☐ "painted in large characters"
☐ "decorated with a cocked hat"
☐ "strange and incomprehensible "
☐ "singularly metamorphosed"

3. Compare the image on the Union Hotel sign described in the excerpt to the image of George Washington on a one-dollar bill, shown above. Which of the following describes a noteworthy difference?

A. While the dollar bill was drawn to depict George Washington, the face on the Union Hotel sign was originally that of King George.
B. The facial expression of George Washington is serious in the image on the dollar bill but smiling in the image on the Union Hotel sign.
C. George Washington's hair is powdered in the image on the dollar bill, but dark brown on the Union Hotel sign.
D. The portrait on the Union Hotel sign includes a pipe, while the portrait on the dollar bill does not.

READING LITERATURE PRACTICE QUESTIONS

Questions 1 through 3 refer to the following excerpt from a story.

EXCERPTED FROM *SHILOH & OTHER STORIES*

1   Leroy Moffitt's wife, Norma Jean, is working on her pectorals. She lifts three-pound dumbbells to warm up, then progresses to a twenty-pound barbell. Standing with her legs apart, she reminds Leroy of Wonder Woman.

2   "I'd give anything if I could just get these muscles to where they're real hard," says Norma Jean. "Feel this arm. It's not as hard as the other one."

3   "That's cause you're right-handed," says Leroy, dodging as she swings the barbell in an arc.

4   "Do you think so?"

5   "Sure."

6   Leroy is a truckdriver. He injured his leg in a highway accident four months ago, and his physical therapy, which involves weights and a pulley, prompted Norma Jean to try building herself up. Now she is attending a body-building class. Leroy has been collecting temporary disability since his tractor-trailer jackknifed in Missouri, badly twisting his left leg in its socket. He has a steel pin in his hip. He will probably not be able to drive his rig again. It sits in the backyard, like a gigantic bird that has flown home to roost. Leroy has been home in Kentucky for three months, and his leg is almost healed, but the accident frightened him and he does not want to drive any more long hauls. He is not sure what to do next. In the meantime, he makes things from craft kits. He started by building a miniature log cabin from notched Popsicle sticks. He varnished it and placed it on the TV set, where it remains. It reminds him of a rustic Nativity scene. Then he tried string art (sailing ships on black velvet), a macramé owl kit, a snap-together B-17 Flying

Fortress, and a lamp made out of a model truck, with a light fixture screwed in the top of the cab. At first the kits were diversions, something to kill time, but now he is thinking about building a full-scale log house from a kit. It would be considerably cheaper than building a regular house, and besides, Leroy has grown to appreciate how things are put together. He has begun to realize that in all the years he was on the road he never took time to examine anything. He was always flying past scenery.

Excerpt from *Shiloh & Other Stories* by Bobbie Ann Mason. Reprinted by permission of International Creative Management, Inc. Copyright © 1982 by Bobbie Ann Mason.

1. Which of the following best describes Leroy's wife, Norma Jean?

   A. shy
   B. loving
   C. self-concerned
   D. grumpy

2. By comparing Leroy's truck to a bird that has flown home to roost, the author suggests that Leroy _____.

   A. comes and goes as he pleases
   B. always preferred to be at home "nesting"
   C. won't be driving his truck for a while
   D. is a bit "flighty" and unpredictable

3. Why might Leroy be continually making things from craft kits?

   Because he

   A. is impatient with his leg healing
   B. has always enjoyed working with his hands
   C. grew tired of bodybuilding
   D. doesn't want to consider what to do next

Questions 4 through 7 refer to this excerpt from a story.

EXCERPTED FROM *WINTER'S TALES*

1   A small sailor-boy, named Simon, stood on the wet, swinging deck, held on to a shroud, and looked up towards the drifting clouds, and to the upper top-gallant yard of the main-mast.

2   A bird, that had sought refuge upon the mast, had got her feet entangled in some loose tackle-yarn of the halliard, and, high up there, struggled to get free. The boy on the deck could see her wings flapping and her head turning from side to side.

3   Through his own experience of life he had come to the conviction that in this world everyone must look after himself, and expect no help from others. But the mute, deadly fight kept him fascinated for more than an hour. He wondered what kind of bird it would be. These last days a number of birds had come to settle in the barque's rigging: swallows, quails, and a pair of peregrine falcons; he believed that this bird was a peregrine falcon. He remembered how, many years ago, in his own country and near his home, he had once seen a peregrine falcon quite close, sitting on a stone and flying straight up from it. Perhaps this was the same bird. He thought: "That bird is like me. Then she was there, and now she is here."

4   At that a fellow-feeling rose in him, a sense of common tragedy; he stood looking at the bird with his heart in his mouth. There were none of the sailors about to make fun of him; he began to think out how he might go up by the shrouds to help the falcon out. He brushed his hair back and pulled up his sleeves, gave the deck round him a great glance, and climbed up. He had to stop a couple of times in the swaying rigging.

5   It was indeed, he found when he got to the top of the mast, a peregrine falcon. As his head was on a level with hers, she gave up her struggle, and looked at him with a pair of angry, desperate yellow eyes.

6   He had to take hold of her with one hand while he got his knife out, and cut off the tackle-yarn. He was scared as he looked down, but at the same time he felt that he had been ordered up by nobody, but that this was his own venture, and this gave him a proud, steadying sensation, as if the sea and the sky, the ship, the bird and himself were all one.

From *Winter's Tales* by Isak Dinesen, Random House, Inc. ©1942.

4. What can you infer about the boy's decision to climb the rig?

A. It took some courage.
B. It was a familiar task.
C. It felt like a chore.
D. He was ordered to do it.

5. Which of the following best describes both the boy and the bird at the beginning of the excerpt?

A. confident
B. alone
C. scared
D. wary

6. Which ideas are most clearly contrasted in this excerpt?

A. love and hate
B. youth and experience
C. fear and fearlessness
D. loneliness and sense of belonging

7. The word _____ best describes the mood created by the author in this excerpt.

A. mournful
B. nostalgic
C. peaceful
D. triumphant

EXCERPTED FROM "THE LEGEND OF SLEEPY HOLLOW"

1   "Who are you?" He received no reply. He repeated his demand in a still more agitated voice. Still there was no answer. Once more he cudgelled the sides of the inflexible Gunpowder, and, shutting his eyes, broke forth with involuntary fervor into a psalm-tune. Just then the shadowy object of alarm put itself in motion, and, with a scramble and a bound, stood at once in the middle of the road. Though the night was dark and dismal, yet the form of the unknown might now in some degree be ascertained. He appeared to be a horseman of large dimensions, and mounted on a black horse of powerful frame. He made no offer of molestation or sociability, but kept aloof on one side of the road, jogging along on the blind side of old Gunpowder, who had now got over his fright and waywardness.

2   Ichabod, who had no relish for this strange midnight companion, and bethought himself of the adventure of Brom Bones with the Galloping Hessian, now quickened his steed, in hopes of leaving him behind. The stranger, however, quickened his horse to an equal pace. Ichabod pulled up, and fell into a walk, thinking to lag behind—the other did the same. His heart began to sink within him; he endeavored to resume his psalm-tune, but his parched tongue clove to the roof of his mouth, and he could not utter a stave. There was something in the moody and dogged silence of this pertinacious companion, that was mysterious and appalling. It was soon fearfully accounted for. On mounting a rising ground, which brought the figure of his fellow-traveller in relief against the sky, gigantic in height, and muffled in a cloak, Ichabod was horror-struck, on perceiving that he was headless!—but his horror was still more increased, on observing that the head, which should have rested on his shoulders, was carried before him on the pommel of the saddle: his terror rose to desperation; he rained a shower of kicks and blows upon Gunpowder, hoping, by a sudden movement, to give his companion the slip—but the spectre started full jump with him.

3   Away then they dashed, through thick and thin; stones flying, and sparks flashing at every bound. Ichabod's flimsy garments fluttered in the air, as he stretched his long lank body away over his horse's head, in the eagerness of his flight.

From "The Legend of Sleepy Hollow" by Washington Irving.

8. What is meant by "he endeavored to resume his psalm-tune" (paragraph 2)?

Ichabod Crane tried to

A. recite religious doctrine
B. ride more steadily
C. start singing again
D. think of a realistic solution

9. What is the effect of the author's use of words such as "dashed," "stones flying," and "sparks flashing" (paragraph 3)?

The words create a feeling of

A. panic
B. clumsiness
C. playfulness
D. magic

10. Which of the following best describes the mood of this excerpt?

A. angry
B. sorrowful
C. suspenseful
D. sentimental

11. Later in the story, the narrator implies that the horseman had a pumpkin on the pommel of his saddle. Given this additional information, Ichabod can best be described as _____ given his actions in the excerpt.

A. brave in the face of great danger
B. too scared to think rationally
C. moving too quickly
D. quick thinking in his escape

Questions 12 through 14 refer to this excerpt from a play.

A man named John Wright has been murdered, and the County Attorney and Sheriff are trying to determine whether Wright's wife might have had a motive.

EXCERPTED FROM *TRIFLES*

COUNTY ATTORNEY: Well, that's interesting, I'm sure. [*Seeing the birdcage.*] Has the bird flown?

MRS. HALE: [*Putting more quilt pieces over the box.*] We think the—cat got it.

COUNTY ATTORNEY: [*Preoccupied.*] Is there a cat?

[*MRS. HALE glances in a quick covert way at MRS. PETERS.*]

MRS. PETERS: Well, not now. They're superstitious, you know. They leave.

COUNTY ATTORNEY: [*To SHERIFF PETERS, continuing an interrupted conversation.*] No sign at all of anyone having come from the outside. Their own rope. Now let's go up again and go over it piece by piece. [*They start upstairs.*] It would have to have been someone who knew just the—

[*MRS. PETERS sits down. The two women sit there not looking at one another, but as if peering into something and at the same time holding back. When they talk now it is in the manner of feeling their way over strange ground, as if afraid of what they are saying, but as if they cannot help saying it.*]

MRS. HALE: She liked the bird. She was going to bury it in that pretty box.

MRS. PETERS: [*In a whisper.*] When I was a girl—my kitten—there was a boy took a hatchet, and before my eyes— and before I could get there—. [*Covers her face an instant.*] If they hadn't held me back I would have— [*Catches herself, looks upstairs where steps are heard, falters weakly.*]—hurt him.

MRS. HALE: [*With a slow look around her.*] I wonder how it would seem never to have had any children around. [*Pause.*] No, Wright wouldn't like the bird—a thing that sang. She used to sing. He killed that, too.

MRS. PETERS: [*Moving uneasily.*] We don't know who killed the bird.

MRS. HALE: I knew John Wright.

MRS. PETERS: It was an awful thing was done in this house that night, Mrs. Hale. Killing a man while he slept, slipping a rope around his neck that choked the life out of him.

MRS. HALE: His neck. Choked the life out of him. [*Her hand goes out and rests on the birdcage.*]

MRS. PETERS: [*With rising voice.*] We don't know who killed him. We don't know.

MRS. HALE: [*Her own feeling not interrupted.*] If there'd been years and years of nothing, then a bird to sing to you, it would be awful—still, after the bird was still.

Excerpted from *Trifles*, by Susan Glaspell, published by Penguin Putnam, Inc.

12. Who does Mrs. Hale think killed the bird?

A. John Wright
B. Mrs. Peters
C. the cat
D. Mrs. Wright

13. Based on the excerpt, which of the following best describes John Wright?

A. a person who is loving and attentive
B. someone who smothers all the joy in another person
C. a person capable of murder
D. someone devoted to law and order

14. Which of the following conclusions can you draw about Mrs. Peters and Mrs. Hale?

A. Together they committed murder.
B. Each one thinks the other one is the murderer.
C. They are eager to tell the police all they know.
D. They understand how someone could be driven to murder.

LANGUAGE ARTS: READING ANSWERS AND EXPLANATIONS

Interpreting Informational Text

Lesson 1: Main Ideas and Details

Practice 1

1. **A. searching for a place to call home** The author states this feeling directly in the first two lines and in the last paragraph.
2. **D. the gods** The second sentence in the second paragraph says, "It was ordained by the deities."
3. **D. It was simply part of their beliefs to follow the pole** The meaning of the pole is explained beginning with the fourth sentence of the second paragraph. The last sentence explains that the Chickasaws lacked sorrow because they trusted the pole's command.
4. **C. understands that her tendency to search is part of her Chickasaw heritage** The details about the author's search for a home, combined with the information that "the search for a homeland is part of the Chickasaw migration legend," helps you understand this main idea.
5. **D. accepts that she is Chickasaw** You can see that the writer is saying that her Chickasaw heritage is an inescapable part of who she is.

Lesson 2: Rephrasing and Summary

Practice 2

1. **C. lack of proper paperwork** As the writer discusses the problems, he states that he wants an "itemized list" and "a proper bill of sale." He does mention the premium price, choice (D), but that price is the reason he expects proper paperwork and is not a complaint in and of itself.
2. **B. the car to be repaired free of charge if the cause of the problem is discovered** This expectation is stated in the fifth paragraph of the letter.
3. **C. The service and warranty on the customer's car have been unacceptable.** The letter is a detailed list of the customer's complaints. They can be summed up by saying that both the service and the warranty have not been as promised.

Lesson 3: Application of Ideas

Practice 3

1. **A. overcoming a bad habit** The writer advises those trying to break free of credit card debt: "Stick with it until you're free again."
2. **B. never use the credit cards** The last paragraph implies that the author approves of using credit cards only once you have already gotten out of debt, and then only for convenience. Thus, if you are in debt, you should stop using your credit cards.
3. **C. losing weight by avoiding all-you-can-eat buffets** Basically, the advice is that you gradually lose your debt by not adding anything to it. This is similar to helping yourself lose weight by not adding to it with portions of food you don't need.
4. **C. "Live within your means."** This statement can be inferred from the advice "Don't borrow any more," and "What I'm against is buying more on your credit cards than you can pay for at the end of the month."

Lesson 4: Cause and Effect

Practice 4

1. **C. It affected nearly everyone.** This answer summarizes the meaning of the first two sentences of the passage.
2. **A. Many people lost the mortgages on their homes.** This answer is stated in the first paragraph: "men and women who saw their mortgages foreclosed." Choices (B) and (D) are both mentioned as causes, not effects, of the depression.
3. **B. low worker incomes** The second paragraph states, "but the actual cause of the collapse was an unhealthy economy. . . . Most laborers . . . could not afford to buy the automobiles . . . because their incomes were too low."
4. **B. They had little effect.** The writer tells what Herbert Hoover did as president to curb the depression ("loans to businesses and banks") but then states that "his efforts proved to be too little and too late."
5. **D. The depression left people emotionally scarred.** The first paragraph states, "No one who lived through those years . . . could ever completely forget." The statement about eating mustard that is provided in the question addresses this emotional effect rather than issues related to farmers, workers, the economy, or the number of individuals affected.

Lesson 5: Comparison and Contrast

Practice 5

1. **D. leave some of his possessions behind** This answer is found in the seventh and eighth lines of paragraph 1.
2. **C. They provided milk and pulled wagons.** The selection states that "cows . . . gave milk all the way to the sink of the Humboldt where they died, having acted as draught animals for several weeks after the oxen had perished."
3. **A. the provisions of each group of travelers** Each paragraph talks about a different group and what it had to offer the wagon train. For example, "Much in contrast to these men were four batchelors . . . , who had a wagon drawn by four oxen . . . cows following behind."
4. **A. be happy to have people who could cook and sew** The writer was interested in assessing how self-sufficient the group could be and what each group could offer the entire wagon train. For example, she writes, "but as he was a wagon maker and his companion a blacksmith by trade and both were accommodating there were always ready hands to 'pry the wheel out of mire.'"
5. **A. They must cooperate and work together.** Throughout the excerpt, there is evidence that all the travelers depended on each other for animals, food, and physical help, such as pulling wagons out of the mud.

Lesson 6: Conclusions and Generalizations

Practice 6.1

1. **A. It is rewarding and one of life's joys.** The passage states that "my teacher's genius . . . made the first years of my education so beautiful." She also delights in observing and learning from the tadpole.

2. **D. insightful and grateful** The writer has insight about the connection between herself and the tadpole: "Thus I learned from life itself. At the beginning I was only a little mass of possibilities." The writer is also grateful to her teacher: "nor has she ceased trying . . . to make my life sweet and useful."

3. **C. show Helen how addition is used in everyday life** You can apply what you learn in the diary entry: "Thus I learned from life itself. . . . She has never since let pass an opportunity to point out the beauty that is in everything. . . ." The teacher would therefore probably use everyday life situations to teach.

4. **D. as an anecdote followed by a generalization based on the anecdote** The writer tells the story of the tadpoles (an anecdote) and relates it to her attitude toward life and learning.

5. **D. Their development is not entirely smooth.** The writer describes the tadpole having difficulty after leaping out of the bowl. This is similar to the quotation about "the stony course" of a child's education.

Practice 6.2

1. **C. On the whole, temperatures are not rising.** The writer states that rising temperatures are "quite simply not what is happening," based on the cold temperatures of the day before.

2. **A. Shady Hollow was hit with a record cold temperature yesterday.** This one piece of information is the example the author uses to support the generalization that temperatures, generally speaking, are not rising.

3. **D. worldwide data tables of temperatures from the 1980s through today** The author's generalization suffers from being based on one temperature reading. His generalization would be more likely to be valid if informed by many temperature readings over time.

Lesson 7: Word Choice

Practice 7

1. **D. the CoolForter blanket** The first sentence of paragraph 2 tells you two things about the CoolForter blanket: that "it works like an electric blanket" and that "it feels like a dream."

2. **B. to show that the blanket is a pleasant indulgence** To "coddle" is to treat gently or take care of a person. Choice (B) describes this idea.

3. **A. fluid** Many people associate the word *chemical* with toxicity or harm. A more neutral word to describe the cooling substance without inaccurate specificity is *fluid*.

4. **C. bland** The word *bland* indicates a lack of interesting features. Unlike the word *neutral*, which also indicates a lack of characteristic features, the word *bland* can carry a negative connotation.

5. **D. It allows the consumer to compare the CoolForter's energy usage to that of a familiar item.** The author's choice of a light bulb, an item with which most readers are probably familiar, emphasizes that the CoolForter blanket will not use excessive amounts of energy.

Lesson 8: Defining a Word Using Context

Practice 8

1. These are sample answers; your answers may differ somewhat.
   a. Amelia's hat and mittens are at the back of the closet, so perhaps she does not have to wear them often. The snowstorm is described as *freak*—that is, unusual. Amelia is cheered up by the idea that the snowstorm is an anomaly, so that must be a good thought.
   b. *Anomaly* means *a very unusual event.*

2.

	Suggests Jo's has good clothes	Suggests Jo's has bad clothes
Nevertheless,		X
Accordingly,	X	
Not surprisingly,	X	
However,		X
Therefore,	X	
Yet		X
That's why	X	

Words that indicate a contrast would suggest that Jo's has bad clothes. Contrast words include *nevertheless, however, yet, but, regardless, on the contrary,* and others. Words that indicate similarity or that two things go together logically would suggest that Jo's has good clothes. Such words would include *accordingly, not surprisingly, therefore, that's why, indeed, hence, similarly,* and others.

3. **C. argument** Context clues from the passage include the fact that the MacAllisters were not speaking to each other much and that their silence was tense. Therefore, they probably had an argument or disagreement before their guests arrived.

4. **B. arrogance** Focus on what you learn about the professor: he sneers and insults his students' work. That suggests that he is unpleasant and arrogant. While a student might be disappointed if her professor was ignorant (D) or provided poor instruction (A), this professor's lectures were "educational." Therefore, choices (A) and (D) are incorrect. Choice (C) is unsupported: just because the professor is unpleasant, he is not necessarily distant.

Lesson 9: Writer's Tone and Point of View

Practice 9

1. **C. the Internet writers** The writer mentions "Internet sass" and then goes on to say that "you gotta love it" because it keeps writers "off the street and out of trouble."

2. **A. The Internet reviews were much more interesting than the TV show.** The review states, "They [Internet writers] were taking hours and hours of

primetime dross and turning it into decadent, amoral, sharp, electronic gold."

3. **A. The show was boring.** The reviewer's main opinion of the show is that it was bad and boring ("non-goings-on of the non-people in the non-house"). Someone yawning supports the idea of boredom.

4. **C. informal and hip** Phrases such as "the dude" and "you gotta love it" contribute to an informal and modern, or hip, tone.

5. **C. someone knowledgeable about the media** The reviewer talks knowledgeably about both television and the Internet.

Lesson 10: Text Structure

Practice 10

1. **B. exposure to the cowpox disease** As seen in the text, James's recovery from cowpox followed his exposure to it. Note that choice (D) refers to Jenner exposing James to smallpox, not cowpox.

2. **C. "After being exposed to the disease"** The transition word *After* tells the reader that James's exposure came before his catching cowpox and recovery from it. Thus, it gives the reader explicit information about the order of the steps in the process.

3. **B. A number of factors can damage a garden.** As discussed in the passage, factors such as weather, pests, and diseases can affect plants and cause damage, undoing the time and work that have been invested.

Interpreting Informational Text Practice Questions

1. **D. hit a boy in the arm to get his attention** The writer talks about breaking a ruler over the head of a boy she likes; you can therefore conclude that she would hit a boy in the arm to get his attention. She responds physically and without much thought to consequences.

2. **B. She was just pretending she didn't want to go to the principal's office.** The circumstances of Brer Rabbit pretending he was afraid to go into the briar patch where he was born and raised are similar to the speaker pretending to be afraid to go to the principal's office.

3. **C. unusual** From the different examples of how Frank Doleman behaved (allowing a young girl to play chess in his office and not punishing boys sent to his office), you can conclude that he was an unusual principal.

4. **A. confident** The additional information you get from the new quotation and the examples of her behavior, plus the overall tone of the excerpt, suggest a confident young girl.

5. **C. concerned but hopeful.** The author is worried about the health impact of soda consumption on teenagers. But she is also hopeful; in the last sentence, she states that more "can" be done to reduce the consumption of sugary beverages.

6. **D. Young people will choose healthier beverages if they are better educated about the dangers of regular soda consumption.** The last paragraph supports this choice. Choice (A) is unsupported by the passage: even though the author does not condemn the legal measures mentioned in paragraph 2, you

do not know whether she would support an overall ban. Choice (B) is unsupported also; the author never mentions diet soda.

7. **C. Young people who drink these beverages regularly will eventually suffer from the same ailments as those who drink soda regularly.** The author points out that, even though juice and energy drinks have somewhat less sugar than soda, regular consumption of those products "is likely to be just as damaging in the long term."

8. **B. effective to some extent.** After describing the measures, the author begins paragraph 3 by stating, "These efforts appear to be paying off" but goes on to explain why they may not fully solve the problem of sugar consumption among teenagers.

9. **C. Reducing excessive consumption of soda.** The author is referring to the efforts described in paragraph 2, all of which attempted to reduce soda consumption.

10. **C. The cost of mandated coverage will lessen the ability of NATS to hire and supply temporary workers.** This question is basically answered in paragraph 2: "the cost of mandates could weaken the ability of the temporary help industry to act as a 'jobs bridge.'"

11. **A. Many workers are losing their jobs and need temporary jobs until they find permanent work again.** The third paragraph explains this reason.

12. **D. to raise awareness of one side of an issue** The whole passage—plus knowledge of who Edward A. Lenz is—helps you see that its purpose is to explain the position of the NATS.

13. **B. Women will not resort to wearing pants or other restrictive men's clothing.** This statement and the lines that follow it help you see that Stanton is saying men can wear their restrictive clothing; women want no part of it.

14. **D. a cloth worn around the neck** By looking at the context clues—or words around the word *stock*—you can see that it is something worn around the neck.

15. **B. speak up about current events** This very direct speech of Stanton's indicates her straight-to-the-point personality. She is not interested in criticism for its own sake but rather speaks up about issues she strongly believes in.

16. **A. Women are fighting for the right to vote.** The phrase "over the horns of bigotry" helps you see that women are fighting for something. The last paragraph of the excerpt helps you see that they are fighting for the right to vote.

Analyzing Informational Text

Lesson 1: Purpose of Text

Practice 1

1. **B. tell how creative engineers saved astronauts** This passage is a narrative about the process of saving the lives of the Apollo 13 astronauts, including, in particular, the role of engineers. Choices (A), (C), and (D) are all far too broad.

2. **B. supports the writer's main recommendation** The writer recommends that the state cut sales taxes on new vehicles. Preventing deaths with the modern

safety features on new cars is one of the reasons for this recommendation.

3. **D. inform about the historical importance of silk** The passage begins by discussing the "historical importance" of silk, and continues throughout to introduce new points about this topic.

4. **C. It provides examples of silk's historical importance in trade and culture.** Nomads traveling to China for silk and the creation of the "Silk Road" are examples of silk's importance.

Lesson 2: Effectiveness of Argument

Practice 2

1. **B. The federal government should automatically raise the minimum wage to match price increases.** The author states that "[s]everal states have taken the sensible step of automatically raising their minimum wage to adjust for inflation and consumer price increases." Later, she also states that "the federal government should follow the lead of the states." Thus, the author is recommending that the federal government should adjust the minimum wage for price increases. The rest of the passage serves to support this recommendation.

2. **D. Those states have systems superior to the federal system of manual increases.** The author's main point is that the federal government should adopt automatic minimum wage increases, as some states currently have done. Thus, she believes that the states' systems are better than the current federal system.

3. **C. Over the past 40 years, the federal minimum wage has not kept pace with inflation.** Choice (C) is a historical fact provided in the second paragraph as evidence to support the writer's argument.

4. **B. Ensuring sustainable incomes for hardworking citizens is a responsibility of lawmakers.** The author states that lawmakers must ensure stability for workers but does not justify why they must do so. She assumes that this is part of the job lawmakers should do.

Lesson 3: Validity of Arguments

Practice 3

1. **C. DRE systems offer more security and accuracy than other voting systems.** The writer introduces DRE voting, describes several voting systems, and concludes by suggesting that DRE prevents the problems associated with these systems and is therefore better.

2. **B. DRE voting avoids problems associated with other voting systems.** The writer supports the assertion that DRE voting is the most accurate and secure voting system by listing problems that might be encountered with other voting systems and then stating that DRE voting avoids such problems.

3. **A. Each voter's choices are recorded in the DRE voting system.** This is one of the facts that the writer cites in support of the assertion that DRE is secure and accurate. The other three answer choices cite facts that are included in the passage, but those facts are all background information and do not give direct support to the writer's main point.

4. **C. The writer fails to consider that even if DRE voting addresses all the flaws of previous systems, it may introduce unique flaws of its own.** The writer's conclusion is based solely on the fact that DRE voting avoids problems that have been associated with the other systems mentioned in the passage. Because no information is given about possible flaws of DRE voting, the reader has no way to verify the writer's claim that DRE voting is the most accurate and secure system.

Lesson 4: Text Related by Theme or Topic

Practice 4

1. **C. online piracy of music files** Both passages are focused on reasons why online piracy is harmful and the need to take further action.

2. **B. additional action to combat online piracy is warranted because piracy causes financial loses to the music industry.** The first passage concludes that more must be done to prevent online piracy. The main factual information the writer uses to support this thesis is information about the financial damage that piracy causes.

3. **A. Fear of piracy makes it difficult for new, experimental acts to get signed.** Both passages reach the same conclusion: more must be done to prevent piracy of music files. Choice (A) is the only answer choice that provides direct support for the conclusion of Passage 2, and, therefore, also for that of Passage 1.

4. **A. Online piracy of digital files has a harmful effect on the music industry.** Both authors provide different reasons as to why piracy is potentially harmful, but both agree that it has a negative effect on the industry.

Lesson 5: Text with Opposing Arguments

Practice 5

1. **C. the MPAA movie rating system** Each writer is making an argument about the relevance and trustworthiness of the MPAA rating system.

2. **B. The MPAA rating system is a useful tool for parents.** The writer of the Argument (Passage 1) uses information about the MPAA rating system to support her argument that the system helps parents to make sound decisions.

3. **D. The MPAA rating system should not be trusted.** In the second sentence, the writer indicates that the MPAA rating system is not a useful guide, and concludes by recommending that parents use a different source of advice.

4. **A. She largely approves of the MPAA rating system as a guideline for parents.** The passage provides no information about the writer's own child-rearing decisions, choice (B), or about her opinion of the effect of the Hays Code on the movie industry, choice (D). Also, her statements about the rating system are uniformly positive, making choice (C) incorrect.

Lesson 6: Texts with Related Graphic Information

Practice 6

1. **D. Governing parties can use their power to shape electoral districts to their advantage.** The passage and the figures focus on demonstrating how gerrymandering works. Choices (A) and (B) are not supported at all by the passage, and choice (C) is far too extreme.

2. **B. Through gerrymandering, a governing party can be elected to a greater number of seats than its voter support might otherwise allow.** The second paragraph describes how the second grid figure shows one party winning 75 percent of the seats from 60 percent of the vote, rather than the 50 percent of seats shown in the first grid figure.

3. **A. They illustrate the advantages a party can obtain through gerrymandering.** As discussed in the passage's second paragraph, the figures show how a party can benefit from the process. While choices (C) and (D) may or may not be true statements, they do not describe how the figures support the passage.

Analyzing Informational Text Practice Questions

1. **D. to discuss whether communication technology helps or hurts relationships** This answer choice reflects the scope of the article introduced at the end of the first paragraph.

2. **B. how technology affects interpersonal connections** The question at the end of paragraph 1 introduces this topic. Paragraph 2 discusses positive effects of communication technology while paragraph 3 discusses a negative effect.

3. **D. The caption reveals that the woman's friends will use their phones during their visit.** The caption is similar to a scenario described in the first paragraph of the passage. In both cases, people are choosing to use technology rather than to enjoy the company of those with whom they have an established relationship.

4. **B. New communication technologies may adversely impact important human relationships.** The author's concluding paragraph discusses how communication technology can connect us with so many people that we have less time and energy to spend on relationships with friends and family, and the caption of the image reveals that the visiting friends plan to spend time on their phones rather than in conversing with one another.

5. **B. the giant squid is the world's longest cephalopod** The author's introduction and conclusion both raise this point, and the evidence in the paragraph supports this thesis.

6. **D. The giant squid is longer than the colossal squid.** The author provides scientific evidence about the colossal squid to support the passage's main idea about the giant squid.

7. **C. The length of the longest known colossal squid specimen is ten meters.** This factual evidence supports the author's main idea.

8. **A. The longest known colossal squid is ten meters long, so there is no colossal squid longer than the**

longest giant squid. According to paragraph 2, there are very few samples of colossal squid, and all of them have been juveniles. It is improper to draw a conclusion about the entire colossal squid species on the basis of such limited evidence.

9. **B. mercury dental amalgam** Though the authors have somewhat different opinions on the subject, both passages are centrally about mercury dental amalgam.

10. **C. Mercury amalgam fillings should be banned because they are unhealthy and bad for the environment.** The first sentence of Passage 1 states that mercury amalgam should be banned for use in dental fillings. The first paragraph cites health reasons for this opinion. The second paragraph cites environmental reasons. Choice (D) is mentioned in Passage 1, but it serves as support for the author's main point.

11. **D. It is a convincing statistic from a reliable source.** The statement that 40–50 percent of mercury in wastewater is from an easily preventable source is a convincing statistic. The EPA is a large non-political government agency and so is likely to provide reliable information.

12. **A. Consumers have no other reason, such as cost or durability, to prefer mercury amalgam to composite fillings.** The author of Passage 1 states that "banning mercury amalgam would draw no consumer backlash" because resin composite fillings are better for cosmetic reasons. The author assumes that there is no other reason to prefer mercury amalgam.

13. **B. Resin composite fillings look better than mercury amalgam fillings when each is used on visible tooth surfaces.** The author of Passage 2 states that amalgam is preferable to resin composite whenever there is no cosmetic need for a tooth-colored filling. Thus, you can infer that he believes that resin composite fillings look more like natural teeth than mercury amalgam.

14. **A. Passage 1, because it cites no sources for the study or the statistic it cites** The author of passage 1 says that "it has been estimated" that 4 percent of the mercury in Lake Superior comes from dental amalgam, but the author cites no source. The author also gives no source for the 2001 study that is cited in the first paragraph.

15. **D. Mercury that accumulates in body tissues causes a variety of health problems.** The study cited in the first paragraph of passage 1 found a correlation between mercury amalgam fillings and a number of health conditions. A correlation does not prove causation, but the author of passage 1 states that "this accumulated mercury causes a variety of health problems."

Reading Literature

Lesson 1: Plot Elements

Practice 1

1. **B. swearing that he was telling the truth** The following statement in the excerpt gives the context and meaning: "It is nevertheless God's own truth, the sacred truth. I repeat it on my soul and my salvation."

2. **D. confronted him and then asked to be searched** According to the excerpt, when the harness-maker

comes in and repeats his story, the two "abused each other for an hour. At his own request, Maître Hauchecorne was searched."

3. **C. A peasant is accused of taking a pocket-book.** As you read the excerpt, you understand that a harness-maker has accused a peasant of taking a pocket-book, and the mayor of the town believes the harness-maker.

4. **C. The harness-maker is higher in social status than the peasant.** The harness-maker is characterized as "a man we can believe." The countryman is referred to as a "peasant." You can infer that the difference in the two men's social status affects the way their statements are viewed.

Lesson 2: Inferences

Practice 2

1. **A. had always loved her** In the first paragraph, Louise recalls her husband's face: "the face that had never looked save with love upon her." The term *save* means "except."

2. **C. spread her arms out in welcome** The first paragraph explains that although Louise knew she would cry at the sight of her dead husband, "that bitter moment" would soon give way to years of freedom, which she welcomed.

3. **A. she was overcome and thrilled to see her husband** The doctors assumed that Louise was so glad to learn her husband had not died in an accident that she was shocked and overjoyed to see him walk in the door.

4. **B. She was shocked that she would not be free.** Much of the excerpt is about Louise looking forward to the freedom of being without her husband. When she learns that her husband is alive, she also learns that she will not be free.

Lesson 3: Character

Practice 3

1. **B. He is reluctant to see the ghost of his wife.** The witch, supposedly speaking as Yaji's wife, says that she lies in her grave longing for Yaji to die and join her. She then asks, "Shall I come to meet you?" Throughout the passage, Yaji seems uncomfortable. At this moment you can infer that he is reluctant.

2. **C. untrustworthy** The witch is tricking Yaji. The witch has her own interests at heart when she pretends it is the wife requesting, "Give this witch plenty of money."

3. **D. neglectful** The information we are given about Yaji suggests that he treated his wife poorly when she was alive and now does not tend her grave.

Lesson 4: Theme

Practice 4

1. **B. finds a new explanation** After his father tells the boy he is dreaming, the boy states, "I decided that it was a magic horse and man that I'd seen."

2. **B. imaginative** The detailed description of the dream and the boy's insistence on believing in it are signs of his imaginative powers.

3. **A. He wants to reconcile what he saw with what his father told him.** Initially the boy seems to think that he saw a real, ordinary horse, but his father explains why this is unlikely. However, the boy does not accept the explanation that he was merely dreaming. Thus, he thinks of a new explanation.

4. **B. having enough money to pay some bills** The father is a practical man, a realist—"where were poor people like us going to find big gray stallions?" Because of the family's poverty, the father would probably enjoy having money to pay bills.

5. **D. Morning and youth are full of possibility.** The end of the excerpt states, "I believed that magic hides in the early morning. . . . you might find something so beautiful . . . nothing else in life could ever be better."

Lesson 5: Style and Point of View

Practice 5

1. **B. He takes things in stride.** When Coach chides Bobby for having three malts, Bobby jokes with him and then pretends to hide them. Bobby is not angry or defensive in a way that could justify choice (D).

2. **C. the actions and speech of the characters** The narrator reports only what can be seen or heard by any observer. As a reader, you don't learn anyone's thoughts or feelings. You must infer them from their actions and speech.

3. **A. informal** Throughout the excerpt, people speak and act quite informally: Daphne washes up in a drinking fountain, Coach speaks with a spoon in his mouth, Bobby jokes with Coach, and so on.

4. **D. not entirely honest about his feelings** In his discussion with Daphne, Coach tries to explain his wife's need for an apartment of her own. Yet he sounds hostile and cuts his wife off when she speaks of her apartment. You can conclude he was hiding his real feelings from Daphne.

Lesson 6: Figurative Language

Practice 6

1. **B. rain clouds approaching** Lines 8–9 state, "patch of cloud spreads, darkening/Like a water-stain on silk." The following line mentions the coming rain: ". . . *quickly, before the rain!*"

2. **C. The rain caused their makeup to run.** The previous two lines mention "soaked by the shower" and "drenched." Immediately preceding the mention of "ruined faces" is a description of "streaked mascara." The girls' makeup is streaked because of the rain.

3. **B. the wind is so strong that it is blowing spray from the river into the boat** The figurative language helps you "see" the effects of the strong wind by painting a picture of curtains embroidered with white foamy water blown from the river.

4. **A. quick and easy** A knife cuts through a melon quickly and easily, and that is how cold, wet autumn weather has cut through the warm summer day.

5. **C. wry and observant** Throughout the poem the speaker observes and comments on what is going on around him with a dryly humorous, or wry, attitude.

Lesson 7: Literary Text with Related Images

Practice 7

1. **B. the Flemish painter** In the excerpt, an old Flemish painting is mentioned; the painter, however, is neither an important character nor one depicted in the painting.

2. **Part One: B. He finds the changes unsettling.** Rip Van Winkle has "smoked so many a peaceful pipe" outside the "quiet little Dutch inn of yore." He was comfortable in his old village and is disturbed by the changes to it.
   Part Two: "strange and incomprehensible"; "singularly metamorphosed" The phrase "strange and incomprehensible" helps to draw the conclusion that Rip's observations are jarring to him. The phrase "singularly metamorphosed" indicates that Rip thinks that the changes in the town are odd.

3. **A. While the dollar bill was originally intended to depict George Washington, the face on the Union Hotel sign was originally that of King George.** Rip recognizes the face of King George. Someone has painted over portions of the sign to change the clothing and substitute a sword for King George's scepter, but the face remains the same.

Reading Literature Practice Questions

1. **C. self-concerned** Leroy's condition inspires Norma Jean to care for herself. She discusses herself and her body, and the passage gives no indication that any of the other answers fit her character.

2. **C. won't be driving his truck for a while** The passage tells us Leroy is injured and probably won't drive, so describing the truck as roosting, or sleeping, implies it will not be used.

3. **D. doesn't want to consider what to do next** The passage says that Leroy is "not sure what to do next" and is making his crafts "in the meantime."

4. **A. It took some courage.** The fourth paragraph says the boy's "heart was in his mouth" and the sixth paragraph explains the boy was "scared as he looked down."

5. **B. alone** The boy has come to believe that you cannot rely on anyone but yourself. He is alone on the deck and sees the bird alone atop the mast. Even though it needs help, he is not going to help it at first.

6. **D. loneliness and sense of belonging** The sailor-boy begins the excerpt believing that everyone must look after himself. The final sentence of the excerpt states that his adventure leaves him with the belief that "the sky, the ship, the bird and himself were all one."

7. **D. triumphant** The mood of the piece rises as the boy climbs the mast to save the bird. At the top, he feels proud of what he has chosen to do and succeeded at doing and feels at one with everything.

8. **C. start singing again** A clue is given in the phrase "but his parched tongue clove to the roof of his mouth, he could not utter a stave." His mouth, dry from fear, could not utter a note of the song.

9. **A. panic** Reading those words both alone and in context gives you a sense of Ichabod's panic-stricken haste to get away.

10. **C. suspenseful** There is mystery and tension over whether the headless horseman will catch up with Ichabod and, if so, what he will do. The events that are happening and the way they are told create suspense.

11. **B. too scared to think rationally** When you realize that Ichabod mistakenly thought he saw a head when it was, in reality, a pumpkin, you can see that he was letting his fear get the better of his judgment.

12. **A. John Wright** Although Mrs. Peters insists they don't know who killed the bird, Mrs. Hale states, "Wright wouldn't like the bird—a thing that sang. She used to sing. He killed that, too. . . . I knew John Wright."

13. **B. someone who smothers all the joy in another person** Mrs. Hale says: "No, Wright wouldn't like the bird—a thing that sang. She used to sing. He killed that, too." From these comments, you can conclude that John Wright was capable of discouraging a person from singing, something that would have made that person happy.

14. **D. They understand how someone could be driven to murder.** The two women seem nervous and are evasive about the bird's death. But they are not protecting themselves. You can tell they suspect who might have murdered Wright and what might have driven the person to murder. References to "she," someone who liked to sing but stopped because of Wright ("He killed that, too"), someone who lived in loneliness and had only the bird as pleasure until the bird was killed, indicate that the women suspect that Mrs. Wright killed her husband.

Language Arts: Writing

The TASC Writing Test assesses your language skills in two different ways. You will have 105 minutes to complete the Writing Test.

1. Expect to spend around 55 minutes answering 50 items that assess language skills. These questions will target skills such as:

   - constructing sentences
   - using grammar correctly
   - using words correctly
   - organizing ideas into paragraphs
   - connecting ideas

2. You will have around 50 minutes to write one essay in response to a passage or pair of passages. You will read the passage or passages and then write an essay that either:

   - argues for one side of a debate and against the other side or
   - explains something from the passage(s)

If you are taking the paper version of the TASC test, you will write your essay on paper. If you are testing on computer, you will type your essay into a box on the screen. On the computer-based TASC test, you will not have spelling- and grammar-check functions. Thus, you should practice spelling and grammar prior to taking the test. However, a small number of minor spelling and grammatical errors will not ruin your essay score, as long as those errors do not interfere with your meaning.

This unit is organized into skills needed to write effective sentences and paragraphs, skills required to write the essay, and skills needed to edit writing and correct mistakes in grammar and usage. Be aware that the skills you will practice in this unit in multiple-choice questions will also be useful to you as you edit your essay for the TASC Writing Test.

See the "TASC Blueprint Alignment: Tables and Notes" section in the online chapter "About the TASC" for more information about how material in this unit aligns to CTB/McGraw-Hill's published TASC test blueprints.

LANGUAGE ARTS: WRITING PRETEST
PART I: LANGUAGE SKILLS

Directions: You may fill in the circles next to the correct answers or write your answers on a separate piece of paper.

Questions 1 through 6 refer to the following paragraphs.

To: Parents and Guardians
From: Sonia Vasquez, School Nurse

(A)

(1) A student in your child's class have been diagnosed with strep throat. (2) Strep throat is a highly contagious disease and a common illness in children. (3) Unlike most sore throats, which are caused by viruses, strep throat is caused by bacteria and is treatable with antibiotics. (4) The time between exposure to the disease and the appearance of symptoms is usually one to three days. (5) To safeguard your child's health, please take the following precautions. (6) Watch your child for strep symptoms. (7) Such as sore throat, fever, swollen glands, and headache. (8) If your child developed any of these symptoms, take him or her to the doctor. (9) If a throat culture is positive, treatment can be started. (10) It is extremely important to take all the prescribed medicine until it is gone.

(B)

(11) Children should get immediate treatment for several reasons. (12) For one, treatment reduces spread of the disease. (13) In addition antibiotics may prevent rheumatic fever. (14) Treatment also prevents other rare but possibly dangerous complications.

(C)

(15) Your child may return to school after taking medicine for 24 hours and the fever must be gone. (16) Please call us with any questions or concerns you have.

1. Sentence 1: **A student in your child's class have been diagnosed with strep throat.**

   Which correction should be made to sentence 1?

   ○ A. replace your with you're
   ○ B. change child's to children
   ○ C. insert a comma after class
   ○ D. change have to has

2. Sentences 6 and 7: **Watch your child for strep symptoms. Such as** sore throat, fever, swollen glands, and headache.

   Which is the best way to write the underlined portion of these sentences?

   ○ A. symptoms. Such as
   ○ B. symptoms, the best known are
   ○ C. symptoms, such as
   ○ D. symptoms examples are

3. Sentence 8: **If your child developed any of these symptoms, take him or her to the doctor.**

   Which correction should be made to sentence 8?

   - A. replace your with you're
   - B. change developed to develops
   - C. remove the comma
   - D. replace him or her with them

4. Which revision would improve the effectiveness of the passage?

   Begin a new paragraph with

   - A. sentence 3
   - B. sentence 4
   - C. sentence 5
   - D. sentence 6

5. Sentence 13: **In addition antibiotics may prevent rheumatic fever.**

   Which correction should be made to sentence 13?

   - A. insert a comma after addition
   - B. insert a comma after antibiotics
   - C. change may prevent to are preventing
   - D. change rheumatic fever to Rheumatic Fever

6. Sentence 15: **Your child may return to school after taking medicine for 24 hours and the fever must be gone.**

   The most effective revision of sentence 15 would begin with which group of words?

   - A. After the fever is gone and your child has taken
   - B. Having taken medicine for 24 hours and the fever
   - C. Your child, once having taken medicine for 24 hours, may
   - D. The fever being gone and the medicine being finished,

Compulsive Gambling

(A)

(1) Most of us can bet on a football game, or buy a lottery ticket with little damage to our finances. (2) In contrast, compulsive gamblers cannot stop even when their behavior had threatened to ruin their lives.

(B)

(3) Gambling frequently occupies the thoughts of compulsive gamblers. (4) For instance, they may be reliving past gambling experiences or coming up with schemes to get more money for gambling. (5) Although they may have tried several times to stop gambling, their efforts met with failure. (6) When trying to stop gambling, they feel irritable and restless. (7) They need to gamble with more and more money in order to enjoy it, losing money increases their desire to gamble. (8) They may even commit fraud forgery, or theft to get the funds to continue their habit. (9) Many of them have lost jobs, important relationships, or career opportunities because of their involvement with gambling.

(C)

(10) Compulsive gambling is like any other addiction. (11) As gamblers lose control over gambling, they lose control over their lives as well. (12) They may become anxious and depressed or they may fail to live up to their obligations, causing others to stop trusting them.

7. Sentence 1: **Most of us can bet on a football game, or buy a lottery ticket with little damage to our finances.**

Which correction should be made to sentence 1?

○ A. insert a comma after <u>us</u>
○ B. change <u>bet</u> to <u>be betting</u>
○ C. remove the comma
○ D. insert a comma after <u>ticket</u>

8. Sentence 2: **In contrast, compulsive gamblers cannot stop even when their behavior <u>had threatened</u> to ruin their lives.**

Which is the best way to write the underlined portion of this sentence?

○ A. had threatened
○ B. will threaten
○ C. threatens
○ D. having threatened

9. Which sentence would be most effective if inserted at the beginning of paragraph B?

    ○ A. Compulsive gamblers have a lot of problems.

    ○ B. Some people engage in compulsive gambling.

    ○ C. Gamblers escape from negative emotions.

    ○ D. Compulsive gamblers display a number of consistent traits.

10. Sentence 7: **They need to gamble with more and more money in order to enjoy it, losing money increases their desire to gamble.**

Which is the best way to write the underlined portion of this sentence?

    ○ A. it. Losing

    ○ B. it but losing

    ○ C. it, now that losing

    ○ D. it and losing

11. Sentence 8: **They may even commit fraud forgery, or theft to get the funds to continue their habit.**

Which correction should be made to sentence 8?

    ○ A. insert a comma after fraud

    ○ B. insert a comma after theft

    ○ C. replace their with there

    ○ D. replace their with they're

12. Sentence 12: **They may become anxious and depressed or they may fail to live up to their obligations, causing others to stop trusting them.**

Which is the best way to write the underlined portion of this sentence?

    ○ A. depressed, or they

    ○ B. depressed, they

    ○ C. depressed. And they

    ○ D. depressed and they

Questions 13 through 18 refer to the following paragraphs.

Choosing a Pet

(A)

(1) People often make impulse buys at Pet Stores just because they see an adorable puppy or kitten. (2) Unhappily, these poor creatures are likely to end up at animal shelters when the owners find he can't care for them. (3) To avoid this outcome, choose your pet wisely. (4) Remember that your pet will become a member of your family and a daily responsibility.

(B)

(5) There's several factors to consider when selecting a pet. (6) First of all, do you have the time to care for a pet? (7) While some pets require little care, puppies and kittens need to be housebroken and to train them. (8) If the animal needs exercise, is your home large enough? (9) Would you enjoy taking your pet outdoors for exercise? (10) Do you think people should get a lot of exercise? (11) Can you afford the costs of food, vaccinations, and health check-ups? (12) Does your building allow pets? (13) Finally, if you must leave home for a few days, can you find someone to care for your pet?

(C)

(14) Once you choose a pet that is appropriate for your lifestyle, bring the animal to a veterinarian for examination. (15) You should be able to return the pet if he or she was unhealthy.

13. Sentence 1: **People often make impulse buys at Pet Stores just because they see an adorable puppy or kitten.**

Which correction should be made to sentence 1?

○ A. change buys to bys
○ B. change Pet Stores to pet stores
○ C. insert a comma before because
○ D. insert a comma before or

14. Sentence 2: **Unhappily, these poor creatures are likely to end up at animal shelters when the owners find he can't care for them.**

Which correction should be made to sentence 2?

○ A. remove the comma
○ B. change animal shelters to Animal Shelters
○ C. insert a comma after shelters
○ D. replace he with they

15. Sentence 5: **There's several factors to consider when selecting a pet.**

Which correction should be made to sentence 5?

- A. change There's to There are
- B. insert a comma after factors
- C. replace to with too
- D. insert a comma after consider

16. Sentence 7: **While some pets require little care, puppies and kittens need to be housebroken and to train them.**

Which is the best way to write the underlined portion of the sentence?

- A. be housebroken and to train them
- B. housebreaking and training
- C. be housebroken and trained
- D. be housebroken and training

17. Which revision should be made to the placement of sentence 10?

- A. move sentence 10 to the beginning of paragraph B
- B. move sentence 10 to follow sentence 6
- C. move sentence 10 to the beginning of paragraph C
- D. remove sentence 10

18. Sentence 15: **You should be able to return the pet if the animal was unhealthy.**

Which correction should be made to sentence 15?

- A. change You to One
- B. insert a comma after pet
- C. replace if with and
- D. change was to is

LANGUAGE ARTS: WRITING PRETEST
PART II: ESSAY

Directions: Read both the selection and the writing prompt and answer the questions that follow.

<u>Questions 1–10</u> are based on the process of writing a response to a reading selection.
Note: Do not start writing your response until you are asked to do so at question 9.

Essay Prompt

The following passage is from Helen Keller's autobiography. Keller was the first deaf and blind person to earn a college degree. She went on to become a leading author, lecturer, and political activist for the rights of the disabled and for peace and human rights.

Before working with her teacher, Helen did not understand what language was. Write an essay explaining how Helen's teacher helped her to come to understand what language was. Include several specific details from the passage to support your explanation.

Excerpted from *The Story of My Life*

The morning after my teacher came she led me into her room and gave me a doll. The little blind children at the Perkins Institution had sent it and Laura Bridgman had dressed it; but I did not know this until afterward. When I had played with it a little while, Miss Sullivan slowly spelled into my hand the word "d-o-l-l." I was at once interested in this finger play and tried to imitate it. When I finally succeeded in making the letters correctly I was flushed with childish pleasure and pride. Running downstairs to my mother I held up my hand and made the letters for doll. I did not know that I was spelling a word or even that words existed; I was simply making my fingers go in monkey-like imitation. In the days that followed I learned to spell in this uncomprehending way a great many words, among them pin, hat, cup and a few verbs like sit, stand and walk. But my teacher had been with me several weeks before I understood that everything has a name.

One day, while I was playing with my new doll, Miss Sullivan put my big rag doll into my lap also, spelled "d-o-l-l" and tried to make me understand that "d-o-l-l" applied to both. Earlier in the day we had had a tussle over the words "m-u-g" and "w-a-t-e-r." Miss Sullivan had tried to impress it upon me that "m-u-g" is mug and that "w-a-t-e-r" is

water, but I persisted in confounding the two. In despair she had dropped the subject for the time, only to renew it at the first opportunity. I became impatient at her repeated attempts and, seizing the new doll, I dashed it upon the floor. I was keenly delighted when I felt the fragments of the broken doll at my feet.

Neither sorrow nor regret followed my passionate outburst. I had not loved the doll. In the still, dark world in which I lived there was no strong sentiment of tenderness. I felt my teacher sweep the fragments to one side of the hearth, and I had a sense of satisfaction that the cause of my discomfort was removed. She brought me my hat, and I knew I was going out into the warm sunshine. This thought, if a wordless sensation may be called a thought, made me hop and skip with pleasure.

We walked down the path to the well-house, attracted by the fragrance of the honeysuckle with which it was covered. Someone was drawing water and my teacher placed my hand under the spout. As the cool stream gushed over one hand she spelled into the other the word water, first slowly, then rapidly. I stood still, my whole attention fixed upon the motions of her fingers. Suddenly I felt a misty consciousness as of something forgotten—a thrill of returning thought; and somehow the mystery of language was revealed to me. I knew then that "w-a-t-e r" meant the wonderful cool something that was flowing over my hand. That living word wakened my soul, gave it light, hope, joy, set it free! There were barriers still, it is true, but barriers that could in time be swept away.

I left the well-house eager to learn. Everything had a name, and each name gave birth to a new thought. As we returned to the house every object which I touched seemed to quiver with life. That was because I saw everything with the strange, new sight that had come to me. On entering the door I remembered the doll I had broken. I felt my way to the hearth and picked up the pieces. I tried vainly to put them together. Then my eyes filled with tears; for I realized what I had done, and for the first time I felt repentance and sorrow.

From *The Story of My Life* by Helen Keller

Unpack the Writing Prompt

1. What is the topic of the writing prompt?

   _____

2. What does the prompt ask you to do?

   _____

3. What does the prompt tell you that you need to include in the response?

   _____

4. Are you being asked to argue for your opinion or to explain something from the passage?

   _____

Develop Your Topic Sentence and Supporting Details

5. Write a sentence that introduces the topic of your essay. This will be the first sentence of your essay.

   _____

6. What are three details from the passage you will use to develop your explanation?

   _____

   _____

   _____

7. Write a concluding sentence that summarizes your explanation.

   _____

Plan, Draft, Revise, and Edit Your Response

8. On a piece of paper, make a plan for your response.

9. On a computer or on a piece of paper, write a response to the prompt that includes an introduction, a body, and a conclusion.

10. On the computer or on the paper, make revisions to improve your response and edit to correct errors in grammar, usage, spelling, capitalization, and punctuation.

STOP. Congratulations! You have completed the Writing pretest. Your next step is to check your answers with the Writing Pretest Answers and Explanations that begin on the next page and then fill in the study planner that appears on page xvii.

WRITING PRETEST ANSWERS AND EXPLANATIONS

PART I: LANGUAGE SKILLS

1. **D. change have to has** The third-person singular subject "student" requires the verb form has.

2. **C. symptoms, such as** This links a fragment to an independent clause to form a complete sentence.

3. **B. change developed to develops** The verb should be in the present tense because the action is occurring in the present. Moreover, the present tense is consistent with the majority of verbs in the passage.

4. **C. sentence 5.** Sentences 1–4 explain basic facts about strep throat. Sentences 5–10 explain what parents should do if their child has strep throat.

5. **A. insert a comma after addition** Generally, an introductory phrase is followed by a comma.

6. **A. After the fever is gone and your child has taken** Combining the detail about taking medicine and the second independent clause about the fever into an introductory subordinate clause results in a smooth, effective sentence.

7. **C. remove the comma** No comma is needed between two verbs in a compound predicate ("bet on a football game or buy a lottery ticket").

8. **C. threatens** The action is always true, so the present tense is correct. Moreover, the present tense is consistent with the majority of verbs in the passage.

9. **D. Compulsive gamblers display a number of consistent traits.** This is the only topic sentence that sums up the main point and is neither too specific nor too general.

10. **A. it. Losing** Choice (A), which forms two complete sentences, is the only choice given that properly corrects the comma splice here. Choice (D) is incorrect because a comma must precede *and* in a compound sentence.

11. **A. insert a comma after fraud** Commas are required between items in a series.

12. **A. depressed, or they** A comma should precede a coordinating conjunction that joins independent clauses.

13. **B. change Pet Stores to pet stores** This term is not capitalized because it is not the name of a store; it is just a type of a store.

14. **D. replace he with they** The antecedent "owners" is plural, so *they* is the correct pronoun to use.

15. **A. change There's to There are** The verb agrees with the subject, "several factors", which is plural.

16. **C. be housebroken and trained** Only option (C) has both verbs in parallel structure and creates a correct sentence.

17. **D. remove sentence 10** The sentence about exercise and people is not relevant to pets, the topic of the article.

18. **D. change was to is** The statement is always true, so the present tense is correct. Moreover, the present tense is consistent with the majority of verbs in the passage.

Part II, Essay

Your responses to items 1 through 4 may vary but should be similar to the following.

1. Helen Keller's coming to understand what language is

2. Explain how her teacher helped her understand what language is

3. Several specific details from the passage

4. Explain something from the passage; no opinion called for

Your responses to items 5 through 7 may vary. The following are sample responses.

5. This essay will explain how Helen Keller's teacher helped her understand what language is.

6. Helen's teacher taught her to spell words for *doll*, *mug*, and *water*. Helen's teacher ran water over one of Helen's hands while repeatedly spelling "w-a-t-e-r" into the other hand. Helen wrote that "suddenly" she understood something.

7. Although Helen did not initially understand that language relates to things in the world, Helen's teacher patiently taught words to Helen until Helen had a flash of insight about what language is.

8. Responses to item 8 might vary quite a bit. You may have written a rough outline or a map of ideas you wished to include in your essay.

9. **Drafting Checklist** Check off each task that you performed. Give yourself a score of 0–5 based on how many checks you made.

    _____ I wrote a first sentence that clearly introduced my explanation.

    _____ I developed several paragraphs responding to the prompt.

    _____ In my response, I cited specific details from the text to support my central idea.

    _____ In my response, I provided additional relevant information based on my own knowledge and perspectives.

    _____ I wrote a conclusion that summarized my explanation.

10. **Revising and Editing Checklist** Give yourself a score of 0–6 based on how many checks you made.

    _____ My piece was well organized, or I improved its organization so that one idea relates to another.

    _____ I made sure that my sentences were complete, clear, and correct.

    _____ Each of my paragraphs has a central idea and supporting details from the text.

    _____ My piece has a clear beginning, middle, and ending.

    _____ I corrected subject-verb agreement, pronoun agreement, and verb tense errors.

    _____ I have corrected punctuation, capitalization, and spelling.

Simple Sentences

A complete simple sentence has at least one subject and one verb. The **subject** is the person, place, or thing that the sentence is talking about. The subject performs an action or is described. The **verb** is the word that tells what action the subject is doing or links the subject to a modifier.

Action verb: Elaine took notes on the meeting.
     subject verb

Linking verb: They were long.
     subject verb modifier

If a sentence is missing either the subject or the verb, it is incomplete. An incomplete sentence is called a **fragment.**

EXAMPLES
No subject: Typed up her notes.
Complete sentence: Elaine typed up her notes.

No verb: The computer in the main office.
Complete sentence: The computer in the main office crashed several times.

A complete sentence must also express a complete thought. The reader should not be left asking questions.

Incomplete thought: When she lost her work. (What happened when she lost her work?)
Complete thought: Elaine was very frustrated when she lost her work.

Incomplete thought: The person in charge of computer support. (What about that person?)
Complete thought: Elaine called the person in charge of computer support.

Incomplete thought: By replacing the hard drive.
Complete thought: Elaine can fix the computer by replacing the hard drive.

Finally, a complete sentence should have correct end punctuation. A statement should end with a period, and so should a command. A question should end with a question mark. An exclamation should end with an exclamation point.

Statement: Elaine has lost several files this way.
Command: Turn off the computer.
Question: Will the computer ever be fixed?
Exclamation: What a mess we're in!

If you find a fragment in your writing, rewrite it to make it a complete sentence.

- If the sentence does not have a subject, add a subject.
- If the sentence does not have a verb, add a verb.
- If the thought is incomplete, add words or combine the incomplete thought with a complete sentence.

KEY IDEAS

- Make sure each sentence has a subject and verb and expresses a complete thought.
- If a sentence doesn't express a complete thought, you may need to add a subject, verb, or other words.
- Use correct end punctuation.

TASC TEST TIP

Read each sentence in a TASC passage to yourself and pause at its end. That may help you "hear" whether the sentence is actually an incomplete thought or a sentence fragment.

A. **Directions:** Write *C* if the sentence is complete or *F* if the sentence is a fragment. Rewrite any fragments to make them complete.

EXAMPLE: Talks all the time on the telephone.
F Dave talks all the time on the telephone.

1. Drives his girlfriend crazy. _____

2. As soon as he comes home from work. _____

3. He calls everyone he knows. _____

4. Dave's sister and his best friend. _____

B. <u>Questions 5 through 7</u> refer to the following advertisement.

What Is Three-Way Calling?

(A)

(1) Three-way calling is a unique service that enables you to conduct a conference call. (2) From the privacy of your own home. (3) You can talk to your sister in Florida and your mother in Nebraska at the same time. (4) It's even possible to seek a third person's advice when you're in the middle of a regular call. (5) For instance, if you're closing a deal, can bring your lawyer into the conversation.

(B)

(6) Why wait? (7) This useful and convenient service. (8) Can be yours for only pennies a month.

5. Sentences 1 and 2: Three-way calling is a unique service that enables you to conduct a conference <u>call. From</u> the privacy of your own home.

Which is the best way to write the underlined portion of these sentences?

A. call. And from
B. call. It from
C. call from
D. calling from

6. Sentence 5: For instance, if you're closing a deal, can bring your lawyer into the conversation.

Which correction should be made to sentence 5?

A. remove the comma after <u>instance</u>
B. change <u>closing</u> to <u>close</u>
C. insert <u>you</u> before <u>can</u>
D. replace <u>lawyer</u> with <u>closing</u>

7. Sentences 7 and 8: This useful and convenient <u>service. Can</u> be yours for only pennies a month.

Which is the best way to write the underlined portion of these sentences?

A. service is
B. service it can
C. service can
D. service. That can

STUDY ADVICE

Remember that you will use grammar skills in two ways on the TASC Writing Test. You will answer multiple-choice questions about grammar, and you will also be expected to use correct grammar in your essay. Learn to recognize grammatical mistakes not only in others' writing but also in your own.

Compound and Complex Sentences

Compound Sentences

The simple sentences described in Lesson 1 are also called **independent clauses.** An independent clause has a subject and a verb and expresses a complete thought. You can join two or more independent clauses in one **compound sentence.** To make a compound sentence, you should:

- Choose a logical **coordinating conjunction** to join the independent clauses. The most common coordinating conjunctions are *and, but, or, nor, for, so,* and *yet.*
- Insert a comma before the coordinating conjunction.

EXAMPLES

Two independent clauses: Sam saw a design flaw. He wrote a memo.
Joined correctly: Sam saw a design flaw, so he wrote a memo.

No coordinating conjunction: Sam asked his boss, she told him to send it.
Correct: Sam asked his boss, and she told him to send it.

No comma: Sam's boss was busy so she asked Sam to write the memo.
Correct: Sam's boss was busy, so she asked Sam to write the memo.

Be sure the coordinating conjunction expresses the correct relationship between the ideas in the two independent clauses.

Relationship between Ideas	Coordinating Conjunction
join two equally important ideas	and
contrast two ideas	but, yet
show a cause	for
show an effect	so
give a choice	or
give no choice	nor

Incorrect conjunction: Sam showed initiative, **yet** his boss praised him.
Correct conjunction: Sam showed initiative, **so** his boss praised him.

Be sure that you are actually joining two independent clauses and not just two subjects or two verbs.

Incorrect: The designers, and the builders got the memo.
Correct (no comma): The designers and the builders got the memo.

Incorrect: The designers needed the information, and appreciated the memo.
Correct (two independent clauses): The designers needed the information. They appreciated the memo.
Correct (no comma): The designers needed the information and appreciated the memo.

A. Directions: Using the list on the previous page, choose a coordinating conjunction for each sentence. On a separate sheet of paper, rewrite the sentence using the conjunction preceded by a comma.

EXAMPLE

I didn't want to seem timid, _____*so*_____ I didn't tell anyone about my experience.

1. It was late _____ I was walking home from work.

2. My coworker, Judy, had offered to drive me _____ I had refused.

3. It was a warm night _____ I decided to get some fresh air.

4. It was really my choice. I could have taken a cab _____ I could have walked.

5. I heard a loud noise _____ I ran the last block to my house. Later, I learned that it was only a car backfiring.

B. <u>Questions 6 through 8</u> refer to the following paragraph.

Air Couriers

(1) If you want to travel abroad but don't have a lot of money, one option is to be an air courier. (2) An air courier carries shipping documents on an international flight, and gets a cheap ticket in return. (3) Companies use couriers because it often costs less to check freight as baggage than to ship it as cargo. (4) Air couriers fly on the major airlines, so sometimes they can't check any baggage of their own. (5) Couriers usually book their trips in advance but they get their tickets on the day of the flight.

6. Sentence 2: An air courier carries shipping documents on an international flight, and gets a cheap ticket in return.

Which correction should be made to sentence 2?

A. change <u>carries</u> to <u>carry</u>
B. remove the comma
C. replace <u>and</u> with <u>but</u>
D. insert <u>so</u> after <u>and</u>

7. Sentence 4: Air couriers fly on the major <u>airlines, so</u> sometimes they can't check any baggage of their own.

Which is the best way to write the underlined portion of this sentence?

A. airlines, but
B. airlines but
C. airlines nor
D. airlines, or

8. Sentence 5: Couriers usually book their trips in advance but they get their tickets on the day of the flight.

Which correction should be made to sentence 5?

A. replace <u>usually</u> with <u>never</u>
B. insert a comma after <u>advance</u>
C. insert a comma after <u>but</u>
D. replace <u>they</u> with <u>she</u>

Complex Sentences

A **complex sentence** is made up of an independent clause and a **subordinate clause**. A subordinate clause has a subject and verb, but it does not express a complete thought.

EXAMPLES

Subordinate clause: Because their pay was too low.
Complex sentence: Teachers went on strike <u>because their pay was too low</u>.
                independent clause   subordinate clause

Every subordinate clause begins with a **subordinating conjunction** that shows the relationship between the subordinate clause and the independent clause. Below is a list of common subordinating conjunctions.

Relationship between Clauses	Subordinating Conjunction
cause/reason	because
effect/result	in order that, so that
time	after, as, before, once, since, until, when, whenever, while
place	where, wherever
choice	if, whether
contradiction	although, even though, though

Choose the subordinating conjunction that conveys the meaning you are trying to express.

Incorrect meaning: The strike continued for more than a month <u>once</u> it finally ended.
Correct meaning: The strike continued for more than a month <u>before</u> it finally ended.

When a subordinate clause comes at the beginning of a sentence, put a comma after it. If the subordinate clause comes at the end of a sentence, you generally don't need a comma before it.

At beginning of sentence: <u>While teachers were on the picket line</u>, kids stayed home.
At end of sentence: Kids stayed home <u>while teachers were on the picket line</u>.

However, when a subordinate clause at the end of a sentence begins with *although, though,* or *even though,* put a comma before the clause.

At beginning of sentence: <u>Even though the public supported the teachers</u>, the school board did not concede to the teachers' demands.
At end of sentence: The school board did not concede to teachers' demands, <u>even though the public supported the teachers</u>.

A subordinate clause cannot stand independently. By itself, a subordinate clause is a sentence fragment. Make sure that every subordinate clause is joined to an independent clause.

Incorrect: After the strike finished. The school year began.
Corrected by joining independent and subordinate clauses: After the strike finished, the school year began.

Compound-Complex Sentences

Some sentences incorporate two independent clauses and one or more subordinate clauses. The rules about independent and subordinate clauses still apply, no matter how many clauses the sentence has.

Incorrect: Because the temperature dropped below zero, the streets froze over and we didn't leave the house.
Correct: Because the temperature dropped below zero, the streets froze over, and we didn't leave the house.

Incorrect: The amusement park opened early on Thursday, extended its hours on Friday evening, even though the rainy weather made it unlikely that crowds would be drawn to the park.
Correct: The amusement park opened early on Thursday and extended its hours on Friday evening, even though the rainy weather made it unlikely that crowds would be drawn to the park.

A. Directions: Join the clauses to form complex sentences. Use the subordinating conjunctions in parentheses.

EXAMPLE: (if) You buy a smoke detector. You can protect your family.
If you buy a smoke detector, you can protect your family.

1. Most fatal fires occur. (when) A family is asleep.

_____

2. (because) A smoke alarm wakes you up. It can allow you to escape.

_____

3. Try to replace the smoke detector's battery. (before) It goes dead.

_____

4. (although) Smoke detectors cost money. The expense is worth it.

_____

B. For <u>questions 5 through 7</u>, read each sentence and answer the question that follows.

5. When you are making business call, it's wise to keep a few key rules in mind.

Which correction should be made to the sentence above?

A. change <u>are making</u> to <u>is making</u>
B. insert <u>a</u> after <u>making</u>
C. remove the comma
D. change <u>it's</u> to <u>its</u>

6. Whenever you identify yourself, ask the person whether this is a good time to talk.

Which correction should be made to the sentence above?

A. replace <u>Whenever</u> with <u>After</u>
B. remove the comma
C. insert a comma after <u>person</u>
D. replace <u>the person</u> with <u>them</u>

7. Before you hang _____ the person for his or her time.

Choose the option that correctly completes the sentence.

A. up and then thank
B. up and thank
C. up thank
D. up, thank

Run-Ons and Comma Splices

Run-Ons

There are two errors people commonly make when they join independent clauses to form a sentence. The first type of error is called a **run-on.** In a run-on, two independent clauses are combined without proper punctuation.

Run-On: Banks offer many helpful services you should check them out.

You can correct a run-on in one of several ways:

- Break the run-on into two separate sentences.

  Correct: Banks offer many services. You should check them out.
- Make a compound sentence (add a coordinating conjunction and a comma).

  Correct: Banks offer many services, <u>so</u> you should check them out.
- Make a complex sentence (add a subordinating conjunction and, if necessary, a comma).

  Correct: <u>Because</u> banks offer many services, you should check them out.

A run-on can also consist of independent clauses strung together with *and.* Correct this kind of run-on by dividing it into one or more compound sentences or by combining ideas into one sentence.

Run-On: Banking is getting more and more convenient and you can check on your account using bank-by-phone services and it's possible to do your banking on the Internet.
Correct: Banking is getting more and more convenient. <u>You</u> can check on your account using bank-by-phone services, <u>and</u> it's possible to do your banking on the Internet.

Run-On: Friday I got paid and I went to the bank and I cashed my check.
Correct: Friday I got paid, went to the bank, <u>and</u> cashed my check.

Comma Splices

The second type of error people sometimes make when joining independent clauses is called a **comma splice.** A comma splice occurs when two sentences are joined with just a comma. To correct a comma splice, add a coordinating conjunction after the comma:

Comma splice: You can check on your account using bank-by-phone services, it's possible to do your banking on the Internet.
Correct: You can check on your account using bank-by-phone services, <u>and</u> it's possible to do your banking on the Internet.

You can also correct a comma splice using the methods described above for correcting a run-on. You can also join two related ideas with a semicolon.

Comma splice: There are fewer bank tellers today, banks do offer other services.
Corrected by creating a complex sentence: <u>Although</u> there are fewer bank tellers today, banks do offer other services.

KEY IDEAS

- A run-on sentence is two or more sentences that are connected without correct punctuation.
- In a comma splice, two sentences are joined with only a comma.
- To correct a run-on or comma splice, make a compound or complex sentence or separate the sentences.

TASC TEST TIP

When you read a run-on sentence or a comma splice, look for the place where you would pause if you read the sentence aloud. That is where you should make the correction.

PRACTICE 3

A. Directions: Correct the following run-ons and comma splices using the methods explained on the previous page.

1. Jeff just got his driver's license, he's very excited.

_____

2. He bought a car that has a lot of miles on it it wasn't very expensive.

_____

3. He doesn't have a lot of free time, he'd like to take a car trip.

_____

4. He needs to find out about car insurance and he needs to get a good map and he needs to join an auto club.

_____

B. **Questions 5 through 7** refer to the following paragraph.

Photography Tips

(A)

(1) It's not hard to take great pictures just keep these tips in mind. (2) For one thing, you need to get close to your subject, or you won't get a good shot. (3) Be patient, wait for the right moment to shoot. (4) Make sure the lighting is sufficient. (5) Even outdoors, you can use a flash to fill in shadows.

(B)

(6) Think about what you want to emphasize in your picture. (7) You don't have to use the autofocus option, most cameras allow you to select the focus point you prefer. (8) For example, many photographs of people focus on the eyes.

5. Sentence 1: It's not hard to take great <u>pictures just</u> keep these tips in mind.

Which is the best way to write the underlined portion of the sentence?

A. pictures if you just
B. pictures if you just that
C. pictures, if you just
D. pictures that just

6. Sentence 3: Be patient, wait for the right moment to shoot.

Which correction should be made to sentence 3?

A. remove the comma
B. insert <u>and</u> in place of the comma
C. insert <u>but then</u> after the comma
D. insert a comma after <u>moment</u>

7. Sentence 7: You don't have to use the autofocus option, most cameras allow you to select the focus point you prefer.

Which correction should be made to sentence 7?

A. delete the comma after <u>option</u>
B. insert <u>and</u> after <u>option</u>
C. insert <u>because</u> in place of the comma
D. delete <u>you</u> after <u>allow</u>

LESSON 4

Subordinate Ideas

Writing is more effective when it flows smoothly. Therefore, try to elimi-nate short, choppy sentences whenever possible. You can do this by using **subordination**, that is, making one clause dependent on another instead of using two independent clauses.

EXAMPLES

Short and choppy: Carla ran for the bus. She missed it.
Complex sentence: <u>Although</u> Carla ran for the bus, she missed it.
Compound sentence: Carla ran for the bus, <u>but</u> she missed it.

If two sentences have the same subject, you can combine them to form one sentence with a compound predicate. The **predicate** includes the verb, the object of the verb, and any words or phrases that modify the verb.

Short and choppy: Carla sat on the bench. She looked at her watch.
With compound predicate: Carla <u>sat on the bench and looked at her watch</u>.

Likewise, when two sentences have the same predicate, you can combine them to form one sentence with a compound subject.

Short, choppy, and repetitive: Carla missed the bus. Dave missed the bus, too.
With compound subject: <u>Carla and Dave</u> missed the bus.

Sometimes ideas can be expressed by adding a **phrase** to a sentence. The table below gives some examples of types of phrases and how they can be used.

Type of phrase	Function	Examples
Adjectival	a phrase that modifies a noun	The Andersons' dog, *an affectionate, playful mop of fur,* greeted Sheila as she walked up the drive.
Adverbial	a phrase that modifies a verb, adjective, or another adverb	Sheila stopped *halfway up the driveway* and stooped to pet the dog. (The phrase modifies the verb "stopped" by explaining where Sheila stopped.)
Participial	a verb phrase that is used to modify a noun or another verb	*Being careful,* Anesha checked the records twice. The bird, *perched atop the old oak tree,* sang cheerfully.
Prepositional	a phrase that begins with a preposition and explains when, where, what kind, whose, or why	The top *of the tower* loomed *above the city's rooftops* and reminded me *of fairy tales.* The farmhouse stood *in a field of ripe wheat* and was shuttered tight *against the autumn wind.*
Absolute	a phrase that contains both an noun and a verb and describes the circumstances in which the main action of the sentence happens	*The snow having melted,* John decided to venture out. *All things considered,* we should probably buy extra supplies.

PRACTICE 4

A. Directions: Write each set of short, choppy sentences as one longer, smooth sentence.

EXAMPLE: If you are in a tornado, keep the windows closed. You should go to a safe place.
<u>If you are in a tornado, keep the windows closed and go to a safe place.</u>

1. Tornadoes can cause a lot of damage. Earthquakes are also capable of causing a lot of damage.

_____

2. Earthquakes are somewhat common in California. Many Californians do not seem to mind.

_____

3. On May 20, 2013, there was a tornado. It happened in Oklahoma. Twenty-four people were killed. Almost 400 people were injured.

_____

4. Tornadoes can occur anywhere in the United States. They can happen any time of year.

_____

B. Questions 5 through 7 refer to the following warranty.

Limited Warranty

(1) If there is any defect, Pantronics will repair this unit free of charge. (2) Audio components will be repaired. (3) Repairs will take place up to one year after the date of purchase. (4) The unit may be brought to the service center. (5) It can also be mailed. (6) A proof of purchase, such as a receipt, must be presented in order to receive service. (7) This warranty does not cover damage due to accidents. (8) It does not cover damage due to mishandling or faulty installation.

5. Sentences 2 and 3: Audio components will be _____ to one year after date of purchase.

Which is the best way to fill in the blank?

A. repaired. Repairs will then take up
B. repaired and repairs will take place up
C. repaired, the repairs will take place up
D. repaired up

6. Sentences 4 and 5: The unit may be brought to the service center. It can also be mailed.

The most effective combination of sentences 4 and 5 would include which group of words?

A. brought or mailed to
B. once brought to the service center,
C. units that are mailed to the service center
D. bringing it to the service center, or mailing

7. Sentences 7 and 8: This warranty does not cover damage due to accidents. It does not cover damage due to mishandling or faulty installation.

The most effective combination of sentences 7 and 8 would include which group of words?

A. accidents, and it
B. accidents, and this warranty
C. accidents, and, in addition, it
D. accidents, mishandling, or faulty installation

Modify Ideas

Modifiers are words and phrases used to add descriptive details. A modifier might be a word like *sweaty*, a verb phrase like *dragging the heavy box*, a prepositional phrase like *from the storage room*, or a clause like *that we packed this morning*. Modifiers make writing clearer, more specific, and more interesting.

EXAMPLES

Without modifiers: Our friends Jack and Tina helped us while we were moving.
With modifiers: Our <u>good</u> friends Jack and Tina helped us while we were moving, <u>watching our baby in their home</u>.

Without modifiers: We realized the weather would not cooperate.
With modifiers: <u>Sweating profusely at 9 A.M.,</u> we realized the weather would be <u>uncooperatively hot</u>.

Use modifiers carefully, or your meaning will be unclear. A **dangling modifier** is a word or phrase at the beginning of the sentence that has no clear subject to describe. To correct a dangling modifier, turn it into a subordinate clause, or make the word that the modifier describes into the subject of the sentence.

Dangling modifier: Driving the truck, one of the boxes fell out. (Who was driving the truck—one of the boxes?)
Correct: <u>As we were driving the truck,</u> one of the boxes fell out.
Correct: Driving the truck, <u>we heard</u> one of the boxes fall out.

Dangling modifier: Parking in a tow zone, a police officer gave us a ticket. (It sounds as if the police officer were parking in the tow zone.)
Correct: <u>Because we parked in a tow zone,</u> a police officer gave us a ticket.

Dangling modifier: Never having planned a move before, the real estate agent gave us some tips. (It sounds as if the real estate agent is the one who had never planned a move.)
Correct: Never having planned a move before, <u>we asked</u> the real estate agent for some tips.

A **misplaced modifier** is poorly placed in the sentence. It is not clear which word it modifies, or it modifies the wrong word in the sentence. To correct a misplaced modifier, put the modifier next to the word it describes.

Misplaced modifier: The moving van was just large enough <u>that we rented</u>.
Correct: <u>The moving van that we rented</u> was just large enough.

Misplaced modifier: We hoisted and lugged all our furniture up two flights of stairs <u>panting heavily</u>. (What was panting heavily—*we* or *the stairs*?)
Correct: <u>Panting heavily, we</u> hoisted and lugged all our furniture up two flights of stairs.

KEY IDEAS

- Modifiers make writing clearer and more interesting.
- Correct a dangling modifier by turning it into a subordinate clause or by making the word that is modified the subject of the sentence.
- Place a modifier as near as possible to the word or phrase it describes.

TASC TEST TIP

When a modifying phrase is at the beginning of a sentence, use a comma to separate it from the rest of the sentence.

PRACTICE 5

A. Directions: Revise each sentence, correcting the misplaced or dangling modifier.

1. Trent's sister encouraged him to become a nurse, who is a health professional.

_____

2. Waking up the patients to take their blood pressure, they get rather annoyed.

_____

3. He writes their temperature and blood pressure on their charts carefully.

_____

4. Talking with the patients, it is hard to make visitors leave at 9 p.m.

_____

B. Questions 5 through 7 refer to the following passage about adoption.

Adoption

(A)

(1) Adoption is a legal procedure that gives a person the rights of a son or daughter who is not the birth child of the adopter. (2) This practice dates back to ancient Greece. (3) People without heirs used it to perpetuate their estates.

(B)

(4) Adoptions may be handled through an agency or by independent placement. (5) Going through an agency, a "home study" to decide whether prospective parents will be fit is required. (6) In an independent placement, there is no study. (7) Lawyers handle these adoptions when parents ask them to frequently.

5. Sentence 1: Adoption is a legal procedure that gives a person the rights of a son or daughter who is not the birth child of the adopter.

The most effective revision of sentence 1 would include which group of words?

A. a legal procedure, adoption that gives
B. a person who is not the birth child
C. the son or daughter of the adopter
D. the birth child, who is a son or daughter

6. Sentence 5: Going through an agency, a "home study" to decide whether prospective parents will be fit is required.

The most effective revision of sentence 5 would begin with which group of words?

A. For parents, going through an agency
B. Requiring a "home study"
C. An agency requires a "home study"
D. Deciding whether a parent is fit

7. Sentence 7: Lawyers handle these adoptions when parents ask them to frequently.

Which correction should be made to sentence 7?

A. insert a comma after <u>adoptions</u>
B. replace <u>to</u> with <u>too</u>
C. insert a comma after <u>to</u>
D. move <u>frequently</u> to follow <u>Lawyers</u>

STUDY ADVICE

Keep in mind that people often do not correctly use modifiers when speaking. Learn the rules in this lesson and don't rely on your ear for modifiers.

Parallel Structure

When you write a sentence that lists two or more words, phrases, or clauses, the elements in the list must be in the same grammatical form. In other words, the sentence must have **parallel structure.** Writing that has parallel structure is clearer and easier to follow.

Examples
Not parallel: Jim wants to eat less, exercise more, and be getting more sleep.
Parallel: Jim wants to <u>eat</u> less, <u>exercise</u> more, and <u>get</u> more sleep.

Not parallel: Walking and to swim are good aerobic exercises.
Parallel: <u>Walking</u> and <u>swimming</u> are good aerobic exercises.

Not parallel: Try to lose weight slowly, sensibly, and be careful.
Parallel: Try to lose weight <u>slowly</u>, <u>sensibly</u>, and <u>carefully</u>.

To be sure that your sentences have parallel structure, follow the guidelines below.

Make sure that verbs in a list are in the same form and tense:

Not parallel: Jim went to the store, bought an exercise mat, and is doing exercises.
Parallel: Jim <u>went</u> to the store, <u>bought</u> an exercise mat, and <u>did</u> exercises.

Be sure that phrases in a list are parallel in form and wording. For example, if one phrase in a list begins with a preposition, the others should, too. If one phrase begins with the word *the*, the others should, too.

Not parallel: Avoid exercising on busy streets, near traffic jams, and polluted areas.
Parallel: Avoid exercising <u>on busy streets</u>, <u>near traffic jams</u>, and <u>in polluted areas</u>.

Not parallel: He left the gym shoes, sweatpants, and the shirt in the gym.
Parallel: He left <u>the</u> gym shoes, <u>the</u> sweatpants, and <u>the</u> shirt in the gym.

Each list must have single words, short phrases, or clauses. Don't put single words and clauses together in the same series:

Not parallel: The most effective fitness programs are low impact, informal, and you can do them at home.
Parallel: The most effective fitness programs are <u>low impact</u>, <u>informal</u>, and <u>home based</u>.

Finally, notice that a comma separates each item within a list of three or more: *low impact, informal, and home based.*

KEY IDEAS

- Listed items should be parallel in form and structure.
- Each phrase should have the same elements as other phrases in the series.
- A list may consist of individual words or full clauses, but never a mixture of both.

TASC TEST TIP

When you revise a sentence to use parallel structure, use the comma to separate each element as shown in these examples.

PRACTICE 6

A. Directions: Rewrite each sentence to make the structure parallel.

EXAMPLE: Jenna works quickly, carefully, and is thorough.
Jenna works quickly, carefully, and thoroughly.

1. Jenna has worked in a factory, a store, and has a waitressed.

   _____

2. She would like putting her kids in a better school and to get a better job.

   _____

3. She thinks the kids' father is irresponsible, lazy, and doesn't care about them.

   _____

4. He doesn't have the time, the energy, or money to give them what they deserve.

   _____

B. Questions 5 through 7 refer to the following memo.

TO: All Employees

(A)

(1) A new alarm system has been installed. (2) It is designed to make our workplace safer, more comfortable, and pleasant. (3) However, we need everyone's cooperation.

(B)

(4) If you are the last one to leave, turn off all lights, computers, and check the coffee makers. (5) Then go to the alarm system located by the door. (6) Punch in the secret code, press ON, and be leaving immediately. (7) Lock the door behind you.

5. Sentence 2: It is designed to make our workplace safer, more comfortable, and pleasant.

Which correction should be made to sentence 2?

A. replace <u>our</u> with <u>are</u>
B. remove the comma after <u>safer</u>
C. insert <u>more</u> before <u>pleasant</u>
D. no correction is necessary

6. Sentence 4: If you are the last one to leave, turn off all lights, _____ coffee makers.

Choose the option that correctly completes the sentence.

A. and computers, and the
B. computers, and check the
C. computers, and checking the
D. computers, and

7. Sentence 6: Punch in the secret code, press ON, and be leaving immediately.

Which correction should be made to sentence 6?

A. change <u>punch</u> to <u>punching</u>
B. remove the comma after <u>ON</u>
C. change <u>be leaving</u> to <u>leave</u>
D. insert a comma after <u>leaving</u>

STUDY ADVICE

Love reading novels or comic books? That's fantastic, because you're building your language skills every time you read. However, sometimes authors deliberately break the rules of grammar to create an artistic effect. So don't mimic your favorite writer on the TASC; rather, use the rules in this chapter when you write your essay.

WRITING EFFECTIVE SENTENCES PRACTICE QUESTIONS

Questions 1 through 5 refer to the following paragraphs.

Conserving Household Energy

(A)

(1) According to the Department of Energy, many families spend an average of 14 percent of their yearly income on heating and cooling costs. (2) Although you can't do much about high fuel prices, you can try some energy-saving measures.

(B)

(3) To reduce wintertime energy costs, keep the shades drawn at night. (4) Seal your windows, so that cold air can't get through the cracks. (5) You can use sealing material available at any hardware store. (6) If you have an air conditioner, cover it with thick plastic. (7) Keep your thermostat at 68°F during the day. (8) Keep it at 62°F at night.

(C)

(9) In the summer, use fans and natural breezes rather than air-conditioning whenever possible. (10) If you have windows that get direct sunlight. (11) Keep the shades down during the day. (12) Don't leave your air conditioner running when you're not at home, change the filter every summer. (13) With a clogged filter, the air conditioner's energy use can go up as much as 5 percent. (14) Put your air conditioner on a low setting. (15) Your home will not cool down when your air conditioner is on full blast any faster.

1. Sentence 4: **Seal your windows, so that cold air can't get through the cracks.**

   Which correction should be made to sentence 4?

   A. change <u>seal</u> to <u>sealing</u>
   B. remove the comma
   C. change <u>can't</u> to <u>couldn't</u>
   D. change <u>through</u> to <u>out</u>

2. Sentences 7 and 8: **Keep your thermostat at 68°F during the day. Keep it at 62°F at night.**

   The most effective combination of sentences 7 and 8 would include which group of words?

   A. keeping your thermostat at
   B. during the day and 62°F
   C. the day, keeping it at
   D. at night, it should be kept

3. Sentences 10 and 11: **If you have windows that get direct <u>sunlight. Keep</u> the shades down during the day.**

   Which is the best way to write the underlined portion of these sentences?

   A. sunlight and
   B. sunlight and to keep
   C. sunlight keep
   D. sunlight, keep

4. Sentence 12: **Don't leave your air conditioner running when you're not at <u>home, change</u> the filter every summer.**

   Which is the best way to write the underlined portion of the sentence?

   A. home and change
   B. home change
   C. home, so change
   D. home. Do change

5. Sentence 15: **Your home will not cool down when your air conditioner is on full blast any faster.**

   The most effective revision of sentence 15 would begin with which group of words?

   A. Your home will not cool down any faster
   B. Having the air conditioner on full blast, it
   C. When your home will not cool down,
   D. Air-conditioning your home on full blast,

Questions 6 through 10 refer to the following letter of complaint.

Cole Electronics
2514 Broadway
New York, NY 10057

Dear Manager:

(A)

(1) On August 2, I purchased a television at your store. (2) When I got the television home I discovered that the picture was fuzzy. (3) Returning to the store to see if the problem could be fixed easily. (4) I assumed that there would be no problem because I had just purchased the set.

(B)

(5) The customer service personnel said they had no time to handle my complaint. (6) They were extremely rude and unprofessional. (7) Finally, a salesman told me that I would have to send the TV to a service center in Detroit. (8) At that point, I demanded a refund. (9) Claiming that the TV had been used, it could not be returned.

(C)

(10) I am angry about the treatment I received and I am also very frustrated. (11) I would now like to receive a full refund or getting the TV repaired locally. (12) Please contact me to let me know what action will be taken. (13) My phone number is (212) 555-2719.

Sincerely,
Jeffrey Barnes

6. Sentence 2: **When I got the television home I discovered that the picture was fuzzy.**

Which correction should be made to sentence 2?

A. replace When with Since
B. insert a comma after home
C. insert a comma after discovered
D. change was to be

7. Sentence 3: **Returning to the store to see if the problem could be fixed easily.**

Which correction should be made to sentence 3?

A. replace Returning with I returned
B. add a comma after store
C. change could to can
D. change easily to easy

8. Sentence 9: **Claiming that the TV had been used, it could not be returned.**

The most effective revision of sentence 9 would begin with which group of words?

A. He claimed that because
B. The TV was claimed to
C. Returning the TV,
D. Making a claim about the TV

9. Sentence 10: **I am angry about the treatment I received and I am also very frustrated.**

The most effective revision of sentence 10 would include which group of words?

A. angry and frustrated about the
B. feeling angry about the treatment
C. being the recipient of such treatment
D. the manner in which I was treated

10. Sentence 11: **I would now like to receive a full _____ the TV repaired locally.**

Choose the option that correctly completes the sentence.

A. refund, getting
B. refund, or getting
C. refund or get
D. refund to getting

Questions 11 through 15 refer to the following paragraphs.

Workplace Friendships

(A)

(1) Should you make friends at work or keep your distance? (2) Most experts agree that it's not wise to get too chummy with your boss. Relationships with coworkers, however, are a more complex matter. (3) Although workplace friendships between peers can be beneficial, they can also cause problems.

(B)

(4) Workplace friendships have many positive aspects. (5) It's hard to work if you feel alone and in a productive way. (6) Having friends at work can make your day more pleasant, and give you energy. (7) Friends can serve as a sounding board for problems and help you succeed.

(C)

(8) However, like any other friendship, workplace friendships can turn sour. (9) Things get messy, when the friendship unravels in plain view of your boss and coworkers. (10) Discrimination and harassment suits have even been brought in some cases.

(D)

(11) Experts recommend keeping your social life with work friends out of the workplace. (12) For instance, don't exchange presents at work or talking about your evening out. (13) Avoid praising a friend publicly if it could make someone else resentful. (14) Keeping your work life separate from your social life may be hard but it's worth the effort.

11. Sentence 5: **It's hard to work if you feel alone and in a productive way.**

    The most effective revision of sentence 5 would include which group of words?

    A. work productively if you
    B. to work, it isn't easy if
    C. if you feel alone and productive
    D. work, feel alone, and be productive

12. Sentence 6: **Having friends at work can make your day more pleasant, and give you energy.**

    Which correction should be made to sentence 6?

    A. change Having to Have
    B. insert a comma after work
    C. remove the comma
    D. change give to giving

13. Sentence 9: **Things get messy, when the friendship unravels in plain view of your boss and coworkers.**

    Which correction should be made to sentence 9?

    A. change get to are getting
    B. remove the comma
    C. insert a comma after unravels
    D. insert a comma after boss

14. Sentence 12: **For instance, don't exchange presents at _____ about your evening out.**

    Choose the option that correctly completes the sentence.

    A. work or talk
    B. work, or talk
    C. work, or talking
    D. working or talking

15. Sentence 14: **Keeping your work life separate from your social life may be hard but it's worth the effort.**

    Which correction should be made to sentence 14?

    A. insert it after social life
    B. insert a comma after hard
    C. insert a comma after but
    D. replace it's with its

Questions 16 through 19 refer to the following paragraphs.

Computer Virus Hoaxes

(A)

(1) If you use email, you've probably received at least one message warning you of a terrible virus that will ruin your computer. (2) Most of these messages are hoaxes. (3) Designed to scare you. (4) Though some messages about viruses are accurate, most are just inaccurate rumors.

(B)

(5) Virus hoax messages are similar to one another. (6) Frequently, they describe viruses that will destroy your hard drive or computer. (7) These hoaxes also claim that a respected authority, such as a government agency, has issued a warning about the virus. (8) You can check a claim like this. (9) Contacting the agency is a good way to check. (10) Finally, hoaxes urge you to send the message to everyone you know, this just creates panic.

(C)

(11) If you receive a virus warning, don't pass it on. (12) However, you don't have to worry about opening the email message itself. (13) Your computer can't get a virus that way. (14) Don't open any suspicious attachments, though, as you might infect your computer with a real virus. (15) By following these guidelines, you can keep your computer equipment safe, and avoid spreading hysteria.

16. Sentences 2 and 3: **Most of these messages are _____ to scare you.**

Choose the option that correctly completes the sentence.

A. hoaxes and they are designed
B. hoaxes and they designed
C. hoaxes, designing
D. hoaxes designed

17. Sentences 8 and 9: **You can check a claim like this. Contacting the agency is a good way to check.**

The most effective combination of sentences 8 and 9 would include which group of words?

A. checking a claim like this
B. to check a claim like this, contact
C. the agency in question can check
D. a good way to check, contacting

18. Sentence 10: **Finally, hoaxes urge you to send the message to everyone you _____ just creates panic.**

Choose the option that best completes the sentence.

A. know and this
B. know, this
C. know. This
D. know that this

19. Sentence 15: **By following these guidelines, you can keep your computer equipment safe, and avoid spreading hysteria.**

Which correction should be made to sentence 15?

A. change By following to To follow
B. replace these with this
C. remove the comma after guidelines
D. remove the comma after safe

STUDY ADVICE

Congratulations on completing another practice set! If you are struggling with a topic and don't feel you have more time to spend on it right this second, flag it for later. Keeping a list of what you should come back to will save time and guide your future studies.

Organize Ideas into Paragraphs

Effective Paragraphs

A **paragraph** is a group of sentences that relate to one main idea. If the sentences do not help develop the same main idea, the paragraph seems disorganized, and the writer's meaning is unclear.

Incorrect:

> Houseplants make a home more beautiful, but many people find them difficult to take care of. I water my houseplants once a week. There are many different kinds of houseplants. If you are buying a houseplant as a gift, consider how much light the person's home gets.

In the example above, each sentence is about houseplants, but there is no main idea. In the paragraph below, however, each sentence supports one idea: *helping houseplants adjust to a new home.*

Correct:

> Houseplants need help to adjust to a new environment. Your home is probably less bright and humid than a greenhouse or plant store. Therefore, when you get a new houseplant, keep it near a south-facing window at first. Move it away from the light over a period of four weeks. Use a humidifier to make the air in your home more humid. These actions will help avoid the loss of foliage that often occurs when plants change locales.

One paragraph should stop and a new one begin when the main idea shifts. In the example below, the first four sentences describe what road rage is, while the last four sentences tell how to react to road rage. The writer should have started a new paragraph with sentence 5.

Incorrect:

> (1) Road rage is an episode of violent behavior that takes place when one driver's actions anger another driver. (2) Young males are the most likely to lose their cool on the road. (3) Most road rage incidents take place during rush hour, when people often get frustrated. (4) Warm weather is another factor in road rage. (5) If you're a victim of an aggressive driver, try to stay calm. (6) Don't react or make eye contact. (7) Try not to brake or swerve in retaliation. (8) These actions will only infuriate the other driver, and you might lose control of your car.

Sometimes the ideas in two paragraphs really belong in one paragraph:

Incorrect:

> To make chicken broth, boil a pot of water. Take some chicken, onions, parsnips, carrots, and herbs, and wrap them up in cheesecloth.
>
> Make sure it is real cotton cheesecloth, or you won't be able to eat the broth! Simmer the cheesecloth-wrapped vegetables and chicken in the water for several hours; then remove them. Add salt and pepper to taste.

KEY IDEAS

- Each paragraph should have one main idea.
- Each sentence in a paragraph should relate to the main idea.
- Join short paragraphs if they both relate to the same main idea.

TASC TEST TIP

If a paragraph is especially long, check to see if the main idea shifts at some point. If so, that is where the paragraph should be divided in two.

A. Directions: Read each group of sentences. If there is a main idea, underline it. If there is no main idea, write "No MI."

_____ 1. The pharmacist at the local drugstore is very helpful. She can always get the medicines we need. She arranges deliveries of our prescriptions when we're sick. When we don't have money, she lets us pay the next time. Many people have written to thank her.

_____ 2. Keep your toolbox well equipped, and you'll always be able to make home repairs. Common home repairs include replacing lighting fixtures and fixing furniture. The community center offers a class on this subject. You can pay someone to do home repairs.

_____ 3. Some people don't vote because they think their vote doesn't count. However, elections have been won by just a few hundred votes. If people don't vote, they are giving up their voice. Every vote counts, so let your voice be heard and vote!

_____ 4. When you are traveling, it's a good idea to mark your luggage clearly. Put a luggage tag on every piece you intend to bring, including hand luggage like backpacks. To recognize your luggage quickly, put a brightly colored ribbon on it.

_____ 5. Listening to music can benefit you in many ways. When you are feeling stressed, music can help soothe and relax you. When you need energy, rock 'n' roll or hip-hop can give you a boost. If you have a baby or small child, soft music can help lull the child to sleep.

B. Questions 6 and 7 refer to the following paragraphs.

The Common Cold

(A)

(1) How frequently you get colds depends on your age. (2) The average young adult gets two to four colds a year. (3) Adults over 60 have fewer than one cold a year, while children have six to ten colds annually. (4) Colds are caused by viruses. (5) Contrary to popular belief, being cold will not cause you to get a cold. (6) Vitamin C is thought to prevent colds, but there is no proof.

(B)

(7) Because there is no cure for the common cold, prevention is key. (8) Washing your hands is the best way to avoid getting a cold. (9) Encourage others who have colds to sneeze into a tissue and throw it away immediately.

(C)

(10) Refrain from touching your eyes and nose, and stay far from people who have colds.

6. Which revision would improve the effectiveness of the article?

Begin a new paragraph with

A. sentence 2
B. sentence 3
C. sentence 4
D. sentence 5

7. Which revision would improve the effectiveness of the article?

A. remove sentence 1
B. remove paragraph (B)
C. remove paragraph (C)
D. join paragraphs (B) and (C)

Topic Sentences in Paragraphs

Every paragraph should have a **topic sentence** that states the main idea. The other sentences in the paragraph are **supporting details.** These details tell more about the topic sentence. The topic sentence usually appears at the beginning of the paragraph, though it may appear elsewhere.

A topic sentence must do two things:

- Identify the topic, or subject, of the paragraph
- State the central point that the writer wants to make about the topic

In the paragraph below, the topic sentence is underlined. Notice how the topic sentence tells the subject of the paragraph (*graffiti in our neighborhood*) and states the central point about the topic (*graffiti is a serious problem in the neighborhood and should be addressed*).

EXAMPLE

<u>We need to do more to stop the problem of graffiti in our neighborhood.</u> Recently, several bus stops and the exterior walls of many buildings have been defaced with unsightly graffiti. The neighborhood is fast becoming a much less desirable place to live. As a result, prospective renters feel frightened and look elsewhere.

A topic sentence should not be too specific or too general. If it is, readers won't know what the overall point is. A topic sentence like "The market is covered with gang symbols," would be too specific for the paragraph above. "There is graffiti in our neighborhood," would be too general.

Main Idea Statements in Essays

Just as every paragraph should have a topic sentence, every essay should have a **main idea statement**. Whereas a topic sentence states the main idea, or "point," of a single paragraph, a main idea statement expresses the central point of all the paragraphs in an essay. In the essay below, the main idea statement is underlined. Notice that while the main idea statement appears in the first paragraph, it is not the first sentence.

EXAMPLE

While graffiti is indeed a serious problem facing our neighborhood, other issues also need to be addressed. <u>Two of the most pressing neighborhood issues are the crime rate and the lack of decent housing.</u>

In recent months, crime has increased. For example, a number of muggings have occurred. As a result, residents are nervous about going out at night. The number of apartment break-ins has increased as well. We need a stronger police presence to combat the crime problem.

In addition, much of the housing in this neighborhood is in poor condition. Every day, residents are put in danger by loose roof tiles, broken locks, and rundown fences. We must put pressure on landlords to resolve their tenants' complaints, perhaps by showing them that, in the long run, it is in their financial interest to do so.

If we do not act immediately, our neighborhood will decline even more. Therefore, I recommend that we form a community task force to tackle these issues. We should ask our city councilwoman to be an advocate for us. With full participation of community members, we will be on our way to a safer, more livable neighborhood.

PRACTICE 1.2

A. Directions: Write topic sentences for each of the following paragraphs.

1. _____

Weather satellites send us information about weather around the world. Thanks to satellite TV, we have an ever-widening range of programs to choose from. Satellites even play a role in long-distance telephone communication.

2. _____

First of all, stock prices are falling. Second, home sales have slowed to a crawl. Finally, many consumers have cut back on big purchases such as cars, home improvements, and vacations.

3. _____

According to the new dress code, employees of the library may now wear "semi-casual" clothing. Khakis, blue jeans with no holes, and other slacks are acceptable for men and women. Skirts must be knee-length or longer. Sandals are acceptable in the summer. Employees are requested not to wear gym shoes.

B. Questions 4 and 5 refer to the following paragraphs.

Repetitive Strain Injury

(A)

(1) Repetitive strain injury is a problem. (2) The injury can affect factory workers, computer users, and meatpackers, among others. (3) Anyone who uses his or her hands all day may be affected, even if the work does not seem to require a lot of physical effort. (4) When fine hand movements are repeated for many hours a day, they eventually strain the forearms, wrists, and fingers.

(B)

(5) Maintaining a stiff and constrained posture, as is required for working at a computer, places a lot of stress on the body. (6) Likewise, holding muscles still for long periods causes fatigue and discomfort. (7) In addition, many jobs require workers to work at top speed all day long. (8) Consistently working quickly deprives the body of natural rest breaks, forcing workers to push themselves to the limit.

4. Which is the most effective revision of sentence 1?

A. Some workers get repetitive strain injury.
B. Just what, you may ask, is repetitive strain injury?
C. Workers suffer many injuries on the job, and repetitive strain injury is just one of them.
D. Repetitive strain injury is a painful condition resulting from repeated use of the hands.

5. Which sentence would be most effective if inserted at the beginning of paragraph (B)?

A. Repetitive movements cause muscle strain.
B. A number of factors contribute to repetitive strain injury.
C. Watch your posture as you work.
D. Repetitive strain injury is very common.

STUDY ADVICE

Remember that practice has three levels: Learn and Review, Practice and Review, Assess and Review. For each lesson, absorb the concepts on the left side of the page. Then practice using the page on the right, and carefully review the explanations in the back of the book. Afterwards, you'll be able to assess your comprehension by completing the practice set and reviewing the explanations. By following these steps, you'll learn a great deal about how the questions work and what you're doing well.

Use Logical Order and Relevant Ideas

When you are writing a paragraph, it is important to put your sentences in a logical order. For instance, you may choose to sequence supporting details from most important to least important, from least important to most important, or in time order. All the sentences in the paragraph should follow the same order. If not, your readers may get confused.

Incorrect:

> To clear a clogged drain using a plunger, fill the sink with enough water to cover the plunger cup. Put petroleum jelly on the rim of the cup to form a tight seal. Before you begin, check to make sure that the plunger's suction cup is big enough to cover the drain. Block the sink overflow with rags. Plunge 15 or 20 times.

Correct:

> To clear a clogged drain using a plunger, <u>first check to make sure that the plunger's suction cup is big enough to cover the drain</u>. Fill the sink with enough water to cover the plunger cup. Put petroleum jelly on the rim of the cup to form a tight seal. Block the sink overflow with rags. Plunge 15 or 20 times.

The reasons and examples you use to support your points should come immediately after you make each point. If they come later, they will be less effective.

Incorrect:

> Don't make a habit of using chemicals to clear your drain. Always wear rubber gloves to protect your hands when using chemical drain cleaners. These powerful cleaners can damage the pipes.

Correct:

> Don't make a habit of using chemicals to clear your drain. <u>These powerful cleaners can damage the pipes</u>. Always wear rubber gloves to protect your hands when using chemical drain cleaners.

Sometimes a sentence in a paragraph relates to the topic in a general way but does not support the topic sentence. This mistake is a type of **irrelevant detail**, as shown in the paragraph below:

> In many cultures, blonde is considered a desirable hair color. Perhaps blonde hair is valued because few people are naturally blonde. The practice of bleaching one's hair blonde is very old, dating back to ancient Roman times, and it continues to be popular today. <u>My sister dyed her hair last year</u>. A number of hair-bleaching products are sold in drugstores and supermarkets.

The sentence "My sister dyed her hair last year," is an irrelevant detail. While it relates to the topic of bleaching one's hair, it does not support the idea that blonde is a popular hair color in many cultures. This sentence should be deleted.

PRACTICE 2

A. Directions: Cross out the irrelevant detail in each paragraph.

1. Why do people blame themselves when things go terribly wrong? Some psychologists believe that by blaming themselves, people find a reason for the upsetting event. Getting very ill is one bad thing that could happen. Finding a reason is more comforting than believing that the event took place for no reason at all.

2. It's almost time for the back-to-school rush. This year, come to Wunnzie's to make sure that your child is outfitted with all the things that he or she needs. We have school supplies at rock-bottom prices. Adult students can also use school supplies. Check out our backpacks and lunch boxes in colors your kids will love. At Wunnzie's, we have everything your kids will ever need!

3. Tenants: On Friday, April 23, the boiler in this building will be fixed. This job will be extremely expensive! There will be no water from 8 a.m. to 5 p.m. Please plan in advance, and draw out water the night before to be used the next day. We apologize for the inconvenience.

B. Questions 4 through 6 refer to the following cover letter.

(A)

Dear Mr. Soros:

(1) Thank you very much for taking the time to speak with me about the carpentry position. (2) It was a pleasure to meet you and to learn about your organization. (3) I enjoyed meeting you and learning about your organization.

(B)

(4) As you will see from the enclosed resume, I recently completed a program in carpentry at Dade Community College. (5) I have also worked in the carpentry field. (6) In addition, I held a secretarial job.

(C)

(7) With my education and experience, I believe that I could make a valuable contribution to your company. (8) Thank you for considering me for this position. (9) I look forward to hearing from you soon. (10) I would be honored to take the job if it were offered to me.

Sincerely,

Sandra Barnes

4. Which revision would improve the effectiveness of paragraph (A)?

A. remove sentence 1
B. move sentence 1 to follow sentence 2
C. move sentence 2 to the beginning of paragraph B
D. remove sentence 3

5. **Sentence 6: In addition, I held a secretarial job.**

Which revision should be made to the placement of sentence 6?

A. move sentence 6 to follow sentence 4
B. move sentence 6 to follow sentence 8
C. move sentence 6 to follow sentence 10
D. remove sentence 6

6. **Sentence 10: I would be honored to take the job if it were offered to me.**

Which revision should be made to the placement of sentence 10?

A. move sentence 10 to follow sentence 2
B. move sentence 10 to follow sentence 4
C. move sentence 10 to follow sentence 5
D. move sentence 10 to follow sentence 8

Relate Sentences and Paragraphs

Good writing flows smoothly and logically from one sentence to the next and from one paragraph to the next. To make your writing flow, use **transitions** to show how ideas are related. Here are some common transitions and their uses.

Transitional word or phrase	Use it to . . .
for example, for instance	give an example
also, furthermore, in addition, in the same way, likewise, moreover, similarly	compare ideas or add to an idea
however, nevertheless, on the other hand, in contrast	contrast ideas
first, second, then, next, after that, later, at last, finally, in conclusion	show steps in a process or time order
because	show a cause
as a result, consequently	show a result
therefore, thus	draw a conclusion

KEY IDEAS

- Use transitions to help your writing flow from sentence to sentence and from paragraph to paragraph.
- Choose the transition that expresses the correct relationship between ideas.

TASC TEST TIP

When you use a transition at the beginning of a sentence, be sure you put a comma after the transition.

You can link two sentences using transitions in the following ways:

EXAMPLES

Begin the second sentence with a transition followed by a comma: Raquel has many hobbies. For example, she paints furniture and sews clothes.

Put the transition within the second sentence and set it off with commas: Raquel has many hobbies. She paints furniture, for example, and sews clothes.

Combine the two sentences into one. Put a semicolon before the transition and a comma after it: Raquel has many hobbies; for example, she paints furniture and sews clothes.

Transitions can also be used to link one paragraph to another, highlighting the relationship between the two paragraphs.

EXAMPLE

Top performance in sports depends on "mental economy." Mental economy involves focusing the mind on the task at hand. When athletes think too much about what they're doing or worry about the outcome, they interfere with the communication between the brain and the muscles.

In addition, athletes must strive for "physical economy." Although athletes put forth a tremendous amount of effort, they must take care to pace themselves in order to conserve energy for the end of the event.

To decide which transition to use, see how the paragraph is organized and what you are trying to accomplish. For example, are you comparing two things? If so, you will want to use transitions that compare ideas. Similarly, when choosing transitions to introduce paragraphs, consider the organization of the entire essay.

A. Directions: Rewrite each pair of sentences using a transition from the chart on the previous page. Change the punctuation if necessary. Write your answers on a separate sheet of paper.

EXAMPLE: We have worked very hard this year. Sales are at an all-time high.
We have worked very hard this year. As a result, sales are at an all-time high.

1. Our marketing efforts need to be enhanced. We will soon begin another marketing initiative.

2. Sales representatives say their jobs are extremely demanding. The salary is attractive.

3. The marketing director has instructed sales representatives to try some new ideas. Sales representatives can give away free samples.

4. A new ad campaign will be launched in just a few weeks. We expect sales to increase.

B. Questions 5 through 7 refer to the following paragraphs.

Library Cafés

(A)

(1) Until very recently, eating was not something that most people associated with libraries. (2) A patron would likely be chased out for munching on a sandwich in a corner. (3) Times are changing, and these days patrons can even buy coffee and a croissant in some public libraries.

(B)

(4) Following the lead of successful bookstores, libraries across the country are installing cafés. (5) Some library cafés have menus that offer just as much variety as a regular restaurant. (6) In addition, one of them offers 20 varieties of coffee, hot cider, and muffins. (7) These refreshments make going to the library more pleasant and may therefore increase library patronage.

(C)

(8) To have a café may benefit a library financially. (9) The income from the café adds to library revenues. (10) Also, as more people enjoy coming to the library, they may be more likely to approve tax increases for it.

STUDY ADVICE

The way your ideas relate to each other may be obvious to you, but it won't be to your readers. It's your job to make it clear how sentence 2 relates to sentence 1, and how sentence 3 relates to sentence 2. As you write, think about how you can make it *really easy* for your readers to follow the flow of your ideas.

5. **Sentence 3:** Times are changing, and these days patrons can even buy coffee and a croissant in some public libraries.

Which correction should be made to sentence 3?

A. insert <u>however</u> after <u>Times</u>
B. insert <u>however,</u> after the comma
C. insert , <u>however</u> after <u>these days</u>
D. insert , <u>however</u> after <u>coffee</u>

6. **Sentences 5 and 6:** Some library cafés have menus that offer just as much variety as those of a regular _____ one of them offers 20 varieties of coffee, hot cider, and muffins.

Choose the best option that correctly completes the sentence.

A. restaurant, in addition,
B. restaurant. For example,
C. restaurant. Nevertheless,
D. restaurant. Thus,

7. **Sentence 8:** <u>To have a café</u> may benefit a library financially.

Choose the best option that corrects the sentence.

A. In addition, having a café
B. On the other hand, having a café
C. A café, by benefiting a library,
D. Financially a café

Connecting Ideas Practice Questions

Questions 1 through 5 refer to the following paragraphs.

The Effects of Lack of Sleep

(A)

(1) Research shows that about 70 million North Americans have experienced the problem of sleep disruption. (2) Losing sleep is more than just an annoyance. (3) In some cases, it can have catastrophic results. (4) In the United States, sleepy drivers are responsible for at least 100,000 car crashes each year. (5) Most people need at least eight hours of shut-eye a night but get only six or seven. (6) Their fast-paced lives leave them little time for sleep. (7) Another factor is poor bedtime habits. (8) Family stresses may also cause sleep loss.

(B)

(9) A study of high school students showed that students with low grades went to bed 40 minutes later and got 25 minutes less sleep than students with high grades. (10) On the other hand, another study shows that when one gets fewer than six to eight hours of sleep, it is harder to learn new skills.

(C)

(11) If you have trouble sleeping, avoid caffeine and alcohol. (12) Get regular exercise during the day, when it won't make you too energized to sleep. (13) Exercise can also help you lose weight.

(D)

(14) Set times for going to bed and getting up each day, and stick to them. (15) Don't watch TV or use a computer late at night, since these stimulate visual response and interfere with sleep. (16) If you find you still can't sleep, get up and do something.

1. Which revision would improve the effectiveness of the article?

   Begin a new paragraph with

   A. sentence 3
   B. sentence 4
   C. sentence 5
   D. sentence 6

2. Which sentence would be most effective if inserted at the beginning of paragraph (B)?

   A. Some high school students get better grades than others.
   B. High-achieving students get more sleep.
   C. Lack of sleep interferes with mathematical ability.
   D. People need more sleep than they used to.

3. Sentences 9 and 10: **A study of high school students showed that students with low grades went to bed 40 minutes later and got 25 minutes less sleep than students with high _____ another study shows that when one gets fewer than six to eight hours of sleep, it is harder to learn new skills.**

   Choose the best option that correctly completes the sentence.

   A. grades. Similarly,
   B. grades, likewise,
   C. grades. As a result,
   D. grades. Therefore,

4. Sentence 13: **Exercise can also help you lose weight.**

   Which revision should be made regarding sentence 13?

   A. move sentence 13 to follow sentence 11
   B. move sentence 13 to follow sentence 14
   C. move sentence 13 to follow sentence 15
   D. remove sentence 13

5. Which revision would improve the effectiveness of the article?

   A. join paragraphs (B) and (C)
   B. move sentence 11 to the end of paragraph (B)
   C. remove sentence 14
   D. join paragraphs (C) and (D)

Questions 6 through 10 refer to the following paragraphs.

Getting Out Those Troublesome Stains

(A)

(1) Have you ever ruined a nice piece of clothing by staining it? (2) If so, the following information on stain removal may interest you. (3) By learning a few simple rules and keeping some household cleaners on hand, you can preserve your clothing. (4) First of all, the faster you act, the better. (5) With time, the stain will set. (6) Be sure to blot the stain rather than scrubbing it. (7) Scrubbing can actually drive the stain into the fabric.

(B)

(8) Use hot water on a grease stain such as salad dressing and cold water on a water-based stain such as wine, pasta sauce, or blood. (9) If you don't know what the stain is or where it came from, use room-temperature water. (10) Otherwise you might set the stain.

(C)

(11) Sometimes other liquids are more effective than water. (12) Lemon juice, for example removes ink, rust, and iodine. (13) White vinegar takes out alcohol, coffee, deodorants, and glue. (14) Liquid shampoo can be used on oil, tar, and grease. (15) Not surprisingly, it works the same way on an oil stain as it does on oil in your hair. (16) Rubbing alcohol removes stains from grass and soft drinks.

(D)

(17) If you find that a stain is not going away or is getting worse, stop and take your clothes to a dry cleaner. (18) Professionals know best. (19) Home remedies may not work on every stain.

6. Which revision would improve the effectiveness of the article?

Begin a new paragraph with

A. sentence 3
B. sentence 4
C. sentence 5
D. sentence 6

7. Which sentence would be most effective if inserted at the beginning of paragraph (B)?

A. Hot and cold water have many uses.
B. Choose the right water temperature for cleaning each stain.
C. Hot water takes out tough stains.
D. The second step is to determine the proper use of hot water.

8. Sentence 12: **Lemon _____ ink, rust, and iodine.**

Choose the option that correctly completes the sentence.

A. juice, for example removes
B. juice, for example. Removes
C. juice for example removes
D. juice, for example, removes

9. Which revision would improve the effectiveness of paragraph (C)?

A. move sentence 11 to follow sentence 12
B. move sentence 12 to follow sentence 14
C. remove sentence 14
D. remove sentence 15

10. Sentence 19: **Home remedies may not work on every stain.**

Which revision should be made to the placement of sentence 19?

A. move sentence 19 to the beginning of paragraph (C)
B. move sentence 19 to follow sentence 13
C. move sentence 19 to the beginning of paragraph (D)
D. move sentence 19 to follow sentence 17

Questions 11 through 14 refer to the following memo.

To: All Employees
From: Denise Ellis, Benefits Manager

(A)

(1) Starting on January 1, Allcity will no longer be our insurance carrier. (2) Instead, you will have a choice of two other insurance carriers: HealthPlan and Rainbow Insurance Company.

(B)

(3) HealthPlan is an HMO. (4) You will not have to pay any money to doctors in advance with this plan, but you must go to doctors listed with the insurance company. (5) HMOs are becoming increasingly popular. (6) With Rainbow Insurance, you may choose any doctor you wish. (7) However you must pay the health providers when you receive the service. (8) Afterwards, you submit the receipts to Rainbow Insurance. (9) Representatives of both companies will be here on December 2 to discuss the details of their plans. (10) Please sign up for an informational session on that day. (11) The sign-up sheet is on the door of the conference room, where the meetings will take place.

(C)

(12) At the meeting, you will receive a card on which you must indicate your choice of company. (13) Please mark your choice in the appropriate box and submit it to me by December 5.

(D)

(14) If you do not submit your card in time, you may not be insured for the month of January. (15) If you are not able to attend any of the informational sessions, please let me know right away. (16) Feel free to contact me at ext. 2453 with any questions you may have about this process.

11. Which revision would improve the effectiveness of paragraph (B)?

   A. remove sentence 3
   B. move sentence 5 to the beginning of paragraph (B)
   C. remove sentence 5
   D. remove sentence 10

12. Sentence 7: **However you must pay the health providers when you receive the service.**

   Which correction should be made to sentence 7?

   A. insert a comma after <u>However</u>
   B. Insert a comma after <u>pay</u>
   C. insert a comma after <u>when</u>
   D. change <u>receive</u> to <u>receives</u>

13. Which revision would improve the effectiveness of the memo?

   Begin a new paragraph with

   A. sentence 7
   B. sentence 8
   C. sentence 9
   D. sentence 10

14. Sentence 14: **If you do not submit your card on time, you may not be insured for the month of January.**

   Which revision should be made regarding sentence 14?

   A. move sentence 14 to the end of paragraph (C)
   B. move sentence 14 to follow sentence 15
   C. move sentence 14 to follow sentence 16
   D. remove sentence 14

Questions 15 through 19 refer to the following paragraphs.

Repairing a Flat Bicycle Tire

(A)

(1) The first step in fixing a flat bicycle tire is to remove the wheel. (2) Next, release the brake. (3) Before you begin, let out any air in the tire. (4) If you are removing the back wheel, put the derailleur in high gear. (5) Then take off the axle nuts by unscrewing counterclockwise. (6) If your bike has safety washers, remove these also. (7) Then remove the wheel.

(B)

(8) Remove the tire, and mark the valve stem position on it. (9) If possible, remove the tire without using tools, because the inner tube punctures easily. (10) Use tire levers or the backs of forks and spoons if necessary. (11) When you find the leak, scrape the spot with sandpaper. (12) Remove the inner tube and inflate it, listening and feeling for air leaks. (13) Then apply cement to the tube, and let it dry completely before putting the patch on.

(C)

(14) First, inflate the tube and make sure the leak has been fixed. (15) Next, slip the inner tube back into the tire, and put the tire back on the rim. (16) Then inflate the tube to the correct pressure. (17) The pressure is right when there is enough air to steady the tire but not so much air that the tire cannot be squeezed between the brake pads.

(D)

(18) Put the bike back on its wheels, and then tighten the wheel nuts. (19) Moreover, readjust the tire pressure, and you're ready to ride!

15. Which revision would improve the effectiveness of paragraph (A)?

    A. move sentence 2 to follow sentence 3
    B. begin a new paragraph with sentence 5
    C. move sentence 5 to follow sentence 7
    D. remove sentence 6

16. Which revision would improve the effectiveness of paragraph (B)?

    A. move sentence 11 to follow sentence 8
    B. move sentence 11 to follow sentence 9
    C. move sentence 11 to follow sentence 12
    D. move sentence 11 to follow sentence 13

17. Which sentence would be most effective if inserted at the beginning of paragraph (C)?

    A. All you have to do now is take care of the tire pressure.
    B. Fixing a flat tire is a long process that requires a lot of patience.
    C. The next step is to put the tire and tube back onto the rim.
    D. Patching the leak properly is also very important.

18. Which sentence would be most effective if inserted at the beginning of paragraph (D)?

    A. The final step is to reinstall the wheel.
    B. Fixing a flat tire requires careful planning.
    C. Whether you are an experienced cyclist or just a beginner, you can fix a flat tire.
    D. Try not to use sharp tools to fix a flat tire.

19. Sentence 19: **Moreover, readjust the tire pressure, and you're ready to ride!**

    Which correction should be made to sentence 19?

    A. replace Moreover, with Then
    B. change readjust to readjusting
    C. remove the comma after pressure
    D. replace you're with your

Noun and Pronoun Agreement

Using Nouns and Pronouns

A **noun** names a person (such as *woman* or *Anne*), a place (such as *drugstore* or *Florida*), a thing (such as *car* or *Titanic*), or an idea (*truth* or *Buddhism*). A **proper noun** refers to a specific person, place, thing, or idea; a **common noun** is more general. For example, *Anne* is a proper noun; *woman* is a common noun.

A **pronoun** is a word that replaces a noun. The **antecedent** is the noun that is being replaced, as shown below:

EXAMPLE

Steven lost his <u>address book</u>. <u>It</u> held many important phone numbers.
             antecedent   pronoun

There are three types of pronouns: subject, object, and possessive.

EXAMPLES

A **subject pronoun** replaces the subject of a sentence.

<u>Steven</u> called home. <u>He</u> was very worried.
subject   subject pronoun

An **object pronoun** replaces the object of a verb or of a preposition.

Steven's wife called him. She asked <u>him</u> what the problem was.
          object pronoun (object of a verb)

She and Steven looked for <u>it</u>.
      object pronoun (object of a preposition)

A **possessive pronoun** replaces a possessive noun.
Steven needed <u>Kelly's</u> number. He called 411 to get <u>her</u> number.
     possessive noun   possessive pronoun

Use this chart for help in remembering the three types of pronouns:

Subject pronoun: replaces subject	Object pronoun: replaces object	Possessive pronoun: shows ownership
I	me	my, mine
you	you	your, yours
he	him	his
she	her	her, hers
it	it	its
we	us	ours
they	them	their, theirs

Avoid these mistakes with pronouns in compound subjects and objects:

Incorrect pronoun in compound subject: Linda and <u>me</u> went to the movies.
Correct: Linda and <u>I</u> went to the movies.

Incorrect pronoun in compound object: We saw Kareem and <u>he</u> at the theater.
Correct: We saw Kareem and <u>him</u> at the theater.

KEY IDEAS

- A noun names a person, place, thing, or idea.
- A pronoun takes the place of a noun.
- Use subject, object, and possessive pronouns in the proper places.

TASC TEST TIP

To choose the option with the correct pronoun in a compound like "They went to the party with James and I," take out "James and" and ask yourself whether the sentence still sounds correct.

PRACTICE 1.1

A. Directions: Write the correct pronoun to replace each underlined noun.

1. <u>Laurie and Paul</u> just moved to California. _____

2. A neighbor told Laurie and <u>Paul</u> that saving water was important there. _____

3. He said they should turn <u>the water</u> off when brushing their teeth. _____

4. <u>Laurie's</u> sister suggested getting a special shower head that saves water. _____

5. Laurie and <u>Laurie's sister</u> will go shopping for it on Sunday. _____

B. <u>Questions 6 through 8</u> refer to the following letter.

To Whom It May Concern:

(A)

(1) I am writing to recommend Bonetta Williams for the position of managerial assistant in your firm. (2) I believe that she is highly qualified for the position, and I urge you to strongly consider her candidacy.

(B)

(3) Bonetta and me have worked together for three years. (4) As my secretary, she has proven to be responsible and efficient. (5) She always getting her work done on time and looks for ways to help others. (6) In addition, I find her extremely intelligent and likable. (7) I will be sorry to see her go.

(C)

(8) My supervisor, Walter Constantine, has also worked with Bonetta and would be happy to speak with you if necessary. (9) Please contact Walter or I if you need any further information.

Sincerely,

Carol Rhodes

6. Sentence 3: Bonetta and me have worked together for three years.

Which correction should be made to sentence 3?

A. replace <u>me</u> with <u>I</u>
B. replace <u>Bonetta</u> with <u>She</u>
C. insert a comma after <u>me</u>
D. change <u>have worked</u> to <u>been working</u>

7. Sentence 5. She always getting her work done on time and looks for ways to help others.

Which correction should be made to sentence 5?

A. replace <u>She</u> with <u>Her</u>
B. insert a comma after <u>time</u>
C. change <u>looks</u> to <u>looking</u>
D. change <u>getting</u> to <u>gets</u>

8. Sentence 9: Please contact <u>Walter or I</u> if you need any further information.

Which is the best way to write the underlined portion of the sentence?

A. Walter and I
B. Walter or me
C. him or I
D. he or me

Pronoun-Antecedent Agreement

Pronouns should agree with their antecedents, or the nouns they refer to. For example, a pronoun and its antecedent must agree in number. If the antecedent is singular, the pronoun should be singular. If the antecedent is plural, the pronoun should be plural.

EXAMPLES

Andy's <u>company</u> is very progressive. <u>It</u> pays for his college classes.
    singular antecedent   singular pronoun

Many <u>employees</u> want to learn more skills, so <u>they</u> take classes.
    plural antecedent   plural pronoun

Incorrect: Any <u>employee</u> who is interested should submit <u>their</u> application.
Correct: Any <u>employee</u> who is interested should submit <u>his or her</u> application.
Correct: <u>Employees</u> who are interested should submit <u>their</u> applications.

Note that for collective nouns (such as *company, jury, family, team, committee, union*), you generally use the singular pronoun *it*.

Incorrect: The <u>committee</u> announced that <u>they</u> will hold weekly meetings.
Correct: The <u>committee</u> announced that <u>it</u> will hold weekly meetings.

A pronoun and its antecedent must agree in person. To agree, they both must be first person (referring to the speaker), second person (the person spoken to), or third person (the person or thing spoken about).

First person	Second person	Third person
I, me, my, mine	you, your, yours	he, him, his
we, us, our, ours		she, her, hers
		it, its
		they, them, their, theirs

The indefinite pronoun *one* is like a third-person personal pronoun. A common error in writing is an incorrect shift between the third-person *one* and the second-person *you*.

Incorrect shift: If <u>one</u> attends college classes, <u>you</u> can be reimbursed.
Correct: If <u>one</u> attends college classes, <u>one</u> can be reimbursed.
Correct: If <u>one</u> attends college classes, <u>he or she</u> can be reimbursed.
Correct: If <u>you</u> attend college classes, <u>you</u> can be reimbursed.

It must be clear which antecedent a pronoun refers to. If necessary, use a noun in place of the pronoun, or reconstruct the sentence.

Unclear: Carlos spoke to his boss, and he told him about the program.
Clear (noun replaces pronoun): Carlos spoke to his boss, and <u>his boss</u> told him about the program.
Clear (different construction): Carlos spoke to his boss, <u>who told him</u> about the program.

Unclear: Michelle helped Shania fill out the financial aid application that she had picked up.
Correct (different construction): After picking up a financial aid application for Shania, Michelle helped her fill it out.

KEY IDEAS

- A pronoun should match its antecedent in person and number.
- Make sure it is clear which antecedent a pronoun refers to.
- If necessary, use a noun in place of a pronoun, or construct the sentence differently so that the antecedent is clear.

TASC TEST TIP

Take into account the whole passage when you are determining which pronoun is correct. A common error to watch for is when a paragraph begins with the third-person form one *and then shifts to the second-person form* you.

A. Directions: Correct any errors in pronoun use. If there are no errors, write C. You may also have to change some verbs.

EXAMPLE: People who live in small towns know ~~one has~~ *they have* access to fewer amenities than big-city dwellers.

___ **1.** Sally is moving to a small town. Her mother is concerned about the health-care options they offer.

___ **2.** Sally tried to reassure her mother, but it was hard for her to believe her.

___ **3.** Sally asked a friend who lives in the town for information about it's health-care facilities.

___ **4.** The town has a freestanding clinic where a person can go when they are sick.

___ **5.** There is also a nearby hospital, and they have a very good reputation.

___ **6.** If one is concerned about health care, you should sign up for a good insurance plan.

B. Questions 7 through 9 refer to the following paragraphs.

The Best Discipline

(A)

(1) What should parents do when their children act up? (2) Parents often like the idea of punishment, but punishment may not be the most effective solution. (3) If the punishment results from the parent's anger, it won't work. (4) Instead, children will learn only that they shouldn't make one's parents angry.

(B)

(5) One parenting expert feels that they should be clear about their expectations from the outset so that children will not unknowingly violate rules. (6) They should respond to children's misbehavior in a calm and neutral fashion. (7) It's also important to choose a consequence related to the action. (8) If a child hits or bites in a play group, for example, it would be most appropriate not to allow the child to play with them for a short time. (9) He or she will begin to see the connection.

7. Sentence 4: Instead, children will learn only that they shouldn't make one's parents angry.

Which correction should be made to sentence 4?

A. remove the comma after <u>Instead</u>
B. change <u>learn</u> to <u>have learned</u>
C. replace <u>they</u> with <u>you</u>
D. replace <u>one's</u> with <u>their</u>

8. Sentence 5: One parenting expert feels that <u>they</u> should be clear about their expectations from the outset so that children will not unknowingly violate rules.

Which is the best way to write the underlined portion of this sentence?

A. he
B. we
C. one
D. parents

9. Sentence 8: If a child hits or bites in a play group, for example, it would be most appropriate not to allow the child to play with them for a short time.

Which correction should be made to sentence 8?

A. insert a comma after <u>hits</u>
B. replace <u>the child</u> with <u>them</u>
C. replace <u>them</u> with <u>the group</u>
D. change <u>it</u> to <u>you</u>

LESSON 2

Verb Forms and Tenses

Regular Verbs

An important part of writing correctly is using the right verb forms. A **verb** is a word that indicates action or being. Each verb has a base form and four other forms. A **regular verb** follows a consistent pattern to create each verb form.

Base form: look

Tense	Verb form	How to write it
Present	look/looks	with *I, you, we, they*: use the base form
		with *he, she, it*: add *-s* to the base form
Present participle	looking	add *-ing*
Past	looked	add *-ed* (*-d* if verb ends with *e*)
Past participle	looked	add *-ed* (*-d* if verb ends with *e*)

The forms are used to create different **verb tenses**, or times. The table below shows how verb tense and form are related. Notice that when you use certain tenses, you must also use a **helping verb**—often a form of *be* or *have*.

Tense	Verb form	Use
Present	look/looks	a habitual action, general truth, or state of being: *I look at the newspaper every day.*
Past	looked	an action that has been completed: *I looked at it this morning.*
Future	will look	an action that has not yet happened: *I will look at it tonight, too.*
Present progressive	am/is/are looking	an action in progress: *I am looking at it right now.*
Present perfect	have/has looked	an action that began in the past and continues until now: *I have looked at it every day this week.*
Past perfect	had looked	an action that was completed before a specific time in the past: *I had looked at it before it got wet.*
Future perfect	will have looked	an action that will be completed by a specific time in the future: *I will have looked at it by the time I get home.*

Sentences often contain clues that tell you which tense to use. For instance, time words and phrases like *yesterday* or *last week* show that the past should be used, *tonight* and *next month* indicate the future, and *by tonight, since 2000,* and *for seven years* indicate the perfect tenses.

Other verbs in the sentence can be clues: *I* look *at the newspaper whenever I* get *the chance.* Finally, verbs in other sentences also can be clues. The verbs in a paragraph or passage are generally in the same tense.

PRACTICE 2.1

A. Directions: Rewrite each verb in its correct tense. Use clues in each sentence for help in choosing the tense.

EXAMPLE: Between 1892 and 1924, about 12 million immigrants *entered* (enter) the U.S. through Ellis Island in New York.

1. By the 1950s, Ellis Island _____ (cease) to be an important immigration checkpoint.

2. The government _____ (close) Ellis Island to immigration in 1954.

3. Now Ellis Island _____ (function) as a national monument.

4. Since the island was reopened as a museum in 1990, many tourists _____ (visit) it.

5. Soon, a genealogical center _____ (open).

6. The island _____ (look) different than it did originally because 24 acres of landfill have been added.

7. Now we _____ (think) about taking a trip to Ellis Island next month.

B. Questions 8 through 10 refer to the following advertisement.

Don't Miss Your Chance!

(A)

(1) The Express Lane credit card has offered a fantastic deal right now, for a limited time only. (2) If you are signing up for Express Lane before April 9, you will receive a 20 percent discount on your first five purchases!

(B)

(3) The Express Lane card carries no monthly charge. (4) You'll pay a low $35 fee just once a year. (5) Become an Express Lane member now. (6) Your savings opportunities will be amazing you!

8. Sentence 1: The Express Lane credit card <u>has offered</u> a fantastic deal right now, for a limited time only.

Which is the best way to write the underlined portion of the sentence?

A. offered
B. is offering
C. offers
D. will offer

9. Sentence 2: If you are signing up for Express Lane before April 9, you will receive a 20 percent discount on your first five purchases!

Which correction should be made to sentence 2?

A. change <u>are signing</u> to <u>have signed</u>
B. change <u>you will</u> to <u>one will</u>
C. change <u>will receive</u> to <u>receive</u>
D. change <u>are signing</u> to <u>sign</u>

10. Sentence 6: Your savings opportunities will be amazing you!

Which correction should be made to sentence 6?

A. change <u>Your</u> to <u>You're</u>
B. change <u>Your</u> to <u>One's</u>
C. insert a comma after <u>opportunities</u>
D. change <u>will be amazing</u> to <u>will amaze</u>

STUDY ADVICE

Remembering the *names* of verb tenses (in the first column of the second table on page 124) isn't nearly as important as remembering how to use them. You may want to make flash cards out of the second and third columns of the tables on page 124. On one side of each card, put a time frame and an action word (such as "an action that has been completed; look"). On the other side, put the verb form that matches (in this case, "looked").

Irregular Verbs

Most verbs are regular verbs; their past and participle forms follow the same pattern. Some verbs, however, are **irregular verbs.** Although some irregular verbs follow a pattern, most do not.

A common error with irregular verbs is using the past participle in place of the past—for instance, *I been there* instead of *I was there*. Discover which irregular verb forms, if any, give you problems. Then learn the correct forms. Here are some tips for learning the forms of irregular verbs:

- If you find two verbs that rhyme in the present form (for example, *grow* and *throw*), check to see if they have the same forms in the past and past participles (*grew, grown; threw, thrown*). If so, learn them together.
- Learn which verbs follow the *i, a, u* pattern: *sing, sang, sung; drink, drank, drunk; sink, sank, sunk.* However, be aware that there are exceptions (*bring, brought, brought*).

Here is a list of common irregular verbs.

Present Form	Past Form	Past Participle Form
am, are, is	was, were	been
become	became	become
begin	began	begun
blow	blew	blown
break	broke	broken
bring	brought	brought
buy	bought	bought
choose	chose	chosen
come	came	come
do	did	done
drink	drank	drunk
eat	ate	eaten
fall	fell	fallen
fly	flew	flown
freeze	froze	frozen
get	got	gotten
give	gave	given
go	went	gone
grow	grew	grown
have, has	had	had
know	knew	known
leave	left	left
lose	lost	lost
ride	rode	ridden
run	ran	run
see	saw	seen
shake	shook	shaken
show	showed	shown
speak	spoke	spoken
steal	stole	stolen
take	took	taken
throw	threw	thrown
wear	wore	worn
write	wrote	written

PRACTICE 2.2

A. Directions: Write the correct form of the verb shown in parentheses.

EXAMPLE: Since November, the school's heating system ___*has broken*___ (break) down several times.

1. Yesterday the technician _____ (come) to resolve the problem once and for all.

2. School employees _____ (show) him the boiler.

3. The technician said, "If you _____ (speak) to me about this sooner, it would have been easier to fix."

4. He _____ (take) parts out of the heating system and replaced them with new ones.

5. He said, "I've never _____ (see) such a poorly installed system."

B. Questions 6 through 8 refer to the following paragraphs.

TV Rating Systems

(A)

(1) In 1996, television industry representatives announced that the industry had formed TV Parental Guidelines. (2) This rating system, designed to give parents advance warning about the content of TV shows, begun to appear on TV in 1997. (3) The ratings system was broke down into six different categories, ranging from "All Children" to "Mature Audiences Only."

(B)

(4) Six months later, after pressure from advocacy groups, the television industry agreed to include additional labels to advise viewers if a show they were about to view contained violence, sexual activity, coarse language, or sexually suggestive language. (5) These labels now given viewers more specific and therefore more helpful information about an upcoming show.

6. Sentence 2: This rating system, designed to give parents advance warning about the content of TV shows, begun to appear on TV in 1997.

Which correction should be made to sentence 2?

A. remove the comma after <u>system</u>
B. change <u>give</u> to <u>be giving</u>
C. change <u>begun</u> to <u>had begun</u>
D. change <u>begun</u> to <u>began</u>

7. Sentence 3: The ratings system <u>was broke</u> down into six different categories, ranging from "All Children" to "Mature Audiences Only."

Which is the best way to write the underlined portion of this sentence?

A. broke itself
B. broke
C. was broken
D. had broken

8. Sentence 5: These labels now given viewers more specific and therefore more helpful information about an upcoming show.

Which correction should be made to sentence 5?

A. change <u>given</u> to <u>will give</u>
B. change <u>given</u> to <u>give</u>
C. insert a comma after <u>information</u>
D. insert a comma after <u>specific</u>

Subject-Verb Agreement

Agreement with a Simple Subject

In the present tense, subjects and verbs must agree in number. To understand the basics of subject-verb agreement, study the chart below. Notice that present tense verbs take an –s ending when they are used with the pronoun subjects *he*, *she*, and *it* or their noun equivalents.

Verb Forms for Singular Subjects	Verb Forms for Plural Subjects
I jump	*we* jump
you jump	*you* jump
he, she, it jumps	*they* jump

To master subject-verb agreement for the Writing Test, be aware of these special nouns and pronouns:

Collective nouns are usually singular, even though they may seem plural. A collective noun names a group, such as *army, crew, crowd, staff, family, herd,* or *flock*. If the group is considered to be a single unit, it is singular.

EXAMPLES

The army is a good place to learn discipline.
The church choir sings each Sunday.

Some nouns that end in –s may look plural, but in fact they are not.

EXAMPLE

Politics is an interesting topic.

Indefinite pronouns do not refer to a specific person. Some indefinite pronouns are singular, some are plural, and some may be either.

Singular	anyone, everyone, someone, no one, one, anybody, everybody, somebody, nobody, anything, everything, something, nothing, another, other, either, neither, each, much
Plural	many, several, few, both
Singular or plural	all, none, some, any, part, most

EXAMPLES

Singular: These days, it seems as if almost everyone is joining a health club.
Singular: Most of the equipment is easy to use.
Plural: Most of the exercise classes are fun
Plural: A few are advanced classes for those already in great shape.

PRACTICE 3.1

A. Directions: Underline the correct verb form to complete each sentence.

EXAMPLE: Every Monday, the National Orchestra (perform, <u>performs</u>) live on the radio.

1. The public (is, are) invited to listen free of charge.

2. Free tickets (becomes, become) available one hour before the performance.

3. The performance (is, are) usually held in Barnes Hall.

4. Many well-known musicians (has, have) played there.

5. Everyone (seem, seems) to enjoy these concerts very much.

6. The concert series (is, are) very popular.

B. Questions 7 through 9 refer to the following article.

The Speed of Sound

(A)

(1) Most of us has heard airplane noise that is so loud it sounds like an explosion. (2) That noise occurs when a plane start to fly faster than the speed of sound. (3) Listeners on the ground hear the noise, but it is not audible to passengers.

(B)

(4) The speed of sound is 1,088 feet per second at 32°F at sea level. (5) It is different at other temperatures and in other substances. (6) For example, sound travels faster in water than in air. (7) Sound takes about one second to move a mile under water, but five seconds to move a mile through air. (8) It travels through ice cold vapor at 4,708 feet per second and through ice cold water at 4,938 feet per second. (9) Surprisingly, some other materials conducts sound very well. (10) For instance, sound travels through glass at speeds up to 19,690 feet per second.

STUDY ADVICE

How long are your study sessions at this point? Remember to push yourself, little by little, until you can focus on the material for two to three hours at a time. It may take weeks or months to get there, but don't give up. Remember: You need to train yourself so that you can focus for a few hours on Test Day.

7. Sentence 1: Most of us <u>has heard</u> airplane noise that is so loud it sounds like an explosion.

Which is the best way to write the underlined portion of this sentence?

A. were hearing
B. have heard
C. having heard
D. hears

8. Sentence 2: That noise occurs when a plane start to fly faster than the speed of sound.

Which correction should be made to sentence 2?

A. change <u>occurs</u> to <u>occur</u>
B. change <u>occurs</u> to <u>occurred</u>
C. change <u>start</u> to <u>starts</u>
D. replace <u>than</u> with <u>then</u>

9. Sentence 9: Surprisingly, some other materials conducts sound very well.

Which correction should be made to sentence 9?

A. replace <u>some</u> with <u>any</u>
B. change <u>conducts</u> to <u>conduct</u>
C. change <u>conducts</u> to <u>conducted</u>
D. insert a comma after <u>sound</u>

Agreement with a Compound Subject

A compound subject is made up of two or more subjects joined by *and* or *or*. To make a verb agree with a compound subject, follow these guidelines:

When two or more subjects are joined by *and*, the compound subject is plural. Use the correct verb form for the plural.

EXAMPLE: Tricia and her sister are caring for their mother.

If two subjects are joined by *or*, the verb agrees with the subject closer to it:

EXAMPLE: A health aide or a nurse visits each day.

When subjects are joined by *either . . . or* or *neither . . . nor*, the verb agrees with the subject closer to it.

EXAMPLE: Neither the brother nor his sisters have medical training.

Interrupting Words

Sometimes a word or group of words comes between the subject and the verb. In that case, locate the subject by asking yourself, "What is this sentence really about?" Mentally cross out the interruptor. Then make the verb agree with the subject.

EXAMPLE: The medicine ~~prescribed by the doctors~~ is on a high shelf.
      subject   interruptor   verb

Interrupting phrases often begin with prepositions, such as *of, in, on, from, with, to,* and *for.*

EXAMPLE: A pile ~~of medical supplies~~ rests in the front hallway.

Interrupting phrases may be set off by commas. Watch especially for phrases beginning with words like *along with, as well as, besides,* and *in addition to.*

EXAMPLES
Dr. Silva~~, who is one of the surgeons,~~ consults with the family.
The sisters~~, along with the medical team,~~ keep the patient comfortable.

Inverted Structure

Checking subject-verb agreement can be tricky when the sentence structure is **inverted**—that is, when the subject comes after the verb. Most questions and sentences that begin with *here* or *there* are inverted.

EXAMPLES
Does the pharmacy have enough medicine to fill the prescription?
Here are the hospital supplies that Tricia ordered.

Incorrect: What is Tricia and her family going to do?
Correct: What are Tricia and her family going to do?

Incorrect: Do Tricia want to send her mother to a hospital?
Correct: Does Tricia want to send her mother to a hospital?

Incorrect: There's the bandages. (Remember that *There's* is short for *There is.*)
Correct: There are the bandages.

PRACTICE 3.2

A. Directions: If a sentence contains an interrupting phrase, cross out the interruptor. Then underline the correct verb to complete the sentence.

EXAMPLE: Brushing and flossing ~~with regularity~~ (is, <u>are</u>) key to good dental health.

1. Many toothpastes on the market (carry, carries) a seal of approval from the American Dental Association.

2. Products carrying the seal (are, is) tested to guarantee that they are safe and effective.

3. Fluoride, an important ingredient in many toothpastes, (strengthens, strengthen) teeth and (attacks, attack) bacteria that cause tooth decay.

4. There (is, are) toothpastes that claim to have special benefits, like tartar control or whitening.

5. Some pharmacies and supermarkets (offers, offer) store-brand toothpaste at a low price.

6. Any toothpaste with fluoride and good flavor (is, are) fine to use, even if it's not a brand-name toothpaste.

B. Questions 7 through 9 refer to the following paragraphs.

Unemployment Insurance

(A)

(1) Unemployment insurance provides workers who have lost their jobs with partial replacement of their salary. (2) Each state administers its own program and have its own laws. (3) The amount received is determined by wage level and the length of employment. (4) When the unemployment rate rises above a certain level, states are required to extend the benefits. (5) The state and federal governments share the cost of the additional benefits.

(B)

(6) In most states, employer contributions pay for this program. (7) Unemployed workers who wish to draw benefits reports regularly to their public employment office to learn about job openings.

7. Sentence 2: Each state administers its own program and have its own laws.

Which correction should be made to sentence 2?

A. change <u>administers</u> to <u>administering</u>
B. change <u>administers</u> to <u>administer</u>
C. change <u>have</u> to <u>has</u>
D. replace <u>its</u> with <u>it's</u>

8. Sentence 3: The amount received is determined by wage level and the length of employment.

If you rewrote sentence 3 beginning with

<u>Wage level and the length of employment</u>

the next word(s) should be

A. determine
B. determines
C. is determined
D. was determined

9. Sentence 7: Unemployed workers who wish to draw benefits reports regularly to their public employment office to learn about job openings.

Which correction should be made to sentence 7?

A. change <u>wish</u> to <u>wishes</u>
B. insert a comma after <u>benefits</u>
C. change <u>reports</u> to <u>report</u>
D. replace <u>their</u> with <u>there</u>

Verb Moods

In addition to **tenses**, which indicate time, verbs also have several **moods**, which indicate how a speaker feels about what she is saying. For example, making a statement is different from asking a question, which in turn is different from expressing a wish. The verb's mood conveys these different attitudes.

There are five verb moods in English.

1. Indicative mood. The indicative is the most common verb mood. It is used when making a statement of fact.

Example: "The weather *is* pleasant today."

2. Interrogative mood. The interrogative is used to ask a question.

Example: "*Is* the weather pleasant today?" Note that in the interrogative, the helping verb ("is") comes before the subject ("weather").

3. Imperative mood. The imperative is used for commands or requests.

Example: "Please *shut* the door."

Sentences in the imperative often leave out the subject being asked to perform the action; in the sentence "Please shut the door," the word "you" is understood.

4. Conditional mood. The conditional is used to make hypothetical statements. The conditional mood typically uses the words *might, should, could,* or *would.*

Example: "If you really wanted to lose weight, you *would* exercise more."

The conditional mood can also be used in the past tense—"If you had wanted to lose weight, you *would have* exercised more"—as well as in the future tense—"If you want to lose weight next year, you *will* exercise more," or "you *might* exercise more."

5. Subjunctive mood. The subjunctive is the least-often used verb mood. It is used in two situations: (a) to express a wish or hypothetical (in this usage, it overlaps with the conditional mood) or (b) to express an order or recommendation. The words *were* and *would* are common in both usages.

Examples (hypothetical): "I wish that I *owned* a speedboat." "If I *were* rich, I would buy a speedboat."

Examples (recommendation): "The dealer recommended that I *purchase* a rowboat instead." "It is important that I *budget* carefully so that I can afford the rowboat."

Note that the subjunctive is often used with verbs such as *order, recommend, demand, insist,* etc. When used with these verbs, the subjunctive verb is often part of a clause beginning with the word *that.*

1. Rewrite the indicative sentence "You will leave me alone," in the (a) interrogative mood and (b) imperative mood. Write your answers on the lines below.

a. _____

b. _____

2. Write the correct form of the verb provided in each blank.

Example: Please _take_ (take) out the trash.

a. _____ (Be) you going to the soccer match?

b. I insist that she _____ (leave) immediately.

c. Jane said that she wished she _____ (be) able to come along, but a previous commitment prevented her from doing so.

d. If you want to get there on time, you _____ (shall) get going as soon as possible.

e. You're blocking two other cars, so _____ (move) your vehicle!

f. Sloths _____ (live) in trees and are among the slowest-moving land mammals.

Questions 3 through 5 are based on the passage below.

(1) In hot, arid weather, snails and other invertebrates keep from drying out by lowering their metabolic rate. (2) This slowed state, similar to hibernation, is called estivation. (3) For one to observe estivation in snails, it is essential that one chooses a hot, dry day. (4) Otherwise, one is unlikely to find any estivating snails. (5) When it is cool and damp, snails are not entering a dormant state.

(6) If one has patiently waited until a hot, dry day, then look for estivating snails on trees or tall plants, or in the deep shade under leaf litter. (7) Snails will also climb structures made by humans, such as telephone poles or fence posts.

3. Sentence 3: For one to observe estivation in snails, it is essential that one chooses a hot, dry day.

Which is the best way to rewrite the underlined portion of the sentence?

A. that one chooses
B. to be choosing
C. that one choose
D. to have chosen

4. Sentence 5: When it is cool and damp, snails are not entering a dormant state.

Which is the best way to rewrite the underlined portion of the sentence?

A. snails are not entering
B. snails will not be entering
C. snails would not enter
D. snails do not enter

5. Sentence 6: If one has patiently waited until a hot, dry day, then look for estivating snails on trees or tall plants, or in the deep shade under leaf litter.

Which is the best way to rewrite the underlined portion of the sentence?

A. then look
B. one might consider looking
C. think to look
D. look

Using Grammar Correctly

Verb Voices and Verbals

Verb Voices

Verbs can be used in the **active voice** or the **passive voice**. Active voice constructions emphasize the subject performing the action, while passive voice constructions emphasize the target of the action. If you have to ask, "Who performed the action?" then the verb is in passive voice.

Examples: The companies that make incandescent light bulbs *design* them to have a short life span. (active voice)
Incandescent light bulbs *are designed* to have a short life span. (passive voice)

Note that in these examples, the passive voice construction allows the actor to avoid taking responsibility for the action. For this reason, and because they are more concise, active voice constructions are preferable in most situations. However, passive voice is appropriate and useful when the target of the action is more important than the entity that performs the action. Also, passive voice can be used to express an opinion that the author doesn't agree with.

Examples: After the wallpaper *is stripped*, the walls *are sanded* before paint *is applied*.

It is sometimes said that Jenkins is a bad writer, but I find his writing delightful.

Verbals

Verbals are words that are created from verbs but that function as nouns, adjectives, or adverbs. There are three types of verbals: gerunds, participles, and infinitives.

Gerunds are verbals that end in *–ing*. They function as nouns.

Examples: *Swimming* is Joey's favorite pastime. Eva's favorite pastime, on the other hand, is *reading*.

Participles are verbals that function as adjectives. They are formed exactly like the present and past participles explained on page 126.

Examples: Ed poured *boiling* water into his glass, causing the glass to break. This *broken* glass will need to be thrown away.

Infinitives are verbals formed by adding the word "to" before the simple form of the verb: *to run, to drive, to dream, to shout, to eat, to leave, to be*, etc. Infinitives can be used as nouns, adjectives, or adverbs.

Examples: After an exhausting day of shepherding children through the museum, Diane's only wish was *to sleep*. (Here, the infinitive functions as a noun.)

Early morning is a good time *to exercise*. (Here, the infinitive functions as an adjective modifying the word "time.")

It takes a great deal of practice *to learn* a new language. (Here, the infinitive functions as an adverb modifying the verb "takes.")

PRACTICE 5

1. Use check marks or X's to indicate whether each of the following sentences is phrased in the active voice or in the passive voice.

Sentence	Active voice	Passive voice
a. The judges awarded the skater first place in the competition.		
b. The Perseid meteor shower can be observed in August of each year.		
c. Joseph's entire family watched the Perseid meteor shower this year.		
d. This orchestra plays phenomenally well.		
e. The last piece on the program has been played three times this week.		
f. Normally, the school is cleaned thoroughly at least twice per week.		

2. Write the correct verbal in each blank, using the verb provided.

   Example: The tennis player needs to break the tie _to win_ (win).

   a. The _____ (cry) child had to be taken to the emergency room for stitches.
   b. Remarkably, the athletic bicyclist was given a ticket for _____ (speed).
   c. The newly _____ (open) public library will hold a children's story hour every Friday afternoon.
   d. Tomorrow will be an excellent day _____ (travel).
   e. _____ (Take) a road trip is a great way _____ (meet) new people.
   f. Beth has continued _____ (work) at the same office even after _____ (move) to a different town.

Questions 3 through 5 are based on the passage below.

(1) The <u>acclaiming</u> Hayao Miyazaki is a Japanese director known for his animated films. (2) His movies often feature female protagonists. (3) While some of Miyazaki's films, such as *Howl's Moving Castle*, are adaptations of preexisting works of fiction, others, such as *Princess Mononoke*, are written by Miyazaki himself. (4) Miyazaki learned early in his career not <u>being</u> fashionable and follow the crowd. (5) His work departs from both Japanese and Western animation in a number of <u>interest</u> ways.

3. **Sentence 1:** The <u>acclaiming</u> Hayao Miyazaki is a Japanese director known for his animated films.

   Which is the best way to rewrite the underlined portion of the sentence?

   A. acclaimed
   B. to acclaim
   C. having acclaimed
   D. being acclaimed

4. **Sentence 4:** Miyazaki learned early in his career not <u>being</u> fashionable and follow the crowd.

   Which is the best way to rewrite the underlined portion of the sentence?

   A. becoming
   B. to be
   C. will be
   D. has been

5. **Sentence 5:** His work departs from both Japanese and Western animation in a number of <u>interest</u> ways.

   Which is the best way to rewrite the underlined portion of the sentence?

   A. interested
   B. having interest
   C. being interested
   D. interesting

USING GRAMMAR CORRECTLY PRACTICE QUESTIONS

Questions 1 through 5 refer to the following paragraphs.

Unorthodox Tennis Stars

(A)

(1) Venus and Serena Williams are not your typical tennis stars. (2) For one thing, they are African Americans in a game that few African Americans have become famous for playing; those who preceded them were Althea Gibson, Arthur Ashe, and Zina Garrison. (3) For another, Venus and Serena are sisters.

(B)

(4) Tennis players often receive hours of instruction from highly paid coaches, but it doesn't happen that way for Venus and Serena. (5) Instead, their father, the former owner of a security-services business, taught them how to play on public courts, after teaching himself through books and films. (6) The family lived in a rough neighborhood, and gang members watched over the girls while she practiced.

(C)

(7) The practice paid off. (8) Venus had won 63 tournaments by the time she turned 12, and she became a professional at 14. (9) In just a few years, she earns millions of dollars in endorsements and prizes. (10) Serena, turning professional a year after Venus, had a slower start. (11) However, some experts think she may now be better than her sister.

(D)

(12) The two sisters, who live in Palm Beach Gardens, Florida, is best friends. (13) Though they sometimes face each other on the court, there been no trace of sibling rivalry.

1. Sentence 4: **Tennis players often receive hours of instruction from highly paid coaches, but it doesn't happen that way for Venus and Serena.**

   Which correction should be made to sentence 4?

   A. change receive to receives
   B. remove the comma
   C. change doesn't to didn't
   D. insert a comma after Instruction

2. Sentence 6: **The family lived in a rough neighborhood, and gang members watched over the girls while she practiced.**

   Which is the best way to write the underlined portion of the sentence?

   A. they
   B. the girls
   C. each
   D. them

3. Sentence 9: **In just a few years, she earns millions of dollars in endorsements and prizes.**

   Which is the best way to write the underlined portion of the sentence?

   A. is earning
   B. earned
   C. earn
   D. will earn

4. Sentence 12: **The two sisters, who live in Palm Beach Gardens, Florida, is best friends.**

   Which correction should be made to sentence 12?

   A. remove the comma after sisters
   B. change live to lives
   C. remove the comma after Florida
   D. change is to are

5. Sentence 13: **Though they sometimes face each other on the court, there been no trace of sibling rivalry.**

   Which correction should be made to sentence 13?

   A. change face to faced
   B. remove the comma after court
   C. change been to was
   D. change been to is

Questions 6 through 10 refer to the following paragraphs.

Getting the Best Service for Your Car

(A)

(1) Have you had trouble finding a good mechanic? (2) By following these tips, you can improve your chances of getting quality service.

(B)

(3) Even before your car breaks down, look for a shop you like and trust. (4) Ask people where they will receive good service at a reasonable price. (5) Don't have picked a shop just because it's close to home, for another shop may have a better deal. (6) Be wary of ads that offer rock-bottom prices. (7) Specials like these often comes with restrictions attached.

(C)

(8) Be as specific as possible when you describe your car's problem to the mechanic. (9) If the technician must spend time trying to determine what's wrong, it will cost more. (10) You also need to request information about both estimates and guarantees before the repair work starts. (11) Ask for a price range rather than an exact estimate. (12) Find out how long the guarantee lasts and whether there's any time or mileage limits.

(D)

(13) If you don't understand a repair explanation, ask for clarification right away. (14) In addition, keep records of all repairs and billing in case of a dispute.

6. Sentence 4: **Ask people where they will receive good service at a reasonable price.**

   Which correction should be made to sentence 4?

   A. change <u>Ask</u> to <u>To ask</u>
   B. change <u>will receive</u> to <u>have received</u>
   C. change <u>will receive</u> to <u>receiving</u>
   D. change <u>people</u> to <u>them</u>

7. Sentence 5: **Don't have picked a shop just because it's close to home, for another shop may have a better deal.**

   Which correction should be made to sentence 5?

   A. change <u>have picked</u> to <u>pick</u>
   B. change <u>have picked</u> to <u>be picking</u>
   C. replace <u>it's</u> with <u>its</u>
   D. remove the comma

8. Sentence 7: **Specials like these often comes with restrictions attached.**

   Which correction should be made to sentence 7?

   A. replace <u>these</u> with <u>this</u>
   B. insert a comma after <u>these</u>
   C. change <u>comes</u> to <u>came</u>
   D. change <u>comes</u> to <u>come</u>

9. Sentence 9: **If the technician must spend time trying to determine what's wrong, it will cost more.**

   Which correction should be made to sentence 9?

   A. change <u>must spend</u> to <u>spent</u>
   B. change <u>what's</u> to <u>what are</u>
   C. remove the comma
   D. replace <u>it</u> with <u>the repair job</u>

10. Sentence 12: **Find out how long the guarantee lasts and whether <u>there's</u> any time or mileage limits.**

    Which is the best way to write the underlined portion of the sentence?

    A. there is
    B. there be
    C. there are
    D. there were

Questions 11 through 15 refer to the following letter.

Taxpayer Notification

(A)

(1) We have received your tax return and have noted some inconsistencies in it. (2) We are therefore proposing a number of changes to your return. (3) These changes and its effect on your refund are outlined below.

(B)

(4) First, the amount you claimed for self-employed income differs from our records. (5) If you wish to contest this change, please send photocopies of one's records. (6) Second, you have made an error in your calculations. (7) Please review our calculations, which is appended to this letter.

(C)

(8) These changes having been made to your return, there is an increase in the amount of taxes you owe. (9) Your refund has therefore been reduced accordingly.

(D)

(10) Contact us if you have any questions about these specific problems or about the documents you must send to contest the changes. (11) Be sure to send the last page of this letter when replying by mail. (12) If we determine that your return was correct as filed, we have credited your account.

11. Sentence 3: **These changes and its effect on your refund are outlined below.**

    Which correction should be made to sentence 3?

    A. insert a comma after changes
    B. replace its with their
    C. insert a comma after refund
    D. change are to is

12. Sentence 5: **If you wish to contest this change, please send photocopies of one's records.**

    Which correction should be made to sentence 5?

    A. change wish to wishes
    B. change send to to send
    C. replace one's with your
    D. change you to one

13. Sentence 7: **Please review our calculations, which is appended to this letter.**

    Which correction should be made to sentence 7?

    A. change review to reviewing
    B. replace our with are
    C. remove the comma
    D. change is to are

14. Sentence 8: **These changes having been made to your return, there is an increase in the amount of taxes you owe.**

    If you rewrote sentence 8 beginning with

    Because of these changes to your return, the amount of taxes you owe

    the next words should be

    A. has increased
    B. have increased
    C. is increasing
    D. are increasing

15. Sentence 12: **If we determine that your return was correct as filed, we have credited your account.**

    Which is the best way to write the underlined portion of the sentence?

    A. are crediting
    B. will credit
    C. will have credited
    D. had credited

Questions 16 through 20 refer to the following paragraphs.

Disability Etiquette

(A)

(1) Many of us doesn't know how to act when meeting someone who has a disability. (2) The main thing to remember is that people with disabilities has feelings just like everyone else. (3) They want to be treated with respect and dignity. (4) Beyond that, try the following tips.

(B)

(5) When you meet a person with a disability, speak and act with he or she as you would with anyone else. (6) Use your usual tone of voice. (7) A person who has trouble hearing you will let you know. (8) Don't talk down to the person or stare. (9) Refrain from using a term like handicap, which focuses on the disability rather than on the person. (10) Instead, use a term such as physically disabled or say, "He uses a wheelchair."

(C)

(11) Any assistive equipment, such as a wheelchair, cane, or communication board, are the person's property. (12) Unless you have the person's express permission, you should not touch it. (13) Also, distracting a blind person's guide dog could put the owner in danger, so do not pet it.

(D)

(14) Finally, if you have a child with you, don't prevent him or her from talking to the person or asking questions. (15) Children are often more accepting than adults.

16. Sentence 1: **Many of us doesn't know how to act when meeting someone who has a disability.**

    Which is the best way to write the underlined portion of the sentence?

    A. does not
    B. don't
    C. didn't
    D. never does

17. Sentence 2: **The main thing to remember is that people with disabilities has feelings just like everyone else.**

    Which correction should be made to sentence 2?

    A. add a comma after remember
    B. change is to are
    C. change has to have
    D. change people to them

18. Sentence 5: **When you meet a person with a disability, speak and act with he or she as you would with anyone else.**

    Which is the best way to write the underlined portion of the sentence?

    A. he or her
    B. him or her
    C. him or she
    D. them

19. Sentence 11: **Any assistive equipment, such as a wheelchair, cane, or communication board, are the person's property.**

    Which correction should be made to sentence 11?

    A. remove the comma after wheelchair
    B. change are to is
    C. change person's to persons
    D. insert a comma after assistive

20. Sentence 13: **Also, distracting a blind person's guide dog could put the owner in danger, so do not pet it.**

    If you rewrote sentence 13 beginning with

    Also, don't pet a blind person's guide dog because distracting

    the next word(s) should be

    A. a blind person's guide dog
    B. it
    C. her
    D. them

Comma Use

As a general rule, **commas** indicate where readers would pause in a sentence if they were reading it aloud. Below are specific guidelines for using commas.

Commas in Compound Sentences

In a compound sentence, place a comma immediately before the coordinating conjunction.

EXAMPLES

Some people are insecure about hosting a party, but others are relaxed and confident.

Many hosts have years of practice, and they have some organizational tips.

Watch out, though, for sentences that appear to be compound but are not. Some sentences have one main clause but have a compound subject or a compound predicate. If a sentence does not have two independent clauses, a comma is not needed before the coordinating conjunction.

Incorrect: Planning, and list making are two key organizational techniques.
Correct: Planning and list making are two key organizational techniques.

Incorrect: Making a list reduces disorganization, and helps you feel in control.
Correct: Making a list reduces disorganization and helps you feel in control.

Commas after Introductory Elements

In general, a comma should follow an introductory word, phrase, or clause to separate the introductory element from the main part of the sentence.

EXAMPLES

Introductory words:
Yes, listing your ideas can be very helpful.
However, making a list is only the first step.

Introductory phrases:
Giving it some thought, carefully draw up a guest list.
For a casual feel, have an open house.
On the day of the party, do as much as you can first thing in the morning.
By party time, you should be able to relax.

Introductory clauses:
Before you make a list, decide what kind of party you will have.
If you are a good cook, you might choose to have a dinner party.

Remember that only a subordinate clause at the beginning of a sentence requires a comma after it. A subordinate clause at the end of the sentence generally does not.

No comma: Decide what kind of party you will have before you make a list.

KEY IDEAS

- In a compound sentence, use a comma before the coordinating conjunction.
- Be careful not to use a comma when only two words or phrases are joined by *and*.
- Insert a comma after an introductory word, phrase, or clause.

TASC TEST TIP

Read a sentence out loud to see if you hear a pause. Before you insert a comma, be sure that you can base your decision on a comma rule.

PRACTICE 1.1

A. Directions: Insert commas where needed in the sentences below. If no commas are required, write *NC*.

_____ 1. Train travel is more pleasant than riding a bus but it can be more expensive.

_____ 2. When you're on a train you can stand up and stretch if you need to.

_____ 3. Most trains have club cars where passengers can get snacks and sometimes even sit at tables.

_____ 4. Unlike buses trains sometimes have seats that face each other.

_____ 5. Traveling through a scenic area you may find that your train has a double-decker car that offers a better view.

_____ 6. Lowered airfares and many people's unwillingness to spend long hours in a train have contributed to the declining popularity of rail travel.

B. Questions 7 through 9 refer to the following paragraphs.

Low-Fat Cooking

(A)

(1) To have a more healthful diet, try cooking with less fat. (2) It's not as hard as you think! (3) For starters use cooking methods that require little or no oil or butter, such as steaming, poaching, or baking. (4) When you do include oil in the preparation of your dish, use less of it. (5) Vinegar can be used without oil in salad dressing and the flavor can be enhanced with fresh herbs.

(B)

(6) Another tactic is to cut down on dairy fat. (7) Avoid regular milk, cream, and sour cream. (8) Add low-fat dairy products or another liquid to your dish instead. (9) Many dairy foods come in a low-fat version, and though, not all of them may be pleasing to the palate, some are.

7. **Sentence 3:** For starters use cooking methods that require little or no oil or butter, such as steaming, poaching, or baking.

Which correction should be made to sentence 3?

A. insert a comma after <u>starters</u>
B. remove the comma after <u>butter</u>
C. remove the comma after <u>steaming</u>
D. insert a comma after <u>little</u>

8. **Sentence 5:** Vinegar can be used without oil in salad <u>dressing and</u> the flavor can be enhanced with fresh herbs.

Which is the best way to write the underlined portion of the sentence?

A. dressing, and
B. dressing and,
C. dressing, or
D. dressing, for example

9. **Sentence 9:** Many dairy foods come in a low-fat version, and though, not all of them may be pleasing to the palate, some are.

Which correction should be made to sentence 9?

A. remove the comma after <u>version</u>
B. insert a comma after <u>pleasing</u>
C. remove the comma after <u>palate</u>
D. remove the comma after <u>though</u>

Commas in a Series

When three or more items are listed in a series, place commas *between* the items:

EXAMPLES

Keith, Darnelle, Marisol, and Doug are ready to take the TASC Test.
They have taken a class, studied together, and prepared well.

The comma before the final *and* or *or* is optional (for example, *March 7, March 14 or March 21*), but using one there will help you place commas correctly in the series.

Just as with any other series, use commas to separate two or more adjectives: *the intelligent, curious child* or *the abandoned, dilapidated, and moldy house.* However, there is one exception to this rule: when the adjective closest to the noun is important for defining it (rather than just describing it), that adjective should not be preceded by a comma. An example: *the lazy hound dog.* In that example, *hound* is important to the definition of the dog.

A good way to tell whether a comma should separate adjectives is to ask yourself: "Would the phrase sound equally right if the adjectives were reversed in order?" If so, put a comma between them. For example:

The intelligent, curious child and *the curious, intelligent child* both sound equally natural. Use a comma.

The lazy hound dog sounds fine, whereas *the hound lazy dog* sounds unnatural. Do not use a comma.

Commas with Appositives

An **appositive** is a word or group of words that gives more information about a noun by renaming it.

EXAMPLES

Marisol, an experienced writer, feels confident about the essay.
Doug's only sister, Gina, was the first in the family to receive a high school equivalency degree.

To decide whether to set off an appositive with commas, mentally cross out the appositive. Then ask, "Can I still identify the person, place, or thing described in the sentence?" If you can, use commas around the appositive.

EXAMPLES

Mann College, a local community college, offers TASC courses.
Keith, who attended TASC classes for a year, has done well there.

Here you can identify the noun without the appositive. Each appositive adds more information, but it is not essential to your understanding. Usually when an appositive is renaming a proper noun, it is not essential.

On the other hand, if you cannot identify the person, place, or thing without the appositive, do not set off the appositive with commas.

EXAMPLES

Keith and his friend Antoine plan to work in construction.
Students who study faithfully usually do well on the test.

In these examples, you cannot identify the nouns without the appositives. You would ask, "Which friend?" and "Which students?" The appositives are essential to your understanding and should not be set off by commas.

PRACTICE 1.2

Comma Errors to Avoid

Do not use a comma between the subject and the verb.

Incorrect: Park College, is the school Doug hopes to attend.

Do not use a comma between two subjects, two verbs, or two other items joined by *and* or *or*.

Incorrect: Science, and math are hard subjects for Keith.
Incorrect: Darnell writes practice essays, and reads literature.
Incorrect: They will review his application, and transcript.

A. Directions: Insert commas where needed in the sentences below. If no commas are required, write *NC*.

_____ 1. Kwanzaa is a week-long African American holiday that celebrates culture community and family.

_____ 2. Kwanzaa a wintertime holiday is based on an ancient African harvest celebration.

_____ 3. It was developed in modern times by scholar Maulana Karenga.

_____ 4. Kwanzaa celebrations include rituals such as singing dancing drumming and poetry reading.

_____ 5. The family lights one candle every day for each of seven principles: unity self-determination responsibility cooperative economics purpose creativity and faith.

B. Questions 6 through 8 refer to the following paragraphs.

Childproofing Your Home

(1) If you have small children, you no doubt appreciate the need to make your home as safe as possible. (2) It is a fact that home accidents, are responsible for more children's injuries than all childhood diseases combined. (3) Taking a few simple measures might reduce the number of times you take your kids to the emergency room.

(4) Start by putting childproof locks on all cupboards in which medicines poisons, or fragile objects are stored. (5) To keep babies and toddlers from entering dangerous areas, put baby gates in doorways and install sleeves on doorknobs. (6) Install safety locks on doors and windows. (7) Make sure that older children, those ten and up can open them in an emergency.

6. Sentence 2: It is a fact that home accidents, are responsible for more children's injuries than all childhood diseases combined.

Which correction should be made to sentence 2?

A. remove the comma after <u>accidents</u>
B. change <u>are</u> to <u>is</u>
C. insert a comma after <u>injuries</u>
D. insert a comma after <u>diseases</u>

7. Sentence 4: Start by putting childproof locks on all cupboards in which medicines poisons, or fragile objects are stored.

Which correction should be made to sentence 4?

A. change <u>Start</u> to <u>Starting</u>
B. insert a comma after <u>medicines</u>
C. insert a comma after <u>objects</u>
D. change <u>are</u> to <u>is</u>

8. Sentence 7: Make sure that older <u>children, those ten and up</u> can open them in an emergency.

Which is the best way to write the underlined portion of this sentence?

A. children those ten and up
B. children, those ten, and up,
C. children, those ten and up,
D. children those ten and up,

Colons and Semicolons

Colons

Colons (:) have many uses. A colon can be used to separate two independent but related clauses. The first clause introduces a topic, and the second clause explains, illustrates, restates, emphasizes, or expands upon the first clause. In a way, colons are shorthand for *such as*, *for instance*, *in other words*, *in addition*, or similar phrases.

Incorrect: Bees are an important component of plant reproduction: the price of new cars is expected to increase next year.
Correct: Bees are an important component of the plant reproduction process: they carry pollen from one plant to another.

Colons can also be used before lists. When used to introduce a list, the colon should not be placed immediately after a verb or preposition.

Incorrect: When I went to the hardware store I bought: a hammer, nails, and sandpaper.
Correct: When I went to the hardware store I bought three items: a hammer, nails, and sandpaper.

Colons can also be placed before long quotations.

Semicolons

A common use of semicolons (;) is to separate long items in a list, particularly if the items contain commas.

Incorrect: I bought a ball-peen hammer, steel, inch-long nails, and large grit, heavy-duty sandpaper.
Correct: I bought a ball-peen hammer; steel, inch-long nails; and large grit, heavy-duty sandpaper.

Semicolons also can be used to separate independent clauses that are related but do not meet the requirements of a colon. Semicolons can be used to replace a comma plus a conjunction such as *and* or *but*.

Example: Luis bought tickets to a football game; Jenna used her allowance to buy tickets to a rock concert.

Because these are independent clauses, they could be written as two sentences. The use of semicolons often is a matter of style more than grammar. Rather than writing a series of short, choppy sentences, an author might choose to combine related sentences by using a semicolon.

Note: In your own writing, it is usually preferable to join two sentences using transitional words such as *and, but, such as, for instance, however,* etc. These words make the relationships between your ideas much clearer to the reader than colons and semicolons with no transitional words do.

KEY IDEAS

- Colons have a number of uses, many of which are related to formatting.
- Colons can be used to join two related sentences or to introduce lists.
- Semicolons can be used to join two related sentences or to separate items in a list, if those items contain commas.

TASC TEST TIP

When joining two sentences with a colon or semicolon, ask yourself, "How would I phrase this connection in words?" If the two sentences could be joined with "such as" or "in other words," use a colon. If the two sentences could be joined with "and" or "but," use a semicolon.

PRACTICE 2

1. Insert colons in the proper place in the following sentences. In some cases, you may need to replace other punctuation with a colon. If no colon is needed, write NC on the line provided.

_____ a. She said the meeting would start at 1230 p.m.

_____ b. After the concert, George exclaimed "That was the group's best performance ever. I want to see them again."

_____ c. Annika's generous parents offered her a graduation present new clothes, furniture, a computer, or a resort vacation were her choices.

_____ d. Ricardo's schedule today includes two meetings, a business lunch, and a charity gala.

_____ e. There are four states that begin with the letter *I*, Idaho, Illinois, Indiana, and Iowa.

2. Insert semicolons in the proper place in the following sentences. In some cases, you may need to replace other punctuation with a semicolon. If no semicolon is needed, write NS. Some sentences may require more than one semicolon.

_____ a. The class went on a field trip and spotted a long, brown snake, two small, noisy finches, and a skittish, furry raccoon.

_____ b. My favorite sports are lacrosse, football, and basketball.

_____ c. Sue ate bacon, and Robert had eggs. Jane's choice was doughnuts.

_____ d. Ernest did well on his TASC test he was accepted by his favorite college.

Questions 3 through 5 refer to the following paragraph.

(1) Customer Service Representatives (CSRs) can be much more valuable to companies than many employers realize. (2) CSRs can perform many valuable functions resolving customer problems, creating additional sales, and providing valuable feedback to management. (3) Some companies only consider the first of these functions and miss out on the additional value that CSRs can add if they receive proper, thorough training, are provided with versatile, reliable technology, and are rewarded for performing all three important, but often neglected, roles. (4) Employers can reward CSRs by increasing compensation, recognition, and a sense of accomplishment are important as well.

3. **Sentence 2:** CSRs can perform many valuable functions resolving customer problems, creating additional sales, and providing valuable feedback to management.

Which correction should be made to sentence 2?

A. Split it into two sentences.
B. Insert a colon after <u>functions</u>.
C. Insert a comma after <u>functions</u>.
D. Insert a semicolon after <u>sales</u>.

4. **Sentence 3:** Some companies only consider the first of these functions and miss out on the additional value that CSRs can add if they receive proper, thorough training, are provided with versatile, reliable technology, and are rewarded for performing all three important, but often neglected, roles.

Which correction should be made to sentence 3?

A. Replace the commas after <u>training</u> and <u>technology</u> with semicolons.
B. Replace the commas after <u>proper</u> and <u>versatile</u> with semicolons.
C. Split it into three sentences.
D. Insert a colon after <u>receive</u>.

5. **Sentence 4:** Employers can reward CSRs by increasing compensation, recognition and a sense of accomplishment are important as well.

Which correction should be made to sentence 4?

A. Insert a colon after <u>increasing</u>.
B. Insert a hyphen after <u>increasing</u>.
C. Change the comma after <u>compensation</u> to a semicolon.
D. No changes are needed.

Capitalization

To recognize capitalization errors on the TASC Writing Test and to use capital letters correctly in your response, follow these guidelines.

Capitalize proper nouns. A **proper noun** is the name of a specific person, place, thing, or idea. If a proper noun has two or more words, capitalize each word.

EXAMPLES
Claude Normand is a major contributor to Portland Community Hospital. The hospital is located on Camden Road in Portland, Maine.
The hospital and charities such as the American Cancer Society rely on contributions from citizens.
All major religions, from Islam to Christianity, support giving to charity.

Note that the key words in addresses are proper nouns and are capitalized. The key words include the names of streets, cities, states, and countries.

Do not capitalize common nouns, which do not refer to a specific person, place, or thing.

EXAMPLE
Incorrect: Many Doctors volunteer at Clinics in the City.
Correct: Many doctors volunteer at clinics in the city.

Capitalize the names of proper adjectives. A **proper adjective** is formed from a proper noun.

EXAMPLE
Mr. Normand has a French-Canadian heritage.

Capitalize a title before a person's name. Do not capitalize a title when it appears without a person's name unless it is used in direct address.

EXAMPLES
Title before name: Mr. Normand met recently with Dr. Halverson and Mayor Maresky.
Title without name: The doctor and mayor were very receptive to his ideas.
Direct address: He said, "Thank you, Mayor, for listening to my proposal."

Capitalize names of holidays, days of the week, and months. Do not capitalize the names of seasons.

EXAMPLES
Memorial Day is always the last Monday in May and is a paid holiday. The project will be completed by the end of spring.

Capitalize names of specific school courses and all languages.

EXAMPLE
I am taking Introduction to Computers 101, English, and math.

KEY IDEAS

- Capitalize proper nouns and adjectives.
- Capitalize days of the week, months, and names of holidays but not seasons.
- Capitalize titles if they come before a person's name or are used to address the person.

TASC TEST TIP

Use the "proper noun" test to determine if a word should be capitalized. To capitalize, make sure the word or phrase is the name of a person, place or thing: "my uncle" is fine, and so is "Uncle Leo."

PRACTICE 3

A. Directions: Correct the capitalization errors in the sentences below.

EXAMPLE: I am writing to thank the ~~S~~taff of the Waterside Physical Therapy ~~c~~enter.

1. Last Spring, I broke my arm in a car accident.

2. My internist, doctor claudia McNally, referred me to Waterside.

3. The center's Director, Ilana Harris, assigned me a physical therapist named Ellie Royce.

4. Ellie studied physical therapy in her native London and used british methods of treatment that relieved my pain quite effectively.

5. She also did therapy with me in the pool at Rainbow health club.

6. I finished my treatments just before labor day, and I feel 100 percent better, thanks to Ellie.

B. Questions 7 through 9 refer to the following paragraphs.

An Unusual Breed

(A)

(1) The Akita is a Japanese dog breed that dates to ancient times. (2) The breed has a special spiritual meaning for many. (3) For example, when a child is born, well-wishers give the family small statues of Akitas to express hopes for future happiness and health. (4) In the past, only Emperors and nobles were allowed to own this breed.

(B)

(5) Akitas are massive, powerful dogs, used for hunting game and guarding. (6) Starting in the 17th century, they were trained to hunt game and waterfowl in the Mountains of Japan. (7) In 1937, Akitas were brought to america by author Helen Keller.

7. Sentence 4: In the past, only Emperors and nobles were allowed to own this breed.

Which correction should be made to sentence 4?

A. remove the comma
B. change Emperors to emperors
C. change nobles to Nobles
D. change were to are

8. Sentence 6: Starting in the 17th century, they were trained to hunt game and waterfowl in the Mountains of Japan.

Which correction should be made to sentence 6?

A. change Starting to Started
B. remove the comma
C. change Mountains to mountains
D. insert a comma after game

9. Sentence 7: In 1937, Akitas were brought to america by author Helen Keller.

Which correction should be made to sentence 7?

A. remove the comma
B. change america to America
C. change author to Author
D. change Helen Keller to helen keller

Possessives and Contractions

Some of the most common spelling errors involve possessives and contractions. Follow these guidelines when spelling these words:

A **possessive** shows ownership. Use apostrophes with possessive nouns. Do not use apostrophes with possessive pronouns.

EXAMPLES
Possessive nouns: friend's car   Marta's map   the dogs' leashes
Possessive pronouns: his, hers, ours, yours, theirs, its
Correct: The car's tires are new. The map is hers.

If a noun is singular or if it is plural but does not end in s, add an apostrophe + s to form the possessive.

Singular possessive: cat's   boss's   women's

If a noun is plural and ends in s, add an apostrophe after the final s.

Plural possessive: workers'   ladies'

A singular possessive often sounds like a plural noun. Use an apostrophe only with the possessive.

Correct: My company's benefits (possessive) make it one of the best companies (plural) to work for.

A **contraction** shortens two words by combining the second word with the first and leaving out one or more letters. An apostrophe takes the place of the missing letters. Some contractions combine pronouns with verbs.

EXAMPLES
here is → here's   there is → there's   I am → I'm

Other contractions combine verbs with the word *not*.

EXAMPLES
have not → haven't   do not → don't   will not → won't

Be careful to use the apostrophe in place of the missing letter or letters. Notice that the correct position is not necessarily the point at which the two words come together.

Incorrect: You do'nt have to come with us tonight. (*do'nt* should be *don't*)

Some possessives and contractions sound the same (*your* and *you're*, *its* and *it's*, *their* and *they're*). To determine whether to use a possessive or a contraction, substitute the two words that make up the contraction. If the substitution makes sense, the contraction is correct. If not, use a possessive.

PRACTICE 4

A. Directions: Underline the correct word or words to complete each sentence.

EXAMPLE: I'm (<u>your</u>, you're) downstairs neighbor, and (<u>I've</u>, Iv'e) been having trouble sleeping lately because of noise late at night.

1. (Theirs, There's) a noise that sounds like the thumping beat of rock music.

2. I (ca'nt, can't) be sure (who's, whose) responsible, but (its, it's) coming from your apartment.

3. My roommates and I have discussed this, and (were, we're) running out of patience.

4. You should talk to your children if the stereo is (theirs, there's).

5. Please be considerate of your neighbors just as we are considerate of (our's, ours).

B. <u>Questions 6 through 8 refer to the paragraphs that follow.</u>

Sales Trainees Wanted

(A)

(1) Do you have a warm smile? (2) Do people feel comfortable with you? (3) Do you have a friendly phone manner? (4) Do you have good organizational skills? (5) Are you good at solving problems? (6) If you've answered yes to these questions, we need you're skills at Macro Software.

(B)

(7) Macro Software is one of the industry leaders in software distribution. (8) In addition to our chain of stores, were proud to offer a mail order service that was the first of its kind. (9) We pride ourselves on our high-quality products, quick delivery times, and excellent customer service.

(C)

(10) We are currently hiring sales trainees for our Miami office. (11) Interested parties should send they're resumes to Jim Burns, Macro Software, 904 Ocean Drive, Miami, Florida.

6. Sentence 6: If you've answered yes to these questions, we need you're skills at Macro Software.

Which correction should be made to sentence 6?

A. insert a comma after <u>yes</u>
B. remove the <u>comma</u>
C. change <u>need</u> to <u>needs</u>
D. replace <u>you're</u> with <u>your</u>

7. Sentence 8: In addition to our chain of stores, were proud to offer a mail order service that was the first of its kind.

Which correction should be made to sentence 8?

A. replace <u>our</u> with <u>hour</u>
B. change <u>were</u> to <u>we're</u>
C. insert a comma after <u>service</u>
D. replace <u>its</u> with <u>it's</u>

8. Sentence 11: Interested parties should send they're resumes to Jim Burns, Macro Software, 904 Ocean Drive, Miami, Florida.

Which correction should be made to sentence 11?

A. replace <u>parties</u> with <u>party's</u>
B. replace <u>they're</u> with <u>their</u>
C. replace <u>resumes</u> with <u>resume's</u>
D. replace <u>Burns</u> with <u>Burn's</u>

Homonyms

Homonyms are words that sound alike but are spelled differently and have different meanings. The following chart lists homonyms and other commonly confused words that people often misspell.

Word	Meaning	Word in Sentence
accept	to receive willingly	I accept responsibility for my actions.
except	excluding	Everyone went except Molly.
affect	to have an impact	Did the medicine affect you?
effect	a result	The effects will wear off soon.
board	a piece of wood	Nail that board to the other one.
bored	not interested	Rami was bored in wood shop class.
brake	to stop; something that stops	Put your foot on the brake!
break	to shatter in pieces	Be careful, or you'll break your arm.
close	to shut	Please close that bag.
clothes	something to wear	I'm going to return those clothes.
desert	to leave behind; arid land	Don't desert a friend in need.
dessert	sweet food served after dinner	They offer dessert to their guests.
fare	money paid by a passenger	The subway fare was just raised.
fair	just, right	A lot of people think it's not fair.
forth	forward	Let's go forth!
fourth	in the 4th position	It is our fourth trip in three days.
grate	to shred	We need to grate some potatoes.
great	fantastic; of large size	It's going to be a great casserole.
hole	opening	There's a hole in the sweater.
whole	entire	Soon the whole thing will fall apart.
know	to understand	I don't know what's wrong with him.
no	opposite of *yes*	He has no sense.
led	past tense of the verb *lead*; brought	He led the worker to the supply room.
lead	a material in pencils	They gave her some lead pencils.
lessen	to decrease	Will you lessen the sugar in the recipe?
lesson	something you learn; moral	That will teach him a lesson.
male	a boy or man	There are both females and males in the Army.
mail	to send a message through the post office; a message sent	Send the letter through the mail.
passed	went by	Have you passed the post office?
past	opposite of *future*	Yes, in the past.
peace	opposite of *war*	When will there be world peace?
piece	a part	That's only a piece of the problem.
principal	head of a school	The principal has called a meeting.
principle	a guiding rule; a moral	He has no principles.
than	compared with	I used to have more money than you.
then	after that; at that time	Then I spent most of mine.
there	at that place	The car is over there.
their	belonging to them	It is their car.
they're	they are	They're going to sell it.
to	indicates a direction	Go to the grocery store.
too	also, in addition	Sharmaine will go, too.
two	the number 2	Buy me two loaves of bread.

PRACTICE 5

A. Directions: Underline the correct word or words to complete each sentence.

EXAMPLE: The chairman of the (<u>board</u>, bored) has called this meeting.

1. This is our (fourth, forth) meeting on the topic of funding.

2. We don't (no, know) any other sources of funding.

3. The director of the organization brought up this (whole, hole) issue.

4. Next (weak, week), we plan to submit a proposal.

5. We worry that a request for funding may (affect, effect) our nonprofit status.

6. In the (past, passed), we could rely on government funding.

B. <u>Questions 7 through 9</u> **refer to the paragraphs that follow.**

Equal Pay for Equal Work?

(A)

(1) In 1963, women earned only 59 percent of the wages men earned. (2) In 1997, the figure was still just 74 percent. (3) Women have logged great achievements in the workforce, so why don't they receive fare pay?

(B)

(4) One explanation is that the statistics include older women. (5) In principal, the age gap could account for the wage gap because older women still work in jobs in which attitudes and conditions of the past prevail. (6) In contrast, women under the age of 25 earn about 92 percent of what men earn. (7) However, upon closer examination, this theory falls flat. (8) Women in entry-level jobs have always earned salaries similar to those of their male peers. (9) The problem is that women don't receive the same raises and promotions that men get. (10) The affect is that, as women get older, the gap between men's and women's salaries becomes greater.

7. Sentence 3: Women have logged great achievements in the workforce, so why don't they receive fare pay?

Which correction should be made to sentence 3?

A. change <u>have</u> to <u>has</u>
B. replace <u>great</u> with <u>grate</u>
C. replace <u>fare</u> with <u>fair</u>
D. replace <u>Women</u> with <u>Woman</u>

8. Sentence 5: In principal, the age gap could account for the wage gap because older women still work in jobs in which attitudes and conditions of the past prevail.

Which correction should be made to sentence 5?

A. change <u>principal</u> to <u>principle</u>
B. change <u>work</u> to <u>working</u>
C. replace <u>past</u> with <u>passed</u>
D. replace <u>for</u> with <u>four</u>

9. Sentence 10: The affect is that, as women get older, the gap between men's and women's salaries becomes greater.

Which correction should be made to sentence 10?

A. replace <u>affect</u> with <u>effect</u>
B. change <u>becomes</u> to <u>become</u>
C. replace <u>greater</u> with <u>grater</u>
D. remove the comma after <u>that</u>

STUDY ADVICE

Homonyms can be tricky. If you are unsure whether you are using the correct word during your practice, be sure to look it up in a dictionary afterward. If you are unsure when writing an essay on Test Day, try to pick a completely different word to avoid an error.

Hyphens

Hyphens (-) have a variety of uses. (Hyphens are sometimes incorrectly referred to as dashes. A dash, which looks like this: – or this: — is longer than a hyphen.) For example, hyphens are used to connect two words to form a compound adjective *before* a noun but are not used *after* a noun.

Examples: The race was won by a well-bred horse.

The horse that won the race was well bred.

You should also use hyphens in compound numbers.

Examples: sixty-two, thirty-three, one hundred twenty-five, fourteen

Use hyphens with the prefixes *ex-*, *self-*, and *all-* unless they are part of a word listed in the dictionary. Hyphens are generally not used before suffixes, with notable exceptions being *-elect and -free*.

Examples: ex-spouse, exfoliate

self-funded, selfless

all-inclusive, altogether

congresswoman-elect, toll-free

Use hyphens with capitalized words, single letters, abbreviations or acronyms, and numbers.

Examples: anti-European, mid-January, V-formation, T-shirt, ex-CIA,

pre-2000, post-1800s

Hyphens are inserted where an awkward combination of letters could be confusing.

Examples: anti-inflammatory, mega-ampere, semi-incomplete

If a word has two very different meanings, a hyphen is sometimes used to clarify the intended meaning.

Examples: re-sign (sign again) and resign (quit)

re-form (make again) and reform (change behavior)

re-create (create again) and recreate (have fun)

When two or more compound terms share the same second segment, that segment need only be included in the last term; the differing first terms use a "hanging" hyphen.

Examples: short-, intermediate-, and long-term results

5- and 10-day periods

KEY IDEAS

- Hyphens are used to indicate that a word has been divided between two lines of text, but there are a few rules that govern how this can be done.
- Hyphens can clarify meaning in a variety of ways.
- Hyphens and dashes are not the same: a dash is longer than a hyphen and is used differently.

TASC TEST TIP

When using a hyphen in a compound adjective, such as "a well-thought-out idea," remember that hyphens are only appropriate if the compound adjective comes before the noun it modifies.

PRACTICE 6

1. Match each word or compound word with its closest definition:

un-ionized		a. in favor of healing
unionized		b. something that used to be a tent
ex-tent		c. organized in a group
extent		d. to obtain
pro-cure		e. scope
procure		f. not having the properties of an ion

2. Insert hyphens where needed in the following sentences. Some sentences may require more than one. If none is required, write NH on the blank provided.

_____ a. Sarah was happy to see many of her long lost friends at her reunion.

_____ b. The thunderstorm caused a 10 minute delay in the game.

_____ c. Josh was very pleased with his new V neck sweater.

_____ d. The police were suspicious of all the ex offenders in the area.

_____ e. The young man was overzealous in his pursuit of the prize.

_____ f. Micah thanked Julia for her selfless act.

_____ g. The members of the self actualization group held a rally yesterday.

_____ h. There are twentysix students in the introductory economics class.

_____ i. The company's subsidiary acted in a semiindependent manner.

_____ j. The contest was open to one, two, or three person teams.

For questions 3 and 4, choose the one best answer to each question.

3. This bookcase costs more because it has hand carved decorations and a set of glass doors.

Which correction should be made to the sentence above?

A. Change bookcase to book-case.
B. Insert a comma after more.
C. Insert a hyphen between hand and carved.
D. Insert a hyphen between glass and doors.

4. The experienced scientists tested the effects of the antidepressant drug on patients over three, five, and ten year timespans.

Which correction should be made to the sentence above?

A. Change experienced to ex-perienced.
B. Change antidepressant to anti-depressant.
C. Insert hyphens after three, five, and ten.
D. Change timespans to time-spans.

USING WRITING MECHANICS PRACTICE QUESTIONS

Questions 1 through 5 refer to the following paragraphs.

Single Parents and Relationships

(A)

(1) Children of single parents don't exactly cheer their parents on at the start of a new relationship. (2) Instead, children may have tantrums erase phone messages, and generally try to ruin their parents' chances. (3) If you are a parent in this situation, you need to understand, and show your children that you love them. (4) However, also let your kids know, that you feel you're doing the right thing.

(B)

(5) Your children may become quickly attached to a new date, even within the course of an evening. (6) Alternatively, they may fear that you plan to marry each potential partner you bring home. (7) For these reasons, it makes sense not to introduce all your dates to your children. (8) Try to see your dates at times when your children are'nt at home.

(C)

(9) Once you become committed to a particular person, it's important to include your partner in family events gradually. (10) Don't be surprised if your children have a negative reaction to your new partner. (11) This time may be difficult for your kids. (12) They're not used to seeing you with a new partner, and they may be realizing that a reconciliation with your exspouse is impossible. (13) If communication breaks down consider family counseling. (14) Children may be more willing to share their worries and complaints in that setting.

1. Sentence 2: **Instead, children may have tantrums erase phone messages, and generally try to ruin their parents' chances.**

   Which correction should be made to sentence 2?

   A. remove the comma after <u>Instead</u>
   B. insert a comma after <u>tantrums</u>
   C. change <u>their</u> to <u>they're</u>
   D. change <u>have</u> to <u>has</u>

2. Sentence 3: **If you are a parent in this situation, you need to understand, and show your children that you love them.**

   Which is the best way to write the underlined portion of this sentence?

   A. understand, and showing
   B. understand. And show
   C. understand and show
   D. understand, and you show

3. Sentence 4: **However, also let your kids know, that you feel you're doing the right thing.**

   Which correction should be made to sentence 4?

   A. remove the comma after <u>However</u>
   B. replace <u>your</u> with <u>you're</u>
   C. replace <u>you're</u> with <u>your</u>
   D. remove the comma after <u>know</u>

4. Sentence 8: **Try to see your dates at times when your children are'nt at home.**

   Which correction should be made to sentence 8?

   A. replace <u>your</u> with <u>you're</u>
   B. insert a comma after <u>times</u>
   C. change <u>are'nt</u> to <u>aren't</u>
   D. change <u>are'nt</u> to <u>isn't</u>

5. Sentence 13: **If communication breaks <u>down consider</u> family counseling.**

   Which is the best way to write the underlined portion of this sentence?

   A. down will consider
   B. down, consider
   C. down. Consider
   D. down, and consider

Questions 6 through 10 refer to the following paragraphs.

The History of Daylight Saving Time

(A)

(1) We set our clocks forward every spring and back every fall, but few of us stop to think about why we do this. (2) One of the main reasons for daylight saving time, is to save energy. (3) In the evening, we use lights, TVs, and electrical appliances. (4) Daylight saving time makes the period between sunset and bedtime one hour shorter, and therefore less electricity is used.

(B)

(5) With daylight saving time, each time zone changes it's standard time by an hour. (6) Time zones were introduced by the railroads to make schedules standard across the country. (7) In 1918, congress passed a law making the rail time zones official. (8) That same year, a second law put the country on daylight saving time for the rest of World War I. (9) The law was unpopular, however, and it was repealed seven months later. (10) Daylight saving time was also in force during most of World War II.

(C)

(11) From 1945 to 1966, each state and town could decide whether to observe daylight saving time. (12) The resulting inconsistencies created a great deal of confusion. (13) For example radio and TV stations had to put out new schedules every time a state started or ended daylight saving time. (14) Then came the Uniform Time Act of 1966, which established starting and ending dates for daylight saving time, in the spring and fall. (15) This law was amended in1986, when the starting date was moved almost a month earlier to save energy.

6. Sentence 2: **One of the main reasons for daylight saving time, is to save energy.**

Which correction should be made to sentence 2?

A. insert a comma after reasons
B. remove the comma
C. change is to are
D. change main to mane

7. Sentence 5: **With daylight saving time, each time zone changes it's standard time by an hour.**

Which correction should be made to sentence 5?

A. remove the comma
B. replace it's with its
C. replace hour with our
D. insert a comma after standard time

8. Sentence 7: **In 1918, congress passed a law making the rail time zones official.**

Which correction should be made to sentence 7?

A. remove the comma
B. change congress to Congress
C. replace passed with past
D. change making to made

9. Sentence 13: **For example radio and TV stations had to put out new schedules every time a state started or ended daylight saving time.**

Which correction should be made to sentence 13?

A. insert a comma after example
B. change had to have
C. change schedules to schedule's
D. insert a comma after schedules

10. Sentence 14: **Then came the Uniform Time Act of 1966, which established starting and ending dates for daylight saving time, in the spring and fall.**

Which correction should be made to sentence 14?

A. change Act to act
B. replace dates with date's
C. remove the comma after time
D. change spring and fall to Spring and Fall

Questions 11 through 15 refer to the following paragraphs.

Rules and Regulations

(A)

(1) Thank you for joining Spring Valley Community center. (2) Before using our facility, please read these rules and regulations carefully.

(B)

(3) Please have your membership card with you at all times when your in the building. (4) When you enter the pool or exercise room, a security guard will request to see your card and will deny you entrance without it.

(C)

(5) Guests are welcome to use the pool and exercise room, but only when accompanied by members. (6) The guest fee is $10 per day. (7) When bringing guests, please have them sign in at the desk in the lobby. (8) They will be given a guest card for the day.

(D)

(9) Pool safety is very important. (10) If you are a week swimmer, life jackets and other flotation devices are available for your use. (11) Do not hesitate to ask lifeguards for help. (12) Children under the age of 12 must swim in the children's pool, unless they're supervised by an adult. (13) Swimming classes are available to help both children and adults improve their skills.

(E)

(14) You must register, and pay for any class you wish to take. (15) Members receive a significant discount. (16) Registration may be limited to a certain number of participants.

11. Sentence 1: **Thank you for joining Spring Valley Community center.**

    Which correction should be made to sentence 1?

    A. insert a comma after <u>you</u>
    B. change <u>Community</u> to <u>community</u>
    C. change <u>center</u> to <u>Center</u>
    D. change <u>you</u> to <u>You</u>

12. Sentence 3: **Please have your membership card with you at all times when your in the building.**

    Which correction should be made to sentence 3?

    A. insert a comma after <u>Please</u>
    B. replace <u>have your</u> with <u>have you're</u>
    C. replace <u>times</u> with <u>times'</u>
    D. replace <u>when your</u> with <u>when you're</u>

13. Sentence 10: **If you are a week swimmer, life jackets and other flotation devices are available for your use.**

    Which correction should be made to sentence 10?

    A. replace <u>week</u> with <u>weak</u>
    B. remove the comma
    C. insert a comma after <u>available</u>
    D. change <u>your</u> to <u>you're</u>

14. Sentence 12: **Children under the age of 12 must swim in the children's pool, unless they're supervised by an adult.**

    Which correction should be made to sentence 12?

    A. insert commas after <u>Children</u> and <u>12</u>
    B. change <u>children's</u> with <u>childrens'</u>
    C. replace <u>they're</u> to <u>their</u>
    D. remove the comma after <u>pool</u>

15. Sentence 14: **You must <u>register, and pay</u> for any class you wish to take.**

    Which is the best way to write the underlined portion of this sentence?

    A. register, pay
    B. register and pay
    C. register. And pay
    D. register. Pay

Questions 16 through 20 refer to the following paragraphs.

Racial Profiling

(A)

(1) African American and Hispanic motorists are much more likely to be stopped by police then their white counterparts, often for no apparent reason. (2) What's their offense? (3) It may be that these individuals have been targeted because of their race.

(B)

(4) Blacks and Hispanics, who some police officers believe are more likely to commit crimes, have been systematically targeted by police. (5) Police statistics from 23 states show that this policy, called racial profiling occurs in every geographic location. (6) Motorists, pedestrians, and airline passengers have been searched. (7) The police do not make class distinctions for nonwhites of every station in life have been victims of this practice.

(C)

(8) The statistical evidence shows a clear pattern. (9) On one Maryland highway, 73 percent of those stopped by police were African American, even though blacks represented only 17 percent of all drivers. (10) Hispanics make up only 8 percent of the population in illinois, yet 30 percent of drivers stopped there are Hispanic. (11) However, police superintendents chiefs of police, and other law enforcement officials dispute the studies that document racial profiling. (12) They maintain that the problem has been confined to a small number of officers and can be remedied easily.

16. Sentence 1: **African American and Hispanic motorists are much more likely to be stopped by police then their white counterparts, often for no apparent reason.**

Which correction should be made to sentence 1?

A. change motorists to Motorists
B. insert a comma after then
C. replace then with than
D. replace for with four

17. Sentence 5: **Police statistics from 23 states show that this policy, called racial profiling occurs in every geographic location.**

Which correction should be made to sentence 5?

A. change states to States
B. insert a comma after states
C. insert a comma after profiling
D. remove the comma

18. Sentence 7: **The police do not make class distinctions for nonwhites of every station in life have been victims of this practice.**

Which is the best way to write the underlined portion of this sentence?

A. distinctions. For nonwhites
B. distinctions, for nonwhites
C. distinctions moreover nonwhites
D. distinctions nonwhites

19. Sentence 10: **Hispanics make up only 8 percent of the population in illinois, yet 30 percent of drivers stopped there are Hispanic.**

Which correction should be made to sentence 10?

A. change make to makes
B. change illinois to Illinois
C. remove the comma
D. replace yet with and

20. Sentence 11: **However, police superintendents chiefs of police, and other law enforcement officials dispute the studies that document racial profiling.**

Which correction should be made to sentence 11?

A. remove the comma after However
B. insert a comma after superintendents
C. insert a comma after officials
D. change studies to studies'

LANGUAGE ARTS: WRITING ANSWERS AND EXPLANATIONS

Writing Effective Sentences

Lesson 1: Simple Sentences

Practice 1

A. The revisions are samples. Your rewrites may differ.
1. **F** It drives his girlfriend crazy.
2. **F** As soon as he comes home from work, he starts talking on the telephone.
3. **C**
4. **F** Dave's sister and his best friend like to talk on the telephone, too.
B. 5. **C. call from** Choice (C) joins a sentence fragment to a complete sentence. "A calling conference" in choice (D) is badly worded.
6. **C. insert you before can** Choice (C) adds a subject to a sentence fragment, thus creating a complete sentence.
7. **C. service can** Choice (C) joins a sentence fragment to a complete sentence and makes sense.

Lesson 2: Compound and Complex Sentences

Practice 2.1

A. 1. It was late, and I was walking home from work.
2. My co-worker, Judy, had offered to drive me, but I had refused.
3. It was a warm night, so I decided to get some fresh air.
4. It was really my choice. I could have taken a cab, or I could have walked.
5. I heard a loud noise, so I ran the last block to my house. Later, I learned that it was only a car backfiring.
B. 6. **B. remove the comma** A comma is required when two independent clauses are joined but not when two verbs are joined (*carries . . . gets*).
7. **A. airlines, but** *But* is the most logical coordinating conjunction here. Most travelers on major airlines can check baggage. Because there are two clauses (*couriers . . . fly, . . . they can't check*), a comma is needed.
8. **B. insert a comma after advance** A comma precedes a coordinating conjunction joining two independent clauses.

Practice 2.2

A. 1. Most fatal fires occur when a family is asleep.
2. Because a smoke alarm wakes you up, it can allow you to escape.
3. Try to replace the smoke detector's battery before it goes dead.
4. Although smoke detectors cost money, the expense is worth it.
B. 5. **B. insert a after making** An indefinite article is needed.
6. **A. replace Whenever with After** *Whenever* is used inappropriately; it does not convey the intended meaning.
7. **D. up, thank** Choice (D) correctly combines a sentence fragment and an independent clause to form a complex sentence.

Lesson 3: Run-Ons and Comma Splices

Practice 3

A. There are several possible correct answers. There may be other correct answers in addition to those listed.
1. Jeff just got his driver's license, and he's very excited. OR Jeff just got his driver's license. He's very excited.
2. He bought a car that has a lot of miles on it, so it wasn't very expensive. OR Because he bought a car that has a lot of miles on it, it wasn't very expensive.
3. He doesn't have a lot of free time, but he'd like to take a car trip. OR Although he doesn't have a lot of free time, he'd like to take a car trip.
4. He needs to find out about car insurance, get a good map, and join an auto club.
B. 5. **A. pictures if you just** Choice (A) turns a run-on sentence into a complex sentence by adding a subordinating conjunction. The comma in choice (C) is unnecessary because the subordinate clause is the second half of the sentence.
6. **B. insert and in place of the comma** Choice (B) turns a comma splice into a compound sentence by adding a coordinating conjunction. Don't be misled by the apparent lack of a subject; both clauses are commands, meaning the subject, *you*, is implied but unstated.
7. **C. insert because in place of the comma** Choice (C) turns a run-on sentence into a compound sentence with a subordinating conjunction and a comma.

Lesson 4: Subordinate Ideas

Practice 4

A. There are several possible answers for each question. Sample answers:
1. Tornadoes and earthquakes can cause a lot of damage.
2. Earthquakes are somewhat common in California, but many Californians do not seem to mind.
3. On May 20, 2013, a tornado in Oklahoma killed 23 people and injured almost 400.
4. Tornadoes can occur anywhere in the United States and at any time of year.
B. 5. **D. repaired up** Choice (D) combines two short, choppy sentences into one smooth sentence. The other choices are run-ons, excessively wordy, or both.
6. **A. brought or mailed to** Choice (A) forms a compound predicate and combines two short, choppy sentences into one smooth, effective sentence.
7. **D. accidents, mishandling, or faulty installation** Choice (D) combines two wordy, repetitive sentences into one smooth, detailed sentence by forming a compound predicate.

Lesson 5: Modify Ideas

Practice 5

A. There are several possible answers for each question. Sample answers:
1. Trent's sister, who is a health professional, encouraged him to become a nurse.
2. When he wakes up the patients to take their blood pressure, they get rather annoyed.

3. He carefully writes their temperature and blood pressure on their charts.
4. It is hard to make visitors who are talking with patients leave at 9:00 p.m.

B. 5. **B. a person who is not the birth child** The phrase *not the birth child* is a misplaced modifier in the original sentence; choice (B) moves the modifier so it modifies the correct noun.

6. **C. An agency requires a "home study"** In the original sentence, it is not clear who is going through an agency.

7. **D. move <u>frequently</u> to follow <u>Lawyers</u>** Choice (D) moves the modifier to show that it is the lawyers who frequently handle adoptions, not the parents who frequently ask about them.

Lesson 6: Parallel Structure

Practice 6

A. There are multiple ways to revise these sentences. An example of each is listed below.
1. Jenna has worked in a factory, a store, and a restaurant.
2. She would like to put her kids in a better school and to get a better job.
3. She thinks the kids' father is irresponsible, lazy, and uncaring.
4. He doesn't have the time, the energy, or the money to give them what they deserve.

B. 5. **C. insert <u>more</u> before <u>pleasant</u>** Choice (C) correctly makes all the adjectives into comparatives (*safer, more comfortable,* and *more pleasant*).

6. **D. computers, and** The original sentence combined single words and clauses in the same series. Choice (D) corrects the error by turning the last item in the list from a clause to a noun phrase (*lights, computers, and coffee makers*).

7. **C. change <u>be leaving</u> to <u>leave</u>** Choice (C) makes all the verbs in the sentence (*punch, press,* and *leave*) parallel.

Writing Effective Sentences Practice Questions

1. **B. remove the comma** When an independent clause comes before a subordinate clause in a complex sentence, there is no need to use a comma.
2. **B. during the day and 62°F** Choice (B) is the most concise.
3. **D. sunlight, keep** Choice (D) combines a subordinate clause sentence fragment and an independent clause to form a complex sentence.
4. **D. home. Do change** Choice (D) corrects the comma splice by adding a period, and is consistent with the theme of the paragraph as being a list of recommendations.
5. **A. Your home will not cool down any faster.** *Any faster* should be placed next to the phrase it modifies, *cool down.*
6. **B. insert a comma after <u>home</u>** In this sentence, *When* begins a subordinate clause. A comma should be placed after a subordinate clause that begins a complex sentence.
7. **A. replace <u>Returning</u> with <u>I returned</u>** Choice (A) adds a subject to a sentence fragment and corrects the verb form to make a complete sentence.

8. **A. He claimed that because** There is no clear subject for the verb phrase at the beginning of the sentence to modify. By adding the subject *He,* choice (A) makes it clear who was claiming that the TV had been used.
9. **A. angry and frustrated about the** Choice (A) makes a smooth complex predicate out of a choppy run-on sentence.
10. **C. refund or get** Choice (C) puts both verbs in the same form. Choice (A) is grammatically correct but illogically suggests that Jeffrey will return *and* repair the TV.
11. **A. work productively if you** This choice moves the idea of being productive closer to the word it modifies, *work.* It also reduces wordiness by using the adverb form *productively.*
12. **C. remove the comma** A comma is not required before a coordinating conjunction that joins two verbs.
13. **B. remove the comma** A comma is not required in a complex sentence when the subordinate clause follows the independent clause.
14. **A. work or talk** Both verbs in the sentence should be in the same form. There is no need for a comma when a coordinating conjunction joins two verbs.
15. **B. insert a comma after <u>hard</u>** A comma is required before the coordinating conjunction that joins the two independent clauses in a compound sentence.
16. **D. hoaxes designed** This choice joins a sentence fragment to an independent clause.
17. **B. To check a claim like this, contact** Choice (B) combines two choppy sentences into one smooth, effective sentence.
18. **C. know. This** Choice (C) splits a comma splice into two independent, correct sentences.
19. **D. remove the comma after <u>safe</u>** A comma is not needed in a compound predicate.

Connecting Ideas

Lesson 1: Organize Ideas into Paragraphs

Practice 1.1

A. 1. The pharmacist at the local drugstore is very helpful.
2. No MI
3. Every vote counts, so let your voice be heard and vote!
4. When you are traveling, it's a good idea to mark your luggage clearly.
5. Listening to music can benefit you in many ways.

B. 6. **C. sentence 4** Sentences 1–3 explain who gets colds and how frequently. Sentences 4–6 are about the causes and prevention of colds.

7. **D. join paragraphs B and C** Sentence 10 in paragraph C is related to the main idea of paragraph B, the prevention of colds.

Practice 1.2

A. Your topic sentences should be similar to these:
1. Satellites have many different functions in today's world.
2. All signs show that the economy is headed for a slump.
3. The library has adopted a new dress code for employees.

B. 4. D. Repetitive strain injury is a painful condition resulting from repeated use of the hands. The original topic sentence is too general. The other options don't tell the central point: what repetitive strain injury is.

5. **B. A number of factors contribute to repetitive strain injury.** This sentence covers the three causes of repetitive strain injury mentioned in the paragraph.

Lesson 2: Use Logical Order and Relevant Ideas

Practice 2

A. 1. Irrelevant detail: Getting very ill is one bad thing that could happen.
2. Irrelevant detail: Adult students can also use school supplies.
3. Irrelevant detail: This job will be extremely expensive!
B. 4. **D. remove sentence 3** This sentence adds no new information to what was given in the previous sentences.
5. **D. remove sentence 6** The information about the secretarial job is not relevant to getting a job in carpentry.
6. **D. move sentence 10 to follow sentence 8** It would be more logical to place sentence 9 at the end of the letter.

Lesson 3: Relate Sentences and Paragraphs

Practice 3

A. Your transitions should be similar to these:
1. Our marketing efforts need to be enhanced. Therefore, we will soon begin another marketing initiative.
2. Sales representatives say that their jobs are extremely demanding. However, the salary is attractive.
3. The marketing director has instructed sales representatives to try some new ideas. For example, sales representatives can give away free samples.
4. A new ad campaign will be launched in just a few weeks. As a result, we expect sales to increase.
B. 5. **B. insert _however,_ after the comma** This position is the most logical for the transition. Also, because it is in the middle of a sentence, it should be set off by commas.
6. **B. restaurant. For example,** Sentence 6 offers an example of the broad menu described in sentence 5.
7. **A. In addition, having a cafe** This option inserts a helpful transition to move the reader smoothly from paragraph B to paragraph C.

Connecting Ideas Practice Questions

1. **C. sentence 5** Sentences 1–4 are about the general problem of sleep disruption, whereas sentences 5–8 are about reasons why people don't get enough sleep.
2. **B. High-achieving students get more sleep.** Both studies relate to the impact of lack of sleep on learning.
3. **A. grades. Similarly,** The ideas in the two sentences are similar, so they can be connected this way.

4. **D. remove sentence 13** The paragraph is about sleep, not losing weight.
5. **D. join paragraphs (C) and (D)** Both paragraphs contain tips for getting more sleep.
6. **B. sentence 4** Sentences 1–3 introduce the purpose of the passage. Sentences 4–7 contain general rules for stain removal.
7. **B. Choose the right water temperature for cleaning each stain.** This sentence is appropriate since the paragraph discusses hot, cold, and room-temperature water.
8. **D. juice, for example, removes** When a transition is placed in the middle of a sentence, commas should both precede and follow it.
9. **D. remove sentence 15** Sentence 15 explains a minor detail and moves away from the main idea of the paragraph.
10. **C. move sentence 19 to the beginning of paragraph D** Putting sentence 19 at the beginning of the paragraph lets readers know in advance what point the paragraph will make.
11. **C. remove sentence 5** Sentence 5 is a general statement about HMOs. It is not relevant to the explanation of which insurance carriers are being made available.
12. **A. insert a comma after _However_** A comma should follow when a transition begins a sentence.
13. **C. sentence 9** Until sentence 9, paragraph B is about the differences between the two insurance plans. Sentence 9 introduces the idea of the informational sessions.
14. **A. move sentence 14 to the end of paragraph C** Sentence 14 refers to the card that was mentioned in paragraph C and so continues that idea.
15. **A. move sentence 2 to follow sentence 3** The description of removing the wheel should start with the initial step.
16. **C. move sentence 11 to follow sentence 12** Sentence 11 tells what to do with the spot where there is a leak, so it should follow the information on finding that spot.
17. **C. The next step is to put the tire and tube back onto the rim.** Paragraph C describes the process of putting the tire and tube back on the rim.
18. **A. The final step is to reinstall the wheel.** Paragraph D describes the final step in the process: putting the wheel back on the bike.
19. **A. replace _Moreover,_ with _Then_** _Then_ is a more appropriate transition for describing steps in a process.

Using Grammar Correctly

Lesson 1: Noun and Pronoun Agreement

Practice 1.1

A. 1. They
2. him
3. it
4. Her
5. she
B. 6. **A. replace _me_ with _I_** _Bonetta and I_ is a compound subject, so a subject pronoun is required.

7. **D. change getting to gets** The simple present tense is appropriate here.
8. **B. Walter or me** The phrase *Walter or me* is an object, so an object pronoun is required.

Practice 1.2

A. 1. Sally is moving to a small town. Her mother is concerned about the health care options it offers.
2. Sally tried to reassure her mother, but it was hard for her mother to believe Sally.
3. Sally asked a friend who lives in the town for information about its health care facilities. OR the town's health care facilities.
4. The town has a freestanding clinic where a person can go when he or she is sick. OR where people can go when they are sick.
5. There is also a nearby hospital, and it has a very good reputation.
6. If one is concerned about health care, one should sign up for a good insurance plan. OR If you are concerned about health care, you should sign up for a good insurance plan.

B. 7. **D. replace one's with their** The word *children* earlier in the sentence is the antecedent to the pronoun; *their* agrees correctly with that antecedent, while the singular *one's* does not.
8. **D. parents** Only choice (D) correctly identifies who should be clear about their expectations.
9. **C. replace them with the group** The term *play group* is a collective noun, so the plural *them* should not be used to refer to it. In this case, repeating the word *group* is the best way to make the meaning clear.

Lesson 2: Verb Forms and Tenses

Practice 2.1

A. 1. had ceased
2. closed
3. functions
4. have visited
5. will open
6. looks
7. are thinking

B. 8. **B. is offering** The action is taking place right now, so the present progressive is the correct tense.
9. **D. change are signing to sign** The present-tense verb *sign* in the subordinate clause is appropriate, given the the future-tense verb *will receive* in the main clause.
10. **D. change will be amazing to will amaze** The verb *will amaze* is in the simple future tense. The future progressive tense in *will be amazing* is incorrect and overcomplicated.

Practice 2.2

A. 1. came
2. showed
3. had spoken
4. took
5. seen

B. 6. **D. change begun to began** The action takes place in the past tense, so the verb should be in its past form, *began*. *Begun* is the past participle.
7. **C. was broken** *Broken* is the correct past participle.
8. **B. change given to give** The clue word *now* tells you that the action is still true, so the present-tense form of *give* is correct.

Lesson 3: Subject-Verb Agreement

Practice 3.1

A. 1. is
2. become
3. is
4. have
5. seems
6. is

B. 7. **B. have heard** In this sentence, the indefinite pronoun *most* is plural ("most of us"). The verb *have heard* agrees with the plural subject.
8. **C. change start to starts** The verb *starts* agrees with the singular subject *plane*.
9. **B. change conducts to conduct** The verb *conduct* agrees with the plural subject *materials*.

Practice 3.2

A. 1. ~~on the market~~   carry
2. ~~carrying the seal~~   are
3. ~~an important ingredient in many toothpastes~~ strengthens, attacks
4. are
5. offer
6. ~~with fluoride and good flavor~~ is

B. 7. **C. change have to has** The verb *has* agrees with the singular subject *state*.
8. **A. determine** The verb *determine* agrees with the compound subject *Wage level and the length of employment*.
9. **C. change reports to report** The verb *report* agrees with the plural subject *workers*.

Lesson 4: Verb Moods

Practice 4

1. a. Will you leave me alone?
   b. Leave me alone!
2. a. Are (interrogative mood)
   b. leave (subjunctive mood)
   c. were (subjunctive mood)
   d. should (conditional)
   e. move (imperative)
   f. live (indicative)
3. **C. that one choose** This is a recommendation, so the verb must be in the subjunctive.
4. **D. snails do not enter** This sentence states a fact, so the verb must be in the indicative.
5. **B. one might consider looking** This sentence states a hypothetical situation, so it requires the conditional mood.

Lesson 5: Verb Voices and Verbals

Practice 5

1.

Sentence	Active Voice	Passive Voice
a. The judges awarded the skater first place in the competition.	X	
b. The Perseid meteor shower can be observed in August of each year.		X
c. Joseph's entire family watched the Perseid meteor shower this year.	X	
d. This orchestra plays phenomenally well.	X	
e. The last piece on the program has been played three times this week.		X
f. Normally, the school is cleaned thoroughly at least twice per week.		X

2. a. crying (present participle; adjective)
b. speeding (gerund; noun)
c. opened (past participle; adjective)
d. to travel (infinitive; adverb modifying "excellent")
e. Taking (gerund; noun); to meet (infinitive; adverb modifying "great")
f. to work (infinitive; noun); moving (gerund; noun)

3. A. acclaimed The past participle functions as an adjective to describe Miyazaki.

4. B. to be The infinitive functions as a noun, specifically, as the direct object of the verb "learn."

5. D. interesting The present participle functions as an adjective to describe the word "ways."

Using Grammar Correctly Practice Questions

1. C. change doesn't to didn't The past tense is required because the second clause in the sentence is discussing what happened in the past.

2. A. they The antecedent of the underlined pronoun is *girls*, so it should be plural. *They* is clear; repeating *the girls* (B) is unecessary. Choice (D) *them* is incorrect because the pronoun is the subject of the dependent clause *while they practiced*.

3. B. earned The past tense is correct here because the action happened in the past over the course of a few years.

4. D. change is to are The verb *are* agrees with the plural subject *sisters*.

5. D. change been to is The main clause needs the present tense verb *is* because the introductory subordinate clause has a present-tense verb, *face*. *Been* is an incomplete verb form.

6. B. change will receive to have received The present perfect is correct here because the point is to find out about other people's past experiences with auto shops, not their predictions about them.

7. A. change have picked to pick Because this sentence is a command, the simple present tense is necessary.

8. D. change comes to come The verb *come* agrees with the plural subject *specials*. The agreement error could also be fixed with *came*, choice (C), but doing so would introduce a tense error in its place.

9. D. replace it with the repair job The pronoun *it* had no clear antecedent, so replacing it with a noun corrects the sentence.

10. C. there are The verb *are* agrees with the plural subject *limits*. The present tense is correct and should not be changed.

11. B. replace its with their The antecedent *changes* is plural, so the plural possessive *their* should be used.

12. C. replace one's with your *Your* is used in the rest of the paragraph, so it is appropriate here.

13. D. change is to are The word *which* is the subject of a subordinate clause. It refers to the plural noun *calculations*. Therefore, the verb *are*, not *is*, is required.

14. A. has increased The interrupting phrase *of taxes* does not change the fact that the subject of the new independent clause is *amount*, which is singular. The verb *has increased* therefore agrees with it.

15. B. will credit The future tense indicates an action that will take place at a later time, which is appropriate in this sentence.

16. B. don't The plural indefinite pronoun *many* is the subject of the sentence; the verb *don't* (don't=do+not) agrees with it. Changing to the past tense, choice (C), would be incorrect.

17. C. change has to have The verb *have* agrees with the plural subject *people*.

18. B. him or her The pronouns are objects of the preposition *with*, so the objective forms *him* and *her* are needed. The antecedent is *a person*, so the plural *them* in choice (D) cannot be used.

19. B. change are to is The verb *is* agrees with the singular subject *equipment*, and the interrupting phrase listing examples of assistive equipment is properly punctuated.

20. B. it *It* is the proper pronoun to use to refer to a dog.

Using Writing Mechanics

Lesson 1: Comma Use

Practice 1.1

A. 1. Train travel is more pleasant than riding a bus, but it can be more expensive.
2. When you're on a train, you can stand up and stretch if you need to.
3. NC
4. Unlike buses, trains sometimes have seats that face each other.
5. Traveling through a scenic area, you may find that your train has a double-decker car that offers a better view.
6. NC
B. 7. A. insert a comma after starters A comma is required after an introductory phrase.
8. A. dressing, and A comma should come before a coordinating conjunction in a compound sentence.
9. D. remove the comma after though The words *though not all of them may be pleasing to the palate* form a subordinate clause, and no commas are necessary in that clause.

Practice 1.2

A. 1. Kwanzaa is a week-long African American holiday that celebrates culture, community, and family.

2. Kwanzaa, a wintertime holiday, is based on an ancient African harvest celebration.

3. NC

4. Kwanzaa celebrations include rituals such as singing, dancing, drumming, and poetry reading.

5. The family lights one candle every day for each of seven principles: unity, self-determination, responsibility, cooperative economics, purpose, creativity, and faith.

B. 6. A. remove the commas after accidents The subject and verb of a sentence should not be separated by a comma.

7. B. insert a comma after medicines Commas should be placed between items in a series.

8. C. children, those ten and up, You can mentally omit the phrase *those ten and up* and still understand the meaning of *older children*. Therefore, the appositive *those ten and up* should be set off by commas.

Lesson 2: Colons and Semicolons

Practice 2

1. a. She said the meeting would start at 12:30 p.m.

b. After the concert, George exclaimed: "That was the group's best performance ever. I want to see them again."

c. Anika's generous parents offered her a graduation present: new clothes, furniture, a computer, or a resort vacation were her choices.

d. NC A colon is not needed because the verb *includes* comes directly before the list.

e. There are four states that begin with the letter *I*: Idaho, Illinois, Indiana, and Iowa.

2. a. The class went on a field trip and spotted a long, brown snake; two small, noisy finches; and a skittish, furry raccoon.

b. NS

c. Sue ate bacon, and Robert had eggs; Jane's choice was doughnuts.

d. Ernest did well on his TASC test; he was accepted by his favorite college.

3. B. Insert a colon after functions. Everything that follows "functions" details what those functions are.

4. A. Replace the commas after training and technology with semicolons. This is a list with complex terms which contain commas and requires semicolons for clarity between items in the list.

5. C. Insert a semicolon after compensation. As written, this is a run-on sentence. The intent of the sentence is that compensation is important but so are recognition and a sense of accomplishment. The semicolon correctly separates these two clauses containing related ideas.

Lesson 3: Capitalization

Practice 3

A. 1. Last spring, I broke my arm in a car accident.

2. My internist, Doctor Claudia McNally, referred me to Waterside.

3. The center's director, Ilana Harris, assigned me a physical therapist named Ellie Royce.

4. Ellie studied physical therapy in her native London and used British methods of treatment that relieved my pain quite effectively.

5. She also did therapy with me in the pool at Rainbow Health Club.

6. I finished my treatments just before Labor Day, and I feel 100 percent better, thanks to Ellie.

B. 7. B. change Emperors to emperors A title should be capitalized only when it comes directly before a person's name or is used in direct address.

8. C. change Mountains to mountains A geographic feature is capitalized only when it is part of the name of a specific place, like *Rocky Mountains*.

9. B. change america to America Proper nouns should be capitalized.

Lesson 4: Possessives and Contractions

Practice 4

A. 1. There's

2. can't, who's, it's

3. we're

4. theirs

5. ours

B. 6. D. replace you're with your In this sentence, the pronoun in question is showing ownership, so *your* is correct.

7. B. change were to we're *Were* is a verb and is incorrect in this sentence. Rather, an apostrophe should be inserted to create the contraction *we're*, the combined form of *we are*.

8. B. replace they're with their In this sentence, the pronoun is possessive, so *their* is correct.

Lesson 5: Homonyms

Practice 5

A. 1. fourth

2. know

3. whole

4. week

5. affect

6. past

B. 7. C. replace fare with fair A *fare* is what you pay to get on the subway; *fair* means *just*.

8. A. change principal to principle A *principal* is the head of a school; *principle* means *a guiding rule*.

9. A. replace affect with effect *Affect* is a verb meaning *to influence*; *effect*, which means *result*, is required here.

Lesson 6: Hyphens

Practice 6

1.

un-ionized	f. not having the properties of an ion
unionized	c. organized in a group
ex-tent	b. something that used to be a tent
extent	e. scope
pro-cure	a. in favor of healing
procure	d. to obtain

2. a. Sarah was happy to see many of her long-lost friends at her reunion.

b. The thunderstorm caused a 10-minute delay in the game.

c. Josh was very pleased with his new V-neck sweater.

d. The police were suspicious of all the ex-offenders in the area.

e. NH

f. NH

g. The members of the self-actualization group held a rally yesterday.

h. There are twenty-six students in the introductory economics class.

i. The company's subsidiary acted in a semi-independent manner.

j. The contest was open to one-, two-, or three-person teams.

3. **C. Insert a hyphen between <u>hand</u> and <u>carved</u>**. The phrase *hand carved* is a compound adjective and appears before the noun it describes (*decorations*). Thus, it needs a hyphen.

4. **C. Insert hyphens after <u>three</u>, <u>five</u>, and <u>ten</u>**. The phrase *ten year* is a compound adjective appearing before the noun it describes (*timespans*), so it takes a hyphen. The words *three* and *five* also go with the word *year* to make a series of compound adjectives, so they take hyphens, too. None of the words *experienced*, *antidepressant*, or *timespans* need hyphens, because their meaning is not changed when a hyphen is inserted.

Using Writing Mechanics Practice Questions

1. **B. insert a comma after <u>tantrums</u>** The phrase *have tantrums* is the first item in series, so it should be followed by a comma.

2. **C. understand and show** A comma should not be used between two verbs, and removing the comma is simpler and cleaner than adding a new subject as in incorrect choice (D).

3. **D. remove the comma after <u>know</u>** All the possessives, contractions, and homonyms in the sentence are spelled correctly. The comma following the introductory transition *However* cannot be removed, but the comma after *know* is incorrect.

4. **C. change <u>are'nt</u> to <u>aren't</u>** The apostrophe in a contraction must be placed in the spot where a letter has been removed.

5. **B. down, consider** An introductory subordinate clause should be followed by a comma.

6. **B. remove the comma** The subject (*One*) and its verb (*is*) should not be separated by a comma.

7. **B. replace <u>it's</u> with <u>its</u>** The sentence is about ownership: each time zone has its own standard time. The possessive form *its* is correct.

8. **B. change <u>congress</u> to <u>Congress</u>** The name *Congress* refers to a specific body of lawmakers and should therefore be capitalized.

9. **A. insert a comma after <u>example</u>** An introductory phrase must be followed by a comma.

10. **C. remove the comma after <u>time</u>** There is no need to separate the final phrase from the rest of the sentence with a comma.

11. **C. change <u>center</u> to <u>Center</u>** When a proper name consists of more than one word, all the words should be capitalized.

12. **D. replace <u>when your</u> with <u>when you're</u>** The sentence is saying, "when you are in the building," so the contraction *you're* is needed.

13. **A. replace <u>week</u> with <u>weak</u>** A *week* is seven days. *Weak*, meaning *not strong*, is appropriate for this sentence.

14. **D. remove the comma after <u>pool</u>** The clause beginning with *unless* does not need to be set off with commas.

15. **B. register and pay** Two items joined by *and* do not require a comma unless both are independent clauses.

16. **C. replace <u>then</u> with <u>than</u>** The word needed in the sentence is *than*, meaning *compared with*. *Then* means *after that* or *at that time*.

17. **C. insert a comma after <u>profiling</u>** The phrase *called racial profiling* is an appositive but is not essential to understanding the sentence. It needs a comma before (which is already given) and after it.

18. **B. distinctions, for nonwhites** The conjunction *for* is connecting two independent clauses in a compound sentence, so it must be preceded by a comma.

19. **B. change <u>illinois</u> to <u>Illinois</u>** Names of states should be capitalized.

20. **B. insert a comma after <u>superintendents</u>** Three items are listed in the series: *police superintendents, chiefs of police, and other law enforcement officials*. There should be commas separating them.

ABOUT THE TEST

Mathematics

The TASC Mathematics Test assesses your ability to reason with numbers. On the Mathematics Test, you will have 105 minutes to answer approximately 52 questions. You will spend 50 minutes answering questions with the aid of calculator and 55 minutes answering questions for which you may not use a calculator. You may take a 15-minute break between those two sections. Questions on this test will target skills such as:

- Performing number operations to solve problems
- Solving word problems
- Understanding proportions and percentages
- Interpreting graphic representations of data
- Finding averages
- Understanding and performing operations with algebraic expressions
- Solving linear and quadratic equations
- Solving problems using geometric formulas

See the "TASC Blueprint Alignment: Tables and Notes" section in the online chapter "About the TASC" for more information about how material in this unit aligns to CTB/McGraw-Hill's published TASC test blueprints.

Most questions on the Mathematics Test will be multiple choice. Some of the questions will ask you to bubble a numerical answer into the grid below:

If you are taking the computer-based TASC test, you may also see drag-and-drop items, in which you are asked to arrange items on the computer screen using your mouse. You will learn more about filling in these grids and interacting with drag-and-drop items in the "Question Formats on the TASC" section in the online chapter "About the TASC."

Tools

On the TASC Mathematics Test, two tools will be available to you to help you answer questions.

Calculator: Whether you take the paper or computer versions of the TASC, you will have access to a scientific calculator for part of the Mathematics Test. See the next page for more information on how to use the calculator.

Formula sheet: You will also be provided with a two-page formula sheet that lists common mathematical formulas. Become familiar with this sheet, which is reproduced on pages 168–169. If a formula is discussed in this book but not listed on the formula sheet, you will need to memorize it.

About Calculators

If you take the computer version of the TASC, you will have access to an on-screen version of the Texas Instruments TI-30XS MultiView™ calculator. For more information on using the online calculator, see below on this page.

If you are taking the paper version of the test, there are a variety of calculators that will be acceptable to use. Please check your state's guidelines before you purchase a calculator for your practice. While the test maker has decided that all of the following calculators are acceptable, each individual state has the right to limit this list and your state might have done so. Once you have determined which calculators are allowed in your state, choose which one will work best for you and start practicing with it right away. The calculator options are listed here.

TI-30XS MultiView™

On this calculator, you use the white numeric keypad to enter numbers, the decimal point, and the negative sign (–) for a negative number such as –213. The operation keys, on the right, allow you to add, subtract, multiply, and divide. The four arrows at the top right of the calculator allow you to move the onscreen cursor up, down, left, or right as needed. The delete key to the left of the arrows allows you to correct mistakes as you work.

The following Casio® calculators have the same basic key functions as the TI-30XS MultiView™, but some of the keys are in different locations and/or have slightly different symbolic representation for various functions. For example, the Casio® calculators use an "equals" key, whereas the TI-30XS MultiView™ has a button that says "enter," which performs the same function.

- **Casio FX-115ES PLUS**
- **Casio FX-115MS PLUS**
- **Casio FX-300ES PLUS**

TI-30Xa™

This calculator has the same basic key functions as the TI-30XS MultiView™ with some distinct differences. The screen does not show as much information and there are no arrows to move your cursor within the display and thus correct work you have previously entered. Additionally, while all basic key functions are present, some of them are in different locations and/or have slightly different symbolic representation on the keys. This calculator is battery powered.

The following calculator has the same basic key functions as the TI-30Xa™ but some of the keys are in different locations and/or have slightly different symbolic representations.

- **Casio FX-260 Solar**

HP 35s Scientific Calculator

This calculator defaults to Reverse Polish Notation, which is different from the algebraic notation you are likely used to entering when using a handheld calculator. However, the user does have the ability to switch to algebraic data entry. As with the other calculators in this section, the same basic key functions are present, but some of the keys are in different places and/or have slightly different symbols to represent various functions.

Because the TI-30XS MultiView™ is the calculator used for the computer test, and because it is one of the calculators that you may use on the paper test, you will see practice tips for using this calculator throughout the Mathematics unit. (See, for example, page 198.) Please practice using your chosen calculator to gain familiarity with what you will see on Test Day. Remember: You do not have to use the calculator to solve problems; only use it if it is relevant to the problem or if you believe it will be helpful.

A Note about the Mathematics Reference Sheet

On the next two pages, you will find mathematical formulas that will be provided to you on Test Day. *Do not* attempt to absorb and memorize these formulas immediately. Skip to page 170 to begin your math studies. Periodically you will refer back to these pages as you work through practice problems.

MATHEMATICS REFERENCE SHEET

Volume

Cylinder: $V = \pi r^2 h$

Pyramid: $V = \frac{1}{3}Bh$

Cone: $V = \frac{1}{3}\pi r^2 h$

Sphere: $V = \frac{4}{3}\pi r^3$

Coordinate Geometry

Midpoint formula:

$$\left(\frac{x_1 + x_2}{2}, \frac{y_1 + y_2}{2}\right)$$

Distance formula:

$$d = \sqrt{(x_2 - x_1)^2 + (y_2 - y_1)^2}$$

Slope: $m = \frac{y_2 - y_1}{x_2 - x_1}, x_2 \neq x_1$

Special Factoring

$a^2 - b^2 = (a - b)(a + b)$

$a^2 + 2ab + b^2 = (a + b)^2$

$a^2 - 2ab + b^2 = (a - b)^2$

$a^3 + b^3 = (a + b)(a^2 - ab + b^2)$

$a^3 - b^3 = (a - b)(a^2 + ab + b^2)$

Quadratic Formula

For $ax^2 + bx + c = 0$

$$x = \frac{-b \pm \sqrt{b^2 - 4ac}}{2a}$$

Interest

Simple interest Formula:
$I = prt$

Interest Formula (compounded n times per year):

$$A = p\left(1 + \frac{r}{n}\right)^{nt}$$

A = Amount after t years.

p = principal

r = annual interest rate

t = time in years

I = Interest

Trigonometric Identities

Pythagorean Theorem: $a^2 + b^2 = c^2$

$\sin \theta = \dfrac{opp}{hyp}$

$\cos \theta = \dfrac{adj}{hyp}$

$\tan \theta = \dfrac{opp}{adj}$

$\sin^2 \theta + \cos^2 \theta = 1$

$Density = \dfrac{Mass}{Volume}$

Central Angle

$m\angle AOB = m\overset{\frown}{AB}$

Inscribed Angle

$m\angle ABC = \dfrac{1}{2}m\overset{\frown}{AC}$

Intersecting Chords Theorem

$A \cdot B = C \cdot D$

Probability

Permutations: $\quad {}_nP_r = \dfrac{n!}{(n-r)!}$

Combinations: $\quad {}_nC_r = \dfrac{n!}{(n-r)!\,r!}$

Multiplication rule (independent events): $P(A \text{ and } B) = P(A) \cdot P(B)$

Multiplication rule (general): $P(A \text{ and } B) = P(A) \cdot P(B)$

Addition rule: $P(A \text{ or } B) = P(A) + P(B) - P(A \text{ and } B)$

Conditional Probability: $P(B|A) = \dfrac{p(A \text{ and } B)}{p(A)}$

Arithmetic Sequence: $a_n = a_1 + (n-1)d$ where a_n is the nth term, a_1 is the first term, and d is the common difference.

Geometric Sequence: $a_n = a_1\, r^{(n-1)}$ where a_n is the nth term, a_1 is the first term, and r is the common ratio.

MATHEMATICS PRETEST

PART I: QUANTITATIVE REASONING—18 QUESTIONS

Directions: You may fill in the circles next to the correct answers or write your answers on a separate piece of paper. You MAY use a calculator.

<u>Questions 1–2</u> refer to the following information and graph.

Video Warehouse has divided the surrounding community into four advertising zones. The graph shows the total number of customers from each zone for a three-week period.

1. During the three weeks, how many customers came from Zones 3 and 4?

   ○ A. between 900 and 1,000
   ○ B. between 1,000 and 1,100
   ○ C. between 1,100 and 1,200
   ○ D. between 1,200 and 1,300

2. Approximately what is the ratio of customers from Zone 1 to customers from Zone 3?

   ○ A. 3:5
   ○ B. 3:2
   ○ C. 2:1
   ○ D. 1:2

3. A potter uses $\frac{3}{5}$ of a pound of clay to make a bowl. How many bowls could the potter make from 10 pounds of clay?

   ○ A. 6
   ○ B. 8
   ○ C. 16
   ○ D. 17

4. Janelle has recently been hired for the job of library assistant. The following graph shows what percent of her time will be spent on each of five tasks each day.

The number of hours that Janelle will spend working at the counter is about how many times the number of hours that she will spend processing new books and repairing bindings?

   ○ A. 2
   ○ B. 3
   ○ C. 4
   ○ D. 6

5. Fifteen percent of the workers at Nationwide Industries earn minimum wage. If 24 workers earn minimum wage, how many total workers are there at Nationwide Industries?

   ○ A.   4
   ○ B.   36
   ○ C. 160
   ○ D. 360

6. An accountant is going to pay the following four bills:

Bill	Amount
W	$27.10
X	$261.00
Y	$2.80
Z	$27.20

   The accountant will pay the bills in order from smallest to largest. In what order will he pay them?

   ○ A. W, X, Z, Y
   ○ B. X, W, Z, Y
   ○ C. Y, X, W, Z
   ○ D. Y, W, Z, X

7. A jar holds 16 ounces of honey. A cook is going to make two recipes. One of the recipes calls for 2.5 ounces of honey, and the other calls for 4.25 ounces of honey. After the cook has made those two recipes, how many ounces of honey will be left in the jar?

   ○ A.   6.75
   ○ B.   9.25
   ○ C. 10.00
   ○ D. 11.75

8. All numbers that are evenly divisible by both 6 and 14 are also divisible by which of the following numbers?

   ○ A.   8
   ○ B. 12
   ○ C. 21
   ○ D. 28

9. Alice, Kathy, and Sheila work as medical assistants at Valley Clinic. Alice has worked 8 years longer than Kathy. Kathy has worked half as long as Sheila. If Sheila has worked at the company for 10 years, how many years has Alice worked there?

   ○ A.   5
   ○ B.   8
   ○ C. 10
   ○ D. 13

Question 10 is based on the spinner below.

10. The spinner shown in the drawing is divided into eight equal sections. If you spin the spinner one time, what is the probability of not getting blue?

   ○ A. $\frac{1}{8}$
   ○ B. $\frac{1}{4}$
   ○ C. $\frac{3}{4}$
   ○ D. $\frac{7}{8}$

11. A computer monitor is regularly priced at $320. During a two-day sale, the price was decreased to $240. Which of the following is the percentage decrease of the monitor's price during the sale?

- A. 25%
- B. 33%
- C. 75%
- D. 80%

12. For a 10-day period, a bank kept track of the number of new accounts opened each day. The results are shown in the table below. What is the median number of accounts opened per day during this 10-day period?

Day	Accounts	Day	Accounts
May 7	6	May 14	4
May 8	2	May 15	8
May 9	7	May 16	6
May 10	5	May 17	4
May 11	4	May 18	7

- A. 5
- B. 5.3
- C. 5.5
- D. 6

13. Jim is a salesperson, and his employers expect him to sell at least $12,000 in merchandise per month. In April, Jim sold $2,500 in the first week of the month and twice that much in the second week. How much must he sell in the rest of April combined in order to sell the minimum expected of him?

- A. $4,500
- B. $5,500
- C. $9,500
- D. $12,000

14. Angela likes to use two walking sticks when she goes hiking, but the two walking sticks she has been given recently are different lengths. One is $3\frac{4}{5}$ feet long, and the other is $3\frac{1}{2}$ feet long.

$3\frac{4}{5}$ feet $3\frac{1}{2}$ feet

Angela wants to cut the longer stick to match the shorter one. How much should she cut from the longer stick so that the two walking sticks will be the same length?

- A. $\frac{3}{4}$ feet
- B. $\frac{3}{5}$ feet
- C. $\frac{3}{10}$ feet
- D. $\frac{1}{4}$ feet

Question 15 is based on the following number line.

0   $\frac{1}{2}$ 1 $1\frac{1}{2}$ 2 $2\frac{1}{2}$ 3 $3\frac{1}{2}$ 4 $4\frac{1}{2}$ 5

15. Which of the following is the decimal point value of the dot on the line above?

- A. 3.25
- B. 3.50
- C. 3.75
- D. 4.00

Question 16 is based on the following information and graph.

Marjorie has a class of 35 students, and she tracked their performance on a recent math exam. The graph below represents how their scores were distributed along the range of possible scores, from F to A.

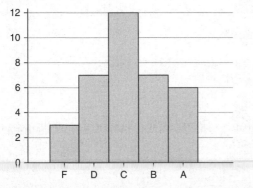

16. Based on the graph, which of the following is a true statement?

○ A. None of Marjorie's students received an F on the exam.
○ B. Most of Marjorie's students received either an A or a B on the exam.
○ C. If Marjorie gave the same exam again to another group of students, most of those students would receive a C.
○ D. More students received either an A or a B than received either a D or an F.

17. Jason deposits $5,000 in a bank account that will pay him 4% simple interest annually. If Jason deposits no more than the initial $5,000, how much money will be in the account at the end of five years? (The formula for simple interest is $I = prt$ or *interest = principal × rate × time*. Use a decimal to express the interest when using that formula.)

○ A. $200
○ B. $1,000
○ C. $5,000
○ D. $6,000

18. A local library shows movies on Thursday evenings. The library administrator has chosen the next six movies he will show, but he has not decided in which order to show them. How many possible orderings of the six movies are there?

○ A.   21
○ B.   36
○ C.   720
○ D. 1,012

MATHEMATICS PRETEST

PART II: ALGEBRAIC REASONING AND GEOMETRY—22 QUESTIONS

The next two pages display formulas that you will be given when you take the TASC test. You can refer to these pages on Part II of this pretest.

Volume

Cylinder: $V = \pi r^2 h$

Pyramid: $V = \frac{1}{3} Bh$

Cone: $V = \frac{1}{3} \pi r^2 h$

Sphere: $V = \frac{4}{3} \pi r^3$

Coordinate Geometry

Midpoint formula:

$$\left(\frac{x_1 + x_2}{2}, \frac{y_1 + y_2}{2} \right)$$

Distance formula:

$$d = \sqrt{(x_2 - x_1)^2 + (y_2 - y_1)^2}$$

Slope: $m = \frac{y_2 - y_1}{x_2 - x_1}, x_2 \neq x_1$

Special Factoring

$a^2 - b^2 = (a - b)(a + b)$
$a^2 + 2ab + b^2 = (a + b)^2$
$a^2 - 2ab + b^2 = (a - b)^2$
$a^3 + b^3 = (a + b)(a^2 - ab + b^2)$
$a^3 - b^3 = (a - b)(a^2 + ab + b^2)$

Quadratic Formula

For $ax^2 + bx + c = 0$

$$x = \frac{-b \pm \sqrt{b^2 - 4ac}}{2a}$$

Interest

Simple Interest Formula:
$I = prt$

Interest Formula (compounded n times per year):

$$A = p \left(1 + \frac{r}{n} \right)^{nt}$$

A = Amount after t years.

p = principal

r = annual interest rate

t = time in years

I = Interest

Trigonometric Identities

Pythagorean Theorem: $a^2 + b^2 = c^2$

$$\sin \theta = \frac{opp}{hyp}$$

$$\cos \theta = \frac{adj}{hyp}$$

$$\tan \theta = \frac{opp}{adj}$$

$$\sin^2 \theta + \cos^2 \theta = 1$$

$$Density = \frac{Mass}{Volume}$$

Central Angle

$m\angle AOB = m\overset{\frown}{AB}$

Inscribed Angle

$m\angle ABC = \dfrac{1}{2} m\overset{\frown}{AC}$

Intersecting Chords Theorem

$A \cdot B = C \cdot D$

Probability

Permutations: $\quad _nP_r = \dfrac{n!}{(n-r)!}$

Combinations: $\quad _nC_r = \dfrac{n!}{(n-r)!\,r!}$

Multiplication rule (independent events): $P(A \text{ and } B) = P(A) \cdot P(B)$

Multiplication rule (general): $P(A \text{ and } B) = P(A) \cdot P(B|A)$

Addition rule: $P(A \text{ or } B) = P(A) + P(B) - P(A \text{ and } B)$

Conditional Probability: $P(B|A) = \dfrac{p(A \text{ and } B)}{p(A)}$

Arithmetic Sequence: $a_n = a_1 + (n-1)d$ where a_n is the nth term, a_1 is the first term, and d is the common difference.

Geometric Sequence: $a_n = a_1\, r^{(n-1)}$ where a_n is the nth term, a_1 is the first term, and r is the common ratio.

Directions: You may fill in the circles next to the correct answers or write your answers on a separate piece of paper. Refer to the formula sheet on the previous pages as needed. You <u>MAY</u> use your calculator.

1. Which point on the number line below represents the value $-\frac{16}{6}$?

- ○ A. Point A
- ○ B. Point B
- ○ C. Point C
- ○ D. Point D

2. Evaluate the expression $2x - (4y - 3) + 5xz$, when $x = -3$, $y = 2$, and $z = -1$.

- ○ A.   45
- ○ B.   16
- ○ C.   4
- ○ D. −10

3. On April 1 of this year, the high temperature in Northville was 46 degrees Fahrenheit. Then a sudden snowstorm arose, and the temperature dropped sharply to a low of −8 degrees Fahrenheit. What was the magnitude of the change in temperature on that day?

- ○ A.   54
- ○ B.   46
- ○ C.   36
- ○ D. −36

Question 4 refers to the following drawing.

4. A tower casts a shadow 11 feet long. The distance from the top of the tower to the end of the shadow is 61 feet. How many feet tall is the tower?

- ○ A. 50
- ○ B. 60
- ○ C. 61
- ○ D. 72

Question 5 is based on the following information.

Designer Furnishings sells premade cabinets and cupboards, as shown below.

Model	Dimensions (in inches)
411R	32 by 22 by 10
412R	28 by 36 by 15
413S	24 by 72 by 18
414S	25 by 24 by 6

5. Each face of cabinet 413S is in the shape of a rectangle. What is the volume of Model 413S in cubic feet?

○ A.   18
○ B.   31
○ C.   36
○ D.   108

6. Together, Levy and Matthew earn $4,680 per month. Levy earns $520 more per month than Matthew earns. How much does Levy earn per month?

○ A. $2,080
○ B. $2,340
○ C. $2,600
○ D. $4,160

7. The design for a new cone-shaped closed container is shown below. What is the surface area of this container, in square inches?

slant height 6 in

diameter 4 in

○ A. 4π
○ B. 12π
○ C. 16π
○ D. 28π

8. Simplify this polynomial:
$3x^3 + x + 2x^3 - 4x^2 + 14y - 2(y + x)$.

○ A. $3x^3 - 3x^2 + 14(-2y + 2x)$
○ B. $5x^3 - 3x^2 + 14y - 2y - 2x$
○ C. $3x^3 - x + 4x^2 + 12y$
○ D. $5x^3 - 4x^2 - x + 12y$

9. A rectangle is drawn on a coordinate grid. Three of its four vertices are located at points $(-1, -2), (-1, 4)$, and $(2, -2)$ What is the location of the fourth vertex?

   A. $(-2, -4)$
   B. $(-1, -4)$
   C. $(1, 4)$
   D. $(2, 4)$

10. Which of the following expressions is equal to the expression $4x - 2(3x - 9)$?

   A. $18 - 2x$
   B. $-10x - 18$
   C. $-2x - 18$
   D. $10x - 18$

11. In the equation $3x^2 - 10x = 8$, which of the following values for x will make the equation true?

   A. -4
   B. -3
   C. 3
   D. 4

12. Solve for x: $12(x - 2) < 24$

   A. $x < 0$
   B. $x > 0$
   C. $x < 12$
   D. $x < 4$

13. Scientists estimate that Earth is 4,540,000,000 years old. What is that number expressed in scientific notation?

   A. 4.54×10^7
   B. 4.54×10^9
   C. 454×10^{10}
   D. $2(127 \times 10^7)$

14. Joe just purchased an oddly shaped piece of property, depicted in the figure below.

What is the area, in square yards, of Joe's new property?

○ A. 120
○ B. 134
○ C. 140
○ D. 204

15. The XYZ Company sells hats and will mono-gram them if customers choose. The price for each monogram varies depending on how many hats a customer would like to have monogrammed. The monogram prices for several order sizes are shown below:

Number of hats to be monogrammed (n)	Price per monogram (p)
1	$5
2	$4.50
3	$4.00
4	$3.50
5	$3.00
6	$2.50

Which of the following best expresses the relationship of price per monogram (for all nonnegative values of p) to number of hats monogrammed shown in the table above?

○ A. $p = \$5.00 - (n - 1)\$0.50$
○ B. $p = \$5.00 - n(\$0.50)$
○ C. $p = (n - 1)\$5.00$
○ D. $p = \$0.50(10n)$

16. A parallelogram has two obtuse angles and two acute angles. If the measure of one of the obtuse angles is 110°, what is the measure, in degrees, of one of the acute angles?

○ A. 10°
○ B. 70°
○ C. 110°
○ D. 240°

Question 17 refers to the following graph.

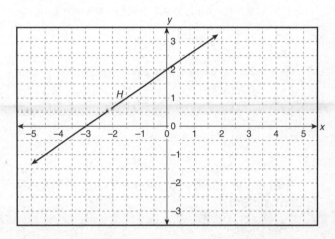

Line *H* is the graph of which of the following equations?

○ A. $y = \frac{1}{3}x + 2$
○ B. $y + 2 = \frac{2}{3}x$
○ C. $y = \frac{2}{3}x + 2$
○ D. $y = 3(x - 2) + 2$

18. A fountain's pool is enclosed by a circular plastic tank. The distance from the center of the pool to the wall of the tank is 10 feet. How long is the wall of the tank in feet?

○ A. 20π
○ B. $\frac{20}{\pi}$
○ C. 25π
○ D. 100π

19. Line *W* passes through the following points on the coordinate grid: (0, – 9) and (4, –1). What is the slope of line *W*?

   A. –2

   B. $-\frac{1}{2}$

   C. $\frac{1}{2}$

   D. 2

20. Beansey's Baked Beans, Inc., has developed a new can for its baked beans, shown below:

8 cm

12 cm

   What is the volume of the new can, in cubic centimeters?

   A. 48π

   B. 96π

   C. 192π

   D. 768π

21. Tina is considering renting a commercial space for her business. The space is shown below.

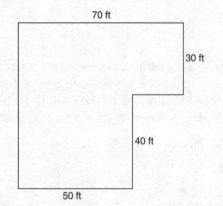

70 ft

30 ft

40 ft

50 ft

   What is the area of the commercial space, in square feet?

   A.   290

   B. 2,100

   C. 2,800

   D. 4,100

22. In the system of equations $3x - 3y = -9$ and $2x + y = 9$, solve for both *x* and *y*. You may use the coordinate grid below to help your work.

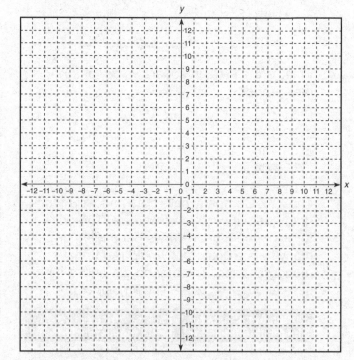

What is the solution set for *x* and *y*?

   A. (2, – 5)

   B. (0, 3)

   C. (0, 9)

   D. (2, 5)

STOP. Congratulations! You have completed the Math pretest. Your next step is to check your answers with the Math Pretest Answers and Explanations that begin on the next page and then fill in the study planner that appears on page xvii.

MATHEMATICS PRETEST ANSWERS AND EXPLANATIONS

PART I: QUANTITATIVE REASONING

1. **D. between 1,200 and 1,300** The graph shows that roughly 900 customers came from Zone 3 during this period and that somewhere between 300 and 400 customers came from Zone 4 during the same period. Thus, adding them together will result in a number between 1,200 and 1,300.

2. **D. 1:2** The bar for Zone 1 is a little less than halfway between 400 and 500; round to 450. The best estimate for the bar for Zone 3 is 900. Make sure you write the ratio in the order stated in the problem. Zone 1: Zone 3 = 450:900, which simplifies to 1:2.

3. **C. 16** Divide 10 by $\frac{3}{5}$. The answer is 16 with a remainder. Since the question asks for how many bowls the potter can complete, ignore the remainder.

4. **B. 3** The graph doesn't give the actual number of hours Janelle will work, but it does show how her time spent at one activity compares to another. If she works 100 hours, she will spend 44 hours working at the counter, 9 hours processing new books, and 6 hours repairing bindings. Compare 44 to 15. The number 44 is about 3 times as great as 15.

5. **C. 160** To solve, set up a ratio. 15 percent = $\frac{15}{100}$. Set that equal to the ratio of employees who make minimum wage to the total number of employees, and use a variable to represent the total number of employees. $\frac{15}{100} = \frac{24}{x}$. Cross multiply: $24 \times 100 = 2400$. Divide: $2400 \div 15 = 160$.

6. **D. Y, W, Z, X** Compare the numbers and list in order from smallest to largest: $2.80, $27.10, $27.20, $261.00.

7. **B. 9.25** Add together the amounts of honey the cook will use in the two recipes: $2.5 + 4.25 = 6.75$. Subtract that amount from the total amount of honey in the jar. $16 - 6.75 = 9.25$.

8. **C. 21** One way to solve the problem is to find a number that is evenly divisible by 6 and 14, and then try dividing that number by each of the answer choices. Go through the multiples of 14 until you find one that is divisible by 6: 14, 28, 42. The number 42 is divisible by both 14 and 6. Then review the answer choices. 42 cannot be evenly divided by 8, 12, 28, or 35. It can be evenly divided by 21.

9. **D. 13** Work backward through the facts. Sheila has worked 10 years. Kathy has worked half as long as Sheila, which equals 5 years. Alice has worked 8 years longer than Kathy. $5 + 8 = 13$ years.

10. **C. $\frac{3}{4}$** Two sections, which equal $\frac{2}{8}$ or $\frac{1}{4}$, are marked "blue." Thus, the chance of not getting blue is $1 - \frac{1}{4} = \frac{3}{4}$.

11. **A. 25%** To find percent of change, divide the amount of change by the original price. Then multiply by 100 to change the result from a decimal to a percent: $\frac{\$320 - \$240}{\$320} \times 100 = \frac{\$80}{\$320} \times 100 = 0.25 \times 100 = 25\%$.

12. **C. 5.5** The median is the middle number of a group of numbers. Arrange the numbers of accounts in order: 2, 4, 4, 4, 5, 6, 6, 7, 7, 8. The middle numbers are 5 and

6. When there are two numbers in the middle, find the mean of those two numbers: $\frac{5+6}{2} = 5.5$.

13. **A. $4,500** Add together the amounts that Jim has sold so far in April: $2,500 + $5,000 = $7,500. Then subtract that amount from the minimum his employers expect him to sell: $12,000 - $7,500 = $4,500.

14. **C. $\frac{3}{10}$ feet** Subtract the length of the shorter stick from the length of the longer one: $3\frac{4}{5} - 3\frac{1}{2}$. To solve, find a common denominator: $3\frac{8}{10} - 3\frac{5}{10} = \frac{3}{10}$.

15. **C. 3.75** The number line is divided into increments, each of which equals one-fourth, or .25. The dot is three increments to the right of the number 3, so its value is 3.75.

16. **D. More students received either an A or a B than received either a D or an F.** Based on the graph, 6 students received an A and 7 students a B. $7 + 6 = 13$. Also, 7 students received a D, and 3 received an F. $7 + 3 = 10$. Since 13 is greater than 10, the A-and-B group is larger than the D-and-F group. Choice (A) is not supported because some students did fail the exam. Choice (B) suggests that most—more than half—of Marjorie's students received an A or B. However, the A-and-B group (13 students) is smaller than the total number of students who got a C (12 students), a D (7 students), or an F (3 students). Choice (C) is unsupported because the graph has no information about how any other group of students would perform.

17. **D. $6,000** Use the formula provided to find the interest Jason's deposit would earn over the five years. As directed, express the percent interest as a decimal, 0.04. 5000×5 (years) $\times 0.04 = $1000. Then, to find out how much is in the account at the end of the five years, add that interest to Jason's original deposit: $5,000 + $1,000 = $6,000.

18. **C. 720** To find out how many possible orderings, or sequences, of six items are possible, multiply. There are six possibilities for the first movie. Then after the first movie has been chosen, there are five possibilities for the second movie, then four for the third movie, and so on: $6 \times 5 \times 4 \times 3 \times 2 \times 1 = 720$.

PART II: ALGEBRAIC REASONING AND GEOMETRY

1. **B. Point B** Convert the improper fraction to a mixed fraction:
$-\frac{16}{6} = -2\frac{4}{6} = -2\frac{2}{3}$, which is the value of Point B.

2. **C. 4** Substitute and simplify:
$= 2x - (4y - 3) + 5xz$
$= 2(-3) - (4[2] - 3) + 5(-3)(-1)$
$= -6 - (8 - 3) + 15$
$= -6 - 5 + 15$
$= -11 + 15$
$= 4$

3. **A. 54** To find the magnitude of the change in temperature, subtract the lowest temperature from the highest temperature: $46 - (-8) = 46 + 8 = 54$.

4. **B. 60** The tower, its shadow, and the distance between them form a right triangle. Use the Pythagorean relationship to find the missing distance:
$$61^2 = 11^2 + h^2$$
$$3721 = 121 + h^2$$
$$3600 = h^2$$
$$60 = h$$

5. **A. 18** To find the volume of a rectangular prism, multiply *base × width × height*. Here, however, the question asks for the volume in feet, while the measurements are given in inches. Therefore, start by converting the inches of model 413S to feet: 24 in × 72 in × 18 in = 2 ft × 6 ft × 1.5 ft = 18 ft^3.

6. **C. $2,600** The question stem gives us two equations. First, we know that $M + L = 4,680$. Also, since Levy earns $520 more than Matthew earns, that can be expressed as $L = M + 520$, or, put another way, $M = L - 520$. Since the question asks for a solution for Levy, substitute the value of M from the second equation in the first equation:
$$(L - 520) + L = 4,680$$
$$2L - 520 = 4,680$$
$$2L = 5,200$$
$$L = 2,600$$

7. **C. 16π** The formula for the surface area of a cone is: $SA = \pi rs + \pi r^2$. In that formula, *SA* means *surface area*, *r* represents the *radius*, and *s* is the *slant height*, or the distance from the bottom of one side of the cone to the point. The diagram indicates that the diameter of the base is 4, so its radius is 2. The slant height is 6. Substitute and simplify:
$$SA = \pi(2)(6) + \pi(2)^2$$
$$SA = 12\pi + 4\pi = 16\pi$$

8. **D. $5x^3 - 4x^2 - x + 12y$** Start by removing the parentheses: $3x^3 + x + 2x^2 - 4x^2 + 14y - 2(y + x) = 3x^3 + x + 2x^3 - 4x^2 + 14y - 2y - 2x$. Then, identify like terms that can be combined:
$3x^3$ and $2x^3$, which add to $5x^3$. $-4x^2$ cannot be combined with any other term.
x and $-2x$ add to $-x$.
$14y$ and $-2y$ add to $12y$.
Combine into a new expression: $5x^3 - 4x^2 - x + 12y$.

9. **D. (2, 4)** On scratch paper, draw the three points given in the question stem:

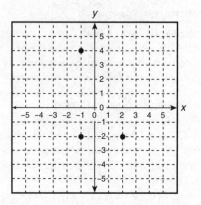

The fourth corner of the rectangle will be at (2, 4).

10. **A. 18 – 2x** Simplify: $4x - 2(3x - 9) = 4x - 6x + 18 = -2x + 18$. That can also be expressed as $18 - 2x$.

11. **D. 4** The simplest way to solve this problem is to try the values of *x* given in the answer choices in the equation. Starting with (A), where *x* equals –4: $3(4)^2 - 10(-4) = 3(16) + 40 = 88$. That's a great deal more than 8. That result suggests that (B), where *x* equals –3, would also be likely to yield a result that's far too large. Try (C) or (D) to see what result a positive number yields. In (C), *x* equals 3: $3(3)^2 - 10(3) = 3(9) - 30 = -3$. That's a little too small, so the answer must be (D), *x* equals 4. Try it to confirm: $3(4)^2 - 10(4) = 3(16) - 40 = 8$. (D) is correct.

12. **D. x < 4** Simplify the expression:
$$12(x - 2) < 24$$
$$12x - 24 < 24$$
$$12x < 48$$
$$x < 4$$

13. **B. 4.54 × 10⁹** Writing a number in scientific notation involves expressing it as the product of two terms: one term is a number and the other is 10 raised to some power. To find how large the power of ten should be, imagine counting spaces to the left of the decimal point. Choice (B) reflects the correct number and the correct power of 10, or places to the left of the decimal point.

14. **D. 204** The shape of Joe's new property is a trapezoid, and the formula for the area of a trapezoid is $A = \frac{1}{2}h(b_1 + b_2)$. In that formula, *A* is area, and *h* means the height, which is 12 yards here. The variables b_1 and b_2 are the two bases, which here are 10 yards and 24 yards. Plug those values into the formula: $A = \frac{1}{2}(12)(10 + 24) = (6)(34) = 204$. (You can tell that Joe's property is a trapezoid because the two bases are parallel; the right angles indicated at the two ends of the *height* line indicate this.)

15. A. $p = \$5.00 - (n-1) \$0.50$ If a customer requests only one monogram, the fee is $5.00. However, if a customer requests 2, the price per monogram drops by $0.50 (which you can think of as $1 \times \$0.50$). If a customer requests 3 monograms, the price per monogram drops another $0.50, or $2 \times \$0.50$ in total. Thus, the price per monogram is $5.00 minus a multiple of $0.50. The multiple is one less than the number of hats ordered.

16. B. 70° In any four-sided figure, all four interior angles add up to 360°. In a parallelogram, the two obtuse angles are equal to one another, and the two acute angles are equal to one another. Here, you know that the two obtuse angles add up to 220°. 360° − 220° = 140°. Since there are two acute angles, divide that number by two.

17. C. $y = \frac{2}{3}x + 2$ The answer choices are in slope-intercept form, so begin by finding the y-intercept, which is 2. Then find the slope, which represents $\frac{rise}{run}$. Find two points on line H, and count the difference between the y-coordinates for those two points in order to find the *rise*. Then count the difference between the x-coordinates for those two points to find the *run*. For each vertical increase of two (*rise*), the line moves three numbers on the horizontal axis (*run*). Thus, the slope is $\frac{2}{3}$, and the equation is $y = \frac{2}{3}x + 2$.

18. A. 20π The question asks for the circumference of the pool. The question stem gives the distance from the middle of the pool to the edge—that's the radius of the circle, which is half the diameter. Thus, the diameter of the circle is 20 ft. Plug that into the formula for the circumference of a circle: $C = d\pi$. $C = 20\pi$.

19. D. 2 The slope of a line can be expressed as $\frac{rise}{run}$. To find the slope using two points, subtract one y-coordinate from another to find the *rise*, and subtract one x-coordinate from another to find the *run*. It does not matter which point you subtract from the other, as long as you are consistent about which point you are subtracting when finding both rise and run.
$\frac{-1-(-9)}{4-0} = \frac{8}{4} = 2$.

20. C. 192π The formula for the volume of a cylinder is $V = \pi r^2 h$. In that formula, V is volume, r is the radius of the base, and h is height. In this case, you know that the diameter of the base of the can is 8, so the radius is 4. Plug in the values: $V = \pi \times (4 \text{ cm})^2 \times (12 \text{ cm}) = \pi \times 16 \text{ cm}^2 \times 12 \text{ cm} = 192\pi \text{ cm}^3$

21. D. 4,100 To find the area of a compound figure like this one, split it up into simpler shapes. Here, the space can be split into two rectangles:

Find the area of the two rectangles and add those two areas together: $(70 \times 50) + (30 \times 20) = 3,500 + 600 = 4,100$.

22. D. (2, 5) There are two ways to solve this problem. First, you could graph both lines. After doing so, your scratchwork should have looked like this:

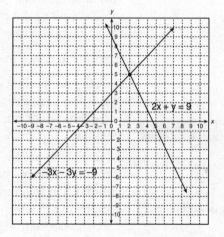

Based on that sketch, the two lines intersect at (2, 5), which means that those coordinates are the solution to the system of equations.

Alternatively, you could also have plugged each answer choice into both equations in order to find the answer choice that works in both equations. For example, to test choice (A) in this way:

Plug (2, −5) into the first equation: $-3x - 3y = -9$.

$-3(2) - 3(-5) \stackrel{?}{=} -9$

$-6 + 15 = -9$. So choice (A) works fine in the first equation. Now try the second: $2x + y = 9$

$2(2) + (-5) \stackrel{?}{=} 9$

$4 - 5 \neq 9$. Answer choice (A) does *not* work in the second equation. Therefore, it is incorrect. Try the other answer choices in a similar way. Only (D) will work in both equations.

LESSON 1

Compare and Order Numbers

Place Value

Numbers are part of your everyday life. Whether you're paying with cash, reading bus schedules, or changing television channels, you're using numbers.

The value of a number depends on the **place value** of its digits. On the place-value chart below, note that the value of a digit increases as you move to the left.

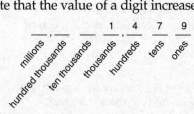

In the whole number shown on the chart, 1 has the greatest value. The number would be read as "one thousand four hundred seventy-nine."

Comparing and Ordering Values

To **order** numbers, you need to compare the value of their digits. Align the place values of the numbers you are comparing. Start at the left and compare the value of the first digit of each number.

Example 1: Place the numbers 342, 98, and 317 in order from least to greatest.

1. Compare the first digit in each number. Since 98 is a two-digit number, and the other numbers are three-digit numbers, 98 has the smallest value.

2. Next, compare the first digit of the remaining numbers. Since both numbers have the same digit (3) in the hundreds place, compare the digits in the tens place. Since 1 is less than 4, 317 is less than 342.

hundreds tens ones

342
98
317

From least to greatest:
98, 317, 342

Rounding Numbers

Place value is also essential to **rounding** numbers. To round a number, adjust it to a specific place value. For example, 40.8 rounded to the nearest ones digit is 41. The number 678 rounded to the nearest ten is 680. When rounding, if the digit to the right of the specified place value is 5 or greater, round up. If it's less than 5, then don't change the number in the specified place value.

Example 2: Round 2451 to the nearest hundred.

1. Locate the place value that you want to round to. Then look at the place value to the right.

2. Round up the digit in the hundreds place. Then change the digits to the right of the hundreds place to zeros.

24**5**1

The value to the right of the hundreds place is a 5. Round up.

2451 rounds up to **2500**

KEY IDEAS

- When ordering numbers, compare the same place values between numbers.
- Round numbers to estimate answers or eliminate answer choices in multiple-choice questions.

TASC TEST TIP

When ordering a list of numbers, rewrite the given list on your scratch paper. Then rewrite them in order, crossing out each number as you go.

PRACTICE 1

A. Write the digit from the number below that corresponds to the listed place value. The first one is done for you.

1,436,879

__4__ **1.** hundred thousands   ____ **5.** thousands

____ **2.** hundreds   ____ **6.** tens

____ **3.** ones   ____ **7.** ten thousands

____ **4.** millions

B. Round these numbers as directed.

8. Round 544 to the nearest hundred.   **11.** Round 11,632 to the nearest thousand.

9. Round 76 to the nearest ten.   **12.** Round 1525 to the nearest thousand.

10. Round 1058 to the nearest hundred.   **13.** Round 84 to the nearest hundred.

C. In each of the following pairs, which number is greater?

14. 100 or 89   **16.** 1099 or 1145

15. 339 or 341   **17.** 125,391 or 119,450

D. Write these numbers in order from <u>least to greatest</u>.

18. 23 18 45 39   **21.** 1429 1420 1432 1425

19. 111 89 109 91   **22.** 12,071 11,098 12,131

20. 1087 932 909 1139   **23.** 15,356 15,309 15,298

E. Choose the <u>one best answer</u> to each question.

24. When stacking items, the heaviest items should be placed at the bottom. Starting at the bottom, in what order should items weighing 45 pounds, 40 pounds, 50 pounds, and 48 pounds be stacked?

  A. 40, 45, 48, 50
  B. 45, 50, 40, 48
  C. 50, 48, 45, 40
  D. 50, 40, 45, 48

25. Which of the following correctly shows 1,543,976 rounded to the nearest hundred thousand?

  A. 2,000,000
  B. 1,600,000
  C. 1,500,000
  D. 1,540,000

STUDY ADVICE

Not a math person? Have no fear! The math concepts tested on the TASC Mathematics Test are covered in this book; you just need to plan your study schedule to include plenty of time to master these topics.

Whole Number Operations

Addition and Subtraction

You use **addition** when you need to combine amounts. The answer in an addition problem is called the **sum,** or **total.** When you are adding, it's helpful to stack the numbers in a column. Be sure to line up the place-value columns and then work from right to left, starting with the ones column.

Sometimes the digits in a place-value column add up to 10 or more. When this happens, you will need to **regroup** to the next place value.

Example 1: Add $40 + 129 + 24$.

1. Align the numbers you want to add on the ones column. Working from right to left, add the ones column first. Since the ones column totals 13, write the 3 in the ones column and regroup, or **carry,** the 1 ten to the tens column.

$$\begin{array}{r} 1 \\ 40 \\ 129 \\ + 24 \\ \hline 3 \end{array}$$

2. Add the tens column, including the regrouped 1.

$$\begin{array}{r} 1 \\ 40 \\ 129 \\ + 24 \\ \hline 93 \end{array}$$

3. Then add the hundreds column. Since there is only one value, write the 1 hundred in the answer.

$$\begin{array}{r} 1 \\ 40 \\ 129 \\ + 24 \\ \hline 193 \end{array}$$

You **subtract** when you want to find the **difference** between amounts. Write the number being subtracted on the bottom and the other number on top, and align the amounts on the ones column. You may also need to regroup as you subtract.

Example 2: If Sue is 57 and Kathy is 38, how many years older is Sue?

1. Find the difference in their ages. Start with the ones column. Since 7 is less than the number being subtracted (8), regroup, or **borrow,** 1 ten from the tens column. Add the regrouped amount to the ones column. Now subtract $17 - 8$ in the ones column.

$$\begin{array}{r} 4\,17 \\ \cancel{5}\cancel{7} \\ - 38 \\ \hline 9 \end{array}$$

2. Regrouping 1 ten from the tens column left 4 tens. Subtract $4 - 3$ and write the result in the tens column of your answer. Check: $19 + 38 = 57$.

$$\begin{array}{r} 4\,17 \\ \cancel{5}\cancel{7} \\ - 38 \\ \hline 19 \end{array}$$

Sue is **19 years older** than Kathy.

Example 3: Find the difference between 205 and 67.

1. Subtract. Start with the ones column. Since 5 is less than the number being subtracted (7), regroup. Since there are 0 tens in the tens column, regroup 1 hundred from the hundreds column. From 10 tens, regroup 1 ten to the ones column. Now subtract 15 − 7 in the ones column.

$$
\begin{array}{r}
\overset{9}{\underset{1\ \ 10\ 15}{\cancel{2}\ \cancel{0}\ \cancel{5}}} \\
-\ 6\ 7 \\
\hline
8
\end{array}
$$

2. Regrouping 1 ten from the tens column left 9 tens. Subtract 9 − 6, and write the result in the tens column of your answer.

$$
\begin{array}{r}
\overset{9}{\underset{1\ \ 10\ 15}{\cancel{2}\ \cancel{0}\ \cancel{5}}} \\
-\ 6\ 7 \\
\hline
3\ 8
\end{array}
$$

3. Regrouping 1 hundred from the hundreds column left 1 hundred. Subtract the hundreds column: 1 − 0. Check: 138 + 67 = 205.

$$
\begin{array}{r}
\overset{9}{\underset{1\ \ 10\ 15}{\cancel{2}\ \cancel{0}\ \cancel{5}}} \\
-\ 6\ 7 \\
\hline
\mathbf{1\ 3\ 8}
\end{array}
$$

A. Solve.

1. $\begin{array}{r} 54 \\ + 23 \\ \hline \end{array}$

3. $\begin{array}{r} 73 \\ - 21 \\ \hline \end{array}$

5. $\begin{array}{r} 105 \\ + 85 \\ \hline \end{array}$

7. $\begin{array}{r} 100 \\ - 57 \\ \hline \end{array}$

2. $\begin{array}{r} 46 \\ + 54 \\ \hline \end{array}$

4. $\begin{array}{r} 55 \\ - 19 \\ \hline \end{array}$

6. $\begin{array}{r} 2386 \\ + 1692 \\ \hline \end{array}$

8. $\begin{array}{r} 2500 \\ - 383 \\ \hline \end{array}$

B. Rewrite the problems in columns before solving.

9. $20 + 12 + 33 =$

10. $245 - 131 =$

11. $30 + 75 + 75 =$

12. $378 - 85 =$

13. $144 + 238 + 101 =$

14. $545 - 89 =$

15. $2095 + 324 =$

16. $1250 - 350 =$

17. $10,326 + 982 =$

18. $15,890 - 705 =$

19. $108,755 + 22,442 =$

20. $44,789 - 13,890 =$

C. Choose the one best answer to each question.

21. What is the total weight of the boxes below, in pounds?

A. 78
B. 88
C. 150
D. 160

22. Celia's share for lunch is $7. If she pays with a $20 bill, how much change should she get?

A. $3
B. $7
C. $13
D. $27

Multiplication and Division

You **multiply** to combine the same amount multiple times. For example, instead of adding $24 + 24 + 24$, you could multiply 24 by 3. If a problem asks you to find the **product** of two or more numbers, you must multiply.

Example 4: Find the product of 24 and 63.

1. Align place values as you rewrite the problem in a column. Multiply the ones place of the top number by the ones place of the bottom number: $4 \times 3 = 12$. Write the 2 in the ones place in the first partial product. Regroup the 1 ten.

$$\begin{array}{r} 1 \\ 24 \\ \times 63 \\ \hline 2 \end{array}$$

2. Multiply the tens place in the top number by 3: $2 \times 3 = 6$. Then add the regrouped amount: $6 + 1 = 7$. Write the 7 in the tens place in the partial product.

$$\begin{array}{r} 1 \\ 24 \\ \times 63 \\ \hline 72 \end{array}$$

3. Now multiply by the tens place of 63. Write a **placeholder** 0 in the ones place in the second partial product, since you're really multiplying by 60. Then multiply the top number by 6: $4 \times 6 = 24$. Write 4 in the partial product and regroup the 2. Multiply $2 \times 6 = 12$. Add the regrouped 2: $12 + 2 = 14$.

$$\begin{array}{r} 2 \\ 24 \\ \times 63 \\ \hline 72 \\ 1440 \\ \hline \mathbf{1512} \end{array}$$

4. Add the partial products to find the total product: $72 + 1440 = \mathbf{1512}$.

To **divide** means to find how many equal parts an amount can be divided into. The amount being broken into parts is called the **dividend.** The number you are dividing by is the **divisor,** and the answer to a division problem is the **quotient.**

Example 5: At a garage sale, 3 children sold their old toys for a total of $54. If they share the money equally, how much money should each child receive?

1. Divide the total amount ($54) by the number of ways the money is to be split (3). Work from left to right. How many times does 3 go into 5? Write the answer 1 directly above the 5 in the dividend. Since $3 \times 1 = 3$, subtract $5 - 3 = 2$.

$$\begin{array}{r} 1 \\ 3\overline{)\$54} \\ -3 \\ \hline 2 \end{array}$$

2. Continue dividing. Bring down the 4 from the ones place in the dividend. How many times does 3 go into 24? Write the answer 8 directly above the 4 in the dividend. Since $3 \times 8 = 24$, subtract $24 - 24 = 0$.

Each child should receive **$18.**

$$\begin{array}{r} \mathbf{18} \\ 3\overline{)\$54} \\ -3 \\ \hline 24 \\ -24 \\ \hline 0 \end{array}$$

Example 6: Divide $1006 \div 4$.

1. Divide the total amount (1006) by 4. Work from left to right. Since 4 doesn't divide into 1, use the next place value in the dividend. How many times does 4 go into 10? Write the answer 2 directly above the first 0 in the dividend. Since $4 \times 2 = 8$, subtract $10 - 8 = 2$.

$$\begin{array}{r} 2 \\ 4\overline{)1006} \\ -8 \\ \hline 2 \end{array}$$

2. Continue dividing. Bring down the 0 from the tens place in the dividend. How many times does 4 go into 20? Write the answer 5 directly above the second 0 in the dividend. Since $4 \times 5 = 20$, subtract $20 - 20 = 0$. Bring down the 6 from the ones place in the dividend. How many times does 4 go into 6? Write the answer 1 above the 6 in the dividend. Since $4 \times 1 = 4$, subtract $6 - 4 = 2$. Write the **remainder** of 2 as part of the quotient.

```
      251 r2
4)1006
 −8
  20
 −20
  06
  −4
   2
```

By reviewing and memorizing multiplication tables, you can save yourself precious time on the TASC Mathematics Test. Multiplication tables can be found online or at your local library.

A. Solve.

1. 121
   $\times 4$

2. 250
   $\times 4$

3. 342
   $\times 8$

4. $5\overline{)65}$

5. $7\overline{)735}$

6. $9\overline{)189}$

7. 45
   $\times 30$

8. 105
   $\times 25$

9. 211
   $\times 16$

10. $10\overline{)280}$

11. $15\overline{)225}$

12. $19\overline{)114}$

B. Solve. If multiplying more than two numbers, find the product of two numbers before multiplying by the next number, and so on.

13. $50 \times 5 =$

14. $179 \div 4 =$

15. $5 \times 6 \times 10 =$

16. $1004 \div 5 =$

17. $25 \times 3 \times 2 =$

18. $7452 \times 9 =$

19. $10{,}760 \div 20 =$

20. $12 \times 8 \times 4 =$

21. $144{,}140 \div 12 =$

C. Choose the one best answer to each question.

22. A fruit juice container holds 16 servings. If the serving size is 6 ounces, how many ounces does the container hold in all?

    A. 10
    B. 22
    C. 76
    D. 96

23. A cashier has fifteen $5 bills. How much money does he have?

    A. $15
    B. $25
    C. $75
    D. $150

24. How many 2-foot lengths can be cut from the string shown below?

    _____
            12 ft

    A. 2
    B. 6
    C. 12
    D. 24

LESSON 3

The Number Line and Signed Numbers

Understanding Signed Numbers

Signed numbers include zero, all positive numbers, and all negative numbers. Zero is neither positive nor negative. On a number line, the positive numbers are shown to the right of zero, and the negative numbers are shown to the left.

A positive number may be written with a plus (+) symbol. If a number has no symbol at all, we assume that it is positive. A negative number *must* be preceded by a minus (−) symbol.

A signed number provides two important facts. The sign tells the direction from zero, and the number tells you the distance from zero. For example, −5 lies five spaces to the left of zero, and +4 lies four spaces to the right of zero.

Adding and Subtracting Signed Numbers

You can use a number line to model the addition of signed numbers.

Examples: $1 + (-4) = -3$ Begin at +1; move 4 in the negative direction (left).

$-5 + 4 = -1$ Begin at −5; move 4 in the positive direction (right).

$-2 + (-3) = -5$ Begin at −2; move 3 in the negative direction (left).

To add without a number line, follow these steps:

• If numbers have like signs, add the numbers and keep the same sign.

• If the numbers have unlike signs, find the difference between the two numbers and use the sign of the larger number.

Example 1: Add $15 + (-25)$.

1. Since the numbers have unlike signs, subtract. $25 - 15 = 10$

2. Use the sign from the larger number. $15 + (-25) = \mathbf{-10}$

Subtraction is the opposite of addition. To rewrite a subtraction problem as an addition problem, change the operation symbol to addition and change the sign on the number you are subtracting. Then apply the rules for adding signed numbers.

Example 2: Subtract 3 – 8.

1. Change the operation symbol and the sign of the number you are subtracting.	3 – 8 becomes 3 + (–8)
2. Add.	3 + (–8) = **– 5**

You can use the same rules to combine several signed numbers.

Example 3: (–5) + 6 – 4 – (–2) = ?

1. Rewrite each subtraction as addition.	(–5) + 6 + (–4) + 2
2. Add the positive terms:	6 + 2 = 8
Add the negative terms.	–5 + (–4) = – 9
3. Combine the results.	8 + – 9 = –1

A. Solve.

1. 8 + (–3)
2. 50 – 5
3. 11 – (–2)
4. –1 + 2
5. –4 – (–5)
6. 8 – (–2)
7. 6 – 9
8. 2 + 11

9. (–7) – (–3)
10. (–4) + 6
11. –15 + (–7)
12. 36 – 4
13. –60 – (–10)
14. –5 – 6
15. 12 + 13
16. –55 + 20

17. 7 + (–3) + (–5) – 10
18. 66 + (–22) – 33
19. –14 – (–6) + 18
20. 80 – (–15) – 20
21. 6 – (–3) + (–5) + 8
22. –23 + (–11) – (–15) + 21
23. 3 + 9 – 5 + 12 – 9 – 11
24. –7 – 20 – (–14)

B. Choose the one best answer to each question.

Question 25 refers to the following number line.

25. The number line above shows which of the following expressions?
    A. 2 + (–3)
    B. 2 + (–5)
    C. –3 + 2
    D. –3 – (+2)

26. At noon, the temperature in the high desert was 92°F. A scientist observed the following temperature changes over the course of the next two hours: +12°, –5°, +6°, –3°, and +13°. What was the temperature in degrees Fahrenheit at the end of the two-hour period?
    A. 95°
    B. 103°
    C. 115°
    D. 131°

STUDY ADVICE

Number lines are very useful for understanding numerical information. They help you visualize the relationship between numbers and quantities. To review and learn about other uses for number lines, turn to pages 196 and 236.

Multiplying and Dividing Signed Numbers

In algebra, multiplication is usually not shown using the times sign ($\times$) because the symbol could be easily mistaken for the variable x. Instead, multiplication is shown using a dot or by placing two numbers next to each other. To avoid confusion, one or both of the numbers may be enclosed in parentheses. For example, the expressions $-5 \cdot 6$ and $-5(6)$ and $(-5)(6)$ all mean "-5 times 6."

In algebra, division can be written with the $\div$ symbol, but it is usually shown with a line that means "divided by." The expression $\frac{20}{-5}$ means "20 divided by -5," as does 20/-5. When multiplying or dividing signed numbers, use the following rules:

• If the signs are the same, the answer is positive.
• If the signs are different, the answer is negative.

Example 4: Multiply $4(-25)$.

1. Multiply the numbers only. $\hfill 4 \times 25 = 100$

2. Determine the sign. Since the signs on the numbers are different, the answer is negative:
$$4(-25) = -\mathbf{100}$$

Example 5: Divide $\frac{-160}{-8}$.

1. Divide the numbers only. $\hfill 160 \div 8 = 20$
2. Determine the sign. Since the signs on the numbers are the same, the answer is positive:
$$\frac{-160}{-8} = \mathbf{20}$$

A problem may contain more than two factors. Remember that each pair of negative factors will equal a positive product. Therefore, if there is an even number of negative terms, the product will be positive. If there is an odd number of negative terms, the product will be negative.

Example 6: $(-5)(6)(-1)(-2)(2) = ?$

1. Multiply. $\hfill 5 \times 6 \times 1 \times 2 \times 2 = 120$

2. There are three negative terms. Since 3 is an odd number, the product is negative: $-\mathbf{120}$.

When a problem contains more than one operation, follow the correct **order of operations**. First, solve any terms inside parentheses, and then solve any terms involving exponents (which you will learn about shortly). Then perform multiplication and division operations first, working from left to right. Do addition and subtraction operations last, also working from left to right. If a problem contains division presented with a division bar, do any operations above and below the bar first, then divide.

Example 7: $(-4)(6) - \dfrac{3 + (-9)}{-2}$

1. Multiply. $\hfill -24 - \dfrac{3 + (-9)}{-2}$

2. Do the operation above the fraction bar. $\hfill -24 - \dfrac{-6}{-2}$

3. Divide. $\hfill -24 - (+3)$

4. Subtract. $\hfill -24 - (+3) = -24 + (-3) = -\mathbf{27}$

Note: *Notice how parentheses clarify meaning:* $4 - 5$ means "four minus five," but $4(-5)$ means "four times negative five."

PRACTICE 3.2

A. Solve. You MAY NOT use a calculator.

1. $(5)(4)$
2. $(7)(-3)$
3. $(-8)(6)$
4. $(-2)(-9)$
5. $(-10)(1)$

6. $9 \div 3$
7. $12 \div (-4)$
8. $-25 \div 5$
9. $(-18) \div (-9)$
10. $\dfrac{40}{-8}$

11. $(14)(-2)$
12. $(-75) \div 25$
13. $13 \div (-13)$
14. $(-5)(15)$
15. $\dfrac{18}{3}$

B. Solve. You MAY use a calculator.

16. $\dfrac{25(4)}{-5}$
17. $(-3)(-5)(2)(-10)$
18. $20 \div (-5) \div (-2)$
19. $\dfrac{6(5)}{(-3)(2)}$

20. $(-11)(2)(-5)(6)$
21. $(12)(-2) \div (-2)$
22. $(-4)(-6)(-5)$
23. $50 \div (2)(-5)$

24. $(-1)(2)(-3)(2)(-1)$
25. $\dfrac{(3)(-4)(2)(5)}{-6}$
26. $\dfrac{4(\;1)}{-8(-2)}$
27. $(-5)(-2)(0)(-1)$

C. Choose the one best answer to each question.

28. Janice is creating a computer spreadsheet. A portion of her work is shown below.

	A	B	C
1	-3	4	7
2	2	-5	-8
3	-1	3	-2

Using the information from the spreadsheet, what is the value of the expression A1*C1*A3/(B3*A3)? (*Hint*: In a spreadsheet, the symbol * means multiplication.)

A. -21
B. -7
C. -1/7
D. 21

29. The product of 2 and 8 is divided by -8. Which of the following expressions could be used to find the value of the statement?

A. $\dfrac{\frac{2}{8}}{-8}$
B. $2(8)(-8)$
C. $\dfrac{2(8)}{(-8)}$
D. $\dfrac{2(-8)}{8}$

30. Which of the following is a true statement about the value of the expression $(52)(-103)(-45)(-8)(3)$?

A. The result is a fraction.
B. The result is greater than 1.
C. The result is a negative number.
D. The result is a positive number.

STUDY ADVICE

Approximately 25% of questions on the Mathematics Test will target algebra skills. Therefore, even though this chapter is long, working your way through it will really pay off on Test Day. Concepts covered in the chapter will increase in difficulty as you go, so be sure to review previous lessons anytime you need to.

LESSON 4

Order of Operations

When a mathematical expression contains more than one operation, its value may depend upon the order in which the operations are performed. To avoid confusion, mathematicians have agreed to perform operations in a certain order.

The Order of Operations
1. Parentheses or any other grouping symbols that enclose operations
2. Exponents and roots
3. Multiplication and division, working from left to right
4. Addition and subtraction, working from left to right

Study the following example to see how to apply the order of operations. Notice that parentheses are used in two places in the expression; however, only the first set of parentheses encloses an operation.

Example 1: Evaluate the expression $\dfrac{(5+3)^2}{4} + 3(-1)$.

1. Perform the addition operation in parentheses. $\dfrac{(8)^2}{4} + 3(-1)$

2. Raise 8 to the second power. $\dfrac{64}{4} + 3(-1)$

3. Divide, then multiply. $16 + (-3)$

4. Add. 13

The value of the expression $\dfrac{(5+3)^2}{4} + 3(-1)$ is **13**.

In more complicated expressions, one set of grouping symbols may be nested within another set. To avoid confusion, you can also use brackets [ ] or braces { } to group operations. To evaluate an expression with more than one set of grouping symbols, work from the inside to the outside.

Example 2: Evaluate the expression $4[5(-4+3)+2]$.

1. Perform the operation in the inner set of grouping $4[5(-4+3)+2]$
symbols: $(-4+3)$. $4[5(-1)+2]$

2. Do the operations inside the brackets. Since multiplication $4[-5+2]$
comes before addition in the order of operations, $4[-3]$
multiply 5 by −1 and then add 2.

3. Multiply 4 and −3.   **−12**

The division bar is also a grouping symbol. Before you divide, perform any operations shown above and below the bar.

KEY IDEAS

- To evaluate an expression correctly, you must follow the order of operations.
- If an expression uses more than one set of grouping symbols, start with the inside set and work to the outside.
- The division bar may be used as a grouping symbol.

TASC TEST TIP

You can use the parentheses keys on your online calculator to help you follow the order of operations.

PRACTICE 4

Example 3: Evaluate the expression $\dfrac{15+25}{2(5)}+6$.

1. Perform the operations above and below the fraction bar.

$$\dfrac{15+25}{2(5)}+6$$

2. Divide, then add.

$$\dfrac{40}{10}+6$$

$$4+6=\mathbf{10}$$

A. Solve. You <u>MAY NOT</u> use a calculator.

1. $4(3)-2+(6+4\cdot 2)$

2. $16\div(10-6)^2$

3. $5^2-(5-7)(2)$

4. $3(-3)+(7+4)$

5. $\dfrac{3^3}{5-2}-\dfrac{(4-2)^2}{2}$

6. $\dfrac{25}{(4+1)}\cdot 3+(6-1)$

7. $2^3+(8-5)^2-3$

8. $(4-12)(-6)+(10-3)$

9. $30\div 3(5-4)$

10. $15+(4)(3)-2^2$

11. $(4+2)^2+(7-2)^3$

12. $7^2\div(11-4)+(9+14)$

13. $2\left[(17-11)^2\cdot\dfrac{(15-5)}{2}\right]$

14. $(5^2+6-3)\div(16-3^2)$

15. $150-4\left[\dfrac{3+9}{4-1}\cdot(14-11)^2\right]$

B. Choose the <u>one best answer</u> to each question.

<u>Question 16</u> refers to the following information.

Susan is in charge of planning Midvale Hospital's parent education classes. The table below shows the cost of each class to the hospital.

Type of Workshop	Cost
Childbirth Classes	$35 per couple
Infant Care	$30 per person
Teaching Your Child to Read	$60 per person

16. A local foundation has offered to pay 75% of the cost of infant care classes. The hospital will cover any remaining costs. There are 28 parents enrolled in the upcoming infant care class. Which of the following expressions could be used to find the amount the hospital will pay?

A. $(75)(28)(30)$

B. $(28)(30)-(0.75)(30)$

C. $(1-0.75)(28)(30)$

D. $(1-0.75)(30)+28$

17. In the expression

$$5+2\left[7\left(\dfrac{10^2}{10}\right)+(6-2)(3)\right],$$

what is the last operation you should perform to find the value of the expression?

A. Subtract 2 from 6.

B. Add 5.

C. Multiply by 2.

D. Find the square of 10.

18. Find the value of the expression $22+6[(14-5)\div 3(17-14)]$.

A. 2.73

B. 28

C. 76

D. 97

STUDY ADVICE

An easy way to remember the order of operations is to memorize the phrase *"Please excuse my dear Aunt Sally. Love, Ron."* The first letters of that phrase correspond to the order of operations: Parentheses, Exponents, Multiply, Divide, Add, Subtract, and work Left to Right.

Absolute Value

The **absolute value** of a number is its distance from zero on the number line. For example, the absolute value of 5 is 5, since 5 is five spaces away from zero on the number line. But the absolute value of −5 is also 5, since −5 is also five spaces away from zero on the number line. Because **distance** is always **positive**, the absolute value of any positive or negative number is always positive.

Absolute value is written as two straight lines around a number, like this: |−5|.

$$|-5| = 5 \qquad\qquad |5| = 5$$

Example 1: Which of the following is equal to |−13|?

    (1)   13

    (2)   −13

The correct answer is **(1)**. Absolute value is always positive.

Treat the absolute value sign as you would treat parentheses in the order of operations. If numbers inside the absolute value sign are being added, subtracted, multiplied, or divided, then do that operation before you do anything else.

Example 2: Which of the following is equal to $-20\,|17-34|$?

    (1)   340

    (2)   −340

The correct answer is **(2)**. First perform the subtraction within the absolute value sign. Because you first found the absolute value, change −17 to 17. Then multiply by −20, like this:

$$-20\,|17-34| = -20\,|-17| = -20\,(17) = -\textbf{340}.$$

We often think in terms of absolute value in real life, though we might not bother to call it that. For example, imagine that you have $314 in a checking account but you write a check for $400. You've overdrawn your account by $86. The bank will record your balance as −$86.00. But you'll probably think, "I'm $86 short." You'll just think of the absolute value, or **magnitude**, of the overdraft, without the negative sign.

KEY IDEAS

- The magnitude of a number, without a sign, is called the absolute value.
- Absolute value is used to determine distance of a positive or negative number from zero.
- In the order of operations, absolute value is treated the same as a set of parentheses.

TASC TEST TIP

A signed number, positive or negative, is used to show its direction in relation to zero. However, when you see a number inside two straight lines, you are working with its distance from zero—which is always positive.

PRACTICE 5

A. Find the absolute values.

1. $|18|$
2. $|-107|$
3. $|423|$

4. $|95|$
5. $|-7026|$
6. $|-18|$

7. $|-5,708,432|$
8. $|-85.6|$
9. $|42|$

10. $|10.5|$
11. $|-163.24|$
12. $|-3.14|$

B. Use absolute value to find the solutions.

13. $5 + |-6|$
14. $-3 |52|$
15. $3 |-52|$
16. $12 \div |-4|$

17. $-|110 - 201|$
18. $-14 + |-28 \div 2|$
19. $706.2 - |-86.4 + 0.2|$
20. $49 \div (-|-7|)$

21. $-5 |-4|$
22. $|-6| - |-7|$
23. $|17| \div |-8|$
24. $|-5.5| \times (-2)$

C. Choose the <u>one best answer</u> to each question.

25. The temperature in Northville at 9:00 p.m. was –5°F. By 5:00 a.m. the following morning, the temperature was –15°F. By how many degrees did the temperature change?

    A. –15 degrees
    B. –5 degrees
    C. 5 degrees
    D. 10 degrees

26. Bob has errands to run. He walks 5 blocks east from his apartment to the barber shop, then walks 6 blocks west to the grocery store, then walks another 2 blocks west to the post office, and finally walks back home. Assuming that Bob's apartment, the barber shop, the grocery store, and the post office are all located on the same street, how many blocks did Bob walk in completing his errands?

    A. 6
    B. 11
    C. 13
    D. 16

27. Milania has a score of –65 points, and Chris has a score of 55 points. By how many points is Milania losing to Chris?

    A. 55
    B. 65
    C. 120
    D. 150

28. Absolute error is the absolute value of the difference between an actual value and its measurement. A deli scale gives a measurement of 25 ounces for a cut of meat that actually weighs only 23.5 ounces. What is the absolute error, in ounces, of the deli scale in this instance?

    A. 1.5
    B. 23.5
    C. 25
    D. 48.5

LESSON 6

TASC Test Calculator Skills

If you take the paper version of the TASC, you will be able to use a hand-held scientific calculator. See pages 166–167 for more information on the various calculator options for the paper-and-pencil test. If you take the computer version of the TASC, you will have access to an on-screen version of the Texas Instruments TI-30XS MultiView™. Whenever the word *Calculator* appears on the screen, you can click on that link to open the calculator. If necessary, use your mouse to move the calculator so that it does not cover the problem. When you are finished with a calculation, click on the *X* at the top of the window to close the calculator.

Some things to keep in mind when using the TI-30XS MultiView™:

- When you are finished with a calculation, use the enter button. (There is no "equal sign" button on this calculator.)
- Every time you begin a calculation, press the clear button above the operation keys to clear the calculator's memory.

Look at the reproduction of the calculator below and follow the examples that demonstrate how to use the calculator's **operation keys**.

Calculations you enter appear here.

Solution to a problem displays here.

Delete key

Arrows (allow you to navigate in the display)

Clear key

Digit keys

Operations keys

On

Enter key

Example 1: Add 63 + 97 + 58 + 32 + 81.

1. Always clear a calculator before starting a new computation. On the TI-30XS MultiView™, use the *clear* key.

   (clear)

2. Enter each number followed by the plus sign. As you type, the numbers and plus signs will appear on the calculator's screen. If you make a mistake, press *delete* to go back and reenter a number.

   63⊕97⊕58⊕32⊕81

3. Press *enter* to find the total.

   (enter)

The total, **331**, will appear on the right-hand side of the display:

   331

PRACTICE 6.1

Example 2: Find the difference between 15,789 and 9,332.

1. Always clear a calculator before starting a new computation.   (clear)
2. Enter the greater number first, followed by the minus operator.   15789 (−)
   NOTE: Use the minus key that is on the right side of the calculator
   with the other operation symbols. Don't use the (−) key at the bottom of the calculator; that key is used to enter a negative number.
3. Enter the number being subtracted.   9332
4. Press the *enter* key to find the answer.   (enter)

The answer **6457** will appear on the right-hand side of the display.   **6457**

Example 3: Find the product of 309 and 68.

1. Always clear a calculator before starting a new computation.   (clear)
2. Enter the first number, followed by the multiplication operator. (The   309 (×)
   multiplication sign will appear in the display as an asterisk rather
   than an ×, but the *multiplication key* looks like an ×.)
3. Enter the next number.   68
4. Press the *enter* key to find the product.   (enter)

The answer **21012** will appear on the right-hand side of the display.   **21012**

Example 4: Divide 12,456 by 12.

1. Always clear a calculator before starting a new computation.   (clear)
2. Enter the number to be divided first, followed by the division operator.   12456 (÷)
3. Enter the number you are dividing by.   12
4. Press the *enter* key to find the quotient.   (enter)

The answer **1038** will appear on the right-hand side of the display.   **1038**

A. Practice solving the following problems on your calculator.

1. $19 + 26 + 85 + 23 =$

2. $2579 - 1392 =$

3. $4 \times 28 \times 7 =$

4. $2568 \div 107 =$

5. $12,356 + 14,728 =$

6. $107,899 - 93,457 =$

7. $209 \times 56 =$

8. $972 \div 18 =$

9. $20,540 \div 13 =$

B. Choose the one correct answer to each question.

10. Dan bought a used car with 16,741 miles on it. If the car now has 42,920 miles on it, how many miles has Dan put on the car?

    A. 16,741
    B. 26,179
    C. 42,920
    D. 59,661

11. A shipment of 20 computers arrived at a warehouse. If each computer is valued at $995, what is the total value of the shipment?

    A. $995
    B. $1015
    C. $1990
    D. $19,900

Using the *2nd* Key for a Second Function

To access some of the functions on the TI-30XS MultiView™, you need to press the *2nd* key in the upper left corner of the keypad. This bright green key will activate the second function also shown in green above the corresponding key. To access the second function of a key, press the *2nd* key first—do not press it at the same time as the function key. Highlighted below are two commonly used second functions—square root and percent. Use the process shown here for all *2nd* function keys.

2nd key

Square root (√ ̄) is the 2nd function of the *x²* key.

Percent (%) is the 2nd function of the left parenthesis key.

Example 5: Find the square root of 169.	**Keys to Press**	**On the Display**
1. Always clear a calculator before starting a new computation.	(clear)	
2. Recognize that square root is a *2nd* function over the *x²* key. Press the *2nd* key. (Note that the term *2nd* now appears in the upper left corner of the display.)	(2nd)	2nd
3. Next, press the *x²* key to activate the square root function in green over the key. You will see a blinking cursor under the square root.	$\frac{\sqrt{}}{x^2}$	$\sqrt{\square}$
4. Now that you have the square root function, enter the number. The number will appear under the square root symbol in the display.	169	$\sqrt{169}\blacktriangleright$
5. Press the *enter* key to find the square root. The answer, **13**, will appear on the right-hand side of the display.	(enter)	$\sqrt{169}$ 13

For more information about square roots, see page 202.

Remember: For all *2nd functions*, (1) press the *2nd* key first to activate the *2nd* function, (2) press the key, and (3) enter the numbers.

PRACTICE 6.2

Example 6: Find the part if you are given the percent and the whole. Find 10 percent of 500.

1. Always clear a calculator before starting a new computation.   clear

2. Enter the number you want to find the percent of.   500

3. Press the multiplication sign. $\times$

4. Enter the percent number.   10

5. Press the *2nd* key and then press the open, or left, parenthesis key to activate the percent function.   2nd % (

6. Press the *enter* key to find the answer.   enter

The answer, **50**, will appear on the right-hand side of the display. Ten percent of 500 is 50.   **50**

Example 7: Find the percent if you are given the whole and the part. What percent of 240 is 60?

1. Always clear a calculator before starting a new computation.   clear

2. Enter the part.   60

3. Press the division sign. $\div$

4. Enter the whole.   240

5. Press the *2nd* key and then press the close, or right, parenthesis symbol. This tells the calculator to translate the answer into a percent.   2nd ▶%)

6. Press the *enter* key to find the answer.   enter

The answer, **25%**, will appear on the right-hand side of the display. Sixty is 25% of 240.   **25%**

For more information about percents, see pages 250–261.

A. Practice solving the following problems on your calculator.

1. $\sqrt{625}$

2. $\sqrt{324}$

3. $\sqrt{1225}$

4. Find 20% of 680.

5. Find 10% of 1250.

6. 15 is what percent of 300?

7. Find 5% of 40.

8. Find 30% of 450.

9. 20 is what percent of 400?

B. Choose the one best answer to each question.

10. Tanya paid 20% of $1680 as a down payment. How much was the down payment?

   A. $20
   B. $168
   C. $336
   D. $840

11. Aaron received a credit of $48 on a purchase of $960. What percent of $960 is $48?

   A.   5%
   B.   20%
   C.   48%
   D.   912%

LESSON 7

Powers and Roots

Powers are a special way to show repeated multiplication. For example, suppose you needed to multiply $5 \times 5 \times 5 \times 5$. This series of operations can be expressed as "five to the fourth power." In other words, the number 5 appears in the multiplication problem four times.

We can write the operations algebraically using **exponents**. In the expression $5 \times 5 \times 5 \times 5$ above, the number 5 is the base. The exponent, a small number written above and to the right of the **base**, tells how many times the base is repeated: $5 \times 5 \times 5 \times 5 = 5^4$.

To evaluate an expression, perform the multiplication indicated by the exponent.

Example 1: Find the value of 2^5.

Write the base the number of times indicated by the exponent and then multiply:

$$2^5 = 2 \times 2 \times 2 \times 2 \times 2 = \textbf{32}.$$

You may encounter some special uses of exponents on the TASC Mathematics Test. An exponent can be any positive number, or it can be 0, or a negative number. Memorize the situations described below.

1. A number raised to the first power equals itself: $8^1 = 8$.

2. A number other than zero raised to the power of zero equals 1: $6^0 = 1$.

3. A number raised to a negative exponent is equal to a fraction with a numerator of 1: $4^{-2} = \dfrac{1}{4^2} = \dfrac{1}{4 \times 4} = \dfrac{1}{16}$.

You can use a calculator to raise numbers to any power. Use the $\boxed{x^2}$ or $\boxed{\wedge}$ key. The following examples are worked out using the keys on the TI-30XS MultiView™. Remember, your calculator may differ if you are taking the TASC on paper.

Example 2: What is the value of 24^2?

Press: $24\boxed{x^2}$ $\boxed{\text{enter}}$. The right side of the display reads 576.

The square of 24 is **576**.

Example 3: Find the value of 9^4.

Enter the base, press $\boxed{\wedge}$, and enter the exponent. Then press $\boxed{\text{enter}}$.

Press: $9\boxed{\wedge}4$ $\boxed{\text{enter}}$. The right side of the display reads 6561.

Nine raised to the fourth power is **6561**.

Note: To raise a negative number to a power using the TI-30XS MultiView™ calculator, you must enter that number in parentheses: $\boxed{(}\boxed{(-)}4\boxed{)}\boxed{x^2}\boxed{\text{enter}}$.

To **square** a number, multiply the number by itself. For example, $6^2 = 6 \times 6 = 36$. In the expression $6 \times 6 = 36$, the number 36 is the **square**, and the number 6 is the **square root** of 36.

PRACTICE 7

The symbol for square root is $\sqrt{\ }$. To find a square root, think, "What number multiplied by itself is equal to the number beneath the square root symbol?"

Example 4: Find the value of $\sqrt{144}$.

You know that $12 \times 12 = 144$, so the square root of 144 is **12**. Although $(-12) \times (-12)$ also equals 144, you will only be expected to find positive roots on the TASC Mathematics Test.

You may have to approximate the value of a square root.

Example 5: The square root of 90 falls between which two whole numbers?

You know that $9 \times 9 = 81$ and $10 \times 10 = 100$. Therefore, the square root of 90 is **between 9 and 10**.

You can also use your calculator to find a square root. On the TI-30SX MultiView™, you must first press the (2nd) key to access the square root function. The $\sqrt{\ }$ function is directly above the x^2 key. (Other calculators may not require the use of the (2nd) key.)

Example 6: Use your calculator to find $\sqrt{90}$ to the nearest tenth.

On the TI-30SX MultiView™, press (2nd) x^2 90 (enter). The right side of the display reads $3\sqrt{10}$.

Press the toggle key, ◄►, to change the format of the answer into a decimal. The right side of the display now reads 9.486832981. Rounding to the tenths place, $\sqrt{90} \approx$ **9.5**.

A. Solve each expression. You MAY NOT use a calculator.

1. 3^2
2. 4^1
3. $\sqrt{9}$
4. 25^0
5. $(-3)^2$
6. $\sqrt{49}$
7. 5^3
8. 4^{-2}

B. Solve each expression below. You MAY use your calculator. Round your answer to the nearest tenth.

9. 3^8
10. $(-6)^4$
11. $\sqrt{150}$
12. 20^3
13. 1^{15}
14. $(-4)^{-2}$
15. $\sqrt{242}$
16. $(3.3)^2$
17. $\sqrt{57}$
18. $\sqrt{536}$
19. 112^0
20. $(-2)^8$

C. Choose the one best answer to each question.

21. The cube shown below measures 6 inches on each side. You can find the volume of the cube by multiplying length × width × height. Which of the following expressions represents the volume of the cube?

    A. 6^1
    B. 6^2
    C. 6^3
    D. 6^6

22. Which of the following expressions has the least value?

    A. 3^{-3}
    B. 4^0
    C. 4^1
    D. 2^{-4}

LESSON 8

Scientific Notation

Scientific notation uses the powers of ten to express very small and very large numbers. In scientific notation, a decimal number (greater than or equal to 1 and less than 10) is multiplied by a power of ten.

Look for patterns as you review these powers of ten.

$10^1 = 10$ $10^2 = 100$ $10^3 = 1,000$ $10^4 = 10,000$ and so on.

$10^{-1} = 0.1$ $10^{-2} = 0.01$ $10^{-3} = 0.001$ $10^{-4} = 0.0001$ and so on.

Did you find the patterns? In the row with positive exponents, the exponent is the same as the number of zeros in the number written in standard form. In the row with negative exponents, the exponent is the same as the number of decimal places in the number.

You can use these patterns to change scientific notation to standard form.

Example 1: Write 6.2×10^5 in standard form.

6.20000

Move the decimal point five places to the *right* (the same number as the exponent). Add zeros as needed.

620,000

Example 2: Write 3.82×10^{-3} in standard form.

Move the decimal point three places to the *left* (the same number as the exponent). Add zeros as needed.

0.00382

Work backward to write large and small numbers in scientific notation.

Example 3: To reach Mars, the Viking 2 spacecraft traveled 440,000,000 miles. What is the distance traveled in scientific notation?

1. Move the decimal point to the left until there is only a single digit in the ones place.

4.40000000

2. Multiply by 10 raised to a power equal to the number of places you moved the decimal point.

4.4×10^8

Example 4: Scientists find that a certain kind of bacteria moves at a rate of 0.00016 kilometers per hour. Write the measurement in scientific notation.

1. Move the decimal place to the right until there is a single digit in the ones place.

0001.6

2. Multiply by 10 raised to a negative exponent equal to the number of places you moved the decimal point.

1.6×10^{-4}

KEY IDEAS

- In scientific notation, a number equal to or greater than 1 and less than 10 is multiplied by a power of ten.
- Very small numbers are expressed by multiplying by a negative power of ten.
- In scientific notation, the number with the greatest power of ten has the greatest value.

TASC TEST TIP

Always try to save time. Suppose the multiple-choice answers are written in scientific notation. Instead of changing each choice to standard notation, change your answer to scientific notation.

PRACTICE 8

You may be asked to compare numbers in scientific notation.

Example 5: Which is greater: 4.5×10^3 or 9.8×10^4?

You don't need to change the numbers to standard notation. Simply consider the powers of ten. Multiplying by 10^4, or 10,000, must have a greater result than multiplying by 10^3, which equals 1,000. In scientific notation, the number with the greater power of 10 has the greater value. Therefore, **9.8×10^4 is greater than 4.5×10^3.**

A. Write each number in scientific notation.

1. 2300
2. 0.00042
3. 12,400,000

4. 14,320,000,000
5. 36,000,000
6. 0.0095

7. 0.00000058
8. 150,000,000,000
9. 0.000000009

B. Convert from scientific notation to standard notation.

10. 5.173×10^{-4}
11. 3.7×10^6

12. 4.8×10^8
13. 1.7×10^{-5}

14. 7.2×10^{-3}
15. 9.16×10^5

16. 8.591×10^7
17. 9.56×10^{-6}

C. Answer the following questions.

18. Many domestic satellites maintain an orbit approximately 23,500 miles above Earth. What is that distance in miles in scientific notation?

19. Modern technology measures very fast transactions in nanoseconds. One nanosecond equals 1.0×10^{-9} of a second. How many seconds is a nanosecond, in standard notation?

20. The average distance of Neptune from Earth is 2.67×10^9 miles. Write the distance, in miles, in standard notation.

21. Light in the vacuum of space travels at a speed of nearly 300 million meters per second. Write the speed, in meters per second, in scientific notation.

D. Choose the one best answer to each question.

Questions 22 and 23 refer to the following table.

Unit	U.S. Equivalent	Metric Equivalent
1 ton	2,000 lb	0.907 metric ton
1 acre	43,560 sq ft	4,047 square m

22. What is the number of square feet in an acre, written in scientific notation?
   A. 0.4356×10^6
   B. 4.356×10^4
   C. 4.356×10^3
   D. 43.56×10^3

23. A shipment of goods weighs 5 tons. Which of the following expressions could be used to express the weight in metric tons?
   A. $5 \times 0.907 \times 10^{-1}$
   B. $5 \times 9.07 \times 10^1$
   C. $5 \times 9.07 \times 10^{-2}$
   D. $5 \times 9.07 \times 10^{-1}$

LESSON 9

Word Problems

To pass the Mathematics Test, you will need to solve word problems. These questions are easier to manage if you use a **five-step problem-solving process**. Practice this process with word problems in this book.

Step 1. What is the **question** asking me to find?

Read the problem carefully. State the question in your own words.

Step 2. What **information** from the problem do I need?

Select only the information you need to answer the question.

Step 3. Which **operation** do I need to perform—addition, subtraction, multiplication, or division?

Choose from one of the four operations above based on your understanding of the question.

Step 4. What is my **solution**?

Carry out the operation with the numbers you chose in step 2.

Step 5. Does my answer **make sense**?

Look back to make sure that you answered the question. Check that your answer makes sense.

To help you decide which operation to use, keep the following ideas in mind.

You...	in order to...
add	combine amounts
subtract	find the difference between amounts
multiply	combine the same amount multiple times
divide	separate one amount into equal-sized groups

Example 1: To cover a sofa, Sophia needs 12 yards of fabric that costs $14 per yard. How many yards does Sophia need for 3 sofas?

    A.   4
    B. 36
    C. 42
    D. 168

The correct answer is **B. 36 yards** of fabric. The question asked you to find the total number of yards of fabric Sophia needs for 3 sofas. Note that the cost of a yard of fabric is not needed to answer the question.

Since you were asked to find the amount of fabric for 3 sofas, you should multiply 12 yards × 3 sofas = 36 yards. Here are two common errors to avoid:

- If you had mistakenly divided, you would have gotten the incorrect answer of 4 yards of fabric for 3 sofas.

- If you had used the $14 price per yard and multiplied by either 3 sofas or 12 yards, you would have been tempted by wrong answers 42 or 168. However, the cost per yard is not needed.

KEY IDEAS

- Successful math problem solvers use a five-step process.
- Read carefully to understand the question and select only the information needed to answer it.
- When you have found an answer, check that it makes sense.

TASC TEST TIP

Some questions on the Mathematics Test may include information that is not needed to answer the specific question. In multiple-choice questions, wrong answer choices may be based on mistakenly using this "extra" information, so read carefully.

PRACTICE 9.1

1. Peter wants to repaint his 700-square-foot apartment. He calculates that he has 3500 square feet of wall space to paint. (He will not paint the floor or the ceiling.) If each gallon of paint will cover 350 square feet of wall space, how many gallons will Peter need?

   A. 2
   B. 5
   C. 10
   D. 15

2. For a family get-together, Darryl wants to be sure that each child gets 2 party favors. The party favors cost $3 each, and there are 11 children coming. How many party favors will Darryl need?

   A. 9
   B. 11
   C. 18
   D. 22

3. Sarah and Kate live 18 miles apart, and they both work at the same office. If Sarah lives 25 miles from the office and Kate lives 30 miles from the office, how many miles farther from the office does Kate live than Sarah?

   A. 5
   B. 7
   C. 12
   D. 15

4. The Navarro family uses an average of 225 gallons of water per day, 5 gallons of which goes through the family's water filter. The Navarros' water filter can process 450 gallons before it needs to be replaced. After how many days of average water use will the family need to replace their filter?

   A. 9
   B. 45
   C. 90
   D. 225

Questions 5 and 6 are based on the following information.

Joyce owns a beauty salon, and she has posted the following information in her salon.

Service	Minutes to Complete	Price
Manicure	30	$15
Pedicure	30	$25
Manicure & Pedicure	45	$35
Facial	45	$45
Makeover	60	$60

5. How many minutes will it take Joyce to give 3 pedicures?

   A. 30
   B. 55
   C. 75
   D. 90

6. How much more does a customer pay for the makeover than for the manicure & pedicure combination?

   A. $15
   B. $20
   C. $25
   D. $35

7. Brandon is planning his part of the local community garden. He has calculated that he can plant 6 seedlings per row, and the garden allots 7 rows to each gardener. What is the maximum number of seedlings Brandon could plant?

   A. 7
   B. 13
   C. 24
   D. 42

Multi-Step Word Problems

The word problems on the previous two pages involved only one operation to solve. However, on the TASC Mathematics Test and other tests, you may need to do several math processes to solve a problem. These are called **multi-step problems**.

When you are working on multi-step problems, there are two important ideas to keep in mind. *What is the question asking me to find?* and *Did I answer the question?*

Review this example of a multi-step problem and the problem-solving process below.

Example 1: To win a prize, Sarah's daughter has to sell 75 boxes of cookies in 3 days. If she sold 16 boxes on day 1 and 34 boxes on day 2, how many boxes would she need to sell on day 3 to win the prize?

        (1) 18
        (2) 25
        (3) 50

Step 1. What is the question asking me to find?

The question asks me to find how many boxes Sarah's daughter needs to sell on the third day to make her goal of 75 boxes.

Step 2. What information from the problem do I need?

I know the total number of boxes she needs to sell (75 boxes).

I know how many boxes she sold on day 1 (16 boxes) and day 2 (34 boxes).

Step 3. Do I need to do only one operation, or do I need to do more than one?

I can add to find how many boxes Sarah's daughter has sold so far: 16 + 34 = 50.

However, that doesn't tell me how many boxes she needs to sell on day 3. I need one more step.

Step 4. What is my solution?

75 boxes total − 50 boxes sold = 25 boxes for day 3. The correct answer is (2) 25.

Step 5. Does my answer make sense? Did I answer the question?

By taking the additional step, I answered the question of how many boxes need to be sold on day 3.

This sample multi-step problem involved only two operations: adding and subtracting. On the actual test, you may need to do three or more operations to answer a question, so read and think carefully about each problem.

As you think about the example, note the most common mistake people make with multi-step problems. Often they stop short of answering the question. Notice that choice (3) 50 is a **partial solution**, but it is not the answer to the question. Using the five-step problem-solving process will help you avoid that mistake.

PRACTICE 9.2

Questions 1–3 are based on the information below.

Farhana's produce company distributes to several restaurants. The table below shows how many cases of different produce each restaurant ordered from Farhana's company in July.

Produce Orders in July					
	Asparagus	**Boston Lettuce**	**Carrots**	**Romaine Lettuce**	**Tomatoes**
Restaurant A	2	3	1	4	3
Restaurant B	4	4	2	2	1
Restaurant C	0	0	3	4	3
Restaurant D	1	2	2	3	4
Restaurant E	3	0	3	2	1

1. If Boston lettuce costs $17 per case and romaine lettuce costs $23 per case, how much did Restaurant D spend on lettuce ordered from Farhana in July?
   A. $85
   B. $93
   C. $103
   D. $143

2. Delivery costs $2 per case for the first 5 cases and $1 per case for each additional case of produce. What was Restaurant B's delivery charge in July?
   A. $13
   B. $18
   C. $20
   D. $26

3. If asparagus costs $22 per case and tomatoes cost $15 per case, which of the following restaurants spent the most on asparagus and tomatoes combined?
   A. Restaurant A
   B. Restaurant B
   C. Restaurant C
   D. Restaurant D

4. At a certain store, loose-leaf paper comes only in packages of 400 sheets. If a student buys enough paper at this store to fill 3 binders with 150 sheets of paper each, how many sheets will be left over?
   A. 17
   B. 50
   C. 350
   D. 450

5. Three friends are baking cupcakes for a bake sale. Each batch of 24 cupcakes requires 2 cups of flour. The friends have a single 5-pound bag of flour that contains 19 cups of flour. How many whole batches of cupcakes can they bake?
   A. 9
   B. 38
   C. 216
   D. 228

6. A certain health insurance plan costs $3000 per year for a family of six. If each member of the family has $750 in medical expenses in a year, and the plan pays 100% of those expenses, how much will the family save by purchasing the plan?
   A. $1500
   B. $2000
   C. $2500
   D. $3000

STUDY ADVICE

Word problems frequently involve rates, which you will read about next. Just remember: You frequently deal with rates in real life, e.g., miles per hour, miles per gallon. Your doctor may measure your heart rate in beats per minute. At your job, you may be paid in dollars per hour. TASC problems simply ask you to apply these real-life concepts, so don't let them throw you off.

LESSON 10

Distance and Cost

Distance

On the Mathematics Test, you'll see questions that will require you to apply formulas. When a relationship is constant, use a formula to set up the information about how the different parts relate to each other. One of the most commonly tested formulas deals with distance, rate, and time. Distance is a product of the rate at which something travels and the amount of travel time:

$$\text{distance} = \text{rate} \times \text{time}, \quad \text{or} \quad d = rt$$

Notice that letters, or variables, can be used to represent the different parts of a formula. A formula allows you to substitute known values for certain variables and solve for the unknown variable.

Example 1: How many miles can you travel if you drive at an average speed of 55 miles per hour for 3 hours?

1. You know the rate (55 miles per hour) and the time (3 hours). Substitute the values in the distance formula.

   $\text{distance} = 55 \times 3$

2. Multiply to find the distance.

   $55 \times 3 = \textbf{165 miles}$

Cost

Another helpful formula is the cost formula. It expresses the relationship between cost, the number of units, and rate (price per unit). Note: The word *per* means for every one unit. The cost formula can be written as follows:

$$\text{total cost} = (\text{number of units}) \times (\text{price per unit}), \quad \text{or} \quad c = nr$$

Example 2: At a bakery, a package of frosted cookies is priced at $3 per package. If a teacher treats her class by buying 4 packages, how much would the cookies cost before tax?

1. You know the number of units (4 packages) and the price per unit ($3 per package). Substitute the values in the cost formula.

   $c = nr$
   $\text{total cost} = 4 \times \$3$

2. Multiply to find the total cost.

   $4 \times \$3 = \textbf{\$12}$

If you know any two of the three variables in a formula, you can solve for the third variable.

Example 3: Max bought a set of 4 floor mats for $44. How much was the price per floor mat?

1. You know the total cost ($44) and the number of units (4 floor mats). Rewrite the formula to solve for the price per unit (r).

   $c = nr$
   $r = \dfrac{c}{n}$

2. Substitute the known values in the cost formula. Divide to find the price per unit.

   $\dfrac{\$44}{4} = \textbf{\$11}$

KEY IDEAS

- The following all indicate multiplication:

  $$n \times r \quad nr \quad n(r) \quad n \cdot r$$

- The following indicate division:

  $$c \div n \quad \dfrac{c}{n}$$

- A formula can be rewritten to solve for each of its variables.

  $$c = nr \quad \dfrac{c}{n} = r \quad \dfrac{c}{r} = n$$

  $$d = rt \quad \dfrac{d}{r} = t \quad \dfrac{d}{t} = r$$

TASC TEST TIP

Substitute all of the values for variables back into a formula to check your answer.

PRACTICE 10

A. Each problem below includes two of the three variables from either the distance formula or the cost formula. Write the missing variable you need to solve for. Then decide which of the following formula variations you would use in each situation. The first one is done for you.

$$d = rt \qquad \frac{d}{r} = t \qquad \frac{d}{t} = r \qquad c = nr \qquad \frac{c}{n} = r \qquad \frac{c}{r} = n$$

1. Given: distance and time

   Solve for: rate

   Formula: $\frac{d}{t} = r$

2. Given: rate and time

   Solve for: _____

   Formula: _____

3. Given: distance and rate

   Solve for: _____

   Formula: _____

4. Given: cost and number of units

   Solve for: _____

   Formula: _____

5. Given: number of units and price per unit

   Solve for: _____

   Formula: _____

6. Given: cost and price per unit

   Solve for: _____

   Formula: _____

B. Use the formulas provided in part A above to help you set up the problems. Solve for the unknown variable.

7. Find the total cost of 4 flats of plants at $12 per flat.

8. Find the total cost of 12 boxes of cookies if each box costs $3.

9. If 4 tires cost $320, how much does a single tire cost?

10. How many tickets would you get for $25 if raffle tickets cost $5 apiece?

11. If you paid $20 for 10 bus transfer tickets, how much did you pay per ticket?

12. Find the distance traveled by a car averaging 60 miles per hour for 3 hours.

13. Find the distance traveled by a train averaging 50 miles per hour for 4 hours.

14. How long does it take for a bus to travel 25 miles at an average rate of 25 miles per hour?

15. If a train travels 270 miles in 3 hours, what is the train's average speed?

16. How long does it take to complete a delivery route of 75 miles at a rate of 25 miles per hour?

C. Choose the <u>one best answer</u> to each question.

17. A company sold a total of $640 in gift boxes. If the gift boxes cost $20 apiece, how many gift boxes did the company sell?

    A. 32
    B. 320
    C. 660
    D. 1280

18. A truck driver traveled 275 miles in 5 hours. What was his average speed in miles per hour?

    A. 1375
    B. 280
    C. 270
    D. 55

LESSON 11

Measurement

The English System of Measurement

Measurements are used to describe an object's length, weight, or volume. We also use measurement to describe a quantity of time. Many people and institutions in the United States use the English system of measurement.

Measurement Equivalencies	
Length 1 foot (ft) = 12 inches (in) 1 yard (yd) = 3 ft 1 mile (mi) = 5280 ft	**Weight** 1 pound (lb) = 16 ounces (oz) 1 ton (t) = 2000 lb
Time 1 minute (min) = 60 seconds (sec) 1 hour (hr) = 60 min 1 day = 24 hr 1 week = 7 days 1 year (yr) = 12 months (mo)	**Volume** 1 cup (c) = 8 fluid ounces (fl oz) 1 pint (pt) = 2 c 1 quart (qt) = 2 pt 1 gallon (gal) = 4 qt

To solve problems, you will need to change from one unit of measure to another. If you need to *change a larger unit of measure to a smaller one,* you need to *multiply.* To change a *smaller unit of measure to a larger one,* you *divide.* Use the measurement equivalencies provided in the chart.

Example 1: A picture frame is 3 ft 8 in long. What is the length of the frame in inches?

1. Change 3 feet to inches using the fact that 1 foot = 12 inches. $3 \text{ ft} \times 12 = 36 \text{ in}$
2. Add the remaining 8 inches. $36 + 8 = 44 \text{ in}$

The picture frame is **44 inches** in length.

Example 2: A package weighs 84 ounces. What is the weight of the package in pounds?

$$\begin{array}{r} 5 \\ 16\overline{)84} \\ -80 \\ \hline 4 \end{array}$$

1. Change 84 ounces to pounds. Because 1 pound = 16 ounces, divide by 16.
2. The remainder is in ounces, the same unit you started with. Therefore, the package weighs **5 lb 4 oz,** or you can express the remainder as a fraction, $5\frac{4}{16} = 5\frac{1}{4}$ **lb.**

You may need to do a series of conversions.

Example 3: A container holds 1.5 gallons. How many cups does the container hold?

1. Change 1.5 gallons to quarts. (Use the fact that 1 gal = 4 qt.)
   $$1.5 \text{ gal} \times 4 = 6 \text{ qt}$$
2. Change 6 quarts to pints. (Use the fact that 1 qt = 2 pt.) $6 \text{ qt} \times 2 = 12 \text{ pt}$
3. Change 12 pints to cups. (Use the fact that 1 pt = 2 c.) $12 \text{ pt} \times 2 = 24 \text{ c}$

The container holds **24 cups.**

In a measurement problem, you may need to add, subtract, multiply, or divide measurements. You can only perform mathematical operations on measurements that use the same unit.

Example 4: A deck requires pieces of railing that are 5 ft 9 in, 15 ft 4 in, and 8 ft 6 in. What is the total length of railing needed?

$$\begin{array}{r} 5 \text{ ft } \ 9 \text{ in} \\ 15 \text{ ft } \ 4 \text{ in} \\ 8 \text{ ft } \ 6 \text{ in} \\ \hline 28 \text{ ft } 19 \text{ in} \end{array}$$

1. Write the measurements in a column, aligning like units of measure.
2. Add like units.
3. Simplify the answer. (Change 19 in to 1 ft 7 in, and add to 28 ft.)   28 ft + 1 ft 7 in = 29 ft 7 in
The deck requires **29 ft 7 in** of railing.

To multiply a measurement by a whole number, multiply the units of measure separately. Then simplify the result.

Example 5: Tony has five lengths of plastic pipe, each measuring 6 ft 10 in. What is the combined length of the pipe?

1. Multiply each part of the measurement by 5.
2. Simplify using the fact that 1 ft = 12 in.
The combined length is **34 ft 2 in.**

$$\begin{array}{r} 6 \text{ ft } \ 10 \text{ in} \\ \times \qquad 5 \\ \hline 30 \text{ ft } 50 \text{ in} \end{array} = 30 \text{ ft} + 4 \text{ ft } 2 \text{ in} = 34 \text{ ft } 2 \text{ in}$$

A. Solve.

1. How many inches are equal to 4 feet?
2. How many minutes are equal to 420 seconds?
3. How many hours are in 3 days?
4. Convert 40 fluid ounces to pints.
5. Five gallons are equal to how many quarts?
6. How many tons is 11,000 pounds?
7. Four yards equal how many inches?
8. How many hours are equal to 720 minutes?
9. How many cups are in two gallons?

B. Choose the one best answer to each question. You MAY use a calculator.

Questions 10 and 11 refer to the following information.

```
         Portable Air Cooler
Duracool R612
3.75 gallon capacity
Runs 6 hours without refilling
width: 27 in; depth: 16 in
height: 13 3/4 in
shipping weight: 26 lb
```

11. Which of these measurements is equal to the width of the Duracool R612?

    A. 2 ft 1 in
    B. 2 ft 3 in
    C. 213 ft
    D. 2 ft 7 in

10. Bob wants to buy an air cooler. He knows the capacity of several other models in quarts. Which of the following expressions could he use to find the capacity for this model in quarts?

    A. 3.75 × 2
    B. 3.75 ÷ 2
    C. 3.75 × 4
    D. 3.75 ÷ 4

12. Max needs to ship six identical packages, each weighing 3 lb 12 oz. What is the total weight of the shipment?

    A. 19 lb 2 oz
    B. 22 lb 8 oz
    C. 24 lb 12 oz
    D. 25 lb 2 oz

The Metric System

The metric system is the measurement system used in most of the countries of the world. The main unit of length in the metric system is the **meter** (m). The **gram** (g) is the basic metric measure of mass (or weight). The basic unit of volume is called the **liter** (*l*). To form units of measure, add prefixes to the basic units described above.

milli- (m) means one-thousandth *centi-* (c) means one-hundredth *deci-* (d) means one-tenth	*deka-* (da) means ten *hecto-* (h) means one hundred *kilo-* (k) means one thousand

Therefore, a kilometer (km) equals 1,000 meters, a milligram (mg) equals one one-thousandth gram, and a centiliter (cl) equals one one-hundredth liter.

Memorize the following chart. As in our decimal place-value system, each column on the chart is 10 times the column to its right. To convert between metric units, count the spaces from the unit you are converting from to the unit you are converting to. Then move the decimal point that number of place values in the same direction.

kilo-	hecto-	deka-	meter	deci-	centi-	milli-
(km)	(hm)	(dam)	(m)	(dm)	(cm)	(mm)
1000 m	100 m	10 m	1 m	0.1 m	0.01 m	0.001 m

Although the chart uses the meter as the basic unit, the chart can also be used with liters (*l*) and grams (*g*).

Example 1: How many millimeters (mm) are equal to 3 centimeters (cm)?

1. Find *milli-* and *centi-* on the chart. The prefix *milli-* is one place to the right of the prefix *centi-*; therefore, you need to move the decimal point one place to the right to convert from centimeters to millimeters.

2. For example, 3 cm = 3.0 cm = **30 mm.**

Example 2: How many grams (g) are equal to 6,400 milligrams (mg)?

1. Start in the *milli-* column. The basic unit (or ones column) is three columns to the left. Move the decimal point three place-value columns to the left.

2. For example, 6,400 mg = 6,400. mg = **6.4 g.**

You may want to memorize the following common conversions:

1,000 meters = 1 kilometer	1 meter = 1,000 millimeters
1 meter = 100 centimeters	1 centimeter = 10 millimeters

Solving Problems with Metric Measurement

Metric measurements are written as decimal numbers. Therefore, you can perform operations with metric measurements using the rules for adding, subtracting, multiplying, and dividing decimals.

Example 3: Three metal rods measure 1.5 meters, 1.85 meters, and 450 centimeters. What is the total length of the rods in meters?

1. Read the question carefully. You are asked to find the total length in *meters*.

2. The first two measures are written in meters. Convert the third measure to meters.
   450 cm = 4.5 m

3. Add using the rules for adding decimals. The total is **7.85 m.**

PRACTICE 11.2

Example 4: Alex is a buyer for a rug retail store. He plans to order 25 acrylic rugs to sell in the store. The shipping weight for each rug is 7.8 kilograms. What is the shipping weight in kilograms of the entire order?

1. Multiply the weight of one rug (7.8 kg) by 25.

2. The weight of 25 rugs is **195 kilograms.** Notice that the answer has the same unit of measure as the number you multiplied.

Note: A common mistake when solving metric problems is putting the decimal point in the wrong place. To avoid errors, estimate before you work the problem. Compare your answer to the estimate.

A. Solve.

1. How many meters equal 5 kilometers?
2. 600 centimeters equal how many meters?
3. How many milligrams equal 4 grams?
4. Eight kilograms equal how many grams?
5. How many centiliters is 40.5 liters equal to?
6. How many liters are equal to 1500 ml?
7. How many grams is 250 milligrams equal to?

8. How many meters are in 30 kilometers?
9. How many cl is 0.75 l equal to?
10. Fifty grams equal how many kilograms?
11. How many liters are 35,200 milliliters equal to?
12. How many centimeters are in 15 meters?

B. Choose the one best answer to each question.

13. A can of machine oil holds 118.3 ml. How many liters of machine oil does the can hold?
    A. 0.01183
    B. 0.1183
    C. 1.183
    D. 11.83

14. In a vitamin supplement, each capsule contains 500 milligrams of vitamins. How many grams of vitamins are found in each capsule?
    A. 5,000
    B. 50
    C. 5
    D. 0.5

15. A type of bonding gel comes in a small container that holds 4 g of the gel. How many of the small containers could be filled from 2.5 kg of the gel?
    A. 6,250
    B. 625
    C. 62
    D. 6

16. Sharon buys 4.8 meters of ribbon to use as trim on a set of kitchen curtains. She actually uses 350 centimeters. How many centimeters of the ribbon are left?
    A. 13
    B. 44.5
    C. 130
    D. 302

Filling in the Answer Grid

Most of the questions on the TASC Mathematics Test are multiple choice. However, some questions will require you to indicate your answer by filling in an **answer grid.** Study the image to the right.

The answer grid can be used for answers that are in whole-number, decimal, or fraction form. For further information about using the answer grid with decimals or fractions, see page 240. Examples of using answer grids with whole-number answers follow.

Example 1: Mario drove 280 miles on Monday, 320 miles on Tuesday, and 75 miles on Wednesday. How many total miles did he drive for the 3 days?

1. Decide which operation to use. Since you need to find a total amount, add the three values.

   $280 + 320 + 75 = \textbf{675}$

2. Write your answer in the blank boxes provided at the top of the standard grid.

3. Darken in the matching circle in the column under each digit in your answer.

When filling in a standard grid, you can position your answer all the way to the right edge of the grid or all the way to the left edge of the grid. That is, you can "start from the left" or "start from the right" when using the grid.

Example 2: Angela worked 40 hours every week for 51 weeks. How many hours did she work in all?

1. Decide which operation to use. Since you need to find the total of the same amount multiple times, multiply.
   $40 \times 51 = \textbf{2040}$

2. Write your answer in the blank boxes provided at the top of the grid.

3. Darken in the matching circle in the column under each digit in your answer.

PRACTICE 12

Directions: For each question, mark your answer in the circles in the appropriate grid.

1. A veterinary clinic treated 435 cats over a 3-month period. At this rate, how many cats will the clinic treat in a 12-month period?

2. A quick oil change shop recommends changing a car's oil and filter every 3,500 miles. If a car is driven 35,000 miles, how many times should the oil and filter have been changed?

3. Attendance at a local play was 348 Friday night, 366 Saturday night, and 280 Sunday afternoon. What was the total attendance for the 3 days?

4. A restaurant sells cookies at the price of 3 for $1. How many cookies could you buy for $5?

5. How many sheets of paper would 4 copies of a 617-page document use, if the document is printed so that only one side of each sheet of paper is used?

6. How many months would it take to pay back $1,050 at $50 per month?

NUMBER AND QUANTITY PART I: PROBLEM SOLVING PRACTICE QUESTIONS

Directions: You <u>MAY</u> use your calculator.

1. A beverage container holds 12 servings. If the serving size is 8 ounces, how many ounces does the container hold in all?

   A. 20
   B. 32
   C. 48
   D. 96

2. Sales at 3 concession stands are $839, $527, and $726. What is the total amount in sales?

   A. $1581
   B. $2092
   C. $2178
   D. $2517

3. If you want to cut 24 two-foot braces, how many boards of the length shown below would you need?

   A. 4
   B. 6
   C. 12
   D. 24

4. Using your calculator, find the value of $\sqrt{441}$.

   A. 11
   B. 21
   C. 221
   D. 441

5. What is the product of 700 and 180,000 written in scientific notation?

   A. 12.6×10^9
   B. 1.26×10^8
   C. 1.26×10^9
   D. 1.26×10^{10}

6. Use your calculator to solve this problem. If Emory paid 20% of $3280 as a down payment, how much was the down payment?

   A. $164
   B. $328
   C. $656
   D. $6560

7. Inventory shows that a warehouse has 45 printers in stock. If each printer is valued at $125, what is the total value of the printer inventory?

   A. $5625
   B. $170
   C. $80
   D. $45

8. Linda can drive 180 miles in 3 hours. On Tuesday, she drove for 7 hours at that rate. How many miles did she drive on Tuesday?

   A. 60
   B. 420
   C. 600
   D. 1260

9. Janelle wants to drive from Danville to Brownsville. If she averages 60 miles per hour, how many hours will it take her to drive the distance?

480 miles

Danville   Brownsville

A.   6
B.   8
C. 60
D. 540

10. A company sold a total of $1440 in gift bears for Valentine's Day. If the gift bears cost $15 apiece, how many gift bears did it sell?

A.   15
B.   96
C. 144
D. 1440

11. In addition to interest charges, Richard's credit card company charges a $25 late fee for payments made after the payment due date. If he was charged a late fee for 8 monthly bills, how much could he have saved by paying the bills on time?

A. $200
B. $80
C. $33
D. $25

12. What is the value of the following expression?

$$\frac{4^3 - [3(12 + 2^2)]}{6 + 5(4) - 15}$$

A. 0

B. $\frac{16}{41}$

C. $1\frac{5}{11}$

D. $3\frac{4}{11}$

13. April has taken her car in for the recommended oil and filter change every 3,500 miles. If April bought her car brand-new, and the odometer now shows just over 17,500 miles, how many oil changes has her car received?

A.   5
B.   14
C.   123
D. 1236

14. A clinic treated 536 children over a 4-month period. At this rate, how many children did the clinic treat in 1 month?

A.   134
B.   536
C.   540
D. 2144

For questions 15 and 16, mark your answers in the grids below.

15. Attendance at a local play was 438 Friday night, 820 Saturday night, and 636 Sunday afternoon. How many more people attended the play on Sunday than on Friday?

16. Raquel has 4 payments left on her car. If each payment is $268, how much does she still owe on her car?

15.   16.

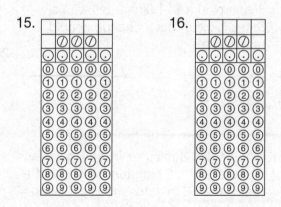

17. In what order should items weighing 51 pounds, 40 pounds, 48 pounds, and 44 pounds be stacked if you want them in order from <u>heaviest to lightest</u>?

    A. 51, 44, 40, 48
    B. 40, 44, 48, 51
    C. 51, 48, 44, 40
    D. 51, 40, 44, 48

18. Which of the following correctly shows 2,354,769 rounded to the nearest ten thousand?

    A. 2,400,000
    B. 2,355,000
    C. 2,350,000
    D. 2,000,000

19. What is the total weight in pounds of the packages below?

18 lb   23 lb   42 lb

    A. 83
    B. 65
    C. 60
    D. 42

20. Jason paid a $14 dinner bill with a $20 bill. How much change should he receive?

    A. $6
    B. $7
    C. $14
    D. $34

21. Maria spent 8 minutes installing a new showerhead, 33 minutes rodding out a drain, and 18 minutes fixing a leaking faucet. <u>About</u> how many minutes did it take Maria to complete all three tasks?

    A. 90
    B. 60
    C. 30
    D. 20

22. Carla drove 248 miles in 4 hours. What was her average rate of speed, in miles per hour?

Mark your answer in the grid below.

23. A bulk bag of nuts contains 144 ounces of nuts. If the nuts are packaged in smaller 8-ounce bags, how many bags will there be?

    A. 8
    B. 12
    C. 18
    D. 136

24. If you drove 299 miles on 9 gallons of gasoline, <u>about</u> how many miles per gallon did the car get?

    A. 10
    B. 30
    C. 270
    D. 300

25. Nydia works in a photo lab. She uses 1 pt 6 fl oz of film developer from a full container. If the capacity of the container is 3 qt, how much developer is left in the container?

    A. 2 qt 10 fl oz
    B. 2 qt 6 fl oz
    C. 2 qt 2 fl oz
    D. 1 qt 10 fl oz

26. A shipment of 33 crates like the one shown below is delivered. <u>Approximately</u> how many pounds did workers unload?

A. 40
B. 120
C. 1200
D. 2000

27. Four friends bought a birthday cake for $21 and balloons for $15. If they divided the cost equally, how much did each friend pay toward the birthday party?

A. $4
B. $5
C. $9
D. $36

28. David paid $20 toward a dinner bill of $128. If the remainder of the bill is divided equally among the remaining 9 people in the group, how much should each person other than David pay?

A. $12
B. $18
C. $20
D. $108

29. A driver traveled 4 hours at an average rate of 65 miles per hour. How many miles did the person drive?

A. 61
B. 69
C. 240
D. 260

30. Using the following information, how much would a large pizza with 3 toppings cost?

| Large 1-Topping Pizza for $14 |
| $2 for Each Additional Topping |

A. $20
B. $18
C. $16
D. $14

31. Bagels are 2 for $1. What is the maximum number of bagels you could buy for $7?

A. 7
B. 10
C. 14
D. 15

For questions 32 and 33, mark your answers in the grids below.

32. How many months would it take to save $1800 at $75 per month?

33. How many 45-page documents would a binder hold if its maximum capacity is 630 sheets of paper?

LESSON 1

Decimal Basics

The Decimal System

Decimals are numbers that use place value to show amounts less than 1. You already use decimals when working with money. For example, in the amount $10.25, you know that the digits to the right of the **decimal point** represent cents, or hundredths of a dollar.

The first four decimal place values are labeled on the chart below.

ten thousands   thousands   hundreds   tens   ones   tenths   hundredths   thousandths   ten-thousandths

2 • 3   7   5

The number 2.375 is shown on the chart. Read *and* in place of the decimal point. After reading the decimal part, say the place value of the last decimal digit. This number would be read "two *and* three hundred seventy-five *thousandths*."

Rounding

Round decimals the same way you round whole numbers.

Example 1: A calculator display reads 3.62835. Round to the hundredths place.

1. Look at the digit to the right of the hundredths place.

   3.62⬚8⬚35

2. If the digit to the right is 5 or greater, round up. If the digit is less than 5, don't change the number. Then drop all digits to the right of the place you are rounding to.

   Since 8 is greater than 5, round up. 3.62835 rounds to **3.63.**

Comparing and Ordering

Comparing decimals is similar to comparing whole numbers.

Example 2: Matt ran the 400-meter race in 45.8 seconds. Alonzo ran the same race in 45.66 seconds. Which runner had the faster time?

1. Line up the decimal points. Add a zero at the **end** of 45.8 so that both times have the same number of digits after the decimal.

   45.80
   45.66

2. Compare the decimal parts of the numbers as though they were whole numbers. **Alonzo's time was faster.**

   80 is greater than 66, so 45.8 is greater than 45.66.

When you compare more than two numbers, it is helpful to compare one place-value column at a time, working from left to right.

Example 3: Arrange the numbers 0.85, 1.8, 0.8, and 0.819 in order from greatest to least.

1. Write the numbers in a column, lining up the decimal points. Add zeros so that the numbers have the same number of decimal places.

0.850
1.800
0.800
0.819

2. Compare the digits, working from left to right. Only 1.8 has a whole number part, so it is greatest. The remaining numbers each have 8 in the tenths column. Looking at the hundredths column, 0.85 is next, followed by 0.819. The least number is 0.8.

In order: **1.8**
0.85
0.819
0.8

A. Round these numbers as directed.

1. Round 3.75 to the tenths place.
2. Round 5.908 to the ones place.
3. A calculator display reads 0.4285714. Round to the nearest hundredth.
4. Round 0.66667 to the nearest thousandth.
5. Round 8.125 to the nearest tenth.
6. A calculator display reads 2.7142857. Round to the nearest thousandth.

B. In each of the following pairs, which number is greater?

7. 0.45 or 0.449
8. 0.008 or 0.08
9. 4.68 or 4.086
10. 0.75 or 1.85
11. 1.0275 or 1.029
12. 0.14 or 0.104

C. Write these numbers in order from least to greatest.

13. 5.6   5.08   5.8   5.802
14. 0.1136   0.12   0.2   0.115
15. 14.005   4.52   4.8   4.667
16. 0.8023   0.8   0.803   0.823

D. Choose the one best answer to each question.

17. In a circuit board assembly, the weights of three parts are 0.572 grams, 0.0785 grams, and 0.6 grams. Which of the following lists the weights in order from greatest to least?

    A. 0.0785 g, 0.572 g, 0.6 g

    B. 0.6 g, 0.0785 g, 0.572 g

    C. 0.6 g, 0.572 g, 0.0785 g

    D. 0.572 g, 0.6 g, 0.0785 g

18. Which of the following correctly shows 1.3815 rounded to the nearest hundredth?

    A. 1.4
    B. 1.382
    C. 1.381
    D. 1.38

LESSON 2

Decimal Operations

Addition and Subtraction

Adding decimals is much like adding whole numbers. The trick is to make sure you have lined up the place-value columns correctly. You can do this by writing the numbers in a column and carefully lining up the decimal points.

Example 1: Add $0.37 + 13.5 + 2.638$.

1. Write the numbers in a column, lining up the decimal points.

2. You may add placeholder zeros so that the decimals have the same number of decimal places.

$$\begin{array}{r} 0.370 \\ 13.500 \\ + 2.638 \\ \end{array}$$

3. Add. Start on the right and add each column. Regroup, or carry, as you would with whole numbers.

4. Place the decimal point in the answer directly below the decimal points in the problem.

$$\begin{array}{r} {}^{1\ 1} \\ 0.370 \\ 13.500 \\ + 2.638 \\ \hline \mathbf{16.508} \end{array}$$

To subtract decimals, write the numbers in a column with the greater number on top. Make sure the decimal points are in a line.

Example 2: Find the difference between 14.512 and 8.7.

1. Write the numbers in a column, lining up the decimal points. Add placeholder zeros so that the numbers have the same number of decimal places.

$$\begin{array}{r} 14.512 \\ - 8.700 \\ \end{array}$$

2. Subtract. Regroup, or borrow, as needed. Place the decimal point in the answer directly in line with the decimal points in the problem.

$$\begin{array}{r} {}^{13\ 15} \\ 14.\cancel{5}12 \\ - 8.700 \\ \hline \mathbf{5.812} \end{array}$$

The greater number may have fewer or no decimal places. In the next example, a decimal is subtracted from a whole number.

Example 3: What does 9 minus 3.604 equal?

1. Line up the place-value columns. Put a decimal point after the whole number 9 and add placeholder zeros.

$$\begin{array}{r} 9.000 \\ -3.604 \\ \end{array}$$

2. Subtract, regrouping as needed. Place the decimal point in the answer.

$$\begin{array}{r} {}^{8\ 9\ 9\ 10} \\ 9.000 \\ -3.604 \\ \hline \mathbf{5.396} \end{array}$$

KEY IDEAS

- Always add and subtract like place-value columns.
- Always line up the decimal points when you write a problem in columns.
- When adding or subtracting, place the decimal point in the answer directly below the decimal point in the problem.

TASC TEST TIP

To make sure that your answer makes sense, mentally round the numbers to the nearest whole number and then add or subtract. The result should be close to your answer.

A. Solve. You MAY NOT use a calculator.

1. 4.025
    $+\,3.971$

2. 6.5
    $+\,4.008$

3. 2.8
    $+\,9.46$

4. 8.04
    $-\,2.19$

5. 8.5
    $-\,1.074$

6. 10
    $-\,7.89$

7. 17.294
    $+\,0.8$

8. 4.07
    $+\,1.047$

9. 17.52
    $+\,3.8$

10. 3.8
    $-\,2.905$

11. 14.64
    $-\,10.8$

12. 100.5
    $-\,98.15$

13. $0.236 + 2.4 + 2.87 =$

14. $38.06 - 16.9 =$

15. $0.006 + 0.09 + 0.549 =$

16. $8.5 - 6.074 =$

17. $1.02 - 0.87 =$

18. $0.45 + 1.8 + 0.07 + 2.56 =$

19. $12.5 - 0.7 =$

20. $25 - 10.984 =$

21. $0.01 + 2.052 + 0.96 + 1.5 =$

22. $12.9 - 10.54 =$

23. $0.68 + 12.3 + 4.9 =$

24. $32.9 - 15.675 =$

B. Choose the one best answer to each question.

25. James ran 3 miles. His times for the individual miles were 7.2 minutes, 6.8 minutes, and 8.25 minutes. How long did it take him, in minutes, to run the 3-mile distance?

    A. 22.25
    B. 22.7
    C. 23.35
    D. 96.5

26. Claudia earns overtime pay when she works more than 40 hours in one week. How many hours of overtime pay did she work for the week of March 4?

    Work Record for March 4–10

March 4	8.5
March 5	Off
March 6	9.25
March 7	8.75
March 8	10
March 9	Off
March 10	7.75

    A. 44.25
    B. 40.0
    C. 4.25
    D. 2.25

27. A plumber cut two lengths of pipe measuring 2.8 and 1.4 meters from a 6-meter length.

    Assuming there was no waste when the cuts were made, what is the length in meters of the remaining piece?

    A. 1.8
    B. 3.2
    C. 4.2
    D. 7.4

28. Mona purchased the following art supplies: a storage box for $16.98, a set of art markers for $31.78, and a pad of paper for $6.50. What was the cost of the three items?

    A. $48.76
    B. $53.26
    C. $55.26
    D. $61.76

Multiplication and Division

The rules you used to multiply whole numbers can be used to multiply decimals. You don't have to line up the decimal points. You will wait until you are finished multiplying before you place the decimal point in the answer. The number of decimal places in the answer equals the total number of decimal places in the numbers you are multiplying.

Example 4: Find the product of 2.6 and 0.45.

$$\begin{array}{r} 2.6 \\ \times\,.45 \\ \hline \end{array}$$

1. Set up the problem as though you were multiplying the whole numbers 26 and 45.

2. Ignore the decimal points while you multiply.

3. Now count the decimal places in the numbers you multiplied. The number 2.6 has one decimal place, and 0.45 has two decimal places, for a total of three.

$$\begin{array}{r} 2.6 \\ \times\,.45 \\ \hline 130 \\ 1\,040 \\ \hline 1.170 \end{array}$$

4. Starting from the right, count three places to the left and insert the decimal point. Thus, the answer is **1.17**.

When you divide decimals, you must figure out where the decimal point will go in the answer before you divide.

Example 5: Divide 14.4 by 6.

$$\begin{array}{r} 2.4 \\ 6\overline{)14.4} \\ -12 \\ \hline 24 \\ -24 \\ \hline 0 \end{array}$$

1. Set up the problem. Since the divisor (the number you are dividing by) is a whole number, place the decimal point in the answer directly above the decimal point in the dividend (the number you are dividing).

2. Divide. Use the rules you learned for dividing whole numbers. The answer is **2.4**.

If the divisor is a decimal, you must move the decimal points in both the divisor and the dividend before you divide.

Example 6: Divide 4.9 by 0.35.

$$.35\overline{)4.90}$$

1. Set up the problem. There are two decimal places in the divisor. Move the decimal point in *both* the divisor and the dividend two places to the right. Note that you need to add a zero in the dividend in order to move the decimal two places.

2. Place the decimal point in the quotient directly above the decimal point in the dividend.

$$\begin{array}{r} 14. \\ 35\overline{)490.} \\ -35 \\ \hline 140 \\ -140 \\ \hline 0 \end{array}$$

3. Divide. The correct answer is **14**.

Note: You may not need to finish dividing in order to choose the correct answer. You may be able to eliminate all but one of the answer choices after only one or two division steps.

PRACTICE 2.2

A. Solve. You __MAY NOT__ use a calculator.

1. $\begin{array}{r} 5.3 \\ \times\, 0.5 \\ \hline \end{array}$

2. $\begin{array}{r} 64 \\ \times\, 0.2 \\ \hline \end{array}$

3. $\begin{array}{r} 12.4 \\ \times\, 0.04 \\ \hline \end{array}$

4. $6\overline{)3.12}$

5. $8\overline{)28.8}$

6. $5\overline{)20.45}$

7. $\begin{array}{r} 6.25 \\ \times\, 1.4 \\ \hline \end{array}$

8. $\begin{array}{r} 13.5 \\ \times\, 0.25 \\ \hline \end{array}$

9. $\begin{array}{r} 9.62 \\ \times\, 1.005 \\ \hline \end{array}$

10. $1.25\overline{)30}$

11. $2.8\overline{)39.76}$

12. $0.003\overline{)47.4}$

13. $15.5 \times 2.2 =$

14. $0.944 \div 0.4 =$

15. $2.05 \times 0.32 =$

16. $1.32 \div 0.5 =$

17. $2.75 \times 0.6 =$

18. $12.825 \div 3 =$

19. $3.36 \times 1.1 =$

20. $15.03 \div 15 =$

21. $0.12 \times 0.06 =$

B. Choose the one best answer to each question.

22. One container of floor cleaner holds 3.79 liters. If Zachary bought 4 containers, how many liters of cleaner did he buy?

    A. 0.9475
    B. 7.79
    C. 12.83
    D. 15.16

23. Ribbon costs $0.45 per foot. A sewing project calls for 20.5 feet of ribbon. To the nearest cent, what will be the cost of the ribbon for the project?

    A. $0.92
    B. $9.23
    C. $9.90
    D. $45.56

24. Armando drove 278.7 miles over a 3-day period. On average, how many miles did he drive each day?

    A. 9.3
    B. 90.3
    C. 92.9
    D. 836.1

Questions 25 and 26 are based on the following information.

Cereal	Net Weight	Servings per Box
Toasted Oats	22.8 oz	19
Crisp Rice	16.9 oz	13
Honey Mix	12.5 oz	10

25. A box of Toasted Oats cereal is priced at $4.94. What is the cost per serving? (*Hint:* Divide the price by the number of servings.)

    A. $0.49
    B. $0.29
    C. $0.26
    D. $0.22

26. Lee bought 4 boxes of Honey Mix cereal. How many ounces of cereal did she buy?

    A. 31.25
    B. 50.0
    C. 67.6
    D. 91.2

STUDY ADVICE

You work with decimals in real life almost every day, because amounts of money are usually expressed in decimal form. *So don't be intimidated* by decimal problems: If you can understand prices, you can work with decimals!

Fraction Basics

A **fraction** uses two numbers to represent part of a whole. The bottom number, called the **denominator,** tells how many equal parts are in the whole group or item. The top number, called the **numerator,** tells how many parts you are working with.

There are 4 equal parts in this rectangle. Since 3 are shaded, we say that $\frac{3}{4}$ of the rectangle is shaded.

In a proper fraction, the numerator is less than the denominator. A **proper fraction** represents a quantity less than 1. An **improper fraction** is equal to or greater than 1.

There are 6 equal parts in the figure, and 6 are shaded; therefore, $\frac{6}{6}$ of the figure is shaded. $\frac{6}{6} = 1$

In this grouping, each figure is divided into 2 equal parts. A total of 3 parts are shaded, so $\frac{3}{2}$ are shaded.

A **mixed number** is another way to show an amount greater than 1. It consists of a whole number and a proper fraction. Another name for the shaded portion in the last figure is $1\frac{1}{2}$. The improper fraction $\frac{3}{2}$ equals $1\frac{1}{2}$.

You can also change an improper fraction to a whole or mixed number.

Example 1: Change $\frac{16}{5}$ to a mixed number.

1. Divide the numerator (16) by the denominator (5). Since 16 is not evenly divisible by 5, there is a remainder of 1. $16 \div 5 = 3 \text{ r } 1$.

2. The answer becomes the whole number, and the remainder becomes the numerator of the proper fraction. The denominator is the same as the one in the original fraction. $\frac{16}{5} = 3\frac{1}{5}$

You can also change a mixed number to an improper fraction.

Example 2: Change $7\frac{2}{3}$ to an improper fraction.

1. Multiply the whole number (7) by the denominator of the fraction (3), and add the numerator (2). $7 \times 3 = 21$ $21 + 2 = 23$

2. Write the sum over the denominator of the original fraction. $7\frac{2}{3} = \frac{23}{3}$

PRACTICE 3

To perform operations with fractions, you need to be able to write equal fractions in higher or lower terms. The **terms** are the numerator and the denominator. A fraction is **reduced to lowest terms** when the two terms do not have any common factor except 1.

To **raise** a fraction, multiply both terms by the same number: $\frac{3}{4} = \frac{3 \times 3}{4 \times 3} = \frac{9}{12}$.

To **reduce** a fraction, divide both terms by the same number: $\frac{10}{15} = \frac{10 \div 5}{15 \div 5} = \frac{2}{3}$.

A. Write a proper fraction for the shaded portion of each figure.

1. **2.** **3.**

B. Write an improper fraction and a mixed number for the shaded portion of each figure.

4. **5.** **6.**

C. Write improper fractions as mixed numbers and mixed numbers as improper fractions.

7. $\frac{17}{3} =$ **9.** $\frac{24}{6} =$ **11.** $\frac{19}{4} =$ **13.** $\frac{43}{9} =$ **15.** $\frac{33}{4} =$

8. $3\frac{3}{5} =$ **10.** $5\frac{2}{9} =$ **12.** $2\frac{5}{12} =$ **14.** $1\frac{3}{4} =$ **16.** $5\frac{7}{10} =$

D. Write an equal fraction with the given denominator.

17. $\frac{3}{4} = \frac{}{16}$ **18.** $\frac{1}{3} = \frac{}{21}$ **19.** $\frac{4}{5} = \frac{}{60}$ **20.** $\frac{3}{8} = \frac{}{40}$ **21.** $\frac{6}{25} = \frac{}{100}$

(Hint for question 17: $4 \times ? = 16$)

E. Reduce each fraction to lowest terms.

22. $\frac{21}{28} =$ **23.** $\frac{4}{24} =$ **24.** $\frac{12}{20} =$ **25.** $\frac{26}{30} =$ **26.** $\frac{60}{90} =$

F. Choose the <u>one best answer</u> to each question.

27. Eighteen out of every 24 people surveyed say they went to at least one movie in December. What fraction of the people surveyed went to at least one movie in December?

A. $\frac{3}{4}$

B. $\frac{2}{3}$

C. $\frac{1}{3}$

D. $\frac{1}{4}$

28. Which of the following fractions equals $\frac{2}{5}$?

A. $\frac{15}{100}$

B. $\frac{30}{100}$

C. $\frac{40}{100}$

D. $\frac{80}{100}$

Fraction Operations

Addition and Subtraction

You can add or subtract **like fractions.** Like fractions have a **common denominator.** In other words, their denominators are the same.

Example 1: Add $\frac{3}{10} + \frac{5}{10}$.

1. Since the denominators are the same, add the numerators.

$$\frac{3}{10} + \frac{5}{10} = \frac{8}{10}$$

2. Reduce the answer to lowest terms.

$$\frac{8}{10} = \frac{8 \div 2}{10 \div 2} = \frac{4}{5}$$

Example 2: Subtract $\frac{2}{9}$ from $\frac{7}{9}$.

Subtract the numerators. The answer is already in lowest terms.

$$\frac{7}{9} - \frac{2}{9} = \frac{5}{9}$$

If the denominators are not the same, raise one or both fractions to higher terms so that they become like fractions.

Example 3: Add $\frac{5}{6} + \frac{1}{4}$.

1. One way to find a common denominator is to think of the multiples of both denominators. The lowest is 12.

Multiples
of 6: 6, $\boxed{12}$, 18
of 4: 4, 8, $\boxed{12}$, 16

2. Raise each fraction to higher terms with a denominator of 12.

$$\frac{5 \times 2}{6 \times 2} = \frac{10}{12}, \frac{1 \times 3}{4 \times 3} = \frac{3}{12}$$

3. Add the like fractions. Rewrite the sum as a mixed number.

$$\frac{10}{12} + \frac{3}{12} = \frac{13}{12} = \mathbf{1\frac{1}{12}}$$

Use the same process to add or subtract mixed numbers. Example 4 shows how to regroup when subtracting mixed numbers.

Example 4: Subtract $4\frac{1}{16} - 1\frac{3}{8}$.

1. Raise the second fraction so that it also has a denominator of 16.

$$\frac{3 \times 2}{8 \times 2} = \frac{6}{16}$$

2. Set up the problem. To subtract the fractions, you need to regroup 1 from the whole number column and add it to the top fraction.

$$4\frac{1}{16} = 3\frac{16}{16} + \frac{1}{16} = 3\frac{17}{16}$$

3. Subtract the fractions and then the whole numbers.

$$3\frac{17}{16} - 1\frac{6}{16} = \mathbf{2\frac{11}{16}}$$

KEY IDEAS

- You can add or subtract fractions, but they must have the same denominator.
- If denominators are not the same, find a common denominator and raise one or both fractions.
- Always reduce answers to lowest terms and change improper fractions to mixed numbers.

TASC TEST TIP

If your solution to a fraction problem is not one of the given answer choices, make sure that you reduced your answer to lowest terms. On the Mathematics Test, answer choices are always written in lowest terms.

A. Solve. Reduce answers to lowest terms. Simplify improper fractions as mixed numbers.

1. $\begin{aligned}&\frac{3}{8}\\+&\frac{1}{8}\end{aligned}$

2. $\begin{aligned}&\frac{1}{6}\\+&\frac{5}{6}\end{aligned}$

3. $\begin{aligned}&\frac{8}{9}\\-&\frac{5}{9}\end{aligned}$

4. $\begin{aligned}&\frac{7}{12}\\-&\frac{5}{12}\end{aligned}$

5. $\begin{aligned}&\frac{1}{4}\\+&\frac{2}{3}\end{aligned}$

6. $\begin{aligned}&\frac{1}{2}\\+&\frac{5}{8}\end{aligned}$

7. $\begin{aligned}&\frac{9}{10}\\-&\frac{3}{5}\end{aligned}$

8. $\begin{aligned}&\frac{7}{9}\\-&\frac{1}{2}\end{aligned}$

9. $\begin{aligned}&2\frac{1}{5}\\+&1\frac{2}{3}\end{aligned}$

10. $\begin{aligned}&4\frac{1}{2}\\-&2\frac{3}{4}\end{aligned}$

11. $5\frac{5}{6}+2\frac{2}{3}=$

12. $6\frac{7}{8}+4\frac{3}{4}=$

13. $12\frac{1}{10}+9\frac{3}{5}=$

14. $2\frac{2}{9}+\frac{2}{3}+4\frac{5}{6}=$

15. $3\frac{1}{3}+5\frac{2}{3}+3\frac{5}{6}=$

16. $\frac{3}{8}+\frac{7}{12}+1\frac{2}{3}=$

17. $16\frac{2}{3}+25\frac{3}{4}=$

18. $10\frac{1}{2}+8\frac{4}{5}+3\frac{1}{4}=$

19. $8\frac{1}{2}-3\frac{4}{9}=$

20. $15-3\frac{7}{8}=$

21. $14\frac{1}{4}-10\frac{3}{7}=$

22. $9\frac{11}{12}-8\frac{5}{8}=$

23. $6-3\frac{4}{7}=$

24. $13\frac{1}{3}-4\frac{4}{9}=$

25. $5\frac{5}{7}-4\frac{4}{5}=$

B. Choose the one best answer to each question.

26. To make the top of a dining room table, Craig glues a piece of oak that is $\frac{5}{16}$ inch thick to a piece of pine that is $\frac{7}{8}$ inch thick. What is the total thickness, in inches, of the tabletop?

    A. $\frac{9}{16}$

    B. $1\frac{3}{16}$

    C. $1\frac{1}{4}$

    D. $1\frac{9}{16}$

27. Carol will use the two bolts shown below to assemble a book cart. How much longer, in inches, is bolt A than bolt B?

    A. $\frac{5}{8}$

    B. $1\frac{3}{8}$

    C. $1\frac{5}{8}$

    D. $1\frac{3}{4}$

28. At a fabric store, Melissa sold $8\frac{7}{8}$ yards of cloth to a customer. If the material was cut from a bolt of fabric containing $23\frac{1}{4}$ yards, how many yards are left on the bolt?

    A. $14\frac{3}{8}$

    B. $15\frac{3}{8}$

    C. $15\frac{3}{4}$

    D. $31\frac{7}{8}$

29. A batch of salad dressing requires $1\frac{2}{3}$ cups of olive oil, $\frac{1}{2}$ cup of vinegar, and $\frac{3}{4}$ cup of water. How many cups of salad dressing will this recipe produce?

    A. $1\frac{2}{3}$

    B. $2\frac{5}{6}$

    C. $2\frac{11}{12}$

    D. $3\frac{7}{12}$

STUDY ADVICE

Remember that practice has three levels: Learn and Review, Practice and Review, Assess and Review. For each lesson, absorb the concepts on the left page. Then practice using the page on the right, and carefully review the explanations in the back of the book. Finally, use the question sets at the end of each chapter to assess your progress. Don't forget to review the explanations for those question sets, too.

Multiplication and Division

It isn't necessary to find a common denominator to multiply and divide fractions. To multiply fractions, simply multiply the numerators and then the denominators. Reduce the answer, if necessary.

Example 5: What is the product of $\frac{7}{8}$ and $\frac{1}{2}$?

Multiply the numerators together, and then the denominators. The answer is in lowest terms.

$$\frac{7}{8} \times \frac{1}{2} = \frac{7 \times 1}{8 \times 2} = \frac{7}{16}$$

Before multiplying a mixed number, change it to an improper fraction.

Example 6: What is $\frac{1}{3}$ of $3\frac{3}{4}$?

1. Change $3\frac{3}{4}$ to an improper fraction.

$$3\frac{3}{4} = \frac{15}{4}$$

2. Multiply the numerators and the denominators.

$$\frac{15}{4} \times \frac{1}{3} = \frac{15 \times 1}{4 \times 3} = \frac{15}{12}$$

3. Change to a mixed number and reduce to lowest terms.

$$\frac{15}{12} = 1\frac{3}{12} = 1\frac{1}{4}$$

You can use a shortcut called **canceling** to reduce the fractions as you work the problem. To cancel, divide both a numerator and a denominator by the same number. The numerator and the denominator can be in different fractions.

Example 7: Multiply $1\frac{1}{2}$ by $1\frac{1}{5}$.

1. Change to improper fractions.

$$1\frac{1}{2} = \frac{3}{2} \text{ and } 1\frac{1}{5} = \frac{6}{5}$$

2. Set up the multiplication problem. Both 6 (a numerator) and 2 (a denominator) are evenly divisible by 2. Divide them by 2. Then multiply using the new numerator and denominator. Finally, change the improper fraction to a mixed number.

$$\frac{3}{2} \times \frac{6}{5} = \frac{3}{\cancel{2}_1} \times \frac{\cancel{6}^3}{5} = \frac{9}{5} = 1\frac{4}{5}$$

The slash marks show that the numbers have been divided.

You will need two additional steps to divide fractions. Before dividing, **invert** the divisor (the fraction you are dividing by). To invert the fraction, switch the numerator and the denominator. Finally, change the division symbol to a multiplication symbol and multiply.

Example 8: Jim has an 8-pound bag of nuts. He wants to fill smaller $\frac{1}{2}$-pound bags using the nuts. How many small bags can he make?

1. Divide 8 by $\frac{1}{2}$. Set up the division problem. Always write whole or mixed numbers as improper fractions.

$$8 \div \frac{1}{2} = \frac{8}{1} \div \frac{1}{2} =$$

2. Invert the fraction you are dividing by. Then change the operation sign to multiplication. Multiply, following the rules for multiplying fractions. **Jim can make 16 small bags.**

$$\frac{8}{1} \times \frac{2}{1} = \frac{16}{1} = 16$$

Note: When you multiply by a fraction less than 1, the answer is smaller than the number you started with because you are finding a "part of." When you divide by a fraction less than 1, the answer is greater than the number.

PRACTICE 4.2

A. Solve. Reduce answers to lowest terms. Simplify improper fractions as mixed numbers.

1. $\frac{2}{3} \times \frac{1}{4} =$

2. $1\frac{5}{6} \times \frac{1}{2} =$

3. $\frac{2}{3} \times 21 =$

4. $50 \times \frac{3}{8} =$

5. $3\frac{1}{2} \times \frac{1}{4} =$

6. $\frac{3}{4} \times \frac{7}{8} =$

7. $2\frac{1}{3} \times 3\frac{2}{5} =$

8. $15 \times 2\frac{3}{4} =$

9. $\frac{5}{8} \times 3\frac{1}{4} =$

10. $\frac{7}{8} \div \frac{1}{16} =$

11. $\frac{4}{5} \div \frac{4}{9} =$

12. $12 \div \frac{1}{4} =$

13. $6 \div 2\frac{1}{2} =$

14. $3\frac{3}{4} \div 1\frac{2}{3} =$

15. $9 \div \frac{1}{3} =$

16. $26\frac{2}{3} \div 3\frac{1}{3} =$

17. $40\frac{3}{8} \div 4\frac{1}{4} =$

18. $3\frac{7}{8} \div 5\frac{1}{6} =$

B. Choose the one best answer to each question.

19. A city is considering raising taxes to build a football stadium. A survey of registered voters yielded the following results:

Position	Fraction of Those Surveyed
Against Tax Hike	$\frac{7}{16}$
For Tax Hike	$\frac{3}{16}$
Undecided	$\frac{3}{8}$

If 400 people were surveyed, how many support the tax hike?

A. 48
B. 75
C. 150
D. 175

20. A tailor has 20 yards of shirt fabric. How many shirts can she complete if each shirt requires $2\frac{3}{4}$ yards of fabric?

A. 6
B. 7
C. 8
D. 10

21. An insurance agent estimates that it takes $\frac{2}{3}$ hour to process a customer's claim. If the agent spends 22 hours per week processing claims, about how many claims does he process in a week?

A. $14\frac{2}{3}$
B. 33
C. 44
D. 66

22. A fluorescent lighting panel is $12\frac{5}{8}$ inches wide. If three of the panels are installed as shown below, what will be the width in inches of the combined panels?

A. $13\frac{7}{8}$
B. $36\frac{5}{8}$
C. $37\frac{7}{8}$
D. $42\frac{7}{8}$

Fraction and Decimal Equivalencies

Fractions and decimals are two ways to show part of a whole. You can change fractions to decimals by dividing.

Example 1: Change $\frac{3}{8}$ to a decimal.

The fraction $\frac{3}{8}$ means $3 \div 8$. Use a calculator to divide. $3 \div 8 = \mathbf{0.375}$

You can also change a decimal to a fraction.

Example 2: Change 0.35 to a fraction.

Write the decimal number over the place value name of the last decimal digit on the right. The last digit, 5, is in the hundredths column. Reduce to lowest terms. $\frac{35}{100} = \frac{35 \div 5}{100 \div 5} = \frac{7}{20}$

You will find it useful to memorize the most common fraction and decimal equivalents. These equivalents will also help you solve percent problems.

Decimal	Fraction		Decimal	Fraction		Decimal	Fraction
0.1	$\frac{1}{10}$		0.375	$\frac{3}{8}$		0.7	$\frac{7}{10}$
0.125	$\frac{1}{8}$		0.4	$\frac{2}{5}$		0.75	$\frac{3}{4}$
0.2	$\frac{1}{5}$		0.5	$\frac{1}{2}$		0.8	$\frac{4}{5}$
0.25	$\frac{1}{4}$		0.6	$\frac{3}{5}$		0.875	$\frac{7}{8}$
0.3	$\frac{3}{10}$		0.625	$\frac{5}{8}$		0.9	$\frac{9}{10}$
$0.33\bar{3}$	$\frac{1}{3}$		$0.66\bar{6}$	$\frac{2}{3}$			

The decimal equivalents for $\frac{1}{3}$ and $\frac{2}{3}$ are marked with a bar. The bar shows that the decimal repeats indefinitely.

You can use fraction and decimal equivalents to save time when solving math problems.

Example 3: Each dose of cough medicine contains 0.25 ounce of medication. How many ounces of medication are in 48 doses?

To solve the problem, you need to multiply 48 by 0.25, a time-consuming calculation. However, since $0.25 = \frac{1}{4}$ you can find $\frac{1}{4}$ of 48 to solve the problem. The answer is **12 ounces**. $48 \times \frac{1}{4} = \frac{48}{4} = \mathbf{12}$

KEY IDEAS

- To change a fraction to a decimal, divide the numerator by the denominator.
- To change a decimal to a fraction, write the number without the decimal point over the place value of the last decimal digit. Reduce.
- Avoid time-consuming calculations by using fraction-decimal equivalents.

TASC TEST TIP

Look at the answer choices before you begin working a multiple-choice problem. Knowing whether you need an answer in fraction or decimal form may affect how you approach the problem.

PRACTICE 5

Knowing fraction-decimal equivalents can also help you interpret remainders when using a calculator.

Example 4: Ray inspects machine assemblies. He must inspect 12 assemblies during his 40-hour workweek. On average, how many hours can he spend on each inspection?

Using a calculator, divide 40 by 12: 40 $\div$ 12 [enter]. The right side of the display reads 3.333333333.

Since you know that $0.33\overline{3} = \frac{1}{3}$, the answer is **$3\frac{1}{3}$ hours.**

Solve. When possible, use fraction and decimal equivalents to make the work easier. You MAY use a calculator on questions 5 and 6.

1. During a 25%-off sale, store clerks find the amount of the discounts by multiplying the regular price by 0.25. What is the discount on an item with a regular price of $80?

   A. $32.00
   B. $20.00
   C. $16.40
   D. $2.00

2. At Linton Products, $\frac{3}{10}$ of the workers are in the company's ride-share program. If there are 480 workers, which of the following expressions could be used to find the number in the ride-share program?

   A. 480×0.7
   B. $480 \div 0.7$
   C. 480×0.3
   D. $480 \div 0.3$

3. Sharon is using a calculator to find out how many hours she has spent on a certain job. She divides, and her display reads:

   $$4.666666666$$

   Assuming her calculations are correct, how many hours did she spend on the job?

   A. $4\frac{1}{6}$
   B. $4\frac{2}{3}$
   C. $4\frac{6}{7}$
   D. 46

4. A gourmet candy company charges the following prices per pound.

Jelly Beans	$9.60
Peanut Brittle	$12.00
Almond Toffee	$28.50

   How much would a customer pay for 1.5 pounds of peanut brittle?

   A. $6.00
   B. $14.40
   C. $18.00
   D. $42.75

5. At 1 p.m., the amount of rain in a rain gauge is 1.125 inches. At 3 p.m., the gauge holds 1.875 inches. What fraction of an inch of rain fell between 1 p.m. and 3 p.m.?

   A. $\frac{7}{8}$
   B. $\frac{3}{4}$
   C. $\frac{7}{10}$
   D. $\frac{1}{8}$

6. A steel rod, 3 meters in length, is cut into 8 equal pieces. What is the length in meters of each piece?

   A. 0.125
   B. 0.333
   C. 0.375
   D. 2.333

STUDY ADVICE

Memorizing some basic fraction-decimal equivalencies can save you time on the TASC Mathematics Test. Consider making flash cards to help you memorize them.

LESSON 6

Decimals and Fractions on the Number Line

On the TASC Mathematics Test you may need to recognize or locate fractions, mixed fractions, or decimals on a **number line**. A number line represents numbers in order from least to greatest. As you move to the left along a number line, numbers decrease in value. As you move to the right, numbers increase in value.

The arrows on the ends indicate that numbers continue forever in both directions. If you imagine zooming in on a portion of that number line, it might look like this:

Thus, a number line can include decimals and whole numbers. For example, the point represents 0.75, which is greater than 0.5 and less than 1.

A number line can also represent fractions and mixed fractions in order from least to greatest:

Use this question to practice working with number lines:

Example 1: John works five shifts per week. His boss asks him to spend exactly half of his time this week working on a specific project. How many work shifts will John devote to that project? Circle the answer on the number line below.

If you circled $2\frac{1}{2}$, you are correct. Multiply 5 by $\frac{1}{2}$ to determine that John will spend $2\frac{1}{2}$ shifts on the project.

PRACTICE 6

A. Choose the one best answer to each question.

1. What is the value of the point on the number line below?

A. 0

B. $\frac{1}{2}$

C. $\frac{2}{3}$

D. $1\frac{1}{3}$

2. What is the value of the point on the number line below?

A. 2

B. 2.5

C. 2.7

D. 2.8

3. In the number line below, what is the value of *A* minus *B*?

```
        B              A
  <──┼──┼──┼──┼──┼──┼──┼──>
     1  1½  2  2½  3  3½
```

A. 1

B. $1\frac{1}{2}$

C. 2

D. $3\frac{1}{2}$

4. Angela baked 24 cookies and gave 16 of them to her neighbor. On the number line below, circle the fraction of Angela's cookies that she gave to her neighbor.

```
  <──┼──┼──┼──┼──┼──┼──┼──>
     0  ¼  ⅓  ½  ⅔  ¾  1
```

B. Write the decimal values of the points on the number lines.

For each of the number lines below, fill in the value of the point using decimals.

5.
```
  <──┼──┼────┼────┼────┼───●───┼─────┼──>
     4  4.125 4.25 4.375 4.5   4.75 4.875  5
                              ↑
                             ( )
```

6.
```
  <──┼──┼────┼────┼───●───┼────┼──>
     8  8.33 8.66  9      9.66  10
                   ↑
                  ( )
```

C. Write the fraction values of the points on the number lines.

For each of the number lines below, fill in the value of the point using mixed fractions.

7.
```
  <──┼──┼────┼────┼───↑───┼────┼──>
     2  2⅓  2⅔   3       3⅔   4
                   ( )
```

8.
```
  <──┼──┼────┼────┼────┼───●───┼────┼──>
     11 11⅙ 11⅓ 11½ 11⅔     12  12⅙
                        ↑
                       ( )
```

LESSON 7

Decimal and Fraction Calculator Skills

Several important calculator keys are used to work with decimals and fractions. Remember, if you are testing on paper, you might use any one of a number of calculators (see pages 166–167 for more information), including the one that follows here. Your state may limit the types of calculators you can use. If you are testing on computer, you will use an on screen version of the calculator below.

Cursor keys move the cursor on the screen up, down, left, and right.

The **fraction key** is used to enter fractions; the **mixed number 2nd function** is in green above it.

The **toggle key** changes between equivalent fraction and decimal forms of a number.

The **decimal point** key enters a decimal point.

Calculator **decimal operations** are performed in the same way that you use operations with whole numbers. You need to use the **decimal point key** ⊙ under the 2 in the white **numeric keypad**. Practice with these examples:

To Solve This Problem...	Press These Keys...	The Right-Hand Side of the Display Reads...
$3.89 + 2.5$	3.89 ⊕ 2.5 enter	6.39
$5.2 - 0.78$	5.2 ⊖ .78 enter	4.42
0.9×15	.9 ⊗ 15 enter	13.5
$1.7 \div 2$	1.7 ÷ 2 enter	0.85

You will use several calculator functions to work with **fractions** and **mixed fraction operations**. First practice entering fractions and converting to decimals.

Example 1: Reduce $\frac{56}{448}$ to lowest terms and then convert to a decimal.

On the Display

1. Clear the calculator.
2. Press the $\frac{n}{d}$ button to enter a fraction. Enter 56 at the blinking cursor, in the numerator.

$$\frac{56}{\vdots}$$

3. Use the down cursor key ▼ to enter 448 in the denominator.

$$\frac{56}{448}$$

4. Press enter to reduce the fraction to lowest terms, which appears on the right of your screen: $\frac{1}{8}$

$$\frac{56}{448} \quad \frac{1}{8}$$

5. To express the fraction as a decimal, press the *toggle* button: ◀▶. The decimal **0.125** appears on the right display.

$$\frac{1}{8} \leftrightarrow 0.125$$

PRACTICE 7

Now practice operations with **mixed fractions** using the *2nd function* key.

Example 2: A plastic pipe is to be cut into pieces measuring $1\frac{7}{8}$ feet. The original pipe was $20\frac{5}{8}$ feet long. How many pieces can be cut from the pipe?

	Keys to Press	**On the Display**
1. Clear the calculator.	clear	
2. Recognize that a mixed fraction is a green *2nd* function: $\bigcup\frac{n}{d}$ over the $\frac{n}{d}$ key. Press the 2nd key and the $\frac{n}{d}$ key. Note both a whole number and a blinking fraction cursor on the display.	2nd $\frac{n}{d}$	▪▪
3. Enter the number being divided first–the whole pipe: $20\frac{5}{8}$. Enter 20, then follow the direction of the onscreen arrow and press the right arrow button to move to the fraction cursors. Enter 5 and then use the down arrow to enter the 8. Exit the fraction by pressing the right arrow again.	20 ▶ 5 ▼ 8 ▶	$20\frac{5}{8}$
4. Press the division key. Then follow the same process with the second number: $1\frac{7}{8}$, starting with the 2nd function: $\bigcup\frac{n}{d}$	÷ 2nd $\frac{n}{d}$ 1 ▶ 7 ▼ 8 ▶	$20\frac{5}{8} \div 1\frac{7}{8}$
5. Press the enter button for the solution. The answer 11 for **11 pieces** appears on the right side of the screen.	enter	$20\frac{5}{8} \div 1\frac{7}{8}$ 11

A. Solve the following problems using your calculator.

1. $3.5 + 1.87 + 2.009$ 2. $3\frac{2}{3} - 1\frac{5}{12}$ 3. $\$25.35 \times 15$ 4. $10\frac{1}{2} \div \frac{1}{4}$

5. Linda earns $95 per day. If she works $\frac{8}{9}$ of a day, how much will she earn?

6. Aaron bought a refrigerator for $956.88. The price includes tax and interest charges. If he makes 12 equal monthly payments, how much will he pay each month?

7. An insurance agent estimates the annual cost of insurance on a home by multiplying the sale price of the home by 0.0125. What will be the yearly cost of insurance on a home priced at $118,000?

8. In a recipe, the total liquid added to a mixture is $1\frac{1}{2}$ cups of water and $2\frac{3}{4}$ cups of chicken broth. How many cups of liquid are used in the recipe?

9. A quilt costs $84.99 and weighs 5.56 pounds. The shipping charge is $1.20 per pound. To the nearest cent, what would be the shipping charge on the quilt?

   A. $5.56
   B. $6.67
   C. $8.26
   D. $10.20

10. A state park contains 64 acres. A wildlife preserve makes up $\frac{3}{8}$ of the park. How many acres are in the preserve?

   A. 8
   B. 21
   C. 24
   D. 27

LESSON 8

Filling in the Answer Grid Using Decimals or Fractions

Some questions on the TASC Mathematics Test may require you to use a bubble grid to answer questions involving decimals or fractions.

Study the following examples. Remember: You should write your answer in the top row of boxes, but this part of the grid will not be scored. You must correctly fill the circles in the grid to receive credit for your answer.

To enter a fraction on the answer grid, bubble in the slash mark to separate the numerator from the denominator.

Example 1: John needs $\frac{3}{4}$ cup of brown sugar for a recipe. If he wants to make only one-half the number of servings, how many cups of brown sugar will he need?

1. Multiply to find the answer. $\frac{3}{4} \times \frac{1}{2} = \frac{3}{8}$

2. Enter the fraction on the grid. Fill in a slash to represent the fraction bar.

You may not enter mixed numbers on the grid. If the answer to a problem is a mixed number, change the mixed number to an improper fraction.

Example 2: Elaine exercised for $1\frac{3}{4}$ hours on Monday and $1\frac{1}{2}$ hours on Tuesday. How many hours did she exercise in all?

1. Add. $1\frac{3}{4} + 1\frac{1}{2} = 1\frac{3}{4} + 1\frac{2}{4} = 2\frac{5}{4}$

2. Change the answer to an improper fraction. $2\frac{5}{4} = \frac{13}{4}$

3. Enter the answer on the grid.

To enter a decimal, fill in a circle on the third row of the grid to show the location of the decimal point.

PRACTICE 8

Example 3: A chemical compound weighs 12.8 kilograms. If the compound is divided equally into five portions, how many kilograms will each weigh?

1. Divide. 12.8 ÷ 5 = **2.56**

2. Write the answer in the blank boxes. Then fill in the appropriate circles in the grid.

Solve. Mark your answers in the grids on the right side of the page. You <u>MAY</u> use your calculator.

1. On a business trip, Alex had to buy gasoline three times. He bought 12.6, 9.8, and 13.2 gallons of gasoline. How many gallons did he buy in all?

2. Aubrey withdraws $150 from her bank account and pays $100 to her day-care provider. What fraction of the withdrawal did she spend on day-care?

3. Colleen worked $9\frac{1}{2}$ hours on Monday and $7\frac{1}{2}$ hours on Tuesday. How many hours more did she work on Monday than on Tuesday?

4. A bottle holds 2.6 ounces of food coloring. How many bottles can be completely filled from 100 ounces of food coloring?

5. For a youth picnic, Leah bought 18 cases of soft drinks: 9 were root beer, 6 were lemon-lime, and 3 were cherry cola. Reduced to lowest terms, what fraction of the cases were cherry cola?

6. A sheet of foam board is 0.5 centimeter thick. How many sheets of the board can be stacked in a space that is 12.5 centimeters high?

STUDY ADVICE

Are you sticking to your study schedule? If not, does it need to be adjusted to make way for other commitments, or can you cut out other activities to make more time to study? You *can* get your high school equivalency degree, but you've got to commit to your studies.

DECIMALS AND FRACTIONS PRACTICE QUESTIONS

Directions: You MAY use your calculator.

1. A wooden flooring strip is $20\frac{1}{2}$ inches long. If you cut off $4\frac{3}{4}$ inches from one end, what will be the new length of the strip in inches?

   A. $16\frac{3}{4}$
   B. $16\frac{1}{4}$
   C. $15\frac{3}{4}$
   D. $15\frac{1}{4}$

2. A box of cereal costs $4.69. The package label says that the box contains 19 servings. What is the cost of 1 serving to the nearest cent?

   A. $0.02
   B. $0.25
   C. $0.47
   D. $2.46

3. How much would a computer system cost if it is priced as shown below?

Pay $200 down and make 12 monthly payments of only $98.85.

   A. $3586.20
   B. $2400.00
   C. $1386.20
   D. $1186.20

4. Unleaded gasoline sells for $2.869 per gallon. How much would $10\frac{1}{2}$ gallons cost? Round your answer to the nearest cent.

   A. $13.40
   B. $28.69
   C. $30.12
   D. $301.20

5. Three packages weigh $1\frac{1}{2}$ pounds, $4\frac{3}{4}$ pounds, and $2\frac{3}{10}$ pounds. What is the average weight, in pounds, of the packages? (*Hint:* Add the weights, then divide by the number of packages.)

   A. 2.14
   B. 2.85
   C. 4.75
   D. 8.55

6. Gina is paid $8 an hour. If she earned $258 in 1 week, how many hours did she work?

   A. $34\frac{1}{2}$
   B. $32\frac{1}{3}$
   C. $32\frac{1}{4}$
   D. $32\frac{1}{5}$

7. A developer plans to build homes on $20\frac{1}{2}$ acres. She estimates that $6\frac{1}{4}$ acres will be used for roads. The remaining land will be divided into $\frac{1}{4}$-acre lots. How many lots can the subdivision include?

   A. 7
   B. 57
   C. 81
   D. 107

8. A school buys 1000 white-board markers. Below is the price per marker for two brands. How much did the school save by buying Brand A instead of Brand B?

   Brand A: $0.27 each
   Brand B: $0.36 each

   A. $0.09
   B. $0.90
   C. $9.00
   D. $90.00

Questions 9 and 10 refer to the following information.

Madison Small Animal Clinic Scheduling Guidelines	
New-Patient Appointment	$\frac{3}{4}$ hr
Immunizations	$\frac{1}{4}$ hr
Routine Physical	$\frac{1}{3}$ hr
Dental Scaling	$\frac{3}{4}$ hr
Sick Animal Visit	$\frac{1}{2}$ hr
Serious-Injury Visit (includes X-rays)	$1\frac{1}{4}$ hr

9. Ray is a veterinarian at the small-animal clinic. He has four appointments scheduled for Monday morning: two new-patient appointments, a serious-injury visit, and a dental scaling. In hours, how much time should these appointments take?

   A. $2\frac{3}{4}$

   B. $3\frac{1}{2}$

   C. $3\frac{3}{4}$

   D. 4

10. Jennifer works $3\frac{1}{2}$ hours each morning at the clinic. How many routine physicals could she complete in one morning?

    A.   4
    B.   9
    C.   10
    D.   11

11. A minor-league baseball stadium has 6000 seats. On Beach Towel Night, the stadium sold 5500 of its available seats. What fraction of the seats were sold?

    A. $\frac{5}{6}$

    B. $\frac{8}{9}$

    C. $\frac{9}{10}$

    D. $\frac{11}{12}$

12. The City Center parking garage charges $3.50 for the first hour and $1.25 for each additional $\frac{1}{2}$ hour. How much would it cost to park at the garage for $2\frac{1}{2}$ hours?

    A. $4.75
    B. $6.25
    C. $7.25
    D. $9.75

For questions 13 and 14, mark your answers in the grids below.

13. Susan scheduled 84 appointments for patients at a hospital outreach clinic. Only 56 patients kept their appointments. What fraction of the scheduled appointments were kept?

14. This portion of a gas bill compares a household's natural gas usage for December of this year and last year.

Gas Bill Comparison Average Daily Usage			
This Year		**Last Year**	
Dec	3.13 therms	Dec	3.97 therms

How many more therms of natural gas did the household use in December of last year than December of this year? Express your answer as a decimal.

15. Jim and Carl have until 1 p.m. to load 250 boxes. By 12:30 p.m., 175 of the boxes are loaded. What fraction of the boxes has not been loaded?

   A. $\frac{1}{5}$

   B. $\frac{3}{10}$

   C. $\frac{3}{5}$

   D. $\frac{7}{10}$

16. On the number line below, what is the value of A minus B?

   A. $\frac{1}{4}$

   B. $\frac{5}{8}$

   C. $\frac{7}{8}$

   D. $1\frac{1}{8}$

17. Scott is driving about 380 miles from Los Angeles to San Francisco. He plans to cover $\frac{3}{4}$ of the distance before noon. How many miles does he plan to drive before noon?

   A. 285
   B. 254
   C. 126
   D. 95

18. A cookie recipe calls for $1\frac{2}{3}$ cups of sugar. If you wanted to make half the quantity shown in the recipe, how many cups of sugar would you use?

   A. $\frac{2}{5}$

   B. $\frac{2}{3}$

   C. $\frac{5}{6}$

   D. $1\frac{1}{6}$

19. How many miles would a map distance of $\frac{5}{8}$ inch represent if $1\,\text{in} = 240\,\text{mi}$?

   A. 40
   B. 130
   C. 150
   D. 200

Question 20 is based on the following information.

Carbide Steel Drill Bits		
Description	Size (inches)	Price
Cutter	$\frac{9}{16}$	$6.19
Core Box	$\frac{5}{32}$	$16.40
Classic	$\frac{3}{8}$	$17.85
Bevel	$\frac{1}{2}$	$10.50

20. Which of the following shows the drill bits arranged in order from least to greatest in size?

   A. cutter, bevel, classic, core box
   B. core box, bevel, classic, cutter
   C. bevel, classic, cutter, core box
   D. core box, classic, bevel, cutter

21. Joe is going to order a pizza. He will eat at least $\frac{1}{2}$ of it. If he's very hungry, he might eat as much as $\frac{7}{8}$ of it. Identify the two points on the number line below that represent the minimum fraction of the pizza Joe might have left over and the maximum fraction of the pizza Joe might have left over.

   A. W and Z
   B. W and Y
   C. X and Z
   D. Y and Z

22. A project should take no more than 60 hours. If John can spare 7.5 hours per day to work on the project, what is the maximum number of days it will take him to finish?

   A. 6
   B. 7
   C. 8
   D. 9

23. A survey shows that $\frac{2}{3}$ of all homeowners have a pet. Of those, $\frac{3}{4}$ have either a dog or cat. Of the homeowners surveyed, what fraction has either a dog or a cat?

  A. $\frac{1}{2}$

  B. $\frac{3}{4}$

  C. $\frac{5}{7}$

  D. $\frac{6}{7}$

24. At Wyman Shipping, 140 employees work during the day shift. At night, the crew is $\frac{2}{5}$ the size of the day shift. How many workers are scheduled to work the night shift?

  A. 28
  B. 56
  C. 70
  D. 94

Question 25 refers to the following map.

The map below shows the distance, in miles, between four stores.

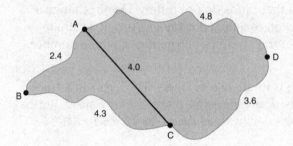

25. Maya drives a van that delivers supplies to each of the stores. On Friday, she traveled the following route.

  Store A to Store B
  Store B to Store C
  Store C to Store D
  Store D to Store C
  Store C to Store A

  How many miles did she drive in all?

  A. 13.9
  B. 15.1
  C. 17.9
  D. 19.1

26. From a wooden dowel $12\frac{1}{2}$ feet long, Jamie cut two pieces, each $3\frac{3}{4}$ feet long. How long, in feet, is the remaining piece?

  A. $8\frac{3}{4}$

  B. $7\frac{1}{2}$

  C. $6\frac{1}{2}$

  D. 5

27. Luis bought 20 shares of stock, priced at $26.38 per share. He also paid an $8 transaction fee. How much did he pay?

  A. $687.60
  B. $535.60
  C. $527.60
  D. $519.60

For questions 28 and 29, mark your answers in the grids below.

28. A mat board is 60 inches wide. How many strips measuring 0.75 inches wide can be cut from the board? (Assume no waste from the cuts.)

29. Of his take-home pay each month, Jerry spends $\frac{1}{6}$ on a car payment and $\frac{1}{4}$ on food. What fraction of his take-home pay is left after paying for these two items?

28.

	⊘	⊘	⊘	
⊙	⊙	⊙	⊙	⊙
⓪	⓪	⓪	⓪	⓪
①	①	①	①	①
②	②	②	②	②
③	③	③	③	③
④	④	④	④	④
⑤	⑤	⑤	⑤	⑤
⑥	⑥	⑥	⑥	⑥
⑦	⑦	⑦	⑦	⑦
⑧	⑧	⑧	⑧	⑧
⑨	⑨	⑨	⑨	⑨

29.

	⊘	⊘	⊘	
⊙	⊙	⊙	⊙	⊙
⓪	⓪	⓪	⓪	⓪
①	①	①	①	①
②	②	②	②	②
③	③	③	③	③
④	④	④	④	④
⑤	⑤	⑤	⑤	⑤
⑥	⑥	⑥	⑥	⑥
⑦	⑦	⑦	⑦	⑦
⑧	⑧	⑧	⑧	⑧
⑨	⑨	⑨	⑨	⑨

LESSON 1

Ratio and Proportion

Ratio

A **ratio** compares two numbers. You can write a ratio using the word *to*, using a colon (:), or using fraction form.

Example 1: A softball pitcher strikes out four batters for every one batter that she walks. What is the ratio of strikeouts to walks?

Always write the numbers in the ratio in the same order in which they appear in the question.

4 to 1   4:1 $\dfrac{4}{1}$

KEY IDEAS

- A ratio has two terms and can be written in words, with a colon, or as a fraction.
- Ratios are simplified by reducing to lowest terms.
- The terms in a ratio can have different labels.

Ratios are similar to fractions. They have two terms, and they can be simplified by reducing to lowest terms.

Example 2: Frank manages a small drugstore. During a two-hour period, he counts 25 cash sales and 15 credit card sales. What is the ratio of credit card to cash sales?

1. Write the ratio as a fraction with the terms in the correct order: credit card to cash sales.

$$\dfrac{\text{credit card sales}}{\text{cash sales}} = \dfrac{15}{25}$$

2. Reduce to lowest terms. The ratio of credit card to cash sales is **3 to 5.**

$$\dfrac{15 \div 5}{25 \div 5} = \dfrac{3}{5}$$

There are some fraction rules that ratios do not follow. Do not change a ratio that is an improper fraction to a mixed number. Also, if a ratio in fraction form has a denominator of 1, <u>do not</u> write it as a whole number. Leave it in fraction form.

TASC TEST TIP

The terms in a ratio must be written in the order given by the words of the question. Don't be fooled by an answer choice on a multiple-choice question that reverses the order of the numbers.

Another important difference is in the use of labels. The terms in a fraction have the same unit labels: $\frac{5}{6}$ *of a pie means 5 slices out of 6 slices.* Ratios <u>may</u> have different labels: *The sale advertised 6 cans for \$1, a 6:1 ratio.*

To write a ratio, you may need to perform one or more basic operations to find one of the terms.

Example 3: A football team won 12 games and lost 8. There were no tied games. What is the ratio of games won to games played?

1. The problem does not tell you the number of games played. Add the games won to the games lost to find the games played.

12 won + 8 lost = 20 played

2. Write the ratio in the correct order and simplify. **The team won 3 games for every 5 games it played, a 3:5 ratio.**

$$\dfrac{\text{games won}}{\text{games played}} = \dfrac{12}{20} = \dfrac{12 \div 4}{20 \div 4} = \dfrac{3}{5}$$

PRACTICE 1.1

A. Write each ratio as a fraction in lowest terms.

1. Stan made 24 sales in 6 hours. What is the ratio of sales to hours?

2. Carol's monthly take-home pay is $1500. She spends $250 a month on food. What is the ratio of food costs to take-home dollars?

3. A toy rocket travels 180 ft in 15 sec. What is the ratio of feet to seconds?

4. At Phil's work, there are 12 part-time workers and 18 full-time workers. What is the ratio of part-time workers to total workers?

5. Juanita drove 336 miles on 14 gallons of gasoline. What is the ratio of miles to gallons?

6. Lynn estimates that a roofing job will cost $1500. Bo estimates that the same job will cost $2400. What is the ratio of Lynn's estimate to Bo's estimate?

7. A basketball player attempted 32 free throws and made 20. What is the ratio of free throws made to free throws missed?

8. There are 10 men and 14 women in Kathleen's math class. What is the ratio of women to the total number of students in the class?

9. To paint his apartment, Alex bought 6 gallons of paint to cover 1440 square feet. What is the ratio of square feet to gallons of paint?

B. Choose the one best answer to each question.

Questions 10 through 12 refer to the following information.

Three candidates are running for mayor. Below are the results of a survey of 600 registered voters.

Candidate	Number of Supporters
Stothard	220
Mesa	180
Newmark	50
Undecided	150

10. What is the ratio of Mesa's supporters to Stothard's supporters?
    A. 9:11
    B. 11:9
    C. 11:20
    D. 20:11

11. What is the ratio of voters who prefer Mesa to the total number surveyed?
    A. 3 to 7
    B. 3 to 10
    C. 3 to 13
    D. 11 to 30

12. What is the ratio of undecided voters to voters who have made a decision?
    A. $\frac{1}{4}$
    B. $\frac{1}{3}$
    C. $\frac{3}{1}$
    D. $\frac{4}{1}$

13. Soan made a $400 down payment on a washer and dryer that cost a total of $1200. What is the ratio of the amount Soan has paid to the amount he still owes?
    A. 1 to 4
    B. 1 to 3
    C. 1 to 2
    D. 2 to 3

14. A team played 77 games and won 56 of them. There were no tied games. What is the ratio of wins to losses?
    A. 3:8
    B. 8:11
    C. 11:8
    D. 8:3

Proportion

A **proportion** is an equation that shows that two ratios are equal. The **cross products** in a true proportion are equal. In other words, when you multiply diagonally across the equal sign, the products are equal.

Example 4: The directions on a can of powdered drink mix say to add 3 cups of water to every 2 scoops of drink mix. Matt adds 12 cups of water to 8 scoops of drink mix. Did he make the drink correctly?

1. Write a proportion, making sure the terms of the ratios are in the same order.

$$\frac{\text{Cups}}{\text{scoops}} \quad \frac{3}{2} \diagup\hspace{-1.1em}\diagdown \frac{12}{8}$$

2. Cross multiply and compare the products. Since the products are the same, the ratios are equal. **Matt made the drink correctly.**

$$3 \times 8 = 24$$
$$2 \times 12 = 24$$

In most proportion problems, you are asked to solve for a missing term.

Example 5: A map scale says that 2 inches = 150 miles. What actual distance would a map distance of 5 inches represent?

1. Write a proportion with both ratios in the same form: inches to miles. The variable x represents the unknown distance.

$$\frac{\text{inches}}{\text{miles}} \quad \frac{2}{150} = \frac{5}{x}$$

2. Locate the term in the first ratio that is diagonal from the known term in the second ratio. Cross multiply.

$$\frac{2}{150} \diagup\hspace{-1.1em}\diagdown \frac{5}{x}$$
$$150 \times 5 = 750$$

3. Divide the result by the remaining known term to find the value of x.

$$750 \div 2 = \textbf{375 miles}$$

Some proportion problems ask you to find a **rate.** A rate compares a quantity to 1. When a rate is written in fraction form, its denominator is always 1. In word form, rates are often expressed using the word *per.*

Example 6: Connie drove 276 miles on 12 gallons of gasoline. How many miles per gallon did she get on the trip?

1. Gas mileage is one kind of rate. You need to find how many miles Connie drove on one gallon of gasoline.

$$\frac{\text{miles}}{\text{gallons}} \quad \frac{276}{12} = \frac{x}{1}$$

2. Solve.

$$276 \times 1 = 276$$
$$276 \div 12 = \textbf{23 miles per gallon}$$

Using your calculator, you can solve proportion problems in one series of calculations.

Example 7: Find the value of x in the proportion $\dfrac{6}{16} = \dfrac{21}{x}$.

You need to multiply 16 and 21, then divide by 6. On the TI-30XS MultiView™ calculator:

1. Press 16 ⊠ 21 ÷ 6.

2. Then press enter. The right side of the display will read 56.

The missing term is **56.**

Note: When working a problem, ask yourself if it can be solved using proportion. This may be possible when two quantities are compared or when three values are given and you are asked to find a fourth.

PRACTICE 1.2

A. Solve for the missing term in each proportion problem. You <u>MAY</u> use your calculator for questions 9 through 16. *Note*: Answers will not always be whole numbers.

1. $\frac{2}{3} = \frac{x}{18}$

2. $\frac{3}{5} = \frac{27}{x}$

3. $\frac{6}{5} = \frac{3}{x}$

4. $\frac{15}{2} = \frac{x}{8}$

5. $\frac{4}{\$212} = \frac{7}{x}$

6. $\frac{25}{6} = \frac{400}{x}$

7. $\frac{7}{30} = \frac{x}{9}$

8. $\frac{0.5}{12} = \frac{3}{x}$

9. $\frac{20}{2.5} = \frac{100}{x}$

10. $\frac{\$5.96}{2} = \frac{x}{3}$

11. $\frac{12}{5} = \frac{3}{x}$

12. $\frac{4}{60} = \frac{2.5}{x}$

13. $\frac{3}{19} = \frac{x}{114}$

14. $\frac{9}{\$80.10} = \frac{x}{\$284.80}$

15. $\frac{\$26.00}{4} = \frac{x}{7}$

16. $\frac{24}{96} = \frac{7}{x}$

B. Choose the <u>one best answer</u> to each question. You <u>MAY</u> use your calculator for questions 20 through 22.

17. A store is advertising the following sale:

Tomato Soup
4 cans for $0.98

    To the nearest cent, how much would five cans of tomato soup cost?

    A. $0.25
    B. $1.23
    C. $2.45
    D. $4.90

18. The Bay City Cardinals have won 5 out of 8 games. At the same rate, how many games will they have to play to win 60 games?

    A. 180
    B. 120
    C. 96
    D. 12

19. Carla drove her truck 414 miles on 18 gallons of gasoline. How many miles did she drive per gallon?

    A. 18
    B. 23
    C. 74
    D. 95

20. The scale on a map reads, "2 cm = 150 km." How many kilometers would be represented by a distance of 4.6 centimeters?

    A. 300
    B. 345
    C. 690
    D. 1380

21. Two ingredients in a recipe are $2\frac{1}{2}$ cups of flour and $1\frac{1}{2}$ cups of sugar. If June keeps the proportion the same, how many cups of flour should she add to 4 cups of sugar?

    A. $6\frac{2}{3}$
    B. 6
    C. 5
    D. $3\frac{3}{4}$

22. Claudia drove 155 miles in 2.5 hours. Which of the following expressions could be used to find how many miles she can drive in 7 hours?

    A. $155 \times 7 \div 2.5$
    B. $2.5 \times 7 \div 155$
    C. $155 \times 2.5 \div 4\,7$
    D. $7 \times 2.5 \times 155$

STUDY ADVICE

Proportions are useful in many ways. If you've ever doubled a recipe or thought about how much it would cost to fill up your car with gas, you've used proportions:

$$\frac{2\,c \text{ flour}}{1 \text{ batch}} = \frac{4\,c \text{ flour}}{2 \text{ batches}} \quad \text{or} \quad \frac{\$3.99}{1 \text{ gallon}} = \frac{\$39.90}{10 \text{ gallons}}$$

Proportions simply ask you to apply these real-world concepts.

LESSON 2

Percents

Percent means "per hundred" or "out of one hundred." For example, if you have $100 and you spend $25, you spent $25 out of $100, or 25% of your money.

Since percent is a way of showing part of a whole, it has much in common with fractions and decimals. To convert a percent to a fraction, write the percent over 100 and reduce. To convert percents to decimals, drop the percent symbol and move the decimal point two places to the left.

<table>
<tr><td>**Percent to Fraction**</td><td>**Percent to Decimal**</td></tr>
<tr><td>$25\% = \frac{25}{100} = \frac{1}{4}$</td><td>$25\% = .25 = 0.25$</td></tr>
</table>

In any percent problem, there are three elements: the base, the part, and the rate. The **base, or the whole,** is the whole quantity, or amount, that the problem is about. The **part** (also called a **percentage**) is a portion of the base. The **rate** is a number followed by the percent symbol (%).

Example 1: At a restaurant, Janice's bill is $20. She gives the waiter a tip of $3, which is 15% of her bill. Identify the base, part, and rate in this situation.

The entire bill of $20 is the whole. The $3 tip is part of the whole, and the rate is 15%.

One way to think of a percent problem is as a proportion. In Example 1, there are two ratios. The $3 tip is part of the $20 total bill, and 15% is the same as $\frac{15}{100}$. Since the two ratios are equal, they can be written as a proportion.

$$\frac{\text{part}}{\text{base}} \quad \frac{3}{20} = \frac{15}{100}$$

Cross multiply to prove the ratios are equal.

$$20 \times 15 = 300$$
$$3 \times 100 = 300$$

You can solve percent problems by setting up a proportion and solving for the missing elements. Just remember to express the percent as a number over 100.

Example 2: At a plant that manufactures lighting fixtures, it is expected that about 2% of the fixtures assembled each day will have some type of defect. If 900 fixtures are completed in one day, how many are expected to be defective?

1. Write a proportion. Remember that 2% means 2 out of 100. Use the variable x to stand for the number of defective fixtures.

$$\frac{\text{part}}{\text{base}} = \frac{\text{rate}}{100}$$
$$\frac{x}{900} = \frac{2}{100}$$

2. Solve for x. Cross multiply and divide by the remaining number. **The company can expect about 18 defective fixtures.**

$$900 \times 2 = 1800$$
$$1800 \div 100 = \mathbf{18}$$

KEY IDEAS

- The percent symbol (%) means "out of 100."
- The three elements of a percent problem are the base (or the whole), the part, and the rate.
- Percent problems can be solved by writing a proportion that has a denominator of 100.

TASC TEST TIP

The word "of" often comes before the base in a percent problem. For example, if you are asked to find 75% of 250, you know that 250 is the base.

PRACTICE 2

A. For each situation, identify and label the base, part, and rate.

1. Victor owes his uncle $1000. Recently, he gave his uncle $200. The payment was 20% of the money he owes.

2. On a test with 80 problems, Sophie got 72 problems right. In other words, she answered 90% of the problems correctly.

3. The Kang family made a down payment of $2,740 on a new car. The down payment was 20% of the purchase price of $13,700.

4. Zoe's take-home pay each month is $2000. She spends $500 on rent each month, which is 25% of her take-home pay.

5. This year, Rafael has 60 regular customers, which is 150% of the 40 regular customers he had last year.

6. Kayla bought a dress for $38. She paid $3.23 in sales tax. The sales tax rate in her state is 8.5%.

7. Misako's employer withholds 15% of her salary each paycheck for taxes. Misako earns $900 each week, and her tax withholding is $135.

8. Harrison got a 10% raise. Before the raise, his hourly wage was $10.70. Now he earns an additional $1.07 per hour.

9. Kim Industries has 800 employees. Of those, 200 workers, or 25%, work part-time.

10. In an election, 5,000 of the 12,500 registered voters actually voted. Only 40% of the registered voters actually voted.

B. Choose the <u>one best answer</u> to each question. Use the proportion $\frac{part}{base} = \frac{rate}{100}$ to solve each problem.

<u>Questions 11 and 12 refer to the following information.</u>

A local newspaper printed the following high school basketball standings:

Team	Wins	Losses
Fairfax	9	3
Hamilton	8	4
Bravo	6	6
Mountain View	4	8
Lincoln	3	9

11. Which of the following expressions could be used to find what percent of its total games Fairfax has won?

   A. $\dfrac{9 \times 100}{12}$

   B. $\dfrac{3 \times 100}{12}$

   C. $\dfrac{12 \times 100}{9}$

   D. $\dfrac{6 \times 100}{12}$

12. What percent of its games did Bravo win?

   A. 100%
   B. 75%
   C. 60%
   D. 50%

13. A jacket with a price tag of $128 is on a rack with the following sign:

   > All Items:
   > 25% off marked price
   > Discount taken at register

   By how much will the price be reduced when the jacket is taken to the register?

   A. $4
   B. $25
   C. $32
   D. $96

LESSON 3

Using the Percent Formula

Solving for Part

You have seen how to use proportion to solve percent problems. You can also solve percent problems using the formula **Base × Rate = Part**. (**Remember that the base can also be referred to as the** *whole*.)

Study the diagram at the right to learn how to use the formula. To use the diagram, cover the element you need to solve for: B = Base, R = Rate (percent), and P = Part. Then perform the operation that connects the remaining elements.

Example 1: A company offers its employees two health plans. In a recent newsletter, the personnel department stated that 70% of the employees chose Plan A. If the company has 320 workers, how many chose Plan A?

1. The rate is 70%, and the base is 320, the total number of workers. You need to solve for the part. Using the diagram, cover P for part. You can see that you need to multiply to solve the problem.

2. Change the percent to a decimal and multiply.
   Out of 320 workers, 224 chose Plan A.

   $70\% = 0.7$

   $320 \times 0.7 = \mathbf{224}$

Solving for Rate

Rewrite the percent formula to solve for rate. Use the formula **Part ÷ Base = Rate**. You can use the diagram to help you remember the formula.

Example 2: A computer system is regularly priced at $1600. On Friday, the manager reduced the price by $640. By what percent did the manager discount the computer system?

1. The base is $1600, the regular price. The part is $640, the amount the price was reduced. You are asked to find the rate of the discount. Cover R for rate (percent). You need to divide the part by the base to solve the problem.

2. Divide 640 by 1600.

3. Convert the decimal answer to a percent by moving the decimal point two places to the right and adding the percent sign. The price reduction was a **40%** discount.

$$\begin{array}{r} 0.4 \\ 1600\overline{)640.0} \\ \underline{640.0} \end{array}$$

$0.4 = 40 = \mathbf{40\%}$

Always ask yourself whether your answer seems reasonable. For example, you know that 40% is a little less than $\frac{1}{2}$, and $\frac{1}{2}$ of $1600 is $800. Since $640 is a little less than $800, it is a reasonable answer.

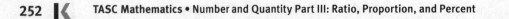

PRACTICE 3.1

A. Solve. You MAY use a calculator for questions 9 through 16.

1. What is 20% of $25?

2. Find 90% of 200.

3. What is 35% of 400?

4. What percent is 19 out of 20?

5. 42 is what percent of 168?

6. What percent is $18 out of $600?

7. Find $33\frac{1}{3}\%$ of 51. (*Hint:* $33\frac{1}{3}\% = \frac{1}{3}$)

8. What is 125% of $48?

9. 240 is what percent of 120?

10. What percent is 3 out of 60?

11. $52 is what percent of $650?

12. Find $8\frac{1}{2}\%$ of $46.

13. $0.65 is what percent of $10.00?

14. Find 28% of $1300.

15. What percent is 2.5 out of 4?

16. Find $66\frac{2}{3}\%$ of 108. (*Hint:* $66\frac{2}{3}\% = \frac{2}{3}$)

B. Choose the one best answer to each question. You MAY use your calculator.

17. Pat called 120 customers to offer a software upgrade. Of those he called, 72 purchased the upgrade. What percent agreed to the purchase?

    A. 40%
    B. 48%
    C. 60%
    D. $66\frac{2}{3}\%$

18. Douglas received a 6% raise. If his old monthly salary was $2,250, what is his monthly salary now? (*Hint:* Find the amount of the raise. Then add the raise to the previous monthly salary.)

    A. $2,256
    B. $2,385
    C. $3,600
    D. $13,500

19. At a restaurant, Levy's total bill is $46. If he wants to tip 15%, how much should he leave as a tip?

    A. $690.00
    B. $31.00
    C. $15.00
    D. $6.90

20. The following advertisement for sporting goods appeared in the newspaper. What percent of the original price is the sale price?

    | Little League Package |
    | Magnum bat, tote bag, and youth cleats |
    | Only $45.50 |
    | Originally $65 |

    A. 20%
    B. 31%
    C. 44%
    D. 70%

21. Lydia pays $3 sales tax on a $50 purchase. Which of the following expressions could be used to find the sales tax rate in her state?

    A. $\dfrac{\$3 \times 100}{\$50}$

    B. $\dfrac{\$3 \times \$50}{100}$

    C. $\$3 \times \$50 \times 100$

    D. $\$3 \div \$50$

STUDY ADVICE

Remember as you study to pay particular attention to words in bold and the Key Ideas on each page on the left. Also, study each worked example to see how to apply the concepts in your own practice.

Solving for Base

Some problems on the TASC Mathematics Test may require you to solve for the base in a percent situation. Remember, the base represents the whole item or group. Read each situation carefully to figure out which element is missing. Then choose the correct method for solving the problem.

Example 3: In a math class, 75% of the students got at least a B grade on the final exam. If 18 students got at least a B, how many students are in the class?

1. Analyze the situation. The 18 students are part of the larger class. You know that the 18 students are 75% of the whole group, so 75% is the rate and the base is unknown.

   Use the diagram. Cover B for base. You need to divide the part by the rate to solve the problem.

2. Convert the rate to a decimal (75% = 0.75) and divide. There are **24 students** in the class.

$$\begin{array}{r} 24 \\ 0.75\overline{)18.00} \\ \underline{150} \\ 300 \\ \underline{300} \\ 0 \end{array}$$

Most of the time, we work with percents that are less than 100%. When a percent is less than 100%, the part is less than the base. However, it is possible to have a situation in which the part is greater than the base. When this occurs, the percent will be greater than 100%.

Example 4: The workforce at Eastland Inc. is growing rapidly. The number of employees this year is 225% of the number last year. If there are 135 employees this year, how many employees did the company have last year?

1. The base is the number of employees the company had last year. This year's number is a percent of last year's number. Therefore, the rate is 225%, the part is 135, and the base is unknown.

2. Convert 225% to a decimal. Drop the % sign and move the decimal point two places to the left.

   $225\% = 2.25 = 2.25$

3. Divide the part (135) by the rate (2.25). Last year, there were only **60 employees**.

$$\begin{array}{r} 60 \\ 2.25\overline{)135.00} \\ \underline{135.0} \\ 0 \end{array}$$

There is often more than one way to approach the solution to a problem. Both the percent formula presented in this lesson and the proportion method from Lesson 1 can be used to solve Example 4.

Formula method: $\dfrac{135}{2.25}$ Proportion method: $\dfrac{135 \times 100}{225}$

If you evaluate both methods using a calculator, both expressions equal 60, the correct solution.

Note: Don't begin calculations before you completely analyze a situation. Every percent problem has three elements. Make sure you know which one is missing before you multiply or divide.

PRACTICE 3.2

A. Find the missing element in each set. You MAY NOT use a calculator.

1. $35 is 20% of what amount?

2. 5% of what number is 14?

3. 3.2 is 50% of what number?

4. $170 is 85% of what amount?

5. 24 is 80% of what number?

6. $105 is 125% of what amount?

7. 190 is 95% of what number?

8. What number is 15% of 60?

9. 90% of $15 is what number?

10. $42 is what percent of $168?

11. $150 is 200% of what amount?

12. 15% of $62 is what amount?

13. 9 is 1% of what number?

14. What percent is 126 of 140?

15. 65% of $1200 is what amount?

16. 5% of an amount is $156. What is the amount?

17. $2\frac{1}{2}$% of a number is 100. What is the number?

18. What percent is $15.60 of $156.00?

B. Choose the one best answer to each question. You MAY use your calculator.

19. Kevin's total payroll deductions are 30% of his earnings. If his deductions add up to $369 for a two-week period, how much were his earnings for the period?

   A. $110.70
   B. $123.00
   C. $1,230.00
   D. $11,070.00

20. A city council established the following budget to improve public transportation.

	Project Budget
Salaries	50%
Office lease	35%
Equipment	6%
Supplies	2%
Miscellaneous	7%

If $72,000 is allotted for equipment, what is the total budget for the project?

   A. $432,000
   B. $940,000
   C. $1,200,000
   D. $120,000,000

21. Jack earns a 5% commission on each sale. If he is paid a $160 commission, which of the following expressions could be used to find the amount of the sale?

   A. $\dfrac{5 \times 100}{160}$

   B. $\dfrac{160 \times 100}{5}$

   C. $\dfrac{5 \times 160}{100}$

   D. $5 \times 100 \times 1.60$

22. American Loan Company mailed 3600 customers an application for a new credit card. Only 20% of the customers returned the application. How many customers returned the application?

   A.   72
   B.   180
   C.   720
   D. 180,000

LESSON 4

Percent Calculator Skills

By changing a percent to either a fraction or decimal, you can use a calculator to solve percent problems. The following examples are worked out using the keys on the TI-30XS MultiView™. Remember, your calculator may differ if you are taking the TASC on paper.

Example 1: What is 25% of 120? Try both decimals and fractions.

Change 25% to the decimal (.25), multiply times 120, and press (enter). **30** is on the right of the display.

Change 25% to the fraction $\frac{25}{100}$ using the $\left[\frac{n}{d}\right]$ key, multiply times 120, and press (enter). **30** is on the right of the display.

On the Display

.25*120	30

$\frac{25}{100}$*120	30

Using either decimals or fractions, you can find that **30** is 25% of 120.

When you use the *percent 2nd* function, you don't have to convert the percent to a fraction or decimal. Practice this function below to multiply to find the **part** when you are given the rate (percent).

Example 2: What is 65% of $360?

Keys to Press

1. Type the base, 360, and press the multiplication sign.

360 [×]

2. Type the rate (65). Press the 2nd function key and engage the percent 2nd function—over the [( ] key. Then press (enter).

65
(2nd) [% ( ] (enter)

On the Display

360*	

360*65%	234

The amount **$234** is 65% of $360.

You can use the percent function to divide to find the **base** when given the rate.

Example 3: Ned paid $150 for a stereo. The amount Ned paid was 20% of the original cost. What was the original cost of the stereo?

Keys to Press

1. Enter the base, 150, and press the division sign.

150 [÷]

2. Enter 20 and press the 2nd function key and the [( ] key. Then press *enter*.

20
(2nd) [% ( ] (enter)

On the Display

150÷	

150÷20%	750

The original cost of the stereo appears on the right of the display: **$750.**

KEY IDEAS

- One way to solve percent problems on the calculator is to change the percent to a decimal or a fraction.
- On the TI-30XS MultiView™ calculator, you can use the percent 2nd function to find the part and the base.
- To create a percent, use the 2nd function, %, which is in green over the left parenthesis [( ] key.

KEY IDEAS

If you are using the TI-30XS MultiView™, practice using the Delete key when you make a mistake in a problem. That will erase your latest entry. The Clear key will erase the entire entry. If you are using a different calculator, find the appropriate keys for these two functions and practice using them.

PRACTICE 4

A. Solve. You <u>MAY</u> use your calculator.

1. Find 46% of $130.

2. 14% of what amount is $13.44?

3. What is 12% of $126?

4. What number is $62\frac{1}{2}$% of 64?

5. 12 is what percent of 400?

6. A number is 32% of 6500. What is the number?

7. 36 is what percent of 144?

8. 90% of what number is 63?

9. Find 7% of 360.

10. What number is $33\frac{1}{3}$% of 237?

11. 25 is what percent of 1000?

12. What is $12\frac{1}{2}$% of 384?

13. 390 is what percent of 500?

14. Find 2% of $800.

15. 32% of what number is 80?

16. What number is $87\frac{1}{2}$% of 16?

17. $112 is what percent of $1600?

18. A number is $66\frac{2}{3}$% of 414. What is the number?

B. Choose the <u>one best answer</u> to each question. You <u>MAY</u> use your calculator.

<u>Questions 19 and 20</u> refer to the following chart.

Shipping and Handling Information	
For Items Costing:	**% of Order + Handling:**
$20 or less	3% + $1.50
$20.01 to $50	4% + $2.50
$50.01 to $100	5% + $4.00
$100.01 or more	8%

19. Chanel placed an $84 order. How much shipping and handling will she be charged on her order?

   A. $4.20
   B. $4.40
   C. $8.20
   D. $8.36

20. Jason placed an order totaling $110. Zola placed a $90 order. How much more did Jason pay in shipping and handling than Zola?

   A. $0.30
   B. $4.30
   C. $4.50
   D. $20.00

21. In an election, 3190 out of 3625 registered voters voted against a tax increase. What percent of the registered voters voted against the increase?

   A. 43%
   B. 83%
   C. 88%
   D. 98%

22. A baseball player has the following statistics. To the nearest percent, what percent of the player's at bats were strikeouts?

At Bats	Hits	Home Runs	Walks	Strikeouts
410	108	2	70	63

   A. 90%
   B. 58%
   C. 26%
   D. 15%

STUDY ADVICE

Remember not to rely too much on the calculator during the TASC Mathematics Test. Not all questions will require you to do lots of math, so don't just start plugging numbers into the calculator. First think about what the problem is asking for.

LESSON 5

Interest

Interest is a fee paid for the use of someone else's money. If you put money in a savings account, you receive interest from the bank. If you borrow money, you pay interest. In each case, the amount that you invest or borrow is called the **principal.**

Simple interest is a percent of the principal multiplied by the length of the loan. This is how simple interest is calculated:

simple interest Interest = principal × rate × time

Or, using abbreviations: $I = prt$

Example 1: Asher borrows $2500 from his uncle for three years at 6% simple interest. How much interest will he pay on the loan?

1. Write the rate as a decimal.   6% = 0.06

2. Substitute the known values in the formula. Multiply.

$$I = prt$$
$$= \$2500 \times 0.06 \times 3$$
$$= \mathbf{\$450}$$

Asher will pay **$450** in interest.

Some problems ask you to find the **amount paid back.** This adds an additional step to an interest problem. In Example 1, Asher will owe $450 in interest at the end of three years. However, he will pay back the interest ($450) plus the principal ($2500): $2500 + $450 = $2950. When he has finished paying the loan, Asher will have paid his uncle $2950.

Most bank accounts, loans, and credit cards do not use simple interest. Instead, they use **compound interest,** which means that the interest is periodically added to the principal. That new total is then used to calculate the interest for that period. The formula for compound interest is as follows:

compound interest $A = p\left(1 + \frac{r}{n}\right)^{nt}$

In the formula, A is the amount that will be in the account or owed on the loan after t years. Again, p is the principal and r is the annual interest rate expressed as a decimal. The letter t stands for the number of years since the principal started earning interest. The letter n represents the number of times per year the interest is **compounded,** or added to the principal.

That formula may look intimidating, but just remember: When you see a compound interest problem, simply figure out which pieces of information in the problem represent p, r, n, and t. Then plug those values into the formula. (Your calculator will be handy here. For more information about exponents, see pages 312–315.)

Notice that the simple interest formula at the top of this page allows you to calculate the interest. The compound interest formula allows you to calculate the total amount of the loan or investment after interest has been added. If a question asks you for just the interest on a loan or investment that has compound interest, use the compound interest formula and subtract the principle from the result.

KEY IDEAS

- Simple interest is found by multiplying principal, rate, and time: $I = prt$.
- The time must be written in terms of years. Write months as a fraction of a year.
- To find the amount paid back, add the principal and the interest.

TASC TEST TIP

A formula sheet is provided when you take the Mathematics Test (see pages 168–169). Every time you see a formula in this book, check to see if it is on the formula sheet. If the formula is not there, you will need to memorize it.

PRACTICE 5

Example 2: Malik takes out a bank loan for $2,000 for a period of two years. The bank will charge him 5% interest, compounded quarterly (that is, four times per year). How much will Malik have to pay the bank back two years from now? Round your answer to the nearest dollar.

Step 1: You are asked to solve for A. Identify the other values.

$$p = 2,000 \qquad r = 0.05$$
$$n = 4 \qquad t = 2$$

Step 2: Plug those values into the formula and solve.

$$A = 2,000\left(1 + \tfrac{.05}{4}\right)^{(4 \times 2)}$$

$$A = 2,000(1.0125)^8$$

$$A = 2,000(1.1045) = 2,208.97$$

Malik will pay the bank **$2209** two years from now.

A. **Solve these problems using the interest formulas on the previous page. You MAY use your calculator. Round your answers to the nearest dollar.**

1. Leah borrows $1500 for 2 years at a 12% *simple* interest rate. Find the interest on the loan.

2. Ricardo borrows $1850 for 8 months at 12% *simple* interest. What is the total amount he will pay back at the end of the loan period?

3. Dominica invested $2000 for 3 years at an interest rate of 7%, compounded annually. How much interest did she earn on her money?

4. If you take out a loan of $800 at 14% interest, compounded annually, for 2 years, how much will you have to pay back at the end of the 2 years?

B. **Choose the one best answer to each question. You MAY use your calculator.**

5. Jean borrowed $1300 to buy tools for her job as an auto mechanic. The loan is for 1 year 6 months at 9% simple interest. Which of the following expressions could be used to find the amount she will pay back at the end of the loan period?
   A. $1300 × 1.5 × 0.09
   B. $1300 × 1.5 × 9
   C. $1300 + ($1300 × 9 × 1.5)
   D. $1300 + ($1300 × 0.09 × 1.5)

Questions 6 refers to the following information.

Option	Length of Loan	Simple Interest Rate
A	$2\frac{1}{2}$ years	12%
B	3 years	10%
C	4 years	9%

6. Charlotte needs to borrow $2400. She is considering the three loan options shown above. How much more interest would Charlotte pay if she takes loan option C instead of option A?
   A. $108
   B. $144
   C. $720
   D. $864

LESSON 6

Percent of Change

Percent is often used to show change.

Example 1: Michelle recently started her own business. Last month, she earned $1000. This month, she earned $2000. How could she describe the increase in her earnings?

All of the following statements accurately describe the change.

- Michelle's earnings doubled from last month to this month.

- This month, her earnings increased by 100%.

- This month's earnings are 200% of last month's earnings.

Percent of change compares a new number, which shows an **increase** or a **decrease**, to the original number—the number before the change.

Example 2: Before her raise, Lisa earned $10.50 per hour. Now she earns $11.34 per hour. What percent raise did her boss give her?

1. Subtract to find the amount of change. $\$11.34 - \$10.50 = \$0.84$

2. Divide the amount of change by $10.50, Lisa's wage before the change. Convert the decimal to a percent. Lisa's hourly wage **increased by 8%.** $\dfrac{\$0.84}{\$10.50} = 0.08 = \mathbf{8\%}$

Think carefully about a situation to decide which number is the original amount.

Example 3: A jacket is on sale for $90. Three days ago, the jacket was on sale for $120. By what percent was the price of the jacket reduced?

1. Subtract to find the amount of change. $\$120 - \$90 = \$30$

2. The price of the jacket was $120 before it was $90, so $120 is the original price. Divide the amount of change by $120. The new price is **25% less** than the price three days ago. $\dfrac{\$30}{\$120} = 0.25 = \mathbf{25\%}$

Percent of increase may be greater than 100%.

Example 4: Calvin started his business with 10 employees. Now he has 60 employees. By what percent has his workforce increased?

1. Subtract to find the amount of change. $60 - 10 = 50$

2. Divide by the original number. Convert the number to a percent. Calvin's workforce has **increased by 500%.** $\dfrac{50}{10} = 5.0 = \mathbf{500\%}$

KEY IDEAS

- The amount of change is the difference between the new number and the original number.
- Find the percent of change by dividing the amount of change by the original number.
- Percent of increase may be greater than 100%.

TASC TEST TIP

You can work backward to check your answers. For example, if a price has decreased by 25%, the new price should be 75% of the original price, since 25% + 75% = 100%.

PRACTICE 6

A. Solve as directed. If necessary, round your answer to the nearest percent. You MAY use your calculator for questions 7 through 10.

1. Find the percent of increase from 2000 to 3000.

2. Find the percent of decrease from $2.00 to $1.25.

3. What is the percent of increase from 30 to 90?

4. Find the percent of decrease from 20 to 11.

5. Find the percent of increase from $25 to $30.

6. What is the percent of decrease from 500 to 340?

7. Find the percent of increase from $1.89 to $2.29.

8. What is the percent of decrease from 21 to 3?

9. Find the percent of increase from 65 to 338.

10. What is the percent of decrease from $1550 to $1025?

B. Choose the one best answer to each question. You MAY use your calculator.

11. Justin recently moved from a part-time to a full-time job. Because of the change, his weekly pay increased from $280 to $448. To the nearest percent, by what percent did his income increase?

   A. 38%
   B. 60%
   C. 168%
   D. 267%

12. David bought a computer game on sale for $36. The game was originally $48. What was the percent of decrease in the game's price?

   A. 12%
   B. 25%
   C. $33\frac{1}{3}$%
   D. 75%

13. The Utleys' rent increased from $600 to $636 per month. By what percent did the rent increase?

   A. 4%
   B. 5%
   C. 6%
   D. 7%

Questions 14 and 15 refer to the following information.

Marc sells computer equipment. He buys printers at wholesale and sells them at retail price. Customers who join his discount club pay the member's price.

Printer Pricing Chart

Model Number	Wholesale Price	Retail Price	Member's Price
L310	$63.00	$141.75	$92.15
L1430	$86.00	$150.50	$105.35

14. What is the percent of increase from wholesale to retail price of the L310 model?

   A. 56%
   B. 78%
   C. 125%
   D. 225%

15. For the L1430 model, what is the percent of decrease from retail price to member's price?

   A. 26%
   B. 30%
   C. 43%
   D. 53%

STUDY ADVICE

Here's a quick rule to remember: When determining percent of change—either increase or decrease—the denominator is always the original value. Study these examples to see percent of change in action.

Ratio, Proportion, and Percent
Practice Questions

Directions: You MAY use your calculator.

1. From a total yearly budget of $360,000, the Kimball Foundation spends $30,000 on leasing office space. What is the ratio of dollars spent on office space to dollars spent on other costs?

   A. 12:1
   B. 11:1
   C. 1:11
   D. 1:12

2. A worker can assemble 5 motors in 2 hours. Which of the expressions below could be used to find how long it would take the worker to assemble 50 motors?

   A. $2 \times \dfrac{50}{5}$

   B. $\dfrac{5 \times 50}{2}$

   C. $\dfrac{5}{2 \times 50}$

   D. $2 \times 5 \times 50$

3. Frank owns a discount music store. The table below shows how much Frank pays for certain merchandise items.

Item	Wholesale Price
CDs	$7.20
Posters	$5.60

   To find his selling price, Frank increases each price by 35%. What is the selling price of a poster?

   A. $9.72
   B. $7.56
   C. $5.95
   D. $1.96

4. Neva's car is now worth $12,000. This is 60% of what she paid for it. How much did she pay for the car?

   A. $7,200
   B. $18,000
   C. $19,200
   D. $20,000

5. At a shop, the ratio of union to non-union workers is 7 to 3. If there are 18 nonunion workers at the shop, how many union workers are there?

   A. 21
   B. 25
   C. 42
   D. 126

6. Camilla earned $954 in commission on $15,900 in sales. What is her rate of commission?

   A. 6%
   B. 9%
   C. $16\frac{2}{3}\%$
   D. 60%

7. John spent the following amounts of time building a workbench:

drawing the plans:	2 hours
cutting the wood:	$1\frac{1}{2}$ hours
assembling the workbench:	2 hours
sanding and sealing:	$3\frac{1}{2}$ hours

   What is the ratio of time spent cutting wood to total time spent on the project?

   A. 1:9
   B. 1:6
   C. 1:5
   D. 3:7

Questions 8 and 9 refer to the following information.

Ford County Farmland Usage Total Acreage: 40,000	
Usage	**Number of Acres**
Dairy	22,000
Nursery/greenhouse	3,600
Vegetables/fruits	5,200
Grains	9,200

8. What percent of Ford County farmland is used for the growing of grains, vegetables, or fruits?

   A. 23%
   B. 36%
   C. 57%
   D. 64%

9. One dairy farmer in Ford County is considering selling her farm to developers, who will convert it from a dairy farm to a resort. If this happens, the amount of farmland devoted to dairy in Ford County will decrease by 20%. How many total acres of farmland will Ford County then have if the dairy farmer decides to sell?

   A. 35,600
   B. 32,000
   C. 17,600
   D. 4,400

10. A serving of peanut butter contains 3 grams of saturated fat and 13 grams of unsaturated fat. This amount of fat is 25% of the recommended amount of fat in a 2000-calorie diet. What is the ratio of grams of saturated fat to total fat in a serving of peanut butter?

   A. $\frac{3}{16}$
   B. $\frac{3}{13}$
   C. $\frac{13}{16}$
   D. $\frac{16}{3}$

11. A drawing of a company logo is 4 inches wide and 5 inches long. If the drawing is enlarged so that it is 12.5 inches long, and the original proportions remain unchanged, how many inches wide will the enlarged drawing be?

   A. 7.5
   B. 10
   C. 15.625
   D. 20

For questions 12 and 13, mark your answers in the grids below.

12. A local hospital currently has 184 male patients. If the ratio of male to female patients is 4:3, how many female patients are there in the hospital?

13. A newspaper advertisement contains the following information.

Busy Body Fitness Center Inventory Reduction Blowout! All sale prices are 20% off original price!	
Equipment	**Sale Price**
Treadmill	$1512
Upright bike	$720
Home gym	$3148

In dollars, what was the original price of the upright bike?

14. The Tigers' ratio of wins to losses is 5 to 4. If the team continues winning at the same rate, how many games will the Tigers win in a 72-game season?

   A. 20
   B. 40
   C. 37
   D. 52

15. A television station called 400 adults and asked the following question: "Do you approve of the governor's new education program?" The table below shows the results of the survey:

Response	Percent
Undecided	16%
Yes	32%
No	52%

   Of the people called, how many did not answer "no"?

   A. 64
   B. 128
   C. 192
   D. 208

16. The price of a carton of computer paper decreased from $25 to $20. What was the percent decrease in the price?

   A. 80%
   B. 50%
   C. 20%
   D. 5%

17. Six months ago, Sandra had 55 regular customers. Now, she has 220% as many regular customers as she had six months ago. How many regular customers does Sandra have now?

   A. 121
   B. 90
   C. 66
   D. 25

18. If 1 gram of fat equals 9 calories, what percent of the calories in a Munchies roast beef sandwich come from fat?

Munchies Sandwich Facts		
Sandwich	Fat (grams)	Calories
Roast Beef	6	300
Club Classic	5	335

   A. 2%
   B. 3%
   C. 6%
   D. 18%

19. For every $8 in their budget, the Parks spend $3 on food. If their weekly budget is $704, how much do they spend on food each week?

   A. $88
   B. $192
   C. $235
   D. $264

20. Suddeth Travel estimates that 80% of its employees have more than 12 days of unused sick leave. If 140 employees have more than 12 days of unused sick leave, how many employees work at the agency?

   A. 112
   B. 164
   C. 175
   D. 700

21. The Gladstone Theater has 900 seats. At a recent show, the ratio of tickets sold to tickets unsold was 11 to 1. How many tickets were sold?

A. 75
B. 810
C. 818
D. 825

22. Matthew put $2200 in a savings account for one year and six months. If he earns simple interest at an annual rate of 8%, how much will he have in the account at the end of the time period?

A. $2212
B. $2376
C. $2464
D. $2640

23. A television set that is regularly priced at $410 is on sale for 20% off. What is the sale price of the television set?

A. $82
B. $328
C. $390
D. $492

24. On a county map shown below, the map scale reads, "0.5 in = 60 mi."

What is the actual distance in miles between Lakeview and Riverside?

A. 23
B. 165
C. 300
D. 330

STUDY ADVICE

Congratulations! You've done a ton of work learning the "number and quantity" skills tested by the TASC. While 15% of the questions on the TASC Mathematics Test directly test number and quantity skills, you will also need these skills to work algebra, geometry, and statistics problems. Keep periodically reviewing the first three chapters of this unit as you work through the remaining chapters.

Question 25 refers to the following information.

Leo's Bookstore kept track of the number of customers who visited the store over a 3-day period and the number of those who made a purchase.

Day	Number of Customers	Number of Customers Who Made a Purchase
Friday	112	83
Saturday	138	45
Sunday	140	91

25. Which of the following could be used to find what percent of Sunday's customers did not make a purchase?

A. $\dfrac{91}{140}$

B. $\dfrac{91}{140} \times 100$

C. $\dfrac{(140 - 91)}{140} \times 100$

D. $\dfrac{(140 - 91)}{91} \times 100$

For questions 26 and 27, mark your answers in the grids below.

26. A school admits 9 out of every 14 who apply. At that rate, how many students will be admitted if 420 apply?

27. In a 40-hour workweek, Marcie spends 15 hours answering telephones. What is the ratio of hours spent answering telephones to hours doing other types of work? (Record your answer as a fraction.)

Tables and Pictographs

Data are facts and information. By analyzing data, we can make predictions, draw conclusions, and solve problems. To be useful, data must be organized in some way. A **table** organizes data in columns and rows. The labels on the table will help you understand what the data mean.

Example 1: The table below shows population figures for selected counties in 2000 and 2010 and the land area in square miles for each county.

County	2000 Pop.	2010 Pop.	Land Area in Sq. Mi.
Adams	11,128	15,295	4,255
Bell	25,199	22,707	2,523
Cook	6,532	6,518	2,398
Davis	82,204	90,834	1,139
Evans	139,510	130,748	921

Which county showed the greatest percent of increase in population from 2000 to 2010?

1. **Read the labels.** The first column shows the county names. The second and third columns show population figures. The fourth column shows land area data. You don't need land area to answer this question.

2. **Analyze the data.** Only Adams and Davis counties show increases from 2000 to 2010.

3. **Use the data.** Find the percent of increase for Adams and Davis counties.

Adams: $\dfrac{15,295 - 11,128}{11,128} \approx 0.374 \approx 37\%$; Davis: $\dfrac{90,834 - 82,204}{82,204} \approx 0.105 \approx 10\%$

Adams County shows the greatest percent of increase in population from 2000 to 2010.

A **pictograph** is another way to display data. Pictographs use symbols to compare data. A key shows what value each symbol represents.

Example 2: A city has three public library branches. A librarian kept track of the numbers of books checked out from each branch in a week. He used the data to create the pictograph below.

PRACTICE 1

From March 4 to March 10, how many books were checked out from the South and West branches combined?

1. There are $4\frac{1}{2}$ symbols for the South Branch and 9 symbols for the West branch. Add: $4\frac{1}{2} + 9 = 13\frac{1}{2}$ symbols.

2. Find the value of the symbols. The key states that each symbol equals 150 books. Multiply by 150: $13\frac{1}{2} \times 150 = $ **2025 books.**

A. Use the table on the previous page to answer questions 1 and 2. Use the pictograph on the previous page to answer questions 3 and 4. You **MAY** use a calculator.

1. On average, how many people were there per square mile in Bell County in 2010?

2. To the nearest percent, what was the percent of decrease in Evans County's population from 2000 to 2010?

3. How many more books were checked out from North Branch than from South Branch during the week of March 4?

4. How many books were checked out from all three branches combined?

B. Choose the **one best answer** to each question.

<u>Questions 5 and 6</u> refer to the following table.

Percent of 3-year-old children with school-readiness skills for the years 2004 and 2010		
	2004	**2010**
Recognizes all letters	11%	17%
Counts to 20 or higher	37%	47%
Writes own name	22%	34%
Reads or pretends to read	66%	67%

5. If 100,000 children were surveyed in each year, which category showed the least percent of increase from 2004 to 2010?

  A. Recognizes all letters
  B. Counts to 20 or higher
  C. Writes own name
  D. Reads or pretends to read

6. A community had 350 three-year-old children in 2010. If the chart is representative of the community, how many were able to write their own name?

  A. 34
  B. 97
  C. 119
  D. 134

<u>Questions 7 and 8</u> refer to the following graph.

Mayfair Parking Garage
Daily Average of Parked Cars by Timed Period

7. How many cars are parked in the garage from 12:01 to 4:30 p.m.?

  A. 275
  B. 350
  C. 375
  D. 650

8. How many more cars are parked from 8 p.m. to noon than are parked after 4:30 p.m.?

  A. 75
  B. 100
  C. 175
  D. 200

Bar and Line Graphs

Working with Bar Graphs

A **bar graph** uses bars to represent values. Bar graphs have two axis lines. One line shows a number scale, and the other shows labels for the bars. By comparing the length of a bar to the scale, you can estimate what value the bar represents.

Example 1: A national corporation made a bar graph (shown below) to show the number of discrimination complaints made by employees during a six-year period. About how many more complaints were made in 2010 than in 2009?

1. **Read the labels.** Each bar represents the number of complaints made within a year. The years are shown beneath the bars.

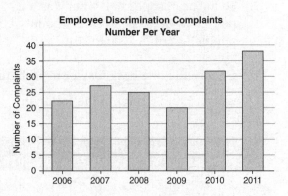

2. **Analyze the data.** Compare the bars for 2009 and 2010 to the scale. There were 20 complaints in 2009 and about 32 complaints in 2010.

3. **Use the data.** Subtract: $32 - 20 = 12$. There were **about 12 more** complaints in 2010 than in 2009.

A **double-bar graph** compares more than one type of data.

Example 2: A studio released four films in one year. The graph below compares the cost of making each movie to its box-office receipts, or ticket sales. Film B's cost is what percent of its box-office receipts?

1. **Read the labels.** Read the key to find the meaning of the bars. Notice that the scale represents millions of dollars.

2. **Analyze the data.** Film B's cost is about $30 million. It brought in about $65 million in receipts.

3. **Use the data.** Find what percent $30 is of $65.

$$\frac{\$30}{\$65} \approx 0.462 \approx \textbf{46\%}$$

A. For questions 1 through 3, use the bar graph entitled "Employee Discrimination Complaints" on the previous page. For questions 4 through 6, use the bar graph entitled "Profit Analysis for Four Films" on the previous page.

1. To the nearest ten, how many employee discrimination complaints were there in 2006 and 2007?

2. To the nearest five, how many more complaints were there in 2011 than in 2006?

3. By what percent did the number of complaints decrease from 2008 to 2009?

4. About how much more did it cost to make Film A than Film D?

5. Which film made the greatest amount of profit? (*Hint:* profit = receipts – cost)

6. Film C's cost was what percent of its box-office receipts?

B. Choose the one best answer to each question.

Questions 7 and 8 refer to the following graph.

Items Sold for the Week of Sept 20

7. Approximately how many more T-shirts were sold than books and toys combined?

A. 40
B. 70
C. 80
D. 90

8. One-half of the games sold during the week of September 20 were on sale for $16. The rest sold for the full price of $24. Approximately how much money did the store take in for games sold during the week of September 20?

A. $400
B. $600
C. $800
D. $1000

Questions 9 and 10 refer to the following graph.

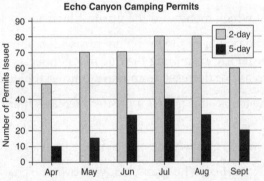

Echo Canyon Camping Permits

9. In May, what was the ratio of the number of 2-day permits to the number of 5-day permits?

A. 2:5
B. 3:17
C. 14:3
D. 14:17

10. In which month was there a total of 80 permits issued?

A. June
B. July
C. August
D. September

Working with Line Graphs

A **line graph** is useful for showing changes over time. By analyzing the rise and fall of the line, you can tell whether something is increasing, decreasing, or staying the same. Like a bar graph, a line graph has two axis lines. One is marked with a scale; the other is marked in regular time intervals.

Example 3: The graph below shows the number of patients who visited an emergency room for the treatment of scooter-related injuries.

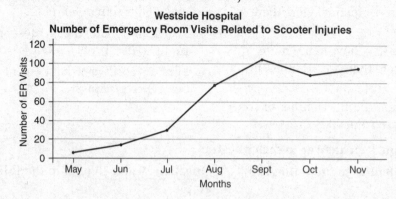

In which month did the greatest increase in scooter-related injuries occur?

The points on the graph are positioned above the months, which are arranged in calendar order. By examining the line that connects the points, you can tell whether there was an increase or decrease from one month to the next.

A steeper line shows a greater increase; therefore, the **greatest increase was from July to August**.

If a line graph has more than one line, a key will tell you what the lines represent.

Example 4: The graph below shows the changes in ticket prices for two amusement parks.

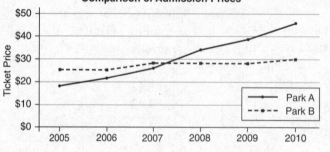

What was the last year in which the admission price to Park B was greater than the admission price to Park A?

The admission prices for Park A are represented by a solid line. Park B's prices are shown with a dotted line. The graph begins in 2005. In 2005, Park B's ticket price is greater than Park A's. Follow the two lines to the right. Between 2007 and 2008, the lines cross, and Park A's prices climb higher than Park B's. **The year 2007** was the last time that Park B charged more than Park A for a ticket.

Note: The steepest line shows the greatest increase or decrease, but it may not show the greatest <u>percent</u> of change. When the original value is small, a small change may result in a high percent of change.

A. For questions 1 through 3, use the graph from Westside Hospital on the previous page. For questions 4 through 6, use the graph "Comparison of Admission Prices" on the previous page.

1. In which month did the number of scooter-related injuries decrease?

2. To the nearest 10, how many emergency room visits were due to scooter injuries in August, September, and October combined?

3. Which of the following shows the greater percent of increase: the change in injuries from June to July or the change from August to September?

4. About how much more did it cost to buy a ticket to Park A than a ticket to Park B in 2009?

5. What was the percent of increase in the ticket prices at Park B from 2005 to 2010?

6. To the nearest 10, how much more did it cost to buy a ticket to Park A in 2010 than in 2005?

B. Choose the **one best answer** to each question.

Questions 7 and 8 refer to the graph below.

Inflation-Adjusted Costs

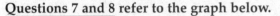

If a purchase cost $100 in the year 2000, what would have been its cost in the past?

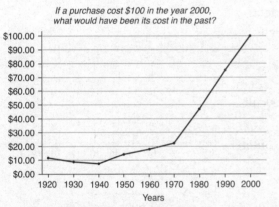

7. Over what period of time did the price of goods actually decrease?

A. 1930 to 1940
B. 1940 to 1950
C. 1960 to 1970
D. 1970 to 1980

8. Goods purchased in 1970 were about what fraction of their cost in the year 2000?

A. $\frac{4}{5}$
B. $\frac{1}{2}$
C. $\frac{1}{3}$
D. $\frac{1}{5}$

Questions 9 and 10 refer to the graph below.

Lamp Depot has two stores. The graph shows the sales data from the two stores for an 8-week period.

9. About how many more sales were there at Store 2 than at Store 1 in week 6?

A. 110
B. 50
C. 40
D. 25

10. During which week did Store 1 experience the greatest increase in sales from the week before?

A. Week 2
B. Week 3
C. Week 4
D. Week 5

STUDY ADVICE

All of the graphics you're learning about in this chapter are simply ways of presenting numbers with pictures. Always begin by getting the big picture. Ask yourself what the graph represents and what you notice most about it. And don't overlook information such as the total represented by the graph.

Box Plots

Box plots are used to depict the median and the spread of a data set. With a box plot you can determine if the data is clustered together or spread out.

Example 1: A new orthodontist in town has recorded the following ages of his first seven patients. Create a box plot to represent the information.

12	16	14	15	15	13	19

1. Arrange the values in numerical order and find the median.

   12　13　14　$\boxed{15}$　15　16　19

2. Find the **first quartile** data point, which is the median of the data points lower than the median.

   12　$\boxed{13}$　14

3. Find the **third quartile** data point, which is the median of the data points higher than the median.

   15　$\boxed{16}$　19

4. Draw a number line and draw a line at the 1st quartile, the median (2nd quartile) and the 3rd quartile.

5. Draw a box connecting the outer two lines.

6. Plot the data set's lowest point and highest point.

7. Using straight lines, connect the two outlying points to the box.

Note that in the box plot, the median appears as the line inside the box. The box contains the middle half of the data set, from the 1st quartile to the 3rd quartile. The 3rd quartile minus the 1st quartile is called the **interquartile range.** The entire plot shows the spread of the data points.

Box plots can be presented horizontally, as above, or vertically.

PRACTICE 3

A. For questions 1 and 2, <u>choose the box plot</u> that matches each data set. Use choices A–D below for <u>both questions</u>.

1. A woman counted the number of birds that ate at her bird feeder every weekday for one week:

   2   6   20   8   3

2. The next week she also counted the number of birds who ate from the feeder on Saturday:

   7   16   8   12   13   15

B. <u>Questions 3 through 6</u> refer to the following two box plots.

Box Plot A

Box Plot B

3. Which box plot represents data with the greater spread?

   A. Box Plot A
   B. Box Plot B
   C. They have the same spread.
   D. Cannot be determined from the information given.

4. What is the greatest data point represented in either of the two box plots?

   A. 0
   B. 14
   C. 18
   D. 20

5. What is the range of the data represented in Box Plot B?

   A. 18
   B. 11
   C. 7
   D. 6

6. What is the interquartile range of the data represented in Box Plot A?

   A. 16
   B. 12
   C. 8
   D. 4

Circle Graphs

A **circle graph** is used to show how a whole amount is broken into parts. The sections of a circle graph are often labeled with percents. The size of each section corresponds to the fraction it represents. For example, a section labeled 25% is $\frac{1}{4}$ of the circle.

Example 1: A graph below shows how a children's sports camp spends its weekly budget.

Sports Camp Weekly Budget $2250

Bus 28%
Permits 8%
Equipment 18%
Umpires 11%
Lunches 35%

How much does the sports camp spend on lunches each week?

1. **Analyze the graph.** According to the heading, the entire circle represents the camp's weekly budget of $2250. Find the section labeled "lunches." According to the section label, lunches make up 35% of the weekly budget.

2. **Use the data.** To find the amount spent on lunches, find 35% of $2250: $2250 × 0.35 = **$787.50.**

A circle graph may also be labeled using fractions or decimals. One common kind of circle graph labels each section in cents to show how a dollar is used.

Example 2: According to the graph, what percent of the average energy bill is spent on drying clothes, lighting, and heating water?

Where Do Your Energy Dollars Go?

Heating and Air-Conditioning $0.60
Clothes Drying $0.03
Other $0.04
Water Heating $0.17
Lighting $0.05
Cooking and Refrigeration $0.11

1. **Analyze the graph.** The entire circle represents $1. The amounts in the sections mentioned in the problem are $0.03, $0.05, and $0.17.

2. **Use the data.** Add the amounts: $0.03 + $0.05 + $0.17 = $0.25. Since $0.25 is 25% of a dollar, **25%** of an average bill is spent on these items.

KEY IDEAS

- In a circle graph, the circle represents a whole amount, and the sections represent parts of the whole.
- Sections are usually labeled with percents, but they can show amounts.
- The size of each section of a circle graph is equal to the fraction or percent it represents.

TASC TEST TIP

Since a circle graph represents a whole, or 100%, amounts can easily be converted to percents. For example, $0.05 on a circle graph can also represent 5%.

PRACTICE 4

A. For questions 1 through 3, use the sports camp budget on the previous page. For questions 4 through 6, use the circle graph on energy on the previous page.

1. What percent of the total sports camp budget is spent on equipment and umpires?

2. What <u>fraction</u> of the sports camp budget is spent on permits?

3. What amount does the camp spend each week on busing?

4. A family's energy bill is $180. Assuming the family's energy use is typical, how much did the family spend on water heating?

5. Which section is greater than 50% of an energy dollar?

6. Which energy cost is about $\frac{1}{10}$ of the energy dollar?

B. Choose the <u>one best answer</u> to each question.

Questions 7 and 8 refer to the following graph.

Average Time Spent on Tasks by Records Clerks, Woods County Recorders Office

Service Desk 25%
Data Entry 44%
Preparing Documents 25%
Filing 6%

7. During a 40-hour workweek, how many hours on average does a records clerk spend preparing documents?

   A. 10
   B. 15
   C. 25
   D. 30

8. What percent of a records clerk's time is spent on tasks other than data entry?

   A. 25%
   B. 31%
   C. 44%
   D. 56%

Questions 9 and 10 refer to the following graph.

The employees of National Bank are given the following graph to explain how their retirement fund is invested.

How Your Retirement Dollar Is Invested

Private Bonds 30 cents
Stock Market 3 cents
Mortgages 20 cents
Public Bonds 40 cents
Real Estate 7 cents

9. What percent of each retirement dollar is invested in real estate and the stock market?

   A. 4%
   B. 10%
   C. 40%
   D. 90%

10. Steve contributes $120 of each paycheck to his National Bank retirement fund. How much of each contribution is invested in public bonds?

   A. $36
   B. $40
   C. $48
   D. $84

Line Plots

A **line plot** shows the frequency of data along a number line. Study the following example.

Example 1: The student health services department at a university surveyed several students, asking them how many times per week they visited the school's gym. The following table shows the results. (Note that in this table and others in this section, the frequency is indicated with tally marks rather than numerals. Tally marks are like the scratch marks you might make when counting items one by one.)

Weekly Gym Visits	Number of Students
0	I
1	II
2	II
3	III
4	I
5	0
6	0
7	I

Next, the health services department decided to create a line plot in order to see the distribution of gym visits. Each *x* represents a student.

You can see from this line plot that there is an uneven **distribution**, or arrangement, of students across the numbers of possible gym visits. Three visits per week has the **highest frequency**, meaning that more students go to the gym three times per week than any other number of visits. You can also see that the data **range** extends from zero visits per week to seven visits per week—no student visits the gym more often than that. The data point showing the one student who visits the gym seven times per week is an **outlier**—that is, a data point that is distant from where most of the data is clustered.

The Mathematics Test may ask you to identify the highest frequency, range, and outliers, or it may give you some data and ask you to identify the line plot that fits the data.

Use the following example to study these concepts further.

Example 2: Students in Ms. Jones's class took a math test. Their scores on the test are displayed on the line plot below. Each dot represents a student. Which grade had the highest frequency? Also, what was the range of the grades?

More students received a C than received any other grade. Therefore, grade **C** has the highest frequency of any grade on the line plot.

The range of grades on the math test was **from D** (the lowest grade received by any student) **to A** (the highest grade received by any student).

PRACTICE 5

For questions 1 and 2, <u>choose the line plot</u> that matches each table. Use choices A–D below for <u>both questions</u>.

1. Zoologists have counted the number of stripes on certain zebras in a zoo. The set of data from these observations is represented by the following table:

Number of stripes per side	Number of zebras with that many stripes
24	I
25	0
26	II
27	0
28	II
29	0
30	II
31	0
32	I

Which line plot represents these data?

2. At a certain elementary school, classes may have different numbers of students. The following table represents how many students are in the classes this year:

Number of students	Number of classes with that many students
24	0
25	0
26	0
27	I
28	I
29	III
30	0
31	I
32	II

Which line plot represents these data?

A.

```
            x
        x   x   x
    x   x   x   x   x   x
    +---+---+---+---+---+---+---+---+---+
    24  25  26  27  28  29  30  31  32
```

B.

```
                    x
                    x
            x   x   x       x   x
    +---+---+---+---+---+---+---+---+---+
    24  25  26  27  28  29  30  31  32
```

C.

```
                x       x       x
        x       x       x       x       x
    +---+---+---+---+---+---+---+---+---+
    24  25  26  27  28  29  30  31  32
```

D.

```
                        x
                x       x       x
        x   x   x       x       x   x   x
    +---+---+---+---+---+---+---+---+---+
    24  25  26  27  28  29  30  31  32
```

Questions 3 and 4 are based on the following information.

Juana runs a community garden. She records how many different types of vegetables garden members are planting. The following line plot is based on Juana's data. Each point represents a member of the community garden. The values on the line plot represent the number of types of vegetables planted by each person.

3. Which of the following can be described as (an) outlier(s)?

   A. the member who plants one type of vegetable
   B. the members who plant three types of vegetables
   C. the members who plant four types of vegetables
   D. the member who plants eight types of vegetables

4. Which value (number of types of vegetables) has the highest frequency in the data?

   A. 2
   B. 3
   C. 4
   D. 8

Histograms

Like line plots, **histograms** display **frequencies**, but they do so in a very different way. Consider the following example:

Example 1: Graham is a veterinarian. Last year he decided to track client appointments for spring shots. The following table and histogram represent his results:

Week of	Number of Appointments
March 1–7	2
March 8–14	4
March 15–21	8
March 22–28	11
March 29–April 4	14
April 5–11	17
April 12–18	13
April 19–25	7
April 26–May 2	5

The **histogram** above on the right has two axes: a **vertical axis** (or *y*-axis) representing numbers of appointments and a **horizontal axis** (also called an *x*-axis) that has increments representing the weeks. The **area** of each bar represents the number of appointments for that week. Thus, you can see not only how many appointments were in any given week but also how the **frequency** of appointments changed over the weeks in the chart.

Finally, histograms can also be used to show percentages. If we alter the histogram about Graham's appointments so that each bar represents the *percent* of total appointments each week, it will look like the one on the right.

Because the percentages add up to 100%, the areas of all the bars add up to 100.

Example 2: What percent of appointments for spring shots occurred during the first two weeks of March?

You can figure this out by adding the percentages for those weeks (you can approximate based on the histogram): for March 1–7, about 2%; for March 8–14, about 5%. Approximately **7%** of appointments for spring shots occurred during those two weeks.

A. Choose the <u>histogram</u> that matches each table. Use choices A–D below for <u>both</u> questions 1 and 2.

1. Josefina runs a retail business. She posted a coupon to a social media site from 9:00 a.m. to 5:00 p.m. The table shows how many people downloaded or printed the coupon.

2. Mike administered a skills assessment to his employees. Possible scores on the skills assessment ranged from 200 to 1800. The following table shows how his employees performed on the assessment:

Hour beginning with:	Number of people who downloaded or printed coupon:
9:00 a.m.	30
10:00 a.m.	56
11:00 a.m.	80
12:00 p.m.	71
1:00 p.m.	56
2:00 p.m.	31
3:00 p.m.	22
4:00 p.m.	14

Score range	Number of employees
200–399	15
400–599	22
600–799	35
800–999	62
1000–1199	80
1200–1399	69
1400–1599	47
1600–1800	20

A.

B.

C.

D.

B. Choose the <u>one best answer</u> to each question.

Question 3 refers to the following histogram and information.

Influenza, or "flu," season in the United States tends to last from fall through spring.

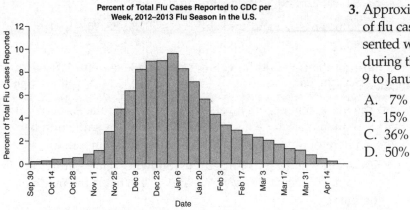

Source: Centers for Disease Control and Prevention

3. Approximately what percent of flu cases in the time period represented was reported to the CDC during the time period of December 9 to January 5?

A. 7%

B. 15%

C. 36%

D. 50%

Measures of Central Tendency

Mean, Median, Mode, and Range

Suppose you were asked how much money you usually spend on groceries in a week. Some weeks, you may spend a great deal; other weeks, much less. You would probably choose an amount in the middle to represent what you typically spend. This middle value is called a **measure of central tendency**. The word *average* is sometimes used for some of these measures.

The most common type of average is the **mean**, sometimes called the *arithmetic mean*. The mean is calculated by adding up all the items in a list and then dividing by the number of items in that list.

Example 1: In five football games, a team scored 14, 21, 3, 20, and 10 points. What is the mean, or average, score per game?

1. Add the values. $14 + 21 + 3 + 20 + 10 = 68$

2. Divide by the number of items in $68 \div 5 = \textbf{13.6 points per game}$
   the data set.

Although it is impossible for a football team to score 13.6 points in a game, the number represents the center of the scores from the five games.

A calculator is useful for finding the mean. Do the calculations in two steps: first the addition, then the division. Try Example 1 above with a calculator.

Another measure of central tendency is the median. The **median** is the middle value in a set of data when the data are put in order.

Example 2: During a 7-hour period, a bookstore recorded the following numbers of sales. Find the median number of sales.

Hour 1	Hour 2	Hour 3	Hour 4	Hour 5	Hour 6	Hour 7
43	28	24	36	28	37	48

1. Arrange the values by size.   24, 28, 28, 36, 37, 43, 48
2. Find the middle number.   24, 28, 28, |36,| 37, 43, 48

If there is an even number of values, the median is the mean of the two middle values.

Example 3: Robert has the following test scores in his math class: 90, 72, 88, 94, 91, and 80. What is the median score?

1. Arrange the values by size and find the   72, 80, |88, 90,| 91, 94
   middle value.

2. Find the mean of the two middle values.   Add: $88 + 90 = 178$
   The median score is **89**.   Divide by 2: $178 \div 2 = \textbf{89}$

The **mode** is the value that occurs most often in a set of data. A set of data could have more than one mode if several items occur the same number of times. If each item of data occurs only once, there is no mode.

Example 4: Six weather stations recorded the following temperatures at 3:00 p.m.: 45°, 44°, 45°, 47°, 46°, and 45°. What is the mode of the data?

The temperature 45° occurs most often (3 times). The mode is **45°**.

PRACTICE 7.1

The **range** of a set of data is the difference between the highest value in the data set and the lowest value in the data set. The range is not a measure of central tendency, but in conjunction with a measure such as mean or median, the range can tell you how far the data spreads on either side of the middle.

Example 5: Over a couple of years, Rogelio had his blood sugar tested several times. His blood sugar readings were 68, 76, 72, 71, 69, 74, 79, and 76 mg/dL. What is the range of Rogelio's blood sugar readings?

Subtract the highest reading from the lowest reading. $\qquad$ $79 - 68 = 11$
The range of the data set is **11**.

A. **For each data set, find the mean, median, mode, and range. Round calculations to the nearest hundredth or cent. You <u>MAY</u> use a calculator.**

1. Golf scores for 7 rounds:
   76, 82, 75, 87, 80, 82, and 79

2. Sales totals for 6 weeks:
   $5,624; $10,380; $8,102; $6,494; $12,008; and $8,315

3. Cost of lunch for 8 days:
   $4.50, $5.25, $4.50, $3.75, $4.50, $5.25, $6.10, and $4.25

4. Scores on 7 quizzes:
   90, 72, 86, 100, 88, 78, and 88

5. High temperatures for 10 days:
   96°, 103°, 98°, 101°, 98°, 100°, 100°, 97°, 98°, and 100°

6. Inches of rainfall over 3-day period:
   2.5, 1.8, and 1.4

B. **Choose the <u>one best answer</u> to each question. You <u>MAY</u> use your calculator.**

Questions 7 and 8 refer to the following information.

Homes Sold in Fairfield Heights in June		
Home	**Asking Price**	**Selling Price**
#1	$124,600	$116,500
#2	$132,400	$124,800
#3	$118,900	$116,500
#4	$98,500	$103,600
#5	$105,800	$109,000
#6	$122,400	$118,400

7. What was the mean asking price of the homes sold in Fairfield Heights in June?

   A. $117,100
   B. $116,500
   C. $115,450
   D. $114,800

8. What was the median selling price of the homes sold in Fairfield Heights in June?

   A. $112,750
   B. $114,800
   C. $116,500
   D. $117,450

9. The numbers of patients enrolled at four health clinics are 790, 1150, 662, and 805. Which expression could be used to find the mean number of patients per clinic?

   A. $\dfrac{790 + 1150 + 662 + 805}{4}$
   B. $790 + 1150 + 662 + 805$
   C. $\dfrac{662 + 1150}{2}$
   D. $(790 + 1150 + 662 + 805) \div 2$

10. What is the median value of $268, $1258, $654, $1258, $900, $1558, and $852?

    A. $1258
    B. $964
    C. $900
    D. $852

11. What is the mode of the following points scored: 14, 17, 14, 12, 13, 15, 22, and 11?

    A. 13.5
    B. 14
    C. 14.75
    D. 16.5

The **standard deviation** (often represented by the Greek letter sigma, σ) of a data set relates to how spread out or close together the data are. The closer together the data points lie, the smaller the standard deviation. Consider the two data sets below:

Set 1: {−1,008; −135; −122; 89; 132; 202; 912}
Set 2: {−2, 6, 7, 10, 14, 16, 19}

Both data sets have the same mean (10), but Set 1 has a larger standard deviation because its data points spread out far on both sides of the mean, whereas more of the data points in Set 2 are close to the mean.

To calculate the standard deviation:

- Find the mean of the data.
- Find the difference between each data point and the mean.
- Square those differences.
- Add up the squares of the differences.
- Divide that sum by the number of data points.
- Take the square root of the result of that.

However, you will probably not be asked to calculate a standard deviation on the TASC test. ***Thus, it is NOT the best use of your time to memorize the steps listed above.*** It is far more likely that you will be asked about your general understanding of what standard deviation is.

Example 1: The standard deviations of four data sets are listed below. Which of the data sets is most tightly clustered together?

Set A = 14, Set B = 10, Set C = 20, Set D = 2.

1. The most clustered data set is the set with the smallest standard deviation.
   Rank the sets from lowest standard deviation to highest.   2, 10, 14, 10

2. The most clustered data set is **Set D**, because it has the lowest standard deviation.

Some types of data, when gathered in large amounts, will fall into a **normal distribution**. This means that the data are centered around one point and are symmetrical. When graphed, the data form a bell-shaped curve. (To imagine how data would be graphed, imagine making a histogram that's so detailed that the "bumps" formed by individual bars are smoothed out into a curved line.) Note that not all data sets form a normal distribution.

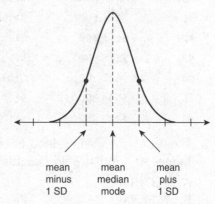

mean
minus
1 SD

mean
median
mode

mean
plus
1 SD

Normal distributions have a number of special traits. For example, the mean, median, and mode of a data set with a normal distribution are all the same value. In addition, when data falls into a normal distribution, the standard deviation has a special usefulness. The area of the normal distribution formed by one standard deviation on both sides of the median encompasses 68% of the data. (This is the area formed by the two dotted lines on either side of the median in the graph above.) When data falls into a normal distribution, 95% of the data will fall within two standard deviations on either side of the mean.

PRACTICE 7.2

Questions 1 through 3 refer to the data sets below. Write your answer on the line below.

Set A: {1, 3, 2, 1, 1, 4, 2, 3, 1}

Set B: {3, 8, 10, 50, 12, 4, 6}

1. Set _____ has data that is more spread out.

2. Set _____ has a larger standard deviation. (*Hint*: You do *not* have to calculate standard deviation in order to answer this question.)

3. Suppose you added a new data point of 13 to both Set A and Set B. Doing so would raise the standard deviation of Set _____ and not have much effect on the standard deviation of Set _____.

---

4. Which one of the following graphs of data displays a normal distribution?

A.

B.

C.

D.

---

5. Stacy measures the height of all students in her class and finds that the data fits a normal distribution. The median height is 60 inches with a standard deviation of 3 inches. In what range will approximately 95% of the data fall?

  A. 57 to 63

  B. 54 to 66

  C. 51 to 69

  D. 48 to 72

6. Jason has collected data about the number of frogs in ponds in a wilderness preserve and has learned that the data form a normal distribution. He knows that the standard deviation of this data is 5, and the median number of frogs per pond is 20. In what range will approximately 68% of the data fall?

  A. 15 to 25

  B. 16 to 24

  C. 17 to 23

  D. 18 to 22

The Basics of Statistical Research

Sampling

It frequently isn't possible or practical to collect data about an entire data set. For example, imagine that a researcher wanted to know how Americans feel about a proposed tax law. Think how difficult it would be to track down every single American and ask him or her! The same problem crops up in many fields of study, including medicine, business, politics, sociology, etc. Thus, researchers often study a **sample**, or just a portion of the population, and use it to make inferences about the entire population.

In order for inferences based on a sample to be valid, the sample must be large enough and also **representative** of (that is, similar to) the entire population of interest. Imagine that the researcher who wants to know how Americans feel about the proposed tax law compiled a sample composed largely of her neighbors, or of Republicans, or of people within a certain income bracket, or of people with children. Her sample would not reflect the variety of views in the population as a whole, and her results would display **bias**. The word *bias* means *slant*, and it also denotes one-sided thinking or not seeing the entire picture. **Randomization**, or compiling the sample at random, helps avoid bias. Researchers use a number of computerized tools to select random samples, but a random sample of a very small population could be selected by drawing names out of a hat—the basic idea is the same.

Descriptive and Inferential Statistics

Sometimes researchers who are using statistics (with or without sampling) simply want to *describe* a population. Examples of questions that can be answered with descriptive statistics are:

How many people in the United States live in small towns?
What is the average fat-to-muscle ratio of American adults?
What is the most common shoe size among women?

At other times researchers want to use statistics in order to make **inferences**—that is, to draw conclusions that aren't obvious from the raw data. Examples of questions that could possibly be answered with inferential statistics include:

Does eating too much fat contribute to liver disease?
Are senior citizens more or less likely than others to vote for a certain candidate?
Can the color of a new product influence whether consumers will purchase it?

Inferential statistical studies employ the **scientific method**. You will read more about the scientific method in the Science Skills chapter, but, in short, the steps are:

- A researcher has a question about the world (such as any of the questions listed above).
- The researcher collects information and data about that question.
- The researcher forms a guess, called a **hypothesis**, about what the answer to the question might be.
- The researcher performs a study to test the hypothesis. (Read more about types of studies below.)
- The researcher interprets the results of the study in order to draw a conclusion.

PRACTICE 8

In the next lesson, you will read more about drawing conclusions from statistical data.

Types of Statistical Studies

There are several different ways in which scientists use statistics to draw inferences. **Experiments** are tightly controlled situations that allow researchers to observe how two things relate. For example, perhaps a doctor wants to know whether people who take vitamin D pills are less likely to develop disease X than are people who don't take vitamin D. The doctor will select a random sample from a larger population and then split that sample into two smaller groups. One group will not engage in the behavior being studied—in this case, that means that group will *not* take vitamin D. This group is called the **control group**. The other group will adopt the treatment or behavior being studied—in this case, that group *will* take vitamin D. This is the **treatment group**. The doctor will monitor the health of both groups. Once the study is completed, the results from the control group and the treatment group will be compared to see whether there is any difference in the incidence of disease X.

By contrast, in an **observational study**, the researcher does not direct the behavior of members of the treatment and control group, and so who falls into those two groups is beyond the researcher's power. For example, suppose that the doctor from the last example wanted to study whether being and remaining overweight correlates with higher risk of disease X. The doctor cannot *make* people be overweight in order to create a treatment group—doing so would be unethical as well as impractical. In this case, the doctor will select a random sample from the population of people who are already overweight and a random sample of people who are not, observe their health over time, and then compare the incidence of disease X in the two groups.

Finally, statisticians sometimes use **surveys** (that is, questionnaires or interviews) instead of observing behavior directly. Surveys can be conducted by phone, online, by mail, or in person. A survey study is similar to an observational experiment in that the participants are already divided into a control group and an experimental group based on their current lifestyle or traits. Surveys have several advantages: they often cost less and take less time than other kinds of studies, and they can record data about things that aren't observable, such as opinions or personal history. Surveys have some disadvantages, too, one of which being that survey respondents may (deliberately or accidentally) misreport facts about themselves.

---

1. Luke is conducting a survey to determine the effectiveness of his high school's tutoring center. Luke sends the survey to the members of his soccer team, many of whom use the tutoring center. If half of the members on the team respond to the survey, will the survey produce reliable data? Why or why not?

   A. no, because the team members may not have confidence that the survey is anonymous
   B. no, because the survey is not a random sample of the relevant population
   C. yes, because at least some of the survey respondents use the tutoring center
   D. yes, because the soccer team members likely come from a variety of backgrounds

2. If Maritsa has little time or money but would like to gauge the effectiveness of a weight loss program offered by her gym, which of the following study types should she most likely choose?

   A. experiment
   B. observational study
   C. sample survey
   D. a combination of techniques

3. A(n) _____ involves directing the behavior of the treatment group, whereas in a(n) _____, the treatment group is based on current behavior.

   A. experiment; observational study
   B. observational study; experiment
   C. sample survey; observational study
   D. experiment; experiment

Making Inferences from Statistical Data

Suppose that you are a researcher, and you have performed an observational study to address the question of whether a trendy diet, Diet Q, contributes to tooth decay. In your study, one group of participants were long-time Diet Q practitioners, the other weren't, and you found that the first group had on average slightly more tooth decay than the second group. Now you have to figure out whether that observed difference is big enough to be informative. After all, when you measure two groups with regard to anything, it's very unlikely that the data for the two groups will be exactly the same. How do you know whether the difference you observed between the two groups is this kind of unimportant random variation or is actually related to Diet Q? In other words, is the difference **statistically significant**?

Calculating statistical significance is pretty complicated, but the idea behind it is simple. If it's very unlikely that you would see your results if your hypothesis were false, then your results are statistically significant. One way that researchers do this is by running **simulations**, or constructing fake scenarios to figure out what truly random results would look like. Then the researchers compare the simulation results with the actual results. (Researchers attach specific numbers to calculating statistical significance, but you will not be asked to calculate these on the TASC test.)

If results are not statistically significant, no conclusions can be drawn from them. If the results of a study are statistically significant, researchers move forward with interpreting them, but there are still challenges. Suppose that you have performed the necessary calculations and determined that your results are statistically significant. Have you *proven* that Diet Q causes tooth decay? By no means! There are two main reasons why.

First, your study has suggested that there is some **correlation** between Diet Q and tooth decay. *Correlation* refers to the tendency of two things to vary together: you've shown that more tooth decay *tends to go along with* practicing Diet Q. Correlation does *not* necessarily mean that one thing causes the other. In this case, maybe Diet Q contributes to tooth decay, or maybe people with more tooth decay become worried about their health generally and decide to try out a trendy diet, like Diet Q, as a result. Or maybe Diet Q adherents tend to come from certain ethnic backgrounds that also display a genetic disposition toward tooth decay. Or maybe . . . the possibilities go on. You haven't proven which of those possibilities is true. What you have done is discredited the idea that there is *no* link between Diet Q and tooth decay. Researchers refer to this as **rejecting the null hypothesis**—that is, rejecting the negation of their starting hypothesis. Rejecting the null hypothesis is considered an important step and is the immediate goal of most research.

Second, in the fields of science and social science, it is generally assumed that valid results can be **replicated**, or repeated in similar studies done by other people using other participants. Thus, people who are interested in the question of Diet Q and tooth decay will pick up where your study left off—repeating it, refining it, studying narrower and narrower questions—until a body of work exists that the community of researchers feels confident in. If your results have been consistently replicated, there may come a day when people consider it more or less proven that there is some link between Diet Q and tooth decay. But *proof* in the world of research is a pretty high standard, and a single study never achieves it.

---

1. Cho has conducted an observational study and finds that the phenomenon she's interested in is, on average, more prevalent in her treatment group than in her control group. What is Cho's very next step?

   A. She must perform the study again in order to check her numbers.

   B. She must determine whether the observed difference is statistically significant.

   C. She must conduct further studies to establish causation.

   D. She must refine her hypothesis to account for these new data.

2. Murad has conducted a survey and found a statistically significant result: survey participants who owned 100 or more books at home tended to have higher-paying jobs than those who did not. Murad concludes from this that having a large personal library leads to a higher-paying job. What is wrong with Murad's conclusion? Select all that apply.

   ☐ Murad overlooked the possibility that having a higher-paying job tends to lead to owning more books.

   ☐ Murad failed to question whether the survey participants who owned many books had actually read them.

   ☐ Murad overlooked the possibility that some other factor, like a college education, tends to lead people to own many books and to have higher-paying jobs.

   ☐ Murad failed to demonstrate that employers know how large their employees' personal libraries are.

Avoiding Mistakes in Statistics

The TASC test may ask you to read about and interpret statistical results. When you do so, be careful to avoid making some common mistakes. If you are asked to evaluate whether a statistical study is valid or not, examine it for bias.

Common Mistakes in Interpreting Studies

In the last lesson, you read about **the difference between correlation** (the tendency of two things to go together) **and causation** (the idea that one thing directly leads to another). Inferring causation when a study has only demonstrated correlation is a very common mistake when interpreting statistics. Now, granted, showing that two things are correlated makes it *somewhat more likely* that there's a causal relationship too, but you don't know for sure. It's also a common mistake to ignore the possibility that some third, possibly hidden factor causes both things. Read this news story and ask yourself what might be wrong with it:

Example 1: News report: "A recent study suggests that brushing teeth often improves academic performance among teenagers. Among the study participants, those who brushed their teeth two to three times per day earned, on average, an entire letter grade higher in core academic subjects than did less-frequent toothbrushers."

The writer of this news report thinks that the correlation between frequent toothbrushing and higher grades means that the first causes the second. But it's equally possible that some third factor, such as a capacity for self-discipline, leads to both frequent toothbrushing and higher grades.

The other mistake people often make when interpreting statistics is **failing to think about scale and proportion**. This mistake stems from the fact that numbers can sound more or less important depending on how they're presented. Consider the following conversation between two friends:

Example 2: Joe said, "You know, it doesn't matter whether you drink regular coffee or decaf coffee. Regular coffee is only 3% caffeine and decaf is 1% caffeine. That's a small difference." Serena replied, "Right, so regular coffee has 300% as much caffeine as decaf. That's a big difference."

In the example above, Joe and Serena agree about the numbers and disagree about the interpretation of them. Joe is failing to think about proportion, which is what matters if the question is about the relative effects of regular and decaf. Think about this example:

Example 3: News report: "A recent study shows that children who pick their noses are 75% more likely to experience disease Z later in life. So parents, break that habit in your children now!"

While nose-picking might not be an attractive habit, is it really going to give your child a disease? Based on the information above, you don't know, because a key piece of information is missing. That missing piece of information is how likely the non-pickers are to get disease Z. If only 0.1% of the general population develops disease Z, then the study has suggested that 0.175% of nose-pickers are likely to contract disease Z. That's still a minimal risk.

Similar misunderstandings can happen when graphs don't show the entire range of possible values or have different scales for their x- and y-axes. Be sure to look carefully at units when interpreting graphs.

Common Mistakes in Conducting Studies

Researchers must avoid bias when selecting samples. One common problem is **selection bias**. Suppose a researcher wanted to know whether a certain household cleaner could cause a certain disease. If the researcher chose her sample just from people who have the disease, she'd be able to tell how many people who got sick used the cleaner, but she wouldn't know how many people used the cleaner and didn't get sick. If she chose her sample just from people who use the cleaner, she could tell how many of those people got the disease, but she wouldn't be able to tell how much *more likely* users of the cleaner are to get the disease than other people. Thus, the researcher needs a random sample of people who use the cleaner and a random sample of those who don't so that she can make comparisons.

A special bias problem in survey research has to do with **self-selection.** Suppose that a store offered its customers a chance to win a new military-themed video game in exchange for filling out a customer satisfaction survey. People who like military-themed video games might be more motivated than others to fill out the survey, and then the survey data would over-represent that group.

---

1. A researcher is presenting his results. He shares the graph below and says, "So, you can clearly see that increases in treatment x correlate with significant increases in outcome y."

You're skeptical about the researcher's claim. Why? Select all that apply.

☐ The graphed line is straight, when you would expect it to be curved.

☐ The y-axis is presented in very small increments, while the x-axis is presented in much larger increments.

☐ The researcher is showing only a portion of values of the y-axis.

☐ The researcher has made an unjustified claim about causation.

2. A political scientist wants to know whether watching local television news programs increases voters' likelihood of voting. To recruit participants for his study, the political scientist posts fliers at polling places on election day, and nowhere else. The political scientist's approach is flawed because it

A. may not reach everyone who voted on election day

B. will over-represent people who are not in a hurry on election day

C. may influence participants to stay at home on election day

D. displays selection bias, in that the fliers will likely not reach those who don't vote

LESSON 11

Probability

Simple Probability

Probability tells whether something is likely or unlikely to happen. The probability of any event can be expressed by a number from 0 to 1. If an event has 0 probability, the event is impossible. An event with a probability of 1 is certain to happen. Most events are somewhere in between.

To find the probability of a simple random event, we must identify favorable and possible outcomes. A **favorable outcome** is the event that we are interested in. The **possible outcomes** are all the possible events that could occur. **Theoretical probability** (sometimes called **simple probability**) is the ratio of favorable outcomes to possible outcomes.

Example 1: The spinner is divided into 8 equal sections. What is the probability of spinning a 4 on the spinner?

1. There are two sections labeled 4 on the spinner, and there are 8 sections in all.

2. Use the probability ratio: $\frac{\text{favorable outcomes}}{\text{possible outcomes}} = \frac{2}{8} = \frac{1}{4}$.

The probability of spinning a 4 on the spinner is **1 out of 4, $\frac{1}{4}$, 0.25, or 25%.**

In Example 1, probability was based on what we knew could happen. Another type of probability, called **experimental probability**, is based on what actually happens during the trials of an experiment. The number of trials are the number of times you try the experiment.

Example 2: Ricardo and Scott used the same spinner to play a game. They kept track of the numbers that they got on each spin for 20 spins. The numbers are shown below.

2, 4, 4, 6, 4, 3, 4, 6, 4, 3, 1, 6, 2, 2, 5, 2, 4, 2, 1, 2

Based on their results, what is the experimental probability of spinning a 4?

1. Ricardo and Scott spun a 4 six times out of twenty.

2. Use this ratio: $\frac{\text{favorable outcomes}}{\text{number of trials in experiment}} = \frac{6}{20} = \frac{3}{10} = $ **0.3, or 30%.**

Notice that experimental probability is not necessarily equal to, theoretical probability. Theoretical probability can tell you what will probably happen, but it can't predict what will actually happen.

PRACTICE 11.1

A. Express probability as a fraction, decimal, <u>and</u> percent for questions 1 through 5. <u>Do not use a calculator.</u>

1. A game has 50 wooden tiles. Players draw tiles to spell words. If 20 of the tiles are marked with vowels, what is the probability of drawing a vowel from the tiles?

2. A spinner has five equal sections colored either red, white, or blue. After 40 spins, a player has the following results:

Color	Frequency
red	⊞⊞
white	⊞⊞ ‖
blue	⊞⊞ ⊞⊞ ⊞⊞ ⊞⊞ ⊞⊞ ‖‖

What is the experimental probability of not spinning blue on the spinner?

3. There are four red, four blue, and two green marbles in a bag. If one marble is chosen at random from the bag, what is the probability that the marble will be green?

4. A movie theater sells 180 adult tickets and 60 children's tickets to a movie. As part of a special promotion, one ticket will be chosen at random, and the winner will receive a prize. What is the probability that the winner will be a child?

5. A spinner has six equal sections numbered from 1 to 6. What is the probability of spinning either a 5 or 6?

B. Choose the <u>one best answer</u> to each question. You <u>MAY</u> use your calculator.

<u>Questions 6 and 7 refer to the following information.</u>

A deck of 12 cards is marked with the following symbols.

6. If a card is chosen at random, what is the probability of selecting a diamond (♦)?

   A. 6%
   B. 12%
   C. 50%
   D. 60%

7. If a card is chosen at random, what is the probability of selecting something other than a club (♣)?

   A. $\frac{3}{4}$
   B. $\frac{2}{3}$
   C. $\frac{1}{3}$
   D. $\frac{9}{100}$

<u>Questions 8 and 9 refer to the following information.</u>

Erin flipped a coin 40 times and made this table to show how many outcomes were "heads" and how many were "tails."

Heads	⊞⊞ ⊞⊞ ⊞⊞ ⊞⊞ ‖‖‖‖
Tails	⊞⊞ ⊞⊞ ⊞⊞ ‖

8. Based on Erin's data, what is the experimental probability of getting tails on a coin flip?

   A. 3 out of 5
   B. 3 out of 4
   C. 2 out of 3
   D. 2 out of 5

9. Based on Erin's data, what is the experimental probability of getting heads on a coin flip?

   A. 3 out of 5
   B. 3 out of 4
   C. 2 out of 3
   D. 1 out of 2

Dependent and Independent Probability

You know how to find the probability of a single event. You can use this knowledge to find the probability of two or more events.

Example 3: Brad tosses two quarters into the air. What is the probability that both will land so that the heads' sides are showing?

One way to solve the problem is to list or diagram all the possible outcomes.

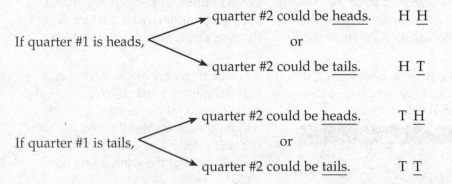

If quarter #1 is heads,
quarter #2 could be <u>heads</u>.   H <u>H</u>
or
quarter #2 could be <u>tails</u>.   H <u>T</u>

If quarter #1 is tails,
quarter #2 could be <u>heads</u>.   T <u>H</u>
or
quarter #2 could be <u>tails</u>.   T <u>T</u>

There are four possible outcomes, and only one is favorable (HH). Therefore, the probability of having both land with the heads side up is $\frac{1}{4}$, or **25%**.

You can also use multiplication to find the probability.

1. Find the probability of the individual events. The probability that one coin will be heads is $\frac{1}{2}$, and the probability that the other will be heads is $\frac{1}{2}$.

2. Multiply to find the probability of both events. $\frac{1}{2} \times \frac{1}{2} = \frac{1}{4}$.

The two coin tosses in Example 3 are **independent events**. When events are independent, one does not affect the probability of another. In Example 4 below, the events are **dependent**. Once the first event takes place, the probability of the second event is changed.

Example 4: A box contains four blue marbles and two red marbles. If you select two marbles, what is the probability that both will be blue?

(*Hint:* Even though the marbles in the box are taken out at the same time, think of one as the first marble and the other as the second marble.)

1. There are six marbles in the box, and four are blue. The probability that the first marble will be blue is $\frac{4}{6}$, which reduces to $\frac{2}{3}$.

2. Assume the first marble selected is blue. Now there are only five marbles in the box, and three are blue. The probability that the second marble will be blue is $\frac{3}{5}$.

3. Multiply to find the probability of the two events. $\frac{2}{3} \times \frac{3}{5} = \frac{6}{15}$, or $\frac{2}{5}$.

The probability that both marbles will be blue is **2 out of 5**.

Note: The events in Example 4 would not be dependent if the first marble were replaced before the second marble was selected. Always think carefully about the situation to decide whether two events are dependent or independent.

PRACTICE 11.2

A. Solve as directed. Express answers as fractions.

1. Kim rolls two standard six-sided dice. What is the chance that both will be 4s?

2. Ten cards are numbered from 1 to 10. Toni draws out a card, replaces it, and then draws another card. What is the probability that both cards will be numbers greater than 5?

3. A spinner has four equal sections. Two sections are red, one is green, and one is blue. If the spinner is spun three times, what is the probability that all three spins will be red?

4. Twenty marbles are placed in a bag. Ten are red, and ten are black. One marble is drawn from the bag and set aside. Another marble is drawn from the bag. What is the chance that both marbles will be red?

5. Allison tosses a coin four times. What is the chance that the coin will be heads all four times?

6. If you roll two standard dice, what is the probability that both will be an odd number?

B. Choose the one best answer to each question. You MAY use your calculator.

Questions 7 and 8 refer to the following information.

In a game a player rolls a die, numbered from 1 to 6, and spins a spinner. The spinner is shown below.

7. What is the probability of rolling a 5 and then spinning an even number?

   A. $\frac{1}{9}$

   B. $\frac{1}{6}$

   C. $\frac{2}{3}$

   D. $\frac{5}{6}$

8. What is the chance that a player will get the same number on both the die and the spinner?

   A. $\frac{5}{6}$

   B. $\frac{2}{3}$

   C. $\frac{1}{3}$

   D. $\frac{1}{6}$

9. Daniel uses the ten cards below in a magic trick.

   Daniel shuffles the cards and asks an audience member to choose and hold two cards. If the cards are chosen randomly, what is the chance that both will be marked with a square?

   A. 8 out of 14
   B. 3 out of 5
   C. 1 out of 3
   D. 1 out of 5

10. There are 15 colored chips in a bag. Eight are green, and seven are white. Five white chips are removed. What is the probability that the next chip selected will be green?

    A. 100%
    B. 80%
    C. 75%
    D. 25%

STUDY ADVICE

Consider making flash cards for some of the mathematical formulas presented in this unit. Then ask a friend to help you do drills using the flash cards.

Combinations

Combinations with One Type of Item

Sometimes the TASC Mathematics Test will ask you how many ways you can combine a set of items. Sometimes you may have only one type of item to combine, and sometimes you may have more than one type to combine. This difference will determine your problem-solving strategy.

Consider an example with *only one type of item:*

Example 1: Pablo is going shopping at a fruit stand that sells apples, bananas, grapes, and pears. Pablo will buy two different kinds of fruit. How many combinations of two kinds of fruit could Pablo buy?

The question is asking you to list possible groups of two out of the overall set of four. Notice that order doesn't matter—that is, *apples and bananas* is no different from *bananas and apples*. To solve this problem, you can make a list. Start with apples, and list all of the **combinations** that include apples: AB, AG, AP. Then make a list of groups that start with bananas and include the remaining fruits: BG, BP. Don't include BA because that's the same as AB. Then make a list of groups that start with grapes and include only the remaining fruits: GP. There are no remaining groups that start with P. You may find it easier to make this list in columns, as follows:

AB

AG   BG

AP   BP   GP

There are **6** possible combinations.

You can also draw a quick table like the following. Include a column for each of the fruits, and let each row represent a possible combination. Place two *x*'s in each row to represent a combination of two fruits.

Apples	Bananas	Grapes	Pears
x	x		
x		x	
x			x
	x	x	
	x		x
		x	x

Notice that you could not draw any more rows with two x's without duplicating some of the existing rows. Count the rows: there are **6** possible combinations of two fruits.

PRACTICE 12.1

If you are asked to find the number of possible combinations ($_nC_r$) in a problem that uses larger numbers, you can use this formula, which appears on the *Mathematics Reference Sheet*:

$$_nC_r = \frac{n!}{(n-r)!r!}$$

In the formula, n is the number of items in the group. The letter r represents the number of items you are asked to combine. The exclamation point indicates a **factorial,** which works like this: Multiply the number by all the smaller whole numbers greater than zero: $6! = 6 \times 5 \times 4 \times 3 \times 2 \times 1$.

Example 2: Maclellan will take 7 of her 9 friends for a fishing weekend. How many combinations of her 9 friends are possible?

Step 1: Plug in the values given in the problem.

$$C = \frac{9!}{(9-7)!7!}$$

Step 2: Either use your calculator, or write out the factorials and cancel.

$$C = \frac{9 \times 8 \times 7 \times 6 \times 5 \times 4 \times 3 \times 2 \times 1}{(2 \times 1)(7 \times 6 \times 5 \times 4 \times 3 \times 2 \times 1)}$$

$$C = \frac{9 \times 8 \times \cancel{7 \times 6 \times 5 \times 4 \times 3 \times 2 \times 1}}{(2 \times 1)(\cancel{7 \times 6 \times 5 \times 4 \times 3 \times 2 \times 1})}$$

$$C = \frac{(9 \times 8)}{2} = 36$$

A. Solve.

1. As a supervisor, Rob is choosing four of his employees to work on a special project. The employees are Angela, Barbara, Colin, David, and Elizabeth. Of those five employees, how many teams of four are possible?

2. Jessica wants to take three books on vacation with her. She has five books to choose from. How many possible combinations of three books could she take on vacation?

3. Grant is cooking a homemade pizza, and he has the following toppings available: anchovies, ham, mushrooms, and sausage. He will choose three of those toppings. How many ways could Grant combine those toppings?

B. Choose the one best answer to each question about combinations.

4. Celia is going to plant a small flower bed with four flowers. She can choose from begonias, fuchsias, hellebore, daisies, and salvia. How many combinations of four flowers are possible?

   A. 5
   B. 20
   C. 24
   D. 120

5. The Sarkesian brothers own a hardware store. There are five items the owners might display in the window. Joe Sarkesian thinks that the window should have two items, but his brother Rick thinks the window should have three items. Counting both Joe's ideas and Rick's ideas for the window, how many possible combinations of the five items are there?

   A. 10
   B. 20
   C. 30
   D. 120

Combinations with More Than One Type of Item

Sometimes you may be asked to count possible combinations with more than one type of item. Consider the following example:

Example 3: Sarah is deciding what to wear. She has three shirts, two pairs of pants, and two pairs of shoes. How many possible outfits does she have, if an outfit is one shirt, one pair of pants, and one pair of shoes?

This question differs from the question about Pablo on page 294. In that question, Pablo was choosing from one overall group of fruits. Here, Sarah is choosing one out of each of three groups—shirts, pants, and shoes. If you are given more than one type of item and must choose one of each type, you can use a tree diagram to figure out all the possible combinations. Study the following example:

Each "branch" of the tree represents a possible combination. The number of branches on the right-hand side represents the possible number of combinations; in this case, there are **12** possible outfits.

However, you can solve the same type of problem (where you have more than one type of item and are choosing one of each type) using the **fundamental counting principle,** which works like this:

Start with shirts: for each shirt, Sarah has two pants options. That's $3 \times 2 = 6$. Additionally, for each of those six options, she has two options for shoes. That's $3 \times 2 \times 2 = \mathbf{12}$.

Use the fundamental counting principle to solve the following problem:

Example 4: Gordon is at a restaurant that serves a three-course meal: an appetizer, an entrée, and a dessert. There are three appetizers, six entrees, and four desserts to choose from. Gordon will order one of each. How many different meals could he order?

Multiply three appetizers by six entrees by four desserts: $3 \times 6 \times 4 = 72$. There are **72** possible ways Gordon could order his meal.

PRACTICE 12.2

A. **Use a tree diagram or the fundamental counting principle to solve the following problems.**

1. Frank is making a sandwich. His sandwich will have one type of bread, one type of meat, and one condiment. He has four types of bread: white, wheat, rye, and a Kaiser roll. Meats he can choose from are chicken, turkey, and roast beef. For condiments, Frank can choose mayonnaise, mustard, vinaigrette, or horseradish. How many ways can Frank make his sandwich?

2. Van Ahn attended a trivia contest and won three rounds. For the first round she won, she could choose one of three restaurant gift certificates. The prize for another round was one of two T-shirts. Winning the third round allowed her to choose one of four souvenir hats. How many possible combinations of prizes were available to Van Ahn?

3. Henry is wrapping a gift for his daughter. He will use one type of wrapping paper, one type of ribbon, and one bow. He has three different types of wrapping paper, three different types of ribbon, and three different bows. How many ways can Henry wrap the gift?

4. Julio is looking forward to a three-day weekend. On Friday, he will either go to the beach or attend a street festival. On Saturday, he plans to visit a museum, but he is trying to decide among three different museums. On Sunday, he will try one of four new restaurants. How many ways could Julio combine these weekend activities?

B. **Choose the one best answer to each question about combinations. Determine whether you are being asked to find possible combinations from one type of item or from multiple types of items. You MAY use your calculator.**

5. The Nu Mu Beta fraternity is deciding what secret passphrase it should require its members to say before being admitted to meetings. The first and third words of the passphrase will be the names of Greek letters. There are 24 letters in the Greek alphabet. The second word will be a number from one to nine. How many possible passphrases are there?

   A.   24
   B.   57
   C.   576
   D. 5,184

6. A video game designer is creating a new superhero, who will have three of five potential superpowers. How many combinations of superpowers could the new superhero have?

   A. 10
   B. 15
   C. 100
   D. 125

7. A chef will make a soup with five ingredients: one of four meats, one of four vegetables, one of four kinds of noodles, one of four kinds of broth, and one of four spices. How many possible combinations of ingredients could the chef put into the soup?

   A.   20
   B.   256
   C. 1,024
   D. 3,125

8. A doctor is deciding how to treat a given disease. The doctor will prescribe one medication, one dietary change, and one type of vitamin supplement. There are five medications, five dietary changes, and five types of vitamins the doctor might prescribe. How many combinations are possible?

   A.   125
   B.   625
   C. 1,250
   D. 3,125

Permutations

On the TASC Mathematics Test, you may be asked how many possible permutations, or sequences, are possible given a group of items. Consider the following example:

Example 1: Eliza is planning her day off. She wants to visit the art museum, try the new coffee shop, call her mom, and take a walk, but not necessarily in that order. How many possible sequences of those four activities are there?

This question asks you for all possible permutations, or ways to sequence the items. Thus, *coffee-art-mom-walk* and *art-coffee-mom-walk* are two different possible outcomes. Consider how this problem differs from the combinations problems on pages 294–297. In those cases, order did not matter; in a permutations problem, order does matter.

Start with how many things could go first: here, there are four possibilities for Eliza's first activity. Once she has done that first activity, three possibilities remain. After she has done a first and second activity, two possibilities remain, and then only one. So you simply multiply: $4 \times 3 \times 2 \times 1$. There are **24** possible permutations.

Some permutations questions may ask you to determine the possible orderings for only some of the items in a list. Consider this example:

Example 2: Ten runners are competing in a race. There are prizes for first, second, and third place. How many possible sequences of the top three prize winners are there?

Notice that you are not simply figuring out how many groups of three can be made out of the ten. Rather, you are figuring out how many sequences of three can be made out of the ten.

Now, multiplying $10 \times 9 \times 8 \times 7 \times 6 \times 5 \times 4 \times 3 \times 2 \times 1$ would give you all the possible permutations of all ten runners, so that approach will not work here. Instead, start with how many people could win first place: here, ten. Once someone has won first, there are nine possibilities for second place. Once someone has won first and someone else has won second, there are eight possibilities for third place. And then you stop multiplying: $10 \times 9 \times 8 = 720$. There are **720** possible ways that the runners could be arranged in the top three prize-winning slots. (Note that simply multiplying 10 by 3 will not work.)

The *Mathematics Reference Sheet* contains a formula that can be helpful if the question involves larger numbers. To find the number of possible permutations $\left(_nP_r \right)$:

$$_nP_r = \frac{n!}{(n-r)!}$$

In that formula, n is the number of items in the group, and r is the number of items you are asked to include in the permutations. To solve Example 2 using the formula, plug in the values and cancel out the values that appear in both the numerator and the denominator:

$$P = \frac{10!}{(10-3)!} = \frac{10 \times 9 \times 8 \times \cancel{7 \times 6 \times 5 \times 4 \times 3 \times 2 \times 1}}{\cancel{7 \times 6 \times 5 \times 4 \times 3 \times 2 \times 1}} = 10 \times 9 \times 8$$

PRACTICE 13

A. Read the problems and decide whether you are being asked to find combinations or permutations. Then solve.

1. Noemi is trying to remember the password for her email. She knows that it has the following characters in it: M, Q, $, L, 7. But she can't remember the order they go in. How many possible sequences of those five characters are there?

2. Five students in a class have volunteered for a special project. Only three can actually help with the project. How many possible groupings of three out of the five are possible?

3. Tyrell is the curator at a gallery and is deciding how to arrange six paintings that will be displayed in a line along one wall. All six paintings will be included. How many possible sequences could Tyrell choose?

B. Choose the <u>one best answer</u> to each question about combinations or permutations. You <u>MAY</u> use your calculator.

4. Soraya has been given six tasks to do at work, but she has time to complete only four of them. She must decide in what order to do the tasks. How many possible orderings of four tasks are available to Soraya?

   A. 24
   B. 36
   C. 360
   D. 720

5. In a certain public garden, the gardener wanted to show the different visual effects that arranging flowers in different sequences can have. So he chose three kinds of flowers and planted flower beds showing each of the possible sequences of the three kinds. How many such flower beds did the gardener plant?

   A. 3
   B. 6
   C. 9
   D. 12

6. Ten people hope to become extras in a movie. The movie's casting director will choose four people to fill the following specific roles in the movie: Bystander #1, Bystander #2, Bystander #3, and Bystander #4. How many ways could those four roles be filled?

   A. 24
   B. 40
   C. 540
   D. 5,040

<u>Questions 7 and 8 refer to the following information:</u>

Clark and his daughter are at the amusement park, and Clark is offering his daughter a choice. They don't have time to ride all six rides at the amusement park, but they can ride three of them.

7. How many combinations of three rides could Clark's daughter choose?

   A. 18
   B. 20
   C. 120
   D. 720

8. Clark's daughter can also choose the order in which she wants to enjoy the rides. How many possible orderings of three out of the six rides are possible?

   A. 18
   B. 20
   C. 120
   D. 720

STATISTICS AND PROBABILITY PRACTICE QUESTIONS

Directions: You <u>MAY</u> use your calculator.

Questions 1 and 2 refer to the following graph.

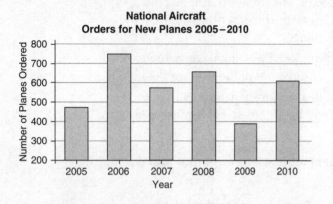

1. The mean number of aircraft orders for the six years shown on the graph is 573 planes. In which year was the number of orders closest to the mean?

   A. 2006
   B. 2007
   C. 2008
   D. 2009

2. By about what percent did orders at National Aircraft decrease from 2008 to 2009?

   A. 30%
   B. 40%
   C. 68%
   D. 75%

3. At a convention, Jim and his three friends each bought three raffle tickets. At the time of the drawing, 400 tickets had been sold. What is the probability that either Jim or one of his friends will win?

   A. $\frac{3}{100}$
   B. $\frac{1}{25}$
   C. $\frac{3}{50}$
   D. $\frac{9}{100}$

Questions 4 through 6 are based on the following table.

Southland Weather March 9			
Area	**High Temp.**	**Low Temp.**	**Precipitation (in Inches)**
Downtown	65° F	53° F	0.45
Airport	62° F	50° F	0.63
Woodland Hills	68° F	50° F	1.34
East Village	56° F	48° F	3.53
Ventura	62° F	49° F	2.57
Highland Park	64° F	55° F	0.84

4. Based on the data in the table, what was the median low temperature for March 9?

   A. 62.8°
   B. 51.5°
   C. 50.8°
   D. 50°

5. What was the mean amount of precipitation (in inches) on March 9 for the areas listed in the table?

   A. 0.65
   B. 1.09
   C. 1.56
   D. 1.99

6. For which area on the table was there the greatest range, or difference, between the high and low temperatures?

   A. Ventura
   B. East Village
   C. Woodland Hills
   D. Downtown

STUDY ADVICE

On the next few pages, you'll practice the statistics and probability skills you learned in this chapter. Remember, only about 10% of questions on the Mathematics Test will be about statistics and probability. So, definitely review these concepts if you need to, but also leave yourself time to study algebra, functions, and geometry (the next three chapters) in depth.

Questions 7 and 8 refer to the graph.

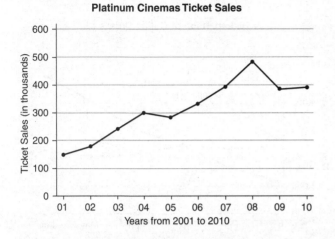

Platinum Cinemas Ticket Sales

Ticket Sales (in thousands)

Years from 2001 to 2010

7. Platinum Cinemas opened its first theaters in 2001. The company's ticket sales increased steadily until what year, when there was a drop in sales?

A. 2004
B. 2005
C. 2008
D. 2009

8. Which year had the sharpest increase in ticket sales over the previous year?

A. 2002
B. 2006
C. 2008
D. 2009

9. At Nelson Stationers, the first 25 customers who visited the store on Monday morning received their choice of a gift. The table below shows how many customers chose each gift.

pen and pencil set	ʮʮ
calculator	ʮʮ ʮʮ ‖
mouse pad	ʮʮ ‖‖

What percent of the customers chose a mouse pad?

A. 17%
B. 25%
C. 32%
D. $33\frac{1}{3}\%$

10. A standard deck of playing cards has 52 cards, with 13 cards each of hearts, diamonds, clubs, and spades. If a card is drawn randomly from the deck, what is the probability that it will be either hearts or diamonds?

A. 1 in 2
B. 1 in 4
C. 1 in 8
D. 1 in 16

For questions 11 and 12, mark your answers in the grids below.

11. Nita worked the following overtime hours over a six-week period.

Week 1: 5 hours

Week 2: $3\frac{1}{2}$ hours

Week 3: 4 hours

Week 4: 0 hours

Week 5: $1\frac{1}{2}$ hours

Week 6: 7 hours

What is the mean number of overtime hours Nita worked each week?

12. A spinner has five equal sections, and they are numbered from 1 to 5. What is the probability of spinning a number greater than 3? (Express the answer as a fraction.)

11.

12.

Questions 13 through 15 refer to the following graph.

In a recent election, five candidates ran for the city council seat from District 11. The results of the race are shown in the graph below.

City Council Election Results

Grace Reiner 9%

Scott Kang 14%

Amos Lee 18%

John Bowen 24%

Barbara Utley 35%

13. The three city council candidates who received the fewest votes received what percent of the total vote?

A. 23%
B. 41%
C. 56%
D. 77%

14. Which two candidates combined received about $\frac{3}{5}$ of the votes cast?

A. Grace and Utley
B. Kang and Utley
C. Bowen and Utley
D. Lee and Bowen

15. If 5100 votes were cast in the election, which of the following expressions could be used to find out how many votes Grace Reiner received?

A. 5100×0.9
B. $\dfrac{5100}{0.9}$
C. $\dfrac{5100}{0.09}$
D. 5100×0.09

Questions 16 through 18 refer to the following graph.

Comparison of Online Orders

16. In which month did Company A and Company B receive about the same number of online orders?

A. February
B. March
C. April
D. May

17. Based on the trends shown by the data, what would be the best prediction for the number of online orders in July for Company A?

A. 7200
B. 5900
C. 5200
D. 4900

18. About 18% of the online orders in April at Company A are returned for credit or exchange. How many orders at Company A were returned for credit or exchange in the month of April?

A. 180
B. 360
C. 540
D. 600

Questions 19 and 20 are based on the following information.

A basketball player's statistics for an eight-game series are shown in the table below.

Game	Shots Attempted	Shots Made
1	25	10
2	23	12
3	26	10
4	24	13
5	29	15
6	18	7
7	24	12
8	27	10

19. What was the median number of shots attempted by this player in the series?

   A. 24
   B. 24.5
   C. 25
   D. 26.5

20. What is the mode of the shots made by this player during the series?

   A. 12
   B. 11
   C. 10 and 12
   D. 10

21. A bag contains 24 marbles. Eight are red, six are blue, and ten are white. A marble is drawn from the bag and replaced. A second marble is chosen at random from the bag. What is the probability that the first marble is red and the second is white?

   A. $\frac{2}{5}$
   B. $\frac{5}{36}$
   C. $\frac{5}{48}$
   D. $\frac{1}{48}$

22. A company has 36 employees. For three months, the owner has kept track of the number of sick days used by her employees per month.

Month	Sick Days
Sept.	34
Oct.	31
Nov.	42

Which expression could be used to find the average number of sick days taken each month?

   A. $\dfrac{34 + 31 + 42}{36}$

   D. $\dfrac{34 + 31 + 42}{3}$

   C. $\dfrac{34 + 31 + 42 + 36}{4}$

   D. $(34 + 31 + 42) \times 3$

For questions 23 and 24, mark your answers in the grids below.

23. Andy rolls two standard six-sided dice. What is the probability of rolling two 1s? Express your answer as a fraction.

24. Angelique, a teacher, is making a reading list for her students. She wants to include one historical novel, one work of science fiction, one book of poetry, and one graphic novel. She has five of each type of book to choose from. How many possible combinations of books could she include in her reading list?

23.

24.

25. A charity's board has ten members. One of the members will be elected president, then another will be elected treasurer, and then a third will be elected secretary. If no member can hold more than one position, how many ways can the members fill those positions?

A.   27
B.   30
C.   720
D. 5,040

Questions 26 and 27 are based on the following information.

The table below displays the reasons why patients visited a walk-in clinic during a certain week.

Reason	Number of Patients
Colds and Flu	卌 卌 卌 I
Cuts and Scrapes	卌 卌 III
Sprained Muscles	卌 卌 II
Tetanus Shots	卌 II
Severe Headaches	卌 卌 II

26. What percent of the patients represented in the table visited the walk-in clinic because of sprained muscles?

A. 17%
B. 20%
C. 24%
D. 75%

27. In the week represented in the table, what was the ratio of the number of patients with colds or flu to the number of patients with severe headaches?

A. 4:15
B. 4:3
C. 3:4
D. 1:5

Questions 28 and 29 are based on the following information and graph.

A hundred people are participating in a medical study. As a first step, the researchers collected information about participants' weight. The graph below represents how many people fell into each weight category.

28. Which weight category displays the highest frequency?

A. 120–139 lbs
B. 180–199 lbs
C. 200–219 lbs
D. 260–279 lbs

29. Consider only the 100 individuals represented in the graph. Which one of the following groups contains the most people?

A. Participants weighing 200 lbs or more
B. Participants weighing less than 200 lbs
C. Participants weighing 180–199 lbs
D. Participants weighing less than 180 lbs

30. There are four children in Mr. Martin's class. Three of them will be selected to be hall monitors. How many combinations of hall monitors are possible?
A.   3
B.   4
C.   9
D. 12

Questions 31 through 33 refer to the following information and table.

The owner of a taxi company measures the gas mileage of each of the cars in her fleet. The table below shows her results.

Average miles per gallon	Number of cars
15	I I
20	ﬔ I I
25	ﬔ
30	ﬔ I
35	I

31. Which of the values (average miles per gallon) displays the highest frequency?
   A. 15 miles per gallon
   B. 20 miles per gallon
   C. 30 miles per gallon
   D. 35 miles per gallon

32. What is the ratio of taxis that get 35 miles per gallon on average to the number of taxis that get 15 miles per gallon on average?

   A. $\frac{1}{2}$

   B. $\frac{3}{2}$

   C. $\frac{4}{5}$

   D. $\frac{1}{10}$

33. Choose the line plot that represents the information in the table.

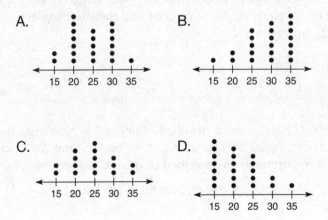

34. Ahmed works at the ticket window of a theater, and one night he decides to track when the patrons arrive for a 7:30 p.m. show. The table below represents his data.

Time period	Percent of patrons who arrive
5:30 to 5:59 p.m.	2%
6:00 to 6:29 p.m.	14%
6:30 to 6:59 p.m.	25%
7:00 to 7:29 p.m.	48%
7:30 to 8:00 p.m.	11%

Which one of the histograms below accurately represents Ahmed's data?

Algebraic Expressions

Writing Algebraic Expressions

An **algebraic expression** uses numbers, operations, and variables to show number relationships. **Variables** are letters (such as x and y) that represent unknown numbers. Each time a letter is used within the same expression, it represents the same number.

To solve algebra problems, you will need to be able to translate number relationships described in words into algebraic expressions. Study the following examples.

Algebraic expressions in words	In symbols
the product of 5 and a number	$5x$
a number decreased by 12	$x - 12$
the sum of 3 and the square of a number	$3 + x^2$
6 less than the quotient of a number and 2	$\frac{x}{2} - 6$
one-half a number increased by 15	$\frac{1}{2}x + 15$
4 times the difference of -3 and a number	$4(-3 - x)$
a number less another number	$x - y$
10 less than a number which is the square root of a number plus 3	$10 - \sqrt{x + 3}$

To do well on algebra questions on the TASC Mathematics Test, you must be able to translate a common life situation into mathematical symbols. You will use this skill to write equations and functions, to apply formulas, and to solve word problems.

Example 1: Kyle processes sales for an online bookstore. The shipping and handling on an order is equal to 4% of the total cost of the order plus $0.95 per book. If c represents total cost and n represents the number of books in an order, which of the following expressions could be used to find the shipping and handling for an order?

(1) $\dfrac{4}{100}nc + 0.95$

(2) $(0.04 + 0.95)n + c$

(3) $0.04c + 0.95n$

This kind of problem is called a **setup problem.** You need to recognize the correct way to find the shipping and handling based on the total cost and number of items. The relationship is described in the second sentence.

shipping and handling = 4% of total cost (c) plus $0.95 per book ($n$)

$$= \qquad 0.04c \qquad + \qquad 0.95n$$

The correct answer is option **(3), $0.04c + 0.95n$.**

A. Write an algebraic expression for each description. Use the variables x and y.

1. a number decreased by 7

2. the product of 3 and the square of a number increased by that number

3. the product of 8 and a number less 10

4. the difference of -3 multiplied by a number and the product of 2 and another number

5. 5 less than the quotient of 10 and a number

6. the sum of -8 and the product of 7 and a number

7. the sum of 16 times a number and the number decreased by 3 times another number

8. a number squared plus the number raised to the fourth power

9. the square of a number plus the quotient of 4 and 7

10. 6 subtracted from the sum of 15 and the square root of a number

11. a number less the sum of another number and 13

12. the square of the sum of a number and 6

13. 17 less the sum of 2 times a number plus another number

14. a number increased by the quotient of 24 and the number

15. the difference of the product of 2 and a number and 15

16. 4 times the difference of two different numbers

17. 5 multiplied by the difference of a number squared and 3

18. the product of a number and the difference of 11 and the square root of 100

B. Choose the one best answer to each question.

19. A minor-league baseball team is giving a local charity the sum of $1500 and $0.50 for each ticket over 2000 sold for one game. Let x represent the number of tickets sold. If the team sells more than 2000 tickets, which of the following expressions could be used to find the amount of the donation?

   A. $1500 + 0.50x$
   B. $1500 + $0.50(2000 - x)
   C. $1500 + $0.50($x$ - 2000)
   D. $1500(2000 - x)($0.50)

20. The sum of 3 times a number and 4 times a second number is divided by the sum of 2 and a third number. Which of the following expressions represents this series of operations?

   A. $(3x + 4y) \div (2 + z)$
   B. $3x + 4y \div (2 + z)$
   C. $3x + 4y \div 2 + z$
   D. $(3x + 4y) \div 2z$

Question 21 refers to the following information.

Appliance City employees earn an hourly wage plus commission. Wage options are shown below.

Option	Hourly Wage	Commission on Sales
A	$7.50	1%
B	$6.00	3%

21. Chandra is paid under Option B. If h represents the number of hours worked and s represents Chandra's total sales, which of the following expressions could be used to find her weekly pay?

   A. $6 + h + 0.03s$
   B. $6h + 0.03s$
   C. $6s + 0.03h$
   D. $0.03(h)(s)$

Simplifying and Evaluating Expressions

Simplifying an expression means to perform all the operations you can within an expression. When working with variables, you must remember an important rule: You can add or subtract like terms only.

A **term** is a number, a variable, or the product or quotient of numbers and variables. A term cannot include a sum or a difference.

Examples: $5x$ $3y^2$ 13 x^3 $\dfrac{x}{2}$

Like terms have the same variable raised to the same power. For example, $3x^2$ and $5x^2$ are like terms. $8y$ and $4y$ are also like terms. However, $6x$ and $2x^2$ are not like terms because the variables are not raised to the same power.

To simplify an expression, combine like terms.

Example 2: Simplify $2x - 5 + 4x^2 - 8 + 6x$.

Combine like terms. It is customary to write the term with the greatest exponent first and to continue in descending order.

$$2x - 5 + 4x^2 - 8 + 6x$$
$$= (2x + 6x) + (-5 + -8) + 4x^2$$
$$= 8x + (-13) + 4x^2$$
$$= \mathbf{4x^2 + 8x - 13}$$

The **distributive property** allows you to remove grouping symbols to simplify expressions. We can state the distributive property using symbols.

$$a(b + c) = ab + ac \quad \text{and} \quad a(b - c) = ab - ac$$

In other words, each term inside the parentheses is multiplied by the term outside the parentheses, and the results are added or subtracted depending on the operation inside the parentheses. Example 3 applies the distributive property.

Example 3: Simplify $4x - 3(x + 9) + 15$.

1. Change subtracting to adding a negative number.

2. Use the distributive property. Multiply -3 by each term in the parentheses.

3. Combine like terms.
   (**Note:** $1x$ means x.)

$$4x - 3(x + 9) + 15$$
$$= 4x + -3(x + 9) + 15$$
$$= 4x + (-3x) + (-3)(9) + 15$$
$$= 4x + (-3x) + (-27) + 15$$
$$= (4x + -3x) + (-27 + 15)$$
$$= \mathbf{x - 12}$$

Evaluating an expression means finding its value. To evaluate an expression, substitute a given number for each variable. Follow the order of operations.

Example 3: Find the value of the expression $\dfrac{3x + 2y}{4}$ when $x = 6$ and $y = 5$.

1. Replace the variables with the values given in the problem.

$$\frac{3x + 2y}{4} = \frac{3(6) + 2(5)}{4}$$

2. Perform the operations above the fraction bar. Then divide.

$$\frac{3(6) + 2(5)}{4} = \frac{18 + 10}{4} = \frac{28}{4} = 7$$

Note: To remove parentheses from an operation that follows a minus sign, imagine that the parentheses are preceded by 1. Then use the distributive property.

$$-(2x + 3)$$
$$= -1(2x + 3)$$
$$= -1(2x) + (-1)(3)$$
$$= -2x + (-3) \text{ or } -2x - 3$$

A. Simplify.

1. $5 + x^2 - 3 + 3x$

2. $2y + 5 + 17y + 8$

3. $3x - 6(x - 9)$

4. $6x^3 + 4 + 2x^2(15) + x^2$

5. $4(y + 8) + 3(y - 6)$

6. $5 - (x - 3) + 4x$

7. $16x + 6(x - 2)$

8. $5y^2 + 4 - 3y^2 + 5 + y$

9. $-3(x + 3) - 2(x + 4)$

10. $5x - (x + 4) - 3$

B. Evaluate each expression as directed.

11. Find the value of $6(x + 2) + 7$ when $x = 2$.

12. Find the value of $3x^2 + 3(x + 4)$ when $x = 3$.

13. Find the value of $\dfrac{(x + y)^2}{2} - 10$ when $x = 2$ and $y = 4$.

14. Find the value of $y^2 + 16 - (y - 5)^2$ when $y = 3$.

15. Find the value of $8x + 9y - (2x + y)$ when $x = 4$ and $y = 6$.

16. Find the value of $x^2 + 3y - 4 + 2(x - z)$ when $x = 7$, $y = 5$, and $z = -3$.

17. Find the value of $(14 - x)^2 + 20\sqrt{x}$ when $x = 9$.

18. Find the value of $\dfrac{3(2x - y)}{3} + 6(y - 5)$ when $x = -2$ and $y = 3$.

19. Find the value of $x^2 - (x^3 + 3)$ when $x = -2$.

20. Find the value of $30x + 2 + 2y^2 - 3(x - 2)^2$ when $x = 1$ and $y = 4$.

C. Choose the <u>one best answer</u> to each question.

21. Which of the following expressions is equal to $3x^2 + 3(x - 3) + x + 10$?

   A. $x^2 + 9x + 1$
   B. $3x^2 + 4x + 19$
   C. $3x^2 - 2x + 19$
   D. $3x^2 + 4x + 1$

22. Given the expression $4x^2 - 3(y + 6)$, which of the following values for x and y will result in a value of -11?

   A. $x = 2, y = 3$
   B. $x = -2, y = 4$
   C. $x = -1, y = 2$
   D. $x = 1, y = 0$

<u>Question 23</u> refers to the following information.

Temperature Conversion Formulas	
To convert Fahrenheit (F) to Celsius (C)	$C = \dfrac{5}{9}(F - 32)$
To convert Celsius (C) to Fahrenheit (F)	$F = \dfrac{9}{5}C + 32$

23. If the temperature is 68° Fahrenheit, what is the temperature in Celsius?

   A. 20°
   B. 36°
   C. 154.4°
   D. 180°

STUDY ADVICE

Algebraic expressions are the foundation for much of the TASC Mathematics Test. In the next chapter, you'll take these skills one step further by working with expressions in word problems, equations, and functions. So, make sure you understand the material so far before moving on.

Expressions and Calculator Skills

Sometimes a calculator may be helpful when you work algebra problems. The following examples are worked using the TI-30XS MultiView™, which you will use if you are taking the TASC on computer, and which you might use if you are taking the TASC on paper. Remember, your calculator may vary if you are testing on paper. Please see pages 166–167 for more information about calculators. The TI-30XS MultiView™, like most scientific calculators, uses algebraic logic, which means that it follows the order of operations that you saw on page 194.

You need to practice using a scientific calculator with algebraic logic. You can find out whether your calculator uses algebraic logic by running this simple test.

Press: $4 \boxed{\times} 3 \boxed{x^2} \boxed{\text{enter}}$. (Your calculator may have an equal sign instead of an *enter* button.) If the display reads **36**, your calculator uses algebraic logic. If the display reads **144**, your calculator does not use algebraic logic. You should find another calculator to practice for the Mathematics Test.

You can use a calculator to evaluate an expression that contains several operations.

Example 1: Find the value of the expression $2x^2 + 3x - 5$ when $x = -4$.

When you come to the variable x, enter -4 by pressing $\boxed{(-)}4$. The $\boxed{(-)}$ key is called the **change sign key**.

Press: $\boxed{2}\ \boxed{(}\ \boxed{(-)}\ \boxed{4}\ \boxed{)}\ \boxed{x^2}\ \boxed{+}\ \boxed{3}\ \boxed{\times}\ \boxed{(-)}\ \boxed{4}\ \boxed{-}\ \boxed{5}\ \boxed{\text{enter}}$

The right side of the display reads **15**.

The value of the expression is **15**.

Expressions sometimes contain grouping symbols to show a different order of operations. You can enter grouping symbols on a scientific calculator. On the TI-30XS MultiView™, the grouping symbols $\boxed{(}$ and $\boxed{)}$ are found above the $\boxed{8}$ and $\boxed{9}$, respectively. When you enter the left, or open, parenthesis, $\boxed{(}$, the calculator waits until you enter the right, or closing, parenthesis, $\boxed{)}$, before it calculates what is inside the symbols.

Example 2: Find the value of the expression $2(x + 4) + \dfrac{5x}{3}$ when $x = 6$.

Press: $2\boxed{\times}\boxed{(}\ 6\ \boxed{+}\ 4\boxed{)}\ \boxed{+}5\boxed{\times}6\boxed{\div}3\ \boxed{\text{enter}}$.

The right side of the display reads **30**.

The value of the expression is **30**.

You can also use your calculator for only part of an expression.

Example 3: Find the value of the expression $\dfrac{3x + 6}{2} + \sqrt{225}$ when $x = 4$.

Substitute 4 for x in the first part of the expression and calculate the results by hand or using your calculator: $\dfrac{3(4) + 6}{2} = \dfrac{12 + 6}{2} = \dfrac{18}{2} = 9$.

Now use your calculator to find the square root of 225.

Press: $\boxed{\text{2nd}}\boxed{x^2}\ 225\ \boxed{\text{enter}}$. The right side of the display reads 15.

Add the results of the two steps: $9 + 15 = \mathbf{24}$.

KEY IDEAS

- On the Mathematics Test, you will use a scientific calculator that follows the order of operations.
- Use the *change sign* key to enter a negative number.
- Use the *grouping symbol* keys to change the order of operations.

TASC TEST TIP

To check your work when using a calculator, enter each calculation twice. If the results are the same, you probably pressed the keys that you intended.

PRACTICE 2

A. Use a calculator as needed to find the value of the expressions as directed.

1. What is the value of $5x^2 - 3x + 5$ when $x = 2$?

2. Find the value of $\sqrt{7x} + 2x$ to the nearest tenth when $x = 5$.

3. If $x = -3$, what is the value of $7x^2 + 2x - 6$?

4. What is the value of $\frac{1}{2}x + 15$ when $x = 3$?

5. Find the value of $3(2x + 3 + y) - 14$ when $x = -2$ and $y = 9$.

6. If $y = -3$, what is the value of $4y^3 + 2(y^2 - 4)$?

7. What is the value of $2(x^2 + 6) + 3(x - 1)$ when $x = 5$?

8. If $x = 4$ and $y = -4$, what is the value of the expression $6x^2 + 3y^2 + 2$?

9. Find the value of $-2(x^3 + 3) + 16x + 2$ when $x = 2$.

10. If $x = 7$, what is the value of the expression $7 + 3(x - 2) - 2x^2$?

11. Find the value of $-(x + y) + 3(2z - y)$ if $x = -5$, $y = -7$, and $z = 4$.

12. What is the value of the expression $x^2 - 7(3 - y) + 4$ when $x = 5$ and $y = 4$?

13. If $x = -2$ and $y = 8$, what is the value of $x^2 + y - 6(y + 3)$?

14. What is the value of $\sqrt{760 - 4x^2}$ to the nearest tenth when $x = 6$?

15. If $x = 20$, what is the value of the expression $4(x + 7) - 3(x - 2)$?

16. Find the value of $\dfrac{x(25 + 2x - y)}{-z}$ when $x = -3$, $y = 4$, and $z = -1$.

17. What is the value of $5y^2 + 4x^2 - 6(x - y)$ when $x = 5$ and $y = -2$?

18. Find the value of $3x^2 \cdot \dfrac{2(x - 3y)}{6}$ when $x = 6$ and $y = 1$.

19. What is the value of the expression $(x^2 + 5)(x^2 - x + 2) - 3$ when $x = -4$?

20. Find the value of $(x + y)(x - y)(2x + y)$ when $x = 9$ and $y = 4$.

B. Choose the one best answer to each question.

Width = 5.6 m
Length = 12.5 m

21. Jake has to buy enough fencing to enclose the rectangular garden shown above.

    The formula for finding the perimeter of (or distance around) a rectangle is $P = 2l + 2w$, where P = perimeter, l = length, and w = width. Using the values from the drawing, what is the perimeter in meters of the garden?

    A. 18.1
    B. 36.2
    C. 70
    D. 140

22. If $x = -5$ and $y = 2$, which of the following expressions has the greatest value?

    A. $x + y$
    B. $-x + y$
    C. xy
    D. $-2xy$

23. What is the value of the expression $2 \div x^{-4}$ when $x = 2$?

    A. 32
    B. 16
    C. 8
    D. -16

Understand Polynomials

The TASC Mathematics *Test* will expect you to understand polynomials. A **polynomial** is made up of terms, and since the prefix *poly-* means "many," a polynomial is a term in which many parts are being combined. Each term in a polynomial may be made up of a combination of coefficients, variables, exponents, and constants.

Coefficients include numbers such as 4, –25, or $\frac{1}{2}$ and will come before the variables. Coefficients can be negative, like –25. If there is no coefficient next to a variable, assume the coefficient is 1. In the expression $x + y + z$, the coefficient in front of each variable is equal to 1.

Variables are letters such as x and y in polynomial terms. In the polynomial $45a^2b$, the variables are a and b.

Exponents, or powers, are a way of showing repeated multiplication. This is also known as raising a number or variable to a power. Polynomials must be raised to whole number exponents. There are no negative or fractional powers in polynomials. In the polynomial $6x^3y^4$, the exponents are 3 and 4. The **degree** of a polynomial with only one variable is the largest exponent of that variable. For example, in the expression $4x^3 + 3x^2 - 5$, the degree is 3 (the largest exponent of x).

A **constant** is a number on its own that will always remain the same. It is not next to a variable. A constant can be either positive or negative, depending on whether it is being added or subtracted. In the expression $4x^3 + 3x^2 + 5$, the constant is 5. No matter what value you substitute for x, 5 will always be just 5.

Polynomials are built out of all of the components above, and there are different types of polynomials, including monomials, binomials, and trinomials. These are important to know.

- A **monomial** is a polynomial with only one term. An example of a monomial is $4xy^2$. This term is made up of a coefficient (4), two variables (x and y), and an exponent (the power of 2).

- A **binomial** is a polynomial with two terms. An example of a binomial is $3x + 2$. The first term is made up of a coefficient (3) and a variable (x), and the second term consists of a constant (2).

- A **trinomial** is a polynomial with three terms. An example of a trinomial is $4x + 3y^2 - 4$. The first term is made up of a coefficient (4) and a variable (x). The second term is made up of a coefficient (3), a variable (y), and an exponent (the power of 2). The third term is made up of a constant, and this time it is a negative number (–4).

A few types of numbers are not categorized as polynomials and cannot be present in polynomial terms. These include the following:

- Division by a variable, such as $\frac{3}{x+3}$ or $\frac{1}{x}$
- Negative exponents, such as $4xy^{-2}$ (exponents can only be 0, 1, 2, etc.)
- Fractional exponents, such as $3a^{\frac{1}{2}}$
- Variables inside radicals, such as $\sqrt{x}$

In a polynomial term, however, you can divide by a constant or have numbers inside a radical. For example, $\frac{4x}{12}$ is allowed, as is $\sqrt{10}$.

A. Identify whether each of the following is a monomial, binomial, or trinomial.

1. $25a$

2. $2xy^2z$

3. $x - 4$

4. $x^3 + y - 1$

5. $7y - 1$

6. $2x^4 + 3x + 4$

7. $\dfrac{x}{3}$

8. y^2

9. $g^2h^2i^2j^2$

10. $x^2 + x^2$

11. $x^2 + 14x + 3$

12. $x^2y + x^2 + y$

13. $g + h$

14. $\sqrt{49}$

15. $3x^2 - 5$

B. For each polynomial, identify the terms. Remember that a coefficient can be positive or negative.

16. $3x^4 - 2x^2 + 3$

17. $12a^2bc$

18. $3g - 4h$

19. $x^2 + y$

20. $-4a - 3b^2 + c$

21. 25

22. $4x^2 + 3x - 7$

23. $\dfrac{3x}{8}$

24. $\sqrt{25}$

25. $\dfrac{x^2}{9}$

26. $49x^2y^2z^2$

27. $18y^2 - 4y^2 + 8$

28. $3h - 4$

29. $x^2 - x + y^2 - 2$

30. $ab + ab^2 + b^2 - 4$

C. Choose the one best answer to each question.

31. What is the sum of the exponents in the expression $4x^3 + 3x^2 + 5$?

    A. 3
    B. 5
    C. 12
    D. 17

32. What is the sum of the coefficients in the expression $a - 3b - c + 2d$?

    A. −3
    B. −1
    C. 2
    D. 3

STUDY ADVICE

If you're having trouble sticking to your study schedule, consider finding a study partner—someone else who is studying for anything (the TASC, the GED® test, or any other exam). The two of you can remind each other to stick to your study schedules, encourage each other, and even have study sessions together.

Simplify Polynomials

Combine Like Terms

When working with polynomials, you must work to combine like terms. **Like terms** have variables that are the same or are terms that have the same variable raised to the same power, or exponent. For example, $8x^3$ and $4x^3$ are like terms, and $5y$ and $3y$ are also like terms.

Unlike terms have variables that are different or have the same variable raised to different powers. For example, $3a$ and $5b$ are unlike terms. The terms $9x$ and $7x^2$ are also unlike terms because the variables are raised to different powers.

You can only combine like terms when simplifying polynomials. Unlike terms cannot be combined. For example, in the polynomial $7x^2 + 4x^3$, you cannot combine the terms because x is raised to different powers in each term. However, in the polynomial $7x^2 + 4x^2$, you can combine terms that all have the same variable and the same exponent: $7x^2 + 4x^2 = 11x^2$.

Example 1: Combine like terms in the polynomial $4y^3 + 2x^3 - 7y^3$.

1. First, identify and group the like terms. $4y^3 - 7y^3 + 2x^3$

The two y^3 terms are alike; the x^3 term cannot be combined with them.

2. Combine the like terms. $-3y^3 + 2x^3$

Simplify Polynomials

Some polynomials may contain both like and unlike terms. The following example shows how like and unlike terms are handled when you have to simplify a polynomial. Start by combining like terms from the exponent with the largest number, or degree, and proceed to the exponent with the smallest number.

Example 2: Simplify the polynomial $7x^4 - 13x^2 + x^4 + 2x^2 + 5x + 3 + x$.

1. Combine like terms with the largest degree, which is 4. Add: $7x^4 + x^4 = 8x^4$.
2. You now have $8x^4 - 13x^2 + 2x^2 + 5x + 3 + x$. Combine like terms from the exponent with the next largest degree, which is 2. Add: $-13x^2 + 2x^2 = -11x^2$.
3. You now have $8x^4 - 11x^2 + 5x + 3 + x$. Finally, combine like terms with the next largest degree, which is 1. Add: $5x + x = 6x$.
4. You now have $\mathbf{8x^4 - 11x^2 + 6x + 3}$.

This is as much as you can simplify this polynomial by combining like terms. The simplified polynomial has no more like terms and must remain as is.

KEY IDEAS

- Like terms can be combined; unlike terms cannot.
- Like terms are either numbers—positive or negative—or variables with the same degree of exponents.
- Polynomials with unlike terms cannot be simplified.

TASC TEST TIP

When working with polynomials, treat the minus sign before a coefficient or constant as an indicator of a negative number. This will help you to combine like terms using the rules of signed numbers that you learned on pages 190–193.

PRACTICE 4

A. For each pair of terms, indicate if they are like terms or unlike terms.

1. $4x^3, x^3$ _____ terms

2. $3x, x$ _____ terms

3. b, b^2 _____ terms

4. $-2x, 7y$ _____ terms

5. $-2x, 7x$ _____ terms

6. $4a, 4$ _____ terms

7. g^2, g^2hi _____ terms

8. $2x^2y, 8x^2y$ _____ terms

9. $-5m, -5m^2$ _____ terms

10. x^2y, xy^2 _____ terms

11. $ab, 8ab$ _____ terms

12. $3y, 3y^2$ _____ terms

13. $14g, \frac{1}{3}g$ _____ terms

14. $12x^2, x^2$ _____ terms

15. a, ab^2 _____ terms

16. $15x^2, -x^2$ _____ terms

17. $10y, 11yz$ _____ terms

18. $x^2, \frac{x^2}{2}$ _____ terms

19. $g, -g^2$ _____ terms

20. $\frac{x}{8}, x^2$ _____ terms

B. Simplify each expression by combining like terms.

21. $3x^2y + 4x^2y$

22. $3b + b$

23. $a - 7a + 3$

24. $14ab + ab^2 + 2ab + 3$

25. $x^2 - 3x^2 + 7$

26. $ab + 2ab + ab$

27. $7g + 7gh + 7g + 7gh$

28. $g^2 + h^2 - 4g^2h^2 + g^2 + h^2 - 4$

29. $9y + y - y^2 - y$

30. $x^2 - 8x^2 + y - 3$

31. $11y + 11y - 7$

32. $9x^2y - 3x^2y + 4y^2 - 21 + y^2 - 2$

33. $8x^2 - 4x + 7 + 4x^3 - x^2 + 7x - 2$

34. $-3x^2 + 6x - 2x^2 - 10x + 5$

35. $9x^2 - 3x^3 + x - 2x^2$

C. Choose the one best answer to each question.

36. What is the simplified form of the expression $3a^2b + 4ab + 3a^2b + 5ab$?

    A. $6a^3b^2 + 8a^3b^2$

    B. $6a^2b + 9ab$

    C. $6a^2b + 8ab$

    D. $15a^6 + b^4$

37. When simplified, how many terms are in the polynomial $j^2 + k^3 - 2j^3 + 5k^3 - 2j^2$?

    A. 2

    B. 3

    C. 4

    D. 5

LESSON 5

Add and Subtract Polynomials

Add Polynomials with One Variable

On the Mathematics Test, you may be required to add polynomials that have one variable. You can add polynomials when they have like terms, including variables and exponents. When you see polynomials within parentheses linked by an addition sign, add them by combining the like terms across the polynomials.

Example 1: Add $(3x^2 + x + 4) + (2x^2 + 2x - 16)$.

1. To add these polynomials, simply combine like terms. Add: $3x^2 + 2x^2 = 5x^2$.
2. Add: $x + 2x = 3x$.
3. Add: $4 + (-16) = -12$.
4. Combine the results into one polynomial: $\mathbf{5x^2 + 3x - 12}$.

Sometimes, an expression needs to be simplified before you add and combine like terms.

Example 2: Add $(5x^2 + 8x - 4) + (2x^2 - 6x + 14x)$.

1. Simplify within the second parentheses. Add: $-6x + 14x = 8x$.
2. Combine like terms across the polynomials. Add: $5x^2 + 2x^2 = 7x^2$.
3. Use the simplified expression from step 1. Add: $8x + 8x = 16x$.
4. Combine the results into one polynomial: $\mathbf{7x^2 + 16x - 4}$.

Subtract Polynomials with One Variable

The only difference between adding and subtracting polynomials is the minus sign between the parentheses. You must distribute the negative sign across the second polynomial. To distribute the negative sign across the second polynomial, simply reverse the signs of each term. Then drop the parentheses and combine like terms across both polynomials.

Example 3: Subtract $(3x^2 + x + 4) - (7x^2 + 2x - 16)$.

1. Distribute the negative sign to everything in the second set of parentheses by reversing the sign of each term: $-7x^2 - 2x + 16$.
2. Drop the parentheses from the entire expression and combine like terms:
$$3x^2 + x + 4 - 7x^2 - 2x + 16$$
$$-4x^2 + x + 4 - 2x + 16$$
$$-4x^2 - x + 4 + 16$$
$$-4x^2 - x + 20$$

Note that subtracting a negative constant or coefficient is the same as adding a positive. In the next example, watch what happens to the negative coefficient inside the second set of parentheses when the sign is distributed.

PRACTICE 5.1

Example 4: Subtract $(x^2 + 2x + 3) - (4x^2 - x + 6)$.

1. Distribute the negative sign to everything in the second set of parentheses by reversing the sign of each term:

$$-4x^2 + x - 6$$

2. Drop the parentheses and combine like terms:

$$x^2 + 2x + 3 - 4x^2 + x - 6$$
$$x^2 - 4x^2 + 2x + x + 3 - 6$$
$$-3x^2 + 3x - 3$$

A. Add the following polynomials.

1. $(3x + 4) + (2x + 2)$

2. $(17y - y + 3) + (4y + 3y + 3)$

3. $(5x^2 - 3x - 4) + (3x^2 - 2x + 6)$

4. $(-a^2 + 2a) + (16a^2 + 6a)$

5. $(9x^2 - 3x - 2) + (2x^2 + 5x + 5)$

6. $(6a + 6) + (-5a - 5)$

7. $(-8g^2 + 7g + 6) + (8g^2 - 7g - 5)$

8. $(2x^2 + 5x) + (2x^2 + 4x + 7x - 9)$

9. $(13y + 4y + 4) + (7y - 7)$

10. $(-a^2 - a^2 - a - 4) + (-a^2 - a^2 - a - 5)$

B. Subtract the following polynomials.

11. $(3y - 4) - (2y - 2)$

12. $(x + 16) - (4x + 3)$

13. $(2a + 1) - (-a - 1)$

14. $(5x^2 + 2x + 4) - (2x^2 + x + 2)$

15. $(7y + 5y + 5) - (2y - 2)$

16. $(9x^2 + 4x + 5x + 4) - (7x^2 + 6x - 9)$

17. $(-g + g - 1) - (-g - g - 2)$

18. $(17a^2 - 4a - 4) - (16a^2 + 6a - 6)$

19. $(7b^2 + b - 8) - (7b^2 + b + 8)$

20. $(21x^2 + 3x^2 - 2x - 4 - 1) - (3x^2 + x^2 + x + 2x - 5 - 1)$

C. Choose the one best answer to each question.

21. What is the sum of the polynomials $(2xy + 3xy^2 - 4x^2y) + (5x^2y - 3xy^2 + 2xy)$?

    A. $x^2y + 4xy$

    B. $4xy + 3x + y$

    C. $7x - 2y$

    D. $7x^2y - 2xy$

22. Which of the following equals $(5x^2 - 2x + 1) - (3x^2 - 3x - 2)$?

    A. $x - 5x - 1$

    B. $2x^2 - x + 3$

    C. $2x^2 + x + 3$

    D. $2x^2 - 5x + 3$

STUDY ADVICE

Look back over your work. If you understood how to add or subtract polynomials, but you made small or careless errors in doing so, give yourself a pat on the back! You've learned the concept, and now you know to watch for small math errors.

Simplifying Polynomials with More Than One Variable

Some polynomials contain terms with different variables—for example, the binomial $2x + 3y$ contains an x term and a y term. You add, subtract, and simplify polynomials with more than one variable just as you do polynomials with just a single variable. However, you have to be careful to add and subtract only like terms. Remember that in all polynomials, like terms have the *same variable* and the *same exponent*. For example, in the polynomial $x^2 + 2x + y^2 + 3x + 2y$, the only like terms are the two x^1 terms. You can combine the $2x$ and the $3x$, but you cannot combine x^2 with any other term, nor can you combine the y^2 or the $2y$ with any other term. The most simplified version of this polynomial is $x^2 + 5x + y^2 + 2y$.

A term that consists of two or more variables multiplied together cannot be combined with terms that contain only one of those variables. For example, you cannot combine $2xy + 7x$. However, you can combine $2xy + 7xy$ to get $9xy$.

Example 5: Simplify $6xy^4 - 20x^2 - 3 + xy^4 + 12x^2 - 30$.

Start by grouping the like terms together. Then add and subtract as appropriate.

$$6xy^4 - 20x^2 - 3 + xy^4 + 12x^2 - 30$$
$$= 6xy^4 + xy^4 - 20x^2 + 12x^2 - 3 - 30$$
$$= 7xy^4 - 8x^2 - 33$$

Adding Polynomials with More Than One Variable

Adding polynomials that contain more than one variable requires the same process as adding polynomials that have only one variable. Just remove the parentheses and combine like terms across both polynomials. Remember that only like terms can be combined.

Example 6: Add $(3x^2 + 6x + 3xy) + (5x^2 - 6xy + 14y)$.

$$(3x^2 + 6x + 3xy) + (5x^2 - 6xy + 14y)$$
$$= 3x^2 + 5x^2 + 6x + 3xy - 6xy + 14y$$
$$= 8x^2 + 6x - 3xy + 14y$$

Subtracting Polynomials with More Than One Variable

Subtracting polynomials that contain more than one variable is exactly the same as subtracting polynomials that contain only a single variable. Remember to distribute the minus sign across the second polynomial when you remove the parentheses. Also remember that only like terms can be combined.

Example 7: Subtract $(3xy^2 + x + 2xy + 4) - (7xy^2 + 2xy - 16)$.

$$(3xy^2 + x + 2xy + 4) - (7xy^2 + 2xy - 16)$$
$$= 3xy^2 + x + 2xy + 4 - 7xy^2 - 2xy + 16$$
$$= -4xy^2 + x + 20$$

Notice that there is no xy term in the final simplified expression because $2xy - 2xy = 0$.

A. Simplify the expressions below.

1. $a^2 + 2a + b^2 + 3a + 3b^2$

2. $x + 3xy + y + 16 - 5x - 4xy$

3. $yz^2 - z^2 + 5 + 3yz - 3z^2 + 4yz$

4. $ab - b + c + 17 + 6ab - 34$

5. $a^4 + c^2 + 3ac - 5a^4 - 2c^2 + 5$

6. $19xyz + x - y + 3xyz + 6 + y$

7. $ef + ef^2 - 10 + 6ef + f$

8. $p + pq - q - p + 3pq - 3 - q + 7$

B. Add the following polynomials.

9. $(ab + b - c + 6) + (3ab - b + c - 6)$

10. $(x^2 + xy - y - 3) + (-x^2 - xy + y + 3)$

11. $(p^6 + p^5 + pq - p^2) + (2p^6 - p^5 + 3pq - q^2)$

12. $(x + xy + 7) + (y - xy + 8)$

13. $(9a + bc + c^2) + (-9a - b + bc - c^2)$

14. $(4xyz + 4x - 4y) + (6xyz - 4x - 4y + 16)$

15. $(5a + 5b + 4c - 6) + (a - b - 4c + d + 6)$

16. $(pq - q + 15) + (6pq - 15)$

C. Subtract the following polynomials.

17. $(ab + a + b + 6) - (8ab + a - b - 6)$

18. $(xy + x + y) - (xy + x + y)$

19. $(p^2 + q^2 + 14) - (3p^2 - 4q^2 + 7)$

20. $(x^4 + yz + z^4) - (yz + z^5)$

21. $(bc^2 + bc + c - 7) - (2bc - c - 7)$

22. $(xy + xz - xyz) - (4xy + xyz)$

23. $(c^3d^7 + c^2 - d + 35) - (2c^2 - 3d + 35)$

24. $(ef^2g - fg + 16) - (ef^2 + fg + 8)$

D. Choose the one best answer to each question.

25. Which of the following equals
$(x + y + z) - (-2x + 2y + z)$?

A. $-x + 3y + 2z$

B. $-2x - y + 2z$

C. $3x - 2y + 2z$

D. $3x - y$

26. Which of the following equals
$(2g^2 + 3h - 5k) + (g^2 + 2h + 3k)$?

A. $g^2 + h - 8k$

B. $3g^2 + 5h - 2k$

C. $2g^2 + 6h^2 - 15k^2$

D. $2g^4 + 5h - 2k$

Multiply Polynomials

Multiply a Monomial by a Monomial

To multiply two monomials, multiply each component separately. Start by multiplying the coefficients (or numbers). If there is no coefficient given, assume that the coefficient is 1 (for example, $xy = 1xy$). Then, multiply each variable separately by adding the exponents of like variables. Remember that a variable with no exponent is a variable raised to the first power (for example, $x = x^1$). So $x(x^3) = x^1(x^3) = x^4$.

Example 1: Multiply $(2ab)(4b)$.

$$2 \times 4 \times a \times b^1 \times b^1 = 8ab^2$$

Multiply a Monomial by a Binomial

To multiply a monomial by a binomial, multiply the monomial by the first term in the binomial, then multiply the monomial by the second term in the binomial. Finally, add the resulting terms.

Example 2: Multiply $-2z^2(z + 3yz)$.

1. Distribute the negative sign:

   $-2z^2(z + 3yz) = 2z^2(-z - 3yz)$.

2. Multiply the monomial by each term in the binomial:

   $2z^2(-z - 3yz) = [2 \times (-1) \times z^2 \times z^1] + [2 \times (-3) \times z^2 \times y^1z^1]$.

3. Add: $-2z^3 + (-6yz^3) = -2z^3 - 6yz^3$.

Multiply Two Binomials

To multiply two binomials, multiply the first terms, then the outer terms, then the inner terms, and, finally, the last terms. Add the results and combine like terms. You can remember this process by the acronym **FOIL**, which stands for First, Outer, Inner, Last.

Example 3: Multiply $(2g^2 + 9)(3g^2 - 4)$.

1. Multiply using FOIL:

   $(2g^2 + 9)(3g^2 - 4) = (2g^2)(3g^2) + (2g^2)(-4) + (9)(3g^2) + (9)(-4)$.

2. Add: $6g^4 - 8g^2 + 27g^2 - 36$.

3. Combine like terms:

   $6g^4 - 8g^2 + 27g^2 - 36 = 6g^4 + 19g^2 - 36$.

KEY IDEAS

- There are a number of ways to multiply polynomials.
- The basic concepts in all involve learning procedures for multiplying constants, variables, and exponents.
- A common method for multiplying binomials is called FOIL for short.

TASC TEST TIP

Always finish the FOIL method by combining like terms after you have multiplied.

PRACTICE 6

A. Multiply the monomials.

1. $(6x)(5x)$

2. $(2xy)(3y)$

3. $(7abc)(4bc)$

4. $(12y)(z)$

5. $(a)(9bc)$

6. $\left(5xyz\right)\left(2xy^2z^4\right)$

7. $(4ab)\left(bc^2\right)$

8. $\left(17f^2gh^3\right)\left(2fh^4\right)$

B. Multiply the binomials by the monomials.

9. $3z^2(6xy + 4z)$

10. $6x(7x - 6z)$

11. $-5ab(3b + 11c)$

12. $-3f^3\left(6h - 8fgh^2\right)$

13. $10z(7x^7 - 5z)$

14. $-z(-z - 6xy)$

15. $8b(9ab + 8a)$

16. $-9(-2x^4 + 3xy^2)$

C. Multiply the binomials by using FOIL. Remember to complete by combining like terms wherever possible.

17. $(x + 5)(x - 6)$

18. $(x + y)(x + y)$

19. $(z + 9)(z - 9)$

20. $(yz^2 + x)(yz^2 - 3x)$

21. $(3x + 3)(3x + 5)$

22. $(x + y)(x - y)$

23. $(y^2 - 6)(y^4 + 10)$

24. $(ab + 3)(ab - 4)$

D. Choose the one best answer to each question.

25. Which of the following expressions is equal to $(4a^3b^2)(3a^2c)$?

   A. $12a^5b^2c$
   B. $7a^5b^2c$
   C. $12a^6bc$
   D. $7a^6b^2c$

26. Martha has $2pc^2$ board games, and John has $6p^2c$ board games. Which of the following expressions represents the product of the number of board games that Martha and John have?

   A. $8p^3c^3$
   B. $8p^2c^2$
   C. $12p^2c^2$
   D. $12p^3c^3$

27. Which of the following expressions is equal to $(4ab + 2)(3ab - 7)$?

   A. $7a^2b^2 + 22ab + 5$
   B. $12a^2b^2 - 22ab - 14$
   C. $12a^2b^2 + 22ab + 14$
   D. $7a^2b^2 - 22ab - 5$

STUDY ADVICE

How's your stress level? As you're working through difficult content, it's especially important to manage your stress. Stay on a regular sleep schedule, exercise, and eat right. Whenever you're stressing out, step away. Remember: You can do this. Just don't let stress get in your way.

Divide Polynomials

Divide Polynomials by a Number

The Mathematics Test will sometimes ask you to simplify a polynomial that is written as a fraction. To simplify, divide the numerator and denominator by a common term. A common term can be the following:

- A number
- A variable with a number as a coefficient
- A more complicated expression

You may need to factor the common term out of the numerator or denominator before you can do the division.

Example 1: Simplify $\dfrac{3x+6}{3}$.

$$\frac{3x+6}{3} = \frac{3(x+2)}{3} = \frac{\cancel{3}(x+2)}{\cancel{3}} = x+2$$

Divide Polynomials by an Expression

Dividing a polynomial by an expression is really no different from dividing by a number. You need a common term in the numerator and denominator, and you may have to factor out that common term (including any variables) before you can do the division.

Example 2: Simplify $\dfrac{25x^3 - 45x^2}{5x}$.

$$\frac{25x^3 - 45x^2}{5x} = \frac{5x(5x^2 - 9x)}{5x} = \frac{\cancel{5x}(5x^2 - 9x)}{\cancel{5x}} = 5x^2 - 9x$$

When the numerator has two added or subtracted expressions that both include the common term, it may be easier to split the polynomial into two separate fractions and simplify them separately. Doing it this way will help you keep straight exactly which terms you can cancel.

Example 3: Simplify $\dfrac{x(x+7) - 3(x+7)}{x+7}$.

$$\frac{x(x+7) - 3(x+7)}{x+7} = \frac{x(x+7)}{x+7} - \frac{3(x+7)}{x+7}$$

$$= \frac{x(\cancel{x+7})}{\cancel{x+7}} - \frac{3(\cancel{x+7})}{\cancel{x+7}} = x - 3$$

A fraction that has an algebraic expression in both its numerator and its denominator, as in the previous examples, is sometimes called a rational expression. Do not be confused if you see this term on the TASC: It simply means that you are being asked to simplify by dividing one expression by another.

PRACTICE 7

A. To simplify, divide each polynomial by a number. (You may need to factor the numerator and/or denominator to find the common term.)

1. $\dfrac{2y + 30}{2}$

2. $\dfrac{7x + 21}{7}$

3. $\dfrac{4x + 20}{4}$

4. $\dfrac{3a + 3b}{3}$

5. $\dfrac{11x^2 + 22x}{11}$

6. $\dfrac{26x^2 + 39x + 13}{13}$

7. $\dfrac{5x + 10y}{5}$

8. $\dfrac{21a + 14b}{7}$

9. $\dfrac{48x + 32y}{32}$

10. $\dfrac{9a - 15b}{12}$

11. $\dfrac{6b + 24c}{18}$

12. $\dfrac{25a + 5b + 15c}{10}$

B. Divide each polynomial. Decide whether it is easier for you to divide the original numerator by the common term (as in Example 2) or whether to split the numerator first (as in Example 3).

13. $\dfrac{18x^2 + 6x}{3x}$

14. $\dfrac{10x^2 + 6x}{2x}$

15. $\dfrac{40y^2 + 10y}{5y}$

16. $\dfrac{42xy + 49x}{7x}$

17. $\dfrac{38xy + 38x}{19x}$

18. $\dfrac{3x + 18}{x + 6}$

19. $\dfrac{x(x + 4) - 6(x + 4)}{x + 4}$

20. $\dfrac{y(y + 3) + 7(y + 3)}{y + 3}$

21. $\dfrac{z(z + 2) - 5(z + 2)}{z + 2}$

22. $\dfrac{22x^2 + 66x}{11x}$

23. $\dfrac{x(y - 2) - 6(y - 2)}{y - 2}$

24. $\dfrac{a(b + 3) + 3(b + 3)}{b + 3}$

C. Choose the <u>one best answer</u> to each question.

25. Which of the following is equal to $\dfrac{21a + 14b}{7}$?

    A. $5a + 5b$
    B. $3a + 14b$
    C. $3a + 2b$
    D. $21a + 2b$

26. James has $27x$ apples, Rachel has $51y$ oranges, and Glen has $60z$ peaches. Which of the following expressions represents the average number of pieces of fruit that James, Rachel, and Glen have in their baskets?

    A. $9x + 51y + 60z$
    B. $46x + 46y + 46z$
    C. $9x + 17y + 60z$
    D. $9x + 17y + 20z$

ALGEBRAIC EXPRESSIONS PRACTICE QUESTIONS

1. Which of the following expressions is equal to $6 - 4(x + 3)$?

   A. $4x + 3$
   B. $4x - 9$
   C. $-4x + 9$
   D. $-4x - 6$

2. If Kris makes d dollars and Heidi makes 75 dollars less than 3 times Kris's wage, what does Heidi make in terms of d?

   A. $d + 75$
   B. $d - 225$
   C. $3d - 75$
   D. $3d - 225$

3. If there are $4x$ identical schools in a region and each school has $3y$ classrooms each with $7x$ desks, how many desks are there in the region?

   A. $11x + 3y$
   B. $28x + 3y$
   C. $84xy^2$
   D. $84x^2y$

4. Which of the following is equivalent to $x^2 - 25$?

   A. $x(x - 25)$
   B. $(x - 5)^2$
   C. $(x + 5)(x - 5)$
   D. $(x - 25)^2$

5. If Tom has $9x$ baseball cards, Adam has 13 more than Tom, and Dave has $2y$ baseball cards, together they would have how many cards?

   A. $9x + 2y + 13$
   B. $18xy + 13$
   C. $18xy + 2y$
   D. $18x + 2y + 13$

Questions 6 and 7 refer to the figure below.

The figure below is a multiplication box. Each place represents the horizontal number multiplied by the vertical number; for example, the 9 in the lower right corner equals 3 multiplied by 3.

	5	y	3
1	5		3
c	20	a	
3	b	d	9

6. Which of the following is equal to ab?

   A. $5y$
   B. $60y$
   C. $100y$
   D. $500y$

7. Which of the following is equal to $a - d$?

   A. b
   B. c
   C. x
   D. y

8. Multiply $7c^2(a^2 + 5b + 7c^2)$.

    A. $7a^2c^2 + 35bc^2 + 49c^4$
    B. $7(ac)^2 + 35(bc)^2 + 49c^4$
    C. $7a^2 + 35b + 49c^4$
    D. $a^2 + 5b + 14c^2$

9. A Little League pie sale fundraiser generated $900. If there were $6x$ pies sold, how much did each pie cost?

    A. $10
    B. $15
    C. $\$\dfrac{x}{150}$
    D. $\$\dfrac{150}{x}$

10. Simplify the expression

$$\frac{(a-4)^2 \, (6b)}{2(3b)\,(a+4)\,(a-4)}.$$

    A. $\dfrac{a-4}{a+4}$
    B. $\dfrac{a+4}{a-4}$
    C. $\dfrac{a-2}{2}$
    D. 1

11. Emilie buys x ounces of chicken for each of her guests at a dinner party. There are $8y$ people coming, and chicken is $\$z$ a pound. How much will the total amount of chicken cost in dollars? (*Hint*: There are 16 ounces in one pound.)

    A. $8xyz$
    B. $16xyz$
    C. $\dfrac{xyz}{2}$
    D. $\dfrac{xyz}{8}$

12. What is the value of the expression $6(x - y) - 8x$ when $x = -2$ and $y = 5$?

    A. -58
    B. -26
    C. 2
    D. 34

13. Which of the following would be equal to $x^2 + 6z$ multiplied by $2y - 4z$ if $x = 2$, $y = 4$, and $z = 3$?

    A. -88
    B. -72
    C. 0
    D. 104

14. If every member of a team is paid $5p$ dollars for his or her participation, and Team Alpha has $6k$ members, Team Beta has $4p$ members, and Team Delta has $9h$ members, which of the following represents the total amount paid to the members of all three teams?

    A. $1080hkp$
    B. $1080hkp^2$
    C. $120p^2k + 45ph$
    D. $30kp + 20p^2 + 45hp$

15. Which of the following is equal to $7x - [(5y)2x - 9y + 8x]$?

   A. $x - 9y + 10xy$
   B. $-3x - 4y$
   C. $-x + 9y - 10xy$
   D. $15x - 9y + 10xy$

16. If Stephanie has $5c$ CDs for every DVD Alyshia has, and Jeff has $4d$ DVDs, which is 15 more than Alyshia has, how many CDs does Stephanie have?

   A. $20cd - 75c$
   B. $20cd + 15$
   C. $80cd - 15$
   D. $80cd - 75c$

17. Divide $\dfrac{56x^4 + 49x^3y^3 - 84x^3 - 7x^2}{7x^2}$.

   A. $8x^2 + 7xy^3 - 12x - 1$
   B. $8x^4 + 7x^3y^3 - 12x^3 - x^2$
   C. $8x^4 + 7y^3 - 5x^3 - 1$
   D. $49x^2 + 42xy^3 - 77x$

18. A charity with a yearly budget of $80d$ gets all of its money from either its yearly ball or from private donations. If the charity raised $64d$ from the silent auction at the ball and $4a$ from ticket sales at the ball, how much will need to be raised in private donations to meet the budget?

   A. $16d$
   B. $16d - 4a$
   C. $16d + 4a$
   D. $144d - 4a$

19. Divide $\dfrac{x^4 + 4x^2y^4 - 8x - y^2}{2y^2}$.

   A. $\dfrac{x^4}{2y^2} + 2x^2y^2 - \dfrac{4x}{y^2} - \dfrac{1}{2}$

   B. $\dfrac{x^2}{2y} + \dfrac{2x^2y^2 - 4x}{y^2 - \dfrac{1}{2}}$

   C. $\dfrac{2x^4y^2 + 8x^2y^2 - 16x}{y^2 + 2y^4}$

   D. $\dfrac{x^4 - 4x}{2y^2 + 2x^2y^2 - \dfrac{1}{2}}$

20. If $12k$ privates, $8f$ lieutenants, and $6r$ captains are divided into $2r$ equal squads, which of the following would express the number of members of one squad?

   A. $6k + 4f + 3r$
   B. $\dfrac{6k + 4f}{r} + 3$
   C. $12k + 8f + 4r$
   D. $12k + 8f + 3r$

21. If $q = 2$ and $r = 4$, which of the following would equal $\dfrac{r^2 x^2 + q^3 x}{(q^2 x)}$?

   A. $4x + 2$
   B. $4x^2 + 2$
   C. $16x^2 + 8x - 2$
   D. $16x^2 + 2$

22. Simplify:

   $$\dfrac{44x^6 + 55x^3y^4 + 88x^2 - 11y^2}{11x^2} - 6x^4 - 8$$

   A. $4x^4 + 5xy^2 + 8x - 1$

   B. $2x^4 + 5xy^3 - y^2 - 8$

   C. $-2x^4 + 5xy^4 - \dfrac{y^2}{x^2}$

   D. $10x^4 + 5y^4 - \dfrac{y^2}{x^2} - 8$

23. Simplify:

$(6x^2 + 5xy^2)(y) - (4xy - 9x)(4xy)$.

A. $5xy^3 - 16x^2y^2 + 42x^2y$
B. $5xy^3 - 16x^2y^2 - 30x^2y$
C. $6x^2y - 11x^2y^2 - 36xy^2$
D. $6x^2y + 5x^2y^2 - 36xy^2 + 16xy$

24. There are $4x$ workers, including managers, in an office. If the salaries of the 3 managers are not included, the average salary of each employee is $5x - 6$. What do the nonmanagerial employees earn in total?

A. $20x^2 - 24x$
B. $20x^2 - 24x - 3$
C. $20x^2 - 9x + 18$
D. $20x^2 - 39x + 18$

25. What is the value of $\dfrac{45xy + 63y^2}{9y}$ if $x = 6$ and $y = 3$?

A. 12
B. 51
C. 108
D. 153

26. Simplify

$\dfrac{3x(x^2 + 3) - 2x(x^2 + 3) - (x^2 + 3)}{x^2 + 3}$

A. $x^3 - 1$
B. $x^3 - 3x - 1$
C. $3x - 1$
D. $x - 1$

27. If the $3h$ people in one country and the $4k$ people in the neighboring country each consume $h - 17$ pounds of rice per year on average, how much rice would be consumed by both countries in one year?

A. $4h + 4k - 17$
B. $4h^2 + 4k - 68k$
C. $12hk + h - 17$
D. $3h^2 + 4hk - 51h - 68k$

28. Simplify:

$\dfrac{4x^2(x + y) - 2(x + y)^2(x - y) - xy(x + y)}{x + y}$

A. $2x^2 + 2y^2 - xy$
B. $4x^2 + xy - 2x - 2y$
C. $4x^2 - xy - 2x - 2y$
D. $3x^2 - 2xy^2 - xy$

Questions 29 and 30 refer to the figure below.

The figure below is a multiplication box. Each place represents the horizontal number multiplied by the vertical number; for example, the 20 in the lower right corner equals 5 multiplied by 4.

	a^2	ab	5
a			ab
c	$8b$		
4		40	20

29. Which of the following is equal to a?

A. 2
B. 4
C. 5
D. 10

30. Which of the following is equal to a^2c?

A. 13
B. 40
C. 42
D. 60

Equations

Writing and Solving One-Step Equations

An **equation** is a mathematical statement that two expressions are equal.

Examples: $3 + 5 = 4 \cdot 2$ $10 - 1 = 3^2$ $5(3 + 4) = 35$

An equation can contain one or more variables. Solving an equation means finding a value for the variable that will make the equation true.

Examples: $4 + x = 11$ $3x = 24$ $x - 5 = -2$

$x = 7$ $x = 8$ $x = 3$

The basic strategy in solving an equation is to isolate the variable on one side of the equation. You can do this by performing **inverse**, or opposite, operations. However, you must always follow one basic rule: whatever you do to one side of the equation, you must also do to the other side.

Example 1: Solve $x - 23 = 45$.

On the left side of the equation, the number 23 is subtracted from x. The inverse of subtraction is addition. Add 23 to both sides of the equation.

$$x - 23 = 45$$
$$x - 23 + \mathbf{23} = 45 + \mathbf{23}$$
$$x = \mathbf{68}$$

To check your work, replace the variable with your solution and simplify.
When $x = \mathbf{68}$, the equation is true.

Check: $x - 23 = 45$
$68 - 23 = 45$
$45 = 45$

The following examples use the inverse operations of multiplication and division.

Example 2: Solve $\frac{x}{2} = 17$.

The variable x is divided by 2. Since multiplication is the inverse of division, you must multiply each side of the equation by 2.

$$\frac{x}{2} = 17$$
$$2\left(\frac{x}{2}\right) = 2(17)$$
$$x = \mathbf{34}$$

When $x = \mathbf{34}$, the equation is true.

Check: $\frac{34}{2} = 17$
$17 = 17$

Example 3: Solve $5x = 75$.

Since the variable x is multiplied by 5, divide both sides of the equation by 5.

$$5x = 75$$
$$\frac{5x}{5} = \frac{75}{5}$$
$$x = \mathbf{15}$$

When $x = \mathbf{15}$, the equation is true.

Check: $5(15) = 75$
$75 = 75$

Sometimes on the TASC, you may be presented with an equation made up entirely of variables. In those cases, you may be asked to "solve for" one of the variables. That means that you must isolate the variable you're solving for on one side of the equation. Study the example below.

Example 4: In physics, *power* is defined as the amount of work done per unit of time. The formula for power is: *power = (force × distance) ÷ time*, or $p = fd \div t$. Rearrange that equation so that you could solve for *f* if you knew the values of *p*, *d*, and *t*.

Step 1. Multiply both sides of the equation by *t*.

Step 2. Divide both sides of the equation by *d*.

$$p = fd \div t$$
$$pt = fd$$
$$\frac{pt}{d} = f$$

A. Solve for the variable in each equation.

1. $7x = 63$
2. $23 + m = 51$
3. $-13 = y - 12$
4. $\frac{x}{4} = -16$
5. $5a = 625$

6. $y - 17 = -30$
7. $x + 6 = 33$
8. $4c = 28$
9. $\frac{12}{x} = 3$
10. $26 = b + 33$

11. $93 = 3x$
12. $s + 16 = 8$
13. $36 = \frac{x}{3}$
14. $t + 14 = 53$
15. $\frac{x}{6} = 8$

16. $16y = -48$
17. $r - 35 = 75$
18. $24 = \frac{120}{x}$
19. $5y = -45$
20. $d + 45 = 20$
21. $16 = 4x$

B. Choose the one best answer to each question.

Questions 22 and 23 refer to the following table.

April Time Sheet Summary
Hours Worked per Week

Week	1	2	3	4
Kayla Sax	36	40	40	y
Erin Grady	x	24	28	38

22. Kayla and Erin worked a total of 77 hours during Week 1. Let *x* = Erin's hours for Week 1. Which of the following equations could be used to solve for Erin's hours during Week 1?

   A. $x - 36 = 77$
   B. $x + 77 = 36$
   C. $x + 36 = 77$
   D. $x - 77 = 36$

23. Erin worked twice as many hours as Kayla did during Week 4. Let *y* = Kayla's hours for Week 4. Which of the following equations could be used to solve for Kayla's hours during Week 4?

   A. $\frac{y}{2} = 38$
   B. $38y = 2$
   C. $2y = 38$
   D. $\frac{1}{2y} = 38$

24. The quotient of a number divided by 4 is 32. What is the number?

   A.   8
   B.   28
   C. 128
   D. 512

25. In electricity, the relationship between voltage, current, and resistance through a wire is summed up in Ohm's law. Ohm's law is represented by the formula: $V = IR$, where *V* is voltage, *I* is current, and *R* is resistance. If you knew both voltage and resistance, how could you rearrange Ohm's law to solve for current? Arrange the boxes below to represent your answer. You may not have to use all the boxes.

   $\boxed{R}$ $\boxed{I}$ $\boxed{V}$ $\boxed{\div}$ $\boxed{\times}$ $\boxed{=}$

26. Mike had \$572.18 in his checking account. After writing a check, he had \$434.68. Which of the following equations could be used to find the amount of the check (*c*)?

   A. $\$572.18 + c = \$434.68$
   B. $\$572.18 - c = \$434.68$
   C. $\$572.18c = \$434.68$
   D. $\frac{\$572.18}{c} = \$434.68$

Solving Multi-Step Equations

Most equations require more than one operation in order to find a solution.

Example 4: Solve $6x + 5 - 2x = 25$.

1. Combine like terms ($6x - 2x = 4x$).

2. Subtract 5 from both sides.

3. Divide both sides by 4.

4. Check by substituting the solution for x in the original equation.

$$6x + 5 - 2x = 25$$
$$4x + 5 = 25$$
$$4x + 5 - 5 = 25 - 5$$
$$4x = 20$$
$$\frac{4x}{4} = \frac{20}{4}$$
$$x = 5$$
$$6(5) + 5 - 2(5) = 25$$
$$30 + 5 - 10 = 25$$
$$25 = 25$$

In this example, the distributive property is used to simplify an expression. As you gain experience, you can perform an operation on both sides of an equation mentally.

Example 5: Solve $-4(x - 6) = 2x$.

1. Use the distributive property to remove the parentheses.
2. Add $4x$ to each side.
3. Divide each side by 6.

$$-4(x - 6) = 2x$$
$$-4x + 24 = 2x$$
$$24 = 6x$$
$$4 = x$$

4. Check.

$$-4(4 - 6) = 2(4)$$
$$-4(-2) = 8$$
$$8 = 8$$

Some of the time you will be expected to write an equation from information given in the problem. The problem will describe two expressions that are equal. Write each expression in symbols and connect the expressions with the equal sign (=). In many problems, the word *is* indicates the = symbol.

Example 6: The product of a number and 6 is 44 more than twice the number. What is the number?

1. Write an equation. The word *is* represents the equal sign.
2. Subtract $2x$ from both sides.
3. Divide both sides by 4.

$$6x = 44 + 2x$$
$$4x = 44$$
$$x = 11$$

4. Check.

The number described in the problem is **11**.

$$6(11) = 44 + 2(11)$$
$$66 = 44 + 22$$
$$66 = 66$$

Note: Subtraction and division operations must be written in the order indicated by the words. "The difference between x and y" must be written $x - y$, not $y - x$. "The quotient of x and y" must be written $\frac{x}{y}$, not $\frac{y}{x}$.

Sometimes you may be asked to solve an equation where one or more of the coefficients is represented by a letter. In these cases, your answer will usually be an expression involving that letter. Study this example:

Example 7: Solve for x: $a(x + 2) - 3 = 14$

1. Add 3 to both sides.

$$a(x + 2) = 17$$

2. Divide both sides by a.

$$x + 2 = \frac{17}{a}$$

3. Subtract 2 from both sides.

$$x = \frac{17}{a} - 2$$

4. Check your work by substituting your answer back into the
   original equation.

$$a\left(\frac{17}{a} - 2 + 2\right) - 3 = 14$$

$$a\left(\frac{17}{a}\right) - 3 = 14$$

$$17 - 3 = 14$$

$$14 = 14$$

A. Solve for the variable in each equation.

1. $3x - 20 = 130$

2. $2y - 8 = -3y - 18$

3. $6m = 14m - 16$

4. $2x + 5 + 6x = -27$

5. $5y + 3(y + 2) = 54$

6. $17 - 4z + 2z = 13$

7. $6m - 4 = m + 11$

8. $35 = x + 7 + 6x$

9. $5p - 2 = 6p - 9$

10. $50 = 3(s + 16) - 2(s - 2)$

11. $\frac{5(2x - 10)}{2} + 14 = 19$

12. $3(3 + r) = 2r + 4$

13. $5y = 2y + 22 + y$

14. Solve for x: $\frac{mx}{2} = 30$

15. Solve for z: $az + bz = 13$

16. Solve for y: $\frac{a}{1 + y} = 10$

B. Choose the one best answer to each question.

17. Three times a number increased by 9 is
    15 less than six times the number. Let
    $x =$ the unknown number. Which of the
    following equations could be used to
    find the value of x?

    A. $3(9x) = 6(15x)$
    B. $3x(9) = 6x - 15x$
    C. $3x + 9 = 15 - 6x$
    D. $3x + 9 = 6x - 15$

18. Dave has 500 baseball cards, which is as
    many as Eric and Travis have combined.
    Eric has three times as many cards as
    Travis has.

Dave	Eric	Travis
500	$3x$	x

    From the information, you can write the
    equation $3x + x = 500$. How many cards
    does Eric have? (*Hint:* Solve for x. Then
    find how many cards Eric has.)

    A. 150
    B. 250
    C. 350
    D. 375

19. The difference of four times a number
    and 7 is 15 plus the quotient of the
    number and 3. Which of the following
    equations could be used to find the
    value of x?

    A. $4x - 7 = \frac{x}{3} + 15$

    B. $7 - 4x = \frac{x}{3} + 15$

    C. $7 - 4x = \frac{3}{x} + 15$

    D. $4x - 7 = \frac{3}{x} + 1$

20. Kim earned x dollars at his part-time
    job on Friday. His wife earned $12 more
    than twice Kim's pay ($2x + 12$). Together,
    they earned $174. How much did Kim
    earn on Friday?
    (*Hint:* Use the equation $x + (2x + 12) =$
    $174.)

    A. $54
    B. $87
    C. $108
    D. $120

Equation Word Problems, Part I

Algebra problems describe how several numbers are related. One number is the unknown, which you will represent with a variable. Using the relationships described in the problem, you can write an equation and solve for the variable.

Example 1: There are twice as many women as men in a class on auto repair. If there are 24 students in the class, how many are women?

1. Express the numbers in the problem in terms of the same variable. Let x represent the number of men. Since there are twice as many women, let $2x$ represent the number of women.

2. Write and solve an equation. The total number of men and women is 24, so $x + 2x = 24$. Solve: $x + 2x = 24$
$$3x = 24$$
$$x = 8$$

Since $x = 8$, $2x = 2(8) = 16$. There are 8 men and **16 women** in the class.

Consecutive numbers are numbers that follow in counting order. For example, 1, 2, and 3 are consecutive numbers. The numbers 2, 4, and 6 are consecutive even numbers, and 1, 3, and 5 are consecutive odd numbers.

Example 2: The sum of three consecutive numbers is 105. What is the greatest of the three numbers?

1. Let x represent the first number and $x + 1$ and $x + 2$ represent the other numbers.

2. Write an equation and solve:
$$x + (x + 1) + (x + 2) = 105$$
$$3x + 3 = 105$$
$$3x = 102$$
$$x = 34$$

3. Find the answer. The variable x represents the first number in the sequence, so the three numbers are 34, 35, and 36. The problem asks for the greatest number, which is **36**.

You may need to use the difference between numbers to write equations.

Example 3: The ticket prices for a play are $12 for adults and $8 for children. One evening, the box office sold 200 tickets. If the total box office receipts were $2240, how many adult tickets were sold?

1. Let x represent the number of adult tickets. Since 200 tickets were sold, the number of children's tickets sold can be written as $200 - x$.

2. Multiply each term by the cost for that type of ticket. Set the total equal to $2240, and solve for x.
$$12x + 8(200 - x) = 2240$$
$$12x + 1600 - 8x = 2240$$
$$4x + 1600 = 2240$$
$$4x = 640$$
$$x = 160$$

3. There were **160 adult tickets** sold.

KEY IDEAS

- To solve a word problem, decide what quantity will be represented by x. Then write expressions for the other quantities in terms of x.
- Write and solve an equation. Answer the question asked in the problem.

TASC TEST TIP

When you find x, you may not be finished solving a problem. Always reread the question. As shown in Example 2, you may need to use the value of x to calculate the solution in a multi-step problem.

PRACTICE 2

A. Solve.

1. Two houses are for sale on the same street. The second house has 1000 square feet less than twice the square feet of the first house. Together the houses have 4400 square feet. What is the square footage of the first house?

2. Julia has 24 coins in her pocket. The coins are either dimes or quarters. The total value of the coins is $4.50. How many coins are dimes? [*Hint:* The value of the dimes is 0.10x, and the value of the quarters is 0.25$(24 - x)$.]

3. The Bulldogs won twice as many games as they lost. If they played a total of 36 games, how many did they win? (There were no tied games.)

4. The sum of four consecutive even numbers is 212. What is the third number? (*Hint:* Let x = the first number, $x + 2$ = the second number, $x + 4$ = the third, and so on.)

5. A children's store is selling pants for $6 each and shirts for $4. Brenda bought 13 items and paid $62. How many shirts did she buy?

6. The sum of three consecutive numbers is 180. What is the least number in the series?

7. In a month Andrew spends twice as much on rent as he does on food for his family. Last month, he spent $1650 on rent and food. How much did he spend on rent?

8. George spends four times as much time helping customers as he does stocking shelves. Last week, he spent 35 hours on the two tasks. How many hours were spent helping customers?

B. Choose the one best answer to each question.

9. Sylvia scored 10 points better than Wiley on their science exam. Greg scored 6 points less than Wiley. Altogether, the students earned 226 points. How many points did Sylvia earn?

   A. 74
   B. 78
   C. 84
   D. 94

10. Two adults and four children paid $48 to get into the fair. A child's ticket is $6 less than an adult's ticket. What is the cost of an adult's ticket?

    A. $15
    B. $12
    C. $9
    D. $6

11. Jenny is four times as old as her niece Tina. In 12 years, Jenny will be only twice as old as Tina. The chart shows expressions for Tina and Jenny's ages now and in 12 years.

	Jenny's Age	Tina's Age
Now	$4x$	x
In 12 Years	$4x + 12$	$x + 12$

    How old is Tina now?

    A. 4
    B. 6
    C. 8
    D. 12

STUDY ADVICE

Remember to include rewards and breaks in your study schedule. Celebrate a job well done with a fun outing. Don't try to study seven days a week—this can lead to burnout. Plan a day off to rest, relax, and reward yourself for the focused studying you have done!

Algebra Problem Solving

One strategy that can help you save time on the more complicated multiple-choice algebra problems is **guess-and-check.** Guess-and-check means selecting one of the answer choices and trying that value in the problem. If you guess correctly, you can move on to the next question. If not, guess again. Guess-and-check is a good strategy for problems involving quadratic equations and expressions.

Example 1: Which of the following is a solution for the equation $2x^2 - 12 = 2x$?

    A.   4
    B.   3
    C.   0
    D. −1

To solve the problem, you would have to rewrite the equation so that the quadratic expression equals zero, factor the expression, and solve.

Instead, substitute each answer choice into the equation.

Option (A): $2x^2 - 12 = 2x$ Option (B): $2x^2 - 12 = 2x$
           $2(4)^2 - 12 = 2(4)$ $2(3)^2 - 12 = 2(3)$
                  $20 \neq 8$ $6 = 6$

Option (B), 3, makes the equation true.

Guess-and-check can also save time when writing an equation seems difficult.

Example 2: Terry is ten years older than his brother Tomas. Twenty years ago, Terry was twice as old as Tomas. How old is Terry now?

    A. 25
    B. 30
    C. 40
    D. 45

Instead of writing an equation, try each age in the answer choices for Terry.

    A. If Terry is 25 now, Tomas is 15. Twenty years ago, Tomas would not have been born.
    B. If Terry is 30 now, Tomas is 20. Twenty years ago, Tomas would have been 0 years old, and Terry would have been 10.
    C. If Terry is 40 now, Tomas is 30. Twenty years ago, Tomas would have been 10, and Terry would have been 20, which is twice as old as 10.

Therefore, **option (C), 40,** is correct.

PRACTICE 3

A. Use guess-and-check to solve the following problems.

1. A number divided by 2 is equal to 12 less than the original number. What is the number?

   A. 12
   B. 20
   C. 24
   D. 28

2. For a fund-raiser, Sandra raised three times as much money as Barbara, and Barbara raised $50 more than Matt. Together they raised $950. How much money did Barbara raise?

   A. $150
   B. $175
   C. $200
   D. $325

3. The three packages below weigh a total of 15 pounds.

   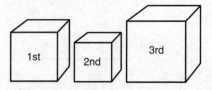

   The first package weighs twice as much as the second package. The third package weighs three times as much as the second package. How many pounds does the first package weigh?

   A. 2
   B. 4
   C. 5
   D. $6\frac{1}{2}$

4. Hannah scored a total of 170 points on two math tests. The score of the first test was 6 points lower than the score of the second test. How many points did Hannah score on the first test?

   A. 76
   B. 82
   C. 88
   D. 90

5. Nelson is twice as old as Maria. Six years ago, Nelson was five times as old as Maria. How old was Nelson six years ago?

   A. 5
   B. 10
   C. 15
   D. 20

6. Which of the following is a solution for the quadratic equation $2x^2 + x - 15 = 0$?

   A. −3
   B. −1
   C. 2
   D. 3

7. An amusement park sells adults' and children's passes. An adult's pass is $25, and a child's pass is $15. A group spent $440 on 20 passes. How many children's passes did the group purchase?

   A. 5
   B. 6
   C. 9
   D. 14

8. The rectangular garden below is twice as long as it is wide. If the total distance around the garden is 120 feet, what is the width of the garden in feet?

   Length = 2 × Width

   Width = ?

   A. 15
   B. 20
   C. 30
   D. 40

The Coordinate Plane

A **coordinate grid** is a way to locate points that lie in a **plane,** or flat surface. The grid is formed by two intersecting lines, an *x*-axis and a *y*-axis. The *x*-axis is actually a horizontal number line, and the *y*-axis is a vertical number line. The point at which the two axes intersect is called the **origin.**

Each point on the grid can be named using two numbers called an **ordered pair.** The first number is the distance from the origin along the *x*-axis. The second number is the distance from the origin along the *y*-axis. The numbers are written in parentheses and are separated by a comma: (*x*, *y*).

Example 1: Write the ordered pairs for points *M* and *P*.

1. Point *M* lies 2 spaces to the right of the origin along the *x*-axis and 3 spaces above the origin along the *y*-axis. The coordinates are **(2, 3).**

2. Point *P* lies 1 space to the left along the *x*-axis and 3 spaces down along the *y*-axis. The coordinates are **(−1, −3).**

To plot points on the grid, use the number lines located at the axes. Remember that right and up are the directions for positive numbers and left and down are the directions for negative numbers.

Example 2: Point *A* is located at (−2, 1), and point *B* is located at (3, −2). Plot these points on a coordinate grid.

1. To plot point *A*, start at the origin. Count 2 spaces left along the *x*-axis. Count 1 space up along the *y*-axis.

2. To plot point *B*, start at the origin. Count 3 spaces right along the *x*-axis. Count 2 spaces down along the *y*-axis.

PRACTICE 4

A. Write the ordered pair for each point.

1. Point *A*
2. Point *B*
3. Point *C*
4. Point *D*
5. Point *E*
6. Point *F*
7. Point *G*
8. Point *H*

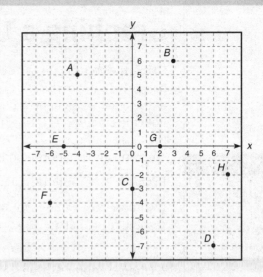

B. Plot the points on the coordinate grid.

9. Plot the following points:

   J at (−3, −2)
   K at (4, 0)
   L at (1, −3)
   M at (−4, 2)

10. Plot the following points:

    N at (0, −1)
    O at (−4, −4)
    P at (3, 1)
    Q at (−3, 0)

C. Choose the one best answer to each question.

11. On the coordinate grid below, a line passes through points *A* and *B*.

Which of the following ordered pairs also lies on the line?

A. (1, 0)
B. (1, −1)
C. (0, −1)
D. (−1, 0)

12. Two of the corners of a triangle are located at (3, −3) and (2, 3). What is the location of the third corner as shown in the diagram below?

A. (−3, −2)
B. (−3, 2)
C. (−2, −3)
D. (3, −2)

Graphing a Line

Using the coordinate system, we can graph equations. When an equation has only two variables, x and y, and neither is raised to a power, the graph of the equation will be a line. When the graph of an equation is a straight line, the equation is a **linear equation.**

To graph an equation, you need to solve for two points on the line.

Example 1: Graph the equation $y = 3x - 4$.

1. Choose any value for x and solve for y. Let $x = 1$.

$$y = 3(1) - 4$$
$$y = 3 - 4$$
$$y = -1$$

If $x = 1$, then $y = -1$. The ordered pair for the first point is $(1, -1)$.

2. Choose another value for x and solve for y. Let $x = 2$.

$$y = 3(2) - 4$$
$$y = 6 - 4$$
$$y = 2$$

If $x = 2$, then $y = 2$. The ordered pair for the second point is $(2, 2)$.

3. Plot the points on a coordinate grid and draw a line through them.

The line is the graph of all the possible solutions for the equation $y = 3x - 4$. Arrows at both ends of the line indicate that the line continues in both directions. From this, you can see that there is an infinite number of solutions to a linear equation.

Some linear equation problems don't require you to draw a graph.

Example 2: Point A lies at $(5, -6)$ on a coordinate grid. The graph of which of the following equations passes through point A?

    (1) $y = -5x + 18$
    (2) $y = -4x + 14$
    (3) $y = -2x - 13$

Use the ordered pair given in the problem. Substitute the x-coordinate, 5, for x in each equation and solve for y. If $y = -6$, the value of the y-coordinate from the ordered pair, you have found the correct equation.

Option (2) is correct.

$$y = -4x + 14$$
$$y = -4(5) + 14$$
$$y = -20 + 14 = -6$$

PRACTICE 5

A. Fill in the y column in each table and graph the equation.

1. $y = \dfrac{1}{2}x + 3$

If	then
$x =$	$y =$
-2	
0	
2	

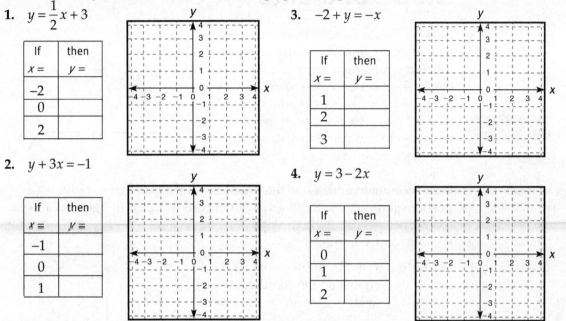

2. $y + 3x = -1$

If	then
$x =$	$y =$
-1	
0	
1	

3. $-2 + y = -x$

If	then
$x =$	$y =$
1	
2	
3	

4. $y = 3 - 2x$

If	then
$x =$	$y =$
0	
1	
2	

B. Choose the _one best answer_ to each question.

<u>**Questions 5 and 6 refer to the following**</u>
coordinate grid.

5. The graph of the equation $y = \dfrac{1}{4}x$ will pass through which of the following pairs of points?

  A. point S and $(-1, 2)$
  B. point S and $(0, -2)$
  C. point T and $(0, 0)$
  D. point T and $(0, -2)$

6. Line P is the graph of which of the following equations?

  A. $y = 4x + 1$
  B. $y = -4x - 1$
  C. $y = 4x + 2$
  D. $y = -4x - 2$

7. Point C is located at $(-3, 5)$. A graph of which of the following equations would pass through point C?

  A. $3x + 2y = 5$
  B. $2x + 3y = 9$
  C. $4x - 2y = 8$
  D. $3x - 3y = 6$

STUDY ADVICE

Hang in there: You're more than halfway through the Mathematics unit! It may feel like a long haul until Test Day, but keep thinking about how good it will feel to have your high school equivalency degree in hand!

Slope of a Line

Slope is the measurement of the steepness of a line. Imagine a road going up a hill. If the road must reach the top of the hill over a short distance, the road will be very steep. Slope measures the relationship between **rise** (how high the road must climb) and **run** (the distance the road goes forward).

On a coordinate grid, a line that moves upward from left to right has a **positive slope.** A line that moves downward from left to right has a **negative slope.** You can find the slope of a line on a coordinate grid by writing the ratio of rise to run.

Example 1: What is the slope of line P shown on the coordinate grid?

1. Find two points on line P. Count to find the rise and run. The line moves up 1 space for every 2 spaces it goes to the right.

2. Write the ratio: $\dfrac{\text{rise}}{\text{run}} = \dfrac{1}{2}$. The slope is $\dfrac{1}{2}$.

Example 2: What is the slope of line S shown on the coordinate grid?

1. Find any two points on line S. The line moves down 6 spaces (a negative direction) and 2 spaces to the right.

2. Write the ratio: $\dfrac{\text{rise}}{\text{run}} = \dfrac{-6}{2} = -3$.

The slope of line S is **–3.**

You can also find slope using the slope formula:

slope of a line $= \dfrac{y_2 - y_1}{x_2 - x_1}$, where (x_1, y_1) and (x_2, y_2) are two points on a line.

Example 3: A line passes through points at coordinates (1, 4) and (–5, 2). What is the slope of the line?

1. Choose one point to be (x_1, y_1). The other will be (x_2, y_2). It doesn't matter which you choose. For this example, $(x_1, y_1) = (1, 4)$ and $(x_2, y_2) = (-5, 2)$.

2. Substitute the values into the slope formula and solve:

$$\frac{y_2 - y_1}{x_2 - x_1} \qquad \frac{2-4}{-5-1} = \frac{-2}{-6} = \frac{1}{3} \quad \text{The slope is } \frac{1}{3}.$$

Since the slope is positive, you know that the line rises from left to right. You also know that it goes up 1 space for every 3 spaces it moves to the right.

In working with slope, there are a few special circumstances that you should memorize. A horizontal line, just like a flat stretch of roadway, has a **slope of 0**. The slope of a vertical line is **undefined**; in other words, our definition of slope will not work for a line that has no run at all.

A. Find the slope of each line.

1. 2. 3.

B. Use the slope formula to find the slope of a line that passes through the following pairs of points.

4. (3, 5) and (−1, 2) 6. (4, 2) and (2, 2) 8. (1, 4) and (−2, −2)

5. (0, 2) and (4, 0) 7. (6, 1) and (0, 3) 9. (4, −2) and (2, 4)

C. Choose the one best answer for each question.

<u>Question 10 refers to the following graph.</u>

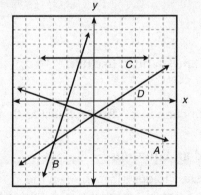

10. Which of the following lines shown on the graph has a slope of $-\frac{1}{3}$?

   A. line A
   B. line B
   C. line C
   D. line D

11. Line N passes through the following points: (0, 4), (1, 2), (2, 0), and (3, −2). What is the slope of line N?

   A. −4
   B. −2
   C. 2
   D. 4

12. Line L passes through point (1, 0) and has a slope of 3. Which of the following points also lies on line L?

   A. (0, 3)
   B. (1, 3)
   C. (2, 3)
   D. (2, 5)

Slope and Equations

Use the Slope-Intercept Form to Find an Equation

Lesson 8 showed how to find the slope of a line and graph it. The examples in this lesson show how you can use the slope and a point on the line to find the equation of a line in two different forms. (You might also need to find the equation of a line from two points. In this case, you would calculate the slope first, then use the slope and one of the points to find the equation.)

The first of these forms is the **slope-intercept form:** $y = mx + b$. In this form of the equation, the variable m stands for the **slope** of the line. The variable b stands for the **y-intercept,** which is the y-value at the point where the line crosses the y-axis. The variables x and y are the **x-** and **y-coordinates** of any point on the line and are usually written as an ordered pair.

Follow these steps to find the equation of a line in the slope-intercept form.

1. Substitute the values that you are given for the slope (m) and the x- and y-coordinates (x, y) into the slope-intercept equation. Be careful not to mix up x and y.

2. Use inverse operations to isolate b.

3. Rewrite the equation in slope-intercept form, leaving x and y as variables and substituting values for m and b.

Example 1: Use the slope-intercept form to find the equation of a line that has the slope $m = 4$ and passes through the point $(-1, -6)$.

1. $-6 = (4) \times (-1) + b$

   $-6 = -4 + b$

2. $-2 = b$

3. $y = 4x - 2$

Note that linear equations are sometimes written like this:

$f(x) = mx + b$

The symbol $f(x)$ simply means "a function of x." Treat $f(x)$ just as though it were the variable y.

Use the Point-Slope Form to Find an Equation

The second important form that is used to describe a line on the Mathematics Test is the **point-slope form:** $y - y_1 = m(x - x_1)$. In this form, (x_1, y_1) is an ordered pair that corresponds to a point on the line. As in the slope-intercept form, m stands for the slope. If you simplify an equation in point-slope form by solving for y, you will get the slope-intercept form of the equation.

Follow these steps to find the equation of a line in the point-slope form.

1. Call the point that you are given (x_1, y_1).

2. Put the x_1 and y_1 values into the point-slope equation.

3. Put the slope value in the point-slope equation for m.

KEY IDEAS

- There are two ways to find an equation if you are given the slope of a line and a point.
- One method is the slope-intercept form.
- The other method is the point-slope form.

TASC TEST TIP

Memorize the formulas for the slope-intercept form and the point-slope form to save time on Test Day.

PRACTICE 7

Example 2: Use the point-slope form to find the equation of the line that passes through the point (4, 3) and has a slope of 2.

1. $(x_1, y_1) = (4, 3)$

2. $y - 3 = m(x - 4)$

3. $y - 3 = 2(x - 4)$

Notice that you can simplify the equation to find the slope-intercept form:

$$y - 3 = 2(x - 4)$$
$$y - 3 = 2x - 8$$
$$y = 2x - 5$$

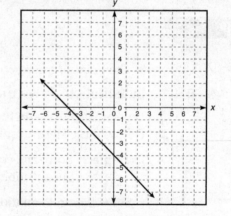

A. Use the slope-intercept form, $y = mx + b$, to find the equation of the line that passes through the given point and has the given slope.

1. $(1, -2); m = -4$　　　　2. $(-1, -4); m = 2$　　　　3. $(-4, 2); m = -\frac{1}{3}$

B. Use the point-slope form, $y - y_1 = m(x - x_1)$, to find the equation of the line that passes through the given point and has the given slope.

4. $(2, 1); m = 3$　　　　5. $(2, 0); m = -\frac{1}{3}$　　　　6. $(1, -2); m = 1$

C. Find the equation of the line that passes through the given points. Write your answer in slope-intercept form.

7. $(-5, 3), (1, 1)$　　　　8. $(-3, 0), (-2, 4)$　　　　9. $(-3, -4), (7, 1)$

D. Choose the **one best answer** for each question.

10. Which of the following is an equation for the line that passes through $(-1, 0)$ and $(2, -3)$?

  A. $y = 3x + 3$
  B. $y = -3x + 9$
  C. $y = -x - 1$
  D. $y = x - 5$

11. Which of the following equations describes the same line as $y - 2 = \frac{1}{2}(x - 6)$?

  A. $y = 3x + 2$
  B. $y = \frac{1}{2}x - 4$
  C. $y = -x + 12$
  D. $y = \frac{1}{2}x - 1$

Question 12 refers to the following graph.

12. Which of the following equations correctly describes the line on the graph?

  A. $y = x - 4$
  B. $y = -x - 4$
  C. $y = x + 4$
  D. $y = -x + 4$

LESSON 8

Systems of Linear Equations

Graph to Solve the System of Equations

The equations in Lessons 7 and 9 are **linear equations:** they have two variables, x and y, and represent straight lines in the coordinate plane. Two or more linear equations make up a **system of linear equations**. Solving a system of two equations means finding the values of both variables. The **solution** will give the x- and y-coordinates of the point at which the two lines intersect. You can express this solution as an ordered pair: (x, y).

One way to solve a system of equations is by graphing each equation using a **T-chart**—like those that you filled in for the Lesson 7 practice. Graphing a system of linear equations provides a picture of the intersection. Follow these steps to solve a system of equations by graphing.

1. Set up an x and y T-chart for each equation. Find two ordered pairs for each equation: use $x = 0$ and find y and then use $y = 0$ and find x.

2. Graph both lines, using the ordered pairs that you generated in step 1.

3. Find the point of intersection and express it in the form (x, y).

Example 1: Graph the equations $6x + 3y = 12$ and $5x + y = 7$ to find the solution.

1.
$6x + 3y = 12$

x	y
0	4
2	0

$5x + y = 7$

x	y
0	7
$\frac{7}{5}$	0

2.

3. The point of intersection—that is, the solution—is **(1, 2)**.

Substitute to Solve the System of Equations

You can also use **substitution** to solve a system of linear equations. Follow these steps to solve a system of linear equations by substitution.

Example 2: Solve the equations $6x + 3y = 12$ and $5x + y = 7$ by substitution.

1. Solve the first equation so that y is expressed in terms of x.

2. Substitute that value of y into the second equation and solve for x.

3. Substitute that value of x into the first equation and solve for y.

The solution is **(1, 2)**.

$$6x + 3y = 12$$
$$3y = 12 - 6x$$
$$y = 4 - 2x$$
$$5x + (4 - 2x) = 7$$
$$3x + 4 = 7$$
$$3x = 3$$
$$x = 1$$
$$6(1) + 3y = 12$$
$$6 + 3y = 12$$
$$3y = 6$$
$$y - 2$$

PRACTICE 8

A. Find two pairs of coordinates for each equation by making a T-chart. Use the coordinates to graph the lines and find the solution.

1. $y = 3x - 15$
   $x + y = 13$

2. $4x + 2y = 10$
   $y = -5x - 4$

B. Find the solution for the two equations by substitution. Express as an ordered pair in the form (x, y).

3. $-7x - y = 22$
   $4x + 2y = 10$

4. $x + y = 9$
   $2x - 3y = 8$

5. $y = 3x + 15$
   $5x - 2y = -26$

6. $10x - y = -1$
   $y = 12x$

C. Choose the <u>one best answer</u> for each question.

7. Where does the line with the equation $x - 2y = 4$ intersect with the line with the equation $6y + 5x = 4$?

   A. $(2, -1)$
   B. $(3, -2)$
   C. $(-2, 1)$
   D. $(-1, 2)$

8. Where does the line with the equation $y = x$ intersect with the line with the equation $y = -x$?

   A. $(1, -1)$
   B. $(-1, 1)$
   C. $(0, 0)$
   D. $(1, 0)$

9. Where does the line with the equation $y = -2$ intersect with the line with the equation $3y = 2x + 3$?

   A. $(-\frac{2}{9}, -2)$
   B. $(-\frac{1}{3}, -2)$
   C. $(-\frac{9}{2}, -2)$
   D. $(\frac{9}{2}, 2)$

10. Which of the following is the equation of a line that intersects $y = 4x + 2$?

   A. $2y = 8x + 2$
   B. $y = 4x - 2$
   C. $y = -4x + 2$
   D. $\frac{1}{2}y = 2x - 7$

Properties of Functions

Writing and Solving Functions

A **function** is an equation that states a relationship between numbers that are put into the function and the numbers that the function outputs. The numbers that can be put into the function are the **domain**. The numbers that the function can output are the **range**.

Functions are often written in the form $f(x)$, meaning "apply the following rule, or function, to some input number." The input number is represented in the function by a variable. In the example $f(x)$, the input number is represented by x.

Example 1: The domain of $f(x) = x + 2$ is {1, 3}. What is the range of $f(x)$?

Substitute 1 for x in the function. $\qquad\qquad\qquad\qquad$ $f(1) = 1 + 3 = 3$

Substitute 3 for x in the function. $\qquad\qquad\qquad\qquad$ $f(3) = 3 + 2 = 5$

The range of $f(x)$ is {**3, 5**}.

The function and input number can be represented by different letters—for example, $g(y)$—but the meaning is exactly the same: apply the following rule to the input number represented by the variable.

Examples: $\qquad f(x) = \frac{x}{2} \qquad g(y) = 2y + 5q \qquad\qquad h(a) = 10 - a$

Some functions have inherently restricted domains.

Example 2: What is the domain of $f(x) = \frac{x}{x^2 - 4}$?

If $x = 2$ or $x = -2$, then $x^2 = 4$, and the denominator of the fraction in the function would be zero. Because division by zero is undefined, 2 and –2 are not part of the domain for $f(x)$. The domain is **all real numbers except 2 and –2**.

Example 3: The amount of money Amanda makes from her job each week is represented by $g(x) = 10x + 5(x - 40)$, where x represents the number of hours Amanda works. What is the domain of x?

No one can work a negative number of hours, and there are only 168 hours in a week, so the domain of the function is $0 \le x \le 16$.

The **solution set** of a function is all ordered pairs of numbers that make the equation true, expressed in the form (domain number, range number).

Example 4: If x is an integer between 1 and 4 inclusive, what is the solution set of $f(x) = x^2 + 2x$?

Solve $f(x)$ for each value of its domain: 1, 2, 3, and 4.
$\quad f(1) = 1^2 + 2 \times 1 = 3$
$\quad f(2) = 2^2 + 2 \times 2 = 8$
$\quad f(3) = 3^2 + 2 \times 3 = 15$
$\quad f(4) = 4^2 + 2 \times 4 = 24$

The solution set of $f(x)$ is {**(1, 3), (2, 8), (3, 15), (4, 24)**}.

PRACTICE 9.1

A. Solve for the value of the function.

1. $f(x) = x + 5$; $x = -2$

2. $g(x) = 10 - 2x$; $x = 5$

3. $f(y) = \frac{18 - y}{-3}$; $y = 9$

B. Solve for the value of x.

4. $f(x) = 14 - x$; $f(x) = 0$

5. $h(x) = 4x + 3$; $h(x) = -5$

6. $f(x) = \frac{x^2}{2x}$; $f(x) = \frac{5}{2}$

C. Answer the questions below.

7. The domain of the function $f(x) = \frac{3x}{x - 3}$ includes all real numbers except _____. Write your answer in the blank.

8. The range of the function $h(x) = |x - 12|$ does NOT include

   A. positive numbers
   B. non-positive numbers
   C. negative numbers
   D. non-integers

9. A restaurant expects that two-thirds of its diners will order coffee. The relationship of coffee orders (C) to diners (d) is represented by

   A. $C(d) = \frac{3}{2}d$

   B. $C(d) = \frac{2}{3}d + 1$

   C. $C(d) = \frac{2}{3} + d$

   D. $C(d) = \frac{2}{3}d$

10. A farmer's order for bags of seed is represented by the function $S(A) = 75A + \frac{1}{10}A$, where A represents the number of acres planted. If the farmer will plant 200 acres this season, how many bags of seed will the farmer buy?

   A. $26\frac{2}{3}$

   B. 1,520
   C. 7,500
   D. 15,020

D. Complete the table as directed.

11. Complete the table with the values of x from the list below, if $f(x) = 2x - 1$.

f(x)	x
21	
5	
3	
-7	

-3
2
3
11

Graphing Functions

A function can be graphed on the coordinate plane. The input values become the x-coordinates, and the output values are the y-coordinates. As a mental shortcut, you can remember that $f(x)$ or $g(x)$ is just like y in the linear equations you've seen.

Example 5: Graph $f(x) = 2x - 1$ for $-2 \leq x \leq 2$.

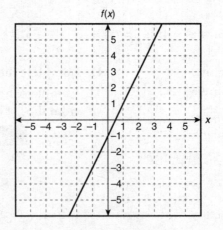

When a function is graphed, certain features become apparent. The **maximum** is the largest value of the range. The **minimum** is the smallest value of the range. The minimum and maximum values are also referred to as the **extreme values** of the function. The **y-intercept** is the point(s) where the line or curve crosses the y-axis, or where $x = 0$. The **x-intercept** is the point(s) where the line or curve crosses the x-axis, or where $y = 0$.

In Example 5, the maximum of $f(x)$ is 3, the minimum is –5, the x-intercept is $\frac{1}{2}$, and the y-intercept is –1.

A function can be described as **increasing** between two points on the x-axis or as **decreasing** between two points on the x-axis. It can also be described as **symmetrical** about a point or a line, such as "symmetrical about the y-axis." That means that the graph to the left of the y-axis and the graph to the right of it are mirror images.

Example 6: The function $g(x)$ increases from $x = 0$ to $x = 2$ and decreases from $x = 2$ to $x = 4$. The y-intercept is 0. The function is symmetrical about the line $x = 2$, and its maximum is $y = 2$. Given this information, graph the function.

Here is a graph that satisfies the given information. This graph represents the function $g(x) = -|x| + 2$.

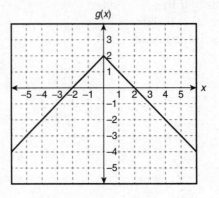

PRACTICE 9.2

A. Draw a rough graph of each of the following functions.

1. $f(x) = 2x - 8$

2. $f(x) = -|x|$

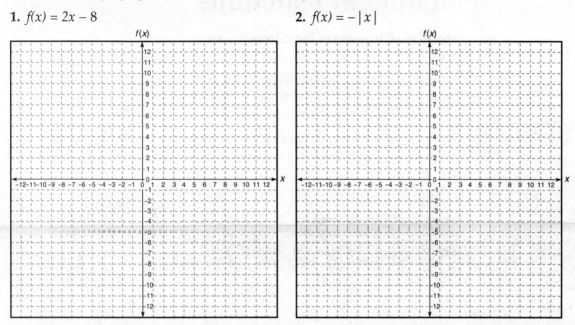

B. Mark the graph or answer the question as directed.

3. On the coordinate plane below, place a dot on the *x*-intercept and the *y*-intercept of the function $f(x) = -4x + 4$.

4. The graph below represents which of the following functions?

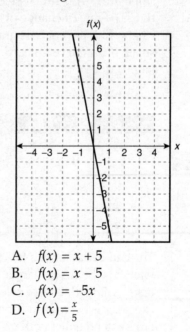

A. $f(x) = x + 5$
B. $f(x) = x - 5$
C. $f(x) = -5x$
D. $f(x) = \frac{x}{5}$

Nonlinear Functions

Features of Nonlinear Functions

A function in which one or more variables are raised to an exponent generates a curve when graphed on the coordinate plane. The slope may be negative or positive or zero at various points along the curve, and it will be steeper through some parts of the curve than others.

To represent the function graphically, you can calculate a few points in the solution set, graph those coordinates, and then draw a curve connecting them.

Example 1: Graph $f(x) = x^2$.

x	f(x)
−2	4
−1	1
0	0
1	1
2	4

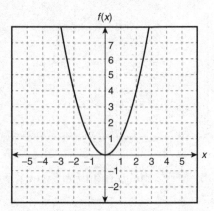

In the graph above, note that the slope at the point (0, 0) is zero, while the slope at (2, 4) is much steeper. The slope at any negative x-value is negative. The rate of change of a function's slope can be estimated from looking at its graph. If the curve is gradual, then the slope's rate of change is relatively small. If the curve is sharp, then the rate of change in the slope is relatively large.

Example 2: Graph $f(x) = x^3$.

x	f(x)
−2	−8
−1	−1
0	0
1	1
2	8

The **end behavior** of a function's graph refers to whether its "arms" go up or down. Memorize these rules: If the exponent is even, as in Example 1, then the arms extend either both up or both down. If the exponent is odd, as in Example 2, then one arm extends upward while the other extends downward.

The right arm of the graph travels upward if the coefficient of the variable with the exponent is positive, as in both Examples 1 and 2 above. The right arm of the graph travels downward if the coefficient of the variable with the exponent is negative.

Example 3: Graph $f(x) = -x^2 + 3$.

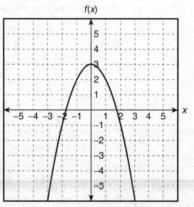

x	$f(x)$
−2	−1
−1	2
0	3
1	2
2	−1

Because the coefficient of the variable is -1, and the exponent is even, both arms of the graph point downward.

---

1. Which of the following describes the end behavior of $f(x) = 5x^3 + x - 10$?

   A. The left arm goes down, and the right arm goes up.
   B. The left arm goes up, and the right arm goes down.
   C. Both arms go up.
   D. Both arms go down.

2. Which of the following describes the end behavior of $f(a) = -7a^4 - 11$?

   A. The left arm goes down, and the right arm goes up.
   B. The left arm goes up, and the right arm goes down.
   C. Both arms go up.
   D. Both arms go down.

3. The graph of $f(x) = Ax^2 - 3.25$ has a maximum and no minimum. The coefficient A must be

   A. positive
   B. negative
   C. even
   D. odd

4. $f(x) = -\dfrac{x^2}{2}$. Match the value of x to the slope of the curve at that point. (*Hint:* You do not have to actually calculate the slope. You can make inferences about where the curve is steeper and which way the "arms" are pointing in order to complete this question.)

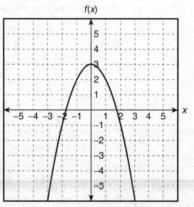

$x = -3$		−4
$x = 0$		−1
$x = 1$		0
$x = 4$		3

5. $f(x) = x^3 - 3x + 2$. Match the value of x to the slope of the curve at that point. (*Hint:* You do not have to actually calculate the slope. You can make inferences about where the curve is steeper and which way the "arms" are pointing in order to complete this question.)

$x = -2$		−3
$x = -1$		0
$x = 0$		9

Periodicity and Local Minima and Maxima

A function may represent a repeating pattern. Such a function is known as **periodic**. The **period** of the function is the length of its cycle. Put another way, the period is the amount of time that elapses before the function begins to repeat itself.

Example 5: John sets his aquarium lighting to brighten during the day and dim at night. He graphs the lighting output in lumens (a unit of the brightness of light) over a week as follows:

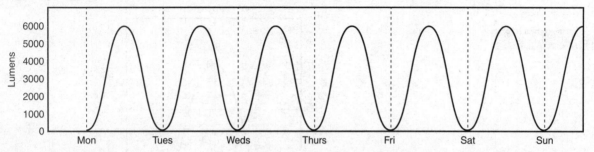

What is the period of this function? What are the maximum and minimum values of this function? If John checks the aquarium light at noon, how many lumens will be it emitting?

The function's period is **1 day**. The maximum value of the function is **6000**, and the minimum value is **0**. At noon on any given day, the light will be emitting **6000 lumens**.

Over any given domain, a function can have a **local maximum** and a **local minimum**. These are the largest and smallest values of the function for the given values of the input variable. They may or may not be the maximum and minimum of the function as a whole. Any point at which the slope changes from negative to positive or vice versa is called an **inflection point**.

Example 6: In the function $f(x) = -(x-1)^5 + 5x$, what are the local maximum and minimum for the domain $0 \leq x \leq 2$?

x	f(x)
0	1
1	5
2	9

The local maximum for the given domain is **9**, and the local minimum is **1**.

Example 7: How many inflection points does the function given in Example 6 have in total?

The graph changes slope in two places: when $x = 0$ and when $x = 2$. The answer is **2**.

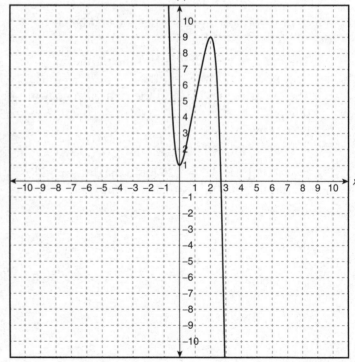

PRACTICE 10.2

Questions 1 through 3 are based on the following information and graph.

MegaStore Corporation hires additional temporary staff when it holds quarterly sales.

1. How long, in months, is the period of Mega-Store's hiring function? Write your answer on the line below.

   _____

2. Approximately, what is the minimum of Mega-Store's hiring function? Write your answer on the line below.

   _____

3. During which of the following months is the staffing level at MegaStore greatest?

   A. February, May, August, November
   B. March, June, September, December
   C. April, July, October, January
   D. January, June, July, December

4. A wave on a lake crests every 5 meters and travels 15 meters per 4 seconds. How many periods of this wave are observed per minute? Write your answer on the line below.

   _____

5. At which of the following values of x is the slope of the function $f(x) = x^2$ greatest?

   A. $x = 10$
   B. $x = 2$
   C. $x = -2$
   D. $x = -10$

6. At which of the following coordinates is the slope of the function $f(x) = -(x - 5)^2$ equal to 0?

   A. $(0, 5)$
   B. $(5, 0)$
   C. $(0, 25)$
   D. $(25, 0)$

7. Place a dot on the coordinate plane at the maximum of $f(x) = -x^4 + 4x$.

Quadratic Equations

A **quadratic equation** contains a squared variable, for example, $x^2 - 3x = 4$. One way to solve quadratic equations is by factoring. This is the simplest method and the one you should use on the TASC Mathematics Test. When you factor an expression, you find the terms that divide evenly into the expression.

Example 1: Factor the expression $15x^2 + 9x$.

1. Look for a term that divides evenly into both $15x^2$ and $9x$. Both terms can be divided by $3x$.

   $15x^2 \div 3x = 5x$
   $9x \div 3x = 3$

2. Factor out $3x$. Write the terms as factors.

   $15x^2 + 9x = \mathbf{3x(5x + 3)}$

Study Example 2 to learn how to multiply factors with more than one term.

$$\overset{\text{(factor)} \quad \text{(factor)}}{\textbf{Example 2:} \ \text{Multiply} \ \underset{\text{four terms}}{(2x + 3)(x - 4)}.}$$

1. Multiply each term in the first factor by each term in the second factor.

   $2x \cdot x = 2x^2$
   $2x \cdot -4 = -8x$
   $3 \cdot x = 3x$
   $3 \cdot -4 = -12$

2. Combine the results.

   $2x^2 + (-8x) + 3x + (-12) =$
   $\mathbf{2x^2 - 5x - 12}$

This method of multiplying factors is called the FOIL method. The letters in FOIL stand for First, Outer, Inner, and Last. Use the word FOIL to make sure you have performed all the necessary operations.

You factor a quadratic equation to solve it. In order to factor it, you must first manipulate the equation so that the quadratic expression is equal to zero. Then, figure out the values the variable could have so that the factors would multiply to zero. One or the other of the two factors, at least, must equal zero. Thus, a quadratic equation may have two solutions.

Example 3: Solve $x^2 - 3x = 4$.

1. Set the equation equal to 0 by subtracting 4 from both sides.

   $x^2 - 3x = 4$
   $x^2 - 3x - 4 = 0$

2. Factor by trial and error. Think: What factors of the last term, –4, when added, will equal –3, the number part of the middle term?
   $-4 \cdot 1 = -4$ and $-4 + 1 = -3$

   $(x \quad)(x \quad) = 0$
   $(x + 1)(x - 4) = 0$

3. If either one of the factors equals 0, then the product of the factors will be 0. Set each factor equal to 0 and solve for x.

   $x + 1 = 0$
   $x = \mathbf{-1}$

   $x - 4 = 0$
   $x = \mathbf{4}$

The solutions to the quadratic equation are **–1 and 4.**

PRACTICE 11

A. Multiply.

1. $(x+4)(x+2)$

2. $(x-3)(x+5)$

3. $(x-1)(x+4)$

4. $(x-6)(x-3)$

5. $(x+8)(x-2)$

6. $(2x+1)(x-2)$

7. $(x-9)(x-5)$

8. $(x+1)(3x-2)$

9. $(x-2)(x+7)$

10. $(3x+8)(x+2)$

11. $(x-6)(x+5)$

12. $(x-10)(x-3)$

13. $(2x+1)(2x+2)$

14. $(x+9)(x-4)$

15. $(x-5)(x-5)$

B. Factor each expression.

16. x^2+4x+3

17. x^2+4x-5

18. $x^2+8x+12$

19. x^2-x-6

20. $x^2+5x-14$

21. x^2-x-12

22. $x^2+2x-35$

23. $x^2-12x+36$

24. x^2-6x-7

25. $x^2+4x-32$

26. $2x^2+5x-3$

27. $2x^2-8x-10$

28. $x^2+5x-50$

29. $4x^2+4x-3$

30. x^2+x-56

C. Choose the one best answer to each question.

31. What are two solutions for the equation $x^2-x=20$?

   A. −4 and 5

   B. 4 and −5

   C. −10 and 2

   D. −2 and 10

32. For which of the following equations is $x=-4$ a solution?

   A. $2x^2-8=0$

   B. $x^2-8x+64=0$

   C. $x^2-2x-15=0$

   D. $2x^2+2x-24=0$

33. What is the only positive solution for the equation $2x^2-7x-30=0$?

   A. 5

   B. 6

   C. 7

   D. 8

34. The area of a rectangle is found by multiplying the length by the width. In the rectangle below, the area of the rectangle is equal to the expression $2x^2-27x+70$.

An expression equal to the length is shown on the diagram. Which of the following expressions is equal to the width of the rectangle?

   A. $x+10$

   B. $x-10$

   C. $2x+10$

   D. $2x-10$

Inequalities

An **inequality** is a mathematical statement that connects two unequal expressions. The inequality symbols and their meanings are:

> greater than   ≥ greater than or equal to

< less than   ≤ less than or equal to

An inequality is solved much like an equation. Use inverse operations to isolate the variable.

Example 1: Solve for x in the inequality $3x + 2 < 8$.

1. Subtract 2 from both sides.
$$3x + 2 < 8$$
$$3x < 6$$

2. Divide both sides by 3.
$$\boldsymbol{x < 2}$$

The solution $x < 2$ states that any number less than 2 makes the inequality true. Check by substituting 1 (a number less than 2) for x: $3(1) + 2 < 8$, which simplifies to $5 < 8$, a true statement.

There is one important difference between solving equalities and inequalities. Whenever you multiply or divide both sides of an inequality by a <u>negative</u> number, you must <u>reverse</u> the inequality symbol.

Example 2: Solve for n in the inequality $-2n - 5 \geq 3$.

1. Add 5 to both sides to remove -5 from the left side of the equation.
$$-2n - 5 + 5 \geq 3 + 5$$
$$-2n \geq 8$$

2. Divide both sides by -2 and *reverse the inequality symbol.*
$$\frac{-2n}{-2} \leq \frac{8}{-2}$$
$$n \leq -4$$

Check your work by substituting a number that is less than or equal to -4 into the <u>original</u> inequality. Here -5 is used for n. Since $5 \geq 3$ is a true statement, the answer is correct.
$$-2n - 5 \geq 3$$
$$-2(-5) - 5 \geq 3$$
$$5 \geq 3$$

When an inequality contains a variable, there is a range of numbers that make the inequality true. For that reason, we often graph the solution. In the examples below, a closed dot means that the number is included in the solution set. An open dot means the number is not included.

Examples: $x < 2$

$x > -3$

$x \leq 1$

$x \geq -2$

KEY IDEAS

- Use <, >, ≤, and ≥ to show the relationship between two unequal expressions.
- The symbol always points to the smaller expression.
- Use inverse operations to solve inequalities. Reverse the inequality sign if you multiply or divide by a negative number.

TASC TEST TIP

Avoid the most common mistake with inequalities: reversing the symbol accidentally. Always check your work by substituting any number that fits the solution into the original inequality.

PRACTICE 12

A **compound inequality** combines two inequalities. To solve a compound inequality, separate the inequalities and solve both. Then combine the solutions.

Example 3: Solve $3x + 4 < 5x < 16 + x$.

1. Write two inequalities and solve each separately.

$$3x + 4 < 5x \qquad\qquad 5x < 16 + x$$
$$4 < 2x \qquad\qquad\quad 4x < 16$$

2. Write the result as a compound inequality. **$2 < x < 4$**

$$2 < x \qquad\qquad\quad x < 4$$

In other words, any quantity that is greater than 2 *and* less than 4 will make the compound inequality true.

A. Solve.

1. $3x - 7 > 5$

2. $13 < 2x - 1$

3. $4 + 2x \le -2$

4. $\dfrac{4+x}{5} \le 8$

5. $2(x + 3) < 4$

6. $3 + 9x \ge 4(x + 7)$

7. $-4(x + 2) < 24$

8. $-2x + 9 < 1$

9. $\dfrac{x-2}{3} > 2x + 11$

10. $6x < 5x + 2$

11. $x + 6 \le 8x - 15$

12. $5x + 14 > 2 + 7x$

13. $13x - 7 \ge 25 - 3x$

14. $x - 6 < 2(x + 2)$

15. $-5 + 3x \ge 4(3x - 8)$

16. $36 > 4(x - 12)$

17. $6 \le 3(x + 3)$

18. $\dfrac{4x}{3} > 8x - 20$

19. $x - 2 < \dfrac{2x+6}{4}$

20. $x \ge 4x - 9$

21. $30 \ge 5(x + 4) \ge 10$

22. $-7x > -2(x + 15) < 10$

23. $3 < 5x - 27 < 53$

24. $22 \le 6x - 2 \le 4x + 16$

B. Choose the <u>one best answer</u> to each question.

25. The perimeter of a square can be found using the formula $P = 4s$, where s is one side of the square.

The perimeter of a square is less than or equal to 64 inches. Which of the following represents the possible measures of the side of the square in inches?

A. $s \le 16$
B. $s \ge 16$
C. $s \ge 8$
D. $s \le 64$

26. Three added to the product of –4 and a number (x) is less than 5 added to the product of –3 and the number. Which of the following is a graph of the solution set of x?

A. ![number line with open circle at 2, arrow left] -5 -4 -3 -2 -1 0 1 2 3 4 5

B. ![number line with open circle at 2, arrow right] -5 -4 -3 -2 -1 0 1 2 3 4 5

C. ![number line with open circle at -2, arrow right] -5 -4 -3 -2 -1 0 1 2 3 4 5

D. ![number line with open circle at -2, arrow right] -5 -4 -3 -2 -1 0 1 2 3 4 5

STUDY ADVICE

Remember to take frequent breaks when studying, at least 10 minutes out of each hour. During your breaks, stand up and move around so you come back to studying refreshed.

Graphing Inequalities

As explained in previous lessons, the process of graphing equations results in a straight or curved line, because any value from the domain has only one unique output value in the range. Graphing inequalities is different, however, because one value in the domain can result in multiple values in the range.

Example 1: Graph the inequality $y \geq 2x - 3$.

1. Draw the line that is defined by the equation $y = 2x - 3$. Using the slope-intercept method, when $x = 0$, $y = -3$, so one point on the line is $(0, -3)$ and the line has a slope of 2. This line depicts the *equation* $y = 2x - 3$.

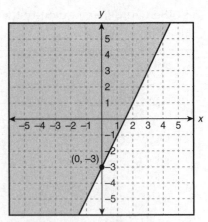

2. Any value of y for a corresponding value of x that is *greater* than the value of y on the line is also an allowable value for the inequality $y \geq 2x - 3$. For instance, if $x = 2$, then $2x - 3 = 4 - 3 = 1$, so any y-value greater than or equal to 1 is a valid solution to the inequality. This process could be repeated for various values of x and all the allowable values for y would be *on or above* the line. Therefore, the graph of an inequality is not just a line but an area. The area of the graph that represents the values of the inequality is usually shaded in some manner and referred to as a **half plane**.

If the inequality had been $y \leq 2x - 3$, then the allowable values for y would have been on or *below* the line.

When graphing, you must also deal accurately with the difference between $\geq$ and $>$ (or $\leq$ and $<$). When the inequality specifies greater (or less) than or equal to, ($\geq$ or $\leq$) the line that forms the border of the solution area is a *solid line* (as drawn above) to indicate that values on the line satisfy the inequality, and the area of the graph is called a **closed half plane**. If the inequality is only $>$ or $<$, the line forming the border of the shaded area is drawn as a *dotted line* to indicate that values on that line do not satisfy the inequality, and the area of the graph is referred to as an **open half plane**.

Graphs of inequalities can be used to help solve problems that involve constraints or limits.

Example 2: Jack is following a diet that allows him to consume 300 calories for lunch. He is going to have soup, which has 30 calories per ounce, and crackers, which have 25 calories per packet. Illustrate graphically what combinations of soup and crackers will total 300 calories or less.

PRACTICE 13

1. Select one axis for soup and one for crackers. If Jack has no crackers, he could eat 10 ounces of soup (30 calories/ounce × 10 ounces = 300 calories). If Jack ate only crackers, 12 packets would be his limit (25 × 12 = 300).

2. Connect these two limits with a straight line; any combination of soup and crackers on the line would be 300 calories. Any values below the line would be less than 300 calories, which is allowable, so shade the area below the line.

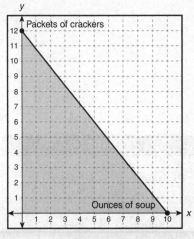

---

1. On the grid below, graph the inequality $y > (x^2 - 2)$.

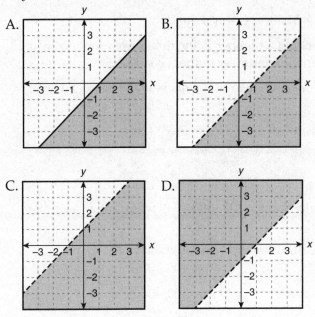

2. Which of the graphs below depicts the inequality $y < x - 1$?

A.   B.

C.   D.

3. Vanessa can spend as much as $3.00 on snacks. She likes Crispy Treats, which sell for 50¢ per ounce, and Grainy Grains, which are priced at 75¢ per ounce. Graphically illustrate the combinations of these snacks that she can afford to buy. Let the y-axis represent Grainy Grains and the x-axis represent Crispy Treats.

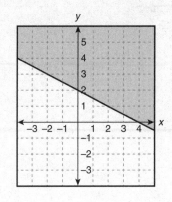

4. What is the inequality shown in the graph below?

A. $y \geq -x + 4$
B. $y \geq x + 2$
C. $y \geq \frac{1}{2}x - 2$
D. $y \geq -\frac{1}{2}x + 2$

Patterns and Functions

A **pattern** is a series of numbers or objects whose sequence is determined by a particular rule. You can figure out what rule has been used by studying the terms you are given. Think: What operation or sequence of operations will always result in the next term in the series? Once you know the rule, you can continue the pattern.

Example 1: Find the seventh term in the sequence: 1, 2, 4, 8, 16, . . .

1. Determine the rule. Each number in the sequence is two times the number before it.

2. Apply the rule. You have been given five terms and must find the seventh. Continue the pattern. The sixth term is $16 \times 2 = 32$, and the seventh term is $32 \times 2 = \mathbf{64}$.

A **function** is a rule that shows how the terms in one sequence of numbers are related to the terms in another sequence. Each distinct number entered into the function produces a unique output. For example, a sidewalk vendor charges $1.50 for a slice of pizza. The chart below shows how much it would cost to buy one to six slices.

Number of Pizza Slices	1	2	3	4	5	6
Cost	$1.50	$3.00	$4.50	$6.00	$7.50	$9.00

Each number in the first row corresponds to a price in the second row. We could say that the amount a customer will pay is a function of (or depends upon) the number of slices the customer orders. This function could be written:

Cost = number of slices $\times$ $1.50, or $C = n(\$1.50)$.

If you know the function and a number in the first set of numbers, you can solve for its corresponding number in the second set.

Example 2: Using the function $y = 3x + 5$, what is the value of y when $x = -3$?

1. Substitute the given value of x. $y = 3(-3) + 5$

2. Solve for y. $y = -9 + 5$

    $y = \mathbf{-4}$

Example 3: Using the function $n = 100 - 4(3 + m)$, what is the value of n when $m = 6$?

1. Substitute the given value of m. $n = 100 - 4(3 + 6)$

2. Solve for n. $n = 100 - 4(9)$

    $n = 100 - 36$

    $n = \mathbf{64}$

KEY IDEAS

- A pattern is a sequence of numbers determined by a mathematical rule.
- A function is a rule that shows how one set of numbers is related to another set of numbers.
- To use a function, substitute values for variables and solve.

TASC TEST TIP

To figure out what rule has been used to form a pattern, begin by finding the difference between each term and the term that follows it in the sequence.

PRACTICE 14

A. Solve.

1. Which number should come next in the following pattern?

   $-12, -9, -6, -3,$ _____

2. What is the next number in the sequence?

   $21, 26, 31, 36,$ _____

3. In the function $y = 4x + 10$, if $x = -2$, what is the value of y?

4. In the function $y = 2x(4 + x) - 2$, if $x = 3$, what is the value of y?

5. Each term in the second row is determined by the function $y = 2x - 1$.

x	1	2	3	4	5	...	12
y	1	3	5	7	9	...	

   What number belongs in the shaded box?

6. In the function $y = \dfrac{x+3}{6} - 8$, if $x = 21$, what is the value of y?

7. What is the next term in the pattern below?

   $1000, 500, 250, 125, 62.5,$ _____

8. What is the next number in the sequence?

   $3, -5, 7, -9, 11,$ _____

9. Each term in the second row is determined by the function $y = 3x + 5$.

x	2	1	0	1	2	...	9
y	-1	2	5	8	11	...	

   What number belongs in the shaded box?

10. In the function $y = (x - 7) + 12$, if $x = -10$, what is the value of y?

B. Choose the one best answer to each question.

Question 11 refers to the following drawing.

1st   2nd   3rd   4th

11. How many blocks would be needed to build the 25th construction in the sequence?

   A. 47
   B. 49
   C. 51
   D. 55

12. What is the sixth term in the sequence below?

   $-14, -8, -2, 4, \ldots$

   A. 10
   B. 14
   C. 16
   D. 22

13. The price per scarf is a function of the number of scarves purchased. The table shows the price per scarf for purchases of up to four scarves.

number (n) of scarves	1	2	3	4
cost (c) per scarf	$5.00	$4.75	$4.50	$4.25

   Which of the following functions was used to determine the prices shown in the table?

   A. $c = n(\$5.00 - \$0.25)$
   B. $c = \$5.00 - \$0.25(n - 1)$
   C. $c = \$5.00 - \$0.25n$
   D. $c = \$5.00n - \$0.25n$

14. Which of the following sequences of values of y could be created using the function $y = 4x - 3$?

   A. $1, 4, 7, 10, 13, \ldots$
   B. $1, 5, 9, 13, 17, \ldots$
   C. $1, 4, 8, 13, 19, \ldots$
   D. $1, -1, -3, -5, -7, \ldots$

Function Applications

Functions are used in many business applications. For instance, they can be used to calculate profit, cost, employee wages, and taxes. On the Mathematics Test, you will read about common work and life situations. The problems may contain or describe a function that you can use to solve the problem.

Example 1: Celino Advertising is finishing a series of print ads for a client. Finishing the project will cost $2000 per day for the first seven days and $3500 per day after seven days. The finishing costs can be found using the function $C = \$2000d + \$1500(d - 7)$, where C = the cost of finishing the project and d = the number of days. If the project takes 12 days to complete, what will the project cost?

Use the function to solve the problem.

$$C = \$2000d + \$1500(d - 7)$$
$$= \$2000(12) + \$1500(12 - 7)$$
$$= \$24000 + \$1500(5)$$
$$= \$24000 + \$7500$$
$$= \mathbf{\$31,500}$$

You may be asked to use functions to make comparisons.

Example 2: Nita decides to join a health club. She gets brochures from two health clubs and compares the plans. Healthstars Fitness charges a one-time membership fee of $250 and $8 per month. Freedom Health Center charges $25 per month. At both health clubs, the price (P) Nita will pay is a function of the number of months (m) she attends the club. The functions are:

Healthstars Fitness $P = \$250 + \$8m$

Freedom Health Center $P = \$25m$

Nita plans to move in 18 months. If she attends a health club until she moves, which one offers the better price?

1. Find the price at Healthstars Fitness: $P = \$250 + \$8m$
$$= \$250 + \$8(18)$$
$$= \$250 + \$144$$
$$= \$394$$

2. Find the price at Freedom Health Center: $P = \$25m$
$$= \$25(18)$$
$$= \$450$$

3. Compare the results. Even though Nita will have to pay a large amount up front, **Healthstars Fitness** offers the better price.

A. Solve. You MAY use a calculator.

1. The Chimney Sweep charges $25 for a chimney inspection. If the customer purchases additional services, $15 of the inspection fee is deducted. Let s = the cost of any additional services. The total cost (C) of an inspection and services can be determined by the function $C = \$25 + (s - \$15)$ where s is not 0.

   a. Jan has her chimney inspected and purchases a smoke guard for $89. How much will she be charged?

   b. After an inspection, Ahmed decides to have a new damper installed for $255. How much will he pay?

2. Ricardo does a great deal of driving for his work. He generally estimates his driving time in hours (t) using the function $t = \frac{m}{60}$, where m = the number of miles.

   a. How many hours will it take Ricardo to drive 330 miles?

   b. How many hours will it take Ricardo to drive 255 miles?

3. A customer's phone charges are a function of the number of minutes of long-distance calls made. The graph shows a comparison of two plans available.

   a. Michelle looks at her previous phone bills and finds that she makes about 350 minutes of long-distance calls per month. Which plan is better for her?

   b. Craig usually makes about 150 minutes of long-distance calls per month. Which plan is better for him?

B. Choose the one best answer to each question. You MAY use a calculator.

Questions 4 and 5 refer to the following information.

Alicia is considering three job opportunities. At all three jobs, weekly pay (P) is a function of the number of hours (h) worked during the week. The functions are shown below:

Job 1	$P = \$9.75h$
Job 2	$P = \$70 + \$8.40h$
Job 3	$P = \$380 \times \frac{h}{38}$

4. If Alicia works 30 hours in a week, how much more will she earn at Job 2 than at Job 1?

   A. $5.33
   B. $29.50
   C. $40.50
   D. $59.00

5. If Alicia works 40 hours per week, which of the following is a true statement?

   A. Alicia will earn the least at Job 3.
   B. Job 1 will pay more than Job 3.
   C. Job 3 will pay more than Job 2.
   D. Alicia will earn the most at Job 2.

6. A company is awarded a $95,000 job that will cost $5,400 per day in expenses. Profits (P) can be calculated using $P = \$95,000 - \$5,400d$, where d = number of days. What is the company's profit if the job takes 14 days to complete?

   A. $10,800
   B. $19,400
   C. $66,100
   D. $75,600

Modeling with Functions

The TASC Mathematics Test may ask you to model real-life situations using functions. Study the example below.

Example 1: Imagine that you open a checking account with an initial deposit of $60. Each month you add $100. Create a function called *f(t)*, where *t* represents the number of months the account has been open, to calculate the amount of money in the account. start a new paragraph here, out-dent and set side-by-side with graph below.

When you first open the account and deposit $60, no time at all has passed yet, so $t = 0$ and $f(0) = 60$. The first month (when $t = 1$), the account contains $60 plus ($100 × 1). The second month (when $t = 2$), it contains $60 plus ($100 × 2), or $200. The third month (when $t = 3$), it contains $60 plus ($100 × 3), or $300, and so on. So $f(t) = \$60 + \$100t$.

The function $f(t) = \$60 + \$100t$ is called a **linear** function because it graphs as a straight line. Not all real-life situations can be represented by linear functions. Sometimes you will need to create an **exponential** function, which graphs as a curve.

Example 2: Imagine a carton of milk going sour. The souring process is caused by bacteria that produce lactic acid. At optimal temperature and pH, these bacteria tend to double once per hour. If there are 100 lactic acid bacteria in a carton of milk initially, create a function $L(t)$ to model the bacterial population as a function of time. At the end of one hour, that is, when $t = 1$, the bacteria have doubled, so there are now 2(100) = 200. At the end of the next hour, when $t = 2$, they have doubled again, so there are now 2(2)(100) = 400. Each hour, the population is multiplied by 2, so that at the end of the tenth hour (when $t = 10$), there will be $2^{10}(100)$ bacteria, and at the end of the twentieth hour (when $t = 20$), there will be $2^{20}(100)$ bacteria, and so on. So we can write $L(t)$ like this:

$$L(t) = 2^t \times 100$$

Note that $L(0) = 100$, which is the number of bacteria at $t = 0$. Look at the above graph to see what $L(t)$ looks like (notice the units on each axis).

KEY IDEAS

- Some real-life situations can be modeled using linear functions. Others will require nonlinear functions.
- You can tell whether you need to use a linear or nonlinear function by looking at a few *x*- and *y*-values. If *y* changes by a constant for each corresponding constant change in *x*, then the function is linear; if not, it is nonlinear.
- The TASC Mathematics Test may describe a real-life situation and ask you to determine whether it would be modeled with a linear function or a nonlinear function.

TASC TEST TIP

When modeling something as a function of time, start by noting the initial situation (at t = 0). Then think about what happens when t = 1, t = 2, t = 3, and so on. Use the pattern you notice to construct the function.

You can determine whether a function is linear or not if you are given sets of data points, or if you use the equation to generate some values for x and y. In a linear function, as the x-value changes by a constant, the y-value also changes by a constant. For example, consider the line represented by the function $f(x) = 2x$. Every time x increases by 1, y increases by 2:

x-value	y-value
1	2
2	4
3	6

However, in a function involving an exponent, each time the x-value increases by a constant, the y-value changes by a non-constant amount. For instance, here are a few x- and y-values for the function $f(x) = x^2$:

x-value	y-value
1	1
2	4
3	9
4	16

1. Consider the x- and y-values for a function, given in the chart below. Is this function linear?

x-value	y-value
2	−8
−1	−1
0	0
1	1
2	8

Questions 2 and 3 refer to the following situation:

A small business has an expense account that contains $6,000 on January 1 of the year. On the first day of each month, the business pays $500 for equipment rental from this account. The expense account does not have overdraft protection, so the business does not allow the account to dip below zero.

2. If the business does not put any money into the account during the year, then which of the following equations describes the expense account balance as a function of time? Assume that t equals the number of months.

   A. $B(t) = \$6{,}000 + \$500t$
   B. $B(t) = \$6{,}000 \times t^2$
   C. $B(t) = \$6{,}000 \times \$500t^2$
   D. $B(t) = \$6{,}000 - \$500t$

3. What is the maximum possible value for t? Write your answer on the line below.

Questions 4 and 5 refer to the following situation:

Ten rabbits are accidentally introduced to a large island that previously had no rabbits at all. The rabbit population triples every four months.

4. Which of the following functions correctly describes the rabbit population as it grows over time, where y represents the number of years that have passed since the rabbits were first introduced?

   A. $P(y) = 10 \times 3^{3y}$
   B. $P(y) = 10 \times 3^y$
   C. $P(y) = 10 \times 4y$
   D. $P(y) = 10 + 30y$

5. If the island can sustain a maximum of 7,300 rabbits before they begin to die due to lack of resources, what is the maximum possible integer value for y?

   A. 0
   B. 1
   C. 2
   D. 3

Parameters of Functions in a Modeling Context

The TASC Mathematics Test may provide you with a function used to model a real-life situation and ask you to interpret the function's parameters, or constants. Study the example below.

Example 3: The rate a certain taxi company charges is given by the function $C(m) = \$2m + \$3$, where m represents length of the trip in miles and $C(m)$ represents the cost of the trip. The \$3 (which is the y-intercept on the graph of this function) represents the flat charge already on the meter before the taxi starts moving. The \$2 (which is the slope of the graph of this function) represents the rate per mile. Look at the graph below, and think about what would happen to the graph if the taxi company charged a different flat fee, or if it charged more or less per mile.

If the taxi company charged more per mile, the slope of the line would increase; if it charged less per mile, the slope would decrease. If the taxi company raised its initial flat charge, the y-intercept would be higher.

The example to the right is a linear function. Some situations must be modeled using a nonlinear function.

Example 4: If a ball is thrown straight up, you need a quadratic function to calculate when the ball will hit the ground given its initial position and velocity. Imagine that a ball is tossed into the air from a height of 3 meters at an initial velocity of 2 m/s. Three things must be included in this model: the ball's initial height, the velocity produced by its being thrown upward (which causes a change in the ball's height), and gravity. Gravity causes objects to fall toward the ground and to accelerate as they do so. Adding its initial height plus its change in height due to its initial velocity plus its change in height due to its acceleration due to gravity (which is approximately $-5m/s^2$) gives its height h at any point in time t:

The ball will hit the ground when $h = 0$: $\qquad 0 = -5t^2 + 2t + 3$

Divide by -1 and solve for t:
$$0 = 5t^2 - 2t - 3$$
$$0 = (5t + 3)(t - 1)$$
$$t = -\frac{3}{5} \text{ or } t = 1$$

A negative value for t would mean a time before the ball was tossed into the air, and that doesn't make sense. So only the positive value, $t = 1$, makes sense. The ball will hit the ground after 1 second.

Consider the graph of this function and think about what would happen to the curve if the ball were thrown from a different height, or if it were thrown with a different velocity.

Both of the examples above involve equations. But sometimes, real-life constraints are not equations, but inequalities. Study the example on the next page.

Example 5: Imagine that a high school theater club needs to raise money to buy costumes for an upcoming production, so the club opens a lemonade stand in the school cafeteria at lunch hour. Each day for a week, the theater club sells both iced tea (at $2.00 per cup) and lemonade (at $1.50 per cup). The theater club members have a total of 500 drink cups at their disposal, so they can sell a maximum of 500 drinks. They must raise a minimum of $850. Which of the following represents the system of inequalities that describes the theater club's constraints?

(1) $2i + 1.5t \geq 850; i + l \leq 500$

(2) $2i + 1.5t \leq 850; i + l \geq 500$

Choice **(1)** is correct. The amount of money the students need to make must be greater than or equal to $850, and the total number of drinks sold must be less than or equal to 500.

---

1. A bakery sells peanut butter cookies according to the following cost function, where d represents the number of cookies in dozens and $C(d)$ represents the total cost of a cookie purchase: $C(d) = \$10 + \$7(d - 1)$. What is the y-intercept of this function, and what does the y-intercept represent?

    A. The y-intercept is 10, which represents the number of cookies in the first dozen sold.
    B. The y-intercept is 7, which represents the cost per dozen after the first dozen.
    C. The y-intercept is 7, which represents the cost per dozen for the first dozen.
    D. The y-intercept is 3, which represents the surcharge for the first dozen cookies sold.

2. If a certain rodent population is allowed to grow without constraints, that population growth can be modeled by the function $P(t) = 100 \times 2^{5t}$, where 100 is the starting population and t represents years. What does the 5 in the exponent signify?

    A. It means that the population study went on for 5 years.
    B. It means that the population doubles 5 times per year.
    C. It means that the population quintuples every year.
    D. It means that the population quintuples every two years.

3. Sascha has at most $30 to spend on chocolate. Her favorite mint chocolate bars cost $3.50 each, while her favorite dark chocolate bars cost $4.50 each. She knows that she will purchase at least one dark chocolate bar and at least two mint chocolate bars. Which system of inequalities best models this situation?

    A. $3.5m + 4.5d \leq 30; d \geq 1; m \geq 2$
    B. $3.5d + 4.5m \leq 30; d \geq 1; m \geq 2$
    C. $3.5m + 4.5d \geq 30; d \geq 2; m \geq 1$
    D. $3.5d + 4.5m \geq 30; d \geq 2; m \geq 1$

4. A rectangular lawn is 10 feet longer than it is wide and has an area of 1,200 square feet. What is the width (that is, the shorter dimension) of the lawn? Write your answer in the space below.

    _____

LESSON 17

Equation Word Problems, Part II

Now that you have learned more about equations and systems of equations, you are ready to apply those skills to solve word problems.

Example 1: Two companies, A and B, charge for shipping by the pound. Company A charges a fixed fee of $3 for any shipment plus $1.50 for each pound in the shipment. Company B charges a fixed fee of $6 for any shipment plus $1 for each pound in the shipment. For what number of pounds would the two companies' shipping charges be the same?

This word problem gives you two equations: one for Company A and one for Company B. Let y represent the shipping charge and x represent pounds in the shipment, and write out the equations:

Company A: $y = 1.5x + 3$ Company B: $y = 1x + 6$

The question asks you what value of x will give the same value of y in both equations. In other words, what is the solution of the system of equations?

Solve by substitution:

$1x + 6 = 1.5x + 3$

$3 = 0.5x$

$6 = x$

The companies would charge the same amount for shipping a **6-pound order.**

You may also be asked to infer an equation from a graphic. Study the following example.

Example 2: A charity was struggling to raise funds. In November of last year it raised only $1500. It then decided to launch a social media campaign. The following graph shows how much money the charity raised for several months, starting with November of last year.

Which of the following equations could be used to find the money raised by the charity in the month x months after November last year? Here, y represents the money raised by the charity.

(1) $y = 1,500x + 500$

(2) $y = 500x + 1,500$

Choice **(2)** is correct: **$1500** is the charity's starting place at the end of November. Each month after that it raises $500 more. In February, which was three months after November, it raised $3000: $500(3) + 1500 = 3000$.

You may also be asked to solve word problems using quadratic equations. Study the following example.

Example 3: Xavier's age times Yelena's age is 120. Xavier is 2 years older than Yelena. How old are Xavier and Yelena?

Write two equations to represent the information given: $\qquad$ $xy = 120$ $\qquad$ $x - y = 2$

Solve using substitution.

1. Isolate a variable in the second equation: $\qquad$ $x = 2 + y$

2. Substitute and simplify: $\qquad$ $(2 + y)y = 120$

$$y^2 + 2y = 120$$

3. Make the equation equal zero and solve by factoring: $\qquad$ $y^2 + 2y - 120 = 0$

$$(y - 10)(y + 12) = 0$$

$$y = 10 \text{ or } -12$$

Now, it doesn't make sense for Yelena to have a negative age. So she must be **10 years old.** Substitute that value back into one of the original equations: $\qquad$ $x - 10 = 2$

Therefore, Xavier is **12 years old.**

---

1. Marguerite, a salesperson, earns a base salary plus a commission based on how much she sells. The following graph represents how much Marguerite can make.

Which of the following equations accurately expresses Marguerite's earnings (e) in terms of her sales (s)?

  A. $e = 30,000s$
  B. $e = 0.3s + 5,000$
  C. $e = 30,250 - 50s$
  D. $e = 0.01s + 30,000$

2. A car dealership is offering a discount on used cars. For sedans, the discount is $1,000 plus $100 for each year of the vehicle's age. For minivans, the discount is $1,500 plus $50 for each year of the vehicle's age. At what age would a vehicle have the same discount whether it were a sedan or minivan?

  A. 10
  B. 12
  C. 14
  D. 16

3. A zoo has contacted two stroller manufacturers to replace its current strollers with upgraded versions. Company A will charge $2,000 initially and $40 per stroller. Company B will only charge $1,550 initially, but $55 per stroller. For what number of strollers will the two companies charge the same price?

  A. 15
  B. 20
  C. 30
  D. 35

FUNCTIONS PRACTICE QUESTIONS

Directions: You MAY use your calculator.

1. Which of the following expressions is equal to $6 - 4(x + 3)$?

   A. $4x + 3$
   B. $4x - 9$
   C. $-4x - 3$
   D. $-4x - 6$

2. Three increased by the product of 4 and a number is equal to the same number decreased by 6. What is the number?

   A. -3
   B. -1
   C. 1
   D. 3

3. What is the equation of a line with a slope of -4 that passes through the point (1, 2)?

   A. $y = -4x + 2$
   B. $y = -4x + 6$
   C. $y = 4x + 1$
   D. $y = 4x + 6$

4. The ordered pair $(-2, -1)$ is a solution to which of the following equations?

   A. $-4x - y = 7$
   B. $4x + y = -7$
   C. $4x - y = -7$
   D. $-4x + y = -7$

5. For a two-week period, Jan earned \$150 less than twice Tom's earnings. Together Jan and Tom earned \$1380. How much did Tom earn?

   A. \$720
   B. \$660
   C. \$510
   D. \$360

Questions 6 and 7 refer to the following graph.

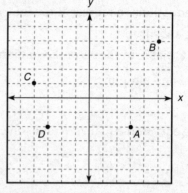

6. If the graph of the equation $y = -x - 5$ were drawn on the grid, which of the points would be on the line?

   A. *A*
   B. *B*
   C. *C*
   D. *D*

7. If a line were drawn through points *B* and *C*, what would be the slope of the line?

   A. -3
   B. $-\frac{1}{3}$
   C. $\frac{1}{3}$
   D. 3

8. Samuel is paid \$350 per month plus a 10% commission on his total sales for the month. If he needs to earn at least \$2100 per month, which of the following expressions represents the total sales for the month (*s*) Samuel needs to achieve?

   A. $s \geq \$17{,}500$
   B. $s \leq \$17{,}500$
   C. $s \leq \$21{,}000$
   D. $s \geq \$21{,}000$

9. For its Checking Plus account, a bank charges $3.95 per month plus $0.10 for each check written after the first ten checks written that month. The function to find the total monthly fee (F) is $F = \$3.95 + \$0.10(n - 10)$, where n = number of checks written.

Greg writes 24 checks in March. How much will he pay in fees for the month?

A. $6.35
B. $5.35
C. $2.40
D. $1.40

10. The sum of four consecutive odd numbers is 104. What is the largest number?

A. 23
B. 25
C. 27
D. 29

11. Which value for x makes the inequality $x > 400$ true?

A. 7^3
B. 4^4
C. 3^6
D. 6^3

12. Four less than the product of a number (x) and 5 is equal to 8 more than 2 added to 3 times the number. Which of these equations could be used to find the value of x?

A. $4 - 5x = 8 + 2 + 3x$
B. $5x - 4 = 8 + 2 + 3x$
C. $5x = 4 - 8 + 2 + 3x$
D. $5x - 4 = 8 + 2 + 3$

13. What is the slope of a line that passes through the points (2, 4) and (4, 6)?

A. -2
B. 1
C. 2
D. 4

14. What is the next number in the sequence?

1, 7, 14, 22, ...

A. 30
B. 31
C. 32
D. 33

15. What is the y-intercept of the line with a slope of 2 that passes through the point (1, 2)?

A. -2
B. $-\dfrac{1}{2}$
C. 0
D. $\dfrac{1}{2}$

16. If the graphs of the equations $y = x + 3$ and $y = -2x - 3$ are drawn on a coordinate grid, at which point do the two lines intersect?

A. $(-3, 2)$
B. $(-2, 1)$
C. $(-2, -1)$
D. $(2, 3)$

17. A hotel is installing a swimming pool that gets deeper as you approach the center. The following graph shows the depth of the pool in relation to the distance from the edge.

Which equation properly represents this relationship if x is the distance from the edge of the pool and y is the depth of the pool?

A. $y = 4.5 + 0.5x$
B. $y = 4.5 + x$
C. $y = 3 + x$
D. $y = 3 + 0.5x$

18. Which of the following shows the product of −7 and x decreased by the sum of 8 and y?

    A. $-7x - (8 + y)$
    B. $-7x - 8 + y$
    C. $(8 + y) - 7x$
    D. $(-7 + x) - (8 + y)$

19. What are the possible solutions for the quadratic equation $x^2 - 5x = 24$?

    A. −8 and 3
    B. −6 and 4
    C. 8 and −3
    D. 4 and −6

20. Cynthia is 6 times as old as Rebecca. In 6 years, Cynthia will be only 3 times as old as Rebecca. How old is Rebecca now?

    A. 3
    B. 4
    C. 8
    D. 12

21. The graph of which equation will pass through points $(0, -3)$ and $(5, 7)$?

    A. $y = \frac{1}{2}x - 3$
    B. $y = 2x - 3$
    C. $y = 2x + 7$
    D. $y = -2x + 3$

22. Which of the following graphs represents the solution set of the inequality $-2(x - 6) > 8$?

    A.
    B.
    C.
    D.

Questions 23 and 24 refer to the following graph.

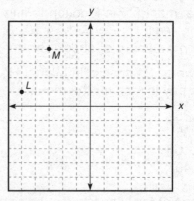

23. Which of the following ordered pairs shows the location of point L?

    A. $(-5, -1)$
    B. $(-5, 1)$
    C. $(-1, 5)$
    D. $(1, -5)$

24. What is the slope of the line that passes through points L and M?

    A. $\frac{-3}{2}$
    B. $\frac{-2}{3}$
    C. $\frac{2}{3}$
    D. $\frac{3}{2}$

25. Bob, Celia, Sam, and Daniel contributed money to buy their boss a retirement gift. Sam and Daniel each gave the same amount of money. Celia gave $12 more than Daniel. Bob gave half as much as Celia gave. If the four workers gave a total of $81, how much did Sam give?

    A. $9
    B. $15
    C. $18
    D. $21

STUDY ADVICE

On Test Day, you will likely see several questions that give you a word problem, a table, or a graph, and ask you to apply an equation or infer an equation from the situation. Carefully review the last three lessons to master those skills.

26. What is the solution set of the inequality $-7x - 4 \geq x - 28$

   A. $x \leq 3$
   B. $x \geq 3$
   C. $x \leq -3$
   D. $x \geq -4$

27. A line goes through the points (0, 2) and (1, 3). What is the equation of the line?

   A. $y = -\frac{1}{2}x + 3$
   B. $y = \frac{1}{2}x + 2$
   C. $y = x + 2$
   D. $y = x + 3$

28. In a recent election, Perez got 5512 more votes than $\frac{1}{3}$ of the leading candidate's votes. Together the two candidates received 18,072 votes. How many people voted for Perez?

   A. 6,024
   B. 8,652
   C. 9,420
   D. 12,560

29. What is the value of x in the equation $-4(x + 2) - 10 = 5x$?

   A. $x = -18$
   B. $x = -2$
   C. $x = 2$
   D. $x = 18$

30. Marcia counts the $5 bills and $10 bills in her cash register drawer. She counts a total of 35 bills with a total value of $240. If $x =$ the number of $5 bills in the drawer, which of the following equations could be used to find the number of $5 bills in the drawer?

   A. $5x + $10x = 35$
   B. $5x + $10x + 35 = 240
   C. $5(35 - x) + $10x = 240
   D. $5x + $10(35 - x) = 240

STUDY ADVICE

Congratulations! You only have one more chapter to go in the Mathematics unit. If you've absorbed the concepts so far, you're almost ready to take the TASC Mathematics Test. Make sure to stick to your study schedule, and you'll soon be ready for Test Day.

For questions 31 and 32, mark your answers in the grids below.

31. The sum of five consecutive numbers is 370. What is the fourth number in the sequence?

32. A baseball pitcher's earned run average (E) is a function of the number of earned runs (r) given up and innings pitched (i). The function is written $E = \dfrac{9r}{i}$. What is the earned run average of a pitcher who gives up 8 runs in 18 innings?

31.

/	/	/	
.	.	.	.	.
0	0	0	0	0
1	1	1	1	1
2	2	2	2	2
3	3	3	3	3
4	4	4	4	4
5	5	5	5	5
6	6	6	6	6
7	7	7	7	7
8	8	8	8	8
9	9	9	9	9

32.

/	/	/	
.	.	.	.	.
0	0	0	0	0
1	1	1	1	1
2	2	2	2	2
3	3	3	3	3
4	4	4	4	4
5	5	5	5	5
6	6	6	6	6
7	7	7	7	7
8	8	8	8	8
9	9	9	9	9

33. Tonya is selling boxes of cookies for charity. She will purchase five boxes of cookies herself and then try to sell more at her office. The following graph represents how many cookies she can sell as a function of how many of her coworkers are willing to purchase cookies.

If x is the number of Tonya's coworkers who are willing to buy cookies and y is the number of boxes of cookies sold, which formula can be used to find the number of boxes of cookies Tonya will sell?

A. $y = 5 + x$
B. $y = 5 + 2x$
C. $y = 7 + x$
D. $y = 7 + 2x$

Points, Lines, and Angles

Basic Definitions

A **point** is a single location in space. We assign a name to a point by writing a letter next to it. A **plane** is a collection of points that extends to form a flat surface. In the drawing, point A lies on plane P.

Much of your work in geometry will be concerned with lines and angles. A **line** is a straight pathway of points that extends indefinitely in two directions. A line may be named by a single letter or by two points on the line.

A **ray** is part of a line that begins at an endpoint and extends indefinitely in one direction. A portion of a line with two endpoints is called a **line segment.** Both rays and line segments are named using two points.

ray: $\overrightarrow{FG}$ segment: $\overline{FG}$

When two rays share an endpoint, they form an **angle.** The shared endpoint is the vertex of the angle. An angle can be named in different ways: by a number written in degrees inside the angle, by the vertex, or by the points on the angle. The symbol $\angle$ means angle.

$\angle 2, \angle E, \angle AEB$

Angles are measured in degrees, indicated by a number and the symbol $°$. We classify angles by their measurement.

A **right angle** forms a square corner and measures 90°. A right angle is often identified by a small square drawn inside it, as shown here.

An **acute angle** is less than 90°.

An **obtuse angle** is greater than 90° but less than 180°.

30°

130°

right angle symbol

A **straight angle** measures 180°.

A **reflex angle** has a measure greater than 180° but less than 360°.

180°

230°

Some Mathematics Test problems are about angle relationships. When the sum of two angles is 90°, a right angle, the angles are **complementary.** When the sum of two angles is 180°, a line or straight angle, the angles are **supplementary.** You can use this information to solve for a missing angle measure.

Example 1: In the drawing, ∠AOB and ∠BOC are complementary. What is the measure of ∠AOB?

The measure of angle BOC is given as 23°, or m∠BOC = 23°. The sum of the angles is 90°. Therefore, ∠AOB measures **67°**.

$$m\angle AOB + 23° = 90°$$
$$m\angle AOB = 90° - 23°$$
$$m\angle AOB = 67°$$

Example 2: In the drawing, ∠1 and ∠2 are supplementary. What is the measure of ∠1?

The measure of ∠2 is 45°. The sum of the angles is 180°. ∠1 measures **135°**.

$$m\angle 1 + 45° = 180°$$
$$m\angle 1 = 180° - 45°$$
$$m\angle 1 = 135°$$

A. Classify each angle based on its angle measure.

1. 55°   **3.** 180°   **5.** 270°   **7.** 30°

2. 95°   **4.** 18°   **6.** 90°   **8.** 110°

B. Choose the one best answer to each question.

Questions 9 and 10 refer to the drawing below.

9. ∠QZR is a straight angle. What is the measure of ∠QZS?

A. 135°
B. 125°
C. 90°
D. 60°

10. What kind of angle is ∠SZT?

A. acute
B. obtuse
C. right
D. straight

Questions 11 and 12 refer to the following drawing.

11. ∠AWD is a straight angle. What is the measure of ∠BWC?

A. 38°
B. 52°
C. 128°
E. 142°

12. What type of angle is ∠AWC?

A. right
B. acute
C. obtuse
D. straight

Parallel Lines and Transversals

Working with Vertical Angles and Transversals

When two lines intersect, they form two pairs of vertical angles. **Vertical angles** have the same angle measure. In the drawing, $\angle 1$ and $\angle 3$ are vertical angles, as are $\angle 2$ and $\angle 4$.

KEY IDEAS

- Vertical angles, which are equal in measure, are formed when two lines intersect.
- When a transversal crosses two parallel lines, special angle relationships form.
- You can find the measure of any angle formed by the transversal if the measure of one angle is known.

Intersecting lines also form adjacent angles. **Adjacent angles** share the same ray. For example, $\angle 1$ and $\angle 2$ are adjacent angles. The adjacent angles in this figure are supplementary angles because their sum is 180°, the measure of a straight angle. If you know the measure of one angle, you can find the measures of the other three angles.

Example 1: In the figure above, $m\angle 1 = 35°$. What are the measures of $\angle 2$, $\angle 3$, and $\angle 4$?

1. The measures of $\angle 1$ and $\angle 2$ are supplementary so their sum equals 180°. Solve for $\angle 2$.

$$m\angle + 35° = 180°$$
$$m\angle 2 = 145°$$

2. Angles 1 and 3 are vertical, so both measure 35°. Angles 2 and 4 are vertical, so both measure 145°.

$$m\angle 1 = 35°, m\angle 3 = 35°,$$
$$m\angle 2 = 145°, m\angle 4 = 145°$$

Parallel lines are lines that are exactly the same distance apart. No matter how far they extend, they will never touch. The symbol for parallel is $\parallel$. A **transversal** is a line that intersects two or more other lines. When a transversal intersects two parallel lines, special angle relationships are formed.

In the drawing, $M \parallel N$. The transversal, line P, forms eight angles.

TASC TEST TIP

You can often tell which angles are equal by looking at a figure. However, you must be able to prove two angles are equal to answer set-up questions and problems on logical reasoning.

Each angle matches another angle in the same position on the transversal. These angles, called **corresponding angles,** always have the same measure. The corresponding angles are $\angle 1$ and $\angle 5$, $\angle 2$ and $\angle 6$, $\angle 3$ and $\angle 7$, and $\angle 4$ and $\angle 8$.

Alternate exterior angles, which are also equal in measure, are on opposite sides of the transversal and are on the outside of the parallel lines. One pair of alternate exterior angles is $\angle 1$ and $\angle 7$. The other is $\angle 2$ and $\angle 8$.

Alternate interior angles are on opposite sides of the transversals and are inside the parallel lines. One pair of alternate interior angles is $\angle 3$ and $\angle 5$. The other is $\angle 4$ and $\angle 6$. Alternate interior angles are always equal in measure.

Example 2: In the figure, $C \parallel D$. If $m\angle 4 = 48°$, what is the measure of $\angle 5$?

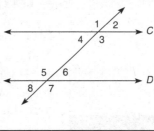

1. There are many ways to solve the problem. Here is one way: $\angle 4$ and $\angle 8$ are corresponding angles, so $m\angle 8 = 48°$.

2. $\angle 8$ and $\angle 5$ are supplementary angles, so $m\angle 5 + 48° = 180°$, and $m\angle 5 = \mathbf{132°}$.

A. Using the figure shown at the right, solve as directed.

1. List one pair of alternate interior angles.

2. Which angle corresponds to $\angle 7$?

3. If $m\angle 3 = 80°$, what is $m\angle 8$?

4. List one pair of alternate exterior angles.

5. List one pair of vertical angles.

6. Which angle corresponds to $\angle 8$?

$g \parallel h$

B. Choose the one best answer to each question.

Question 7 refers to the following figure.

7. The measure of $\angle 3$ is 75°. What is the measure of $\angle 1$?

   A.   15°
   B.   75°
   C.   105°
   D.   115°

8. Which of the following is a true statement about corresponding angles?

   A.   They are also supplementary angles.
   B.   They are in the same position with respect to both parallel lines.
   C.   They are also alternate interior angles.
   D.   They are also alternate exterior angles.

Questions 9 and 10 refer to the following figure.

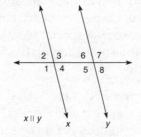

$x \parallel y$

9. The measure of $\angle 7$ is 115°. What is the measure of $\angle 4$?

   A.   25°
   B.   65°
   C.   115°
   D.   245°

10. Which of the following angles is equal in measure to $\angle 2$?

   A. $\angle 1$
   B. $\angle 3$
   C. $\angle 5$
   D. $\angle 8$

STUDY ADVICE

About a quarter of questions on the TASC Mathematics Test are about geometry. If these concepts seem new, take your time absorbing the basics. Geometry is challenging for a lot of people, but you can master these skills with practice.

Plane Figures

Four-Sided Plane Figures

A **plane figure** is a set of line segments, all lying on a single plane. To prepare for the TASC Mathematics Test, learn the properties of each shape. You will need to identify the characteristics of different types of four-sided plane figures and draw conclusions about their angles and sides.

You are already familiar with rectangles and squares. A **rectangle** is a four-sided figure with four right angles. The opposite sides (sides across from each other) are the same length, and they are parallel.

A **square** is actually a kind of rectangle. It, too, has four right angles with parallel opposite sides. However, a square has one additional property: its four sides are all the same length.

A **parallelogram** is a four-sided figure whose opposite sides are parallel and the same length. In addition, its opposite angles (the angles diagonally across from each other) are also equal in measure. A special parallelogram, called a **rhombus** (not shown), has four sides of equal length.

A **trapezoid** is a four-sided figure with exactly one pair of parallel sides. The definition of a trapezoid does not dictate the measure of the angles or the lengths of the sides.

Sides with the same markings are equal.

All four-sided plane figures have one important property in common. The sum of the measures of the interior angles is 360°. You can use this fact to find a missing angle measure.

Example 1: In figure *ABCD*, the opposite sides are parallel. What is the measure of ∠*A*?

1. Identify the figure. The notation on the drawing tells you that the opposite sides are equal in measure. Since they are also parallel, the figure is a parallelogram.

2. Find the measure of ∠*C*. The opposite angles of a parallelogram are equal in measure; therefore, *m*∠*C* = *m*∠*B*. Both ∠*B* and ∠*C* measure 110°.

KEY IDEAS

- Plane figures are classified by the properties of their sides and angles.
- The sum of the interior angles of any four-sided plane figure is 360°.
- By using the properties of any four-sided plane figure and algebraic reasoning, you can find missing angle measures.

TASC TEST TIP

Don't rely on sight alone to identify a geometric figure. Read carefully to see which properties are given. Then identify the figure based on the properties.

3. Find the measure of $\angle A$. You know the measures of $\angle A$ and $\angle D$ are equal and that the sum of all four angles equals 360°. Let $x = m\angle A$. Therefore, $2x$ = the sum of $m\angle A$ and $m\angle D$. Write an equation and solve.

$$2x + 110° + 110° = 360°$$
$$2x + 220° = 360°$$
$$2x = 140°$$
$$x = 70°$$

The measure of $\angle A$ is **70°**.

A. List the names of four-sided plane figures introduced on the previous page that can exhibit the following properties. Write *None* if no four-sided plane figure has the given property.

1. four right angles

2. opposite sides are equal in length

3. exactly one pair of parallel sides

4. all angles are equal in measure

5. only three right angles

6. opposite angles are equal in measure

7. all four sides are equal in length

8. sum of interior angles is 360°

9. sides are all of different lengths

10. four equal angles and four equal sides

B. Choose the one best answer to each question.

Questions 11 and 12 refer to the following figure.

11. Angle F is 20° more than three times the measure of $\angle H$. What is the measure of $\angle F$?

A. 40°
B. 120°
C. 140°
D. 180°

12. In order for figure *EFGH* to be a trapezoid, which of the following must be a true statement?

A. *EF* is the same length as *FH*.
B. *EF* ∥ *GH*.
C. $m\angle F = m\angle H$.
D. $m\angle G = m\angle F$.

Question 13 refers to the following figure.

13. If the opposite sides in figure *RSUT* are parallel, what is the measure of $\angle R$?

A. 5°
B. 20°
C. 90°
D. 270°

14. A four-sided plane figure has sides measuring 10, 15, 10, and 15. The opposite angles are equal, but there are no right angles. What is the figure?

A. rhombus
B. rectangle
C. parallelogram
D. trapezoid

Triangles

The Properties of Triangles

A **triangle** is a closed three-sided plane figure. From the definition, we can infer other properties. Since a triangle has three sides, it must also have three interior angles and three vertices.

A triangle is named by writing its vertices in any order. The triangle shown at right could be named ΔDEF. Its sides are DE, EF, and DF.

Triangles can be classified by the lengths of their sides and by the measures of their angles. In the figures below, sides with the same number of marks are equal.

Classified by Side Lengths

equilateral triangle
All sides are equal in length. Note that the angles also are equal.

isosceles triangle
Exactly two sides are equal in length. Note that the two angles opposite these sides are equal.

scalene triangle
No sides are equal in length, and no angles are equal.

Classified by Angle Measures

right triangle
One angle measures 90°.

acute triangle
All angles measure less than 90°.

obtuse triangle
One angle is greater than 90°.

Each triangle can be classified in two ways.

Example 1: What kind of triangle is ΔPQR?

1. Classify by its sides: Two sides have the same length, so ΔPQR is an isosceles triangle.

2. Classify by its angles: $\angle P$ is a right angle, so ΔPQR is a right triangle.

ΔPQR is a **right isosceles triangle**.

PRACTICE 4

The sum of the measures of the interior angles of any triangle is 180°. We can use this fact to solve for a missing angle.

Example 2: In △ABC, ∠A measures 55° and ∠B measures 100°. What is the measure of ∠C?

Write an equation and solve.

$$55° + 100° + ∠C = 180°$$
$$155° + ∠C = 180°$$
$$∠C = 25°$$

The measure of ∠C is **25°**.

A. Classify each triangle in two ways.

1.

2.

3.

B. Find the measure of the unknown angle in each triangle.

4.

5.

6.

C. Choose the <u>one best answer</u> to each question.

<u>Questions 7 and 8 refer to the following</u>
figure.

7. If ∠DAB measures 115° and ∠DCB measures 95°, what is the length of side AC in centimeters? (*Hint*: Use the facts in the problem to find *m*∠BAC and *m*∠BCA.)

A. 6
B. 8
C. 14
D. 22

8. What kind of triangle is △ACD?

A. isosceles
B. acute
C. right
D. obtuse

---

9. One angle in a scalene triangle measures 38°, and another angle measures 56°. What is the measure of the third angle?

A. 38°
B. 56°
C. 86°
D. 124°

Congruent and Similar Triangles

Comparing Triangles

Figures are **congruent** (indicated by the symbol ≅) when they have exactly the same size and shape. In other words, two figures are congruent if their corresponding parts (the angles and sides) are congruent. In real life, you can often guess that two geometric shapes are congruent by looking. However, in geometry and on the TASC Mathematics Test, you must be able to prove that figures are congruent.

Two triangles are congruent if the following corresponding parts are congruent:

Side-Side-Side (SSS) The side measures for both triangles are the same.

Side-Angle-Side (SAS) Two sides and the angle between them are the same.

Angle-Side-Angle (ASA) Two angles and the side between them are the same.

Example 1: Are triangles *ABD* and *BCD* congruent?

1. Find the known corresponding parts: $\angle ABD \cong \angle CBD$ and $\angle ADB \cong \angle CDB$. Both triangles share side *BD*.

2. Is this enough information to prove the triangles are congruent? Yes, two angles and the side between them are equal. Using the ASA rule, $\triangle ABD \cong \triangle BCD$.

Understanding Similarity

Figures are **similar** (shown by the symbol ~) when the corresponding angles are congruent and the corresponding sides are in proportion. In other words, similar figures always have the same shape, but they do not have to be the same size.

There are two rules that you can use to prove that two triangles are similar:

Rule 1: If two angle measures in the first triangle are equal to two angle measures in the second triangle, the triangles are similar.

Rule 2: If all corresponding sides have the same ratio, the triangles are similar.

Example 2: Are triangles *JKL* and *MNO* similar?

1. Compare corresponding angles. Since only one angle measure is given, you cannot use Rule 1 to prove the triangles are similar.

2. Write ratios comparing the sides in the first triangle to the corresponding sides in the second triangle. Each ratio is equal to $\frac{1}{2}$.

$$\frac{\triangle JKL}{\triangle MNO} \qquad \frac{3}{6} = \frac{4}{8} = \frac{5}{10} = \frac{1}{2}$$

Because the ratios are equal, the triangles are similar: $\triangle JKL \sim \triangle MNO$.

KEY IDEAS

- Congruent figures are the same size and shape. Similar figures are the same shape, but they do not have to be the same size.
- Prove triangles are congruent using the rules SSS, SAS, or ASA.
- Triangles are similar if two angles are congruent or if all corresponding sides are in proportion.

TASC TEST TIP

When a figure is flipped or turned, it may be difficult to identify corresponding parts. Try redrawing one of the figures so that it is turned to match the first figure. Always label your sketch carefully.

PRACTICE 5

If you know that two triangles are similar, you can use proportion to find an unknown measure.

Example 3: $\triangle XYZ \sim \triangle STU$. What is the measure of side ST?

Side SU corresponds to side XZ, and side ST corresponds to side XY. Set up a proportion and solve.

$$\frac{SU}{XZ} = \frac{ST}{XY} \quad \frac{9}{12} = \frac{x}{8} \quad 12x = 72 \quad x = 6$$

Side ST measures **6 units**.

A. For these items, the figures are not drawn to scale. Decide whether the triangles are congruent. Write **Yes**, **No**, or **Not Enough Information**.

B. Choose the <u>one best answer</u> to each question.

<u>Questions 4 and 5</u> refer to the following figure.

$\triangle RST \sim \triangle XYT$

4. What is the measure of side ST if side YT measures 30 units?

   A. 40
   B. 45
   C. 48
   D. 55

5. If $m\angle S = 68°$ and $m\angle T = 48°$, what is the measure of $\angle TXY$?

   A. 48°
   B. 64°
   C. 68°
   D. 116°

<u>Question 6</u> refers to the following figure.

6. What is the measure of the side labeled x?

   A. 2.5
   B. 2.9
   C. 3.2
   D. 3.8

Similar Triangle Applications

Indirect Measurement

Similar triangles are often used to measure objects that would be impossible to measure using ordinary tools. This process is called **indirect measurement.**

One common application involves using shadows to find the height of a tall object. In the diagram, both a man and a tree cast shadows at the same time of day. Since the angle of the sun is the same for both the man and tree, two similar triangles are formed.

We can easily measure the two shadows using ordinary tools. We can also measure the man's height. Using these facts, we can solve for the height of the tree.

Example 1: If the man in the diagram is 6 feet tall, what is the height of the tree?

Write a proportion and solve. $\dfrac{\text{man's shadow}}{\text{tree's shadow}} \quad \dfrac{4}{24} = \dfrac{6}{x} \quad \dfrac{\text{man's height}}{\text{tree's height}}$

$$24(6) = 4x$$
$$144 = 4x$$
$$36 = x$$

The height of the tree is **36 feet.**

We also use indirect measurement to measure distance across a large object.

Example 2: An engineer needs to know the width of a small lake. Using surveyor's tools, she marks off two similar triangles. She measures the distances shown on the diagram. Using her findings, what is the width of the lake?

The 10-ft side corresponds to the 25-ft side. The 24-ft side of the small triangle corresponds to the lake's width.

$$\frac{10}{25} = \frac{24}{x}$$

$$25(24) = 10x$$
$$600 = 10x$$
$$60 = x$$

The lake is **60 feet wide.**

PRACTICE 6

Choose the <u>one best answer</u> to each question.

1. An 8-foot-tall street sign casts a 6-foot shadow at the same time that a building casts a 48-foot shadow. How many feet tall is the building?
   A. 36
   B. 54
   C. 64
   D. 96

Question 2 refers to the following diagram.

2. To find the height of a cliff, a surveyor puts a 10-foot pole in the ground, 80 feet from the base of the cliff. He then determines the point on the ground from which he can sight both the top of the pole and top of the cliff. Using the distances shown in the diagram, what is the height of the cliff?
   A. 32
   B. 42
   C. 105
   D. 200

3. A meter stick is placed in the ground near a flagpole. At the time that the meter stick casts a shadow 2.5 meters in length, the flagpole casts a shadow 22.5 meters long. Which of the following proportions can be used to find the height of the flagpole (x) in meters?
   A. $\frac{2.5}{22.5} = \frac{1}{x}$
   B. $\frac{22.5}{2.5} = \frac{1}{x}$
   C. $\frac{1}{2.5} = \frac{22.5}{x}$
   D. $\frac{22.5}{1} = \frac{x}{2.5}$

Question 4 refers to the following diagram.

4. To find the distance across a river, a surveyor marks off two similar right triangles. Using the distances shown in the diagram, what is the distance, in feet, from one bank of the river to the other?
   A. 36
   B. 39
   C. 42
   D. 49

5. Phil is building a frame to hold a hammock. He wants to place a metal brace across the frame as shown in the drawing below. If he places the brace as shown in the diagram, what will be the length of the brace in feet?

   A. 3
   B. 4
   C. 6
   D. 8

STUDY ADVICE

You will likely see a small number of questions about similar or congruent triangles on Test Day. However, you will see more questions that test area and volume (coming up in the next few lessons). So, review the concepts here but also leave yourself time to study area and volume in depth.

Pythagorean Relationship

As you know, a right triangle has one right angle. The side directly across from the right angle, called the **hypotenuse**, is the longest side of the right triangle. The remaining sides, the rays of the right angle, are the **legs** of the triangle.

Thousands of years ago, people found a special relationship, called the **Pythagorean relationship**, among the sides of a right triangle. You can use this relationship to find the measure of any side of a right triangle if the other two side measures are known.

Pythagorean relationship $a^2 + b^2 = c^2$; a and b are legs, and c is the hypotenuse of a right triangle

In other words, the square of the hypotenuse is equal to the sum of the squares of the two legs of the right triangle.

KEY IDEAS

- The hypotenuse is the longest side of a right triangle. It is found opposite the right angle.
- The sum of the squares of the legs of a right triangle equals the square of the hypotenuse.

Example 1: What is the length of the hypotenuse of the right triangle shown in the diagram?

hypotenuse
3 ft
4 ft

1. The lengths of the legs are 3 ft and 4 ft. Let one leg equal a and the other equal b.

2. Solve for c. Substitute the values.

$$a^2 + b^2 = c^2$$
$$3^2 + 4^2 = c^2$$
$$9 + 16 = c^2$$
$$25 = c^2$$
$$\sqrt{25} = c$$
$$5 = c$$

3. When one side of an equation equals a squared variable, isolate the variable by finding the square root of both sides.

The length of the hypotenuse is **5 feet**.

The Pythagorean relationship can also be used to solve for the length of a leg.

Example 2: If John places a 13-foot ladder 3 feet from the base of a wall, how far up the wall will the ladder reach to the nearest tenth foot?

The wall, ground, and ladder form a right triangle. The hypotenuse is 13 ft in length. One leg is 3 ft. You need to find the length of the other leg.

13 ft
⊢3 ft⊣

$$a^2 + b^2 = c^2$$
$$3^2 + b^2 = 13^2$$
$$9 + b^2 = 169$$
$$b^2 = 160$$
$$b = \sqrt{160}$$
$$b \approx 12.6$$

The ladder will extend **12.6 feet** up the wall.

Note: Most of the time, you will need to use your calculator for the final step when using the Pythagorean relationship. To find the square root of 160 on the *TI-30XS MultiView*™ calculator, press: (2nd)(x²) 160 (enter) (use ◀▶ to convert the result from a radical to a decimal format).

TASC TEST TIP

Watch for right triangles with sides in a 3-4-5 or 5-12-13 ratio. These triangles often appear on math tests because the measures of the sides are all whole numbers.

PRACTICE 7

Some right triangles display special proportions, which are worth memorizing.
A right triangle whose angles are 45°, 45°, and 90° displays the following relationship:
leg : leg : hypotenuse $= x : x : x\sqrt{2}$.
A right triangle whose angles are 30°, 60°, and 90° displays the following relationship:
leg : leg : hypotenuse $= x : x\sqrt{3} : 2x$.

A. The lengths of two sides of a right triangle are given. Find the length of the remaining side to the nearest tenth unit. You may use a calculator.

1. leg a: 8 in
   leg b: 8 in
   hypotenuse c: ? in

2. leg a: 9 yd
   leg b: 12 yd
   hypotenuse c: ? yd

3. leg a: 1.5 cm
   leg b: 2 cm
   hypotenuse c: ? cm

4. leg a: ? m
   leg b: 3 m
   hypotenuse c: 6 m

5. leg a: 6 mm
   leg b: ? mm
   hypotenuse c: 10 mm

6. leg a: ? ft
   leg b: 5 ft
   hypotenuse c: 18 ft

7. leg a: 7 cm
   leg b: 10 cm
   hypotenuse c: ? cm

8. leg a: 15 in
   leg b: ? in
   hypotenuse c: 30 in

9. leg a: 4 km
   leg b: 5 km
   hypotenuse c: ? km

B. Choose the <u>one best answer</u> to each question.

10. On a coordinate plane, points A, B, and C can be connected to form a right triangle.

What is the distance from A to C, to the nearest tenth unit? (*Hint:* Count units to find the lengths of the sides, and use the Pythagorean relationship to find the distance between the points.)

   A. 5.2
   B. 6.7
   C. 8.4
   D. 10.1

11. The two shorter sides of a right triangle measure 18 ft and 24 ft. What is the measure in feet of the third side?

   A. 25
   B. 28
   C. 30
   D. 42

12. Jan has built a rectangular frame out of wood to use for the bottom of a platform. He wants to add a diagonal brace as shown in the drawing below.

5 ft

11 ft

What will the length of the brace be, to the nearest tenth of a foot?

   A. 16.0
   B. 13.7
   C. 12.8
   D. 12.1

13. The hypotenuse of a right triangle measures 39 inches. If one leg measures 15 inches, what is the measure of the other leg, in inches?

   A. 36
   B. 24
   C. 18
   D. 12

Perimeter and Area

Perimeter is the distance around a figure. To find perimeter, simply add the lengths of the sides. For common figures, you can apply a formula to find the perimeter. You need to memorize these formulas.

square	Perimeter = 4 × side	$P = 4s$
rectangle	Perimeter = 2 × length + 2 × width	$P = 2l + 2w$
triangle	Perimeter = side_1 + side_2 + side_3	$P = a + b + c$

Example 1: A rectangle is 16 inches long and 9 inches wide. What is the perimeter of the rectangle?

Use the formula: Perimeter = 2 × length + 2 × width
$$= 2 \times 16 + 2 \times 9$$
$$= 32 + 18$$
$$= \textbf{50 in}$$

Area is the measure of the space inside a flat figure. Area is measured in square units. For example, if the sides of a figure are measured in inches, its area will be measured in square inches. The formulas for finding area are shown below.

square	Area = side^2	$A = s^2$
rectangle	Area = length × width	$A = lw$
parallelogram	Area = base × height	$A = bh$
triangle	Area = $\frac{1}{2}$ × base × height	$A = \frac{1}{2}bh$
trapezoid	Area = $\frac{1}{2}$ × height (base_1 + base_2)	$A = \frac{1}{2}h(b_1 + b_2)$

Three of the formulas mention two new measures: base and height. The **base** is one side of the figure. The **height** is the length from the vertex to the base, forming a right angle to the base.

Example 2: Find the area of figure *ABCD*.

1. Identify the figure. *ABCD* is a parallelogram.

2. Find the facts you need. To use the formula for finding the area of a parallelogram, you need to know the height and the length of the base. Ignore the length of side *BD*.

3. Use the formula Area = base × height.

Area = 12 × 7

= **84 sq cm or 84 cm²**

PRACTICE 8

A. Find the area and perimeter of each figure.

1.

3.

5.

2.

4.

6.

B. Choose the one best answer to each question.

Question 7 refers to the following figure.

7. What is the area in square inches of the shaded portion of the rectangle?

- A. 38
- B. 40
- C. 56
- D. 88

8. The four sides of a rectangle measure 9 feet, 6 feet, 9 feet, and 6 feet. What is the area of the rectangle in square feet?

- A. 30
- B. 36
- C. 54
- D. 81

9. Martin is building a rectangular patio centered on one side of his yard. The rest of his yard, shown in the diagram, is planted in grass.

If the measurements in the diagram are in feet, what is the square footage of the grass portion of Martin's yard?

- A. 108
- B. 162
- C. 324
- D. 432

10. A square measures 6 centimeters on one side. What is the perimeter of the square in centimeters?

- A. 12
- B. 24
- C. 36
- D. 216

Circles

Circumference and Area

A **circle** is a closed set of points that are all the same distance from a single point, the center of the circle. The **circumference** of a circle is its perimeter, or the distance around the circle. The **area** of a circle is the space inside the circle.

To find perimeter and area of a circle, you need to know two other measures of a circle. The **diameter** is a line segment with endpoints on the circle that passes through the center of the circle. The **radius** is a line segment that connects the center of the circle to any point on the circle. As you can see from the diagram, the radius is one-half the diameter.

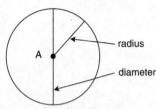

The formulas for circumference and area use a special quantity called **pi** (π). Pi is the ratio of the circumference to the diameter. It is equal to approximately 3.14. The digits for pi continue infinitely, so calculations with pi are always approximations. For the Mathematics Test, you will use 3.14 as the value of pi. Below is the formula for finding the circumference of a circle.

Circumference $= \pi \times$ diameter, or $C = \pi d$

Example 1: A china plate has a gold rim. If the plate's diameter is 10.5 inches, what is the distance around the rim to the nearest tenth of an inch?

Use the formula: $C = \pi d$

$\qquad\qquad\quad = 3.14(10.5)$

$\qquad\qquad\quad = 32.97$, which rounds to **33.0 inches**

Use this formula to find the area of a circle: Area $= \pi \times$ radius^2, or $A = \pi r^2$.

Example 2: The circular surface of a satellite component must be covered with heat-resistant tiles. If the radius of the component is 4 meters, what is the area in square meters?

Use the formula: $A = \pi r^2$

$\qquad\qquad\quad = 3.14(4^2)$

$\qquad\qquad\quad = 3.14(16)$

$\qquad\qquad\quad = $ **50.24 square meters**

In some situations, you may need to solve for either the diameter or radius. Remember, the diameter is twice the radius ($d = 2r$), and the radius is one-half the diameter: $r = \frac{1}{2}d$.

PRACTICE 9.1

Example 3: What is the circumference of circle *B* to the nearest tenth of a centimeter?

1. The radius of the circle is 5 cm. Therefore, the diameter is 2×5, or 10 cm.

2. Use the formula: $C = \pi d$
$$= 3.14(10)$$
$$= 31.4 \text{ cm}$$

A. Find the circumference and area of each circle. Round answers to the nearest tenth.

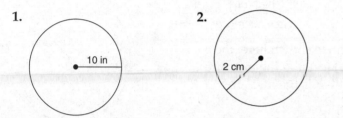

1.　　　　2.　　　　3.

B. Choose the <u>one best answer</u> to each question.

<u>Questions 4 and 5 refer to the following</u> drawing.

4. If workers lay a tile border around the edge of the fountain shown in the diagram, how many feet long will the border be to the nearest foot?

A. 19
B. 36
C. 38
D. 57

5. Which of the following expressions could be used to find the area of the bottom surface of the fountain?

A. 3.14×6
B. 3.14×6^2
C. 3.14×12
D. 3.14×12^2

6. The radius of a circle is 6.5 cm. What is the diameter of the circle in centimeters?

A. 3.25
B. 13.0
C. 33.16625
D. 132.665

7. On the target below, the 5- and 10-point bands are each 2 inches wide, and the inner circle has a diameter of 2 inches.

To the nearest inch, what is the outer circumference of the 10-point band?

A. 6
B. 13
C. 19
D. 113

STUDY ADVICE

Here are two mnemonics (memory tricks) to help you learn the formulas in this lesson:

Circumference: Learn "Cherry pie's delicious" to remember $C = \pi d$.

Area: Learn "Apple pies are too" to remember $A = \pi r^2$.

Interior Angles, Arcs, and Chords

You have learned that angles are measured in degrees. A circle represents 360 degrees. If you draw an angle of x degrees with the vertex at the center of the circle, that pie piece, so to speak, will take up $\frac{x}{360}$ of the circle. Study the following diagram:

The portion of a circle's circumference that forms the outside of a "pie piece" is called an **arc**. The length of an arc has the same proportional relationship to the circumference that its angle does to 360. In the previous diagram:

$$\frac{\text{length of } Y}{\text{circumference}} = \frac{m\angle X}{360}$$

Example 4: In the circle shown here, the circumference is 400 feet and the measure of arc S is 50 feet. What is the measure of angle AOB?

Step 1: Set up the proportion.

$$\frac{50}{400} = \frac{mAOB}{360}$$

Step 2: Cross multiply and divide to solve the proportion.

$$400 \times mAOB = 50 \times 360$$

The measure of angle AOB is **45 degrees.**

$$mAOB = \frac{18,000}{400} = 45$$

Now suppose you drew an angle so that its vertex was not on the center of the circle but on one side of the circle, like this: You could still use a proportion to find the length of arc Q. However, the proportion is different:

$$2 \times \frac{mABC}{360} = \frac{\text{length of arc } Q}{\text{circumference of circle}}$$

Example 5: In the circle shown, what is the length of arc Q? Round your answer to the nearest tenth.

Step 1: First, find the circumference of the circle. The diagram shows that the radius is 10 units.

$$C = 20\pi \approx 62.8$$

Step 2: Set up the proportion. Simplify.

$$2 \times \frac{40}{360} = \frac{\text{length of arc } Q}{62.8}$$

$$\frac{2}{9} = \frac{\text{length of arc } Q}{62.8}$$

Step 3: Cross multiply to solve.

$$62.8 \times 2 \div 9 \approx \mathbf{14}$$

Arc Q is **14 units** long.

KEY IDEAS

- A circle represents 360 degrees.
- An arc is a portion of the circumference of a circle. Its length can be calculated if you know the circumference of the circle and the degree measure of the angle that defines that arc.
- A chord is a straight line whose end points fall on the circumference of a circle.

TASC TEST TIP

The TASC Mathematics Reference Sheet contains key formulas related to chords and arcs (see page 169), so you do not have to memorize these formulas.

PRACTICE 9.2

A **chord** is a straight line that has its endpoints on the circumference of a circle. You can find the length of a chord if you know the circle's radius and how far the midpoint of the chord is from the center of the circle. That's because the radius forms the hypotenuse of a right triangle, as shown in the diagram.

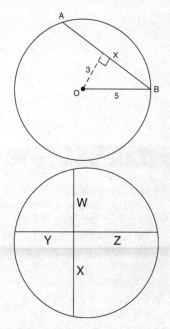

Example 6: In the circle shown, what is the length of chord *AB*?

Step 1: One leg of the right triangle is 3, and the hypotenuse is 5. Set up an equation based on the Pythagorean relationship.

$$(\text{length of } XB)^2 + 3^2 = 5^2$$

Step 2: Solve for the length of *XB*.

$$(\text{length of } XB)^2 = 16$$
$$(\text{length of } XB) = 4$$

Step 3: Because *XB* is only half of chord *AB*, double the result to find the length of chord *AB*. Chord *AB* is **8 units** long.

$$4 \times 2 = 8$$

Two chords that intersect have the following relationship:

length of *W* × length of *X* = length of *Y* × length of *Z*

A. For each of the following circles, find either the measure of the angle marked *X* or the length of the chord marked *Y*. Use 3.14 for pi, and round your answer to the nearest unit.

1.   **2.**   **3.**

B. Choose the one best answer to each question.

4. In the following circle, what is the length of *A* in meters?

A. 4
B. 5
C. 6
D. 10

5. In the following circle, what is the length of chord *LM*?

A. 12
B. 14
C. 24
D. 26

Introduction to Trigonometry

Trigonometry is a mathematical subject that deals with triangles. Trigonometry has many practical applications in the sciences and engineering, but the Mathematics Test will ask you basic questions about trigonometric relationships.

Trigonometric relationships are frequently associated with right triangles, but some applications deal with all types of triangles. Because one of the three angles of a right triangle must be 90°, the size of either of the non-right angles determines the size of the other acute angle and, therefore, the shape of any right triangle. Given the properties of similar triangles, the proportional relationships among the sides must be the same for all right triangles that have the same angles.

The sides are called by the following letters: **O**, the side **opposite** the specified angle in a right triangle; **A**, the side **adjacent** or next to the angle; and **H**, the **hypotenuse**.

There are six trigonometric functions as shown in this table. (The Greek letter theta, θ, is frequently used to represent the measurement of the angle.) Each of these functions is calculated by dividing one side length by another side length, as indicated in the third column:

Name	Symbol	Function
Sine	sin θ	$\frac{O}{H}$
Cosine	cos θ	$\frac{A}{H}$
Tangent	tan θ	$\frac{O}{A}$
Cosecant	csc θ	$\frac{H}{O}$
Secant	sec θ	$\frac{H}{A}$
Cotangent	cot θ	$\frac{A}{O}$

Notice that the last three formulas are merely the reciprocals of the first three. The values of these functions for any angle can be found using an appropriate calculator, in tables, or by division if the lengths of the sides are known. To find the sine of an angle with measure 30°:

sin 30 enter

Another function that can be performed on the calculator is "*arc*," which is the angle that has a given value for a trigonometric function. So, if you knew the value of sine for a given angle, you could find out that angle's measure. For example, *arcsin* 0.5 = 30°. Think of this function as "the measure of the angle whose sine is 0.5 is 30°." The *arcsin*, *arccos*, and *arctan* functions are accessible on the TI-30XS Multiview™ calculator as (2nd) $\sin^{-1}$, (2nd) $\cos^{-1}$, and (2nd) $\tan^{-1}$ respectively. To calculate *arcsin* 0.5:

2nd sin . 5 enter

Example 1: If the sides of a right triangle are 3 cm, 4 cm, and 5 cm, what is the sine of the smallest angle?

1. The shortest side of a triangle will always be opposite the smallest angle, in this case, 3 cm. Thus, you must find the sine of the angle that is opposite the side measuring 3, which will be the opposite side (3) divided by the hypotenuse. And you can deduce the length of the hypotenuse: the hypotenuse will always be the longest side, which is 5 cm.

2. Using the sine formula: $\sin\theta = \frac{O}{H} = \frac{3}{5} = \mathbf{0.6}$

Example 2: The cosine of an angle in a right triangle is 0.75 and the hypotenuse is 10 cm. What is the length of the side adjacent to that angle?

1. $\cos\theta = \frac{A}{H}$, so $A = \cos\theta\,(H)$

2. A (the adjacent side) = 0.75 (10 cm) = **7.5 cm**

There are some special relationships among the trigonometric functions in right triangles. For instance, the sine of one of the acute angles will equal the cosine of the other. Also, the equation $(\sin\theta)^2 + (\cos\theta)^2 = 1$, holds true for all right triangles. These relationships can be useful to help determine unknown values.

You MAY use a calculator for the questions on this page.

1. The sine of a certain angle is 0.6. What is the cosine of that same angle? Write your answer on the line below.

_____

2. Fill in the missing values in the table to the nearest ° (degree) or 0.1 cm based on the triangle shown below (remember that geometric figures are not necessarily drawn to scale). (*Hint*: Use trigonometric relationships. As you use these, round them to the hundredths place.)

Angle ABC	90°
Angle ACB	70°
Angle CAB	
Side AB	
Side BC	10 cm
Side AC	

3. If cos θ = 0.70, then sin (90° − θ) = ?

   A. 0.30
   B. 0.49
   C. 0.70
   D. 1.43

4. Match the values in the second table with the blanks in the first table and place the values in the correct cell for θ = 27°.

sin θ	
cos θ	
tan θ	
csc θ	
sec θ	
cot θ	

0.891
1.122
1.963
0.454
2.203
0.510

5. If sin θ = X and cos θ = Y, then tan θ = ?

   A. $\frac{X}{Y}$

   B. XY

   C. $\frac{Y}{X}$

   D. $\frac{1}{XY}$

Trigonometry in General Triangles

Trigonometric functions in right triangles are based upon geometric relationships among the sides (SOH-CAH-TOA). When applied to non-right triangles, however, the functions can have different characteristics. For instance, cosines and tangents of obtuse angles are actually negative numbers. There are three formulas that use the trigonometric functions in the context of triangles in general.

The first of these formulas, $A = \frac{1}{2} ab (\sin C)$, can be used to calculate the area of any triangle when two sides and the included angle are known. This formula can be derived by creating a perpendicular line from $\angle A$ to side a. The length of this line is $b(\sin C)$. The area of any triangle is one-half the base times the height, in this case $\frac{1}{2} a \times b(\sin C)$ or $\frac{1}{2} ab(\sin C)$.

Example 1: If side $c = 8$ cm, side $a = 12$ cm, and $\angle B = 25°$, what is the area of the above triangle?

1. Since the problem provides values for two sides and the included angle, the above formula will work.

2. The sine of 25° is 0.42262.

3. $A = \frac{1}{2}(12 \text{ cm})(8 \text{ cm})(.42262) = \textbf{20.3 cm}^2$

Another formula that applies to all triangles, $\frac{\sin A}{a} = \frac{\sin B}{b} = \frac{\sin C}{c}$, is called the **Law of Sines**. In the triangle above, the height is either $b(\sin C)$ or $c(\sin B)$. Setting those alternative ways of calculating the height equal to each other, $b(\sin C) = c(\sin B)$. Dividing both sides of the equation by bc and canceling like terms results in $\frac{\sin C}{c} = \frac{\sin B}{b}$. The same process could be repeated for $\angle A$ using a different perpendicular height to derive the Law of Sines.

Example 2: If side $c = 8$ cm, side $b = 10$ cm, and $\angle B = 25°$, what is the measure of $\angle C$?

1. The Law of Sines states that $\frac{\sin B}{b} = \frac{\sin C}{c}$.
2. Substituting the known values ($\sin B = 0.42262$), $\frac{0.42262}{10} = \frac{\sin C}{8}$
3. Solve: $\sin C = 0.33810$, so $\angle C = 19.8°$.

The third generalized function is the **Law of Cosines**, which states that $a^2 = b^2 + c^2 - 2bc (\cos A)$. (And also the counterparts $b^2 = a^2 + c^2 - 2ac (\cos B)$ and $c^2 = a^2 + b^2 - 2ab (\cos C)$.) This law is often referred to as the generalized equivalent of the Pythagorean theorem; if the angle in the equation is 90°, then its cosine is 0 and only $a^2 = b^2 + c^2$ remains. Like the Law of Sines, this formula can be derived by constructing right triangles within the general triangle.

In the right triangle created by the height, the Pythagorean theorem states that $a^2 = h^2 + (b - r)^2$.
Looking at the left triangle, $h = c(\sin A)$ and

PRACTICE 11

$r = c(\cos A)$. Substituting these values into the first equation gives $a^2 = c(\sin A)^2 + (b - c(\cos A))^2$. This simplifies to $a^2 = c^2(\sin^2 A + \cos^2 A) + b^2 - 2bc(\cos A)$. Since $(\sin^2 A + \cos^2 A) = 1$, then $a^2 = c^2 + b^2 - 2bc(\cos A)$.

Example 3: If $\angle A = 20°$, $c = 7$cm, and $b = 10$cm, what is the length of a?

1. Using the Law of Cosines, $a^2 = 7^2 + 10^2 - 2(10)(7)(0.89101) = 149 - 124.7 = 24.3$
2. Taking the square root of both sides, $a = 4.9$ cm.

---

1. Calculate and fill in the areas of the triangles to the nearest 0.1cm² using the sides and angles shown in the table.

$\angle C$	Side A	Side B	Area (cm²)
10°	5 cm	5 cm	
45°	8 cm	3 cm	
60°	10 cm	2 cm	
90°	3 cm	4 cm	

2. Two of the angles of a triangle are 37° and 72°. The side opposite the 37° angle is 4 cm long. Use the Law of Sines to determine the length of the side opposite the third angle.

    A.   3.8 cm
    B.   6.0 cm
    C.   6.3 cm
    D.   8.0 cm

3. What is the length of side x ?

    A.   9.2 cm
    B.   10.9 cm
    C.   12.0 cm
    D.   18.4 cm

4. A triangle has sides of 12 mm, 5 mm, and 8 mm. Use the Law of Cosines to fill in the chart below with the measurements of the angles to the nearest 0.1°.

Side	Opposite $\angle$
12 mm	
5 mm	
8 mm	

5. The table below lists two sides and the included angle of some triangles. For each row, calculate the measurement of the side opposite the given angle.

Side	Angle	Side	Opposite side
6	22°	5	
11	55°	3	
8	100°	7	
10	10°	10	

Geometry

LESSON 12

Volume

Rectangular Solids, Cubes, Cylinders, and Spheres

Volume, also called **capacity**, is the measure of space inside a three-dimensional object. You measure volume in cubic units. In other words, if the sides of an object are measured in inches, the volume is the number of cubes (one inch per side) you would need to fill the object.

Many common three-dimensional objects have at least two identical and parallel faces. Think of a cereal box or a soup can. Both objects have identical faces at the top and bottom of the container. Either of these faces can be called the base of the object. To find the volume of any container with identical bases, multiply the area of one base by the height of the object: Volume = area of base × height.

Another way to find the volume of an object is to use the formula that applies specifically to that object.

rectangular prism	Volume = area of base × height	$V = Bh$
cube	Volume = edge^3	$V = e^3$
cylinder	Volume = pi × radius^2 × height	$V = \pi r^2 h$
sphere	Volume = $\frac{4}{3}$ × pi × radius^3	$V = \frac{4}{3}\pi r^3$

In the examples below, formulas are used to find the answers, but the problems can also be solved by simply multiplying the area of the base by the height.

A **rectangular prism** has two identical rectangular bases. The remaining sides of the figure are also rectangles.

Example 1: A cardboard box has the dimensions shown in the diagram. What is the volume of the box in cubic feet?

Use the formula: $V = Bh$, where B is *length × width*
$$= (4 \times 5)(3) = \textbf{60 cubic feet}$$

A **cube** is a rectangular prism with six identical faces. In a cube, each edge (where the sides meet) is the same length.

Example 2: A wood block measures 2 inches per edge. What is the volume of the block?

Use the formula: $V = e^3$
$$= 2^3 = \textbf{8 cubic inches}$$

A **cylinder** has two circular bases. The bases are connected by a curved surface. Cans, barrels, and tanks are often in the shape of cylinders.

Example 3: A storage tank has a radius of 1.5 meters and a height of 3 meters. What is the volume of the tank to the nearest cubic meter?

Use the formula:

$$V = \pi r^2 h$$
$$= 3.14(1.5^2)(3) = 21.195 \text{ m}^3,$$

which rounds to **21 cubic meters**

A. Find the volume of each object to the nearest whole unit.

1.

3.

5.

2.

4.

6.

B. Choose the <u>one best answer</u> to each question.

<u>Question 7 refers to the following drawing.</u>

4 ft   4 ft

7. A rectangular box with a volume of 80 cubic feet has the length and width shown in the drawing. What is the height of the box?

A. 5
B. 10
C. 16
D. 20

8. A wooden crate measures 5 feet along each edge. What is the crate's volume in cubic feet?

A. 15
B. 25
C. 125
D. 150

<u>Question 9 refers to the following drawing.</u>

12 ft

3 ft

9. Linda adds a water stabilizer to her children's swimming pool once a week. The instructions tell her to add one scoop of the product for every 20 cubic feet of water. About how many scoops should she add per week?

A. 3
B. 6
C. 17
D. 36

Volume of Pyramids and Cones

A **pyramid** is a three-dimensional object with four triangular faces that connect to the same vertex. The base of a pyramid can be any closed figure, but you will likely not see pyramids with complicated bases on the TASC test. Here, we will focus on pyramids with square bases. But remember: If you can find the area of the base, you can find the volume of the pyramid.

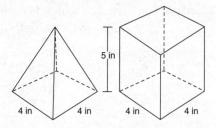

The rectangular prism and the pyramid shown here both have identical square bases and the same height. Compare the two figures. As you can see, the pyramid holds much less than the rectangular prism. In fact, it holds only one-third of the rectangular prism's volume.

The formula for finding the volume of a pyramid is as written below. The height of a pyramid is the perpendicular distance from the base to the vertex at the top.

pyramid   Volume $= \frac{1}{3} \times$ area of base $\times$ height

Example 4: Find the volume of the pyramid shown here.

The length of a base edge is 5 cm. The height of the pyramid is 6 cm. Ignore the diagonal edges.

Apply the formula: $V = \frac{1}{3}Bh$

$\qquad = \frac{1}{3}(5^2)(6)$

$\qquad = \frac{1}{3}(25)(6)$

$\qquad = \mathbf{50\ cm^3}$

While the example above uses a pyramid with a square base, the formula can be applied to any pyramid, including pyramids with rectangular or triangular bases. Use your knowledge of area formulas to calculate the area of the base, multiply it by the height, and multiply that by $\frac{1}{3}$.

A **cone** is similar to a cylinder. Both have a circular base and a curved side. The curved side of a cone slants inward so that it meets at a point, or vertex. The volume of a cone is $\frac{1}{3}$ of the volume of a cylinder with the same size base and height.

Notice that the formula for the volume of a cone contains the formula for finding the area of a circle (πr^2).

cone   Volume $= \frac{1}{3} \times \pi \times$ radius$^2 \times$ height

Example 5: Find the volume of the cone shown here.

The radius of the base is 2 inches, and the height is 9 inches.

Apply the formula: $V = \frac{1}{3}\pi r^2 h$

$\qquad = \frac{1}{3}(3.14)(2^2)(9)$

$\qquad = \frac{1}{3}(3.14)(4)(9)$

$\qquad = \mathbf{37.68\ in^3}$

PRACTICE 12.2

A. Find the volume of each object to the nearest unit.

1.

3 in
3 in   3 in

3.

5 cm

12 cm

5.

2 in   8 in

2 in

2.

6 in

9 in

4.

10 m

12 m   12 m

6.

18 cm

15 cm

B. Choose the one best answer to each question.

7. Advertisers have designed this pyramid-shaped package to hold action figures.

h = 15 cm

10 cm   10 cm

After testing the design, the manufacturer decides to increase both the length and width of the base by 4 cm. How many more cubic centimeters will the new package hold than the package shown above?

A. 480
B. 500
C. 980
D. 2940

8. The height of a cone is half the diameter of its base. If the cone's height is 4 inches, what is the cone's volume to the nearest cubic inch?

A. 21
B. 48
C. 67
D. 201

9. Which of the following is a true statement about the figures shown below?

4 cm

3 cm   2 cm

Figure A

h = 6 cm

3 cm   3 cm

Figure B

A. The volume of A equals the volume of B.
B. The volume of B is greater than the volume of A.
C. Both A and B have a volume greater than 20 cubic centimeters.
D. The volume of B is less than the volume of A.

10. A cone's base is a circle with a radius of 8 inches. The cone's height is 15 inches. What is the cone's approximate volume in cubic inches?

A. 125
B. 250
C. 500
D. 1000

Surface Area

The **surface area** is the total area of the outside **faces** of three-dimensional figures. This is different from the **volume**, which is the capacity of what a figure can hold. Surface area is expressed in square units.

Surface Area of a Square Prism

The surface area of a **square prism (cube)** is the sum of the areas of the six squares that form the prism. The area of one square is s^2. Since these sides are the same, find the area of one side and multiply by 6.

Example 1: Find the surface area of a cube with sides of 3 inches each.

$$SA = 6s^2$$
$$SA = 6(3 \text{ in})^2 = 6\left(9 \text{ in}^2\right) = \textbf{54 in}^2$$

Surface Area of a Rectangular Prism

The surface area of a **rectangular prism** is the sum of the areas of the six rectangles that form the prism.

Example 2: Find the surface area of this box.

$$SA = ph + 2B$$
$$SA = \text{perimeter} \times \text{height} + 2(\text{area of base})$$
$$SA = (5 \text{ m} + 6 \text{ m} + 5 \text{ m} + 6 \text{ m}) \times 7 \text{ m} + 2(6 \text{ m} \times 5 \text{ m})$$
$$SA = (22 \text{ m})7 \text{ m} + 2\left(30 \text{ m}^2\right) = 154 \text{ m}^2 + 60 \text{ m}^2 = \textbf{214 m}^2$$

Surface Area of a Pyramid

The surface area of a **pyramid** is $\frac{1}{2}$ the perimeter of the base (p) times the **slant height** (s) plus the area of the base (B). The slant height is the length of a line segment from the **apex** (top) to the **base**.

slant height

Example 3: What is the surface area of a pyramid with a slant height of 5 feet, a base with a perimeter of 14 feet, and a base with an area of 12 feet?

$$SA = \tfrac{1}{2}\,ps + B$$
$$SA = \tfrac{1}{2}\,\text{perimeter} \times \text{slant height} + \text{base area}$$
$$SA = \tfrac{1}{2}(14 \text{ ft})(5 \text{ ft}) + 12 \text{ ft}^2$$
$$SA = \tfrac{1}{2}\left(70 \text{ ft}^2\right) + 12 \text{ ft}^2 = 35 \text{ ft}^2 + 12 \text{ ft}^2 = \textbf{47 ft}^2$$

PRACTICE 13.1

A. Find the surface area of each object in square units. Use the formulas on the previous page.

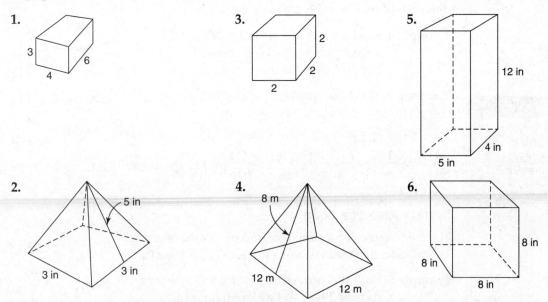

1.

3
6
4

3.

2
2
2

5.

12 in
4 in
5 in

2.

5 in
3 in   3 in

4.

8 m
12 m
12 m

6.

8 in
8 in
8 in

B. Choose the <u>one best answer</u> to each question. Use the formulas on page 402.

7. Which of the following is a true statement about the figures shown below? (Measurements indicated are all in the same units.)

5
5
5

3
10
3

Figure A   **Figure B**

A. The surface area of Figure *A* is equal to the surface area of Figure *B*.

B. The surface area of Figure *A* is half of the surface area of Figure *B*.

C. The surface area of Figure *A* is greater than the surface area of Figure *B*.

D. The sum of the surface areas of both Figure *A* and Figure *B* is greater than 300.

8. If the dimensions of the box below are doubled, by how many square centimeters does the surface area increase?

A.   8
B.   54
C. 162
D. 216

3 cm
3 cm
3 cm

9. All the edges of a metal box are of equal length. If the surface area is 150 square inches, what is the length, in inches, of each edge of the box?

A.   5
B.   6
C. 25
D. 50

STUDY ADVICE

Understanding surface area can be challenging. Be sure to allot ample study time to this important topic! You may see several questions about surface area on Test Day.

Finding the surface areas of cylinders, cones, and spheres involves using some dimensions of circles.

Surface Area of a Cylinder

To find the surface area of a cylinder, multiply the circumference ($2\pi r$) by the **height** (h) and add the product to the area of the two ends of the cylinder, each of which is the area of a circle (πr^2).

Example 4: Find the surface area of a cylinder with a radius (r) of 4 inches and a height (h) of 3 inches.

You may find the on-screen calculator helpful to complete these calculations effectively.

$SA = 2\pi rh + 2\pi r^2$
$SA = (2 \times 3.14 \times 4 \times 3) + (2 \times 3.14 \times 4^2)$
$SA = (6.28 \times 12) + (6.28 \times 16) = 75.36 \text{ in}^2 + 100.48 \text{ in}^2$
$\quad\ = \mathbf{175.84 \text{ in}^2}$

Surface Area of a Cone

The surface area of a **cone** is found by combining the **lateral side surface** (πrs) with the area of its **base** (πr^2).

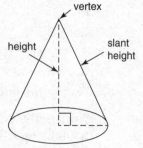

Example 5: Find the surface area of a cone with a radius of 2 feet and a slant height of 5 feet.

$SA = \pi rs + \pi r^2$
$SA = \text{lateral side surface with slant height} + \text{area of base}$
$SA = \pi(2)(5) + \pi(2^2)$
$SA = 10\pi \text{ft}^2 + 4\pi \text{ft}^2 = 14\pi \text{ft}^2 = 14 \text{ ft}^2 \times 3.14 \cong \mathbf{43.96 \text{ ft}^2}$

Surface Area of a Sphere

The surface area of a **sphere** is four times the area of a circle with the same radius as the sphere.

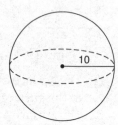

Example 6: What is the surface area of this sphere with a radius of 10 feet?

$SA = 4\pi r^2$
$SA \approx 4 \times 3.14 \times 10^2 \approx \mathbf{1256 \text{ ft}^2}$

A. Find the surface area of each object in square units. Use the formulas on the previous page.

1.

3.

5.

2.

4.

6.

B. Choose the <u>one best answer</u> to each question. Use the formulas on the previous page.

7. If the length of the diameter of a sphere is 8, how many square units is its surface area?

   A. 16π
   B. 64π
   C. 256π
   D. 512π

8. A cone, pictured below, has a slant height of 8 inches and a diameter of 8 inches. If the cone's slant height is doubled, and the diameter is halved, which of the following statements must be true?

   8 in

   8 in

   A. The new cone will have the same surface area as the original cone.
   B. The new cone will have a surface area exactly half of the surface area of the original cone.
   C. The new cone will have a surface area exactly double that of the surface area of the new cone.
   D. The new cone will have a surface area less than the surface area of the original cone.

9. In the cylinder below, the diameter of the circular base is equal to the height of the cylinder. What is the surface area of the cylinder, to the nearest square inch?

   6 in

   A. 57
   B. 113
   C. 170
   D. 339

Combined Figures

Breaking Combined Figures into Parts

A combined figure puts together geometric figures to form a new shape. To find the perimeter of a combined figure, simply add the lengths of the sides. You may need to solve for one or more missing lengths.

Example 1: A family room has the dimensions shown in the diagram. All measures are in feet. What is the perimeter of the room?

1. Find the missing measures. Measurement x equals the combined lengths of the two opposite walls: $x = 8 + 4 = 12$ ft. You also know that $18 - 10 = y$, so $y = 8$ ft.

2. Add all distances to find the perimeter:
$12 + 18 + 8 + 8 + 4 + 10 = \textbf{60 ft.}$

To find the area or volume of a combined figure, break the figure into parts. Then apply the correct formula to each part.

Example 2: What is the area of the figure in square centimeters?

1. Divide the figure into two shapes, and find any missing measurements. Here the figure is divided into a trapezoid and a rectangle.

2. Calculate the area of each shape.
Rectangle: $A = lw$
$= 2(5) = 10 \text{ cm}^2$

Trapezoid: $A = \frac{1}{2}h(b_1 + b_2)$
$= \frac{1}{2}(3)(5 + 7) = 18 \text{ cm}^2$

3. Combine: $10 + 18 = \textbf{28 cm}^2$.

Example 3: Find the volume of the container shown below.

Break the figure into a cylinder and a cone and find the volume of each.

1. Cylinder: $V = \pi r^2 h$
$= (3.14)(1^2)(2) = 6.28 \text{ m}^3$
2. Cone: $V = \frac{1}{3}\pi r^2 h$
$= \frac{1}{3}(3.14)(1^2)(1.5) = 1.57 \text{ m}^3$

3. Combine: $6.28 + 1.57 = \textbf{7.85 m}^3$ or **7.85 cu m.**

PRACTICE 14

A. Find the perimeter and area of each figure.

1.

2.

(*Hint:* Think of the figure as a rectangle and a half circle.)

3.

B. Find the volume of each figure to the nearest cubic unit.

4.

5. $h = 8$

6.

C. Choose the <u>one best answer</u> to each question.

7. A slab of concrete will have four concrete blocks in each corner as shown in the drawing below.

If each corner block has the same dimensions, what is the volume of the structure in cubic feet?

A. 72
B. 168
C. 288
D. 360

8. A candy package is in the shape of a cylinder with a cone on each end.

If the radius of the cylinder is 2 inches and the cones are identical, what is the capacity of the container to the nearest cubic inch?

A. 33
B. 100
C. 134
D. 201

STUDY ADVICE

Any time you are feeling overwhelmed, step away and take a walk (or play basketball, or work on a hobby). Even though there is a great deal of information to absorb to do well on the TASC, you can do it if you maintain focus and be patient with yourself.

Relationships Between 2-D and 3-D Figures

The TASC test may ask you to think about relationships between two-dimensional (flat) figures and three-dimensional figures (figures that have volume). Some questions may ask you what shape a cross section of a solid would have. A cross section is the shape that would result if you cut a solid figure in two and looked at the cut surface. When you answer these questions, it's important to note whether the cut goes straight across or is angled. Study the example below.

Example 1: If the square-based right pyramid pictured were cut along the dotted line, what shape would the cross section have?

The base of the pyramid is a square, so any cut that went straight across the pyramid would also be a square. But that is not the case here. This cut would begin higher on the back of the pyramid and end lower down, closer to the base of the pyramid, in front. Since pyramids are narrower on top than on the bottom, the shape made by the cut would be narrower on the higher side than on the lower side.

The cross section is a **trapezoid**.

Example 2: If the right cylinder shown were cut along the dotted line, what shape would the cross section have?

(1) Circle

(2) Oval

If you answered **(2)**, you are correct. Since the cut is at an angle, the cross section won't be a circle.

Another way the TASC test might ask you to work with 2-D (two-dimensional) and 3-D (three-dimensional) figures has to do with **rotation**, or turning. Some TASC questions may give you a flat shape and ask you what solid shape it would make if it were rotated. Imagine a child blowing bubbles with a loop-shaped bubble wand. The child soaks the wand in bubble solution and then spins completely around in one place, producing one continuous bubble. That bubble would have a large, skinny donut shape

KEY IDEAS

- To visualize the shape of a cross section of a solid, ask yourself whether the "cut" is being made vertically, horizontally, or at an angle.
- Some TASC test questions may ask you what kind of solid would be made by rotating a flat shape in 3-D space. On these questions, pay attention to the axis around which the shape should be rotated.

TASC TEST TIP

If you find this lesson challenging, try practicing in real life: Go to a hobby store and purchase inexpensive foam shapes. Experiment with cutting these in various ways to see what the cross sections look like.

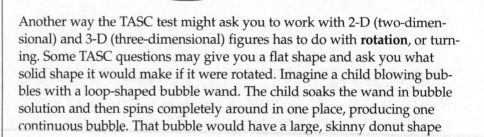

PRACTICE 15

because of the rotation of the bubble wand. When you answer these questions, pay careful attention not only to the shape but also to the *axis around which* it should be rotated. Study the examples below. In each example, the dotted line indicates the axis of rotation. The drawings on the right in each column show the solid shape that would result from the rotation.

A. Match each diagram below with the shape of the cross sections, indicated by dotted lines. Use choices (a) through (h) for all questions. You may or may not use all letters, and you may use some letters more than once. Answer choices are not drawn to scale.

B. The diagrams in questions 9 and 10 below show a shape and an axis (indicated by a dotted line) around which the shape should be rotated. In your own words, write the name of a common object that the resulting figure would resemble.

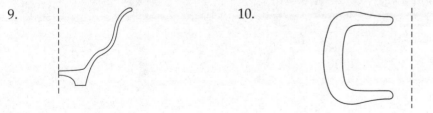

9.
10.

_____   _____

Modeling Density

In physics, **density** is defined as the amount of mass there is in a given volume: $d = \dfrac{m}{v}$. For example, if a small wooden statue has a mass of 500 g and a volume of 670 cm^3, the density of the statue is

$$d = \frac{m}{v} = \frac{500 \text{ g}}{670 \text{ cm}^3} = 0.75 \text{ g/cm}^3.$$

The word "density" can also be used more broadly to mean the amount of something per unit of volume. Examples include the density of a sugar solution (such as a teaspoon of sugar dissolved in a cup of tea) or the density of air pollutants (such as smoke rising from a smokestack: the density of soot particles in the air decreases with distance from the smokestack).

Finally, **surface density** means the amount of something per unit of area. A common example of surface density is population density, which is often given as the number of people per square mile.

Example: In 2013, the state of Tennessee had a population of approximately 6,500,000. The land area of Tennessee is about 41,000 square miles. In the same year, Vermont had a population of approximately 625,000. The land area of Vermont is about 9,200 square miles. Which of these two states was the more densely populated in 2013?

(1) Tennessee

(2) Vermont

The correct answer is **(1)**. To determine which state was more densely populated in 2013, calculate the population density of each separately. Tennessee had a population density of 6,500,000 people per 41,000 square miles. Divide to find the number of people per square mile:

$6,500,000 \div 41,000 \approx 159$

Now do the same calculation for Vermont:

$625,000 \div 9,200 \approx 68$

Because Tennessee had about 159 people per square mile while Vermont only had about 68 people per square mile, Tennessee had the higher population density of the two.

KEY IDEAS

- Density, in a broad sense, is the amount of something in a given volume, such as grams per cubic centimeter.
- Surface density is the amount of something in a given unit of area.
- The Mathematics Test may ask you to use your knowledge of area and volume formulas to calculate density.

TASC TEST TIP

Begin a density problem by setting up a fraction with the quantity of interest in the numerator and units of volume or area in the denominator.

---

1. During an algal bloom (that is, an unusually large growth of algae in ocean water) off the coast of South Korea, scientists took samples of ocean water to determine the density of algal cells present. One such sample contained 40,600 algal cells in 5 ml of water. What was the density of algal cells present per milliliter, rounded to the nearest hundred? Write your answer on the line below.

_____

2. The following table lists the square mileage of three states and the estimated black bear population in each of those states for the year 2011. Which of these three states had the lowest black bear population density in 2011? Place a check in the appropriate box in the left-hand column.

	Estimated black bear population	Land area in square miles
☐ Alaska	200,000	663,267
☐ New York	6,500	54,556
☐ California	30,000	163,696

3. The density of the block of wood depicted below is 0.45 grams per cubic centimeter.

10 cm
10 cm
15 cm

What is the mass of the block in grams? Write your answer on the line below.

_____

4. An ice cube dropped into a glass of water will immediately rise to the surface of the water and float. The ice cube floats because

A. the density of ice is greater than the density of water

B. the density of ice is less than the density of water

C. the density of ice is equal to the density of water

D. the density of ice is inversely proportional to the density of water

5. A customer in an antiques shop is considering purchasing a gold artifact. However, the customer wants to be certain that the artifact is in fact gold, rather than merely gold plated, before finalizing the transaction. The artifact has a volume of 0.002 m³ and a mass of 17.6 kg. The customer calculates the density of the artifact in order to determine whether it is in fact gold.

The table below gives the densities of four types of metal. Place a check in the box in the left-hand column to indicate what kind of metal the statue is made of.

Type of metal	Density
☐ cast iron	7,200 kg/m³
☐ bronze	8,800 kg/m³
☐ silver	10,500 kg/m³
☐ gold	19,300 kg/m³

6. The density of a certain polystyrene foam is approximately 0.03 grams per cubic centimeter. If a block of this polystyrene foam has a mass of 30 kg, then what is its volume?

A. 1 m³

B. 1 cm³

C. 10 m³

D. 10 cm³

Geometry Calculator Skills

When solving problems with formulas, you can generally save time by performing some or all of the operations on a calculator. Remember the order of operations when solving formulas and always check your work, either by reentering the key sequence or by estimating an answer and comparing your answer to the estimate.

Example 1: A pyramid has a height of 81 feet. The base is in the shape of a square with each side measuring 40 feet. What is the volume in cubic feet of the pyramid?

Use the formula for the volume of a pyramid: $\frac{1}{3}Bh$. Begin by calculating the area of the base: 40×40, or 40^2. Multiply that by the height, 81. In the last step, dividing by 3 is the same as multiplying by $\frac{1}{3}$.

Evaluate the exponent.	40 $\boxed{x^2}$
Multiply by 81.	$\boxed{\times}$ 81
Divide by 3.	$\boxed{\div}$ 3 $\boxed{\text{enter}}$
The right side of the display	**43200**

shows the correct answer, **43,200**.

To enter this formula using a fraction using one series of keystrokes on the TI-30XS MultiView™ calculator, enter the following: $\boxed{\frac{n}{d}}$ 1 $\boxed{\blacktriangledown}$ 3 $\boxed{\times}$ 40 $\boxed{x^2}$ $\boxed{\times}$ 81 $\boxed{\text{enter}}$.

The right side of the display shows **43200**.

The volume of the pyramid is **43,200 square feet**.

You may need your calculator to find the exact answer to problems that involve the Pythagorean relationship. These problems can also be done in one series of keystrokes.

Example 2: A right triangle has legs 10 inches and 24 inches in length. What is the length of the hypotenuse?

Use the formula $a^2 + b^2 = c^2$. You will need to add the squares of the legs and then find the square root of the total.

Press: 10 $\boxed{x^2}$ $\boxed{+}$ 24 $\boxed{x^2}$ $\boxed{\text{enter}}$. The display will read 676. Then press $\boxed{\text{2nd}}$ $\boxed{x^2}$ 676 $\boxed{\text{enter}}$. The right side of the display shows **26**.

The hypotenuse is **26 inches** in length.

If you need to include the quantity pi (π) in a calculation, the TI-30XS MultiView™ calculator includes a *pi* key, located three keys below the *2nd* key on the left-hand side of the keypad.

Example 3: What is the area of a circle with radius 2.4 cm? Round your answer to the nearest tenth.

Use the formula Area $= \pi r^2$. Press $\boxed{\pi}$ $\boxed{\times}$ 2.4 $\boxed{x^2}$ and then press $\boxed{\text{enter}}$. The right side of the display reads 18.09557368. Round that to find the answer: **18.1 cm²**.

A. Use your calculator to evaluate each formula.

1. Find the perimeter of a rectangle with a length of 16 inches and a width of 5 inches.
   Perimeter = 2 × length + 2 × width

2. Find the area of a triangle with a base of 26 centimeters and a height of 15 centimeters. Area = $\frac{1}{2}$ × base × height

3. What is the volume of a cube if the edge measures 3.5 feet? Round to the nearest cubic foot. Volume = edge^3

4. What is the measure of the hypotenuse of a right triangle when the legs measure 13 cm and 9 cm? Round your answer to the nearest tenth.
   Pythagorean relationship: $a^2 + b^2 = c^2$

5. Find the circumference of a circle with a diameter of 12 inches. Round to the nearest tenth.
   Circumference = π × diameter

6. Find the volume of a cone with a radius of 12 cm and a height of 20 cm. Round to the nearest cm^3.
   Volume = $\frac{1}{3}$ × π × radius^2 × height

B. Choose the one best answer to each question. You MAY use your calculator.

Question 7 refers to the following drawing.

7. For a woodworking project, Paul cuts the shape shown above from plywood. What is the area in square inches of the piece? (*Hint:* Think of the shape as a triangle removed from a rectangle.)

   A. 400
   B. 480
   C. 520
   D. 640

8. To the nearest cubic meter, what is the volume of a cylinder with a radius of 1.5 meters and a height of 5 meters?

   A. 25
   B. 35
   C. 45
   D. 141

Questions 9 and 10 refer to the drawing.

All measurements are in centimeters.

9. How many cubic centimeters greater is the volume of Box A than the volume of Box B?

   A. 64
   B. 1,448
   C. 4,928
   D. 5,056

10. An advertiser plans to print advertisements on one side panel of each of the boxes (the shaded faces in the drawing). What is the total area, in square centimeters, that the advertiser will cover?

    A. 224
    B. 384
    C. 608
    D. 1448

GEOMETRY PRACTICE QUESTIONS

1. What is the surface area, in square centimeters, of a cube with each edge length of 5 cm?

   A. 15
   B. 25
   C. 125
   D. 150

2. What is the surface area, in square centimeters, of a cylinder with a height of 10 cm and a radius of 6 cm?

   A. 136π
   B. 160π
   C. 192π
   D. 256π

3. What is the surface area, in square centimeters, of a cylinder that measures 8 cm tall with a diameter of 6 cm on its base?

   A. 48π
   B. 57π
   C. 66π
   D. 132π

4. A pyramid has a square base. If each edge of the pyramid is 4, what is the total surface area of the entire pyramid?

   A. $8\sqrt{3}$
   B. $8\sqrt{3} + 16$
   C. $16\sqrt{3} + 16$
   D. $64\sqrt{3}$

Question 5 refers to the following figure.

5. A toy factory paints all of its rubber balls with 2 coats of latex for durability. How many square centimeters of latex are needed to cover a rubber ball with a circumference of 16π cm?

   A. 64π
   B. 128π
   C. 256π
   D. 512π

6. The floor of a walk-in closet measures 7 feet by 4 feet. If the ceiling height is 8 feet, what is the volume in cubic feet of the closet?

   A. 28
   B. 56
   C. 112
   D. 224

Question 7 refers to the following figure.

7. An ice cream cone has a spherical scoop of ice cream placed inside. Exactly one-half of the ice cream is visible above the rim of the cone. What is the surface area of the entire ice cream treat, in units squared?

   A. 24π
   B. 30π
   C. 48π
   D. 60π

8. The radius of Sphere A is 2, and the radius of Sphere B is 1. What is the ratio of the volume of Sphere A to that of Sphere B? (*Hint*: Use the formula for the volume of a sphere on page 168.)

   A. 1:2
   B. 4:1
   C. 8:1
   D. 8:3

Question 9 refers to the following figure.

18 in

9. Three identical rectangular boxes are stacked one on top of another. The total height of all three boxes is the same as the width of one box. The length of the boxes is 18 in, and the width is half the length. What is the combined volume, in cubic inches, of all three boxes?

A. 1458
B. 1800
C. 2124
D. 3136

10. Using a compass, Max hikes 300 yards due north of his campsite. From that point, he hikes 400 yards due east. If he were to hike directly to his campsite from this point, how many yards would he have to hike?

A. 400
B. 500
C. 600
D. 700

11. The rectangular base of a container is 9 inches long and 7 inches wide. By how many cubic inches will the volume of the container increase if you increase the length of the base by 2 inches?

A. 84
B. 126
C. 168
D. 216

12 in

9 in   7 in

12. In a right triangle, the hypotenuse measures 15 inches. If one leg of the triangle measures 6 inches, which of the following equations could be used to find the length of the other leg (x) in inches?

A. $x = \sqrt{15 - 6}$
B. $x = 15 - 6$
C. $x^2 = 15^2 + 6^2$
D. $x^2 = 15^2 - 6^2$

13. The length of a rectangle is three times its width. If the perimeter of the rectangle is 96 inches, what is its length in inches?

A. 12
B. 24
C. 36
D. 48

Question 14 refers to the following figure.

7 cm

16π cm

14. Sarah is making party hats for a birthday party. Each hat is in the shape of a cone and will have a circumference of 16π cm and a slant height of 7 cm. She will be making 20 hats. What is the total surface area, in square centimeters, of all 20 hats combined?

A.   32π
B.   56π
C.   112π
D.   1120π

15. Use your calculator to make the following calculation. In the figure above, a square contains a circle such that each of the sides of the square is touching a point on the circle. What is the area, in square inches, of the shaded portion?

   A. 3.43
   B. 12.57
   C. 16.00
   D. 28.57

Questions 16 and 17 refer to the following.

A classroom is 40 feet long and 25 feet wide. The ceiling height is 12 feet. The school district plans to repaint the room and put in air-conditioning. The ceiling tile will not be painted.

16. What is the approximate total square footage of the four walls of the room? Ignore space taken up by windows and doors.

   A. 1200
   B. 1560
   C. 1920
   D. 4000

17. To choose an air-conditioning system, the school district must know the volume of the room. What is the volume in cubic feet?

   A. 1000
   B. 3120
   C. 12000
   D. 15625

18. Laura is painting model pyramids for an art project. She needs one tube of paint for every 30 square inches of surface area. If Laura paints each pyramid and its base, approximately how many tubes of paint should she buy?

   A. 4
   B. 16
   C. 48
   D. 109

Question 19 refers to the following figure.

19.

A city plans to build a bridge across a local river. To find the width the bridge will span, an engineer stakes out two similar triangles. What is the distance in yards from point *A* to point *B*?

A. 2.4
B. 25.8
C. 148.8
D. 170

Questions 20 and 21 are based on the following figure.

line *P* ∥ line *Q*

20. Which of the following conclusions can you draw based on the information given in the drawing?

A. $m\angle5 = 60°$
B. $\angle7$ is an obtuse angle
C. $m\angle3 = 30°$
D. $\angle2$ must be a right angle

21. Which of the following is a true statement about the figure?

A. $m\angle2 + m\angle7 = 180°$
B. $m\angle4 = m\angle7$
C. $m\angle3 + m\angle4 = 90°$
D. $m\angle3 + m\angle6 = 180°$

For questions 22 and 23, mark your answers in the grids below.

22. The following diagram shows the length of the shadows of a man and a building at 4 p.m.

If the man in the drawing is 6 feet in height, what is the height of the building in feet?

23. A parallelogram has a base of 6 centimeters and a height of 10 centimeters. This parallelogram has the same area as a triangle with a height of 5 centimeters. What is the measure, in centimeters, of the base of the triangle?

22.

```
      ⊘ ⊘ ⊘
    · · · · ·
    0 0 0 0 0
    1 1 1 1 1
    2 2 2 2 2
    3 3 3 3 3
    4 4 4 4 4
    5 5 5 5 5
    6 6 6 6 6
    7 7 7 7 7
    8 8 8 8 8
    9 9 9 9 9
```

23.

```
      ⊘ ⊘ ⊘
    · · · · ·
    0 0 0 0 0
    1 1 1 1 1
    2 2 2 2 2
    3 3 3 3 3
    4 4 4 4 4
    5 5 5 5 5
    6 6 6 6 6
    7 7 7 7 7
    8 8 8 8 8
    9 9 9 9 9
```

STUDY ADVICE

Congratulations! You've made it through the Mathematics unit. Reward yourself! And remember to review these concepts periodically as you continue to study, up until you take the TASC Mathematics Test.

MATHEMATICS ANSWERS AND EXPLANATIONS

Number and Quantity I: Problem Solving

Lesson 1: Compare and Order Numbers

Practice 1

1. 4
2. 8
3. 9
4. 1
5. 6
6. 7
7. 3
8. 500
9. 80
10. 1100
11. 12,000
12. 2000
13. 100
14. 100
15. 341
16. 1145
17. 125,391
18. 18, 23, 39, 45
19. 89, 91, 109, 111
20. 909, 932, 1087, 1139
21. 1420, 1425, 1429, 1432
22. 11,098, 12,071, 12,131
23. 15,298, 15,309, 15,356
24. **C. 50, 48, 45, 40** Arrange weights from heaviest to lightest.
25. **C. 1,500,000** The digit in the ten thousands column is less than 5, so round down.

Lesson 2: Whole Number Operations

Practice 2.1

1. 77
2. 100
3. 52
4. 36
5. 190
6. 4078
7. 43
8. 2117
9. 65
10. 114
11. 180
12. 293
13. 483
14. 456
15. 2419
16. 900
17. 11,308
18. 15,185
19. 131,197
20. 30,899
21. **B. 88** Calculate: $24 + 8 + 56 = 88$
22. **C. $13** Calculate: $20 - 7 = 13$

Practice 2.2

1. 484
2. 1000
3. 2736
4. 13
5. 105
6. 21
7. 1350
8. 2625
9. 3376
10. 28
11. 15
12. 6
13. 250
14. 44 r3
15. 300
16. 200 r4
17. 150
18. 67,068
19. 538
20. 384
21. 12,011 r8
22. **D. 96** Calculate: $16 \times 6 = 96$
23. **C. $75** Calculate: $15 \times 5 = 75$
24. **B. 6** Calculate: $12 \div 2 = 6$

Lesson 3: The Number Line and Signed Numbers

Practice 3.1

1. 5
2. 45
3. 13
4. 1
5. 1
6. 10
7. −3
8. 13
9. −4
10. 2
11. −22
12. 32
13. −50
14. −11
15. 25
16. −35
17. −11
18. 11
19. 10
20. 75
21. 12
22. 2
23. −1
24. −13
25. **B. 2 + (−5)** The operation starts on + 2 and moves 5 units to the left (a negative direction).
26. **C. 115°** Begin with 92°. Then perform the following operations:
$92° + 12° - 5° + 6° - 3° + 13° = 115°$

Practice 3.2

1. 20
2. −21
3. −48
4. 18
5. −10
6. 3
7. −3
8. − 5
9. 2
10. −5
11. −28
12. −3
13. −1
14. −75
15. 6
16. −20
17. −300
18. 2
19. −5
20. 660
21. 12
22. −120
23. −125
24. −12
25. 20
26. −1
27. 0
28. **B. −7** Substitute the numbers from the spreadsheet for the cells in the expression and solve. Note that A1 is column A, row 1; A3 is column A, row 3; and so on. $\frac{(-3)(7)(-1)}{(3)(-1)} = \frac{21}{-3} = -7$
29. **C. $\frac{2(8)}{(-8)}$** To find the product of two numbers, multiply: 2(8). Then divide by −8, as directed in the problem.
30. **C. The result is a negative number.** Do not do any calculations. Instead, examine the factors. Since there is an odd number of negative factors, the answer will be negative.

Lesson 4: Order of Operations

Practice 4

1. 24
2. 1
3. 29
4. 2
5. 7
6. 20
7. 14
8. 55
9. 10
10. 23
11. 161
12. 30
13. 360
14. 4
15. 6

16. **C. (1 − 0.75)(28)(30).** The total cost of the class can be found by multiplying 28 members by $30. Since the foundation pays 75%, or 0.75, the hospital will pay 100% − 75%, or (1 − 0.75). You must multiply the amount the class will cost by the percent that the hospital will pay. Only choice (C) performs these operations.

17. **B. Add 5.** The operations in the brackets must be performed first. Once these are completed, multiply by 2 and then add 5. Notice that it is not necessary to find the value of the expression to answer the question.

18. **C. 76**

$$22 + 6[(14 − 5) ÷ 3(17 − 14)]$$
$$= 22 + 6[9 ÷ 3(3)]$$
$$= 22 + 6[3 × 3]$$
$$= 22 + 6[9]$$
$$= 22 + 54 = 76$$

Lesson 5: Absolute Value

Practice 5

1. 18
2. 107
3. 423
4. 95
5. 7,026
6. 18
7. 5,708,432
8. 85.6
9. 42
10. 10.5
11. 163.24
12. 3.14
13. 11
14. −156
15. 156
16. 3
17. −91
18. 0
19. 620
20. −7
21. −20
22. −1
23. 2.125
24. −11

25. **D. 10 degrees** The change in temperature is the absolute value of the result of the new temperature minus the old temperature: $|(−5) − (−15)| = |10|$, or 10 degrees.

26. **D. 16** In order to find out how many blocks Bob walked in total, you also need to know how long the last leg of his journey (from the post office back to his apartment) was. To find this distance, you can think of movement east as having a positive value and movement west as having a negative value. So, on the first three legs of his journey Bob walked 5 + (−6) + (−2), leaving him 3 blocks from his house. The last leg of his journey is 3 blocks, and you can simply add the absolute values of each part of the trip: $|5| + |−6| + |−2| + |3| = 16$

27. **C. 120** Add the absolute value of Milania's score to the absolute value of Chris's score: $|−65| + |55| = 65 + 55 = 120$

28. **A. 1.5** The question defines absolute error as the absolute value of the difference between the actual and approximate values: 23.5 − 25 = −1.5, and $|−1.5| = 1.5$.

Lesson 6: TASC Test Calculator Skills

Practice 6.1

1. 153
2. 1187
3. 784
4. 24
5. 27,084
6. 14,442
7. 11,704
8. 54
9. 1580
10. **B. 26,179** Press (clear) 42920 (−) 16741 (enter).
11. **D. $19,900** Press (clear) 995 (×) 20 (enter).

Practice 6.2

1. 25
2. 18
3. 35
4. 136
5. 125
6. 5%
7. 2
8. 135
9. 5%
10. **C. $336** Press (clear) 1680 (×) 20 (2nd) ((enter).
11. **A. 5%** Press (clear) 48 (÷) 960 (2nd)) (enter). The right side of the screen will display 5%.

Lesson 7: Powers and Roots

Practice 7

1. 9
2. 4
3. 3
4. 1
5. 9
6. 7
7. 125
8. $\frac{1}{16}$
9. 6561
10. 1296
11. 12.2
12. 8000
13. 1
14. $\frac{1}{16}$
15. 15.6
16. 10.9
17. 7.5
18. 23.2
19. 1
20. 256

21. **C. 6^3** To find the volume, you would need to solve $6 × 6 × 6$, which can be written as 6^3.

22. **A. $3^{−3}$** Examine the choices. Choices (A) and (D) will result in a fraction, a value less than 1. Choices (B) and (C) will each have a value of 1 or greater.

Choice (A): $3^{−3} = \frac{1}{3^3} = \frac{1}{27}$

Choice (D): $2^{−4} = \frac{1}{2^4} = \frac{1}{16}$.

Since $\frac{1}{27} < \frac{1}{16}$, choice (A) is correct.

Lesson 8: Scientific Notation

Practice 8

1. $2.3 × 10^3$
2. $4.2 × 10^{−4}$
3. $1.24 × 10^7$
4. $1.432 × 10^{10}$
5. $3.6 × 10^7$
6. $9.5 × 10^{−3}$
7. $5.8 × 10^{−7}$
8. $1.5 × 10^{11}$
9. $9 × 10^{−9}$
10. 0.0005173
11. 3,700,000
12. 480,000,000
13. 0.000017
14. 0.0072
15. 916,000
16. 85,910,000
17. 0.00000956
18. $2.35 × 10^4$
19. 0.000000001
20. 2,670,000,000
21. $3 × 10^8$

22. **B. 4.356×10^4** In scientific notation, the whole-number portion must be a digit from 1 to 9. Choice (B) is correct because the decimal place must be moved 4 places.

23. **D. $5 \times 9.07 \times 10^{-1}$** In scientific notation, a ton = 9.07×10^{-1} metric tons. Multiply this by 5 to find the equivalent weight of five tons.

Lesson 9: Word Problems

Practice 9.1

1. **C. 10** No paint is needed for the floor, so ignore the 700 square feet. 3500 square feet of wall space ÷ 350 square feet per gallon = 10 gallons.
2. **D. 22** 11 children × 2 party favors per child = 22.
3. **A. 5** Calculate: 30 − 25 = 5. The information that Sarah and Kate live 18 miles apart is not needed.
4. **C. 90** Calculate: 450 gallons ÷ 5 gallons of *filtered* water use per day = 90 days.
5. **D. 90** The table states that it takes Joyce 30 minutes to give a pedicure. 3 × 30 = 90
6. **C. $25** Subtract the cost of the manicure & pedicure combination ($35) from the cost of a makeover ($60). $60 − $35 = $25
7. **D. 42** Calculate: 7 × 6 = 42

Practice 9.2

1. **C. $103** Restaurant D ordered 2 cases of Boston lettuce and 3 cases of romaine lettuce in July. (2 × $17) + (3 × $23) = $103.
2. **B. $18** Calculate: 4 + 4 + 2 + 2 + 1 = 13 total cases, and delivery for the first 5 cases costs $2 each. 13 − 5 = 8 cases remained after the first 5, so delivery for those 8 cases costs $1 each. (5 × $2) + (8 × $1) = $18.
3. **B. Restaurant B** Calculate the totals for each restaurant:

Rest.	Asparagus	Tomatoes	Asparagus + Tomatoes
A	2 × $22	3 × $15	$44 + $45 = $89
B	4 × $22	1 × $15	$88 + $15 = $103
C	0 × $22	3 × $15	$0 + $45 = $45
D	1 × $22	4 × $15	$22 + $60 = $82

4. **C. 350** Calculate: 3 × 150 = 450 sheets will be used. Since the paper sells in packages of 400 sheets, 2 packages are needed, and 2 × 400 = 800. 800 − 450 = 350 sheets left over.
5. **A. 9** Calculate: 19 ÷ 2 = 9 r1, so the friends can make 9 whole batches using 2 cups of flour for each batch (and 1 cup will be left over).
6. **A. $1500** Calculate: (6 × $750) − $3000 = $1500.

Lesson 10: Distance and Cost

Practice 10

1. rate; $\frac{d}{t} = r$
2. distance; $d = rt$
3. time; $\frac{d}{r} = t$
4. price per unit; $\frac{c}{n} = r$
5. cost; $c = nr$
6. number of units; $\frac{c}{r} = n$
7. **$48** $c = nr$
   4 × $12 = $48
8. **$36** $c = nr$
   12 × $3 = $36
9. **$80** $\frac{c}{n} = r$
   $\frac{$320}{4} = 80
10. **5** $\frac{c}{r} = n$
    $\frac{$25}{$5} = 5$
11. **$2** $\frac{c}{n} = r$
    $\frac{$20}{10} = 2
12. **180 miles** $d = rt$
    60 × 3 = 180
13. **200 miles** $d = rt$
    50 × 4 = 200
14. **1 hour** $\frac{d}{r} = t$
    $\frac{25}{25} = 1$
15. **90 miles per hour** $\frac{d}{t} = r$
    $\frac{270}{3} = 90$
16. **3 hours** $\frac{d}{r} = t$
    $\frac{75}{25} = 3$
17. **A. 32** $\frac{c}{r} = n$
    $\frac{$640}{$20} = 32$
18. **D. 55** $\frac{d}{t} = r$
    $\frac{275}{5} = 55$

Lesson 11: Measurement

Practice 11.1

1. 48 in
2. 7 min
3. 72 hr
4. $2\frac{1}{2}$ pt
5. 20 qt
6. $5\frac{1}{2}$ tons
7. 144 in
8. 12 hr
9. 32 c
10. **C. 3.75 × 4** 4 qt = 1 gal, so multiply the number of gallons by 4 to find the number of quarts.
11. **B. 2 ft 3 in** 12 in = 1 ft Divide. 27 ÷ 12 = 2 r3, or 2 ft 3 in
12. **B. 22 lb 8 oz** Multiply. 3 lb 12 oz × 6 = 18 lb 72 oz To simplify, divide. Use the fact that 1 lb = 16 oz. 72 ÷ 16 = 4 r8. 18 lb + 4 lb 8 oz = 22 lb 8 oz

Practice 11.2

1. 5,000 m
2. 6 m
3. 4,000 mg
4. 8,000 g
5. 4,050 cl
6. 1.5 l
7. 0.25 g
8. 30,000 m
9. 75 cl
10. 0.05 kg
11. 35.2 l
12. 1500 cm
13. **B. 0.1183** There are 1,000 milliliters in 1 liter. 118.3 ml ÷ 1,000 = 0.1183 l
14. **D. 0.5** There are 1000 milligrams in 1 gram. 500 ÷ 1,000 = 0.5 g
15. **B. 625** Convert 2.5 kg to grams. 2.5 ÷ 1,000 = 2500 g Divide. 2,500 g ÷ 4 g = 625 containers
16. **C. 130** Convert 4.8 meters to centimeters. 4.8 × 100 = 480 cm Subtract. 480 − 350 = 130 cm

Lesson 12: Filling in the Answer Grid

Practice 12

1. **1740** There are four 3-month periods in a 12-month period, so multiply the number of cats treated in one 3-month period by 4: 435 × 4 = 1,740
2. **10** Divide: 35,000 ÷ 3,500 = 10
3. **994** Add the attendance for each day: 348 + 366 + 280 = 994
4. **15** Multiply the number of cookies you buy with $1 by the number of dollars: 3 × 5 = 15
5. **2468** Multiply: 4 × 617 = 2,468
6. **$21** Divide the amount owed by the amount paid per month: $1,050 ÷ $50 = $21

Problem Solving Practice Questions

1. **D. 96** Multiply: 12 servings × 8 ounces = 96
2. **B. $2092** Add to find the total: $839 + $527 + 726 = $2092
3. **A. 4** Divide the length of the sample board by the length of the brace you want: 12 foot board ÷ 2 feet per brace = 6 braces per board. Since you can get 6 braces from each board, divide the total number of braces you want by 6: 24 ÷ 6 = 4 boards.
4. **B. 21** Use the square root function on your calculator or multiply each answer option by itself to find the square root of 441.
5. **B. $1.26 × 10^8$** Calculate: 700 × 180,000 = 126,000,000. Scientific notation reduces to a single digit in front of the decimal, and to do this requires moving up 8 digits, so it would be $1.26 × 10^8$.
6. **C. $656** You can use your calculator. Multiply: $3280 × 20% = $656
7. **A. $5625** Multiply: $125 × 45 = $5625
8. **B. 420** Divide distance by time to find Lydia's speed per hour: 180 ÷ 3 = 60. Then multiply by the number of hours she drove on Tuesday: 60 × 7 = 420

9. **B. 8** Divide the distance by the speed to find the time: 480 ÷ 60 = 8 hours.
10. **B. 96** Divide the total cost by price per item to find the number of items: $1440 ÷ 15 = $96
11. **A. $200** Multiply the late fee by the number of times Richard has paid his bill late: $25 × 8 = $200
12. **C. $1\frac{5}{11}$** Calculate: $\frac{4^3 - [3(12 + 2^2)]}{6 + 5(4) - 15} =$

    $\frac{64 - [3(12 + 4)]}{6 + 5(4) - 15} = \frac{64 - [3(16)]}{6 + 20 - 15} =$

    $\frac{64 - 48}{6 + 20 - 15} = \frac{16}{11} = 1\frac{5}{11}$

13. **A. 5** Divide. 17,500 total miles ÷ 3,500 miles between oil changes = 5 oil changes.
14. **A. 134** Divide: 536 total children ÷ 4 months = 134 children per month
15. **198** Subtract to find the difference: 636 − 438 = 198
16. **1072** Multiply: $268 per payment × 4 payments left = $1072
17. **C. 51, 48, 44, 40**
18. **C. 2,350,000** Since the digit to the right of the ten thousands place is less than 5, the digit in the ten thousands place remains the same.
19. **A. 83** Add: 18 + 23 + 42 = 83
20. **A. $6** Subtract: $20 − $14 = $6
21. **B. 60** Since the question says "about," you can use approximate, or rounded, figures. Round the amounts and add: 8 + 33 + 18 ≈ 10 + 30 + 20 = 60
22. **62** Divide distance by time to find the rate of speed: 248 ÷ 4 = 62
23. **C. 18** Divide: 144 ÷ 8 = 18
24. **B. 30** Since the question says "about," you can use approximate figures. Round 299 to 300 and 9 to 10 and then divide: 300 ÷ 10 = 30
25. **A. 2 qt 10 fl oz** 3 qt = 2 qt 2 pt = 2 qt 1 pt 16 fl oz Subtract.

    ```
      2 qt 1 pt 16 fl oz
    −      1 pt  6 fl oz
    ───────────────────
      2 qt      10 fl oz
    ```

26. **C. 1200** Use rounded figures: 33 rounds to 30, and 41 pounds rounds to 40: 30 × 40 = 1200.
27. **C. $9** Find the total and divide by 4: $21 + $15 = $36, then $36 ÷ 4 = $9
28. **A. $12** Subtract the amount David paid from the total: $128 − $20 = $108. Then divide the remaining amount by the remaining number of people in the group: $108 ÷ 9 = $12.
29. **D. 260** 65 miles per hour × 4 hours = 260 miles.
30. **B. $18** Add the cost of a 1-topping pizza and $2 for each of the 2 additional toppings: $14 + $2 + $2 = $18
31. **C. 14** Multiply by 2 for each dollar: 2 × 7 = 14
32. **24** Divide: $1800 ÷ $75 per month = 24 months
33. **14** Divide the maximum capacity by the number of pages per document: 630 ÷ 45 = 14

Number and Quantity II: Decimals and Fractions

Lesson 1: Decimal Basics

Practice 1

1. 3.8
2. 6
3. 0.43
4. 0.667
5. 8.1
6. 2.714
7. 0.45
8. 0.08
9. 4.68
10. 1.85
11. 1.029
12. 0.14

13. 5.08, 5.6, 5.8, 5.802
14. 0.1136, 0.115, 0.12, 0.2
15. 4.52, 4.667, 4.8, 14.005
16. 0.8, 0.8023, 0.803, 0.823
17. **C. 0.6 g, 0.572 g, 0.0785 g** The correct answer lists the weights from greatest to least. Since none of the weights has a whole number part, compare the tenths places.
18. **D. 1.38** This is the only choice that is rounded to the hundredths place. Since the number in the thousandths place of 1.3815 is less than 5, round down.

Lesson 2: Decimal Operations

Practice 2.1

1. 7.996
2. 10.508
3. 12.26
4. 5.85
5. 7.426
6. 2.11
7. 18.094
8. 5.117
9. 21.32
10. 0.895
11. 3.84
12. 2.35
13. 5.506
14. 21.16
15. 0.645
16. 2.426
17. 0.15
18. 4.88
19. 11.8
20. 14.016
21. 4.522
22. 2.36
23. 17.88
24. 17.225

25. **A. 22.25** Add the times: $7.2 + 6.8 + 8.25 = 22.25$ minutes. You do not need to use the 3-mile distance to solve the problem.
26. **C. 4.25** Add to find Claudia's total hours for the week: $8.5 + 9.25 + 8.75 + 10 + 7.75 = 44.25$. Then subtract 40 to find the number of overtime hours: $44.25 - 40 = 4.25$ hours.
27. **A. 1.8** Add the lengths cut from the pipe: $2.8 + 1.4 = 4.2$. Then subtract from 6: $6 - 4.2 = 1.8$ meters.
28. **C. $55.26** Add the amounts: $\$16.98 + \$31.78 + \$6.50 = \$55.26$

Practice 2.2

1. 2.65
2. 12.8
3. 0.496
4. 0.52
5. 3.6
6. 4.09
7. 8.75
8. 3.375
9. 9.6681
10. 24
11. 14.2
12. 15,800
13. 34.1
14. 2.36
15. 0.656
16. 2.64
17. 1.65
18. 4.275
19. 3.696
20. 1.002
21. 0.0072

22. **D. 15.16** Multiply 3.79 liters by 4: $3.79 \times 4 = 15.16$ liters.
23. **B. $9.23** Multiply $\$0.45 \times 20.5$: $\$0.45 \times 20.5 = \$9.225$, which rounds to $9.23.
24. **C. 92.9** Divide to find the average daily miles: $278.7 \div 3 = 92.9$ miles.
25. **C. $0.26** There are 19 servings in a box of Toasted Oats. Divide: $\$4.94 \div 19 = \$0.26$.
26. **B. 50.0** Find the weight in the table and multiply: $12.5 \times 4 = 50$ ounces.

Lesson 3: Fraction Basics

Practice 3

1. $\frac{3}{5}$
2. $\frac{2}{4}$; $\frac{1}{2}$
3. $\frac{2}{3}$
4. $\frac{7}{3}$; $2\frac{1}{3}$
5. $\frac{7}{2}$; $3\frac{1}{2}$
6. $\frac{15}{4}$; $3\frac{3}{4}$
7. $5\frac{2}{3}$
8. $\frac{18}{5}$
9. 4
10. $\frac{47}{9}$
11. $4\frac{3}{4}$
12. $\frac{29}{12}$
13. $4\frac{7}{9}$
14. $\frac{7}{4}$
15. $8\frac{1}{4}$
16. $\frac{57}{10}$
17. $\frac{12}{16}$
18. $\frac{7}{21}$
19. $\frac{48}{60}$
20. $\frac{15}{40}$
21. $\frac{24}{100}$
22. $\frac{3}{4}$
23. $\frac{1}{6}$
24. $\frac{3}{5}$
25. $\frac{13}{15}$
26. $\frac{2}{3}$

27. **A. $\frac{3}{4}$** Of those surveyed, $\frac{18}{24}$ went to at least one movie. Reduce the fraction to lowest terms: $\frac{18 \div 6}{24 \div 6} = \frac{3}{4}$.
28. **C. $\frac{40}{100}$** Raise $\frac{2}{5}$ to an equivalent fraction with a denominator of 100 by multiplying both numbers by 20: $\frac{2 \times 20}{5 \times 20} = \frac{40}{100}$.

Lesson 4: Fraction Operations

Practice 4.1

1. $\frac{1}{2}$
2. 1
3. $\frac{1}{3}$
4. $\frac{1}{6}$
5. $\frac{11}{12}$
6. $1\frac{1}{8}$
7. $\frac{3}{10}$
8. $\frac{5}{18}$
9. $3\frac{13}{15}$
10. $1\frac{3}{4}$
11. $8\frac{1}{2}$
12. $11\frac{5}{8}$
13. $21\frac{7}{10}$
14. $7\frac{13}{18}$
15. $12\frac{5}{6}$
16. $2\frac{5}{8}$
17. $42\frac{5}{12}$
18. $22\frac{11}{20}$
19. $5\frac{1}{18}$
20. $11\frac{1}{8}$
21. $3\frac{23}{28}$
22. $1\frac{7}{24}$
23. $2\frac{3}{7}$
24. $8\frac{8}{9}$
25. $\frac{32}{35}$

26. **B.** $1\frac{3}{16}$ Add to find the total: $\frac{5}{16} + \frac{7}{8} = \frac{5}{16} + \frac{14}{16} = \frac{19}{16} = 1\frac{3}{16}$ inches.

27. **C.** $1\frac{5}{8}$ Subtract to find the difference in the lengths: $2\frac{7}{8} - 1\frac{1}{4} = 2\frac{7}{8} - 1\frac{2}{8} = 1\frac{5}{8}$ inches.

28. **A.** $14\frac{3}{8}$ Subtract the amount sold from the amount on the bolt:
$23\frac{1}{4} - 8\frac{7}{8} = 23\frac{2}{8} - 8\frac{7}{8} = 22\frac{10}{8} - 8\frac{7}{8} =$
$14\frac{3}{8}$ yards.

29. **C.** $2\frac{11}{12}$ Add the amounts: $1\frac{2}{3} + \frac{1}{2} +$
$\frac{3}{4} = 1\frac{8}{12} + \frac{6}{12} + \frac{9}{12} = 1\frac{23}{12} = 2\frac{11}{12}$ cups.

Practice 4.2

1. $\frac{1}{6}$
2. $\frac{11}{12}$
3. 14
4. $18\frac{3}{4}$
5. $\frac{7}{8}$
6. $\frac{21}{32}$
7. $7\frac{14}{15}$
8. $41\frac{1}{4}$
9. $2\frac{1}{32}$
10. 14
11. $1\frac{4}{5}$
12. 48
13. $2\frac{2}{5}$
14. $2\frac{1}{4}$
15. 27
16. 8
17. $9\frac{1}{2}$
18. $\frac{3}{4}$

19. **B.** 75 Find $\frac{3}{16}$ of 400 by multiplying:
$$400 \times \frac{3}{16} = \frac{\overset{25}{\cancel{400}}}{1} \times \frac{3}{\underset{1}{\cancel{16}}} = \frac{75}{1} = 75.$$

20. **B.** 7 Divide: $20 \div 2\frac{3}{4} = \frac{20}{1} \div \frac{11}{4} =$
$\frac{20}{1} \times \frac{4}{11} = \frac{80}{11} = 7\frac{3}{11}$. Ignore the remainder since the problem asks how many shirts can be completed.

21. **B.** 33 You need to find how many $\frac{2}{3}$ hours there are in 22 hours. Divide: $22 \div \frac{2}{3} = \frac{22}{1} \div \frac{2}{3} = \frac{11}{1} \times \frac{3}{1} = \frac{33}{1}$.

22. **C.** $37\frac{7}{8}$ Multiply $12\frac{5}{8}$ inches by 3, the number of panels: $12\frac{5}{8} \times 3 = \frac{101}{8} \times \frac{3}{1} = \frac{303}{8} = 37\frac{7}{8}$.

Lesson 5: Fraction and Decimal Equivalencies

Practice 5

1. **B.** $20.00 Instead of multiplying $80 by 0.25, you can also find $\frac{1}{4}$ of $80.
2. **C.** 480×0.3 Find $\frac{3}{10}$ of 480. "Of" in "of the workers" indicates multiplication, and the decimal equivalent of $\frac{3}{10}$ is 0.3.
3. **B.** $4\frac{2}{3}$ The decimal part of the calculator display equals the fraction $\frac{2}{3}$.
4. **C.** $18.00 Multiply 12 by 1.5. The decimal $1.5 = 1\frac{1}{2}$. Convert that fraction to an improper fraction: $\frac{3}{2}$ Now multiply: $12 \times \frac{3}{2} = \frac{36}{2} = 18$.
5. **B.** $\frac{3}{4}$ Subtract: $1.875 - 1.125 = 0.75$, which equals $\frac{3}{4}$ inch.
6. **C.** 0.375 Instead of dividing 3 by 8, think: $3 \div 8$ means $\frac{3}{8}$, which equals 0.375.

Lesson 6: Decimals and Fractions on the Number Line

Practice 6

1. **C.** $\frac{2}{3}$ The number line is in increments of $\frac{1}{3}$, and the value you are asked to identify comes halfway between $\frac{1}{3}$ and 1.
2. **D.** 2.8 The number line is in increments of 0.2, and the value you are asked to identify comes halfway between 2.6 and 3.
3. **C.** 2 A minus B is $3\frac{1}{2} - 1\frac{1}{2} = 2$.
4. $\frac{2}{3}$ Angela gave 16 of 24 cookies to her neighbor: $\frac{16}{24} = \frac{2}{3}$.
5. 4.625 Each increment on this number line is 0.125 greater than the previous increment.
6. $9.3\overline{3}$ Each increment on the number line is $0.3\overline{3}$ greater than the previous increment.
7. $3\frac{1}{3}$ Each increment on the number line is $\frac{1}{3}$ greater than the previous increment.
8. $11\frac{5}{6}$ Each increment on the number line is $\frac{1}{6}$ greater than the previous increment.

Lesson 7: Decimal and Fraction Calculator Skills

Practice 7

1. **7.379**
2. $2\frac{1}{4}$ To work with mixed fractions on the TI-30XS MultiView™, use the (2nd) function above the $\left(\frac{n}{d}\right)$ key: (2nd) $\left[\frac{n}{d}\right]$ 3 ▶ 2 ▼ 3 ▶ ⊟ (2nd) $\left[\frac{n}{d}\right]$ 1 ▶ 5 ▼ 12 (enter). The number $\frac{9}{4}$ will appear on the right-hand side of the display.
3. **$380.25**
4. **42**
5. **$84.44** Multiply: $95 \times \frac{8}{9} = 84.44\overline{4}$. Round to get $84.44.
6. **$79.74** Divide: $956.88 \div 12 = $79.
7. **$1,475** Multiply: $118,000 \times 0.0125 = $1,475
8. $4\frac{1}{4}$ cups Add: $1\frac{1}{2} + 2\frac{3}{4} = 4\frac{1}{4}$
9. **B.** $6.67 Multiply the weight of the quilt by $1.20: $5.56 \times $1.20 = 6.672, which rounds to $6.67.
10. **C.** 24 You need to find $\frac{3}{8}$ of 64. Multiply. $64 \times \frac{3}{8} = 24$ acres.

Lesson 8: Filling in the Answer Grid Using Decimals or Fractions

Practice 8

1. **35.6** Add: $12.6 + 9.8 + 13.2 = 35.6$ gallons of gasoline.
2. $\frac{2}{3}$ Divide the amount spent by the total: $\frac{$100}{$150} = \frac{2}{3}$
3. **2** Subtract: $9\frac{1}{2} - 7\frac{1}{2} = \frac{19}{2} - \frac{15}{2} = \frac{4}{2} = 2$
4. **38** Divide: $100 \div 2.6 = 38.46$ so 38 bottles can be filled.
5. $\frac{1}{6}$ State the number of cherry colas as a fraction: $\frac{3}{18}$ of the cases were cherry cola, which equals $\frac{1}{6}$.
6. **25** Divide: $12.5 \div 0.5 = 25$ sheets of foam board.

Decimals and Fractions Practice Questions

1. **C. $15\frac{3}{4}$** Subtract: $20\frac{1}{2} - 4\frac{3}{4} =$
   $20\frac{2}{4} - 4\frac{3}{4} = 19\frac{6}{4} - 4\frac{3}{4} = 15\frac{3}{4}$

2. **B. $0.25** Divide the cost by the number of servings: $4.69 \div 19 \approx 0.247$, which rounds to $0.25.

3. **C. $1386.20** To find the amount the 12-month plan will cost a customer, multiply $98.85 by 12 and add $200: $(98.85 \times 12) + 200 = 1386.20$.

4. **C. $30.12** Multiply using your calculator. Use 10.5 for $10\frac{1}{2}$: $2.869 \times 10.5 = 30.1245$, which rounds to $30.12.

5. **B. 2.85** Since the answer choices are decimals, use your calculator. Use decimals instead of fractions: $1\frac{1}{2} = 1.5$, $4\frac{3}{4} = 4.75$, and $2\frac{3}{10}$
   $= 2.3$. To find the average, add the three weights and divide the total by 3: $\frac{1.5 + 4.75 + 2.3}{3} = \frac{8.55}{3} = 2.85$,

6. **C. $32\frac{1}{4}$** Divide: $258 \div 8 = 32.25$, which equals $32\frac{1}{4}$.

7. **B. 57** Subtract $6\frac{1}{4}$ from $20\frac{1}{2}$ and divide the difference by $\frac{1}{4}$. To do the work quickly, use the fraction keys on your calculator or change the fractions to decimals: $20\frac{1}{2} - 6\frac{1}{4} = 14\frac{1}{4}$; $14\frac{1}{4} \div \frac{1}{4} = 57$.

8. **D. $90.00** Brand B costs $0.09 more than Brand A, so the school will save $0.09 on each marker. Multiply the savings by 1000: $0.09 \times 1000 = 90.00$.

9. **B. $3\frac{1}{2}$** Add the times for the appointments:
   $\frac{3}{4} + \frac{3}{4} + 1\frac{1}{4} + \frac{3}{4} = 1\frac{10}{4} = 3\frac{2}{4} = 3\frac{1}{2}$

10. **C. 10** Divide $3\frac{1}{2}$ hours by the amount of time needed for a routine physical: $3\frac{1}{2} \div \frac{1}{3} = \frac{7}{2} \div \frac{1}{3} = \frac{7}{2} \times \frac{3}{1} = \frac{21}{2} = 10\frac{1}{2}$. Therefore, Jennifer can complete 10 physicals. Ignore the fraction remainder.

11. **D. $\frac{11}{12}$** Write the fraction and reduce it to lowest terms. You can save time by using the fraction key on your calculator, which automatically reduces a fraction to lowest terms. Press 5500 $\boxed{\frac{n}{d}}$ ▼ 6000 (enter). The right-hand side of the display will read $\frac{11}{12}$.

12. **C. $7.25** The first hour costs $3.50, and there are $1\frac{1}{2}$ hours left. There are 3 half hours, or $1\frac{1}{2}$ hours, so you will pay $3.50 + (3 \times 1.25) = 7.25$.

13. **$\frac{2}{3}$** Write a fraction and reduce: $\frac{56}{84} = \frac{56 \div 28}{84 \div 28} = \frac{2}{3}$

14. **0.84** Subtract to compare: $3.97 - 3.13 = 0.84$.

15. **B. $\frac{3}{10}$** Subtract: $250 - 175 = 75$. Thus, 75 out of 250, or $\frac{75}{250}$, have not been loaded. Reduce: $\frac{75 \div 25}{250 \div 25} = \frac{3}{10}$.

16. **B. $\frac{5}{8}$** $A - B = \frac{7}{8} - \frac{1}{4}$. Find a common denominator and subtract: $\frac{7}{8} - \frac{2}{8} = \frac{5}{8}$.

17. **A. 285** To find $\frac{3}{4}$ of 380, multiply. Change $\frac{3}{4}$ to 0.75. Then $380 \times 0.75 = 285$.

18. **C. $\frac{5}{6}$** To find half of $1\frac{2}{3}$, either multiply by $\frac{1}{2}$ or divide by 2. Both results are the same: $1\frac{2}{3} \times \frac{1}{2} = \frac{5}{3} \times \frac{1}{2} = \frac{5}{6}$.

19. **C. 150** You need to find $\frac{5}{8}$ of 240. Multiply:
    $240 \times \frac{5}{8} = \frac{\overset{30}{240}}{1} \times \frac{5}{\underset{1}{8}} =$
    $\frac{150}{1} = 150$.

20. **D. core box, classic, bevel, cutter** You could change the fractions to decimals to solve the problem, but the quickest method is to rewrite the fractions with a common denominator of 32:
    cutter: $\frac{9}{16} = \frac{18}{32}$;
    core box: $\frac{5}{32}$;
    classic: $\frac{3}{8} = \frac{12}{32}$;
    bevel: $\frac{1}{2} = \frac{16}{32}$.
    Then arrange the like fractions from least to greatest by their numerators.

21. **B. W and Y.** The most Joe will eat will be $\frac{7}{8}$ of his pizza, so the minimum he'll have left over will be $\frac{1}{8}$ of it. The least Joe will eat will be $\frac{1}{2}$, so the maximum he'll have left over will be $\frac{1}{2}$ of the pizza.

22. **C. 8** Divide: $60 \div 7.5 = 8$ days.

23. **A. $\frac{1}{2}$** Multiply: $\frac{2}{3} \times \frac{3}{4} = \frac{\overset{1}{2}}{\underset{1}{3}} \times \frac{\overset{1}{3}}{\underset{2}{4}} = \frac{1}{2}$.

24. **B. 56** Multiply: $140 \times \frac{2}{5} = \frac{\overset{28}{140}}{1} \times \frac{2}{\underset{}{5}} = \frac{56}{1} = 56$.

25. **C. 17.9** Maya travels five segments of the route. Add to find the total distance: $2.4 + 4.3 + 3.6 + 3.6 + 4.0 = 17.9$.

26. **D. 5** Add to find the total amount to be cut off:
    $3\frac{3}{4} + 3\frac{3}{4} = 6\frac{6}{4} = 7\frac{1}{2}$. Subtract from $12\frac{1}{2}$: $12\frac{1}{2} - 7\frac{1}{2} = 5$.

27. **B. $535.60** Multiply $26.38 by 20 and add $8 to the result: $26.38 \times 20 = 527.60$. Then: $527.60 + 8.00 = 535.60$.

28. **80.** Divide: $60 \div 0.75 = 80$.

29. **$\frac{7}{12}$** Add the fractions and subtract the total from 1:
    $\frac{1}{6} + \frac{1}{4} = \frac{2}{12} + \frac{3}{12} = \frac{5}{12}$. Then: $1 - \frac{5}{12} = \frac{12}{12} - \frac{5}{12} = \frac{7}{12}$.

Number and Quantity III: Ratio, Proportion, and Percent

Lesson 1: Ratio and Proportion

Practice 1.1

1. $\frac{24}{6} = \frac{4}{1}$

2. $\frac{\$250}{\$1500} = \frac{1}{6}$

3. $\frac{180}{15} = \frac{12}{1}$

4. $\frac{12}{30} = \frac{2}{5}$ Add $12 + 18 = 30$ to find the total workers.

5. $\frac{336}{14} = \frac{24}{1}$

6. $\frac{\$1500}{\$2400} = \frac{5}{8}$

7. $\frac{20}{12} = \frac{5}{3}$ Subtract $32 - 20 = 12$ to find the free throws missed.

8. $\frac{14}{24} = \frac{7}{12}$ Add $10 + 14 = 24$ to find the total students.

9. $\frac{1440}{6} = \frac{240}{1}$

10. **A. 9:11** Write the ratio in fraction form and reduce:
    $\frac{180}{220} = \frac{9}{11}$.

11. **B. 3 to 10** Calculate: $\frac{180}{600} = \frac{3}{10}$.

12. **B. $\frac{1}{3}$** Subtract to find the voters who have made a decision: $600 - 150 = 450$. Write the ratio and reduce: $\frac{150}{450} = \frac{1}{3}$.

13. **C. 1 to 2** Subtract to find the amount owed: $1200 - $400 = 800. Write the ratio and reduce: 400 to 800 = 1 to 2.

14. **D. 8:3** Subtract to find the number of losses: $77 - 56 = 21$. Write the ratio and reduce: $\frac{56}{21} = \frac{8}{3}$.

Practice 1.2

1. 12
2. 45
3. 2.5 or $2\frac{1}{2}$
4. 60
5. $371
6. 96
7. 2.1 or $2\frac{1}{10}$
8. 72
9. 12.5 or $12\frac{1}{2}$
10. $8.94
11. 1.25 or $1\frac{1}{4}$
12. 37.5 or $37\frac{1}{2}$
13. 18
14. 32
15. $45.50
16. 28
17. **B. $1.23** Calculate: $\frac{4}{\$0.98} = \frac{5}{x}$. $0.98 \times 5 \div 4 = 1.225, which rounds to $1.23.
18. **C. 96** Calculate: $\frac{5}{8} = \frac{60}{x}$; $8 \times 60 \div 5 = 96$.
19. **B. 23** Calculate: $\frac{414}{18} = \frac{x}{1}$; $414 \times 1 \div 18 = 23$.
20. **B. 345** Calculate: $\frac{2\text{ cm}}{150\text{ km}} = \frac{4.6\text{ cm}}{x\text{ km}}$; $150 \times 4.6 \div 2 = 345$.
21. **A. $6\frac{2}{3}$** Write the proportions using fractions. The process is the same: $\frac{2\frac{1}{2}}{1\frac{1}{2}} = \frac{x}{4}$; $2\frac{1}{2} \times 4 \div 1\frac{1}{2} = 6\frac{2}{3}$.
22. **A. $155 \times 7 \div 2.5$** Set up the proportion and think about the order of operations you would need to solve for x: $\frac{155}{2.5} = \frac{x}{7}$; $155 \times 7 \div 2.5 = x$.

Lesson 2: Percents

Practice 2

1. base = $1000
   part = $200
   rate = 20%
2. base = 80
   part = 72
   rate = 90%
3. base = $13,700
   part = $2,740
   rate = 20%
4. base = $2000
   part = $500
   rate = 25%
5. base = 40
   part = 60
   rate = 150%
   60 is 150% *of* 40. The word *of* indicates that 40 is the base.
6. base = $38
   part = $3.23
   rate = 8.5%
7. base = $900
   part = $135
   rate = 15%
8. base = $10.70
   part = $1.07
   rate = 10%
9. base = 800
   part = 200
   rate = 25%
10. base = 12,500
    part = 5,000
    rate = 40%

11. **A. $\frac{9 \times 100}{12}$** Add the wins and losses to find the total games played: $9 + 3 = 12$; then write the proportion: $\frac{9}{12} = \frac{x}{100}$. To solve the proportion, you need to find the expression that multiplies 9 and 100 and divides by 12. Only choice (A) does this.

12. **D. 50%** Bravo played 12 games ($6 + 6 = 12$). Then $\frac{6}{12} = \frac{x}{100}$ and $6 \times 100 \div 12 = 50$.

13. **C. $32** To find 25% of $128, solve the proportion: $\frac{x}{\$128} = \frac{25}{100}$; $128 \times 25 \div 100 = 32. Since $25\% = \frac{1}{4}$, you can also find the answer by dividing $128 by 4.

Lesson 3: Using the Percent Formula

Practice 3.1

1. $5
2. 180
3. 110
4. 95%
5. 25%
6. 3%
7. 17
8. $60
9. 200%
10. 5%
11. 8%
12. $3.91
13. $6\frac{1}{2}\%$ or 6.5%
14. $364
15. 62.5% or $62\frac{1}{2}\%$
16. 72

17. **C. 60%** Calculate: $72 \div 120 = 0.6 = 60\%$.
18. **B. $2,385** Calculate: $2,250 \times 0.06 = 135, and $2,250 + $135 = $2,385$.
19. **D. $6.90.** Calculate: $46 \times 0.15 = 6.90.
20. **D. 70%** Find what percent $45.50 is of $65 by dividing: $45.50 \div $65 = 0.7$, which equals 70%.
21. **A. $\frac{\$3 \times 100}{\$50}$** You need to divide the part ($3) by the whole ($50) to find the rate; however, choice (D) states $3 \div 50, which equals 0.06. You still need to change 0.06 to a percent, which you can do by multiplying by 100. If you write a proportion to solve the problem, you will see that choice (A) is correct.

Practice 3.2

1. $175
2. 280
3. 6.4
4. $200
5. 30
6. $84
7. 200
8. 9
9. $13.50
10. 25%
11. $75
12. $9.30
13. 900
14. 90%
15. $780
16. $3120
17. 4000
18. 10%

19. **C. $1,230.00** Solve for the base: $\frac{\$369}{0.3} = $1,230$.
20. **C. $1,200,000** Solve for the base. $\frac{\$72,000}{0.06} = $1,200,000$.
21. **B. $\frac{160 \times 100}{5}$** Set up the problem as a proportion: $\frac{160}{x} = \frac{5}{100}$. To solve the proportion, you would multiply 160×100 and divide by 5. Only choice (B) carries out those operations.
22. **C. 720.** The base is 3600, the total number who received the application. The part is the unknown number who returned the application. Since $20\% = 0.2$, you can solve for the part by multiplying the base by the rate: 3600×0.2.

Lesson 4: Percent Calculator Skills

Practice 4

1. $59.80
2. $96
3. $15.12
4. 40
5. 3%
6. 2080
7. 25%
8. 70
9. 25.2
10. 79
11. 2.5% or $2\frac{1}{2}$%
12. 48
13. 78%
14. $16
15. 250
16. 14
17. 7%
18. 276

19. **C. $8.20** Chanel's order falls between $50.01 and $100. Find 5% of $84: press: 0.05 ⊠ 84 (enter). The right side of the display reads 4.2, or $4.20. Add $4: $4.20 + $4 = $8.20.
20. **A. $0.30** Find the shipping and handling for Jason's order: 8% of $110 = $8.80. Find the shipping and handling for Zola's order: 5% of $90 = $4.50, and $4.50 + $4.00 = $8.50. Then find the difference: $8.80 − $8.50 = $0.30.
21. **C. 88%** Press: 3190 ÷ 3625 (2nd) (|) (enter). The right side of the display reads 0.88. You could also simply divide: 3190 ÷ 3625 = .88. Then mentally translate .88 into 88%.
22. **D. 15%** Divide strikeouts (63) by at bats (410): press: 63 ÷ 410 (enter). The right side of the display reads 0.153658537, which rounds to 15%.

Lesson 5: Interest

Practice 5

1. **$360**
2. **$1,998** Because 8 months is $\frac{2}{3}$ of a year, use $\frac{2}{3}$ for t in the formula.
3. **$450**
4. **$1,040**
5. **D. $1,300 + ($1,300 × 0.09 × 1.5)** Find the interest by multiplying the amount borrowed ($1300) by the interest expressed as a decimal (0.09) by the time period in years (1.5). To find the amount paid back, the amount borrowed must be added to the interest. Only choice (D) shows this series of operations.
6. **B. $144** Find the interest for each loan option: Option A: $2,400 × 0.12 × 2.5 = $720; Option C: $2,400 × 0.09 × 4 = $864. Subtract to find the difference: $864 − $720 = $144.

Lesson 6: Percent of Change

Practice 6

1. 50%
2. 38%
3. 200%
4. 45%
5. 20%
6. 32%
7. 21%
8. 86%
9. 420%
10. 34%

11. **B. 60%** Subtract: $448 − $280 = $168. Divide by the original weekly pay: $168 ÷ $280 = 0.6, which equals 60%.
12. **B. 25%** Subtract: $48 − $36 = $12. Divide by the original price: $12 ÷ $48 = 0.25, which equals 25%.

13. **C. 6%** Subtract: $636 − $600 = $36. Divide by the original rent: $36 ÷ $600 = 0.06, which equals 6%.
14. **C. 125%** The wholesale price of the model is $63, and the retail price is $141.75. Subtract: $141.75 − $63 = $78.75. Divide by the wholesale price: $78.75 ÷ $63 = 1.25, which equals 125%.
15. **B. 30%** The retail price of the model is $150.50, and the member's price is $105.35. Subtract: $150.50 − $105.35 = $45.15. Divide by the retail price: $45.15 ÷ 150.50 = 0.3, which equals 30%.

Ratio, Proportion, and Percent Practice Questions

1. **C. 1:11** Subtract to find the dollars spent on other costs: $360,000 − $30,000 = $330,000. Write a ratio and reduce: $\frac{\$30,000}{\$330,000} = \frac{1}{11}$.
2. **A. $2 \times \frac{50}{5}$** Write a proportion: $\frac{5}{2} = \frac{50}{x}$. To solve it, multiply 2 × 50 and divide by 5. Only choice (A) performs these operations.
3. **B. $7.56** Find 35% of $5.60: $5.60 × 0.35 = $1.96; add: $1.96 + $5.60 = $7.56. Another way to get the answer is to find 135% of $5.60. $5.60 × 1.35 = $7.56.
4. **D. $20,000** The current worth of the car ($12,000) is part of the base. Solve for the base: $12,000 ÷ 0.6 = $20,000.
5. **C. 42** Solve the proportion: $\frac{7}{3} = \frac{x}{18}$; 7 × 18 ÷ 3 = 42.
6. **A. 6%** The commission is part of the base. Solve for the part: $954 ÷ $15,900 = 0.06 = 6%.
7. **B. 1:6** Add to find the total time spent on the project: $2 + 1\frac{1}{2} + 2 + 3\frac{1}{2} = 9$ hours. $1\frac{1}{2}$ hours = 1.5 hours. Write a ratio using decimals and reduce: $\frac{1.5}{9} = \frac{1}{6}$.
8. **B. 36%** Add to find the acres used for grains, vegetables, or fruits: 5,200 + 9,200 = 14,400. Solve for percent: 14,400 ÷ 40,400 = 0.36 = 36%.
9. **A. 35,600** Calculate the decrease in acres of dairy farmland: 22,000 × 20% = 4,400. Subtract that amount from the total acreage of farmland to determine how many acres of farmland will remain: 40,000 − 4,400 = 35,600.
10. **A. $\frac{3}{16}$** The total fat is 3 + 13 = 16 grams. Write the ratio of saturated fat (3 grams) to the total (16 grams). The ratio cannot be simplified.
11. **B. 10** Write a proportion and solve: $\frac{4}{5} = \frac{x}{12.5}$. Then 4 × 12.5 ÷ 5 = 10 inches.
12. **138** Write a proportion and solve: $\frac{4}{3} = \frac{184}{x}$. Then 3 × 184 ÷ 4 = 138 female patients.
13. **900** If 20% is the amount of the discount, then the sale price must be 80% of the original price. The sale price is the part, and the original price is the base. Solve for the base: $720 ÷ 0.8 = $900.
14. **B. 40** If the ratio of wins to losses is 5:4, then the ratio of wins to games played is 5:9. Write a proportion and solve: $\frac{5}{9} = \frac{x}{72}$; 5 × 72 ÷ 9 = 40 games won.
15. **C. 192** Add to find the number that did not answer "no": 16% + 32% = 48%. Find 48% of 400: 400 × 0.48 = 192.

16. **C. 20%** To find the percent decrease, subtract the lower price from the higher price and divide the difference by the original price. In this case, the original price is $25, the higher price. To change the answer to a percent, you must move the decimal point two places to the right or multiply by 100.

17. **A. 121** When the rate is greater than 100%, the part will be greater than the base. Solve for the part: $55 \times 2.2 = 121$.

18. **D. 18%** There are 6 grams of fat in the roast beef sandwich, so there are $6 \times 9 = 54$ calories in the sandwich from fat. The total number of calories in the sandwich is 300. Find what percent 54 is of 300: $54 \div 300 = 0.18 = 18\%$.

19. **D. $264** Write a proportion and solve: $\frac{\$8}{\$3} = \frac{\$704}{x}$; $\$3 \times \$704 \div \$8 = \$264$.

20. **C. 175** The 140 employees who have more than 12 days of sick leave are part of the whole workforce. You need to solve for the base: $140 \div 0.8 = 175$.

21. **D. 825** If the ratio of sold to unsold tickets is 11 to 1, then the ratio of sold to total tickets is 11 to 12. Write a proportion and solve: $\frac{11}{12} = \frac{x}{900}$; $11 \times 900 \div 12 = 825$.

22. **C. $2464** Use the formula for finding simple interest: $I = prt$: $\$2200 \times 0.08 \times 1.5 = \$264$. To find the amount in the account at the end of the time, add the interest to the original investment: $\$2200 + \$264 = \$2464$.

23. **B. $328** Once you find the discount by multiplying 0.2 by $410, you will need to subtract the discount from $410 to find the sale price.

24. **D. 330** After changing $2\frac{3}{4}$ to the decimal 2.75, write a proportion and solve: $\frac{0.5}{60} = \frac{2.75}{x}$; $60 \times 2.75 \div 0.5 = 330$.

25. **C. $\frac{(140 - 91)}{140} \times 100$** There were 140 customers on Sunday, and 91 made a purchase. Therefore, 140 – 91 did not make a purchase. To find the percent rate, divide the difference by 140, the total number of customers on Sunday (the base). Then move the decimal point two places to the right or multiply by 100 to change the answer to a percent. Only choice (C) shows this sequence of operations.

26. **270** Write a proportion and solve: $\frac{9}{14} = \frac{x}{420}$.

27. **$\frac{3}{5}$** If Marcie spends 15 hours answering telephones, she spends 40 – 15, or 25 hours doing other tasks. Write a ratio and reduce: $\frac{15}{25} = \frac{3}{5}$.

Statistics and Probability

Lesson 1: Tables and Pictographs

Practice 1

1. **9** Calculate: $22{,}707 \div 2523 = 9$

2. **6%** Calculate: $(139{,}510 - 130{,}748) \div 139{,}510 \approx 0.06$, or 6%.

3. **300** There are $6\frac{1}{2}$ symbols in the "North" row and $4\frac{1}{2}$ in the "South" row. Two more symbols translates to 300 more books.

4. **3000** Count the number of symbols, 20, and multiply by 150.

5. **D. Reads or pretends to read** If 100 children were surveyed in each year, then the number of children who recognized all letters increased from 11 to 17. To find the percent change, use the percent change formula: $\frac{\text{amount of change}}{\text{original value}} = \frac{17-11}{11} = \frac{6}{11}$, or a roughly 55% increase. Performing similar calculations for all categories will reveal that "reads or pretends to read" showed the least percent increase: $\frac{67-66}{66} = \frac{1}{66} \approx 2\%$. Note that simply subtracting 66 from 67 does not give you the percent of change.

6. **C. 119** In 2010, 34% of 3-year-old children could write their own names. Find 34% of 350: $350 \times 0.34 = 119$.

7. **C. 375** There are $7\frac{1}{2}$ car symbols. Each symbol represents 50 cars. Multiply: $7\frac{1}{2} \times 50 = 375$

8. **A. 75** Compare the symbols for the two rows. There are $1\frac{1}{2}$ more symbols for 8 a.m. to noon than there are after 4:30 p.m. Multiply: $1\frac{1}{2} \times 50 = 75$

Lesson 2: Bar and Line Graphs

Practice 2.1

1. **50**

2. **about 15** Estimate 38 complaints in 2011 and 22 complaints in 2006. Subtract and round.

3. **20%** The number of complaints decreased by 5, from 25 to 20. This represents a $\frac{5}{25} = 20\%$ decrease.

4. **about $20 million** Estimate values from the graph and subtract. Be sure to use the black bars that represent cost.

5. **Film A** Film A has the biggest difference in size between the bar representing box-office receipts and the bar representing cost.

6. **150%** Calculate: $\frac{60}{40} = \frac{3}{2} = 150\%$

7. **A. 40** There are approximately 110 T-shirts, more than 40 books, and a little fewer than 30 toys sold. Combined, about 70 books and toys were sold. Subtract 70 from 110, and you have about 40.

8. **D. $1000** There were about 50 games sold, so 25 sold for $16 and 25 sold for $24. Calculate: $(25 \times 16) + (25 \times 24) = 1000$.

9. **C. 14:3** Write a ratio and simplify: $\frac{70}{15} = \frac{14}{3}$

10. **D. September** Add the 2-day and 5-day permits for each month. Only September's permits equal 80.

Practice 2.2

1. **October** The point representing October is lower than the point representing the previous month, and the line leading to it slopes downward. This indicates a decrease.

2. **270** Estimate totals for the three months and add.

3. **from June to July** The number of visits increased more from August to September, but because the number in June was so low, the percentage increase from June to July is nearly 100%.

4. **$10** Estimate values and subtract.

5. **20%** The price increased from about $25 to about $30, an increase of $5. $\frac{5}{25} = 20\%$.

6. **$30** The price increased from about $18 to about $45. This increase is almost $30.

7. **A. 1930 to 1940** The price of goods decreased over two decades, 1920 to 1940. Note the downward movement of the line. Only the time period 1930 to 1940 is included among the answer options.

8. **D. $\frac{1}{5}$** The price of the same goods was about $20 in 1970 and $100 in 2000. Write a ratio and simplify: $\frac{\$20}{\$100} = \frac{1}{5}$

9. **B. 50** There were about 390 sales in Store 2 and 340 sales in Store 1 in the sixth week: $390 - 340 = 50$.

10. **D. Week 5** The steepest line segment leads from week 4 to week 5, indicating the largest increase in sales from the previous week.

Lesson 3: Box Plots
Practice 3

1. **A.** Arrange the data set in order: 2, 3, 6, 8, 20. Then find key values:
median = 6, 1st quartile = 2.5, and 3rd quartile = 14
The box plot that displays these values is Box Plot A.

2. **D.** Put the numbers in order: 7, 8, 12, 13, 15, 16. Then find key values:
median = 12.5, 1st quartile = 8, and 3rd quartile = 15
The box plot with these points is Box Plot D. Note that if there is an even number of numbers, the two middle numbers become part of the upper and lower quartile because they are above and below the median, respectively.

3. **A. Box Plot A** The information depicted in Box Plot A is spread across more numbers than in Box Plot B.

4. **C. 18** The largest point represented is in Box Plot B, 18.

5. **B. 11** To find the range of an entire data set, subtract the smallest value from the largest. In a box plot, those largest and smallest values are represented by dots at the two ends of the graph. Here, those dots are 18 and 7. $18 - 7 = 11$

6. **B. 12** In a box plot, the interquartile range of the data is represented by a rectangle. Locate the points that mark the ends of the rectangle to identify the values at the two ends of the interquartile range. Here, the two ends of the rectangle are 16 and 4. $16 - 4 = 12$

Lesson 4: Circle Graphs
Practice 4

1. **29%** Find those two categories on the circle graph and add.

2. $\frac{2}{25}$ $8\% = \frac{8}{100} = \frac{2}{25}$

3. **$630** Use the total budget. $\$2250 \times 28\% = \$630$.

4. **$30.60** 17 cents of every dollar are spent on water heating: $\$180 \times 0.17 = \$30.60$.

5. **Heating and Air-Conditioning** The section labeled "Heating and Air-Conditioning" takes up more than half the circle.

6. **Cooking and Refrigeration** This section is 11 cents of every dollar, which is about 10%.

7. **A. 10** According to the graph, a records clerk spends 25%, or $\frac{1}{4}$, of his or her time preparing documents. Then 25% of 40 hours is 10 hours.

8. **D. 56%** If 44% of the time is spent on data entry, then $100\% - 44\% = 56\%$ spent on other tasks.

9. **B. 10%** Add: 3 cents plus 7 cents in 10 cents. Then 10 cents out of 100 cents is $\frac{10}{100}$, or 10%.

10. **C. $48** 40 cents out of every dollar, or 40%, is spent on public bonds. Then 40% of $120 is found by multiplying: $\$120 \times 0.4 = \$48$.

Lesson 5: Line Plots
Practice 5

1. **C.** Look for a line plot that reflects that two zebras have 26 stripes, two have 28, two have 30, etc.

2. **B.** Look for a line plot that reflects three classes with 29 students, two classes with 32, etc.

3. **D. the member who plants eight types of vegetables** Most of the data points are clustered around the quantities 1 through 4. The member who planted 8 types of vegetables is distant from that cluster of data and so is an outlier.

4. **B. 3** Three people grew three vegetables—that's more people than grew any other specific number of vegetables.

Lesson 6: Histograms
Practice 6

1. **C.** Look for the histogram that begins with 30 and that has a second bar at 56, a third bar at 80, etc.

2. **D.** Look for the histogram that begins with 15 and that has a second bar at 22, a third bar at 35, etc.

3. **C. 36%** Estimate the percentages represented by the four bars that cover the time period of December 9 through January 5: 8%, 9%, 9%, and 10%. Add those estimates to find the approximate percentage of cases reported during that entire time period, resulting in 35%.

Lesson 7: Measures of Central Tendency
Practice 7.1

1. mean: 80.14
median: 80
mode: 82
range: 12

2. mean: $8,487.17
median: $8,208.50
mode: none
range: $6,384

3. mean: $4.76
median: $4.50
mode: $4.50
range: $2.35

4. mean: 86
median: 88
mode: 88
range: 28

5. mean: 99.1°
   median: 99°
   mode: 98° and 100°
   range: 7°
6. mean: 1.9 inches
   median: 1.8 inches
   mode: none
   range: 1.1
7. **A. $117,100** Add the amounts in the column labeled "Asking Price" and divide by 6, the number of prices listed.
8. **C. $116,500** Arrange the selling prices in order: $124,800; $118,400; $116,500; $116,500; $109,000; $103,600. Since the number of items is even, there are two in the middle: $116,500 and $116,500. Since these are the same amount, the average of the two is also $116,500.
9. **A.** To find the mean, add the numbers and divide by the number of items in the set. In this case, there are 4 numbers.
10. **C. $900** The median is the middle amount. Arrange the amounts in order and find the middle amount.
11. **B. 14** The mode is the number that occurs most often. Only 14 occurs more than once in the data.

Practice 7.2

1. **B** The range of Set A is 3, while the range of Set B is 47.
2. **B** The more spread-out data set will have the higher standard deviation.
3. **A; B**

Adding a new data point of 13 to Set A would dramatically increase its range and would impact its standard deviation. On the other hand, a data point of 13 would fall more or less in the middle of Set B and thus would not have much impact on its standard deviation. Note that you did not have to perform any calculations in order to answer this question.
4. **B.** A normal distribution is symmetrical around its mean. Only choice (B) displays that quality.
5. **B. 54 to 66** The area defined by two standard deviations on either side of the mean will encompass 95% of the data. And in a normal distribution, the median is equal to the mean. Since the mean is 60 and the standard deviation is 3, that range will be from (60 − 2(3)) to (60 + 2(3)), or 54 to 66.
6. **A. 15 to 25** The area defined by one standard deviation on either side of the mean will encompass 68% of the data. And in a normal distribution, the median is equal to the mean. Since the mean is 20 and the standard deviation is 5, that range will be from (20 − 5) to (20 + 5), or 15 to 25.

Lesson 8: The Basics of Statistical Research

Practice 8

1. **B. no, because the survey is not a random sample of the relevant population** Luke is interested in the effectiveness of the tutoring center for *all* students, not just soccer players. Thus, he must draw a sample from across the student body.
2. **C. sample survey** A survey is a good way to gather data relatively quickly and cheaply, especially when the participants have access to the data. That is, participants themselves can observe whether they've lost weight. If Maritsa were studying something less easily observed by participants—such as amount of cholesterol in the blood—a survey probably wouldn't work.
3. **A. experiment; observational study** In an experiment, the researcher directs the behavior of both treatment and control groups. In an observational study, those groups are selected based on their current behavior, and that behavior is not directed by the researcher.

Lesson 9: Making Inferences from Statistical Data

Practice 9

1. **B. She must determine whether the observed difference is statistically significant.** Cho has progressed as far as observing a difference. She must determine whether that difference is greater than what could be expected due to unimportant random variation before she does anything else with her results.
2. **Murad overlooked the possibility that having a higher-paying job tends to lead to owning more books. Murad overlooked the possibility that some other factor, like a college education, tends to lead people to own many books and to have higher-paying jobs.** Murad has made the common mistake of inferring causation when in fact his data only show correlation. The two correct answer choices describe two other ways the causal relationships could be playing out in Murad's data. It would not be correct to criticize Murad for not asking whether large-library owners are reading their books, because he has made no claim about the effects of reading. Nor has he made a claim that employers have to know anything about their employees' personal libraries in order for the libraries to cause the higher-paying jobs. When you are critiquing a piece of research, stick to what the researcher has actually claimed, and don't criticize claims the researcher hasn't even made.

Lesson 10: Avoiding Mistakes in Statistics

Practice 10

1. **The y-axis is presented in very small increments, while the x-axis is presented in much larger increments.** Whenever you see a graph, look at scales and at the intervals covered by axes. In this case, the researcher is proudly displaying what looks like a pretty sharp increase in outcome y—in fact, a hasty glance at the graph would suggest that one increment of increase in treatment x correlates with one increment of increase in outcome y. But look more closely at the axes: what the graph actually shows is that 10 units of treatment x correlate with 0.5 units of increase in treatment y. Now, that's still a correlation, so it *may* be important and valuable information. But you probably can't conclude that it's *significant* without more information. The information gives you no reason to expect that the graph would be curved, and the researcher has not made a claim of causation. Thus, the first and fourth answer choices are not reasons to be skeptical. It wouldn't make sense for the researcher to graph negative treatments, and the y-axis logically ends where the number of treatments graphed end, so the third choice isn't a reason to be skeptical.

2. **D. displays selection bias, in that the fliers will likely not reach those who don't vote** The political scientist is making the classic mistake of choosing participants who display the outcome he's interested in. If the participant wants to find out whether people who watch local television news programs are more likely to vote than others, he needs to recruit a group of participants who do watch local television news programs and a group who don't and then compare their voting behavior.

Lesson 11: Probability

Practice 11.1

1. $\frac{2}{5}$, 0.4, 40% Calculate: $\frac{20}{50} = \frac{2}{5}$

2. $\frac{3}{10}$, 0.3, 30% There were 12 non-blue spins out of 40 total spins: $\frac{12}{40} = \frac{3}{10} = 30\%$.

3. $\frac{1}{5}$, 0.2, 20% Calculate: $\frac{2}{2+4+4} = \frac{2}{10} = \frac{1}{5} = 20\%$

4. $\frac{1}{4}$, 0.25, 25% Calculate: $\frac{60}{180+60} = \frac{60}{240} = \frac{1}{4} = 25\%$

5. $\frac{1}{3}$, 0.33, $33\frac{1}{3}$% Calculate: $\frac{2}{6} = \frac{1}{3}$

6. **C. 50%** There are 12 cards in the deck, and 6 are diamonds:
$\frac{6}{12} = \frac{1}{2} = 50\%$

7. **A.** $\frac{3}{4}$ There are 3 clubs, so 9 are not clubs: $\frac{9}{12} = \frac{3}{4}$.

8. **D. 2 out of 5** Sixteen out of 40 trials resulted in tails: $\frac{16}{40} = \frac{2}{5}$.

9. **A. 3 out of 5** Twenty-four out of 40 trials resulted in heads: $\frac{24}{40} = \frac{3}{5}$.

Practice 11.2

1. $\frac{1}{36}$ The events are independent, so multiply.
$\frac{1}{6} \times \frac{1}{6} = \frac{1}{36}$

2. $\frac{1}{4}$ Because the first card is replaced, the two choices are independent. The cards greater than 5 are 6, 7, 8, 9, 10. Multiply: $\frac{5}{10} \times \frac{5}{10} = \frac{1}{2} \times \frac{1}{2} = \frac{1}{4}$

3. $\frac{1}{8}$ Half of the sections are red, so there is a $\frac{1}{2}$ chance that the result will be red. Each spin is independent. Multiply: $\frac{1}{2} \times \frac{1}{2} \times \frac{1}{2} = \frac{1}{8}$

4. $\frac{9}{38}$ The marble is *not* replaced, so the probabilities are not the same. There is a $\frac{1}{2}$ chance the first marble is red. But once one red marble is removed, the odds of a second red become $\frac{9}{19}$. Multiply: $\frac{1}{2} \times \frac{9}{19} = \frac{9}{38}$.

5. $\frac{1}{16}$ Each flip is independent and has a $\frac{1}{2}$ chance of coming up heads: $\frac{1}{2} \times \frac{1}{2} \times \frac{1}{2} \times \frac{1}{2} = \frac{1}{16}$.

6. $\frac{1}{4}$ Half of the numbers on a standard die are odd:
$\frac{1}{2} \times \frac{1}{2} = \frac{1}{4}$.

7. **A.** $\frac{1}{9}$ The probability of rolling a 5 is $\frac{1}{6}$. Of the six equal sections on the spinner, four are even numbers, so there is a $\frac{4}{6}$, or $\frac{2}{3}$, chance of spinning an even number. Multiply the probability of each outcome:
$\frac{1}{6} \times \frac{2}{3} \times \frac{2}{18} = \frac{1}{9}$.

8. **D.** $\frac{1}{6}$ The only numbers that are on the spinner are 2, 3, and 4. There is only one 2 on the die, one 3 on the die, and one 4 on the die. So, no matter what number comes up on the spinner, there is a $\frac{1}{6}$ chance the die rolls that number.

9. **C. 1 out of 3** Of the 10 cards, 6 are marked with a square; therefore, there is a 6 in 10, or $\frac{3}{5}$, chance of getting a square on the first pick. Now there are only 9 cards left, and 5 are squares, so there is a a $\frac{5}{9}$ chance of getting a square on the second pick. Multiply: $\frac{3}{5} \times \frac{5}{9} = \frac{15}{45} = \frac{1}{3}$.

10. **B. 80%** After the five white chips are removed from the bag, the bag contains 10 chips, with 8 green and 2 white. The probability of getting green is $\frac{8}{10}$, which equals 80%.

Lesson 12: Combinations

Practice 12.1

1. **5** Since Rob is choosing 4 team members, each possible team leaves out exactly 1 employee. There are 5 possible employees Rob could leave out, so there are 5 possible teams.

2. **10** Either an organized list or a table will work. To solve this problem using a list organized in columns,

assign the books letters: A, B, C, D, and E. Count possible combinations:

A and B combin-ations	A and C combin-ations	A and D combin-ations	B and C combin-ations	B and D combin-ations	C and D combin-ations
ABC	ACD	ADE	BCD	BDE	CDE
ABD	ACE		BCE		
ABE					

3. **4** Use either a table or an organized list, as above.
4. **A. 5** Use a table, an organized list, or the formula.
5. **B. 20** This question asks you to add the number of possible groups of two out of five to the number of possible groups of 3 out of 5. Perform each of those tasks separately, or realize that they will have the same solution because choosing 3 to be in the group is the same as choosing 2 to be out of the group. Then, add the possible combinations together.

Practice 12.2

1. **48** Use the fundamental counting principle: 4 (types of bread) × 3 (types of meat) × 4 (condiments) = 48.
2. **24** Use the fundamental counting principle: 3 (restaurant certificates) × 2 (T-shirts) × 4 (hats) = 24.
3. **27** Use the fundamental counting principle: 3 × 3 × 3 = 27.
4. **24** On Friday, Julio has 2 choices. On Saturday, he has 3. On Sunday, he has 4 choices. Use the fundamental counting principle: 2 × 3 × 4 = 24
5. **D. 5,184** There are three words in the passphrase: 24 choices for the first, 9 for the second, 24 for the third. Use the fundamental counting principle: 24 × 9 × 24 = 5184.
6. **A. 10.** You are asked for combinations from one set of items. Use either a table or an organized list. You can assign the superpowers letters A–E to make it easier to see how to combine them.
7. **C. 1,024** Use the fundamental counting principle: 4 (meats) × 4 (vegetables) × 4 (noodles) × 4 (broth) × 4 (spices) = 1024.
8. **A. 125** Use the fundamental counting principle: 5 (medications) × 5 (dietary changes) × 5 (vitamins) = 125.

Lesson 13: Permutations

Practice 13

1. **120** This is a permutations problem, because order matters. The question asks how many sequences of five items are possible. 5 × 4 × 3 × 2 × 1 = 120.
2. **10** This is a combinations problem: you are being asked how many groups of three are possible, given five students. Order does not matter. Use a table or an organized list; you may name the students A–E if that is easier.
3. **720** This is a permutations problem, because order matters. 6 × 5 × 4 × 3 × 2 × 1 = 720.
4. **C. 360** This is a permutations problem, in which you are counting possible sequences of four out of six tasks. 6 × 5 × 4 × 3 = 360.

5. **B. 6** This is a permutations problem: the question asks you how many possible sequences of three types of flowers are possible. 3 × 2 × 1 = 6.
6. **D. 5,040** This is a permutations problem, because you are told that the role of Bystander #1 is different from the role of Bystander #4. (Notice the phrase "specific roles" in the question.) Thus, order matters. The question is asking how many sequences of four are possible given ten people. 10 × 9 × 8 × 7 = 5040.
7. **B. 20** This is a combinations problem asking how many groups of three out of six are possible. Use a table or an organized list.
8. **C. 120** This is a permutations problem asking how many sequences of three out of six are possible. 6 × 5 × 4 = 120.

Statistics and Probability Practice Questions

1. **B. 2007** Only the bar for 2007 falls between 500 and 600 on the scale.
2. **B. 40%** Estimate the values for 1998 and 1999. Then find the percent of decrease. Estimate roughly 650 and 390 for 1998 and 1999. Subtract. 650 − 390 = 260. Divide by the original number. 260 ÷ 650 = 0.4 = 40%
3. **A. $\frac{3}{100}$** Jim and his friends bought a total of 12 tickets (4 people × 3 tickets). Then 12 out of $400 = \frac{12}{400} = \frac{3}{100}$
4. **D. 50°** Arrange the low temperatures in order: 55°, 53°, 50°, 50°, 49°, and 48°. Find the middle of the list. Since there are two temperatures in the middle and both are 50°, the mean of the two must be 50°.
5. **C. 1.56** Add the six amounts, and divide by 6: 0.45 + 0.63 + 1.34 + 3.53 + 2.57 + 0.84 = 9.36, and 9.36 ÷ 6 = 1.56 inches. It makes sense to use your calculator on this question.
6. **C. Woodland Hills** Mentally subtract the low temperature from the high temperature for each area. The greatest difference is in Woodland Hills. 68° − 50° = 18°.
7. **B. 2005** Ticket sales increased each year from 2001 through 2004. The first year in which they declined was 2005.
8. **C. 2008** The line graph shows the steepest increase (line rising from left to right) from 2007 to 2008.
9. **C. 32%** Eight customers chose a mouse pad. 8 ÷ 25 = 0.32 = 32%
10. **A. 1 in 2** Of the 52 cards, 26 are either hearts or diamonds. $\frac{26}{52} = \frac{1}{2}$
11. **3.5 or $\frac{7}{2}$** Add the hours, and divide by 6, the number of weeks: 5 + 3.5 + 4 + 0 + 1.5 + 7 = 21 hours, and 21 hours ÷ 6 = 3.5 hours.
12. **$\frac{2}{5}$** Only the numbers 4 and 5 are greater than 3. The probability is 2 out of 5, $\frac{2}{5}$, or 0.4.
13. **B. 41%** The three candidates who received the smallest percentages of the vote also received the smallest number of votes. Add. 9% + 14% + 18% = 41%
14. **C. Bowen and Utley** Since $\frac{3}{5} = 60\%$, look for two candidates whose combined percent is close to 60%. Since 24% + 35% = 59%, the correct answer is choice (C).

15. D. 5100 × 0.09 Grace Reiner received 9%, which equals 0.09. You know the percent and the base. Multiply to find the part.

16. B. March The lines for both companies cross in March.

17. B. 5900 Company A's orders continue to climb at about the same rate. Imagine extending the solid line to the next month. The line would reach to almost 6000. Choice (A) is too high an increase.

18. C. 540 The graph indicates that about 3000 orders were placed in April. Multiply: 3000 × 18% = 540.

19. B. 24.5 Use only the Shots Attempted column. Put the numbers in order, and find the middle: 29, 27, 26, 25, 24, 24, 23, 18. The two in the middle are 25 and 24. Find the mean of those numbers: 25 + 24 = 49, and 49 ÷ 2 = 24.5.

20. D. 10 Use the Shots Made column. The mode is the number that occurs most often. In this case the mode is 10, which occurs three times.

21. B. $\frac{5}{36}$ The probability that a marble is red is $\frac{8}{24}$, or $\frac{1}{3}$. The chance that a marble is white is $\frac{10}{24}$, or $\frac{5}{12}$. Because the first marble is replaced, the two events are independent. Multiply: $\frac{1}{3} \times \frac{5}{12} = \frac{5}{36}$.

22. B. $\frac{34 + 31 + 42}{3}$ To find the mean, add the three numbers and divide by 3, the number of months in the list. There are 36 employees, but you don't need this number to solve the problem.

23. $\frac{1}{36}$ The probability of rolling one "one" is $\frac{1}{6}$. Multiply to find the chance of rolling two ones: $\frac{1}{6} \times \frac{1}{6} = \frac{1}{36}$.

24. 625 Use the fundamental counting principle: 5 × 5 × 5 × 5 = 625.

25. C. 720 This is a permutations question, because the board is not simply picking three members. Rather, those members will also be ordered in a specific way. Multiply: 10 options for president × 9 options for secretary × 8 options for treasurer = 720.

26. B. 20% First find the total number of patients: 16 (colds and flu) + 13 (cuts and scrapes) + 12 (sprained muscles) + 7 (tetanus shots) + 12 (severe headaches) = 60. Now find what percent of 60 is represented by 12: $\frac{12}{60} \times 100 = 20\%$

27. B. 4:3 The ratio of patients with colds or flu to the number of patients with severe headaches is 16:12, which simplifies to 4:3.

28. B. 180–199 lbs The bar corresponding to this weight range is the tallest bar on the graph.

29. B. Participants weighing less than 200 lbs Choices (C) and (D) are both subsets of choice (B), and so cannot be correct. Add the totals of the columns in the graph to reveal that the total for choice (B) is greater than that of (A).

30. B. 4 In each combination, one child is left out. There are 4 ways to leave out one child.

31. B. 20 miles per gallon Seven cars got 20 miles per gallon on average, more than in any other line of the table.

32. A. $\frac{1}{2}$ One car got 35 miles per gallon, and two got 15 miles per gallon.

33. A.

34. D.

Only choice (D) reflects that 48% of visitors arrived during the fourth time period listed.

Algebraic Expressions

Lesson 1: Algebraic Expressions

Practice 1.1

1. $x - 7$
2. $3x^2 + x$
3. $8x - 10$
4. $-3x - 2y$
5. $\frac{10}{x} - 5$
6. $-8 + 7x$
7. $16x + x - 3y$
8. $x^2 + x^4$
9. $x^2 + \frac{4}{7}$
10. $15 + \sqrt{x} - 6$
11. $x - (y + 13)$
12. $(x + 6)^2$
13. $17 - (2x + y)$
14. $x + \frac{24}{x}$
15. $2x - 15$
16. $4(x - y)$
17. $5(x^2 - 3)$
18. $x(11 - \sqrt{100})$

19. **C. $1500 + $0.50(x − 2000)$** Let x represent the number of tickets sold. The expression $x - 2000$ is the number of tickets over 2000 sold. Multiply this expression by $0.50 to find the amount donated based on ticket sales. Then add $1500. Only choice (C) shows this sequence of operations.

20. **A. $(3x + 4y) ÷ (2 + z)$** The sum of 3 times a number and 4 times a second number is represented by the expression $3x + 4y$. The sum of 2 and a third number is represented by $2 + z$. The first expression is divided by the second. Parentheses are necessary to clarify the order of operations.

21. **B. $6h + 0.03s$** The correct sequence of operations shows the sum of 6 multiplied by the number of hours ($6h$) and 3% of the sales, or $0.03s$. Only choice (B) adds these two expressions.

Practice 1.2

1. $x^2 + 3x + 2$
2. $19y + 13$
3. $-3x + 54$
4. $6x^3 + 31x^2 + 4$
5. $7y + 14$
6. $3x + 8$
7. $22x - 12$
8. $2y^2 + y + 9$
9. $-5x - 17$
10. $4x - 7$
11. 31
12. 48
13. 8
14. 21
15. 72
16. 80
17. 85
18. -19
19. 9
20. 61

21. **D. $3x^2 + 4x + 1$** Simplify the expression.
$3x^2 + 3(x - 3) + x + 10$
$= 3x^2 + 3x - 9 + x + 10$
$= 3x^2 + 4x + 1$

22. **A. $x = 2$, $y = 3$** Substitute the values in the choices into the expression. Choice (A) equals -11.
$4x^2 - 3(y + 6)$
$= 4(2^2) - 3(3 + 6)$
$= 4(4) - 3(9)$
$= 16 - 27$
$= -11$

23. **A. 20°** You need to convert a Fahrenheit temperature to Celsius.
$C = \frac{5}{9}(F - 32)$
$C = \frac{5}{9}(68 - 32) = 20$

Lesson 2: Expressions and Calculator Skills

Practice 2

1. 19
2. 15.9
3. 51
4. $16\frac{1}{2}$
5. 10
6. -98
7. 74
8. 146
9. 12
10. -76
11. 57
12. 36
13. -54
14. 24.8
15. 54
16. -45
17. 78
18. 108
19. 459
20. 1430

21. **B. 36.2** Use the formula stated in the problem.
$P = 2l + 2w$
$= 2(12.5) + 2(5.6)$
$= 25 + 11.2$
$= 36.2$

22. **D. $-2xy$** Try each expression: $x + y = -3$; $-x + y = 7$; $x - y = 3$; $xy = -10$; and $-2xy = 20$. The value of choice (D) is greatest.

23. **A. 32** If $x = 2$, then $2 \div x^{-4} = 2 \div \frac{1}{2^4} = 2 \div \frac{1}{16} = 32$.

Lesson 3: Understand Polynomials

Practice 3

1. Monomial
2. Monomial
3. Binomial
4. Trinomial
5. Binomial
6. Trinomial
7. Monomial
8. Monomial
9. Monomial
10. Binomial
11. Trinomial
12. Trinomial
13. Binomial
14. Monomial
15. Binomial

16. First term: $3x^4$, second term: $-2x^2$, third term: -3
17. First term: $12a^2bc$
18. First term: $3g$, second term: $-4h$
19. First term: x^2 second term: y
20. First term: $-4a$, second term: $-3b^2$, third term: c
21. First term: 25
22. First term: $4x^2$, second term: $3x$, third term: -7
23. First term: $\frac{3x}{8}$
24. First term: $\sqrt{25}$
25. First term: $\frac{x^2}{9}$
26. First term: $49x^2y^2z^2$
27. First term: $18y^2$, second term: $-4y^2$, third term: 8
28. First term: $3h$, second term: -4
29. First term: x^2, second term: $-x$ third term: y^2, fourth term: -2
30. First term: ab, second term: ab^2, third term: b^2, fourth term: -4
31. **B. 5** Two variables in the expression have exponents: x^3 and x^2. Add the values of the exponents: $3 + 2 = 5$
32. **B. -1** The coefficients in this expression are $1, -3, -1$, and 2. Add those values: $1 + (-3) + (-1) + 2 = -1$

Lesson 4: Simplify Polynomials

Practice 4

1. Like
2. Like
3. Unlike
4. Unlike
5. Like
6. Unlike
7. Unlike
8. Like
9. Unlike
10. Unlike
11. Like
12. Unlike
13. Like
14. Like
15. Unlike
16. Like
17. Unlike
18. Like
19. Unlike
20. Unlike

21. $7x^2y$
22. $4b$
23. $-6a + 3$
24. $ab^2 + 16ab + 3$
25. $-2x^2 + 7$
26. $4ab$
27. $14g + 14gh$
28. $-4g^2h^2 + 2g^2 + 2h^2 - 4$
29. $-y^2 + 9y$
30. $-7x^2 + y - 3$
31. $22y - 7$

32. $6x^2y + 5y^2 - 23$

33. $4x^3 + 7x^2 + 3x + 5$

34. $-5x^2 - 4x + 5$

35. $-3x^3 + 7x^2 + x$

36. **B. $6a^2b + 9ab$** Identify and group like terms. Then combine:
$3a^2b + 4ab + 3a^2b + 5ab$
$= 3a^2b + 3a^2b + 4ab + 5ab$
$= 6a^2b + 9ab$

37. **B. 3** Identify and group like terms. Then combine:
$j^2 + k^3 - 2j^3 + 5k^3 - 2j^2$
$= j^2 - 2j^2 + k^3 + 5k^3 - 2j^3$
$= -j^2 + 6k^3 - 2j^3$
The expression has three terms.

Lesson 5: Add and Subtract Polynomials

Practice 5.1

1. $5x + 6$
2. $23y + 6$
3. $8x^2 - 5x + 2$
4. $15a^2 + 8a$
5. $11x^2 + 2x + 3$
6. $a + 1$
7. 1
8. $4x^2 + 16x - 9$
9. $24y - 3$
10. $-4a^2 - 2a - 9$
11. $y - 2$
12. $-3x + 13$
13. $3a + 2$
14. $3x^2 + x + 2$
15. $10y + 7$
16. $2x^2 + 3x + 13$
17. $2g + 1$
18. $a^2 - 10a + 2$
19. -16
20. $20x^2 - 5x + 1$
21. **A. $x^2y + 4xy$** Identify, group, and combine like terms:
$(2xy + 3xy^2 - 4x^2y) + (5x^2y - 3xy^2 + 2xy)$
$= 2xy + 2xy - 4x^2y + 5x^2y + 3xy^2 - 3xy^2$
$= 4xy + x^2y$
22. **C. $2x^2 + x + 3$** Distribute the negative sign to everything in the second polynomial. Then group and combine like terms:
$(5x^2 - 2x + 1) - (3x^2 - 3x - 2)$
$= 5x^2 - 2x + 1 - 3x^2 + 3x + 2$
$= 5x^2 - 3x^2 - 2x + 3x + 1 + 2$
$= 2x^2 + x + 3$

Practice 5.2

1. $a^2 + 5a + 4b^2$
2. $-4x - xy + y + 16$
3. $yz^2 - 4z^2 + 7yz + 5$
4. $7ab - b + c - 17$
5. $-4a^4 - c^2 + 3ac + 5$
6. $22xyz + x + 6$
7. $7ef + ef^2 + f - 10$
8. $4pq - 2q + 4$

9. $4ab$
10. 0
11. $3p^6 + 4pq - p^2 - q^2$
12. $x + y + 15$
13. $2bc - b$
14. $10xyz - 8y + 16$
15. $6a + 4b + d$
16. $7pq - q$
17. $-7ab + 2b + 12$
18. 0
19. $-2p^2 + 5q^2 + 7$
20. $x^4 + z^4 - z^5$
21. $bc^2 - bc + 2c$
22. $-3xy + xz - 2xyz$
23. $c^3d^7 - c^2 + 2d$
24. $ef^2g - ef^2 - 2fg + 8$
25. **D. $3x - y$** Distribute the negative sign. Then identify, group, and combine like terms:
$(x + y + z) - (-2x + 2y + z)$
$= x + y + z + 2x - 2y - z$
$= x + 2x + y - 2y + z - z$
$= 3x - y$
26. **B. $3g^2 + 5h - 2k$** Identify, group, and combine like terms:

$(2g^2 + 3h - 5k) + (g^2 + 2h + 3k)$
$= 2g^2 + g^2 + 3h + 2h - 5k + 3k$
$= 3g^2 + 5h - 2k$

Lesson 6: Multiply Polynomials

Practice 6

1. $30x^2$
2. $6xy^2$
3. $28ab^2c^2$
4. $12yz$
5. $9abc$
6. $10x^2y^3z^5$
7. $4ab^2c^2$
8. $34f^3gh^7$
9. $18xyz^2 + 12z^3$
10. $42x^2 - 36xz$
11. $-15ab^2 - 55abc$
12. $-18f^3h + 24f^4gh^2$
13. $70x^7z - 50z^2$
14. $z^2 + 6xyz$
15. $72ab^2 + 64ab$
16. $18x^4 - 27xy^2$
17. $x^2 - x - 30$
18. $x^2 + 2xy + y^2$
19. $z^2 - 81$
20. $y^2z^4 - 2xyz^2 - 3x^2$
21. $9x^2 + 24x + 15$
22. $x^2 - y^2$
23. $y^6 - 6y^4 + 10y^2 - 60$
24. $a^2b^2 - ab - 12$
25. **A. $12a^5b^2c$** The coefficients of each term are 4 and 3, so the coefficient of their product is 12. The product of a^3 and a^2 is a^5. Only choice A contains both of these elements.

26. D. $12p^3c^3$ You need the product of $2pc^2$ and $6p^2c$, which can be calculated as $(2pc^2)(6p^2c)$. The product of the coefficients 2 and 6 is 12, the product of p and p^2 is p^3, and the product of c and c^2 is c^3. Only choice (D) has all three of these elements.

27. B. $12a^2b^2 - 22ab - 14$ Use FOIL:
$(4ab \times 3ab) + (4ab \times [-7]) + (2 \times 3ab) + (2 \times [-7])$
$= 12a^2b^2 - 28ab + 6ab - 14$
$= 12a^2b^2 - 22ab - 14$

Lesson 7: Divide Polynomials

Practice 7

1. $y + 15$
2. $x + 3$
3. $x + 5$
4. $a + b$
5. $x^2 + 2x$
6. $2x^2 + 3x + 1$
7. $x + 2y$
8. $3a + 2b$
9. $\frac{3x}{2} + y$
10. $\frac{3a}{4} + \frac{5b}{4}$
11. $\frac{b + 4c}{3}$
12. $\frac{5a + b + 3c}{2}$
13. $6x + 2$
14. $5x + 3$
15. $8y + 2$
16. $6y + 7$
17. $2y + 2$
18. 3
19. $x - 6$
20. $y + 7$
21. $z - 5$
22. $2x + 6$
23. $x - 6$
24. $a + 3$
25. **C.** $3a + 2b$ Break the fraction up into two separate fractions:
$\frac{(21a + 14b)}{7} = \frac{21a}{7} + \frac{14b}{7}$
Then divide each numerator by 7 to get $3a + 2b$.
26. **D.** $9x + 17y + 20z$ The average of a set of terms is equal to the sum of the terms divided by the number of terms in the set. In this case, that can be represented by the expression
$\frac{(27x + 51y + 60z)}{3}$
Break this up into three separate fractions:
$\frac{27x}{3} + \frac{51y}{3} + \frac{60z}{3}$
Then divide each numerator by 3 to get $9x + 17y + 20z$.

Algebraic Expressions Practice Questions

1. **D.** $-4x - 6$
2. **C.** $3d - 75$ Since Heidi makes 75 less than 3 times Kris's wage, multiply Kris's wage, d, by 3 and subtract 75 to get $3d - 75$.
3. **D.** $84x^2y$ Total desks = schools × rooms per school × desks per room. $4x \times 3y \times 7x = (4)(3)(7)(x)(x)(y) = 84x^2y$.

4. **C.** $(x + 5)(x - 5)$ Multiply the monomials and polynomials in the answer choices until you find an answer choice that results in the expression in the question stem. For answer choice (C), use FOIL: $(x + 5)(x - 5) = x^2 - 5x + 5x - 25 = x^2 - 25$.

5. **D.** $18x + 2y + 13$ Tom has $9x$, Adam $9x + 13$, and Dave $2y$: $9x + (9x + 13) + 2y = 18x + 2y + 13$.

6. **B.** $60y$ The diagram shows multiplication problems done using a table, so the horizontal number times the vertical number will yield the value in the table. The table tells you that $a = yc$ and $b = 5 \times 3 = 15$. So $ab = 15yc$. Now look for a value for c. Since $20 = 5c$, c must equal 4, and you have $ab = (15)(4)y = 60y$. There is not enough information to deduce the value of y, but since y appears in all the answer choices, you do not need to try to find its value.

7. **D.** y The diagram shows multiplication problems done using a table, so the horizontal number times the vertical number will yield the value in the table. $d = 3y$ and $a = 4y$, so $a - d = 4y - 3y = y$.

8. **A.** $7a^2c^2 + 35bc^2 + 49c^4$ Multiply each term by $7c^2$. $7c^2(a^2) + 7c^2(5b) + 7c^2(7c^2) = 7a^2c^2 + 35bc^2 + 49c^4$.

9. **D.** $\$\frac{150}{x}$ To figure out the individual pie cost, divide $900 by the number of pies, $6x$: $\frac{900}{6x} = \frac{150}{x}$.

10. **A.** $\frac{a - 4}{a + 4}$ Cancel out $6b$ in the numerator and $2(3b)$ (which equals $6b$) in the denominator. Then, one $(a - 4)$ will cancel, leaving $\frac{a - 4}{a + 4}$.

11. **C.** $\frac{xyz}{2}$ To find the total cost, multiply ounces per guest by the number of guests by the cost per ounce. Since $\$z$ is the cost per pound, the result needs to be divided by 16. $\frac{(x)(8y)(z)}{16} = xyz\left(\frac{8}{16}\right) = \frac{xyz}{2}$.

12. **B.** -26 Substituting -2 for x and 5 for y leads to $6(-2 - 5) - 8(-2) = 6(-7) - (-16) = -42 + 16 = -26$.

13. **A.** -88 Substituting 2 for x, 4 for y, and 3 for z leads to a product of $[2^2 + 6(3)] \times [2(4) - 4(3)] = (4 + 18) \times (8 - 12) = 22 \times -4 = -88$.

14. **D.** $30kp + 20p^2 + 45hp$ Because $5p$ is paid to every member, each number of team members would be multiplied by $5p$, and the team totals would be added. $5p(6k) + 5p(4p) + 5p(9h) = 30kp + 20p^2 + 45hp$

15. **C.** $-x + 9y - 10xy$ Solve: $7x - [(5y)2x - 9y + 8x] = 7x - [10xy - 9y + 8x] = 7x - 10xy + 9y - 8x = -x - 10xy + 9y$.

16. **A.** $20cd - 75c$ Alyshia has $4d - 15$ DVDs. Multiply $5c$ by Alyshia's DVD total: $(4d - 15)$: $5c(4d - 15) = 5c(4d) - (5c)(15) = 20cd - 75c$

17. **A.** $8x^2 + 7xy^3 - 12x - 1$ Factor out $7x^2$: $\frac{56x^4 + 49x^3y^3 - 84x^3 - 7x^2}{7x^2}$
$= \frac{(7x^2)(8x^2 + 7xy^3 - 12x - 1)}{7x^2}$
$= 8x^2 + 7xy^3 - 12x - 1$

18. **B.** $16d - 4a$ The amount $80d$ is needed. Anything earned at the ball will be subtracted, and $64d$ and $4a$ were both earned: $80d - 64d - 4a = 16d - 4a$ left to raise.

19. A. $\frac{x^4}{2y^2} + 2x^2y^2 - \frac{4x}{y^2} - \frac{1}{2}$ Split the fraction:

$$\frac{x^4 + 4x^2y^4 - 8x - y^2}{2y^2}$$

$$= \frac{x^4}{2y^2} + \frac{4x^2y^4}{2y^2} - \frac{8x}{2y^2} - \frac{y^2}{2y^2}$$

$$= \frac{x^4}{2y^2} + 2x^2y^2 - \frac{4x}{y^2} - \frac{1}{2}.$$

20. B. $\frac{6k + 4f}{r} + 3$ The total of the three groups ($12k + 8f + 6r$) should be divided by the number of squads, $2r$:

$$\frac{12k + 8f + 6r}{2r} = \frac{12k}{2r} + \frac{8f}{2r} + \frac{6r}{2r}$$

$$= \frac{6k}{r} + \frac{4f}{r} + 3$$

$$= \frac{6k + 4f}{r} + 3.$$

21. A. $4x + 2$ Substitute 2 for q and 4 for r in the expression:
$\frac{4^2x^2 + 2^3x}{2^2x} = \frac{16x^2 + 8x}{4x} = 4x + 2.$

22. C. $-2x^4 + 5xy^4 - \frac{y^2}{x^2}$ Split the fractions and then simplify by factoring out $11x^2$:

$$\frac{11x^2(4x^4 + 5xy^4 + 8)}{11x^2} - \frac{11y^2}{11x^2} - 6x^4 - 8$$

$$= 4x^4 + 5xy^4 + 8 - \frac{y^2}{x^2} - 6x^4 - 8$$

$$= -2x^4 + 5xy^4 - \frac{y^2}{x^2}$$

23. A. $5xy^3 - 16x^2y^2 + 42x^2y$ Distribute:
$(6x^2 + 5xy^2)(y) - (4xy - 9x)(4xy)$
$= 6x^2(y) + 5xy^2(y) - (4xy(4xy) - 9x(4xy))$
$= 6x^2y + 5xy^3 - (16x^2y^2 - 36x^2y)$
$= 42x^2y + 5xy^3 - 16x^2y^2$

24. D. $20x^2 - 39x + 18$ The question states that the average salary of the non-managerial employees is $(5x - 6)$. That means that

$$5x - 6 = \frac{\text{Total of non-managers' salaries}}{\text{Number of non-managers}}$$

The question also states that the number of non-managers in the office is $4x - 3$. So,

$$5x - 6 = \frac{\text{Total of non-managers' salaries}}{4x - 3}$$

Then $(5x - 6)(4x - 3) = $ total of non-managers' salaries $= 20x^2 - 39x + 18$

25. B. 51 Factor before substituting.
$\frac{45xy + 63y^2}{9y} = \frac{(9y)(5x + 7y)}{9y} = (5x + 7y).$
Substitute 6 for x and 3 for y: $5(6) + 7(3) = 30 + 21 = 51.$

26. D. $x - 1$ Split the fraction:

$$\frac{3x(x^2 + 3) - 2x(x^2 + 3) - (x^2 + 3)}{x^2 + 3}$$

$$= \frac{3x(x^2 + 3)}{x^2 + 3} - \frac{2x(x^2 + 3)}{x^2 + 3} - \frac{x^2 + 3}{x^2 + 3}$$

$$= 3x - 2x - 1 = x - 1.$$

27. D. $3h^2 + 4hk - 51h - 68k$ Add the populations of both countries ($3h + 4k$) and multiply by the rice consumption: ($h - 17$): $(3h + 4k)(h - 17)$
$= (3h)(h) + (3h)(-17) + (4k)(h) + (4k)(-17)$
$= 3h^2 - 51h + 4hk - 68k.$

28. A. $2x^2 + 2y^2 - xy$ Split the fraction:

$$\frac{4x^2(x+y)}{(x+y)} - \frac{2(x+y)^2(x-y)}{(x+y)} - \frac{xy(x+y)}{(x+y)}$$

$$= 4x^2 - 2(x + y)(x - y) - xy$$

$$= 4x^2 - 2(x^2 - y^2) - xy$$

$$= 2x^2 + 2y^2 - xy$$

29. A. 2 The diagram shows multiplication problems done using a table, so the horizontal number times the vertical number will yield the value in the table. To figure out a, first look at the top right term. Since $5 \times a = ab$, $b = 5$. Another term with only a and b is the bottom middle, $4 \times ab = 40$. Substituting 5 for b shows that $20a = 40$, so $a = 2$.

30. B. 40 The table tells you that $a^2 \times c = 8b$. Use the table to find a value for b. Since the top right cell of the table shows that $5 \times a = ab$, b must equal 5, and $8b = 40$.

Functions

Lesson 1: Equations

Practice 1.1

1. $x = 9$	12. $s = -8$
2. $m = 28$	13. $x = 108$
3. $y = -1$	14. $t = 39$
4. $x = -64$	15. $x = 48$
5. $a = 125$	16. $y = -3$
6. $y = -13$	17. $r = 110$
7. $x = 27$	18. $x = 5$
8. $c = 7$	19. $y = -9$
9. $x = -4$	20. $d = -25$
10. $b = -7$	21. $x = 4$
11. $x = 31$	

22. C. $x + 36 = 77$ Erin's hours (x) plus Kayla's hours (36) = 77 hours.

23. C. $2y = 38$ Erin worked twice as many hours as Kayla ($2y$), and Erin worked 38 hours, so $2y = 38$.

24. C. 128 A number (x) divided by 4 is 32. Solve for x: $\frac{x}{4} = 32$, $x = 128$.

25. $\boxed{I} \boxed{=} \boxed{V} \boxed{\div} \boxed{R}$
The question gives you the formula $V = IR$. To rearrange the formula in order to solve for current (I), divide both sides of the equation by R.

26. B. \$572.18 $- c = $ \$434.68 When you subtract the check from the amount in the checking account, the result will be the current balance.

Practice 1.2

1. $x = 50$	9. $p = 7$
2. $y = -2$	10. $s = -2$
3. $m = 2$	11. $x = 6$
4. $x = -4$	12. $r = -5$
5. $y = 6$	13. $y = 11$
6. $z = 2$	14. $x = \frac{60}{m}$
7. $m = 3$	15. $z = \frac{13}{a+b}$
8. $x = 4$	16. $y = \frac{a-10}{10}$ or $y = \frac{a}{10} - 1$

17. D. $3x + 9 = 6x - 15$ "Three times a number" is $3x$ and "increased by 9" means to add 9. "Six times the number" is $6x$, and "15 less than" means to subtract 15. The word "is" shows that the two expressions should be connected by the = symbol.

18. D. 375 Solve:
$3x + x = 500$
$\quad 4x = 500$
$\quad\ \ x = 125$
The variable x is the number of cards that Travis has. Eric has $3x$, or 3×125, which equals 375.

19. **A.** $4x - 7 = \frac{x}{3} + 15$ Remember that differences and quotients must be written in the order stated in the problem. The difference of four times a number and 7 is $4x - 7$. The quotient of the number and 3 plus 15 is $\frac{x}{3} + 15$.

20. **A. $54** Solve:
$$x + (2x + 12) = \$174$$
$$3x + 12 = \$174$$
$$3x = \$162$$
$$x = \$54$$

Lesson 2: Equation Word Problems, Part I

Practice 2

1. **1800 sq. ft.** Let the square footage of the first house be h, and the second house's square footage will then be $(2h - 1000)$. Then write an equation that combines both houses. The equation is $h + (2h - 1000) = 4400$. Solve for h.

2. **10 dimes** Let x equal the number of dimes in Julia's pocket. The equation is $0.10x + 0.25(24 - x) = 4.50$.

3. **24 games** Let w represent the number of wins, and then the number of losses will be half of w. Write an equation:
$$w + \frac{1}{2}w = 36$$
$$1\frac{1}{2}w = 36$$
$$\frac{3}{2}w = 36$$
$$3w = 72$$
$$w = 24$$
Alternatively, you could solve the equation by calculating the number of losses. Let l = losses. Wins will be twice that much. Then the equation would read $l + 2l = 36$. Once you find l, remember to multiply it by two to find the number of wins.

4. **54** The equation is $x + (x + 2) + (x + 4) + (x + 6) = 4x + 12 = 212$. Solve for $x + 4$, the third number.

5. **8 shirts** Let s represent the number of shirts Brenda bought, and then the number of pants she bought will be equal to $13 - s$. Then, write an equation using the dollar amount she spent: $\$6(13 - s) + \$4s = \$62$. Solve for s.

6. **59** Let x equal the smallest of the three consecutive numbers. Then: $x + (x + 1) + (x + 2) = 180$. Solve for x.

7. **$1100** Andrew spends twice as much on rent, which means he spends half as much as his rent on food. The equation is $r + \frac{1}{2}r = \$1650$. Solve for r.

8. **28 hours** Let h represent the time he spends helping customers, and then stocking shelves will be one-fourth of h. Write an equation:
$$h + \frac{1}{4}h = 35$$
$$1\frac{1}{4}h = 35$$
$$\frac{5}{4}h = 35$$
$$5h = 140$$
$$h = 28$$

9. **C. 84** Let w = Wiley's points, $w + 10$ = Sylvia's points, and $w - 6$ = Greg's points. Write and solve an equation:
$$w + w + 10 + w - 6 = 226$$
$$3w + 4 = 226$$
$$3w = 222$$
$$w = 74$$
Wiley scored 74 points, so Sylvia scored $74 + 10 = 84$ points.

10. **B. $12** Let a = the price of an adult's ticket and $a - \$6$ = the price of a child's ticket. The question states that the cost of 2 adults' tickets and 4 children's tickets is $48. Write and solve an equation:
$$2a + 4(a - 6) = 48$$
$$2a + 4a - 24 = 48$$
$$6a - 24 = 48$$
$$6a = 72$$
$$a = 12$$

11. **B. 6** You know that in 12 years, Jenny will be twice as old as Tina. Therefore, if you multiply Tina's age in 12 years by 2, it will equal Jenny's age in 12 years. Write and solve an equation:
$$4x + 12 = 2(x + 12)$$
$$4x + 12 = 2x + 24$$
$$2x = 12$$
$$x = 6$$

Lesson 3: Algebra Problem Solving

Practice 3

1. **C. 24** Take each answer choice and divide it by 2. Then, check to see if the resulting number is 12 less than the answer choice. For example, choice (A) 12: $12 \div 2 = 6$. And 6 is not 12 less than 12. Thus, choice (A) is incorrect. Only choice (C) works: $24 \div 2 = 24 - 12$.

2. **C. $200** Try each number. Choice (A) says Barbara raised $150. If she did, Sandra would have raised $450, and Matt would have raised $100. Also, the three of them together would have raised $150 + $450 + $100 ≠ $950. Since those numbers don't total to $950, (A) must be incorrect. Only (C) works: $200 + $600 + $150 = $950.

3. **C. 5** The answer choices represent possible weights for the first package. Try (A): if the first package weighs 2, the second package would weigh 1, and the third package would weigh 3. Add them together to see if they total 15: $2 + 1 + 3 ≠ 15$. So (A) is incorrect. Only (C) works: $5 + 2.5 + 7.5 = 15$.

4. **B. 82** The answer choices represent possible scores for the first test. If (A) 76 is Hannah's score on the first test, then her score on the second test would be 82, and $76 + 82 ≠ 170$. Only choice (B) works: $82 + 88 = 170$.

5. **B. 10** The answer choices represent how old Nelson might have been six years ago. If (A) were correct, then Nelson would have been 5 six years ago, and he would be 11 now. Also, six years ago Maria would have been 1 year old, and today she would be 7. Now, the question is, is Nelson's current age

twice Maria's age? $11 \neq 2 \times 7$. So (A) is incorrect. Choice (B) does work: if Nelson was 10 six years ago, then Maria would have been 2. Today Nelson would be 16 and Maria would be 8, and 16 is two times 8.

6. **A. –3** To solve by guessing, plug each answer choice into the equation. Try (A):
$2(-3)^2 + (-3) - 15 = 0.$
$\qquad 2(9) - 18 = 0.$
$\qquad\quad 18 - 18 = 0.$

7. **B. 6** If the group purchased 5 children's passes, as (A) suggests, then they would have purchased 15 adult's passes. Multiply each amount by the cost of that type of ticket, to see if the total equals $440: $(5 \times \$15) + (15 \times \$25) = \$450$. Thus, (A) is incorrect. Choice (B) works: $(6 \times \$15) + (14 \times \$25) = \$440$.

8. **B. 20** The answer choices represent possible values for the width. If (A) were correct, then the width would be 15 and the length would be 30. Add to find out whether choice (A) would give the value of 120 for the perimeter: $15 + 15 + 30 + 30 = 90$. Thus, (A) is incorrect. Choice (B) works: $20 + 20 + 40 + 40 = 120$.

Lesson 4: The Coordinate Plane

Practice 4

1. $(-4, 5)$
2. $(3, 6)$
3. $(0, -3)$
4. $(6, -7)$
5. $(-5, 0)$
6. $(-6, -4)$
7. $(2, 0)$
8. $(7, -2)$

9.

10.

11. **D. (–1, 0)** Plot each point in the answer choices. Only choice (D) lies on the line that passes through points A and B.

12. **A. (–3, –2)** Find the two points discussed in the problem. Then locate the third corner of the triangle, and find the coordinates of the corner. The missing corner is 3 spaces to the left of the origin and 2 spaces down: $(-3, -2)$.

Lesson 5: Graphing a Line

Practice 5

1.

If $x =$	Then $y =$
–2	2
0	3
2	4

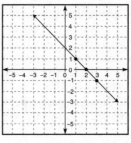

2.

If $x =$	then $y =$
–1	2
0	–1
1	–4

3.

If $x =$	then $y =$
1	1
2	0
3	–1

4.

If $x =$	then $y =$
0	3
1	1
2	–1

5. **C. point T and $(0, 0)$** Try the coordinates for points S and T in the equation. Both lie on the graph of the equation. Check the remaining points in the answer choices. Only $(0,0)$ will make the equation $y = \frac{1}{4}x$ true.

6. **D. $y = -4x - 2$** Choose two points on line P. The easiest points to work with are the ones represented by dots: $(-1,2)$ and $(0,-2)$. Try one of those points in the equations. If the point works in the equation, try the other point as well. (You must try both because any number of lines may pass through a single point. To establish that the equation represents line P, it must fit both points.) Both points work only in choice (D): $y = -4x - 2$.

7. **B. $2x + 3y = 9$** Try the coordinates $(-3, 5)$ in each equation. Only choice (B) is true.
$$2x + 3y = 9$$
$$2(-3) + 3(5) = 9$$
$$-6 + 15 = 9$$
$$9 = 9$$

Lesson 6: Slope of a Line

Practice 6

1. 1
2. −2
3. 0
4. $\frac{3}{4}$
5. $-\frac{1}{2}$
6. 0
7. $-\frac{1}{3}$
8. 2
9. −3

10. **A. line A** Of the answer choices, only line A has a negative slope, so it must be the correct answer. Line A moves down 1 space each time it goes 3 spaces to the right, a ratio of −1 to 3 or $-\frac{1}{3}$.

11. **B. −2** You have more information than you need. Choose any two points and use the slope formula to solve for the slope. For example, if you choose points $(0, 4)$ and $(1, 2)$, your calculations would be: $\frac{2-4}{1-0} = -\frac{2}{1} = -2$.

12. **C. $(2, 3)$** The best way to solve the problem is probably to make a quick sketch. Because the line has a slope of 3, start at point $(1, 0)$ and count 3 spaces up and 1 space to the right. You are now at point $(2, 3)$, which is choice (C). You can check your work using the slope formula.

Lesson 7: Slope and Equations

Practice 7

1. $y = -4x + 2$
$x = 1; y = -2; m = -4$
$-2 = -4(1) + b$
$b = 2$

2. $y = 2x - 2$
$x = -1; y = -4; m = 2$
$-4 = 2(-1) + b$
$b = -2$

3. $y = -\frac{1}{3}x + \frac{2}{3}$
$x = -4; y = 2; m = -\frac{1}{3}$
$2 = -\frac{1}{3}(-4) + b$
$b = \frac{2}{3}$

4. $y - 1 = 3(x - 2)$
$x_1 = 2; y_1 = 1; m = 3$

5. $y = -\frac{1}{3}(x - 2)$
$x_1 = 2; y_1 = 0; m = -\frac{1}{3}$

6. $y + 2 = x - 1$
$x_1 = 1; y_1 = -2; m = 1$

7. $y = -\frac{1}{3}x + \frac{4}{3}$
First, find the slope:
$m = \frac{3-1}{-5-1} = -\frac{1}{3}$.
Choose either ordered pair to substitute for x and y:
$m = -\frac{1}{3}; x = 1; y = 1$
Follow the steps to find the equation of a line in the slope-intercept form.
$1 = -\frac{1}{3}(1) + b$
$b = \frac{4}{3}$

8. $y = 4x + 12$
$m = \frac{4-0}{-2-(-3)} = 4$
$0 = 4(-3) + b$
$b = 12$

9. $y = \frac{1}{2}x - \frac{5}{2}$
$m = \frac{1-(-4)}{7-(-3)} = \frac{1}{2}$
$1 = \frac{1}{2}(7) + b$
$b = -\frac{5}{2}$

10. **C. $y = -x - 1$** Plug both points into the slope formula.
$m = \frac{-3-0}{2-(-1)} = -1$. Then, use m and one of the points to solve for b.
$0 = -1(-1) + b$
$b = -1$

11. **D. $y = \frac{1}{2}x - 1$** To answer this question, simplify the equation in the question to find an answer that matches:
$y - 2 = \frac{1}{2}(x - 6)$
$y - 2 = \frac{1}{2}x - 3$
$y = \frac{1}{2}x - 1$

12. **B. $y = -x - 4$** Because the line on the graph slopes down from left to right, its slope is negative, so you can eliminate choices (A) and (C) immediately. Then note that the line crosses the y-axis at $(0, -4)$, so the y-intercept is −4. Therefore, the correct choice is (B).

Lesson 8: Systems of Linear Equations

Practice 8

1. **(7, 6)**

$$y = 3x - 15 \qquad x + y = 13$$

x	y
0	−15
5	0

x	y
0	13
13	0

2. **(−3, 11)**

$$4x + 2y = 10 \qquad y = -5x - 4$$

x	y
0	5
$\frac{5}{2}$	0

x	y
0	−4
$-\frac{4}{5}$	0

3. **(3, −1)**

Isolate y:
$$-y = -7x + 22$$
$$y = 7x - 22$$

Substitute:
$$4x + 2(7x - 22) = 10$$

$$4x + 14x - 44 = 10$$
$$18x = 54$$
$$x = 3$$

Substitute back:
$$y = 7(3) - 22$$
$$y = -1$$

4. **(7, 2)**

Isolate y:
$$y = 9 - x$$

Substitute:
$$2x - 3(9 - x) = 8$$
$$2x - 27 + 3x = 8$$
$$5x = 35$$
$$x = 7$$

Substitute back:
$$y = 9 - 7$$
$$y = 2$$

5. **(−4, 3)**

y is already isolated.
$$y = 3x + 15$$

Substitute:
$$5x - 2(3x + 15) = -26$$
$$5x - 6x - 30 = -26$$
$$-x = 4$$
$$x = -4$$

Substitute back:
$$y = 3(-4) + 15$$
$$y = 3$$

6. **$(\frac{1}{2}, 6)$**

y is already isolated.
$$y = 12x$$

Substitute:
$$10x - (12x) = -1$$
$$-2x = -1$$
$$x = \tfrac{1}{2}$$

Substitute back:
$$y = 12\left(\tfrac{1}{2}\right)$$
$$y = 6$$

7. **A. (2, −1)** Isolate x in the first equation. $x = 2y + 4$. Then, substitute into the second equation to find a value for y.
$$6y + 5(2y + 4) = 4$$
$$16y + 20 = 4$$
$$y = -1$$

Finally, use that value of y in the first equation to find a value for x. $x = 2(-1) + 4 = 2$

8. **C. (0,0)** The equation $y = x$ represents a line whose x-coordinate is always equal to the y-coordinate. The equation $y = -x$ represents a line whose y-coordinate is always equal to the negative of the x-coordinate. Neither line has a b term in its equation, so both lines have a y-intercept of zero, meaning that they both cross the y-axis at (0,0).

9. **C. $\left(-\frac{9}{2}, -2\right)$** Since the only possible y-value for the line $y = -2$ is -2, simply substitute that value for y in the equation $3y = 2x + 3$ to find the intersection:
$$3(-2) = 2x + 3$$
$$-9 = 2x$$
$$x = -\tfrac{9}{2}$$

10. **C.** $y = -4x + 2$ Two different lines cannot intersect if they are parallel. Lines are parallel if they have the same slope. Only choice (C) does not have a slope of 4, so this is the correct choice.

Lesson 9: Properties of Functions

Practice 9.1

1. $f(x) = 3$
2. $g(x) = 0$
3. $f(y) = -3$
4. $x = 14$
5. $x = -2$
6. $x = 5$
7. **3** If x were equal to 3, then the denominator would be $3 - 3 = 0$, and division by zero is undefined (that is, not permitted).
8. **C. negative numbers** The absolute value of an expression can be 0 or positive; it cannot be negative.
9. **D.** $C(d) = \frac{2}{3}d$ The number of coffee orders is a function of the number of diners, so coffee orders is $C(d)$, and that number is $\frac{2}{3}d$.
10. **D. 15,020** Substitute 200 for A:
    $f(200) = 75 \times 200 + \frac{1}{10} \times 200 = 15,000 + 20 = 15,020$.
11.

$f(x)$	x
21	11
5	3
3	2
–7	–3

Practice 9.2

For questions 1 and 2, your hand-drawn graphs may be rougher but should resemble the following.
1. The graph of $f(x) = 2x - 8$ is below.

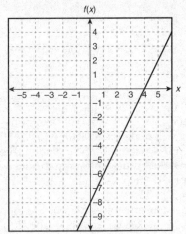

2. The graph of $f(x) = -|x|$ is below.

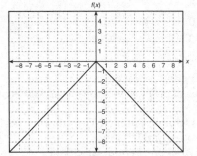

3. *x*-intercept = (1,0); *y*-intercept = (0,4)

4. **C.** $f(x) = -5x$ First look for the function's y-intercept. The line crosses the y-axis at 0, so that allows you to eliminate answer choices (A) and (B). Then look for the slope. The slope is negative, and that eliminates answer choice (D).

Lesson 10: Nonlinear Functions

Practice 10.1

1. **A. The left arm goes down, and the right arm goes up.** The odd exponent 3 means the arms go in opposite directions; the positive coefficient 5 means the right arm goes up.
2. **D. Both arms go down.** The even exponent 4 means the arms go in the same direction; the negative coefficient –7 means the arms go down.
3. **B. negative** The even exponent 2 means both arms go in the same direction. The fact that the function has a maximum means the arms go down. The coefficient of the squared term must be negative.
4.

$x = -3$	3
$x = 0$	0
$x = 1$	–1
$x = 4$	–4

5.

$x = -2$	9
$x = -1$	0
$x = 0$	−3

Practice 10.2

1. **3** The hiring function repeats every 3 months.
2. **500** The number of employees drops to approximately 500.
3. **C. April, July, October, January.** The graph peaks in April, July, October, and January.
4. **45** Each crest marks one period. Calculate:
   $\frac{15\text{ m}}{4\text{ sec}} \times \frac{1\text{ crest}}{5\text{ m}} = \frac{3\text{ crest}}{4\text{ sec}}; \frac{3\text{ crest}}{4\text{ sec}} \times \frac{60\text{ sec}}{1\text{ min}} = 45$ crests/minute.
5. **A.** $x = 10$ Consider this graph of the function:

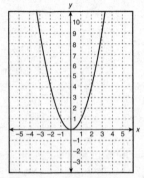

The curve rises fastest when x is greatest. Notice that when x is negative, the slope is negative.
6. **B. (5, 0)** Consider this graph of the function:

7. The function $f(x) = -x^4 + 4x$ reaches its maximum at $x = 1$. The first graph below represents the correct answer to the question; the second graph below shows the graph of the function.

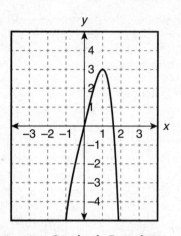

Lesson 11: Quadratic Equations

Practice 11

1. $x^2 + 6x + 8$
2. $x^2 + 2x - 15$
3. $x^2 + 3x - 4$
4. $x^2 - 9x + 18$
5. $x^2 + 6x - 16$
6. $2x^2 - 3x - 2$
7. $x^2 - 14x + 45$
8. $3x^2 + x - 2$
9. $x^2 + 5x - 14$
10. $3x^2 + 14x + 16$
11. $x^2 - x - 30$
12. $x^2 - 13x + 30$
13. $4x^2 + 6x + 2$
14. $x^2 + 5x - 36$
15. $x^2 - 10x + 25$

For questions 16–30, the order of the factors does not matter: for example, $(2x - 1)(x + 3) = (x + 3)(2x - 1)$

16. $(x + 1)(x + 3)$
17. $(x - 1)(x + 5)$
18. $(x + 2)(x + 6)$
19. $(x - 3)(x + 2)$
20. $(x - 2)(x + 7)$
21. $(x - 4)(x + 3)$
22. $(x - 5)(x + 7)$
23. $(x - 6)(x - 6)$
24. $(x - 7)(x + 1)$
25. $(x - 4)(x + 8)$
26. $(2x - 1)(x + 3)$
27. $(2x - 10)(x + 1)$ or $(2x + 2)(x - 5)$ or $(2)(x - 5)(x + 1)$
28. $(x - 5)(x + 10)$
29. $(2x - 1)(2x + 3)$
30. $(x - 7)(x + 8)$
31. **A. −4 and 5** Get 0 on one side of the equation: $x^2 - x - 20 = 0$. Then, factor: $(x + 4)(x - 5) = 0$. Determine which values of x will make each factor equal to 0. The solutions 5 and −4 will make the equation true.
32. **D. $2x^2 + 2x - 24 = 0$** Substitute −4 for x in the answer choices. Only choice (D) works. $2(-4)^2 + 2(-4) - 24 = 2(16) + (-8) - 24 = 32 - 32 = 0$
33. **B. 6** Substitute the answer choices for x in the equation. Only choice (B) makes the equation true: $2(6)^2 - 7(6) - 30 = 2(36) - 42 - 30 = 72 - 72 = 0$. You can also factor the original equation: $(x - 6)(2x + 5)$, so $x = 6$ or $x = -\frac{5}{2}$.
34. **B. $x - 10$** You know that length × width = area. You need to factor the expression $2x^2 - 27x + 70$, and you know that one of the factors is the length, $(2x - 7)$. So $2x^2 - 27x + 70 = (2x - 7)(x - 10)$. The width is $(x - 10)$.

Lesson 12: Inequalities

Practice 12

1. $x > 4$	**13.** $x \geq 2$
2. $x > 7$	**14.** $x > -10$
3. $x \leq -3$	**15.** $x \leq 3$
4. $x \leq 36$	**16.** $x < 21$
5. $x < -1$	**17.** $x \geq -1$
6. $x \geq 5$	**18.** $x < 3$
7. $x > -8$	**19.** $x < 7$
8. $x > 4$	**20.** $x \leq 3$
9. $x < -7$	**21.** $-2 \leq x \leq 2$
10. $x < 2$	**22.** $-20 < x < 6$
11. $x \geq 3$	**23.** $6 < x < 16$
12. $x < 6$	**24.** $4 \leq x \leq 9$

25. A. $s \leq 16$ The perimeter must be less than or equal to 64, so solve the inequality: $4s \leq 64$, which leads to $s \leq 16$.

26. D.

Solve the inequality:
$-4x + 3 < -3x + 5$
$-x < 2$
$x > -2$

To graph the solution $x > -2$, place an open circle at -2, because -2 is not included in the solution. Then, extend the line to the right to include all values greater than -2.

Lesson 13: Graphing Inequalities

Practice 13

1. The same logic for graphing inequalities applies to nonlinear functions as well. Since the graph will not be a straight line, a table can be used to determine some representative values for $y = x^2 - 2$.

x	x^2	y
0	0	-2
±1	1	-1
±2	4	2
±3	9	7

Use these representative points to draw the curve for $y = x^2 - 2$ using a *dotted* line because the inequality does not include values on the line. Shade in the area above the curve to create the open half plane.

2. B.

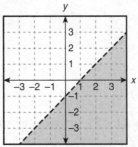

Because the inequality is "less than" rather than "less than or equal to," the line that forms the limit to the open half plane should be dotted rather than solid.

3. Since the term "as much as" includes the value itself, the graph will have a solid line connecting the limits of 6 ounces of Crispy Treats ($3.00/$0.50) and 4 ounces of Grainy Grains ($3.00/$0.75) and the closed half-plane will be below the line connecting those two points.

4. D. $y \geq -\frac{1}{2}x + 2$ Check by evaluating two representative points on the graph such as (0,2) and (4,0). The slope of the line connecting those two points is $\frac{0-2}{4-0}$ $= -\frac{1}{2}$. Therefore the coefficient of x must be $-\frac{1}{2}$. No other answer choice has that coefficient, so there is no need to solve for the y-axis intercept.

Lesson 14: Patterns and Functions

Practice 14

1. 0	**6.** -4
2. 41	**7.** 31.25
3. 2	**8.** -13
4. 40	**9.** 32
5. 23	**10.** -5

11. B. 49 To highlight the pattern, it might be useful to make a table or list:

1st	2nd	3rd	4th
1 block	3 blocks	5 blocks	7 blocks

The number of blocks in each construction equals $2n - 1$, where n is the number in the sequence. The 25th construction would require $2(25) - 1 = 49$ blocks.

12. C. 16 Each term is 6 greater than the term before it. The next (that is, the fifth) term in the sequence is 10, and the sixth term is 16.

13. B. $c = \$5.00 - \$0.25 \, (n - 1)$ The original price per scarf ($5) is reduced by 25 cents starting with the second scarf.

14. B. 1, 5, 9, 13, 17, . . . Try the numbers 1, 2, and 3 for x in the function. This will result in the first three terms of the pattern: 1, 5, and 9. Only choice (B) contains these three terms.

Lesson 15: Function Applications

Practice 15

1. a. $99
   b. $265
2. a. 5.5 hours
   b. 4.25 hours
3. a. Plan A
   b. Plan B
4. **B. $29.50** Use the functions for the two jobs, substituting 30 hours for h:
   Job 1: $P = \$9.75h = \$9.75(30) = \$292.50$
   Job 2: $P = \$70 + \$8.40h = \$70 + \$8.40(30) = \$70 + \$252 = \$322$
   Subtract: $\$322 - \$292.50 = \$29.50$
5. **D. Alicia will earn the most at Job 2.** Use the functions to find Alicia's wages at all three jobs based on 40 hours:
   Job 1: $P = \$9.75h = \$9.75(40) = \$390$
   Job 2: $P = \$70 + \$8.40h = \$70 + \$8.40(40) = \$70 + \$336 = \$406$
   Job 3: $\$380 \times \frac{h}{38} = \$380 \times \frac{40}{38} = \$10 \times 40 = \$400$
   Compare the three results. Alicia will earn the most at Job 2.
6. **B. $19,400** Use the function to calculate the profit:
   $P = \$95,000 - \$5,400d$
   $P = \$95,000 - \$5,400(14)$
   $P = \$95,000 - \$75,600$
   $P = \$19,400$

Lesson 16: Modeling with Functions

Practice 16.1

1. **No** From the first to the second data point, x increases by 1, while y increases by 7. After that, each time x increases by 1, y increases by 1 as well. So the change in y is not constant, and this cannot be a linear function.
2. **D. $B(t) = \$6,000 - \$500t$** At $t = 0$, there is $6,000 in the account. Start with $6,000 and subtract $500 for each month.
3. **12** The question states that the small business does not allow its account balance to dip below zero. The amount of money in the account decreases each month and becomes zero when $t = 12$. $B(12) = \$6,000 - \$500 \times 12 = \$6,000 - \$6,000 = 0$.
4. **A. $P(y) = 10 \times 3^{3y}$** The population is 10 initially, and it triples 3 times each year. When $y = 1$, it will have tripled three times, or increased by a factor of 3^3. When $y = 2$, it will have tripled 6 times, or increased by a factor of $3^{3 \times 2}$, and so on.
5. **C. 2** $10 \times 3^{3 \times 2} = 7,290$, which is less than 7,300. $10 \times 3^{3 \times 3} = 196,830$, which is far too big. So the greatest possible value for y is 2. Notice that the question called for the greatest possible *integer* value, but even if it had not, you could have inferred that the answer would be a whole number. After all, it does not make sense to speak in terms of fractions of rabbits.

Practice 16.2

1. **D. The y-intercept is 3, which represents the surcharge for the first dozen cookies sold.** To find the y-intercept, rewrite the function in the form $y = mx + b$:
   $C(d) = 10 + 7(d - 1)$
   $C(d) = 10 + 7d - 7$
   $C(d) = 7d + 3$
   The y-intercept is 3. Each dozen cookies costs $7, but there is a surcharge of $3 no matter how many dozens one buys. So the y-intercept represents the flat fee added to the cost of the first dozen cookies.
2. **B. It means that the population doubles 5 times per year.** The base 2 means that the population is multiplied by 2, or doubles, at certain intervals. The exponent signifies how often the population doubles. The exponent is $5y$, so the population doubles 5 times each year.
3. **A. $3.5m + 4.5d \leq 30; d \geq 1; m \geq 2$** The mint chocolate bars cost $3.50 each and the dark chocolate bars cost $4.50 each, and the total expenditure must be less than or equal to $30. The correct way to express this situation is $3.5m + 4.5d \leq 30$. The second and third inequalities in the answer choice give Sascha's stated constraints: she will buy at least one dark chocolate bar and at least two mint chocolate bars. Only choice (A) gives this inequality.
4. **30 feet** Call the width of the lawn x and the length $x + 10$. $A = wl = x(x + 10) = 1,200$, so $x^2 + 10x - 1,200 = 0$. Factor: $(x + 40)(x - 30) = 0$. So $x = -40$ or $x = 30$. Because distances are always positive, the natural constraint in this situation is that $x > 0$. There is only one solution that meets this constraint, so the width of the lawn is 30 feet.

Lesson 17: Equation Word Problems, Part II

Practice 17

1. **D. $e = 0.01s + 30,000$** Marguerite's base salary is $30,000 and increases by 0.01 times the amount of her sales.
2. **A. $10** Set up two equations using the given information: $\$1,000 + \$100x$ for sedans and $\$1,500 + \$50x$ for minivans, where x represents the vehicle's age. Set the two equations equal to each other: $\$1,000 + \$100x = \$1,500 + \$50x$. Then subtract $50x from both sides: $\$1,000 + \$50x = \$1,500$. Next, subtract $1,000 from each side: $\$50x = \$500$. Divide both sides by $50 to solve.
3. **C. $30** Set up two equations using the given information. For company A, the cost is $\$2,000 + \$40x$ where x represents the number of strollers. For company B, the cost is $\$1,550 + \$55x$. Set the two equations equal to each other: $\$2,000 + \$40x = \$1,550 + \$55x$. Subtract $40x from both sides: $\$2,000 = \$1,550 + \$15x$. Next, subtract $1,550 from each side: $\$450 = \$15x$. Divide both sides by $15 to solve.

Functions Practice Questions

1. **D. $-4x - 6$** Use the order of operations: $6 - 4(x + 3) = 6 - 4x - 12 = -4x - 6$
2. **A. -3**
   $3 + 4x = x - 6$
   $3x = -9$
   $x = -3$
3. **B. $y = -4x + 6$** Choices (A) and (B) are the only two choices with the correct slope. Plug in $x = 1$ and $y - 2$ into both equations; only (B) works.

4. **C. $4x - y = -7$** Try $x = -2$ and $y = -1$ in each equation. Only choice (C) is true: $4(-2) - (-1) = -8 + 1 = -7$

5. **C. \$510** Let t = Tom's earnings and $2t - \$150$ = Jan's earnings.
$$2t - \$150 + t = \$1380$$
$$3t - \$150 = \$1380$$
$$3t = \$1530$$
$$t = \$510$$

6. **D. D** The coordinates of D are $(-3, -2)$, which make the equation $y = -x - 5$ true.
$$y = -x - 5$$
$$-2 = -(-3) - 5$$
$$-2 = 3 - 5$$
$$-2 = -2$$

7. **C. $\frac{1}{3}$** Count the rise and run from C to B. The line moves up 3 spaces as it moves 9 to the right: $\frac{3}{9} = \frac{1}{3}$.

8. **A. $s \geq \$17,500$** Samuel's earnings can be represented by the expression $\$350 + 0.1s$, where s represents total sales for the month. Since Samuel needs to earn at least $2,100, this expression must be greater than or equal to $2,100. Solve:
$$\$350 + 0.1s \geq \$2,100$$
$$0.1s \geq \$1,750$$
$$s \geq \$17,500$$

9. **B. \$5.35** Substitute 24 for n and solve:
$$F = \$3.95 + \$0.10(24 - 10)$$
$$F = \$3.95 + \$0.10(14)$$
$$F = \$3.95 + \$1.40$$
$$F = \$5.35$$

10. **D. 29** Let x = the first number. The remaining numbers are $x + 2$, $x + 4$, and $x + 6$. Solve:
$$x + (x + 2) + (x + 4) + (x + 6) = 104$$
$$4x + 12 = 104$$
$$4x = 92$$
$$x = 23$$
The numbers are 23, 25, 27, and 29. The problem asks for the largest of these numbers.

11. **C. 3^6** Calculate: $3 \times 3 \times 3 \times 3 \times 3 \times 3 = 729$. The other expressions are less than 400. You could also use estimation to help with this problem. For example, to evaluate choice (A), remember that $7 \times 7 = 49$. Then, since 49 is almost 50, round up to make the calculation easier: $7 \times 50 = 350$. So $7^3 < 350$, and it is definitely less than 400.

12. **B. $5x - 4 = 8 + 2 + 3x$** Translate each part of the problem to numbers and symbols and then connect the parts with the = symbol.

13. **B. 1** To find the slope of a line that crosses two points, find the difference between the y-coordinates and then divide by the difference in the x-coordinates: $\frac{6-4}{4-2} = \frac{2}{2} = 1$.

14. **B. 31** From 1 to 7, there is a difference of 6. From 7 to 14, there is a difference of 7. From 14 to 22, there is a difference of 8. To find the next term, add 9 to 22: $22 + 9 = 31$.

15. **C. 0** To find the y-intercept of a line when given the slope and a point, plug the x- and y-coordinates and the slope into the point-slope form, $y = mx + b$. This results in $2 = 2(1) + b$. Solve for b.

16. **B. $(-2, 1)$** Create tables for each linear equation to find values of y when substituting values for x:

$y = x + 3$ 　　　　 $y = -2x - 3$

x	y
0	3
-3	0

x	y
0	-3
$-\frac{3}{2}$	0

17. **D. $y = 3 + 0.5x$** Start with what is given: around the edge the pool is 3 feet deep. Then add another 0.5 feet of depth for every foot you walk from the edge, which is represented by $0.5x$. Putting the two pieces of information together yields the equation $y = 3 + 0.5x$

18. **A. $-7x - (8 + y)$** The word *product* indicates multiplication, and the word *sum* indicates addition. Choice (B) means that y is added, rather than subtracted, from the product (due to order of operations), so it is incorrect.

19. **C. 8 and –3** Either solve by factoring or by trying each option in the equation. The correct factorization is as follows:
$$x^2 - 5x - 24 = 0$$
$$(x - 8)(x + 3) = 0$$
$$x = 8 \text{ or } x = -3$$

20. **B. 4** Cynthia's age right now is six times Rebecca's, or $6r$. Thus, in six years, Cynthia will be $6r + 6$ years old, and Rebecca will be $r + 6$ years old. Write an equation and solve for r:
$$6r + 6 = 3(r + 6).$$

21. **B. $y = 2x - 3$** Try the given points in the equations in the answer options. Only choice (B) works with both points.

22. **B.**
$$-2(x - 6) > 8$$
$$-2x + 12 > 8$$
$$-2x > -4$$
$$x < 2$$

Remember to reverse the inequality symbol when you divide both sides by a negative number.

23. **B. $(-5, 1)$** Point L is 5 spaces to the left of the origin along the x-axis and 1 space above the origin along the y-axis.

24. **D. $\frac{3}{2}$** The coordinates of point L are $(-5, 1)$, and the coordinates of point M are $(-3, 4)$. Find the slope by finding the difference of the y-coordinates, and divide by the difference of the x-coordinates: $\frac{1-4}{-5-(-3)} = \frac{-3}{-2} = \frac{3}{2}$.

25. **C. \$18** Let s = Sam's gift. Then:
Daniel's gift = s.
Celia's gift $s + 12$ (since Sam and Daniel gave the same amount).
Bob's gift = $0.5(s + 12)$ (that is, one-half of Celia's gift). Add those four quantities together and set the sum total to $81:
$$s + s + (s + 12) + .5(s + 12) = 81$$
$$3.5s + 18 = 81$$

$$3.5s = 63$$
$$s = 18$$

26. **A.** $x \leq 3$ Remember to reverse the inequality sign when dividing by a negative number.
$$-7x - 4 \geq x - 28$$
$$-8x \geq -24$$
$$x \leq 3$$

27. **C.** $y = x + 2$ Start by finding the slope: $\frac{3-2}{1-0} = 1$. Now you know that the equation will be $y = x + b$, and you can eliminate choices (A) and (B). And in this case, no calculations are required to find the y-intercept, because one of the points given in the question is (0, 2)—the point where the line crosses the y-axis.

28. **B.** 8,652 Let $x =$ votes for the leading candidate and $p =$ votes for Perez. Write an equation: $p = \frac{1}{3}x + 5,512$. Additionally, you can say that $p + x = 18,072$, or $p = 18,072 - x$ Substitute for p:
$$18,072 - x = \tfrac{1}{3}x + 5,512$$
$$12,560 = \tfrac{4}{3}x$$
$$x = 9420$$
That number represents the number of votes the opposing candidate received. Now, substitute that value back into the simpler of the two original equations:
$$p + 9,420 = 18,072$$
$$p = 8,652$$

29. **B.** $x = -2$ Simplify:
$$-4(x + 2) - 10 = 5x$$
$$-4x - 8 - 10 = 5x$$
$$-4x - 18 = 5x$$
$$-18 = 9x$$
$$-2 = x$$

30. **D.** $5x + 10(35 - x) = \$240$ The total value of the \$5 bills is \$5x. Since there are 35 bills, the number of \$10 bills must be $35 - x$. The value of the \$10 bills is \$10(35 $- x$). The sum of the value of the \$5 bills plus the value of the \$10 bills is \$240.

31. **C.** 75 Let $x =$ the first number in the sequence. Then write an equation:
$$x + (x + 1) + (x + 2) + (x + 3) + (x + 4) = 370$$
$$5x + 10 = 370$$
$$x = 72$$
The first number in the sequence is 72. That means the fourth number (which equals $x + 3$) is 75.

32. **4** Substitute and solve: $E = \frac{9(8)}{18} = 4$.

33. **B.** $y = 5 + 2x$ Because Tonya initially purchases five boxes of cookies, the equation will start out with 5. Each coworker can be counted on to purchase two boxes, written as $2x$. Thus, the amount of cookies sold can be represented with the function $y = 5 + 2x$.

Geometry

Lesson 1: Points, Lines, and Angles

Practice 1

1. acute
2. obtuse
3. straight
4. acute
5. reflex
6. right
7. acute
8. obtuse
9. **A.** 135° $m\angle RZS + m\angle QZS = 180°$. Because $\angle RZS$ measures 45° $\angle QZS$ must measure 135°
10. **C.** **right** Because $m\angle RZQ = 180°$, subtract the two known angles to find the measure of $\angle SZT$. 180° $-$ 45° $-$ 45° $=$ 90°. Because $\angle SZT$ measures 90°, it is a right angle.
11. **A.** 38° $\angle AWB + \angle BWC + \angle CWD = \angle AWD$, a straight angle with a measure of 180°. You know that $m\angle AWB = 90°$ and $m\angle CWD = 52°$, so substitute those values in the first equation: 90°$+ m\angle BWC+$ 52°$= 180°$, which results in $\angle BWC = 38°$.
12. **C.** **obtuse** $m\angle AWC$ is greater than the right angle $\angle AWB$ and less than the straight angle $\angle AWD$. $\angle AWC$ must be obtuse.

Lesson 2: Parallel Lines and Transversals

Practice 2

All possible answers are shown.
1. $\angle 4$ and $\angle 6$, $\angle 3$ and $\angle 5$
2. $\angle 3$
3. 100°
4. $\angle 1$ and $\angle 7$, $\angle 2$ and $\angle 8$
5. $\angle 1$ and $\angle 3$, $\angle 2$ and $\angle 4$, $\angle 5$ and $\angle 7$, $\angle 6$ and $\angle 8$
6. $\angle 4$
7. **B.** 75° $\angle 3$ and $\angle 1$ are vertical angles. Therefore, $m\angle 3 = m\angle 1$. $m\angle 3 = 75°$, so $m\angle 1 = 75°$.
8. **B. They are in the same position from one parallel line to the other.** The transversal and the parallel lines form eight angles. Corresponding angles lie on the same side of the transversal and have the same relationship to the nearest parallel line.
9. **B.** 65° Angle $\angle 7$ and $\angle 3$ are corresponding angles, so $m\angle 7 = m\angle 3$; therefore, $m\angle 3 = 115°$. Angle $\angle 3$ and $\angle 4$ are adjacent angles, which means 115°$+ m\angle 4 = 180°$ and $m\angle 4 = 65°$.
10. **D.** $\angle 8$ Angle $\angle 2$ and $\angle 8$ are alternate exterior angles. Therefore, they are equal.

Lesson 3: Plane Figures

Practice 3

1. rectangle, square
2. parallelogram, rectangle, square, rhombus
3. trapezoid
4. rectangle, square
5. none
6. rectangle, square, parallelogram, rhombus
7. square, rhombus
8. rectangle, square, parallelogram, rhombus, trapezoid
9. trapezoid
10. square
11. **C.** 140° Let $h =$ the measure of $\angle H$. Then $3h + 20° = m\angle F$. The sum of the angles of a quadrilateral is 360°, so $3h + 20° + h + 90° + 90° = 360°$

Solve the equation:
$4h + 200° = 360°$, so $4h = 160°$, $h = 40°$, and $3h + 20° = 140°$.

12. **B.** $EF \parallel GH$ In other words, line EF is parallel to line GH. A trapezoid is a quadrilateral with exactly one pair of parallel sides.

13. **C.** **90°** If the opposite sides of a figure are parallel and all four sides are equal, then the figure is either a square or rhombus. Since $\angle T$ is a right angle, the figure is square. Therefore, all the angles measure 90°.

14. **C.** **parallelogram** This quadrilateral has opposite sides that are equal and opposite angles that are equal. It has no right angles, and the two sets of sides are different lengths. The quadrilateral must be a parallelogram.

Lesson 4: Triangles

Practice 4

1. equilateral, acute
2. scalene, obtuse
3. isosceles, acute
4. 64°
5. 45°
6. 97°
7. **C.** **14** Solve for $\angle BAC$: $m\angle BAC + 55° = 115°$, so $m\angle BAC = 60°$. Solve for $\angle BCA$: $\angle BCA + 35° = 95°$, so $\angle BCA = 60°$. If two of the angles of $\triangle ABC$ each measure 60°, the third angle also measures 60°. The triangle is equilateral, and all the sides of ABC are equal to side AB.
8. **C.** **right** $55° + 35° + m\angle D = 180°$. Solve for the missing angle: $m\angle D = 90°$. Therefore, the triangle is a right triangle.
9. **C.** **86°** The angles of a triangle add up to 180°. 38° + 56° = 94°, so the third angle can be found by subtracting 94° from 180°: $180° - 94° = 86°$.

Lesson 5: Congruent and Similar Triangles

Practice 5

1. No
2. Yes
3. Not enough information
4. **C.** **48** Because the triangles are similar, the sides must be proportional. Set up the ratio $\frac{25}{40} = \frac{30}{x}$ where x equals the length of ST. Solve: $x = 48$
5. **B.** **64°** Similar triangles have equal angle measures. If $m\angle S = 68°$, then $m\angle TYX = 68°$. $m\angle TYX + m\angle T + m\angle TXY = 180°$. Substitute and solve: $68° + 48° + m\angle TXY = 180°$ so $m\angle TXY = 64°$.
6. **C.** **3.2** The two triangles are similar because two of the angle measures in one triangle are equal to two of the angle measures in the other triangle. The side labeled x corresponds to the side with length 4.8. The side of length 2.8 corresponds to the side with length 4.2. Solve the ratio $\frac{x}{4.8} = \frac{2.8}{4.2}$: $x = 3.2$.

Lesson 6: Similar Triangle Applications

Practice 6

1. **C.** **64** Set up a proportion comparing the sign's shadow to the building's shadow and the sign's height to the building's height. $\frac{6}{48} = \frac{8}{x}$: so $x = 64$.

2. **B.** **42** The 10-ft pole is 25 ft from the vertex of the angle; the base of the cliff is 80 + 25, or 105 ft from the vertex of the angle. Set up a proportion. $\frac{105}{25} = \frac{x}{10}$: so $x = 42$.

3. **A.** $\frac{2.5}{22.5} = \frac{1}{x}$ Set up a proportion comparing the meter stick's shadow to the flagpole's shadow and the meter stick's height to the flagpole's height.

4. **D.** **49** Examine the two triangles to find corresponding sides. The 8-ft side of the smaller triangle corresponds to the 28-ft side of the larger triangle. Write a proportion and solve: $\frac{8}{28} = \frac{14}{x}$: so $x = 49$.

5. **B.** **4** If you imagine a line drawn at the bottom of the frame, you will have two similar triangles. The base of the large triangle is 6 ft, and the base of the small triangle is unknown. The side of the large triangle is 12 ft and the side of the small one is 12 − 4 = 8 ft. Write a proportion and solve: $\frac{8}{12} = \frac{x}{6}$, so $x = 4$.

Lesson 7: Pythagorean Relationship

Practice 7

1. $c = 11.3$ in
2. $c = 15$ yd
3. $c = 2.5$ cm
4. $a = 5.2$ m
5. $b = 8$ mm
6. $a = 17.3$ ft
7. $c = 12.2$ cm
8. $b = 26.0$ in
9. $c = 6.4$ km

10. **B.** **6.7** The distance from A to C is 3 units, and the distance from B to C is 6 units.
$$c^2 = a^2 + b^2$$
$$c^2 = 3^2 + 6^2$$
$$c^2 = 9 + 36$$
$$c^2 = 45$$
$$c = \sqrt{45} \cong 6.7$$

11. **C.** **30** The shorter sides are the legs. Solve for the hypotenuse.
$$c^2 = a^2 + b^2$$
$$c^2 = 18^2 + 24^2$$
$$c^2 = 324 + 576$$
$$c^2 = 900$$
$$c = \sqrt{900} = 30$$

12. **D.** **12.1** The brace divides the rectangle into two right triangles with the brace as the hypotenuse of each. Solve for the hypotenuse of one of the triangles:
$$c^2 = a^2 + b^2$$
$$c^2 = 5^2 + 11^2$$
$$c^2 = 25 + 121$$
$$c^2 = 146$$
$$c = \sqrt{146} \cong 12.08, \text{ which rounds to 12.1.}$$

13. **A.** **36** Calculate:
$$c^2 = a^2 + b^2$$
$$39^2 = 15^2 + b^2$$
$$1,521 = 225 + b^2$$
$$1,296 = b^2$$
$$b = \sqrt{1,296} = 36$$

Lesson 8: Perimeter and Area

Practice 8

1. area: 39 sq units
   perimeter: 30.8 units
2. area: 16 sq units
   perimeter: 16 units

3. area: 640 sq units
   perimeter: 104 units
4. area: 29.6 sq units
   perimeter: 24.6 units
5. area: 616 sq units
   perimeter: 109 units
6. area: 38 sq units
   perimeter: 32 units
7. **C. 56** The shaded portion is a trapezoid:
   $\frac{1}{2} \times (5 + 9) \times 8 = 56$.
8. **C. 54** The area of a rectangle is its base times its height. $9 \times 6 = 54$.
9. **C. 324** Subtract the area of the patio from the area of the entire yard. Both are rectangles, so multiply length and width to find the area: $(24 \times 18) - (12 \times 9) = 324$.
10. **B. 24** Add all four sides: $6 + 6 + 6 + 6 = 24$ centimeters.

Lesson 9: Circles

Practice 9.1

1. $C = 62.8$ in; $A = 314.2$ in^2
2. $C = 12.6$ cm; $A = 12.6$ cm^2
3. $C = 25.1$ m; $A = 50.2$ m^2
4. **C. 38** Use the formula $C = \pi d$, where $d = 12$. $12 \times 3.14 = 37.7$
5. **B. 3.14×6^2** The formula for the area of a circle is $A = \pi r^2$. The radius of a circle is half of the diameter. Half of 12 is 6. Substitute 6 for r and 3.14 for π. $A = 3.14 \times 6^2$.
6. **B. 13.0** The diameter of a circle is twice the radius. $6.5 \times 2 = 13$.
7. **C. 19** Find the circumference of the 10-point band. First find the diameter, which passes through the 10-point band, the inner circle, and the 10-point band a second time on its way from one edge of the circle to the other. Add the width of the 10-point band twice and the diameter of the inner circle: $2 + 2 + 2 = 6$ inches. Now you can use the formula for circumference: $6 \times 3.14 = 18.84$, which rounds to 19 inches.

Practice 9.2

1. **34.4°**
2. **10.5 m**
3. **106.1 m**
4. **B. 5** To solve for A, use the formula at the top of the practice page.
   $12 \times A = 15 \times 4$
   $A = \frac{60}{12} = 5$
5. **C. 24** Use the Pythagorean theorem to find half the length of LM:
   (half of LM)$^2 + 5^2 = 13^2$
   (half of LM)$^2 = 144$
   half of $LM = 12$
   $LM = 24$

Lesson 10: Introduction to Trigonometry

Practice 10

1. **0.8** Use the relationship $(\sin \Theta)^2 + (\cos \Theta)^2 = 1$ to find the unknown value.
   $(0.6)^2 + (\cos \Theta)^2 = 0.36 + (\cos \Theta)^2 = 1$
   $(\cos \Theta)^2 = 1 - 0.36 = 0.64$

Take the square root of both sides of the equation to determine that $\cos \Theta = 0.8$.

2.

Angle ABC	90°
Angle ACB	70°
Angle CAB	**20°**
Side AB	**27.65 cm**
Side BC	10 cm
Side AC	**29.41 cm**

Because you are given the measures of two angles, you can find the measure of the third by remembering that the interior angles of a triangle add up to 180 degrees. $180 - 90 - 70 = 20$. So the missing angle measure is 20°. Now you can use trigonometric relationships to find the missing leg lengths. There is more than one way to do so; the work below is an example.
If angle CAB's measure is 20, then sin CAB = sin 20 = 0.34. (The question instructed you to round to the hundredths place here.) That means that the side opposite angle CAB divided by the hypotenuse is equal to 0.34. The side opposite angle CAB is side CB, which is equal to 10 (as given in the question). The hypotenuse is side AC.
$\frac{10}{AC} = 0.34$
$10 = 0.34(AC)$
$AC = 29.41$
Now you can fill in that value and keep working.
If angle ACB's measure is 70, then sin ABC = sin 70 = 0.94. That means that the side opposite angle ACB divided by the hypotenuse is equal to 0.94.
$\frac{AB}{AC} = 0.94$
$\frac{AB}{29.41} = 0.94$
$AB = 27.65$
3. **C. 0.70** The sum of the two acute angles in a right triangle must be 90°. The cosine of a non-right angle in a right triangle is equal to the sine of the other acute angle (and vice-versa). If Θ is one of those angles, then $90° - \Theta$ is the other, so $\cos \Theta = \sin (90° - \Theta)$.
4. Use your calculator to find the values.

sin Θ	**0.454**
cos Θ	**0.891**
tan Θ	**0.510**
csc Θ	**2.203**
sec Θ	**1.122**
cot Θ	**1.963**

5. **A.** $\frac{x}{y}$ tangent = sine divided by cosine

Lesson 11: Trigonometry in General Triangles

Practice 11

1.

$\angle C$	Side A	Side B	Area (cm²)
10°	5 cm	5 cm	2.2 cm²
45°	8 cm	3 cm	8.5 cm²
60°	10 cm	2 cm	8.7 cm²
90°	3 cm	4 cm	6.0 cm²

$\sin 10° = 0.17365$ $A = 0.5(5)(5)(0.17365) = 2.2$ cm²
$\sin 45° = 0.70711$ $A = 0.5(8)(3)(0.70711) = 8.5$ cm²
$\sin 60° = 0.86603$ $A = 0.5(10)(2)(0.86603) = 8.7$ cm²
$\sin 90° = 1.00000$ $A = 0.5(3)(4)(1) = 6.0$ cm² Note: This is a right triangle, so the Pythagorean Theorem applies.

2. C. 6.3 cm Since the internal angles of a triangle sum to 180°, the missing angle is $180° - 37° - 72° = 71°$. Use the Law of Sines to set up the proportion: $\frac{\sin 37°}{4} = \frac{\sin 71°}{x}$ or $\frac{0.60182}{4} = \frac{0.94552}{x}$; $x = 6.28$ cm.

3. A. 9.2 cm The problem provides the measurement of an angle and its opposite side plus another angle, so the Law of Sines can be used to solve for the length of the other side. $\frac{\sin 40°}{6} = \frac{\sin 80°}{x} = \frac{0.64279}{6} = \frac{0.98481}{x}$; $x = 9.19$ cm.

4.

Side	Opposite $\angle$
12 mm	133.4°
5 mm	17.6°
8 mm	29.0°

Designating the sides as $a = 12$, $b = 5$, and $c = 8$, the Law of Cosines can be used to calculate each opposite angle individually.

$a^2 = b^2 + c^2 - 2bc(\cos A)$
$12^2 = 5^2 + 8^2 - 2(5)(8)(\cos A)$
$144 = 25 + 64 - 80(\cos A)$
$55 = -80(\cos A)$
$\cos A = \frac{55}{(-80)} = -0.6875$
$\angle A = 133.4°$

$b^2 = a^2 + c^2 - 2ac(\cos B)$
$5^2 = 12^2 + 8^2 - 2(12)(8)(\cos B)$
$25 = 144 + 64 - 192(\cos B)$
$-183 = -192(\cos B)$
$\cos B = \frac{(-183)}{(-192)} = 0.95312$
$\angle B = 17.6°$

$c^2 = a^2 + b^2 - 2ab(\cos C)$
$8^2 = 12^2 + 5^2 - 2(12)(5)(\cos C)$
$64 = 144 + 25 - 120(\cos C)$
$-105 = -120(\cos C)$
$\cos C = \frac{(-105)}{(-120)} = 0.875$
$\angle C = 29.0°$

Check the answers to ensure that the angles total 180°: $133.4 + 17.6 + 29.0 = 180.0$

5.

Side	Angle	Side	Opposite Side
6	22°	5	2.3
11	55°	3	9.6
8	100°	7	11.5
10	10°	10	1.7

The Law of Sines cannot be used to solve for these values since there is not enough information to calculate the common ratio. However, there is sufficient data to use the Law of Cosines. Designating the given angle as $\angle A$ and the two given sides as b and c, the unknown side will be a.

$a^2 = b^2 + c^2 - 2bc(\cos A)$
$a^2 = 6^2 + 5^2 - 2(6)(5)(\cos 22)$
$a^2 = 36 + 25 - 60(0.92718) = 5.37$
$a = 2.3$

$a^2 = 11^2 + 3^2 - 2(11)(3)(\cos 55)$
$a^2 = 121 + 9 - 66(.57358) = 92.14$
$a = 9.6$

$a^2 = 8^2 + 7^2 - 2(8)(7)(\cos 100)$
$a^2 = 64 + 49 - 112(-0.17365) = 132.45$
$a = 11.5$

$a^2 = 10^2 + 10^2 - 2(10)(10)(\cos 10)$
$a^2 = 100 + 100 - 200(0.98481) = 3.04$
$a = 1.7$

Lesson 12: Volume

Practice 12.1

1. 160 cubic units
2. 27 cubic units
3. 141 cubic units
4. 420 cubic units
5. 3 cubic units
6. 236 cubic units
7. **A. 5.** $V = lwh$ You know that the length and width of the box both equal 4 and that the volume equals 80. Solve the equation:
$80 = 4 \times 4 \times h$
$80 = 16h$
$5 = h$
8. **C. 125** If each edge measures 5 feet, then the figure is a cube. $5^3 = 125$.
9. **C. 17** First, you must find the volume of the pool. The radius of the pool is 6 and the height is 3.
$V = \pi r^2 h$
$\approx 3.14 \times 6^2 \times 3$
$\approx 3.14 \times 36 \times 3$
≈ 339.12
Therefore, the volume is about 339. Solve the proportion $\frac{1}{20} = \frac{x}{339}$, where x equals the number of scoops Linda must add: $20x = 339$; $x = 16.95$, about 17.

Practice 12.2

1. 9 in³
2. 127 in³

3. 314 cm^3
4. 480 m^3
5. 11 in^3
6. 1060 cm^3
7. **A. 480** First, find the volume of the original package. Substitute the numbers given into the volume equation: $V = \frac{1}{3} \times 10^2 \times 15 = 500$. Then find the volume of the new package. Add 4 to the length and width of the base to get 14. Substitute into the volume equation again and solve: $V = \frac{1}{3} \times 14^2 \times 15 = 980$. Find the difference of the two volumes: $980 - 500 = 480$.
8. **C. 67** You know that the height of the cone is half of the diameter of the base. Since the radius of the base is also half of the diameter, the radius must equal the height. Therefore, the radius is 4. Now solve the equation: $V = \frac{1}{3} \times \pi \times 4^2 \times 4 \approx 67$.
9. **D. The volume of B is less than the volume of A.** First, find the volumes of the two figures. Figure A is a rectangular solid. Use the formula $V = lwh = 4 \times 3 \times 2 = 24$. Figure B is a pyramid. Use the formula $V = \frac{1}{3}Bh = \frac{1}{3} \times 3^2 \times 6 = 18$. Now compare the two volumes. Since $24 > 18$, choice (D) must be the answer.
10. **D. 1,000** Use the formula $V = \frac{1}{3} \pi r^2 h = \frac{1}{3} \times \pi \times 8^2 \times 15 \approx 1,005$, which is about 1,000.

Lesson 13: Surface Area

Practice 13.1

1. 108
2. 39
3. 24
4. 336
5. 256
6. 384
7. **C. The surface area of Figure A is greater than the surface area of Figure B.** Calculate both surface areas. Figure A: $25 \times 6 = 150$. Figure B: $(30 \times 4) + (9 \times 2) = 138$. Therefore, Figure A's surface area is greater than Figure B's.
8. **C. 162** The original box has a side length of 3 centimeters, so the surface area is 54 square centimeters. When the dimensions are doubled, the new box has a side length of 6 centimeters, so the surface area is 216 square centimeters. The difference in surface areas is $216 \text{ cm} - 54 \text{ cm}$, which is 162 square centimeters.
9. **A. 5** If all the edges are the same length, then the box must be a cube, and each square face has the same area. There are 6 faces. Divide 150 by 6 to get an area of 25 for each face. Then $\sqrt{25} = 5$, so each side has a length of 5 in.

Practice 13.2

1. 168π
2. 40π
3. 36π
4. 378π
5. 400π
6. 96π

7. **B. 64π** The formula for the surface area of a sphere uses the radius, and the radius is half the diameter, so $8 \div 2 = 4 = r$. Now use the formula for the surface area of a sphere: $SA = 4\pi r^2 = 4 \times \pi \times 4^2 = 64\pi$.

8. **D. The new cone will have a surface area less than the surface area of the original cone.** The original cone has a radius of 4, so its surface area is $\pi(4)(8) + \pi(4^2) = 32\pi + 16\pi = 48\pi$. The new cone will have a slant height of 16, a diameter of 4 and a radius of 2, so its surface area is: $\pi(2)(16) + \pi(2^2) = 32\pi + 4\pi = 36\pi$, which is less than 48π.
9. **C. 170** The surface area of the cylinder is $2\pi(3)(6) + 2\pi(3^2) = 36\pi + 18\pi = 54\pi = 54(3.14) \approx 170$ square inches.

Lesson 14: Combined Figures

Practice 14

1. $P = 150$ units
   $A = 1050$ sq units
2. $P = 49.7$ units
   $A = 159.3$ sq units
3. $P = 72$ units
   $A = 168$ sq units
4. $V = 185$ cubic units
5. $V = 278$ cubic units
6. $V = 399$ cubic units
7. **D. 360** Find the volume of the main rectangular slab: $V = lwh$, so $V = 3 \times 8 \times 12 = 288$ cubic feet. Find the volume of one of the blocks: $V = lwh$, so $V = 3 \times 3 \times 2 = 18$ cu ft. Multiply by 4, the number of blocks: $18 \times 4 = 72$ cu ft. Finally, add the main slab to the blocks: $288 + 72 = 360$ cu ft.
8. **C. 134** The radius of both the cones and the cylinder is 2. The height of one cone is 4 inches. Find the volume of one cone: $V = \frac{1}{3}\pi r^2 h = \frac{1}{3} \times 3.14 \times 2^2 \times 4 \approx 16.7$ cu in. Multiply by 2 to find the volume of both cones: $16.7 \times 2 = 33.4$ cu in. Find the volume of the cylinder: $V = \pi r^2 h \approx 3.14 \times 2^2 \times 8 \approx 100.48$ cu in. Add to find the total volume: $33.4 + 100.48 = 133.88$ cu in, which rounds to 134 cu in.

Lesson 15: Relationships between 2-D and 3-D Figures

Practice 15

1. f. triangle
2. e. rectangle
3. c. parabola
4. g. square
5. a. circle
6. b. trapezoid
7. b. trapezoid
8. e. rectangle
9. Your wording may have varied, but it should have described a bowl or basin:

10. Your wording may have varied, but it should have described an automobile tire:

Lesson 16: Modeling Density

Practice 16

1. **8,100** Divide 40,600 by 5 to find the number of cells per ml, then round to the nearest hundred: $40,600 \div 5 = 8,120 \approx 8,100$.

2. **New York** The population density of black bears is the number of bears divided by land area. Here is the calculation for each state:
   a. Alaska: $200,000 \div 663,267 \approx 0.30$
   b. New York: $6,500 \div 54,556 \approx 0.12$
   c. California: $30,000 \div 163,696 \approx 0.18$
   The question asks for the state with the *lowest* population density of black bears, so the correct answer is New York.

3. **675 g** The mass of an object is equal to its volume times its density. Begin by finding the block's volume: $10 \times 10 \times 15 = 1,500$. And $1,500 \times 0.45 = 675$.

4. **The density of ice is less than the density of water.** An object will float in a liquid if its density is less than the density of the liquid.

5. **bronze** Density equals mass divided by volume. $17.6 \div 0.002 = 8,800$.

6. **A. 1 m³.** 30 kg is 30,000 g. Set up a proportion:
   $$\frac{0.03\,\text{g}}{\text{cm}^3} = \frac{30,000\,\text{g}}{x}$$
   Because $0.03\,\text{g} \times 10^6 = 30,000\,\text{g}$, multiply 1 cm³ by 10^6 in order to find the missing quantity: $x = 1\,\text{cm}^3 \times 10^6 = 1,000,000\,\text{cm}^3$. Since that isn't one of the answer choices, you will have to convert that to another unit.
   100 cm = 1 m. Since this question deals with cubed units, cube both sides of that equation:
   $$1,000,000\,\text{cm}^3 \times \frac{(1\,\text{m})^3}{(100\,\text{cm})^3} = 1,000,000\,\text{cm}^3 \times \frac{1\,\text{m}^3}{1,000,000\,\text{cm}^3}$$
   $$= 1\,\text{m}$$

Lesson 17: Geometry Calculator Skills

Practice 17

1. 42 in
2. 195 cm²
3. 43 ft³
4. 15.8 cm
5. 37.7 in
6. 3016 cm³

7. **C. 520** Use the formulas for finding the area of a rectangle and the area of a triangle, and subtract the area of the cut-out triangle from the area of the rectangle. On the TI-30XS MultiView™ calculator, enter the following: 32 ⊗ 20 ⊖ 20 ⊗ 12 ⊗ .5 (enter). The right side of the display will read 520. You can enter the entire calculation in this fashion because

the TI-30XS™ MultiView understands the algebraic order of operations. If you press enter after each of those operations, your answer will be incorrect.

8. **B. 35** Use the formula for finding the volume of a cylinder. Press: (π) ⊗ 1.5 (x²) ⊗ 5 (enter). The right side of the display will read **35.34291735**, which rounds to 35 meters

9. **D. 5,056** Use the formula for finding the volume of a rectangular solid. Subtract the volume of Box B from the volume of Box A. Press: 26 ⊗ 12 ⊗ 32 ⊖ 22 ⊗ 8 ⊗ 28 (enter). The right side of the display will read **5056**.

10. **C. 608** Use the formula for finding the area of a rectangle. Combine the areas of the two faces. Press: 32 ⊗ 12 ⊕ 28 ⊗ 8 (enter). The right side of the display will read **608**.

Geometry Practice Questions

1. **D. 150** If the edge length is 5 cm, then each square surface has an area of 25 cm². There are 6 faces, so multiply by 6 to get 150 cm².

2. **C. 192π** Substitute the values given in the question into the formula for the surface area of a cylinder:
   $SA = 2\pi rh + 2\pi r^2$
   $SA = 2\pi(6)(10) + 2\pi(6^2)$
   $SA = 120\pi + 72\pi = 192\pi$

3. **C. 66π** The surface area of a cylinder is calculated with the formula $SA = 2\pi rh + 2\pi r^2 = (2 \times \pi \times 3 \times 8) + (2 \times \pi \times 9) = 48\pi + 18\pi = 66\pi$.

4. **C. $16\sqrt{3} + 16$** The surface area of a pyramid with a four-sided base is $SA = \frac{1}{2}ps + B$, where p is the perimeter of the base, s is the slant height of a face of the pyramid, and B is the area of the base. The pyramid described in this problem has a square base with sides of length 4, so both the perimeter (p) and the area of its base (B) are 16. Each face of the pyramid is an equilateral triangle, the height of which represents the slant height (s) of the pyramid. Divide one of the equilateral triangles into two 30:60:90 triangles and use the side length ratio $x: x\sqrt{3} : 2x$ to determine the slant height of the pyramid. Since the base of one of these 30:60:90 triangles is 2 (half the length of a side of the pyramid's base) and the hypotenuse is 4 (the length of a side of the equilateral triangles making up the faces of the pyramid), the height of each 30:60:90 triangle (and, therefore, of each equilateral triangle face of the pyramid) is $2\sqrt{3}$. That is the slant height (s) of the pyramid as well.
   Now, plug in all of the relevant measures and solve: $\frac{1}{2}ps + B = \frac{1}{2} \times (16 \times 2\sqrt{3}) + 16 = 16\sqrt{3} + 16$.

5. **D. 512π** The circumference is 16π so the diameter is 16, and the radius is 8. The surface area is $4\pi r^2 = 256\pi$. The paint covers the ball twice, so multiply by 2 to get 512π.

6. **D. 224** A closet is in the shape of a rectangular solid. To find the volume, multiply: $V = lwh = 7 \times 4 \times 8 = 224$ cubic feet.

7. **C. 48π** The cone has a surface area of $\pi rs = \pi \times 3 \times 10 = 30\pi$ (don't include the base of the cone). A sphere with radius 3 has a surface area of $4\pi r^2 = 4 \times \pi \times 3^2 =$

36π. The surface area of the ice cream is half of that, or 18π. Add to get $30\pi + 18\pi = 48\pi$.

8. **C. 8:1** The formula for the volume of a sphere is $V = \frac{4}{3}\pi r^3$. Find the volumes of both spheres and simplify the ratio between those volumes. Or think about it this way: the ratio of the volume of Sphere A to that of Sphere B would be as follows.

$(\frac{4}{3}\pi \times 2^3)$ to $(\frac{4}{3}\pi \times 1^3)$

Find the value of the exponents:

$(\frac{4}{3}\pi \times 8)$ to $(\frac{4}{3}\pi \times 1)$

You know that you can simplify a ratio by dividing both sides of the ratio by a number. Here, divide both sides by $\frac{4}{3}\pi$ to get:

8 to 1.

9. **A. 1458** The height of all three boxes is 9 in, the length is 18 in, and the width is 9 in. The total volume is $18 \times 9 \times 9 = 1458$.

10. **B. 500** Since Max hikes directly east after hiking directly due north, he has made a 90° turn. The distances hiked therefore form a right triangle. The legs are 300 and 400 yards. To solve for the hypotenuse, use the Pythagorean relationship:

$$a^2 + b^2 = c^2$$
$$300^2 + 400^2 = c^2$$
$$90,000 + 160,000 = c^2$$
$$250,000 = c^2$$
$$500 = c$$

A quicker solution would be to notice that the distances form a large triangle with sides in the 3:4:5 ratio. Then it is easy to see that the hypotenuse of a triangle with legs of 300 and 400 yards is 500 yards.

11. **C. 168** The volume of the container as drawn in the diagram is $V = lwh = 9 \text{ in} \times 7 \text{ in} \times 12 \text{ in} = 756 \text{ in}^3$. If you increase the length by 2 inches, the volume is 11 in $\times$ 7 in $\times$ 12 in $= 924 \text{ in}^3$. Find the difference: $924 \text{ in}^3 - 756 \text{ in}^3 = 168 \text{ in}^3$. You can solve the problem more easily by multiplying the added length by the width and height: $2(7)(12) = 168$.

12. **D. $x^2 = 15^2 - 6^2$** Use the Pythagorean relationship. If $a^2 + b^2 = c^2$ and c is the hypotenuse, then $b^2 = c^2 - a^2$, and $x^2 = 15^2 - 6^2$.

13. **C. 36** Use the formula for finding the perimeter of a rectangle. Let $3w = $ length.
$P = 2l + 2w$
$96 = 2(3w) + 2w$
$96 = 8w$
$w = 12$
So the width is 12 inches, and the length is $3 \times 12 = 36$ inches.

14. **D. 1120π** The circumference is 16π, so $r = 8$ cm. A cone-shaped party hat does not have a base, so $SA = \pi rs = 56\pi$. Multiply by 20 to get 1120π.

15. **A. 3.43** To find the area of the shaded region, subtract the area of the circle from the area of the square. One side of the square is equivalent to the diameter of the circle. The radius is 2, so the diameter—and each side of the square—is 4. So $A = 4^2 - \pi \times 2^2 \approx 3.43$.

16. **B. 1,560** You may find it helpful to draw a sketch of the room. Two walls measure 40 by 12 feet. Two walls measure 25 by 12 feet. Find the total area: $2 \times 40 \times 12 + 2 \times 25 \times 12 = 960 + 600 = 1,560$.

17. **C. 12,000** Use the formula $V = lwh$. Multiply: $40 \times 25 \times 12 = 12,000$.

18. **A. 4** Begin by finding the total surface area of all three pyramids. The formula for the surface area of a pyramid is $SA = \frac{1}{2}ps + B$. For each pyramid, plug in the values and calculate:
Top left pyramid:
$SA = \frac{1}{2}(2 + 2 + 2 + 2)(3) + (2 \times 2)$
$\quad = 16$
Top right pyramid:
$SA = \frac{1}{2}(3 + 3 + 3 + 3)(6) + (3 \times 3)$
$\quad = 45$
Bottom pyramid:
$SA = \frac{1}{2}(4 + 4 + 4 + 4)(4) + (4 \times 4)$
$\quad = 48$
Thus, the total surface area for all three pyramids is:
$16 + 45 + 48 = 109$

The problem states that Laura needs one tube of paint for each 30 square inches. Thus, she needs $109 \div 30 \approx 3.6$. In order to finish her project, she should buy four tubes of paint.

19. **C. 148.8** Because the triangles are similar, the lengths of their legs are proportional. Set up a proportion: $\frac{50}{120} = \frac{62}{x}$, where x is the length of the bridge. Then cross-multiply and solve: $x = 120 \times 62 \div 50 = 148.8$.

20. **A. $m\angle 5 = 60°$** $m\angle ABC$ must equal 60° because the sum of the interior angles of a triangle is 180°, and you know that $\angle BAC$ measures 30° and $\angle ACB$ measures 90°. $180° = 30° + 90° + 60°$. Since lines P and Q are parallel, triangles ABC and ADE are similar. Angle 5, or $\angle ADE$, corresponds to $\angle ABC$; therefore, $\angle 5$ measures 60°.

21. **D. $m\angle 3 + m\angle 6 = 180°$** Lines P and Q are parallel, so AD is a transversal. You know that $\angle 3$ and $\angle 4$ are adjacent supplementary angles, so their sum is 180°. $\angle 4$ and $\angle 6$ are corresponding angles, so they have equal measures. Since the sum of $m\angle 3$ and $m\angle 4$ is 180° and $m\angle 6 = m\angle 4$, the sum of $m\angle 3$ and $m\angle 6$ must be 180° as well.

22. **45** Imagine drawing a line from the top of the man to the end of his shadow and another line from the top of the building to the end of the shadow's building. Once you do so, you have two similar right triangles. Let x equal the height of the building, and set up a proportion: $\frac{3.5}{26.25} = \frac{6}{x}$. Cross multiply and solve: $26.25 \times 6 \div 3.5 = 45$.

23. **24** It may help to make a sketch. The area of the parallelogram is $6(10) = 60$ sq cm, so the area of the triangle is also 60 sq cm. To find the base of the triangle, use the formula for finding the area of a triangle and solve for the base.
$60 = \frac{1}{2}b(5)$
$60 = 2.5b$
$24 = b$

ABOUT THE TEST

Social Studies

The TASC Social Studies Test evaluates your ability to understand, interpret, and apply information. You will have 75 minutes to answer 47 items. Most items will be multiple-choice, though you may also see multiple-answer, drag-and-drop, and constructed-response items. (See the "Question Formats on the TASC" section in the online chapter "About the TASC" for more information about question types on the TASC test.)

Content Areas

Civics and Government (25%) topics include modern and historic governments, constitutional government, levels and branches of the U.S. government, the electoral system, and the role of the citizen.

U.S. History (25%) topics stretch from colonialism and the American Revolution through the Civil War and Reconstruction into the modern era of industrialization, immigration, two world wars, the Great Depression and New Deal era, the Cold War, and the movements for equal rights.

Economics (20%) topics include economics concepts and systems, the government and the economy, and labor and consumer economics issues.

Geography (15%) topics cover the relationship among resources, the environment, and societies.

World History (15%) topics include the beginnings and development of human societies as well as political and economic revolutions and the causes and consequences of wars in the modern era.

Social Studies Skills

In addition to testing your understanding of social studies passages, illustrations, graphs, and charts, questions are based on your understanding of major skills. After you study these skills, you will reinforce them as you work through the unit. They include:

- Determining **central ideas and making inferences**
- Analyzing **words, events,** and **ideas** in social studies contexts
- Analyzing authors' **purposes** and **points of view**
- Evaluate authors' **reasoning** and **evidence**
- Analyze **relationships within and between social studies materials**
- Interpret data and statistics in **graphs** and **charts**

Note that while you will be expected to interpret data, you will not have to perform extensive calculations during the TASC Social Studies Test. You will not have access to a calculator during the Social Studies Test.

See the "TASC Blueprint Alignment: Tables and Notes" section in the online chapter "About the TASC" for more information about how material in this unit aligns to CTB/McGraw-Hill's published TASC test blueprints.

SOCIAL STUDIES PRETEST
PART I: SOCIAL STUDIES SKILLS

Directions: You may fill in the circles next to the correct answers or write your answers on a separate piece of paper.

Question 1 refers to the following passage.

With the passage of the Fifteenth Amendment in 1870, all African Americans were given the right to vote throughout the United States. However, many Southern states quickly enacted legislative barriers to disenfranchise these new voters. Provisions such as poll taxes, literacy tests, and the grandfather clause prevented many African Americans from exercising their rights. For nearly one hundred years, these restrictions persisted in many Southern states. The civil rights movement, which gained national momentum in the 1950s, sought to address this unequal treatment in voting rights laws. Finally, in 1965, the Voting Rights Act provided for federal oversight of states that had previously raised unfair barriers to African American voting and outlawed discriminatory measures such as poll taxes and literacy tests. Voter participation among African Americans dramatically increased in the following years.

1. Which of the following describes the author's main idea?

   ○ A. The Voting Rights Act of 1965 ended discrimination in all areas of American society.
   ○ B. The main effect of the Voting Rights Act of 1965 was to empower individual states to end discriminatory measures against African American voting.
   ○ C. The Voting Rights Act of 1965 gave the federal government oversight of state elections to end barriers against African American voting.
   ○ D. The Fifteenth Amendment did not end racism in Southern states.

Question 2 refers to the following passage.

To address the nation's financial insolvency after the Revolutionary War, George Washington turned to his Secretary of the Treasury, Alexander Hamilton. Hamilton proposed creating a national bank, which would help to pay back the nation's debt and stabilize the nation's currency. Immediately, Hamilton faced stiff opposition from those who believed in a **strict construction** of the Constitution; they believed that Congress and the president could only exercise powers specifically written in the Constitution. Because the Constitution did not give the power to create a national bank, Hamilton's actions would be unconstitutional. In response, Hamilton offered a justification for the constitutionality of his bank based on a **loose construction** of the Constitution, meaning that Congress could use the Necessary and Proper Clause of the Constitution to stretch its power beyond what was specified in the words of the document. In Washington's first great test of presidential leadership, he sided with Hamilton and the idea of a national bank.

2. What is meant by the term "construction" in the passage?

   ○ A. building
   ○ B. creation
   ○ C. interpretation
   ○ D. structure

Questions 3 and 4 refer to the following passage.

In an attempt to make consumers more aware of the nutritional value of the foods they purchase, the Food and Drug Administration (FDA) is attempting to impose strict new regulations on all food retailers. These regulations would require that the caloric information of each food product be clearly posted on the premises, typically through signs that would be expensive to create and maintain. While these regulations would place a financial burden on all food retailers—an expense that would necessarily be passed on to consumers—the regulations would be particularly devastating to smaller restaurants, grocery stores, and convenience stores that offer fresh food items. To relieve this burden on smaller businesses, Congress has proposed the Common Sense Nutritional Disclosure Act, which would exempt smaller food establishments that primarily sell prepackaged foods from having to post on-site information. Also, under this legislation, restaurants that take most of their orders remotely can post caloric information online.

3. What is the author's point of view regarding the FDA's new food regulations?

   A. The FDA's new regulations would place a financial hardship on small food retailers.

   B. The FDA's new regulations would help consumers choose foods of a higher nutritional value.

   C. The FDA's new regulations would have a more severe financial impact on chain restaurants than on smaller food retailers.

   D. The FDA's new regulations would give food retailers more diverse options for displaying caloric information.

4. Which one of the following words points to the author's viewpoint regarding the FDA's strict new regulations?

   A. "aware"

   B. "strict"

   C. "devastating"

   D. "remotely"

Questions 5 and 6 refer to the following paragraph.

It is known that a significant quantity of oil exists within the Arctic National Wildlife Refuge (ANWR) of Alaska. Shockingly, there are many who would have us ignore this incredible resource housed right within our national borders. One commonly cited reason against drilling for oil in the ANWR is that the drilling process would endanger the existence of the porcupine caribou, whose calving grounds encompass much of the region. But science has shown us that as many as 99 percent of all the species that once existed on Earth are now extinct, and the vast majority of these extinctions were not caused by humans. Clearly, then, extinctions are a sad but natural aspect of life on Earth, and we have no reason not to drill in the ANWR.

5. Which of the following statements is a correct evaluation of the argument?

   A. The argument is valid, because it relies on scientific evidence that has been shown to be true.

   B. The argument is valid, because extracting oil would bolster the national economy.

   C. The argument is invalid, because it confuses correlation with causation.

   D. The argument is invalid, because it attempts to refute one reason against doing something while ignoring other possible reasons.

6. Which of the following considerations, if true, best illustrates why the author's evidence is inadequate?

   A. Some people depend on the porcupine caribou for food.

   B. People who call themselves "scientists" often make claims that are very persuasive.

   C. There is not enough oil in the ANWR to have a measurable impact on global oil prices.

   D. Extracting oil from the ANWR would reduce the foreign trade deficit.

Questions 7 and 8 are based on the following information and map.

After World War II, Germany was split into two nations: democratic West Germany and communist East Germany. West Germany was under the control of the victorious Allies, who formed an alliance called the North Atlantic Treaty Organization (NATO). In 1955, NATO decided to allow West Germany to join NATO and to rearm. In response, the U.S.S.R. (that is, the Soviet Union) and a number of communist Eastern European countries formed what they called a "Treaty of Friendship, Co-operation, and Mutual Assistance," commonly referred to as the Warsaw Pact. In the Warsaw Pact, the communist countries agreed to band together if one of them was attacked, and the smaller communist countries agreed to put their military forces under the command of the Soviet Union.

Source: Central Intelligence Agency

7. Some historians believe that, in forming the Warsaw Pact, the Soviet Union wanted to create a buffer between itself and NATO countries. How does the map support that view?

  ○ A. The map indicates that many of the World War II Allies joined the Warsaw Pact, but not until the 1960s.

  ○ B. The map shows that most of the Warsaw Pact countries lay between the Soviet Union and Western countries, including France, West Germany, and Great Britain.

  ○ C. The map shows that the Warsaw Pact involved the building of a wall between the Soviet Union and Western Europe.

  ○ D. The map indicates that the Soviet Union was made up of smaller republics on its western border.

8. The map could be used to dispute which one of the following claims?

  ○ A. In forming the Warsaw Pact, the Soviet Union greatly increased its access to oceanic coastline.

  ○ B. In forming the Warsaw Pact, the Soviet Union wished to increase its trade with Africa.

  ○ C. The Warsaw Pact benefitted Bulgaria and Romania no less than the Soviet Union.

  ○ D. The Warsaw Pact initially included Albania.

Question 9 refers to the following table and map.

Average Yearly Rainfall in New England	
State	Avg. Rainfall/Year
Connecticut	47 inches
Maine	41 inches
Massachusetts	45 inches
New Hampshire	42 inches
Rhode Island	44 inches
Vermont	39 inches

Source: netstate.com

9. What is the average (arithmetic mean) yearly rainfall, in inches, of the three northernmost states in New England?

○ A. $40\frac{2}{3}$
○ B. 41
○ C. 42
○ D. $43\frac{1}{3}$

Question 10 refers to the following graph.

The graph below shows the percent of people who voted in presidential elections from 1996 to 2012.

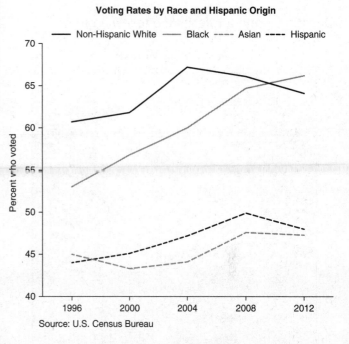

Source: U.S. Census Bureau

10. Over the period illustrated by the line graph, the rate at which eligible black voters participated in presidential elections

○ A. fluctuated up and down, but ended higher than it began.
○ B. steadily increased, surpassing that of white voters in the 2012 elections.
○ C. increased sharply in the middle of the time period shown on the graph before dropping back closer to its original level.
○ D. was consistently lower than the rates of most other races and ethnic groups.

SOCIAL STUDIES PRETEST
PART II: SOCIAL STUDIES CONTENT

Directions: You may fill in the circles next to the correct answers or write your answers on a separate piece of paper.

Question 1 and 2 refer to the following map.

Colonial Triangular Trade

1. Based on this map, what were the three sides of the triangle in the triangular trade?

   ○ A. Europe to the West Indies; the West Indies to Africa; Africa to the British colonies

   ○ B. the West Indies to the British colonies; the British colonies to Africa; Africa to the West Indies

   ○ C. the West Indies to England; England to the British colonies; the British colonies to Africa

   ○ D. South America to Africa; Africa to the West Indies; the West Indies to the British colonies

2. Which statement is a conclusion based on the map rather than a supporting detail from the map?

   ○ A. Cargo ships never had to sail empty on any leg of a profitable triangular journey.

   ○ B. The journey of Africans from Africa to the Americas was called the Middle Passage.

   ○ C. Slaves sometimes were transported on cargo ships from the West Indies to the British colonies.

   ○ D. Rum was shipped from one of the ports on the east coast of North America.

Question 3 refers to the following information.

Several types of U.S. banking institutions and some of their main services are described below.

Federal Reserve banks control the nation's monetary policy and maintain stability of the banking and financial systems.

Commercial banks accept deposits, make loans, and provide related services to corporations and other businesses.

Retail banks provide savings and checking accounts, mortgages, personal loans, and debit and credit cards to consumers.

Community development banks serve residents and spur economic development in low- to moderate-income areas.

Credit unions provide their members with checking and savings accounts, mortgages, and other services at a lower interest rate than other financial institutions.

3. At which type of financial institution would the ABC Printing Company be most likely to take out a loan to finance the purchase of a new printing press?

   ○ A. Federal Reserve bank

   ○ B. commercial bank

   ○ C. retail bank

   ○ D. community development bank

Questions 4 and 5 refer to the following passage.

Somerville has had a long history of corruption. From the 1960s to the 1980s, its mayor, councilors, and tax assessors were involved in a complex network of bribery and favors. The "strong-mayor" system of government is responsible for this corruption; in the history of Massachusetts, all but a single instance of municipal corruption occurred under a strong-mayor government. Because that tainted system is still in place to this day in Somerville, the current mayor must be viewed with strong suspicion.

4. Which of the following words or phrases is based on the author's opinion, not fact?

  ○ A. long history
  ○ B. tainted system
  ○ C. bribery
  ○ D. mayors, councilors, and tax assessors

5. Is the author's conclusion properly supported by evidence?

  ○ A. Yes, because the corruption in Somerville spreads beyond the office of the mayor.
  ○ B. Yes, because 20 years of corruption can accurately be called a "long history."
  ○ C. No, because there is no mention of criminal investigation or charges.
  ○ D. No, because no indication is given that the current mayor will behave as past mayors did.

6. Most Americans believe it is their duty as citizens to take part in our system of government.

Which of the following actions represents participation in government?

  ○ A. pursuing higher education
  ○ B. displaying the American flag
  ○ C. volunteering at a hospital
  ○ D. serving on a jury

7. In many Latin American countries, control passes back and forth between military and civilian rule. Generally, when a civilian government rules, it tries to improve conditions for the nation's citizens, but these attempts lead to turmoil and civil unrest. In response, the military takes power and imposes strict controls on the populace. Such shifts have taken place in Argentina, Peru, and Chile in recent decades.

Which of the following is highly valued by those who favor military rule?

  ○ A. social welfare
  ○ B. freedom
  ○ C. democracy
  ○ D. law and order

Questions 8 and 9 refer to the following chart.

Presidential Powers in Several Nations

Constitutional Power	U.S.A.	South Africa	France	Mexico
Control armed forces	✔	✔	✔	✔
Approve legislation	✔	✔	✔	✔
Appoint executive branch officials	✔	✔	✔	✔
Appoint judges	✔	✔	✔	✔
Appoint prime minister			✔	
Dissolve legislature			✔	

8. Which of the following is a difference between the powers of the U.S. and French presidents?

○ A. The U.S. president controls the armed forces, and the French president does not.

○ B. The U.S. president approves legislation, and the French president does not.

○ C. The French president has the power to dissolve the legislature, while the U.S. president does not.

○ D. The French president has the power to appoint judges, while the U.S. president does not.

9. Which of the following statements is a conclusion based on the chart rather than a detail?

○ A. The president of South Africa cannot dissolve the legislature.

○ B. Of all the presidents shown, the French president has the greatest variety of powers.

○ C. The president of Mexico has the power to appoint judges.

○ D. The U.S. president has the power to approve legislation.

Question 10 refers to the following paragraph.

After the Civil War, southern states passed Jim Crow laws, which kept whites and blacks apart in public places like restaurants, buses, and restrooms. In an 1896 case, *Plessy v. Ferguson*, the U.S. Supreme Court upheld a Louisiana law requiring separate railroad cars for white and black passengers. The Court ruled that it was constitutional to have "separate but equal" facilities for whites and blacks and other minorities. The Court reasoned that "legislation is powerless to eradicate racial instincts or to abolish distinctions." One justice dissented, saying that the decision was "inconsistent with the personal liberty of citizens, white and black."

10. Which of the following statements is an opinion rather than a fact?

○ A. In the late 1800s, many southern states passed Jim Crow laws to keep whites and blacks separate in public places.

○ B. In Louisiana, a law required separate railroad cars for white and black passengers.

○ C. *Plessy v. Ferguson* was an 1896 Supreme Court case that challenged the Louisiana law related to segregated railroad cars.

○ D. The U.S. Supreme Court ruling in *Plessy v. Ferguson* was wrong because it infringed on freedoms guaranteed in the Constitution.

Questions 11 and 12 refer to the following paragraph and chart.

When the U.S. government cannot cover its expenses, it borrows money by selling bonds. It pays back the principal and interest on the bonds over a period of many years. The national debt is the total amount the U.S. government owes at any particular point in time. In 2010, this was about $13.2 trillion.

One way of measuring the national debt is by computing the per capita national debt. The per capita national debt is the total national debt divided by the population of the United States. The graph below shows the per capita national debt every five years from 1990 to 2010.

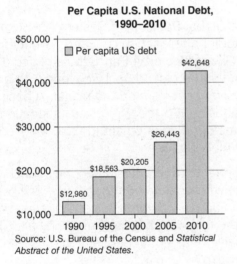

Per Capita U.S. National Debt, 1990–2010

☐ Per capita US debt

- 1990: $12,980
- 1995: $18,563
- 2000: $20,205
- 2005: $26,443
- 2010: $42,648

Source: U.S. Bureau of the Census and *Statistical Abstract of the United States*.

11. Which of the following conclusions is supported by the data in the paragraph and the graph?

- ○ A. The nation's debt increased at a faster rate than did the U.S. population during the period shown on the graph.
- ○ B. Every person in the United States owed an average of $20,000 to the government in the year 2000.
- ○ C. In 1990, the U.S. government owed every American about $13,000.
- ○ D. The U.S. government sold about $5.7 trillion worth of bonds in 2000.

12. Which action would enable the U.S. government to reduce its debt?

- ○ A. Postpone payment of that debt.
- ○ B. Pay interest to foreign investors.
- ○ C. Pay interest to U.S. investors.
- ○ D. Raise taxes and cut spending.

Question 13 refers to the following paragraph.

The ninth-century BCE collapse of the Mayan empire is often attributed to a massive drought. But new geological and archaeological evidence from the Yucatan peninsula in Mexico shows that the Mayans engaged in massive deforestation, clearing land for crops and burning the wood to bake bricks for their cities and temples. Modern weather models show that the destruction of native vegetation could have contributed to as much as 60 percent of the dry weather that is believed to have ended this civilization.

13. According to the theory presented in the paragraph, what was the effect of Mayan deforestation of the Yucatan peninsula?

- ○ A. The Mayans needed more land to grow crops.
- ○ B. Scientists discovered new evidence in the geological record.
- ○ C. A drought was significantly worsened due to lack of native vegetation.
- ○ D. Baking bricks required an enormous amount of wood.

Question 14 refers to the following map.

Great Britain during the Industrial Revolution, 1830

14. Which of the following is a conclusion based on the map rather than a supporting detail from the map?

    ○ A. The Industrial Revolution took place in Great Britain around the year 1830.

    ○ B. More than 300,000 people lived in Sheffield around 1830.

    ○ C. Many cities had large populations because nearby coal and iron ore deposits meant jobs.

    ○ D. There was a large area with coal deposits in southern Wales around 1830.

15. When a nation follows a policy of appeasement, it makes concessions to an aggressor in order to preserve the peace.

Which of the following is an example of appeasement?

    ○ A. Italy's support of Spanish Nationalists in the Spanish Civil War in the late 1930s

    ○ B. Great Britain's acceptance of Germany's takeover of Austria and Czechoslovakia in the late 1930s

    ○ C. Germany's 1939 invasion of Poland, which started World War II

    ○ D. Japan's alliance with Germany and Italy in 1940, which created the Rome-Berlin-Tokyo Axis

16. The Global Positioning System (GPS) can pinpoint any location on Earth. Twenty-four GPS satellites orbit Earth, transmitting signals that can be picked up by anyone with a GPS receiver anywhere on the planet. A basic handheld GPS receiver gives its location in terms of degrees of latitude and longitude on the global grid.

Michael bought a basic handheld GPS receiver because he thought it would help him find his way around Los Angeles. Which of the following best explains why his GPS receiver was not very useful for this purpose?

    ○ A. GPS satellites do not orbit over Los Angeles.

    ○ B. The latitude and longitude grid does not extend over urban areas.

    ○ C. Knowing only latitude and longitude does not help a person get around a city.

    ○ D. Not all of the streets in Los Angeles run in a straight line.

Questions 17 through 19 refer to the following poster.

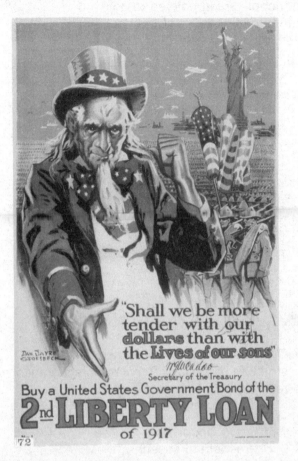

17. The person who designed this poster used irony to make a point. Behind this irony was an assumption with which the designer expected viewers to agree.

    Which of the following statements summarizes this assumption?

    ○ A. People will give to the war effort because they are doing well economically.
    ○ B. Financing the war requires selling bonds and raising taxes.
    ○ C. During wartime, people have little money to spend on their sons.
    ○ D. People value the lives of their children more than they value money.

18. During which war was this poster part of a government advertising campaign?

    ○ A. the Civil War
    ○ B. World War I
    ○ C. World War II
    ○ D. the Vietnam War

19. If the government were running a similar advertising campaign today, which medium would probably reach the most people?

    ○ A. posters
    ○ B. leaflets and brochures
    ○ C. print ads in financial newspapers
    ○ D. television ads on primetime

Question 20 refers to the following table.

The Five Most Populous American Colonies, 1750

Colony	Population (estimate)
Massachusetts	188,000
Pennsylvania	119,700
Connecticut	111,300
Maryland	141,000
Virginia	231,000

Source: U.S. Bureau of the Census

20. Which of the following statements is supported by the data in the chart?

    ○ A. The population of all of the American colonies was less than 700,000.
    ○ B. Virginia had more than twice as many people as Maryland.
    ○ C. Most of the population of Massachusetts was of English origin.
    ○ D. The population of the colony of New York was smaller than that of Connecticut.

Questions 21 through 23 refer to the following paragraph and flowchart.

The U.S. Civil Service system is designed to ensure that people are appointed to government positions because of their skills and abilities rather than because of their political affiliation. Over 90 percent of federal jobs are covered by civil service rules. The typical steps in applying for a civil service job are shown below.

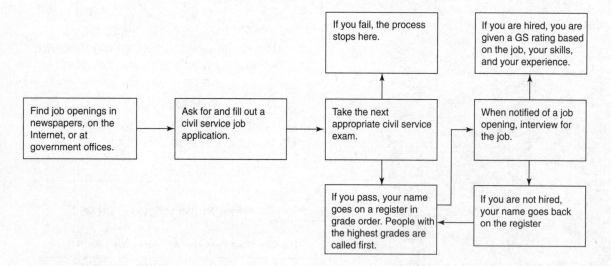

21. Which of the following is the best title for the flowchart?

 ○ A. A History of the Civil Service
 ○ B. The Qualifications of Civil Service Workers
 ○ C. Applying for Civil Service Jobs
 ○ D. Interviewing for a Civil Service Job

22. What does a civil servant's GS rating probably affect most?

 ○ A. salary
 ○ B. length of service
 ○ C. job security
 ○ D. education level

23. On which of the following values does the structure of the Civil Service system primarily rest?

 ○ A. patriotism
 ○ B. equal opportunity
 ○ C. freedom of speech
 ○ D. respect for seniority

Questions 24 and 25 refer to the following graphs.

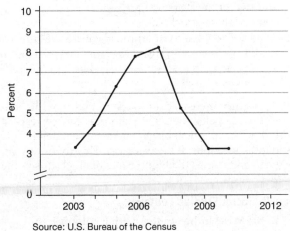

Interest Rates for Conventional Mortgages

Source: U.S. Bureau of the Census

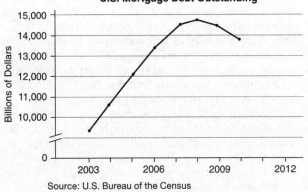

U.S. Mortgage Debt Outstanding

Source: U.S. Bureau of the Census

24. In 2005, what were the approximate interest rate and approximate total mortgage debt outstanding for a conventional mortgage?

○ A. 8 percent and $13,000 billion
○ B. 4 percent and $11,000 billion
○ C. 6 percent and $12,000 billion
○ D. 6 percent and $9,000 billion

25. Based on the graphs, how do mortgage interest rates and total mortgage debt outstanding compare?

○ A. Interest rates rise in direct proportion to decreases in total mortgage debt outstanding.
○ B. The higher the interest rate, the lower the total mortgage debt outstanding.
○ C. The lower the interest rate, the higher the total mortgage debt outstanding.
○ D. As interest rates rise and then fall, the total mortgage debt will move similarly but not at the same rate.

26. A culture hearth refers to the center of a culture—the source of its ideas, values, customs, fashions, and practices. An example of an ancient culture hearth was the area along the Nile River in Egypt. The agricultural, economic, social, artistic, and religious ideas and practices that grew up there spread through trade to other areas of the ancient world.

Which of the following is an example of a modern culture hearth with worldwide influence?

○ A. Pyongyang, capital of North Korea, which has a 95 percent literacy rate
○ B. Ottawa, capital of Canada, with a population of about one million
○ C. New Zealand, which exports wool and textiles
○ D. Hollywood, California, which produces movies and television shows enjoyed around the world

STOP. Congratulations! You have completed the Social Studies pretest. Your next step is to check your answers with the Social Studies Pretest Answers and Explanations that begins on the next page and then fill in the study planner that appears on page xvii.

SOCIAL STUDIES PRETEST ANSWERS AND EXPLANATIONS

Part I: Social Studies Skills

1. **C. The Voting Rights Act of 1965 gave the federal government oversight of state elections to end barriers against African American voting.** The passage described the historical events that led to the Voting Rights Act, and how this legislation ended the voting discrimination that certain states enacted after the passage of the Fifteenth Amendment.

2. **C. interpretation** According to the passage, the terms "strict construction" and "loose construction" refer to different ways in which people interpret the range of powers that the Constitution grants to the federal government.

3. **A. The FDA's new regulations would place a financial hardship on small food retailers.** According to the passage, smaller food retailers would feel more of the burden than larger establishments, and the Common Sense Nutritional Disclosure Act seeks to relieve this burden.

4. **C. "devastating"** This word highlights the author's point of view that the FDA's new regulations would be especially harmful to smaller food retailers.

5. **D. The argument is invalid, because it attempts to refute one reason against doing something while ignoring all the others.** The paragraph states that possible danger to the porcupine caribou is "one commonly cited" reason against drilling in the Arctic National Wildlife Refuge. This implies that there are other reasons as well. Thus, the author's conclusion that "we have no reason not to drill in the ANWR" is unsupported, since the author has attempted to refute only one of the possibly many reasons against drilling in the refuge.

6. **A. Some people depend on the porcupine caribou for food.** The primary evidence in this argument is that almost all of the species that have ever lived on Earth have gone extinct, and the vast majority of these extinctions happened naturally. The author uses this evidence to argue that the human threat to the porcupine caribou isn't a big deal. However, the author fails to consider the possibility that human-caused extinctions are worse than naturally-occurring ones. Choice (A) shows that the loss of the caribou by human hands would cause a severe problem: the loss of a major food source for some people.

7. **B. The map shows that most of the Warsaw Pact countries lay between the Soviet Union and Western countries, including France, West Germany, and Great Britain.** The passage states that the World War II Allies, which included France and Great Britain, formed NATO. It also states that West Germany was allowed to join NATO. And the map makes clear that the smaller Warsaw Pact countries lay geographically between those nations and the Soviet Union.

8. **A. In forming the Warsaw Pact, the Soviet Union greatly increased its access to oceanic coastlines.** Although most of the Warsaw Pact countries touched the ocean, most of their borders were land borders, and two of the Warsaw Pact countries were completely landlocked.

9. **A. $40\frac{2}{3}$** The three northernmost states are Maine (ME), New Hampshire (NH) and Vermont (VT). To find the average, sum the rainfall of each state and divide by 3. $\frac{41+42+39}{3} = 40\frac{2}{3}$.

10. **B. steadily increased, surpassing that of white voters in the 2012 elections.** The solid gray line corresponds to the rate at which black voters participated in presidential elections. It increases consistently from year to year, and shows the highest rate of all groups in the 2012 election.

Part II: Social Studies Content

1. **B. the West Indies to the British colonies; the British colonies to Africa; Africa to the West Indies** According to the map, the West Indies exported sugar and molasses to the British colonies in North America. The British colonies exported rum to Africa. Finally, Africa exported slaves and gold to the West Indies. The trade routes formed a triangle.

2. **A. Cargo ships never had to sail empty on any leg of a profitable triangular journey.** This is a general conclusion that is supported by the details of the map, which show goods traveling along each leg of the triangular trade route. Therefore, a very profitable journey must have meant a ship carried cargo on each leg of the route. The remaining options state details that may or may not be confirmed by the map.

3. **B. commercial bank** According to the descriptions, commercial banks provide services to businesses and other corporations. None of the other descriptions describe financial institutions making loans to companies. They focus either on national financial systems or on individual borrowers.

4. **B. tainted system** "Tainted" is a loaded word that indicates the author's belief that a "strong-mayor" system is inherently corrupt.

5. **D. No, because no indication is given that the current mayor will behave as past mayors did.** A strong-mayor system may enable—but does not guarantee—corruption. Past corruption is not by itself enough reason to have a strong suspicion toward the current government.

6. **D. serving on a jury** Serving on a jury, like voting, is a civic duty of each citizen. It is a way to participate in the judicial branch of government. Note that although choice (B), displaying the American flag, is a patriotic act, it does not involve participating in government in any way and so is not a way of participating in the political system.

7. **D. law and order** The hallmark of military rule is strict control over the citizenry; in other words, law and order.

8. **C. The French president has the power to dissolve the legislature, while the U.S. president does not.** The checkmark in the last row under "France" indicates that the French president can dissolve the legislature. The U.S. president does not have this power.

9. **B. Of all the presidents shown, the French president has the greatest variety of powers.** This statement is a conclusion, a generalization based on the details in the chart. Choices (A), (C), and (D) are specific details from the chart.

10. **D. The U.S. Supreme Court ruling in *Plessy v. Ferguson* was wrong because it infringed on freedoms guaranteed in the Constitution.** This statement is a rephrasing of the dissenting justice's opinion, or belief, about the case. The other statements are all facts from the paragraph.

11. **A. The nation's debt increased at a faster rate than did the U.S. population during the period shown on the graph.** You can tell this is true because the per capita debt figure increased steadily from 1990 to 2010. This would happen only if the debt increased faster than the population of the United States.

12. **D. Raise taxes and cut spending.** You can conclude from the text that to cut the national debt, the U.S. government would have to increase income (raise taxes) and lower costs (cut spending).

13. **C. A drought was significantly worsened due to lack of native vegetation.** According to the passage, the deforestation caused a significant portion of the drought that led to the Mayan collapse. Choices (A) and (D) are both causes, not effects, of the deforestation.

14. **C. Many cities had large populations because nearby coal and iron ore deposits meant jobs.** Coal and iron ore were among the most important raw materials of the Industrial Revolution. By examining the relationship of the location of the cities to that of the coalfields and iron ore deposits, you can conclude that Great Britain's most populous cities (with the exception of London) were large partly because of their proximity to the important raw materials of the Industrial Revolution. The remaining statements are details from the map.

15. **B. Great Britain's acceptance of Germany's takeover of Austria and Czechoslovakia in the late 1930s** Of all the options, this is the only one that has the element of concession without opposition that is the hallmark of appeasement.

16. **C. Knowing only latitude and longitude does not help a person get around a city.** Being able to pinpoint precise location in terms of latitude and longitude is not of much value in a city unless this information is translated into streets and highways. A basic receiver such as the one described in the paragraph does not

do that; however, other more sophisticated models, such as those built into vehicle dashboards or cellular phones, do just that.

17. **D. People value the lives of their children more than they value money.** This is the underlying assumption of the poster: that Americans have been willing to send their sons into battle where they risk their lives, but haven't been donating money to the war cause with equal willingness. The poster thus plays upon their sense of guilt.

18. **B. World War I** The poster is dated 1917, so the war is World War I.

19. **D. television ads on primetime** Today the government could probably reach the most people with TV ads rather than print ads, because so many people watch TV.

20. **D. The population of the colony of New York was smaller than that of Connecticut.** Since the chart shows the five colonies with the largest populations in 1750, it follows that any colony not listed has a population smaller than that of Connecticut, which ranked fifth. The other options are not supported by the data in the table.

21. **C. Applying for Civil Service Jobs.** This title best describes what the flowchart shows—the steps in applying for a civil service job.

22. **A. salary** The GS rating of a job, based on the job description and the candidate's skills and experience, is directly related to the salary level of the position. The other options would not be affected by the GS rating.

23. **B. equal opportunity** Since civil service jobs are open to all who apply and are awarded on merit, they are designed to provide equal opportunity for employment, regardless of gender, race, ethnicity, party affiliation, or other factors.

24. **C. 6 percent and $12,000 billion** Locate 2005 on each graph. (Note that each tic mark on the horizontal axis indicates a year, even if it is not labeled.) The first graph shows the mortgage interest rate was about 6 percent in 2005. The second graph shows the total outstanding mortgage debt was about $12,000 billion in 2005.

25. **D. As interest rates rise and then fall, the total mortgage debt will move similarly but not at the same rate.** Look at the general trend shown by each graph. Note that as interest rates rise and fall, the mortgage debts rise similarly but fall at a different rate.

26. **D. Hollywood, California, which produces movies and television shows enjoyed around the world** The movies and TV shows that originate in Hollywood are distributed worldwide, helping to spread American popular culture to other nations.

Determine Central Idea and Draw Conclusions

The **central idea** of a passage or graphic is the main idea it is intended to convey. This is supported by **details** or **examples**.

> At the outset of the Revolutionary War, the American colonies had a small navy of only 31 ships. To contest the far superior number of vessels in the British fleet, the colonies employed privateers, independent ships authorized to harass and capture enemy merchant and cargo ships. Armed with more than 14,000 guns, American privateers captured well over 2,000 enemy ships. These figures demonstrate how difficult it would have been, without the aid of privateers, for the colonies to win their independence against a larger, better equipped British Navy.

▶ What is the topic of this passage?
  (1) the importance of colonial privateers to winning the Revolutionary War
  (2) the fact that American privateers captured well over 2,000 enemy ships

Choice **(1)** is correct. The main point of the passage is that privateers were crucial to the colonies' success in their war for independence. The number of ships captured by privateers, referred to in choice (2), is used to support that point.

One skill needed to understand social studies information is the ability to **draw conclusions** from what you read or see. This skill requires you to go beyond what is directly stated and make an inference about what is meant or implied.

▶ Which of the following conclusions can be drawn based on this graph?

(1) The productivity of a bakery is based on a number of factors.
(2) The productivity of the bakery rises when more bakers are added.

You were correct if you selected choice **(2)**. As you look at the graph, the line—the number of cakes baked—rises steeply when more bakers are added. This associates the productivity of the bakery with the number of bakers. Choice (1) may well be true, but it is not a conclusion based on this graph.

Questions 1 through 3 are based on the following passage.

Theater was one of the most popular forms of art in ancient Greece, and one form of drama—tragedy—was central to Greek culture. Tragedies told familiar stories from Greek myths and epics, but actors portrayed the main roles, and a chorus narrated the background of the story and commented upon the action. These serious dramas centered on a main character who displayed exceptional attributes but also had a tragic flaw that caused his downfall. This flaw was often hubris, which is excessive pride or overconfidence.

1. Which of the following is the topic of the paragraph?

   A. the superiority of Greek theater
   B. the standard forms of Greek drama
   C. the characteristics of Greek tragedy
   D. the most popular Greek tragedies

2. Which of these details supports the central idea?

   A. Theater was one of the most popular Greek art forms.
   B. Tragedies were more important than comedies in ancient Greece.
   C. Greeks thought flaws other than hubris were not tragic.
   D. The main character in Greek drama has a tragic flaw that causes his downfall.

3. Which of these conclusions is supported by the paragraph?

   A. Ancient Greeks did not expect to see an original story each time they attended the theater.
   B. Playwrights in ancient Greece also wrote myths and epics.
   C. Tragedies in ancient Greece were judged on the basis of how serious their stories were.
   D. Only highly cultured people attended tragedies in ancient Greece.

Questions 4 and 5 are based on this graphic.

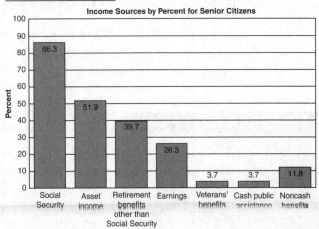

Source: Social Security Administration

4. The graph answers which of the following questions?

   A. What is the dollar value of the income for senior citizens?
   B. How much do senior citizens have in savings accounts?
   C. How many senior citizens are dependent upon veterans' benefits for their retirement income?
   D. Where do the incomes of senior citizens come from?

5. Which of the following conclusions can be drawn from this graph?

   A. More senior citizens need to continue to work in order to make ends meet now than in the past.
   B. Social Security benefits are the most widespread means of support for most senior citizens.
   C. Senior citizens who receive income from veterans' benefits also receive benefits from public assistance.
   D. Senior citizens who do not receive Social Security benefits get income from one or more other sources.

STUDY ADVICE

If you have trouble identifying the central idea of social studies passages, review the *Language Arts: Reading* lessons on pages 12–15. Identifying the main idea of a passage works the same way no matter what type of passage you are reading.

Interpret Words and Ideas

When you interpret social studies materials, you need to understand **key terms** in context. For instance, on page 502, the word *articles* is presented. You already know an everyday use of the word, such as "articles of clothing," but in the context on page 502, an *article* refers to a section of the U.S. Constitution.

Some social studies material is organized in **chronological** or time order. Look at the timeline below and answer a question about the sequence of events.

- Reading social studies materials requires understanding key terms in their context.
- Social studies material is often organized as a sequence of events or as steps in a process.
- Analyzing social studies materials often involves relating causes to effects.

Inventions in the 1870s

		Cylinder phonograph	Cash register
		Carbon arc	Carbon filament
Blasting gel	Telephone	lightbulb	lightbulb
1875	1876	1877	1879

▶ Which of the following events preceded the invention of the carbon arc lightbulb?
   (1) invention of the telephone
   (2) invention of the carbon filament lightbulb

Timelines are read left to right from oldest to most recent, so choice **(1)** is correct. Choice (2) refers to the carbon filament lightbulb, invented in 1879, a year after the carbon arc lightbulb.

Another way that social studies material is organized is by **cause and effect**, which is another way of asking "What resulted from this action?" or "What made this event happen?" Read the following paragraph to practice this skill.

The prices of goods and services are determined by the relationship between supply and demand. When supply exceeds demand, sellers must lower prices to stimulate sales; on the other hand, when demand exceeds supply, consumers bid up prices as they compete to purchase items or services that they desire.

To learn key social studies terms, pay close attention to the meaning of the words in **bold type** *throughout this unit.*

▶ Based on the theory of supply and demand, under which of the following scenarios would prices be most likely to rise?
   (1) The demand for a product exceeds that product's supply.
   (2) Producers and sellers advertise a product in order to stimulate demand for that product.

Choice **(1)** is correct. According to the law of supply and demand, prices rise when demand outpaces supply. Choice (2) describes a situation in which producers and sellers advertise to stimulate demand for their product, but without knowing whether the supply is limited, we cannot conclude that this would cause the price to increase.

Some questions may require you to understand that the fact that two events **correlate**, or happen at the same time, does not necessarily mean that one **caused** the other. Remember that causation can never be deduced from correlation alone.

PRACTICE 2

Questions 1 through 3 are based on this passage.

From 1820 to 1870, more than 7.5 million immigrants arrived on U.S. shores. That was more people than the entire U.S. population in 1810. Almost all of these immigrants came from Northern Europe, and a majority were Catholic. Historians have often focused on what pushed these emigrants out of Europe. During the 1840s, for example, Germany experienced a series of crop failures that, combined with social upheaval triggered by rapid industrialization in urban areas, produced riots, civil unrest, and open rebellion. During the same years, Ireland saw the infamous potato famine strike poor and working class Irish families, killing an estimated 700,000 people.

While those crises spurred Europeans to emigrate, a variety of factors created a simultaneous pull to immigrate to the United States. Letters home from friends and family members who had immigrated earlier often described the United States as a "land of plenty" and related stories of successful employment and plentiful land. Steamship companies offering passage across the Atlantic advertised with posters that showed majestic scenes of American abundance.

1. According to the passage, which of the following was a cause of Northern European immigration to the United States in the 1840s and 1850s?

   A. Americans' desire to double the population of the United States
   B. efforts by Northern European governments to reduce the number of people living in poverty
   C. political and social instability in some Northern European countries
   D. efforts to spread Catholicism to the United States

2. Based on the passage, which one of the following was most likely to have been featured on a steamship company poster?

   A. a folk-art painting depicting the life of the rural poor in the United States
   B. a portrait of an American politician from the 1840s
   C. a poster advertising an American product
   D. a painting of pioneers settling and farming productive prairie land

3. Which of the following results of Northern European immigration to the United States in the mid-1800s can be inferred from the passage?

   A. a spread of poverty in the United States
   B. a decline in political upheaval in Northern Europe
   C. a growth in the population of the United States
   D. a number of Americans converting to the Catholic faith

Questions 4 and 5 are based on this timeline.

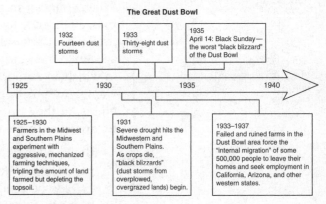

Source: www.pbs.org

4. Given the information in the timeline, which of the following would be a flawed inference?

   A. Mechanized farming contributed to dust storms.
   B. Internal migration led to overgrazing.
   C. Severe drought contributed to "black blizzards."
   D. Some farmers left the Dust Bowl before the worst dust storm hit the region.

5. Which of the following could have been a cause of the Great Dust Bowl?

   A. "black blizzards"
   B. internal migration
   C. depleted topsoil
   D. failed farms

Analyze Author's Purpose and Point of View

Any author of social studies material has a viewpoint and a purpose. Social studies material can have many purposes, such as to inform or educate (for example, a textbook or magazine article). Other materials, such as newspaper editorials and online blogs, are used to convince people of a point of view.

An author's **point of view** is his or her way of looking at the world. Some social scientists follow a method of examining the facts and coming to a conclusion. In other cases, an author may start with a point of view and assemble facts or evidence to support it.

When you read social studies materials, determine whether an author has a **bias**, a tendency to see one point of view. A bias is not a bad thing in and of itself (after all, we all have biases), but you should take the author's bias into account. One kind of material that displays extreme bias is **propaganda**, in which an author tries to convince people to act and think as the author wants. Authors of propaganda selectively include certain facts and ignore others, or they use loaded words to trigger emotional responses. Use the following example to practice finding the author's point of view.

> Until the 1980s, most anthropologists mistakenly estimated the native population in North America at the time of Columbus's expedition in 1492 to be somewhere between 2 million and 7 million people. They based these estimates on the number of Native Americans alive at the time of their first contact with European explorers and settlers. However, the estimates ignored the impact of infectious diseases, such as smallpox, which traveled much faster than humans did and would have decimated the native population before Europeans made contact with native people.

▶ What is the author's point of view about the population of North America in 1492?

   (1) that it was not exactly 2 million people or 7 million people but was somewhere in between those two numbers

   (2) that it was probably much larger than 7 million people

Choice **(2)** is correct. The author points out a reason to think that anthropologists prior to the 1980s undercounted the native population. Answer (1) gives the estimate of most anthropologists prior to the 1980s.

▶ Which of the following words is a clue to the author's viewpoint?

   (1) ignored

   (2) estimated

The correct choice is **(1)**. The author believes that the anthropologists' estimates were flawed because they ignored relevant information about the impact of diseases on the native population. Answer (2) misses the author's point; he doesn't fault them for estimating, but rather for ignoring evidence when they made their estimates.

KEY IDEAS

- Social studies material may be written to inform or to persuade.
- Thoughtful readers need to take an author's purpose and point of view into account.
- Some authors may express a bias or point of view by the selection of supporting details or use of loaded words.

TASC TEST TIP

You may be provided with a newspaper editorial, an online blog commentary, or a speech. Ask yourself, "What is the author's viewpoint? How are facts and evidence organized to be convincing? How are words chosen to have an impact?"

Questions 1 through 3 are based on the paragraph and poster below.

During World War I, the U.S. National War Garden Commission began a campaign to encourage private citizens to grow their own food as a means of supporting the war effort. This practice became very popular. With increased private food production, the government could reserve much of the cheaper, mass-produced food for the troops. The money saved in feeding soldiers freed up resources for other military needs. In addition, planting war gardens, also known as victory gardens, gave American citizens a sense of empowerment.

"Every Garden a Munition Plant"

Source: Library of Congress Poster by James Montgomery Flagg

1. Which of the following best describes the poster's use of the word *Victory*?

   A. ambiguous
   B. informative
   C. propagandistic
   D. impersonal

STUDY ADVICE

If you find it difficult to identify an author's point of view, review the *Language Arts: Reading* lesson on page 30.

2. What is meant by the poster's caption "Every Garden a Munition Plant"?

   A. War gardens require a great deal of time to cultivate.
   B. Citizens who plant war gardens encourage a sense of community in their hometowns.
   C. Citizens who plant war gardens help supply the war effort with essential resources.
   D. War gardens provide an excellent opportunity to learn about gardening, canning, and food drying.

3. The author's primary purpose in writing the paragraph accompanying the poster is most likely to

   A. describe war gardens and explain their popularity in the United States
   B. encourage patriotism and continued support for a strong United States military
   C. distinguish the efforts of American citizens during World War I from those of citizens in other countries
   D. rebut the accusations of those who claimed that civilians did not do enough to support the U.S. war effort in World War I

Question 4 is based on the following dialogue.

Congresswoman Burns: The new organic food safety regulations are likely to increase the average cost of some food staples. The costs are justified, however, by the peace of mind that comes from knowing your food is safe and healthy.

Concerned Citizen: Rising prices are a cancer eating away at our families. High costs will drive people away from healthy foods and wind up harming our children's diets. Instead of buying wholesome, natural products, parents will feed their kids fast food.

4. Which of the following constitute "loaded" words the Concerned Citizen uses to support her point?

   A. high costs
   B. fast food
   C. a cancer
   D. our children's diets

Evaluate Author's Reasoning and Evidence

Social studies authors in print and online publications use a variety of strategies to support their viewpoints. They may use the following:

- **Facts**—information that can be proven to be true
- **Opinions**—beliefs about a concept or situation
- **Judgments**—conclusions that are supported by reasons and evidence

On the TASC Social Studies Test, you need to read carefully to distinguish among these three concepts.

▶ Indicate whether each of the following statements is a fact (F), an opinion (0), or a judgment (J).

(1) ___ Because it raises the amount employers will pay in payroll taxes, the new tax bill may contribute to higher unemployment.

(2) ___ Last year, manufacturing output in our state rose by 4.6 percent over the previous year.

(3) ___ We should limit the role played by the federal government in formulating energy policy for our region of the country.

Statement (1) is a judgment; the author's conclusion (that the bill may increase unemployment) is based on evidence (that the bill raises payroll taxes). Statement (2) is a fact; the truth or falsity of the statement can be checked against empirical data. Statement (3) is an opinion; the author makes a recommendation (limit the role of the federal government) but offers no evidence or reasoning to support it.

To be credible, an author needs to support his or her claims with evidence. Part of your job on the Social Studies Test is to answer questions about whether or not an author's claims are supported.

Delaware was the first state to ratify the U.S. Constitution. Because of its history of favorable corporate tax policies, Delaware is today home to 63 percent of Fortune 500 corporations. There is no doubt then that Delaware's Freedom-of-Information Act, requiring the state government to respond within 15 days of a request, should serve as a model for similar acts in other U.S. states.

▶ Does the author support the claim of the passage?
(1) Yes, because he believes and asserts that there is no doubt about the truth of the claim.
(2) No, because he asserts the truth of the claim without offering evidence relevant to the claim.

Choice **(2)** is correct. The author's claim is that Delaware's Freedom-of-Information Act should serve as a model for similar acts in other states, but the other statements in the passage are irrelevant to that claim. Choice (1) is incorrect because stating a claim firmly ("no doubt") does not provide *support* for the claim.

KEY IDEAS

- An author's point of view may be supported by facts, opinions, and reasoned judgment.
- While reading, analyze whether information is a fact, an opinion, or a conclusion based on reasoning or evidence.
- A careful reader evaluates whether an author supports his or her claims with evidence.

TASC TEST TIP

When you read social studies material, ask yourself, "What is the claim being made? Is evidence provided to support this claim? Is the evidence relevant to the claim and sufficient and credible enough to support it?"

1. Consultant: Finding a reliable energy supply is vital to Cambodia, a country still recovering from decades of civil war and genocide in the late 1970s. Damming the Mekong River could solve Cambodia's energy supply problems. However, since the Mekong flows through China, Myanmar, Laos, and Thailand before it reaches Cambodia, regional cooperation will be necessary.

    Which of the following is an opinion, and not a fact, presented by the consultant?

    A. Damming the Mekong could solve Cambodia's energy problems.
    B. The Mekong River flows through several countries before reaching Cambodia.
    C. Cambodia experienced civil war.
    D. Many Cambodians were killed in the late 1970s.

Question 2 is based on this cartoon referencing the labor movement of the early 20th century.

SPITING HIMSELF.
—Morris for the George Matthew Adams Service.

Source: Literary Digest 9/6/1919. Originally from the George Matthew Adams Service (Morris).

2. Which of the following represents the viewpoint of the cartoonist?

    A. Strikes can achieve better working conditions.
    B. Strikes have a detrimental impact on workers.
    C. Farmworkers are more likely to engage in strikes than are factory workers.
    D. Strikes should hamper production.

3. Historian: Ancient Greece was the greatest of the early civilizations. While the Babylonians may have had arithmetic and ancient Egypt built the pyramids, ancient Greece gave us our first taste of democracy.

    Which of the following is a fact that the historian uses to support her opinion?

    A. Ancient Greece was the greatest early civilization.
    B. Babylonians made use of arithmetic.
    C. The pyramids were built in ancient Egypt.
    D. Ancient Greece pioneered democracy.

Question 4 is based on the following chart.

The Articles of Confederation were the predecessor to the United States Constitution.

	The Articles of Confederation	The Constitution
Federal Court System	No system of federal courts	Court system exists to deal with issues between citizens, states
Regulating Trade	No provision to regulate interstate trade	Congress has the right to regulate trade between states
Executive Power	No executive with power; president merely presided over Congress	Executive branch is headed by president who chooses Cabinet and has checks on power of judiciary and legislature
Raising an Army	Congress could not draft troops; depended on states to contribute forces	Congress can raise an army to deal with military situations
Sovereignty	Sovereignty resides in states	The Constitution is the supreme law of the land
Taxes	Congress could ask states to pay taxes	Congress has the right to levy taxes on individuals

4. Which of the following is a conclusion supported by the table above, rather than a detail stated in the table?

    A. The Constitution allows Congress to enforce collection of taxes, whereas the Articles of Confederation did not.
    B. The Constitution grants more power to the federal government than did the Articles of Confederation.
    C. There were no national armed forces before the Constitution was drafted.
    D. Trade was not nationally regulated by the Articles of Confederation.

Analyze Relationships Between Materials

Content Presented in Graphic Format

Social studies content is often presented in graphic form. Two of the most useful displays are graphs and maps.

Circle graphs are used to show how a whole is divided into parts; they show fractions or percents.

Line graphs and **bar graphs** organize material by using labels on the bottom axis and values on the side.

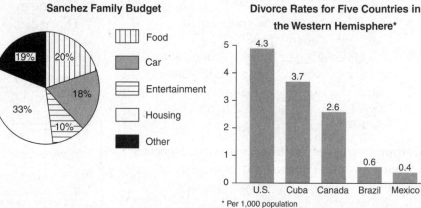

Maps use a **legend** (also called the **key**) to explain symbols, a **compass rose** to indicate directions, and **scales** to determine distances. To interpret information on a map, note any labels printed directly on the map. Then, check the legend to see whether the color, shading, or symbols shown give additional information.

▶ According to the map, what is England's climate?
   (1) mild and humid
   (2) cold and humid

In this map, England appears just to the left and slightly above the center. It is shown in gray, indicating that its climate is "mild and humid." The correct answer here is choice (1).

PRACTICE 5.1

1. According to the circle graph on page 476, the greatest portion of the Sanchez family's budget is spent on which two items?

   A. housing and food
   B. housing and entertainment
   C. food and car
   D. entertainment and other

2. Which of the following statements is supported by the bar graph on page 476?

   A. Cuba has the highest divorce rate in the hemisphere.
   B. Mexico has the lowest divorce rate in the hemisphere.
   C. Mexico's divorce rate is decreasing.
   D. Brazil has a higher divorce rate than Mexico.

Questions 3 and 4 refer to the following graph.

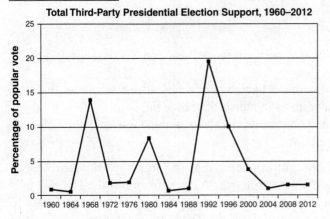

3. Based on the graph, you may validly infer that support for third-party candidates _____ during the 1980s and 1990s.

   A. steadily increased
   B. steadily decreased
   C. neither increased nor decreased
   D. fluctuated

4. The graph can be used to disprove which one of the following claims?

   A. Third-party candidates have not enjoyed significant support in the 21st century.
   B. The third-party candidate who garnered the most support since 1960 was Ross Perot in 1992.
   C. Third party candidates have never captured more than 10 percent of the popular vote in any presidential election.
   D. In most elections, all third-party candidates combined get less than 5 percent of the popular vote.

Questions 5 and 6 are based on the following map.

5. What does this map show?

   A. political boundaries in the ancient Americas
   B. physical features of the Americas
   C. how agriculture spread in the Americas
   D. all ancient civilizations of the Americas

6. Which of the following statements is supported by the information on the map?

   A. Both the Andes civilization and Mesoamerica domesticated maize.
   B. Both the Andes civilization and Mesoamerica domesticated beans.
   C. Agriculture developed in the Andes civilization before it did in Mesoamerica.
   D. Agriculture spread more rapidly northward than southward.

Integrating Text and Graphic Content

In reading social studies materials and the materials you encounter in daily life, you often have to combine text information with a graphic. For example, an online article about a conflict in Africa may have a map. A newspaper graph with information about new immigrants in your community may accompany a story about their contributions to local health care and manufacturing industries.

Practice combining information with the passage and graphic below.

Consumer confidence is an economic indicator that reflects how optimistic consumers are about their personal finances, given the state of the economy. When consumer confidence shows a monthly trend of decline month after month, consumers are pessimistic about their chances of finding and keeping good jobs. When their confidence is low, consumers spend less—especially on nonessential items—and tend to save more of their money. On the other hand, when confidence is high, consumers will make more discretionary, or optional, purchases.

Consumer Confidence by Month in Country X

► Which of the following is a valid inference based on the passage and the graph above?

(1) Consumers in Country X likely spent a higher percentage of their income on luxury items in March than they did in July.

(2) Unemployment in Country X is likely to remain high for the remainder of the year shown.

Choice **(1)** is correct. The graph shows that the trend in consumer confidence has generally been in decline from March through July. The text tells you that when consumer confidence is lower, consumers are less likely to spend, especially on nonessential goods. These two statements combined support choice (1). Choice (2) cannot be inferred from the information in the passage or that in the graph. Neither of those sources provides a basis to make a prediction about future unemployment.

PRACTICE 5.2

Questions 1 through 3 relate to the following passage and map.

The sea otter (*Enhydra lutris*) is a marine mammal native to the coasts of the northern and eastern North Pacific Ocean. At one time, sea otters populated the entire coast of what is now the state of California and farther south along Mexico's Baja California coastline. Prior to 1741, the sea otter population worldwide is estimated to have been 150,000–300,000.

Between 1741 and 1911, however, sea otters were hunted extensively for their fur, and the world population fell to just 1,000–2,000 individuals. By 1911, the wild sea otter population in California was limited exclusively to a small area around Monterey Bay.

Fortunately, an international ban on hunting, conservation efforts, and programs to reintroduce the sea otter into previously populated areas have contributed to numbers rebounding, and the species now occupies about two-thirds of its former range. Despite these successes, sea otter populations in California have declined, and the sea otter remains classified as an endangered species.

Current Range of the Sea Otter in California

* Maps and ranges not to scale

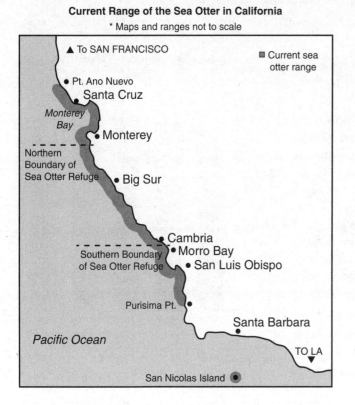

1. According to the passage, which one of the following statements about the sea otter is true?

   A. Sea otter conservation efforts have been more successful in areas outside of California than they have been within California.
   B. Sea otter populations were threatened by water pollution as well as by extensive hunting.
   C. The sea otter population is now about two-thirds of its pre-1741 number.
   D. Sea otters have been able to live in habitats from which they were once eliminated.

2. Which of the following conclusions can be drawn from the information in the passage and the map?

   A. Sea otters will soon have the same range they had prior to 1741.
   B. Sea otter habitat has been restored only within the boundaries of the Sea Otter Refuge.
   C. Sea otters are still hunted in the area north of Point Ano Nuevo.
   D. The current range of the sea otter in California is larger than it was in 1911.

3. The author of the passage would be most likely to agree with which of the following statements about the information in the map?

   A. The range of sea otters shown on the map indicates that sea otter conservation programs are no longer needed.
   B. The range of sea otters shown on the map is identical to the range of sea otters prior to 1741.
   C. Without conservation efforts and reintroduction programs, the range of sea otters in California would be smaller than what is shown on the map.
   D. Ten years from now, the range of sea otters in California will be larger than what is currently shown on the map.

Interpret Data and Statistics

Social studies materials often involve data or statistics. The TASC Social Studies Test will not require you to perform extensive calculations, and you will not use a calculator during the Social Studies Test. However, you may be asked to interpret data to spot **trends,** make **comparisons** or **contrasts,** or make **inferences** from data.

Franklin County Family Finances			
Year	Median income (family of 4)	Average % to taxes	Average % to savings
2009	$40,800	27%	5.2%
2010	$41,500	28%	6.0%
2011	$42,300	29%	5.5%
2012	$44,100	29%	5.1%

▶ Which of the following statements about Franklin County families is supported by the table?

(1) An increase in their median income over the last few years has caused those families to save less.

(2) An increase in their median income has not necessarily resulted in an increase in the percent of their income saved by those families.

Choice **(2)** is correct. As the median income has increased over the last few years, the rate of savings has not, on average increased. Choice (1) is not supported because the table contains no information about what causes Franklin County families to behave in any way.

Some questions may ask you to use graphs to make comparisons or to identify trends.

▶ What of the following trends is indicated by the data in the chart?

(1) Between 2003 and 2007, foreign arrivals from overseas grew at a faster pace than foreign arrivals from North America.

(2) Between 2003 and 2007, foreign arrivals from North America grew at a faster pace than foreign arrivals from overseas.

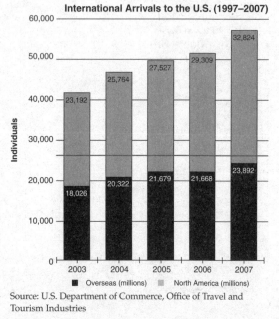

International Arrivals to the U.S. (1997–2007)

■ Overseas (millions) ■ North America (millions)

Source: U.S. Department of Commerce, Office of Travel and Tourism Industries

Choice **(2)** is correct here. Foreign arrivals from North America grew from a little over 23 million in 2003 to almost 33 million in 2007, an increase of around 41 percent. Meanwhile, overseas arrivals rose from roughly 18 million in 2003 to just under 24 million, a change of approximately 33 percent growth.

PRACTICE 6

Question 1 is based on the following table.

New Mexico: Population by Age, 2010	
Under 18	518,672
18–19	61,169
20–24	142,370
25–34	267,245
35–49	393,362
50–64	404,106
65 & over	272,255
Total	**2,059,179**

Adapted from U.S. Census Bureau

1. The table provides data that will allow you to answer which one of the following questions about New Mexico in 2010?

   A. What specific age was the median age?
   B. How many residents were teenagers?
   C. What percent of residents were 50 or older?
   D. Why were individuals over 65 such a small part of the population?

Question 2 is based on the following line graph.

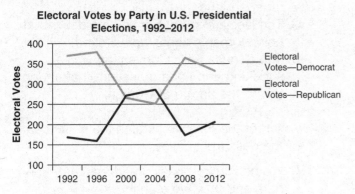

2. The information in the graph supports the conclusion that in the presidential elections from 1992 to 2012,

   A. Democrats and Republicans won the presidency an equal number of times.
   B. the average margin of victory was higher in years when a Democrat won than in years when a Republican won.
   C. the average margin of victory was higher in years when a Republican won than in years when a Democrat won.
   D. more electoral votes were cast in the 2008 presidential election than were cast in the 1996 presidential election.

Questions 3 and 4 are based on the following chart.

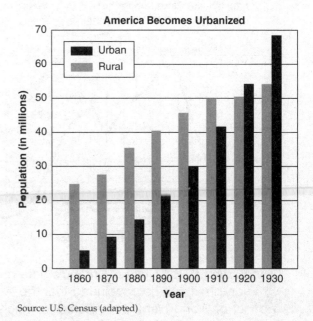

Source: U.S. Census (adapted)

3. According to the bar graph, in what year were there approximately as many Americans living in rural locations as there were in urban settings?

   A. 1860
   B. 1910
   C. 1920
   D. 1930

4. During the decades represented in the graph, the urban population of the United States grew at increasing rates, while the rural population

   A. continued to grow at a steady rate.
   B. grew and then shrank.
   C. continued to grow, but at decreasing rates.
   D. grew at first and then stopped growing.

SOCIAL STUDIES SKILLS PRACTICE QUESTIONS

Questions 1 and 2 are based on the following line graph and timeline.

Unemployment Rates During the New Deal: Percentage of Jobless Nonfarm Workers, 1926–1946

Source: U.S. Census Bureau, Bureau of Labor Statistics

1. According to the Census Bureau's data on the graph, it can be concluded that the onset of World War II contributed to which change in the U.S. unemployment rate?

   A. The unemployment rate stabilized at the beginning of World War II and remained stable until the war's end.
   B. The unemployment rate declined consistently until shortly before the war's end.
   C. The unemployment rate decreased during World War II but remained above the normal rate throughout the war.
   D. The unemployment rate increased gradually throughout the war.

2. According to the graph, the most significant and uninterrupted change in the U.S. unemployment rate between 1926 and 1946 occurred immediately after

   A. the stock market crash
   B. FDR's first New Deal
   C. the New Deal, Part 2, began
   D. the U.S. entered World War II

Questions 3 and 4 are based on the following passage.

The women's rights movement in the United States gained strength with the 1848 Seneca Falls Convention. The defining document of this gathering was the Declaration of Sentiments, which was patterned after the Declaration of Independence but focused on the fact that women lacked basic freedoms that men enjoyed. The revolutionary nature of the Seneca Falls Convention was apparent in the public's response to the event. One newspaper described Seneca Falls as "the most shocking and unnatural event ever recorded in the history of womanity."

3. Which of the following statements based on the passage is an opinion, not a fact?

   A. The Seneca Falls Convention helped the women's rights movement gain strength.
   B. The Declaration of Sentiments was modeled on the Declaration of Independence.
   C. The Declaration of Sentiments described how women's rights were limited.
   D. The Seneca Falls Convention was a shocking and unnatural event that undermined the nature of women.

4. Which of the following states the main idea of the passage above?

   A. Women lacked basic freedoms that men had, and they were angry.
   B. The Seneca Falls Convention was open to both men and women.
   C. The women's rights movement was stronger in Seneca Falls than in the rest of the United States.
   D. The Seneca Falls Convention was important in the fight for women's rights.

Questions 5 and 6 refer to the following map.

Reported Cases of Human Plague—United States, 1970–2010

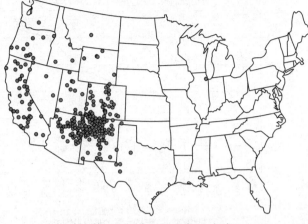

1 dot placed in county of exposure for each plague case

Source: Centers for Disease Control

5. Which of the following conclusions is supported by this map?

   A. More than half of the reported cases of human plague in the United States between 1970 and 2010 were reported in four states.

   B. More than 99 percent of diphtheria-related deaths in the United States between 1970 and 2010 occurred in the western half of the United States.

   C. The majority of reported cases of plague in the American Southwest spread from one infected person.

   D. In the United States, human plague most frequently occurs within larger cities, where the risk of contagion is greatest.

6. The map above could be used to disprove which of the following claims?

   A. There were more cases of plague in the United States between 2000 and 2010 than there were between 1990 and 2000.

   B. Although many cases of plague have been reported in the United States since 1970, no deaths have been reported.

   C. Several cases of plague were reported on the East Coast of the United States between 1970 and 2010.

   D. Plague is less virulent in colder climates than it is in warmer climates.

Question 7 is based on the following passage and chart.

The invention of the cotton gin by Eli Whitney in 1784 revolutionized the cotton industry in the American South. The separation of the cotton seeds and fibers, once a painstaking task that slaves performed by hand, could now be done quickly by machine. This made cotton goods more affordable, thereby increasing international demand for these goods and, consequently, the profits of cotton farmers. Ironically, however, the cotton gin did not reduce the South's reliance on slavery. In fact, with the boom of the cotton industry, more slaves were used to pick the cotton at a faster rate to keep up with the increasing demand for cotton.

7. Which of the following conclusions is supported by the passage?

   A. Eli Whitney invented the cotton gin with the hope that it would reduce slavery.

   B. The cotton gin had little impact on the cotton industry in the South.

   C. After the invention of the cotton gin, many plantation owners found that they needed fewer slaves.

   D. The effects of the cotton gin on the cotton industry actually led to an increased demand for slaves in the South.

Question 8 is based on the following graph.

State Population Change per Year (%)

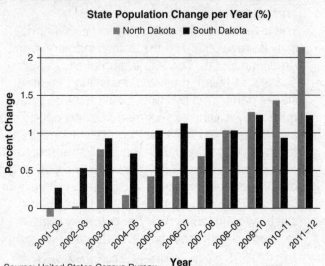

Source: United States Census Bureau

The above graph shows the percent increase, year by year, in the populations of each of North Dakota and South Dakota over eleven years.

8. Which of the following statements about the eleven-year period is supported by the graph above?

   A. North Dakota's population increased every year, while South Dakota's stayed the same.
   B. The population of South Dakota was originally greater than that of North Dakota, but in 2012, the population of North Dakota was greater than that of South Dakota.
   C. In most years, the percent population increase in South Dakota was greater than that in North Dakota.
   D. In most years, the percent population increase in North Dakota was greater than that in South Dakota.

Questions 9 and 10 are is based on the following graphic.

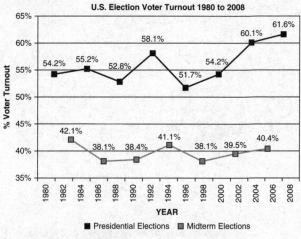

Source: weathertrends360.com

9. Which one of the following statements about elections in the years 1980–2008 is supported by the graph?

   A. Voter turnout for midterm elections displayed a greater range than voter turnout for presidential elections.
   B. The data for voter turnout for presidential elections displayed no mode.
   C. On average, half as many voters turned out for midterm elections as turned out for presidential elections.
   D. A smaller percentage of voters turned out for each midterm election than turned out for each presidential election.

10. The graph provides information that would allow you to answer which one of the following questions?

   A. Why did a greater percentage of voters turn out for the 1994 midterm election than for other midterm elections?
   B. The average voter turnout for midterm elections was approximately how much lower than that for presidential elections for the years 1980–2008?
   C. How does voter turnout for a presidential election affect voter turnout for the midterm election two years later?
   D. How did the presence of a high-profile third party candidate in the 1992 presidential election affect voter turnout?

Questions 11 and 12 are based on the following excerpt from a speech.

Today, 8 million adult Americans, more than the entire population of Michigan, have not finished five years of school. Nearly 20 million have not finished eight years of school. Nearly 54 million—more than one-quarter of all America—have not . . . finished high school.

Each year more than 100,000 high school graduates, with proved ability, do not enter college because they cannot afford it. And if we cannot educate today's youth, what will we do in 1970 when elementary enrollment will be 5 million greater than 1960? . . .

In many places, classrooms are overcrowded and curricula are outdated. Most of our qualified teachers are underpaid, and many of our paid teachers are unqualified. So we must give every child a place to sit and a teacher to learn from. Poverty must not be a bar to learning, and learning must offer an escape from poverty.

—President Lyndon Johnson, May 22, 1964
Great Society Speech, University of Michigan

11. Which of the following statements from the speech is an opinion rather than a fact?

A. Each year more than 100,000 high school graduates do not enter college.
B. 8 million adult Americans have not finished five years of school.
C. Most of our qualified teachers are underpaid.
D. More than one-quarter of Americans have not finished high school.

12. Which of the following would be the best title for this excerpt?

A. "A History of Educational Problems"
B. "Why Michigan Is Falling Behind"
C. "Why College Is Unaffordable"
D. "Our Duty Is to Educate Our Children"

STUDY ADVICE

Many questions on the TASC Social Studies Test will reward you for the skills you just learned. You may sometimes need to combine those skills with some basic knowledge of social studies content. The next five chapters will provide you with an overview of that content.

Questions 13 and 14 are based on the following information and graph.

From 1861 to 1865, the United States fought a devastating Civil War. The Union (the North) eventually defeated the Confederates (the South). The following chart gives facts about the population in both Union and Confederate states in 1860.

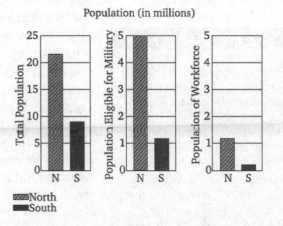

Population (in millions)

13. Which of the following statements is supported by the information and graph?

A. The war was likely to end in a stalemate.
B. Population differences would have no effect on the war's outcome.
C. The Union states had significant population advantages in the war.
D. The population in the Union states grew substantially during the war.

14. The graph provides information that allows you to answer which one of the following questions about the Civil War?

A. What percentage of the total population in the United States fought in the military?
B. What percentage of the total population of the United States was eligible for the military?
C. Why was the population in the workforce much lower than the population eligible for the military?
D. How did differences in skills held by people in the workforce affect the outcome of the Civil War?

Exploration, Colonialism, and the American Revolution

The first Americans traveled from Asia across the Bering Strait into North America and, over many generations, down to South America. Called **Native Americans**, they established extensive tribal cultures and several advanced civilizations.

In the late 1400s, **explorers** from Europe searched for a sea route to Asia so they could trade for Asian gold and spices. They traveled around the tip of Africa. However, in 1492, Christopher Columbus convinced Spain to finance a trip west, across the Atlantic Ocean. When he reached land, he thought he had found India and called the inhabitants Indians. Later explorers realized that they had found a "New World," and many European nations set out to establish **colonies** there. The first explorers were searching for valuable resources and for the glory of conquest. This colonization led to tragedy for many Native Americans who died from diseases or were killed, enslaved, or forced off their lands.

In the 1500s and 1600s, European nations, including Spain, France, England, and the Netherlands, established settlements in North America. Settlements were established to gain power and wealth or to provide colonists a place for permanent residence. The first permanent English settlement was established in Jamestown, Virginia, in 1607. In 1620, the **Pilgrims** sailed to the Americas aboard the *Mayflower* and established a second English colony in Massachusetts. Beginning about 1675, colonists began importing a large number of slaves who had been forcibly taken from Africa. Many were put to work on the plantation system in the Southern colonies.

The colonies grew rapidly in the early 1700s. When England defeated France in the French and Indian War (1754–1763), England acquired many of France's American colonies. After the war, England sought to regain more control over the Thirteen Colonies. It also sought to recover economically from the debts caused by the costly war. New British taxes and policies troubled the colonists; however, it was not until 1775 that a war for independence seemed inevitable. After a series of skirmishes, the **Continental Congress** assigned George Washington to lead the Continental Army and ordered publication of the **Declaration of Independence** on July 4, 1776.

Despite the superiority of the well-trained British forces, the Americans had the advantage of defending their own land and eventually forged a fighting force with strong military leaders. The **American Revolution** lasted until the surrender of the British at Yorktown in 1781. In 1783, the final treaty to end the war resulted in the recognition of American independence. The new nation initially formed a weak national government through the **Articles of Confederation**. This first effort stressed a loose confederation of the states with strong local control. Over time, many colonial leaders recognized the need for a centralized government. The principles of this government were established in the **U.S. Constitution**, which was ratified in 1788. To counter fears of an overly powerful government, the first ten amendments to the Constitution, the **Bill of Rights**, promised many individual freedoms, such as freedom of speech and assembly.

KEY IDEAS

- European explorers sought wealth and conquest in the New World from the 1400s to the 1600s.
- The Thirteen Colonies declared independence from England in 1776.
- America won its independence in 1783 and ratified the U.S. Constitution in 1788.

TASC TEST TIP

Reviewing key vocabulary can help you prepare for the TASC Test. As you review, look up any words that you do not understand. Pay special attention to the words in bold type.

PRACTICE 1

Questions 1 and 2 refer to the following map.

European Colonial Settlements, 1650

St. Lawrence River

Quebec

Montreal

Boston

Plymouth

New Haven

New Amsterdam

Atlantic Ocean

Jamestown

Roanoke Island

St. Augustine

Legend:
- Dutch
- English
- French
- Spanish
- Swedish

N W E S

1. Choose the correct phrase that would fill in the blank.
   Based on the map, _____ had the southernmost colony in 1650.

   A. the Dutch
   B. the English
   C. the Spanish
   D. the Swedish

2. Which of the following conclusions is supported by the map?

   A. By 1650, Spain had conquered most of North America.
   B. The English established several colonies in the New World.
   C. The Dutch established their colonies in the western part of North America.
   D. French colonies extended along the East Coast between Boston and Jamestown.

3. Some of the early colonists did not come to the New World to gain power and wealth. These groups came seeking freedom from persecution.

   Which immigrant group is most similar to those early colonists?

   A. African slaves who were involuntarily brought to work on plantations
   B. Mexican workers who came to the U.S. to earn better wages than they could at home
   C. British businessmen who visited the U.S. to invest in media companies
   D. Haitian refugees who fled to the U.S. to escape a dictatorship

4. Which of the following was a cause of the American Revolution?

   A. France's defeat in the French and Indian War
   B. increased British taxes and restrictions on the colonies
   C. Britain's acquisition of France's colonies in North America
   D. the publication of the Declaration of Independence

5. The first amendment to the U.S. Constitution states: "Congress shall make no law abridging the right of the people peaceably to assemble, and to petition the government for a redress of grievances."

   Based on the passage on page 486, what is the most likely reason the framers of the Constitution included these guarantees?

   A. They were planning to organize assemblies.
   B. They were concerned about the government becoming tyrannical.
   C. They were hoping to petition the government.
   D. They were attempting to prevent a redress of grievances.

Westward Expansion, the Civil War, and Reconstruction

Early in the history of the United States, the North and the South diverged economically. The North developed a varied economy that included industry and commerce as well as agriculture. Slavery had been legal throughout the North during the colonial period. However, by the early 1800s, it was **abolished** in all Northern states. Women and **immigrants**, as well as men, provided labor for the growing economy in the North.

The Southern economy was based largely on agriculture. By the 1800s, there was one major crop in the South: cotton. Southern farmers came to depend on increasing numbers of slaves to do the work of planting and harvesting.

As the United States expanded during the early 1800s, the North and the South struggled to maintain a balance of power. New states were generally added in pairs, one slave and one free. But there was increasing tension over the vast western territory that had become part of the United States by the mid-1800s. In the 1850s, Congress voted that the territories themselves should decide whether or not to allow slavery. This soon led to war in Kansas. The violence in Kansas foreshadowed the violence that soon tore up the nation.

In the late 1850s, political parties fractured over the slavery issue. Four candidates ran for president in 1860. Abraham Lincoln, who promised to halt the spread of slavery (although not abolish it where it already existed), won. Opposed to Lincoln's policies, most slave states **seceded** from the United States. They set up their own government, called the **Confederacy**. By April 1861, the United States (called the **Union**) and the Confederacy were at war.

At first it seemed as if the Confederacy might win. However, by the summer of 1863, the Confederacy began to wear down. Ammunition, uniforms, and shoes were in short supply for Confederate soldiers, because the South lacked industry. There were food shortages for soldiers and civilians alike. The war was fought mostly in the South, and the destruction was terrible. After four long years, in 1865, Confederate general Robert E. Lee surrendered to Union general Ulysses S. Grant. The Civil War ended.

For the next 12 years, federal troops oversaw the rebuilding of the South. This period was called **Reconstruction**. Schools were established for former slaves, who were all freed when the war ended. However, the **sharecropping** system, which kept black farmers enslaved economically, soon came into being. Whites who came back to power as Reconstruction ended in the South in the 1870s prevented African Americans from exercising their right to vote.

The 19th century was also characterized by a wrangle for power and land between the U.S. government and Native Americans. The U.S. government at various times made and broke treaties, waged war, or attempted to absorb Native Americans into European culture. During the early 19th century, the predominant policy was one of relocation. In one famous series of relocations, dubbed the "Trail of Tears," tens of thousands of Native Americans from five tribes were removed on foot from their homeland in the Southeast to territory west of the Mississippi; many thousands died along the way. During the latter part of the 19th century, federal Native American policy shifted toward a focus on *assimilation*, or making Native Americans conform to the customs of European society.

PRACTICE 2

1. Which of the following disagreements was a main cause of the Civil War?

   A. whether cotton should be the main crop in the South
   B. whether slavery should continue to exist
   C. whether the United States should expand westward
   D. whether slavery should be permitted in territories in the West

2. In 1820, Missouri proposed to enter the Union as a slave state. Based on the passage, what do you think was the response of Northerners in Congress?

   A. They supported having another slave state join the Union.
   B. They lobbied against having Missouri join the Union at all.
   C. To balance the admission of Missouri, they agreed to a compromise in which Maine was admitted as a free state.
   D. They started a war to prevent Missouri from attaining statehood.

3. In the mid-1950s, the country of Vietnam was divided. There was a communist government in the North and a noncommunist government in the South. The two fought for control of Vietnam. In 1975, the communists won. Vietnam was united under this form of government.

   Because both wars _____, the Vietnam War and the U.S. Civil War can be said to share some similarities.

   A. involved racial conflict
   B. saw the addition of new territory upset the balance of power
   C. concluded with the formation of new nations
   D. concluded with the reunification of the nation

Questions 4 and 5 refer to the following photographs of people who served in South Carolina's state government in 1868.

Photography by Katherine Wetzel. Reprinted with the permission of The Museum of the Confederacy, Richmond, Virginia.

4. Which of the following is a fact confirmed by information in the photographs?

   A. Southern Democrats were treated very well during Reconstruction.
   B. It was unfair that former Confederate soldiers could vote during Reconstruction.
   C. In 1868, many African Americans served in the government of South Carolina.
   D. The most qualified leaders in South Carolina government in 1868 were African Americans.

5. Which of the following conclusions about the course of Reconstruction is supported by the photographs and the passage on page 488?

   A. African Americans in the South gained and then lost political power.
   B. African Americans in the South lost and then gained political power.
   C. Whites in the South gained and then lost political power.
   D. African Americans served in government in each Southern state.

Industrialization, Immigration, and the Progressive Era

KEY IDEAS

- The U.S. underwent rapid industrialization starting in the mid-1800s.
- Immigrants came from many places to work in the expanding American industries.
- Rapid industrialization brought problems, which labor unions and reformers tried to solve, especially during the Progressive Era.

TASC TEST TIP

The TASC Social Studies Test examines your ability to interpret graphs, charts, maps, and other visual sources of information.

In the mid-1800s, American industries, which had been growing steadily since the late 1700s, began a period of extremely fast growth. This rapid **industrialization** occurred for several interconnected reasons. With the addition of the vast western territories, the United States gained plentiful **natural resources**. Among these resources were materials, such as metals, needed to manufacture new products and machines, and fuels, such as coal, needed to run these machines. Another reason for rapid industrialization was the invention of many new machines and new industrial processes. With these new inventions and processes, manufactured goods could be produced more easily, more efficiently, and less expensively. A third reason for the rapid industrialization was the nation's booming population. The U.S. population more than doubled in the last 40 years of the 1800s. There were more people to buy more goods, spurring commerce and further industrial growth.

Rapid industrialization meant that many new factories were built in the mid- and late-1800s. Most were built in or near the nation's large cities, including New York, Boston, Chicago, Philadelphia, and Pittsburgh. These urban centers had large groups of people who could work in the factories and large groups of people who would buy the goods the factories produced.

U.S. factory jobs drew many **immigrants** to American cities. Although the United States has always been a "nation of immigrants," the late 1800s saw a sharp rise in the number of people moving here from foreign countries. The majority came from Europe, including Germany, Italy, Russia, and Eastern European countries. Many also came from Mexico and Central America. Asian immigration was declining because the government had passed laws barring Chinese from moving to the United States. However, thousands of Japanese came to this country, taking jobs in farm fields and mines.

America's factory workers, whether native- or foreign-born, worked very hard at grueling, dangerous work. Many received low pay for long hours on the job. Over time, workers began to unionize. By joining a **union**, workers pledged to work together for better and safer working conditions and higher wages. They called **strikes** when their employers cut their pay or refused to grant raises. Many of the laws we have today, including the eight-hour workday and the five-day workweek, came about through the bitter struggles for better working conditions that unions waged in the late 1800s and the early 1900s.

Unions weren't the only groups working to solve problems brought on by America's rapid industrialization. Some reformers worked to clean up slums, improve health care, and stop child labor. Others worked to preserve the nation's natural beauty by creating national parks. Still others worked to give more people a voice in government. For example, many women lobbied to gain the right to vote. In the early 1900s, groups were working toward so many sweeping social and political improvements that the time is called the **Progressive Era**.

PRACTICE 3

1. Which of the following likely occurs during a period of rapid industrialization?

   A. the annexation of new territory
   B. an increase in manufacturing
   C. an increase in population
   D. an increase in immigration

2. Which event most likely contributed to the growth of American industries in the mid-1800s?

   A. the passage of the Chinese Exclusion Act, which banned Chinese immigration
   B. the passage of the Sherman Antitrust Act, which helped prevent businesses from forming monopolies
   C. the development of the Bessemer process, which made it easier to produce steel
   D. the development of settlement houses to aid impoverished immigrants and city dwellers

3. Based on the passage, which of the following would early union workers have valued the most?

   A. productivity in the workplace
   B. contact with people of all different backgrounds
   C. cooperation with others to improve worker safety
   D. the freedom to work whenever they pleased

4. What was a strong ideal held by people working toward reforms during the Progressive Era?

   A. efficiency
   B. wealth
   C. artistic beauty
   D. fairness

Questions 5 and 6 refer to the following graphs.

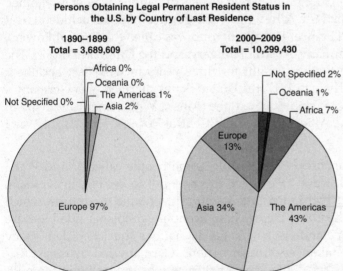

Persons Obtaining Legal Permanent Resident Status in the U.S. by Country of Last Residence

1890–1899
Total = 3,689,609

2000–2009
Total = 10,299,430

6. A student looked at these graphs and said, "So I see that, in the years 1890–1899, roughly seven times as many people came to the United States from Europe than did in the years 2000–2009. After all, 97 is roughly seven times 13."

   Which of the following best describes the flaw in the student's reasoning?

   A. The student failed to differentiate between northern Europe and southern Europe.
   B. The student failed to consider the reasons why people immigrate to the United States.
   C. The student failed to consider the different totals represented by each pie chart.
   D. The student failed to explain what led to a decrease in immigration from Europe.

5. Which of the following best completes this statement? In the 1890s, the vast majority of persons gaining permanent legal residency came from Europe, whereas in the early 2000s, a majority of such persons came from _____.

   A. Europe and Asia
   B. Asia and the Americas
   C. Africa, Oceania, and Europe
   D. Africa and the Americas

LESSON 4

The United States as an Emerging World Power

The expansion of U.S. industries in the mid-1800s had an effect not only on the nation's economy but also on its politics. Business and government leaders wanted access to more natural resources, which industries needed to continue growing. They also wanted to be able to sell more goods overseas. Regions in Africa, Asia, and Latin America had rich natural resources. People in these regions might buy what Americans wanted to sell. To promote industrial growth and increase its power, the United States became imperialistic. **Imperialism** is the policy by which a stronger nation extends economic, military, and/or political control over a weaker nation or region.

European nations had been engaging in imperialism for many centuries. In the late 1800s, the United States joined in. In 1898, the United States fought the Spanish-American War. Ostensibly, the United States declared war on Spain because of Spain's mistreatment of Cuba, which was a Spanish colony. Yet, after winning the war, the United States took over Spain's colonies of Cuba, Puerto Rico, the Philippines, and Guam. It granted independence to none of them.

The next war the United States was involved in was World War I, which began in Europe in 1913. It pitted two groups of nations against each other. One group was called the **Allies;** the leading Allied nations included Great Britain, Russia, and France. The other group was called the **Central Powers,** which included Germany, Austria-Hungary, and the Ottoman Empire. The Allies and Central Powers fought for three years in what fast became a deadly stalemate. Then, in 1917, the United States, alarmed over Germany's sinking of American ships, joined the Allies. With American help, in November 1918 the Allies defeated the Central Powers, and World War I ended.

Because the destruction was so terrible, some people called World War I "the war to end all wars." However, this was not to be. Within 12 years, by 1929, the world had fallen into a serious economic downturn, which Americans called the **Great Depression**. Economic problems aided the rise of **fascism** in Europe and elsewhere. Fascist nations squelched democracy and advocated the takeover of other nations. Germany, led by fascist dictator Adolf Hitler, started attacking smaller nations in Europe in the mid-1930s. Italy fought to take over Ethiopia, in Africa. Japan attacked China. Hitler built an alliance with Italy and Japan, which came to be called the **Axis**. By 1939, war again broke out between the Axis and the Allies.

The United States did not enter World War II until 1941, when the Japanese bombed the U.S. naval base at Pearl Harbor in Hawaii. This time, Americans fought not only in Europe but also in Africa and Asia as well. With its horrific battles, the fire-bombing of cities, the **Holocaust**, and the dropping of two atomic bombs on Japan, World War II led to massive destruction. The United States, which played a major part in the Allied victory in World War II in 1945, also played a major part in helping to rebuild war-scourged nations after the war was over.

Question 1 refers to the following chart.

Factors Related to the Growth of Imperialism

Economic	Desire for greater access to natural resources or new markets
Military	Desire for control of ports that could serve as refueling stations for long sea voyages or air flights
Political	Desire to spread the institutions of democracy or other political systems
Religious	Desire to spread Christianity or other faith
Cultural/Racial	Lack of respect for different cultures or races

1. Cuba lies about 90 miles off the coast of Florida. After the United States freed Cuba from Spanish rule in 1898, the U.S. Navy built an important base there.

   Which of the following factors from the chart best explains the situation in Cuba after 1898?

   A. economic
   B. religious
   C. political
   D. military

2. What assumption do you need to make to fully understand the last sentence in paragraph 4 on page 492?

   A. In World War I, the Allies fought the Central Powers.
   B. In World War II, the Allies included England, France, and Russia.
   C. In World War II, the Allies included the Germans, Austrians, and Ottoman Turks.
   D. In World War II, the Axis included Germany, Italy, and Japan.

3. Franklin D. Roosevelt became president during the height of the Great Depression, in 1933. He soon instituted a set of federal programs called the New Deal to try to lower unemployment.

   Which conclusion about the effectiveness of New Deal programs does the text on page 492 and graph below support?

U.S. Unemployment Rate, 1929–1944

Source: *Historical Statistics of the United States*

   A. Within a year, the New Deal had raised unemployment to its pre-Depression level.
   B. Within a year, the New Deal had lowered unemployment to its pre-Depression level.
   C. Unemployment fell after the start of the New Deal and continued to fall sharply as the U.S. entered World War II.
   D. The New Deal lowered unemployment, but the Allied victory in World War II lowered it further.

4. Which statement best summarizes the main idea of paragraph 5 on page 492?

   A. America entered World War II in 1941.
   B. Americans fought in Europe, Africa, and Asia.
   C. World War II involved more nations than any other war ever fought.
   D. America took a strong leadership role during and after World War II.

STUDY ADVICE

If you feel like you have a good handle on U.S. History topics from the past 100 years, great! The TASC emphasizes these. If not, don't worry. Spend a little more of your time studying these lessons.

The Cold War and the Civil Rights Era

After World War II ended, the capitalist and communist nations soon began engaging in a power struggle called the **Cold War**. Leading the capitalist nations was the United States; leading the communist nations was the Soviet Union. The Cold War never led to direct fighting between these two superpowers, although there was a constant threat of nuclear war. Clashes between communism and capitalism did lead to numerous smaller conflicts. These included the Korean War of the early 1950s and the Vietnam War, which lasted from 1954 to 1975. The United States sent soldiers to both. The Vietnam War was long and difficult and caused deep divisions among Americans. The United States sent massive military aid to the noncommunist South Vietnamese, but they kept losing to the communist North Vietnamese. Although a few Americans wanted to continue fighting, in 1973, America pulled out of Vietnam. In 1975, the communists took over the country.

The Cold War ended in 1991 with the breakup of the Soviet Union and the end of communism there. In the late 1980s, Soviet leader Mikhail Gorbachev had tried to reform the communist government. But the loosening of Soviet control had led to the collapse of many communist governments of Eastern Europe. The Berlin Wall, which had separated East and West Germany, was torn down. With communism no longer so threatening, world politics became less tense but also more unpredictable.

During the second half of the 20th century, the United States continued to face many challenges. In the 1950s, African American leaders launched the **civil rights movement** to try to end segregation and discrimination in the United States. Among their victories included the integration of public schools and other public facilities, the passage of laws protecting the voting rights of minorities, and the striking down of laws that permitted overt discrimination based on race or cultural background. However, minority groups and people of all backgrounds concerned about fair application of the law have continued to be vigilant in insisting that civil rights laws be upheld.

Another area of challenge in recent decades has been **technology**. Technology has led to many advances in science, medicine, and our personal lives. Computers, for instance, make many jobs easier and more productive. They allow almost instantaneous communication with co-workers, family, and friends. Furthermore, they allow people from around the world to share information quickly and easily, giving us the sense that we live in a "global village." However, our reliance on the use of technology has led us to pollute the air with exhaust from a growing number of cars. It has led us to pollute the water with acid rain, resulting from burning coal to generate increased electricity. It has led us to pollute our land with mountains of trash and tons of hazardous wastes.

KEY IDEAS

- The Cold War dominated U.S. foreign policy from the end of WWII until the fall of the Soviet Union.
- Social changes in the U.S. in the mid-1900s included the expansion of civil rights for minorities.
- Technological advances have introduced benefits but also caused problems.

ON THE TASC TEST

The TASC Social Studies Test will include some questions that focus on the role of the United States in the world.

PRACTICE 5

1. The conflict during the second half of the 20th century between the United States and the Soviet Union was called the Cold War because it involved _____.

   A. communists and capitalists
   B. two countries at the far north of Earth
   C. the threat of nuclear war
   D. no direct combat

2. Which of the following best summarizes the message of the cartoon below?

© 1980 Mark Alan Stamaty. Reprinted with permission of the artist.

   A. Nuclear bombs are extremely destructive.
   B. Expanding U.S. nuclear capabilities is a good idea.
   C. The buildup of nuclear arms increases fear and instability, not peace.
   D. The threat of nuclear war is lessened if both superpowers have equally powerful weapons.

3. Which of the following statements about the Vietnam War is a false generalization?

   A. Some Americans served in both Korea and Vietnam.
   B. The United States sent massive military aid to South Vietnam.
   C. Americans were in complete agreement about pulling out of Vietnam.
   D. The Vietnam War lasted much longer than the Korean War.

4. Which of the following goals would a civil rights activist be most likely to pursue?

   A. getting Congress to enact laws to restrict the sale of firearms
   B. petitioning for a city ordinance requiring those selling real estate to select a buyer without regard to race
   C. getting local companies to stop polluting the environment
   D. working with local clergy to publicize a worship service open to people of all religions

5. Which of the following is a conclusion about technology rather than a supporting detail?

   A. Reliance on technology has increased pollution.
   B. Cars cause air pollution.
   C. Coal-generating power plants cause acid-rain pollution.
   D. The ease of manufacturing disposable items has led to land pollution at landfill sites.

U.S. HISTORY PRACTICE QUESTIONS

Questions 1 and 2 refer to the time line below.

Important Events in Early Cherokee History

Cherokee adopt agriculture, with corn as major crop	Europeans first visit Cherokee villages; spread deadly disease, smallpox	White settlers begin to clash with Cherokee over possession of land in the South	Cherokee adopt white farming methods, religion, and life style	Cherokee develop a written language used to this day	Cherokee forced to give up their lands in the South and move to the West
~800	1540	1700	1800	1820	1838

1. Which of the following is a conclusion based on multiple details in the time line?

   A. The Cherokee had begun farming around 800, before Europeans came to America.
   B. Although the Cherokee adopted many aspects of white culture, they were driven off their ancestral lands.
   C. The Cherokee traditionally considered land ownership to be a tribal matter rather than a right of individuals acting on their own.
   D. The Bible was one of the first books the Cherokee translated into their written language.

2. When President Andrew Jackson mandated that the Cherokee move west in 1830, he claimed that the U.S. government would be better able to protect the Cherokee from whites who might try to get their new land in the West. The Cherokee considered this to be illogical.

   Which of the following summarizes the logical fallacy?

   A. If the government can't protect us from white settlers here, now, how could it protect us from whites moving west in the future?
   B. If you ask us to move to the West now, how do we know you won't ask us to move back to the South in the future?
   C. If the land we have in the South is good, why wouldn't the land in the West be better?
   D. If the state governments are protecting us now, why can't the U.S. government help later?

3. In the late 1700s, Abigail Adams—wife of John Adams, who was our nation's second president—wrote the following in a letter to her sister:

   I will never consent to have our sex considered in an inferior point of light. Let each planet shine in their own orbit . . . if man is Lord, woman is *Lordess*—that is what I contend for.

Based on this letter, which of the following principles was Abigail Adams advocating?

   A. the separation of church and state
   B. the abolition of slavery
   C. the promotion of scientific learning
   D. equal rights and opportunities for women

Questions 4 and 5 refer to the following map.

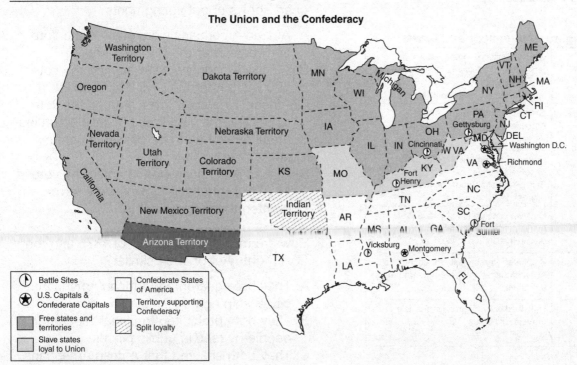

The Union and the Confederacy

4. List four states that permitted slavery but did not join the Confederacy.

_____

_____

_____

_____

5. The loyalty of Maryland was of crucial importance to the Union. Based on the map, which statement best explains why this was so?

A. The nation's capital was located nearby.
B. The Confederate capital was located there.
C. It was close to Fort Sumter, where the Civil War began.
D. Important rail lines ran through Baltimore, Maryland.

6. In the Emancipation Proclamation, issued in 1863, President Lincoln freed all people enslaved in the states that had seceded from the Union. This proclamation was explicitly not to be put into effect in slave states that had remained in the Union. The proclamation went on to say:

I hereby enjoin upon the people so declared to be free to abstain from all violence . . . and make known that such persons of suitable condition will be received into the armed services of the United States to garrison forts, positions, stations, and other places, and to man vessels of all sorts.

Based on the information given about the Emancipation Proclamation and the text of the order itself, which of the following was a major reason Lincoln issued the proclamation?

A. to encourage states to secede from the Union
B. to punish slaveholders throughout the South
C. to weaken the North by enlisting former slaves in the Confederate army
D. to weaken the South by enlisting former slaves in the Union army

Civil Rights Amendment and Laws

14th Amendment (1868)	Granted citizenship and equal protection of the law to all persons born in the United States (not applied to American Indians)
15th Amendment (1870)	Granted voting rights to African Americans
Civil Rights Act of 1875	Gave African Americans the right to serve on juries Banned racial segregation in public places
Civil Rights Act of 1964	Outlawed segregation by race in public places and racial discrimination in employment
Voting Rights Act of 1965	Prohibited literacy tests for voting Allowed the federal government to register voters
Civil Rights Act of 1968	Outlawed discrimination in the sale or rental of homes

7. An Asian American registers to vote and is given a reading test. Which of the following is the civil rights amendment or law relevant to this situation?

A. Civil Rights Act of 1875
B. Civil Rights Act of 1964
C. Voting Rights Act of 1965
D. Civil Rights Act of 1968

8. Which statement best summarizes what this chart shows about voting rights?

A. African Americans were granted the vote five years after the Civil War ended.
B. African Americans were granted the vote 100 years after the Civil War ended.
C. African Americans were granted the vote soon after the Civil War, but laws enforcing these rights had to be passed a century later.
D. African Americans were granted the vote in 1870 but American Indians were never granted these same rights.

9. How are the Civil Rights Act of 1875 and the Civil Rights Act of 1964 similar?

A. They both guaranteed African Americans citizenship rights.
B. They both prohibited the legal separation of people by race in public places.
C. They both ensured that African Americans could serve on juries.
D. They both make job discrimination illegal.

10. Alexander Graham Bell invented the telephone in the spring of 1876. In the fall, he exhibited it at an exposition in Philadelphia. When leading scientists saw Bell's invention, they said, "Here is the greatest marvel ever achieved in electrical science."

Which of the following statements related to the passage is an opinion, not a fact?

A. Bell invented the telephone in 1876.
B. Bell exhibited the telephone at an exposition in Philadelphia.
C. Scientists admired Bell's invention.
D. The telephone was the greatest electrical invention ever.

Questions 11 through 13 are based on the paragraph and the political cartoon below.

In 1974, President Richard Nixon resigned from office. He had been involved in a scandal known as Watergate. The Watergate scandal implicated Nixon in covering up crimes committed by members of his reelection committee. These crimes ranged from illegally harassing political opponents to burglary and bribery. With Congress investigating him, he was sure to be impeached. This cartoon was published before Nixon resigned to avoid impeachment.

Hey guys, do you really think we need that clause about impeachment in there?

Cartoon by Robert Lawlor. Reprinted with permission of the *Philadelphia Daily News*.

11. In this cartoon, whom is Nixon addressing?

    A. the writers of the Declaration of Independence
    B. the framers of the U.S. Constitution
    C. the past presidents of the United States
    D. the present session of Congress

12. Which value was Congress furthering by investigating Nixon and Watergate?

    A. the pursuit of justice
    B. the duty of obedience
    C. loyalty to a friend
    D. love of mercy

STUDY ADVICE

How did this practice set go? If you missed a few questions, go back and review those lessons. Remember as you study to pay particular attention to words in bold and the Key Ideas in each lesson.

13. About Watergate, one historian has written, "In a society in which distrust of leaders and institutions of authority was already widespread, the fall of Richard Nixon seemed to confirm the most cynical assumptions about the character of American public life."

Which of the following was most likely a reason for Americans' growing distrust of their government in the years just prior to Watergate?

    A. mismanagement of the New Deal
    B. the beginning of rock music
    C. the escalation and failure of the Vietnam War
    D. the scandals of previous presidents, including John Kennedy and Bill Clinton

Questions 14 and 15 refer to the graph below.

Hispanic Population by Nationality, 1990

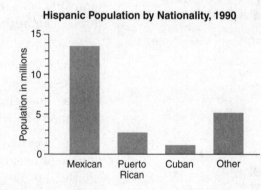

Source: U.S. Census Bureau

14. In 1990, approximately how many people of Cuban nationality lived in the United States?

    A. 100
    B. 100,000
    C. 1,000,000
    D. 5,000,000

15. A Hispanic family moved into an apartment next door to yours in 1990. Based solely on the bar graph, which place was the family most likely to be from?

    A. Cuba
    B. Mexico
    C. Puerto Rico
    D. Spain

Historic Basis for U.S. System

The system of government in the United States is known as **representative democracy**. In this form of government, the citizens vote to elect representatives who make and execute laws. To understand this form of democracy, it is helpful to first distinguish democracy from other types of government. Then, you can trace the historical development of democracy and see how representative democracy differs from other types of democracy employed over time and around the globe.

The origins of **democracy** are ancient. The term *democracy*, which means "rule of the people" in Greek, arose in approximately 500 BCE in the Greek city-state of Athens. The concept of "rule of the people" distinguishes democracy from **monarchy**, the "rule of one person" (such as a king or queen); **aristocracy**, the "rule of an elite class" (lords or barons, for example); **theocracy**, the "rule of the church"; and **anarchy**, rule by no one (arguably not a form of government at all). Democracy is also distinct from forms of **authoritarian rule**, such as dictatorship, military rule, and fascism.

In ancient Athenian democracy, laws were voted upon by a council of all citizens, a system known as **direct democracy**. In ancient Athens, however, a "citizen" was defined as a free male landowner over the age of 20. Women, foreigners, slaves, non-landowners, and minors were excluded from the vote.

For the eventual development of democracy in the U.S., one of the most important events was the signing of the **Magna Carta** (Latin for "Great Charter") in England in 1215. England was a monarchy, but some nobles protested the king's absolute power and forced him to sign the Magna Carta. This document limited the king's rule and subjected his decisions to review. This same period also saw the development of the legal doctrine of **habeas corpus**, which made it illegal for the government to hold or imprison individuals without granting them trials.

Over time, the group allowed by the Magna Carta to review the king's decisions developed into a **parliament** of lawmakers appointed by title and/or elected by citizens. As the power of the parliament grew, England transformed into a **parliamentary democracy**. In this system, a government is formed by the party holding a majority of seats in the parliament. In most parliamentary democracies, the majority party appoints or authorizes the chief executive, such as the prime minister or president.

Known as the Age of Enlightenment, the 17th and 18th centuries saw the spread of democracy to many other European countries. England, France, Holland, and other European powers also adopted **bills of rights** for individuals during this period. The philosophies dominant in this era emphasized reason and individual rights and encouraged government by the people. Enlightenment philosophers such as Adam Smith, John Locke, and Voltaire strongly influenced the founders of the United States.

PRACTICE 1

Directions: Match each choice in the box corresponding to the form of government that best matches the description.

1.

Direct democracy	
Monarchy	
Representative democracy	
Aristocracy	

Choices:

In <u>Country A</u>, laws are made and administered by lords who inherit their lands and titles.
In <u>Country B</u>, laws are made by a sovereign king and are subject to no review.
In <u>Country C</u>, laws are made by Congress, an elected group of representatives.
In <u>Country D</u>, laws are made by the vote of all citizens.

2. Which of following can be inferred about the Founding Fathers of the United States?

   A. They sought to establish the power of the king of England in the United States.
   B. They were concerned about protecting the rights of individuals.
   C. They argued that the United States should adopt a system of direct democracy.
   D. They thought representatives from the United States should sit in England's Parliament.

3. In the United States, laws are enacted by Congress, a group of representatives elected by the people. Which of the following was most likely the chief historical model for the U.S. Congress?

   A. Athenian council of citizens
   B. Magna Carta
   C. Parliament of England
   D. Declaration of the Rights of Man and the Citizen adopted in France in 1789

4. Some nations have been ruled by a form of government known as constitutional monarchy. While a king or queen is the single, sovereign ruler of the country, his or her power is limited by a constitution, a formal document outlining which of the monarch's decisions are subject to review or may be overruled by a court of law.

   Which of the following was most likely a constitutional monarchy?

   A. the ancient city-state of Athens
   B. any country ruled by fascism
   C. the United States at the time of its founding
   D. England during the Age of Enlightenment

5. If the United States were a parliamentary democracy, which of the following would be most likely to occur?

   A. The office of the president would decrease in power.
   B. The office of the president would increase in power.
   C. The president would be elected by a majority vote of all citizens.
   D. The president would be appointed by the majority party in the parliament.

The U.S. Constitution

The Constitution established the American government as a **liberal democracy** and a **republic**. *Liberal* refers to the political philosophy of **liberalism**, which holds that the role of government is to foster the well-being of the individual. The United States also operates on **republican** principles, meaning it is governed by elected representatives rather than by people who inherit political power or seize it by force. The terms *liberal* and *republican* when used to describe our form of government should not be confused with modern political positions or political parties. Abraham Lincoln succinctly and eloquently expressed these ideas in the Gettysburg Address (1863), when he described U.S. government as being "of the people, by the people, for the people."

The authors of the Constitution set out their goals for the new nation in the document's **preamble**, or introduction. They wanted to unite the states under one government and ensure that citizens could pursue prosperity while enjoying safety and freedom under the rule of law.

Following the preamble are the original seven **articles** of the U.S. Constitution. These articles provide for the three branches of government (see page 504), establish the rights of states, and set forth procedures for ratifying and amending the Constitution. Article 6 states that no other laws can contradict any part of the Constitution.

According to Article 5, a constitutional **amendment** can be proposed by Congress if it is supported by two-thirds majorities in both the House and Senate. The proposed amendment then must be ratified by three-fourths of the states. This process ensures that amendments have very broad national support.

The original Constitution did not specifically describe citizens' rights, an omission that was controversial even as the Constitution was being written. However, political leaders agreed to wait to make amendments to the Constitution until after it was **ratified**. The first ten amendments to the U.S. Constitution, passed in 1791, became the **Bill of Rights**. The First Amendment, for example, guarantees freedom of religion, freedom of speech, and freedom of the press. The Sixth and Seventh Amendments guarantee citizens' rights to trial by jury.

As Americans' ideas about citizenship and government have evolved, the amendment process has allowed the Constitution to evolve as well. The Thirteenth Amendment (1865) outlawed slavery; the Fifteenth Amendment (1870) established that the rights of citizens "shall not be denied or abridged … on account of race, color, or previous condition of servitude." The Nineteenth Amendment (1920) gave women the right to vote. The Twenty-fourth Amendment (1964) banned poll taxes, which some states were using to prevent African Americans from voting. The Twenty-sixth Amendment (1971) lowered the voting age to 18.

KEY IDEAS

- The U.S. Constitution is the basis for our government structure and legal system.
- The Bill of Rights—the first ten constitutional amendments—define the rights of citizens.
- Amendments to the Constitution require wide support, but many important amendments have gained enough support to be ratified.

ON THE TASC TEST

The TASC Social Studies Test may include an excerpt from or a reference to one of the following U.S. historical documents:

- *Declaration of Independence*
- *U.S. Constitution, including the Bill of Rights and other amendments*
- *Landmark Supreme Court cases*

PRACTICE 2

1. Which of the following is the main characteristic of a republic?

   A. voting rights extended to few adult citizens
   B. elected representatives exercising government power on behalf of citizens
   C. people governing themselves by voting directly on all issues
   D. power concentrated among a small group

2. The Constitution is a relatively brief document containing only about seven thousand words. It establishes the structure and powers of the U.S. government but does not give many specifics.

   What assumption were the drafters of the Constitution working under as they kept the document general and brief?

   A. There was not enough time to draft a long, detailed document before the states had to ratify it.
   B. Most of the power of the federal government would be reserved to the president, who could govern as he saw fit.
   C. The details of government would be worked out in the future, as the need arose, within the framework of the Constitution.
   D. Written constitutions were an untested basis for democratic government, so it was better to keep such a document brief.

3. Franklin Delano Roosevelt was elected to the presidency four times between 1933 and 1945. In reaction to this, the Twenty-second Amendment, ratified in 1951, allowed presidents a maximum of two terms in office.

   People who favored presidential term limits would most likely have valued which of the following?

   A. responsibility but no authority
   B. authority but no responsibility
   C. the power of an office, not an individual
   D. the power of an individual, not an office

4. The third paragraph of the passage on page 502 includes a summary of Article 6 of the Constitution, also called the supremacy clause.

   _____ is an example of the supremacy clause in action.

   A. Congress voting to appropriate $2 billion for a federal highways program
   B. The Environmental Protection Agency issuing new regulations on a pollutant
   C. The U.S. Supreme Court refusing to hear a case
   D. The U.S. Supreme Court declaring an Illinois state law unconstitutional

Question 5 refers to the following chart.

Methods of Amending the Constitution

Proposal	Ratification Method	When Used
Two-thirds vote in both houses of Congress to propose an amendment	By three-quarters of the state legislatures	For every amendment except one
	By special conventions in three-fourths of the states	Twenty-first Amendment (repealing Prohibition)
Two-thirds of states request Congress to call a constitutional convention to consider an amendment	By three-quarters of the state legislatures	Never used
	By special conventions in three-fourths of the states	Never used

5. Which of the following would best explain why the third and fourth methods of amending the Constitution have never been used?

   A. State governments do not usually act together.
   B. Only Congress can propose amendments.
   C. State legislatures can vote on an amendment.
   D. Conventions meet more frequently than Congress and state legislatures do.

STUDY ADVICE

The TASC places high emphasis on the U.S. Constitution and the foundations of the American political system, so if you have a solid understanding of these topics, congratulations! If you still feel a bit shaky, review this lesson.

LESSON 3

Levels and Branches of Government

The U.S. government works in layers with different responsibilities at the national, or **federal**, level; the state level; and local levels, including cities, villages, and counties. The federal government works across all 50 states, and its decisions and actions affect everyone. States have their own constitutions, similar to the U.S. Constitution. State governments also are quite powerful in shaping the lives of people in their states.

Federalism, which is a basic principle of the U.S. Constitution, means that power is shared between the national and state levels of government. Dividing power between federal and state government protects the rights of individual states, but also allows our national government to enforce certain rights of citizenship. The Constitution gives some powers only to the national government, some only to state government, and some to both. For example, only the federal government can declare war. States are given the power to establish schools. Both federal and state governments can levy taxes and set up court systems.

The Constitution established **separation of powers**, giving three branches of the federal government different roles. The states follow the federal example. On the federal level, the **executive branch** consists of the president and various advisors (including the president's cabinet) and government departments, such as the State Department. The executive branch enforces the nation's laws and provides national leadership, setting goals and policies. The **legislative branch** consists of two houses of **Congress: the Senate** and the **House of Representatives**. Congress is responsible for making laws that all citizens, organizations, and businesses must follow. The **judicial branch**, made up of the federal court system including the Supreme Court, decides disputes related to laws, including the U.S. Constitution.

U.S. citizens vote for the president and all members of Congress. As a result, these politicians have a responsibility to represent and serve their **constituents**—the people who elected them. The president may be elected to only two terms of four years each. Representatives are elected for two years and Senators for six years; these members of Congress may be reelected for any number of terms.

Federal judges, in contrast, are appointed by the president and **confirmed** by the Senate. They can serve in these positions for life. As citizens, we have a right to expect our federal judges to make **impartial** decisions based on the Constitution and the laws of the United States.

The people who wrote the U.S. Constitution were afraid to give any government body too much power. Therefore, not only does each branch have separate powers, but each branch can act in ways that affect the other branches. This system, called **checks and balances**, is also found in state governments. For example, the president can **veto** laws made by Congress. Congress can override a presidential veto by repassing the law with a two-thirds majority. The Constitution is also now interpreted to mean that judges can review laws and declare them **unconstitutional**.

KEY IDEAS

- Under our Constitution, the federal government must share power with the states.
- The federal government has three major branches—executive, legislative, and judicial.
- The three branches of the government balance each other's power.

ON THE TASC TEST

Editorial cartoons like the one on page 505 use pictures and humor to make a political point.

1. What is the key characteristic of federalism?

   A. division of power between national and state governments
   B. concentration of power in one government
   C. concentration of power at the local level
   D. a judicial system with trial, appellate, and supreme courts

2. Which of the following is an example of a government entity that is part of the executive branch?

   A. the Democratic National Committee
   B. Congress's House Rules Committee
   C. the U.S. Court of Appeals
   D. the State Department

3. Why do lifetime appointments help ensure that federal judges rule impartially on legal issues?

   A. Federal judges need not worry about pleasing their constituents in order to be reelected.
   B. Only people who demonstrate loyalty to the ruling political party are appointed.
   C. Lifetime appointments mean that federal judges acquire a great deal of experience.
   D. A federal judge must be impartial or he or she will not be reelected.

4. Match each of the following definitions to the matching term.

Checks and balances	
Veto	
Senators	
Constituents	
Representatives	

| Limits that one branch of government can place on the other branches |
| The people whom political leaders represent |
| The president's power to strike down a law |
| Legislators who serve two-year terms |
| Legislators who serve six-year terms |

5. An example of checks and balances would be

   A. a governor vetoing a law passed by the state legislature
   B. a state determining the highway speed limit
   C. a Senate committee voting not to send legislation to the full Senate for a vote
   D. the House of Representatives holding hearings about a controversial issue

Question 6 refers to the following cartoon.

"Let's never forget that the constitution provides for three equally important branches of government: the legislative and the other two."

6. Which of the following people is most likely depicted in the cartoon?

   A. the president
   B. a member of Congress
   C. the head of a government department
   D. a federal judge

The Electoral System

Two **political parties** dominate the political arena in the United States: the **Democrats** and the **Republicans**. These parties represent different ideas about the role of government in our nation. In each election season, the parties and candidates work to promote their views, or **platforms**—their positions on issues like tax reform, Social Security, education spending, environmental protection, and so on.

The political parties have developed large organizations for raising money and getting their candidates elected. Each party runs its own **primary** election, in which candidates within the party compete with each other for the party's **nomination**. After the primary elections, the winners from each party's primary face off in the general election. In presidential elections, the primary season ends with a party **convention**, where delegates from each state gather to select the party's candidate. Citizens vote in a general election, and the results are tallied by state. Following the general election, electors from each state cast their state's votes in the **Electoral College**. The electors generally must cast their votes for the candidate who won the general election in their state. The candidate who wins the greatest number of electoral votes becomes president.

Although Democrats and Republicans are by far the largest political parties, there are small parties as well. At times, a "third-party candidate" like Ralph Nader or Ross Perot attracts enough support to influence the outcome of the national election. Even when small parties offer interesting new ideas or solutions to problems, they have great difficulty attracting money and public attention because the Democratic and Republican parties are so well established.

Although many voters consider themselves to be either Republicans or Democrats, many others are **independent**. Candidates and their political parties rely heavily on **opinion polls** to find out what voters think; they try to tailor their campaign messages to appeal to large numbers of voters. Groups of voters who might "swing" an election one way or another are particularly important targets for political campaigns.

Political campaigns can be very expensive, and the higher the office, the more expensive the campaign. To reach the public, candidates pay for mailings, TV ads, and events, including personal appearances. They need campaign staff and offices; they must pay for travel expenses. As a result, fund-raising has become a very important part of running for office.

The size of campaign contributions to a candidate or political action committee (PAC) is limited by law. However, since the 2010 Supreme Court ruling in *Citizens United v. Federal Election Commission*, "super PACs" have been able to spend unlimited amounts in support of a candidate, as long as they do not coordinate explicitly with the candidate. Citizens, corporations, and unions have been able to donate unlimited amounts to super PACs. The question of financial influence in politics remains controversial.

KEY IDEAS

- U.S. politics are dominated by the Democratic and Republican parties.
- Political parties hold primaries to select candidates for the general election.
- Political campaigns are very expensive, and campaign financing is a controversial topic.

TASC TEST TIP

When you are asked a question about a circle graph, such as the ones on page 507 remember that it represents a whole, or 100%.

1. Which of the following is necessary for a candidate to win the presidency?

    A. earning a majority of primary wins
    B. receiving a majority of the popular vote
    C. receiving a majority in the Electoral College
    D. having no third-party opponent

2. An exit poll is one that surveys people as they leave a voting location. Instead of waiting for votes to be counted, the media often announce the winners of elections based on exit polls.

    Which of the following is an important drawback of using exit polls?

    A. Exit polls may be inaccurate if the people polled are not representative of the voting public as a whole or if the election is very close.
    B. Exit polls allow the media to present election results during prime time on election night instead of waiting until later in the evening.
    C. Exit polls have undue influence on the way politicians running for office conduct their campaigns.
    D. Exit polls are likely to be unreliable when there is a wide margin between the candidates.

3. Which of the following is an example of a primary election?

    A. A Democrat and a Republican oppose one another in a race for the U.S. Senate.
    B. A Republican and an independent candidate oppose one another in a race for the state senate.
    C. Once presidential candidates are chosen, they select their running mates.
    D. Two city council members are on a ballot to determine which one will run for mayor as a Democrat.

STUDY ADVICE

If you've been working through this book in order, it might be time to review the Reading and Writing units. Don't forget to do periodic reviews of material you haven't seen in a while, so that those skills don't get rusty.

Questions 4 and 5 refer to the following graphs.

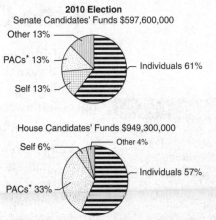

2010 Election
Senate Candidates' Funds $597,600,000
Other 13%
PACs* 13%
Self 13%
Individuals 61%

House Candidates' Funds $949,300,000
Self 6%
Other 4%
Individuals 57%
PACs* 33%

*PACs are Political Action Committees – groups that raise money for candidates.

Source: Federal Election Commission.

4. How do the campaign funding sources of Senate and House candidates compare?

    A. Individual donations provided a larger percentage of funds raised by House candidates than of those raised by Senate candidates.
    B. In total, individuals contributed a greater dollar amount to House candidates than they did to Senate candidates.
    C. Political parties provided a greater percentage of the funds raised by Senate candidates than they did of funds raised by House candidates.
    D. On average, Senate candidates received a greater percentage of their funds from PACs than did House candidates.

5. Which of the following statements is supported by the graphs?

    A. In 2010, self-funding was a larger source of funds for Senate candidates than it was for House candidates.
    B. In 2010, individual donations were the largest source of funds for Senate candidates but not for House candidates.
    C. In 2010, PACs were the largest source of funds for House candidates but not for Senate candidates.
    D. Fund-raising accounts for most of the work on a congressional campaign.

The Role of the Citizen

Citizenship is a special relationship between a person and a nation: the nation owes the person certain rights and guarantees; the person has certain obligations to the nation. Thus, citizens of the United States have both rights and responsibilities.

People born in the United States, no matter what the circumstances, automatically become U.S. citizens. Regardless of where you were born, if one of your parents was a U.S. citizen, then you are also a U.S. citizen. People who **immigrate** to the United States from other countries can become U.S. citizens through a legal process called **naturalization**; underage children are naturalized along with their parents.

Our rights of citizenship are established in the first ten amendments to the U.S. Constitution—the Bill of Rights (see page 502)—and in other sections of the Constitution. One of the most fundamental rights of U.S. citizens is our right to participate in our nation's political life. We are eligible to vote and to hold public office, and we elect representatives to govern us.

In addition to rights, citizens have responsibilities. First and foremost, we must uphold the laws of our country. As citizens, we also make contributions to the national welfare. Our taxes pay for services that the government provides to benefit everyone. By voting, we choose our government representatives and help to make the political process meaningful for everyone. Through national service—such as military service, holding public office, or participating in intensive volunteer programs—citizens may devote years of their lives to the responsibilities of citizenship.

Our **jury** system is an important example of the give-and-take of citizenship. Each of us is guaranteed the right to a fair and speedy trial, heard by "a jury of peers," if we are accused of a crime. However, we are also obligated to serve on juries or as **witnesses** when we are called by the court system. The fairness of our legal system depends on citizens participating in that system. Therefore, our employers are obligated to release us from work at the request of the courts.

In addition to upholding the rights and responsibilities established by law, many citizens contribute their time and money to serve society. Some people volunteer their time and skills, such as by fund-raising for schools, building low-cost homes, or serving meals to the homeless. Others give money to organizations such as political campaigns, environmental groups, and nonprofits that provide social services. Many people also contribute to the general welfare in their daily activities, such as by recycling or helping their neighbors.

A belief in the words written in the Constitution and in the rights and responsibilities of citizenship survived the Civil War and continues to pervade American public life, even as immigration from all over the world makes the country more diverse than ever.

1. _____ outlines the rights of U.S. citizens.

   A. The Declaration of Independence
   B. The U.S. Constitution
   C. A U.S. passport
   D. A person's naturalization papers

Questions 2 and 3 refer to the following information.

Noncitizens can be classified into five groups:

Resident alien A foreigner who has established permanent residence in the United States.

Nonresident alien A foreigner who is staying in the United States for a brief, specified period.

Enemy alien A foreigner who is a citizen of a nation at war with the United States.

Refugee A foreigner fleeing his or her country to escape persecution or danger.

Illegal alien A foreigner who comes to the United States without legal documentation.

2. Louvina married an American and moved to the United States from Trinidad in 2010. Three years later, she filed a legal petition requesting U.S. citizenship. In what category of alien does Louvina belong?

   A. resident alien
   B. nonresident alien
   C. enemy alien
   D. refugee

3. What would happen to the legal status of noncitizens living in the United States if their country declares war on the United States?

   A. They would become nonresident aliens.
   B. They would become resident aliens.
   C. They would become enemy aliens.
   D. They would become refugees.

4. The United States must balance the right of society to protect itself against the rights of an accused criminal. One aspect of this tension is the Fourth Amendment guarantee of "the right of people to be secure in their persons, houses, papers, and effects, against unreasonable searches and seizures."

   Which of the following values is supported by the Fourth Amendment?

   A. free speech
   B. privacy
   C. civic duty
   D. volunteerism

Question 5 refers to the following graph.

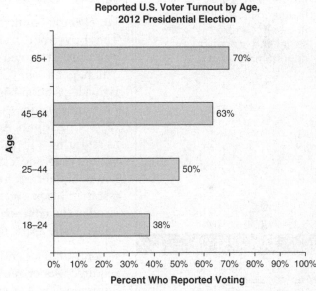

Reported U.S. Voter Turnout by Age, 2012 Presidential Election

Source: United States Census Bureau

5. Which of the following is a conclusion based on the graph rather than a detail of the graph?

   A. About 63 percent of people aged 45 to 64 reported voting in the 2012 presidential election.
   B. Those aged 65+ reported the highest voter turnout in the 2012 presidential election, at 70 percent.
   C. If the 2012 presidential election is representative of elections generally in the United States, voter turnout increases with age.
   D. Only about 38 percent of young people reported voting in the 2012 presidential election.

Contemporary Issues in American Politics

Interactions between Federal and Local Government

Many issues that dominate today's headlines are rooted in the relationship between government operation and constitutional principles.

Federalism is the separation of powers between the states and the federal government. One idea that has been an important part of America's culture of federalism is the idea that states have the right to exercise powers not specifically reserved for the federal government in the Constitution. One cause of the Civil War was that slavery was legal under state laws in the South, and Southerners feared Congress would pass federal laws outlawing slavery nationwide. Since the Civil War, the federal government has exercised ever-increasing influence over state and local matters.

For example, in the 20th century, Congress passed federal civil rights laws. These overrode some state laws (called "Jim Crow" laws) and common practice that denied African Americans the equal opportunity to get an education, get a job, vote, and use public facilities such as hotels. Federal civil rights legislation has also sought to enforce equal treatment of women, people with disabilities, people of different religions, and others. For example, the Voting Rights Act of 1965 prevents states from imposing any law, such as requiring a literacy test, that prevents racial or language minorities from voting. (Literacy tests did so by allowing voting officials to decide who and had not qualified: for example, white voters were often given a much easier test than black voters.) The Voting Rights Act is still relevant today: it is at issue in the controversy over some states' recently passed "voter ID laws," which some argue tend to disenfranchise certain minorities.

Recently, the federal Affordable Care Act (popularly known as Obamacare) required Americans to purchase health insurance or pay a fine. The Supreme Court upheld this law, basing its decision on the constitutional clause given Congress the power to tax. However, health insurance is still regulated by state law, and exchanges where people can purchase health insurance are set up in each state, not nationally.

The federal government also exercises control over state and local governments by helping to fund their operation. For example, a great deal of money to fund schools and highways comes to state and local governments from the federal government, and to receive that money, states and localities must obey certain federal rules. The federal government has the power to borrow very large amounts of money, whereas most other governmental units need to balance their budget each year. Sometimes cities have had to declare bankruptcy, as Detroit, Michigan, did in 2013. Therefore, federal money is especially important during economic downturns and in areas that are chronically economically depressed. It is also important to areas that have suffered a disaster, such as New Orleans, Louisiana after Hurricane Katrina in 2005.

KEY IDEAS

- Tension between which powers are reserved for states and which can be exercised by the federal government plays a significant role in American politics.
- A long-term trend in U.S. law has been to extend the right to vote to more citizens and to attempt to extend equal social and economic opportunity.

TASC TEST TIP

When considering a current political issue, think about what the Constitution says about the role of government in protecting the rights of individuals and how the government may or may not need to limit the freedom of some people to ensure the liberty of others.

1. Which of the following illustrates the idea that states may exercise powers not specifically reserved for the federal government?

   A. The United States decides to send foreign aid to Bangladesh.
   B. Texas sets the rural interstate highway speed limit at 80 miles per hour, and Delaware sets it at 55 miles per hour.
   C. The Supreme Court overturns a law passed by Congress and signed by the president.
   D. Congress increases the top federal income tax rate from 39.6 percent to 50 percent.

2. If a state passed a law requiring citizens to prove they could read and understand the Constitution before registering to vote, that law

   A. would be legal, because states have the authority to decide how to register voters
   B. would be legal, as long as the state makes all prospective voters take the test
   C. would be illegal, because it would violate citizens' Miranda rights
   D. would be illegal, because it would violate the federal Voting Rights Act of 1965

3. In the event of a major disaster, such as an earthquake or drought, an important governmental source of funds to recover from that disaster is

   A. the federal government
   B. local property taxes
   C. individuals' personal savings
   D. state college endowments

4. Match the decision to the level of government that usually makes laws to determine answers to the questions below.

Who can get married?	
Who is a U.S. citizen?	
Which school can a child attend?	

federal
state
local

Government Authority and Individual Rights

Since its 1803 decision in *Marbury v. Madison*, the U.S. Supreme Court has had the right to determine whether laws are constitutional. The Court's opinions have sometimes changed. For example, in 1896 the Court ruled in *Plessy v. Ferguson* that racial segregation was constitutional, but in 1954 in *Brown v. Board of Education*, the Court declared that separate facilities are inherently unequal.

The Supreme Court often evaluates laws in terms of whether they violate the Bill of Rights. For example, in *Mapp v. Ohio* (1961), the Court ruled that obtaining evidence without a search warrant violates the Fourth Amendment and cannot be used to convict someone of a crime. In *Miranda v. Arizona* (1966), the Court said that a suspect must be informed of the right, guaranteed by the Fifth and Sixth Amendments, not to incriminate oneself. When someone is arrested, he or she must be read "Miranda rights." Since September 11, 2001, the question has arisen whether the federal government is violating citizens' right to privacy, implied throughout the Bill of Rights, by collecting large amounts of data in an effort to detect terrorist activity. This question is a matter of ongoing controversy.

Participation in a Democratic Society

The First Amendment protects freedom of speech and freedom of the press, including via television and the Internet. The media can greatly influence people's political views. In recent decades, many more sources of news have appeared, and many of these radio stations, cable television channels, and websites attract audiences by providing news with a distinct political bias. People may choose their news from sources they already agree with and may not be exposed to alternative ideas. This media environment may limit the political debate that informs participation in a democracy.

In addition, many citizens are not motivated to express their views by voting. Turnout—that is, the percent of eligible voters who actually vote—is usually between 50 percent and 60 percent for presidential elections, lower for congressional elections in years when a president is not being elected. Voter turnout is even lower for local elections, such as elections for judgeships, sheriffs, county and city legislators, school boards, and other important roles. There may be many reasons why people don't vote, but voting is an important part of being a responsible citizen.

PRACTICE 6.2

1. Which of the following is true about U.S. Supreme Court decisions?

   A. Once the Court decides an issue, it will never hear another case that raises that issue.
   B. Decisions are based on the justices' interpretation of the articles of the Constitution but not the amendments.
   C. Many important decisions have determined that government must respect citizens' rights as laid out in the Bill of Rights.
   D. The Court bases its decisions on the assumption that individuals do not have a fundamental right to privacy.

2. In the U.S. Supreme Court's decision in *Florida v. Jardines* (2013), Justice Antonin Scalia wrote, "When it comes to the Fourth Amendment, the home is first among equals." What is Scalia most likely to have meant by this?

   A. Law enforcement has a particular interest in investigating criminal acts that take place in people's homes.
   B. The U.S. Supreme Court should not hear cases in which law enforcement officers have searched private homes for evidence.
   C. Individuals have more freedom of speech within their home than outside it.
   D. An individual has a reasonable expectation of privacy in his or her home.

3. In the United States today, a recall election is when a person votes for

   A. a primary candidate to withdraw from the race
   B. a recount for their party representative
   C. a public official to be removed from office
   D. the previous public official to be reinstated

4. Match the type of election to the likely voter turnout (percentage of registered voters).

Election for president	
Election for U.S. House representative and state legislators	
Election for county parks commissioner, school board members, and sheriff	

25%
40%
55%

CIVICS AND GOVERNMENT PRACTICE QUESTIONS

Question 1 refers to the following chart.

Political Divisions in the 113th Congress, 2013

Party	House	Senate
Republicans	234	45
Democrats	201	53
Others	—	2 (In case of a tie, Vice President Joe Biden (D) votes.)
Vacant	—	—

1. Which of the following is the best summary of the chart above?

   A. Congress is made up of the House and the Senate.
   B. In 2013, a different major party controlled the House than controls the Senate.
   C. In 2013, the narrow margin of control in each body of Congress made it difficult to pass legislation.
   D. In 2013, the vice president was likely to cast the deciding vote on many bills before the Senate.

2. In 1215, English nobles limited royal power by forcing King John to accept the Magna Carta. This document gave certain rights to nobles, such as protection of private property, trial by jury, and religious freedoms.

   Therefore, the _____ shares essential characteristics with the Magna Carta.

   A. Mayflower Compact, which established a government for Plymouth colony,
   B. Bill of Rights of the U.S. Constitution, which guarantees citizens certain rights,
   C. Albany Plan of Union, which called for a colonial confederation,
   D. *Federalist Papers*, which encouraged ratification of the U.S. Constitution,

Questions 3 and 4 refer to the following passage.

In 1979, Congress passed legislation to allow political parties to raise unlimited amounts of general-purpose money not designated for particular candidates. In 1991, a lawsuit forced disclosure of such "soft money" contributions, and concern grew about the size of individual donations, the extent of total donations, and the ways in which the money was being spent. During the presidential elections of 1996 and 2000, campaign fund-raising, especially the raising and spending of soft money, was an issue, with the candidates promising reform. Finally, in 2001, after several years of hearings, the Senate passed the McCain-Feingold bill, which would eliminate the unregulated soft money contributions that make up a large proportion of the parties' budgets.

3. Which of the following is an example of a soft money contribution?

   A. a $250 ticket to a fund-raising dinner-dance to benefit a mayoral candidate
   B. a $3,000 donation to the campaign fund of an incumbent senator
   C. a $3,000 contribution to a party fund for TV ads on political issues
   D. a $1,000 gift to a senator's campaign fund in response to a direct mail solicitation

4. Which of the following is the most likely reason soft money was not a major issue in the 1980s?

   A. People were less aware of soft money because disclosure was not required at that time.
   B. Political campaigns were publicly financed, so soft money was not needed.
   C. Most candidates spent part of their campaign funds on television ads.
   D. McCain and Feingold had not submitted their campaign finance reform bill.

Questions 5 and 6 refer to the following paragraph and graphs.

In order to win a presidential election, a candidate must win a majority of the vote in the Electoral College. Each state has as many electors as it has senators and representatives in Congress. In most states, the winner of the popular vote gets all the electoral votes of the state. These graphs show the popular and Electoral College votes in the election of 2012.

5. Which one of the following statements is supported by the information in the paragraph and the graphs?

   A. A presidential candidate will receive the same percentage of electoral votes as he or she received of the popular vote.
   B. Romney won a greater percentage of the electoral vote than of the popular vote in 2012.
   C. Jill Stein won a greater percentage of the popular vote than of the electoral vote in 2012.
   D. The total of popular votes cast for all candidates other than Barack Obama was greater than the total of those cast for Barack Obama.

6. Which of the following would be the best title for the paragraph and the graphs?

   A. 2012 Presidential Election: How Obama Defeated Romney
   B. 2012 Presidential Election: Third-Party Influence
   C. 2012 Presidential Election: Winning the Electoral College
   D. 2012 Presidential Election: Popular and Electoral Votes

Question 7 refers to the following passage.

Where do I vote? Your voting district is determined by your place of residence. Watch your local newspaper for an announcement indicating polling locations and times, or contact your local board of election to determine your voting location.

7. Which of the following is assumed but not stated outright in the voter guide above?

   A. The board of election is the county, city, or town office responsible for local voting.
   B. A voter's polling place is determined by his or her address.
   C. A voter can find his or her polling place on the Internet.
   D. A voter can call the Office of the Secretary of State to find out where to vote.

8. An interest group is an organization with specific goals that seeks to influence government policies.

   Place a ★ into the box next to each entity that constitutes an interest group. There may be more than one.

The Democratic Party, which nominates candidates and tries to win elections	
The National Association of Manufacturers, which lobbies for businesses	
The Federal Communications Commission, which regulates broadcasters	
The Cabinet, an advisory body for the president	
Public Citizen, a nonprofit consumer rights advocacy group	

WAYNE STAYSKAL
Courtesy Tampa Tribune

© 1998 Wayne Stayskal, Tampa Tribune. Reprinted by permission of Wayne Stayskal.

9. What is the main idea of this cartoon?

A. Most voters are working people.
B. Most registered voters don't vote.
C. Voters should establish another political party.
D. A non-voters' party would lose every election.

10. Which of the following values is the cartoonist appealing for?

A. the work ethic
B. majority rule
C. civic duty
D. national pride

11. An oligarchy is a system of government in which a small group of people holds power.

Which of the following is an oligarchy?

A. China, where the top leaders of the communist party control the government
B. Iraq, when it had a dictator, Saddam Hussein
C. Great Britain, with a monarch, a prime minister, and an elected parliament
D. Greece, with a prime minister and an elected parliament

12. Three typical laws from the code of Hammurabi, written about 1700 B.C.E., are "If a son strike his father, his hands shall be hewn off. If a man put out the eye of another man, his eye shall be put out. If he break another man's bone, his bone shall be broken."

What principle underlies these laws?

A. retribution
B. rehabilitation
C. incarceration
D. mediation

Questions 13 and 14 refer to the following map and table.

The Death Penalty in the United States, 2013

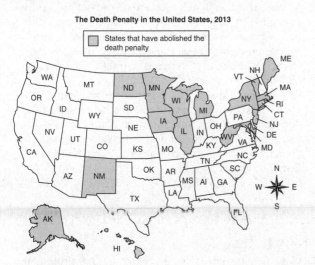

NOTE: Connecticut, Maryland, and New Mexico have abolished the death penalty prospectively. Anyone convicted of a capital offense that occurred prior to abolition of the death penalty in these states may be legally executed.

Homicide Rate per 100,000 Population, 2010

Highest	Lowest
Louisiana, 11.9	Vermont, 1.3
Mississippi, 9.6	New Hampshire, 1.4
Alabama, 8.2	Idaho, 1.5
Maryland, 7.6	Wyoming, 1.6
New Mexico, 7.4	Hawaii, 1.8

Source: National Center for Health Statistics and U.S. Bureau of the Census.

13. How many states have the death penalty?

   A. 12
   B. 18
   C. 32
   D. 40

14. People who favor capital punishment usually argue that it prevents serious crimes like homicide. Based on the map and chart, what is a logical flaw with this argument?

   A. A life sentence without parole costs taxpayers more than executing an inmate.
   B. Some executed inmates turn out to have been innocent based on newly discovered evidence.
   C. Two of the five states with the highest per capita homicide rates have abolished the death penalty.
   D. Two of the five states with the lowest per capita homicide rates have abolished the death penalty.

15. The U.S. Constitution gives the president the power to make treaties with foreign nations, and it gives the Senate the power to "advise and consent" on all treaties. Thus, a two-thirds majority of the Senate must ratify any treaty presented by the president. In 1978, President Jimmy Carter persuaded the Senate to ratify treaties with Panama that transferred control of the Panama Canal from the United States to Panama. Many Americans were outraged and believed that U.S. interests had been given away.

Which of the following is an opinion rather than a statement of fact?

   A. Presidents have the power to enter into treaties with foreign nations.
   B. A two-thirds majority of the Senate is needed to ratify a treaty.
   C. The 1978 Panama treaties sold out U.S. interests to Panama.
   D. The 1978 Panama treaties gave control of the Panama Canal to Panama.

16. In the mayor-council form of city government, voters elect both a mayor and a city council. The mayor is the city's chief executive, operating the city on a day-to-day basis and also serving a ceremonial function. The city council is a legislative body, in charge of the city's finances and passing city laws. In the council-manager form of city government, voters elect a city council that makes city policies and laws. The council may elect a mayor who has a largely ceremonial function. It appoints a professionally trained city manager to oversee day-to-day operations.

What is the main similarity between the mayor's role in the mayor-council and in the council-manager forms of city government?

   A. The mayor sets policy.
   B. The mayor runs day-to-day operations.
   C. The mayor is elected by voters.
   D. The mayor has ceremonial duties.

SOCIAL STUDIES ANSWERS AND EXPLANATIONS

Social Studies Skills

Lesson 1: Determine Central Idea and Draw Conclusions

Practice 1

1. **C. the characteristics of Greek tragedy** The passage describes tragedy as "central to Greek culture" and supports this point with details about the plots, staging, characters, and themes of Greek tragedy.

2. **D. The main character in Greek drama has a tragic flaw that causes his downfall.** Choice (D) cites one of the details the author uses to describe the characteristics of Greek tragedy. The other choices are all too broad (choice (A)) or misrepresent what the passage actually said (choices (B) and (C)).

3. **A. Ancient Greeks did not expect to see an original story each time they attended the theater.** Choice (A) is the only answer choice supported by information in the passage. The writer tells you that tragedies "told stories familiar from myths and epics," so it must have been the case that theatergoers knew the general story that would be acted out.

4. **D. Where do the incomes of senior citizens come from?** Choice (D) is correct because the graph tells you the sources of income for American senior citizens. The graph doesn't give any actual dollar amounts, nor does it state how many senior citizens there are in the U.S. You would need those numbers to answer the questions in choices (A), (B), and (C).

5. **B. Social Security benefits are the most widespread means of support for most senior citizens.** Each bar in the graph represents the percentage of all seniors who receive some of their income from that source. Since the Social Security bar is the tallest (representing more than 86% of all seniors), choice (B) must be true based on the graph.

Lesson 2: Interpret Words and Ideas

Practice 2

1. **C. political and social instability in some Northern European countries** In the first paragraph of the passage, the author mentions "riots, civil unrest, and open rebellion" as some of the factors that pushed German citizens to migrate. Those events are examples of "political and social instability," so choice (C) is correct.

2. **D. a painting of pioneers settling and farming productive prairie land** In the passage, the author discusses "abundance" in the second paragraph, giving examples of the kinds of optimistic messages that attracted people to the U.S. The image of pioneers opening up productive farmland is symbolic of the economic opportunity promised to 19th century immigrants to the U.S., so choice (D) is correct.

3. **C. a growth in the population of the United States** In the first paragraph, the author tells you that the number of immigrants arriving in the U.S. between 1820 and 1870 was greater than the entire U.S. population just 10 years before that time period. You can conclude from the passage that the U.S. population grew.

4. **B. Internal migration led to overgrazing.** According to the timeline, aggressive agriculture occurred prior to 1930 and the "black blizzards," caused in part by overgrazing, began in 1931. Internal migration did not begin until around 1933. Inferring that internal migration (which began later) caused overgrazing (which had already occurred) would be illogical, so choice (B) is correct.

5. **C. depleted topsoil** The "aggressive, mechanized farming techniques" that depleted the topsoil in the American Midwest and Southern plains occurred prior to and contributed to the dust storms and "black blizzards" that characterize the Great Dust Bowl. Internal migration (choice (B)) and failed farms (choice (C)) were results, not causes, of the Dust Bowl.

Lesson 3: Analyze Author's Purpose and Point of View

Practice 3

1. **C. propagandistic** Page 472 explains that propaganda uses emotional language to influence readers' behavior. Here, asking the readers to "have a part in Victory" is just such language.

2. **C. Citizens who plant war gardens help supply the war effort with essential resources.** As the passage explains, war gardens were encouraged so that, with citizens supplying more of their own food, the government could use its limited resources to feed and equip soldiers, sailors, and airmen. Choice (C) paraphrases this nicely.

3. **A. describe war gardens and explain their popularity in the United States** The author's tone is neutral and explanatory; he or she simply wants to explain what war gardens were and why they were popular during the two world wars. The author is not advocating a point of view (choice (B)), trying to compare or contrast the U.S. with any other country (choice (C)), or arguing against anyone else's position (choice (D)).

4. **C. a cancer** By using a frightening and often fatal disease such as "cancer" to describe the impact of the proposed regulations, the citizen is making an emotional comparison. The analogy is especially aggressive given that the issue addresses health and safety.

Lesson 4: Evaluate Author's Reasoning and Evidence

Practice 4

1. **A. Damming the Mekong could solve Cambodia's energy problems.** The author argues for cooperation among Cambodia and its neighboring countries, all of which share the Mekong river. The reason this is important, the author asserts, is because hydroelectric power from the Mekong would help solve Cambodia's energy problems. Nowhere in the argument, however, does the author support this contention.

2. **B. Strikes have a detrimental impact on workers.** The cartoon shows a laborer using a strike as a means of "cutting off" production, depicted as a tree branch. The joke is that the worker sits on the wrong

side of the branch he's cutting. Once the worker is successful in cutting off production, the cartoonist implies, he will fall to the ground along with production. Choice (B) neatly sums up the cartoonist's point.

3. **D. Ancient Greece pioneered democracy.** The one reason the author gives for believing that Ancient Greece was the greatest of the early civilization is that it was the birthplace of democracy. Thus, choice (D) is correct. Choice (A) is the author's opinion, not a fact supporting that opinion. Choices (B) and (C) are both reasons that ancient Babylon and Egypt (and not the author's favorite, Greece) might be considered great.

4. **B. The Constitution grants more power to the federal government than did the Articles of Confederation.** In each category compared in the chart, the federal government has more power under the Constitution than it had under the Articles of Confederation, so choice (B) is a valid inference, though it is not explicitly stated anywhere on the chart. All three wrong answers cite specific facts stated in the chart.

Lesson 5: Analyze Relationships Between Materials

Practice 5.1

1. **A. housing and food** Study the circle graph (pie chart) to see that the two largest portions are labeled with white (33%) and vertical lines (20%). Checking the legend to the right shows that these "slices" correspond to housing and food, respectively.

2. **D. Brazil has a higher divorce rate than Mexico.** This bar chart directly supports choice (D): Brazil's divorce rate is 0.6 per thousand, while Mexico's is 0.4 per thousand. Choice (B) is incorrect because this chart shows five countries in the Western Hemisphere, not all of them. One of the countries not shown on the chart may have a divorce rate even lower than Mexico's. Choice (C) is incorrect because this chart conveys nothing about how divorce rates have changed over time.

3. **D. fluctuated** As you read the line graph left to right, showing the change over time, you see that percentage of votes for third-party presidential candidates went up and down multiple times, so "fluctuated" is accurate.

4. **C. Third party candidates have never captured more than 10 percent of the popular vote in any presidential election.** The statement in choice (C) is disproved by 1968 (14 percent) and 1992 (more than 19 percent).

5. **C. how agriculture spread in the Americas** The map shows two places at which agriculture originated independently (indicated by black stars) and where agriculture spread out from those two points (indicated by the white arrows). The map shows no political boundaries (choice (A)) or physical features (choice (B)) of the Americas, nor does it claim to name all of the ancient civilizations on the two continents (choice (D)).

6. **B. Both the Andes civilization and Mesoamerica domesticated beans.** Check right below the names of the two civilizations named on the map and you'll find the crops they learned to grow. "Beans" is the only crop listed for both the Andes and Mesoamerican groups.

Practice 5.2

1. **D. Sea otters have been able to live in habitats from which they were once eliminated.** Choice (D) is directly supported by the third paragraph of the passage, which refers to successful "programs to reintroduce the sea otter into previously populated areas." Choice (C) is incorrect because, although the passage says that the sea otters in California have regained about two-thirds of their former habitat range, it does not indicate that they have reached two-thirds of their former population numbers. Choices (A) and (B) are not mentioned at all in the passage.

2. **D. The current range of the sea otter in California is larger than what it was in 1911.** According to the passage, the sea otter's range in 1911 "was limited . . . to a small area around Monterrey Bay." The map makes it clear that the sea otter's range now extends significantly to both the north and south of Monterrey Bay. Putting the information from the passage together with that from the map shows that choice (D) must be true.

3. **C. Without conservation efforts and reintroduction programs, the range of sea otters in California would be smaller than what is shown on the map.** In the third paragraph of the passage, the author states that conservation and reintroduction programs "have contributed to" the expansion of the sea otter's habitat range in California. This directly supports the statement in choice (C).

Lesson 6: Interpret Data and Statistics

Practice 6

1. **C. What percent of residents were 50 or over?** To calculate the percentage of New Mexico residents age 50 and over, you first find the number of residents 50 and over and divide that by the total number of residents. You can find the total number of residents who are at least age 50 by adding the categories for 50–64 and 65 & over. You are given the total number of residents so you can solve for this question. Because age brackets are grouped and exact ages aren't given, it is not possible to solve for choice (A). You cannot solve for choice (B) because the bracket "under 18" contains teenagers and non-teenagers with no distinction between the two. The chart gives no reasoning, only numerical information, so choice (D) is also incorrect.

2. **B. the average margin of victory was higher in years when a Democrat won than in years when a Republican won.** In both years in which a Republican won the presidential election (2000 and 2004) the final electoral vote count was very close. In each of the four years in which a Democrat won (1992, 1996, 2008, and 2012) the Democratic candidate

captured a much larger portion of the electoral vote. Thus, choice (B) is supported by the graph.

3. **C. 1920** Of the years shown on the graph, 1920 is the point when the rural and urban populations are closest in number. Prior to 1920, the rural population was much larger than the urban population. After 1920, the urban population begins to be much larger than the rural population.

4. **C. continued to grow, but at decreasing rates** The rural population continued to increase during every decade shown in the graph. However, the increase in population growth was less in the later decades than in the earlier decades, as evidenced by the smaller differences between the heights of the bars in the later decades than the earlier ones.

Social Studies Skills Practice Questions

1. **B. The unemployment rate declined consistently until shortly before the war's end.** Checking the timeline, you can see that World War II began in 1939 and ended in 1945. Unemployment went down every year between 1939 and 1944, and rose just slightly in 1945. Thus, choice (B)'s description of the war's impact on unemployment is correct.

2. **A. the stock market crash** Immediately after the stock market crash in 1929, unemployment increases dramatically and directly until 1933. That makes choice (A) correct. After 1933, unemployment declines gradually until the end of the war, and the decline is interrupted by a small increase during 1937–1938.

3. **D. The Seneca Falls Convention was a shocking event that undermined the nature of women.** There is no objective way to prove that something is "shocking and unnatural." Those words reveal that the statement in choice (D) was the opinion of one newspaper's editors.

4. **D. The Seneca Falls Convention was important in the fight for women's rights.** The passage's primary purpose is to explain how the women's movement "gained strength" at the Seneca Falls Convention.

5. **A. More than half of the reported cases of human plague in the United States between 1970 and 2010 were reported in four states.** Even if you don't recognize the four states in question as Arizona, California, Colorado, and New Mexico, the map clearly shows the overwhelming concentration of reported plague cases as occurring there. Choice (A) is justified by the information in the map.

6. **C. Several cases of plague were reported on the East Coast of the United States between 1970 and 2010.** The statement in choice (C) is clearly false given the information in the map. No cases of plague were recorded east of Illinois during the time period depicted by the map.

7. **D. The effects of the cotton gin on the cotton industry actually led to an increased demand for slaves in the South.** The fact stated in choice (D) is directly supported by the end of the passage where the writer explains the effects of the cotton gin: "with the boom in the cotton industry, more slaves were used to pick cotton at a faster rate."

8. **C. In most years, the percent population increase in South Dakota was greater than that in North Dakota.** Choice (C) is correct. In seven of the eleven years shown (every year from 2001–02 to 2007–08), South Dakota's annual population increase was greater than that of North Dakota. The increases were approximately equal in 2008–09, and North Dakota's increase was greater in the remaining three years. Choices (A) and (B) make statements about the populations of these states, but the graph only contains information about *percent increase*, or proportional increase, of the population.

9. **D. A smaller percentage of voters turned out for each midterm election than turned out for each presidential election.** The entire midterm election line graph falls below the line graph for the presidential elections, meaning that in each instance, the percentage of voters who turned out for the midterm election was smaller than the percentage that turned out for the presidential election.

10. **B. The average voter turnout for midterm elections was approximately how much lower than that for presidential elections for the years 1980–2008?** You can find the average voter turnout for each type of election by taking the average of each line graph. Dividing the average voter turnout for midterm elections by the average voter turnout for presidential elections and multiplying by 100 will answer the question in choice (B). The remaining answer choices all ask for the reasoning behind a given circumstance, and no rationale for the numbers can be determined using only the numbers themselves.

11. **C. "Most of our qualified teachers are underpaid"** Choice (C) is a value judgment. A fact is a statement that can be proven or disproven by direct experience or objective verification. An opinion is a statement of belief or judgment. President Johnson uses both facts and opinions to support his contention that there is a crisis in education, including statistical facts (choices (A), (B), and (D)) and the value judgment that teachers should be paid more.

12. **D. "Our Duty Is to Educate Our Children"** The excerpt is about the importance of educating every child in the country. It does not give a history of education, as stated in choice (A), nor does it mention the specifics of education in Michigan, as stated in choice (B). While the cost of college education is briefly mentioned in the second paragraph, it is simply a detail, not the main topic of the passage, so choice (C) is incorrect.

13. **C. The Union states had significant population advantages in the war.** It is clear that in all three graphs, the Confederate states were at a population disadvantage in comparison to the North at the start of the Civil War.

14. **B. What percentage of the total population of the United States was eligible for the military?** The percentage of the total population eligible for the

military can be found by obtaining the total population and the total population eligible for the military. Both can be found by using the charts. There is no information given about the total number of people that actually fought in the military, so answer choice (A) cannot be determined. Choices (C) and (D) both ask for reasoning behind something, which cannot be determined from the numbers alone.

U.S. History

Lesson 1: Exploration, Colonialism, and the American Revolution

Practice 1

1. **C. the Spanish** According to the map and the key, Spain had the southernmost colony along the east coast of what would eventually become the United States.
2. **B. The English established several colonies in the New World.** The map shows several English colonies along the New England coast and in what is now Virginia and Maryland.
3. **D. Haitian refugees who fled to the U.S. to escape a dictatorship** Like the early colonists, the Haitian refugees of the mid- and late 1900s came to the United States seeking freedom from political persecution.
4. **B. increased British taxes and restrictions on the colonies** The fourth and fifth sentences of paragraph 4 link increased taxes and restrictions to the outbreak of the American Revolution.
5. **B. They were concerned about the government becoming tyrannical.** The first amendment guarantees citizens' rights to pressure their government. The passage explains that the framers of the U.S. Constitution did not want the government to become overly powerful. While choices (A) and (C) were both rights listed amongst the guarantees of the First Amendment, they do not explain *why* the Framers listed them. Choice (B) discusses their motivations and is correct.

Lesson 2: Westward Expansion, the Civil War, and Reconstruction

Practice 2

1. **D. whether slavery should be permitted in territories in the West** This is implied in the third and fourth paragraphs of the passage. Choice (B) is incorrect because the fourth paragraph says that Abraham Lincoln promised to halt the spread of slavery, not to end it where it already existed.
2. **C. To balance the admission of Missouri, they agreed to a compromise in which Maine was admitted as a free state.** The third paragraph of the passage describes how the U.S. government tried to maintain a balance of power between the North and the South by adding states in pairs: one slave state and one free state. Since Missouri was a slave state, the most likely response of Northerners would be to propose the addition of a free state. (Indeed, Maine and Missouri were the 23rd and 24th states to join the United States.)
3. **D. concluded with the reunification of the nation** The information in the question indicates that North and South Vietnam were reunited under the Communists at the end of the Vietnam War. The passage implies that at the end of the U.S. Civil War, the North and the South again were united under the United States federal government.
4. **C. In 1868, many African Americans served in the government of South Carolina.** There are more than 20 African Americans included in this composite photograph of the South Carolina legislature. The other choices are opinions that cannot be confirmed by the photograph.
5. **A. African Americans in the South gained and then lost political power.** The number of African Americans in the composite photograph of the South Carolina state legislature of 1868 indicates that near the beginning of the Reconstruction period, African Americans had considerable political power. Paragraph 6 on page 488 states that by the 1870s, whites were preventing African Americans from exercising their newly won right to vote. This indicates that African Americans were losing political power as Reconstruction ended.

Lesson 3: Industrialization, Immigration, and the Progressive Era

Practice 3

1. **B. an increase in manufacturing** By definition, industrialization is related to increased manufacturing. This meaning is implied in the passage in paragraphs one and two.
2. **C. the development of the Bessemer process, which made it easier to produce steel** The first paragraph of the passage relates rapid industrialization to the invention of new industrial processes. The Bessemer process was one such process. It made steel more readily available for tools, railroads, construction, and other uses.
3. **C. cooperation with others to improve worker safety** The fourth paragraph indicates that union workers pledged to work together (cooperate) for better working conditions. The passage states that better working conditions include improved worker safety.
4. **D. fairness** The fifth paragraph discusses the Progressive Era. The fact that reformers were working to improve conditions for poor people and to give people a greater voice in government indicates that fairness was a strong ideal for them.
5. **B. Asia and the Americas** The second circle graph indicates that, in the years 2000–2009, 77 percent of persons obtaining legal resident status came from Asia and the Americas.
6. **C. The student failed to consider the different totals represented by each pie chart.** When comparing percentages that are based on two different totals, the percentages cannot be directly compared.

Lesson 4: The United States as an Emerging World Power

Practice 4

1. **D. military** The building of a naval base indicates that the correct category is "military."
2. **B. In World War II, the Allies included England, France, and Russia.** The author assumes that you realize that the Allies of World War II included the same major powers as the Allies in World War I. If you do not recognize this unstated assumption, you will not understand who fought whom in World War II.
3. **C. Unemployment fell after the start of the New Deal and continued to fall as the U.S. entered World War II.** The graph shows a decline in the unemployment rate after the New Deal went into effect in 1934. It shows that unemployment went up in 1938 but then dropped after that and dropped considerably after the U.S. entry into World War II in 1941.
4. **D. America took a strong leadership role during and after World War II.** The paragraph focuses on the role the United States played during and after World War II. The other choices are details from the paragraph or they bring up information not included in the paragraph.

Lesson 5: The Cold War and the Civil Rights Era

Practice 5

1. **D. no direct combat** The first paragraph of the passage implies that the name "Cold War" was used because there was no direct fighting.
2. **C. The buildup of nuclear arms increases fear and instability, not peace.** The statement about peace and stability made by the man on the right in the bottom frame of the cartoon is supposed to be ironic. The cartoonist's mention of the man's trembling arms suggests that the situation is not stable, and that perhaps we should be afraid.
3. **C. Americans were in complete agreement about pulling out of Vietnam.** Paragraph one states that even when defeat for South Vietnam seemed fairly certain, a few Americans still wanted to continue contributing to the fighting. Therefore, it is an overstatement to say that Americans were in complete agreement that pulling out of Vietnam was the right thing to do.
4. **B. petitioning for a city ordinance requiring those selling real estate to select a buyer without regard to race** Paragraph three states that the aim of the civil rights movement was to end segregation and discrimination in the United States. Preventing the selective selling of real estate was one important way civil rights activists worked to end discrimination, making decreased segregation possible.
5. **A. Reliance on technology has increased pollution.** This is a conclusion—a general statement about a topic. The other choices are details—facts or examples—that support this conclusion.

U.S. History Practice Questions

1. **B. Although the Cherokee adopted many aspects of white culture, they were driven off their ancestral lands.** This statement is the only one with a large enough scope to be considered a conclusion. The other choices are details that are either included in, related to, or not based on the time line.
2. **A. If the government can't protect us from white settlers here, now, how could it protect us from whites moving west in the future?** This question shows the lack of logic in the government's claim that location was what made it difficult to protect Cherokee rights. Location had nothing to do with the government's lack of protection of Cherokee land in the South. The government did not have the political will to enforce laws protecting the Cherokee.
3. **D. equal rights and opportunities for women** Adams's statements that women are not inferior and her invention of the term *Lordess* both indicate that she advocated equality for women.
4. **You may have listed any four of the following: Delaware, Kentucky, Maryland, Missouri, and West Virginia.** The map shows that these five slave states remained loyal to the Union.
5. **A. The nation's capital was located nearby.** If the nation's capital, located adjacent to the state of Maryland, had been surrounded by Confederate states, it would have been extremely difficult for the U.S. army to defend it. This would have given a great edge to the Confederacy during the Civil War. The other choices are untrue, irrelevant, or not verifiable by the map.
6. **D. to weaken the South by enlisting former slaves in the Union army** This was implied by the text of the Proclamation that is quoted. None of the other choices are supported by the text.
7. **C. Voting Rights Act of 1965.** The chart explains that this act prohibited literacy (reading) tests for voting.
8. **C. African Americans were granted the vote soon after the Civil War, but laws enforcing these rights had to be passed a century later.** This is implied by the passage of the 15th Amendment in 1870 and by the passage of the Voting Rights Act of 1965. Congress would not have passed the later law if the 15th Amendment were being upheld and enforced. Choice (A) is true, based on the chart, but is not a summary of the information in the chart.
9. **B. They both prohibited the legal separation of people by race in public places.** The chart shows that both the 1875 and the 1964 Civil Rights Acts banned racial segregation in public places.
10. **D. The telephone was the greatest electrical invention ever.** This statement is said to have been made by leading scientists of the time; this is not in the author's voice. It is the only opinion. Choices (A), (B), and (C) are all facts stated in the passage.
11. **B. the framers of the U.S. Constitution** The clothes of the men in the picture indicate that this cartoon is set in the late 1700s. Impeachment is discussed in the caption. Impeachment was a provision that the

framers of the Constitution included in order to prevent the kind of abuse of presidential power carried out by Nixon. Impeachment of elected officials was not discussed in the Declaration of Independence, which laid out the reasons for the United States' independence from Great Britain, so choice (A) is incorrect.

12. **A. the pursuit of justice** By investigating the circumstances of Watergate, Congress was trying to make sure that the nation's laws were carried out.

13. **C. the escalation and failure of the Vietnam War** Of the choices listed, only (C) describes an event just prior to the Watergate scandal. The bloodshed and failure of the Vietnam War caused many people to question authority, including the government, and to question decisions made by the government.

14. **C. 1,000,000** The scale on the vertical axis of the bar graph shows that population is measured in millions. The bar for Cuba stands one unit high. This means that about 1,000,000 people of Cuban descent lived in the U.S. in 1990.

15. **B. Mexico** The bar graph shows that most people in the U.S. who are Hispanic originally came from Mexico. Therefore, Mexico is the most likely nation of origin of the unknown family.

Civics and Government

Lesson 1: Historic Basis for U.S. System

Practice 1

1.

Direct democracy	In Country D, laws are made by the vote of all citizens.
Monarchy	In Country B, laws are made by a sovereign king and are subject to no review.
Representative democracy	In Country C, laws are made by Congress, an elected group of representatives.
Aristocracy	In Country A, laws are made and administered by lords who inherit their land and titles.

2. **B. They were concerned about protecting the rights of individuals.** According to the passage on page 500, the Founding Fathers were influenced by the Enlightenment philosophers, who did place importance on the rights of the individual.

3. **C. Parliament of England** Similar to the United States Congress, the parliamentary system in England allows for citizens to elect representatives to a lawmaking body.

4. **D. England during the Age of Enlightenment** According to the passage on page 500, England adopted a bill of rights for the individual during the Enlightenment. This action limited the monarchy's power over the individual.

5. **D. The president would become the chief lawmaker.** In a parliamentary democracy, the majority party in the Parliament appoints the president. Since the Parliament is the lawmaking body of government, the President would become the chief lawmaker.

Nothing in the text indicates whether this would make the office of the president more or less powerful than it currently is, so choices (A) and (B) are unsupported.

Lesson 2: The U.S. Constitution

Practice 2

1. **B. elected representatives exercising government power on behalf of citizens** According to the first paragraph of the passage, the key characteristic of a republic is elected officials governing for the voters.

2. **C. The details of government would be worked out in the future, as the need arose, within the framework of the Constitution.** The leaders who drafted the Constitution were wise enough to realize that they could not anticipate every eventuality, so instead of trying to cover everything in the Constitution, they made it a general framework within which specific future decisions and laws could be made.

3. **C. the power of an office, not an individual** Roosevelt's long tenure worried many people as they saw his power growing with time. They pursued term limits to prevent any individual from amassing too much power as president.

4. **D. The U.S. Supreme Court declaring an Illinois state law unconstitutional** The supremacy clause asserts the supremacy of federal law when it conflicts with state law. Therefore, the declaration that a state law is unconstitutional is an exercise of the supremacy clause.

5. **A. State governments do not usually act together.** The third and fourth methods of passing a constitutional amendment both require concerted action by state governments. Therefore, choice (A) would explain why those methods have never been used. Choices (B) and (D) are contradicted by information in the chart. Choice (C) repeats information in the chart, but does not provide a useful explanation.

Lesson 3: Levels and Branches of Government

Practice 3

1. **A. division of power between national and state governments** According to the second paragraph of the passage on page 504, a federalist form of government divides power between the national and state levels of government.

2. **D. the State Department** The State Department is part of the executive branch; its head is a member of the president's cabinet. The Democratic National Committee, choice (A), is not part of the government at all. Choice (B) is part of Congress, and therefore part of the legislative branch. Courts, choice (C), are in the judicial branch.

3. **A. Federal judges need not worry about pleasing their constituents in order to be reelected.** Because they do not need to please any constituents in order to be reelected, federal judges can preside without worrying about making unpopular decisions. This leaves them freer to be impartial judges of the law.

4.

Checks and balances	Limits that one branch of government can place on the other branches
Veto	The president's power to strike down a law
Senators	Legislators who serve six-year terms
Constituents	The people whom political leaders represent
Representatives	Legislators who serve two-year terms

5. **A. a governor vetoing a law passed by the state legislature** The governor, who heads the state's executive branch, is limiting the power of the state's legislative branch.

6. **B. a member of Congress** Although this person subscribes to the idea that the government is divided into three branches, he can only think of one of them—the one to which he belongs. Since he is probably in the legislative branch, he is likely to be a member of Congress. The way the desks are arranged and the way the man is standing to make his point are visual cues that the setting of the cartoon is Congress.

Lesson 4: The Electoral System

Practice 4

1. **C. receiving a majority in the Electoral College** According to the second paragraph of the passage on page 506 a president must have a majority in the Electoral College to be elected.

2. **A. Exit polls may be inaccurate if the people polled are not representative of the voting public as a whole or if the election is very close.** It is more likely that a poll will be wrong if an unrepresentative sample is used or if the election is very close. Under those circumstances it is hazardous to call an election based on exit poll results, as was shown in the 2000 presidential election, in which the media gave Florida's vote first to Gore, then to Bush, and only hours later declared the state too close to call.

3. **D. Two city council members are on a ballot to determine which one will run for mayor as a Democrat.** A primary is an election to choose among candidates of the same party. The winner of the primary then faces an opponent of another political party in the general election.

4. **B. In total, individuals contributed a greater dollar amount to House candidates than they did to Senate candidates.** Although Senatorial candidates received a higher percentage (greater by 4%) of their contributions from individual donors, the total dollar amount received by the House candidates was much higher (greater by approximately $350,000,000). Therefore, the total dollar amount of individual contributions received by the House candidates was ultimately greater than that received by the Senate candidates.

5. **A. In 2010, self-funding was a larger source of funds for Senate candidates than it was for House candidates.** The Senate candidates' own contributions accounted for 13% of the total Senate Candidates' Funds while the House Candidates' own contributions accounted for only 6% of the total House Candidates' Fund. In addition, calculations based on the total amount of funds reveal that Senate candidates spent more total dollars on self-funding than did House candidates.

Lesson 5: The Role of the Citizen

Practice 5

1. **B. The U.S. Constitution** According to the third paragraph of the passage, the Constitution sets forth the rights of citizens.

2. **A. resident alien** Because she moved here permanently as the wife of an American citizen, Louvina is a resident alien and will remain so until she qualifies for citizenship through naturalization.

3. **C. They would become enemy aliens.** If the country of aliens residing in the United States declares war on the United States, that nation becomes an enemy state, and the aliens become enemy aliens.

4. **B. privacy** The protection against unreasonable search and seizure is essentially a protection of certain aspects of citizens' privacy. The government must demonstrate a good reason before it is allowed to search or seize property.

5. **C. If the 2012 presidential election is representative of elections generally in the United States, voter turnout increases with age.** This is the only statement general enough to be a conclusion. All the other options are details from the graph that support this conclusion.

Lesson 6: Contemporary Issues in American Politics

Practice 6.1

1. **B. Texas sets the rural interstate highway speed limit at 80 miles per hour, and Delaware sets it at 55 miles per hour.** Each state may set its own highway speed limits. (The federal National Maximum Speed Law was in effect from 1974 to 1995, but was then repealed.)

2. **D. would be illegal, because it would violate the federal Voting Rights Act of 1965** The lesson explains that the Voting Rights Act outlawed literacy tests as a qualification for voting.

3. **A. the federal government** To recover from a major disaster, local areas depend heavily on federal assistance.

4.

Who can get married?	state
Who is a U.S. citizen?	federal
Which public school can a child attend?	local

Who can get married (e.g., how old one has to be, whether the couple can be of the same sex) is determined by each state. U.S. citizenship is determined by the Constitution and federal law. Public school attendance is determined by school district regulations.

Practice 6.2

1. **C. Many important decisions have determined that government must respect citizens' rights as laid out in the Bill of Rights.** Supreme Court decisions have played a key role in upholding and fleshing out the Bill of Rights.

2. **D. An individual has a reasonable expectation of privacy in his or her home.** The Fourth Amendment says that people cannot be searched or their property seized unless the government has probable cause, and this freedom from government intrusion is greatest in private spaces such as one's home.

3. **C. a public official to be removed from office** A recall election is when voters decide whether to remove a public official from office. This option allows voters to use a direct vote to end an elected official's term early.

4.

Election for president	55%
Election for U.S. House representative and state legislators in non-presidential-election years	40%
Election for county parks commissioner, school board members, and sheriff	25%

Voter turnout tends to be higher for presidential elections than for congressional elections in years when a president is not being elected. Voter turnout is lowest for local elections.

Civics and Government Practice Questions

1. **B. In 2013, a different major party controlled the House than controlled the Senate.** According to the numbers of the 113th Congress, the Republicans had majority control in the House and the Democrats had majority control in the Senate. Choice (A) is too broad to be a summary of this chart which focuses on political divisions. The conclusions in choices (C) and (D) require more information than the chart provides.

2. **B. Bill of Rights of the U.S. Constitution, which guarantees citizens certain rights,** Like the Magna Carta, the Bill of Rights of the U.S. Constitution accords citizens certain rights and protections. Note that the scope of the Bill of Rights is broader in that it protects the rights of all citizens, not just a special group, as the Magna Carta did.

3. **C. a $3,000 contribution to a party fund for TV ads on political issues** Of all the choices, this is the only donation that is going to a political party fund rather than to a specific candidate, so it is a "soft money" contribution.

4. **A. People were less aware of soft money because disclosure was not required.** During the 1980s, political parties did not have to reveal the amount and sources of their soft money contributions, so the extent of this type of campaign financing was not generally known. Only when a law was passed requiring disclosure did people become aware of the scale of soft money donations and so began to raise their concerns about the issue.

5. **C. Jill Stein won a greater percentage of the popular vote than of the electoral vote in 2012.** Jill Stein won 0.36% of the popular vote, but she did not win any electoral votes in the 2012 election.

6. **D. 2012 Presidential Election: Popular and Electoral Votes** This is the only option that covers the topic of the paragraph as well as that of the graphs.

7. **A. The board of election is the county, city, or town office responsible for local voting.** Nowhere in this excerpt from the voter's guide is the board of election defined or explained; the writer assumes that the reader knows what it is.

8.

The Democratic Party, which nominates candidates and tries to win elections	
The National Association of Manufacturers, which lobbies for businesses	★
The Federal Communications Commission, which regulates broadcasters	
The Cabinet, an advisory body for the president	
Public Citizen, a nonprofit consumer rights advocacy group	★

9. **B. Most registered voters don't vote.** Despite the fact that voting is one of the obligations of citizens, in most elections, less than half of the nation's registered voters actually vote.

10. **C. civic duty** The cartoonist is appealing to voters to take their civic duty to vote more seriously.

11. **A. China, where the top leaders of the Communist party control the government** Of the national governments described, only China is an oligarchy, a government with rule by a small group of people. The other options are not oligarchies; they are either democracies or autocracies.

12. **A. retribution** These laws all embody the urge to take revenge on wrongdoers, or to exact retribution. The other principles underlie the modern criminal justice system and other modern legal systems.

13. **C. 32** Look for the map key to determine the symbol for death penalty states. According to the map, 18 states do not have the death penalty, so 32 out of 50 states have the death penalty.

14. **D. Two of the five states with the lowest per capita homicide rates have abolished the death penalty.** If that argument were correct, then the states with the lowest homicide rates should all be death penalty states, but that is not the case. Two states—Vermont and Hawaii—that have homicide rates among the lowest in the nation do not have the death penalty.

15. **C. The 1978 Panama treaties sold out U.S. interests to Panama.** Choice (C) states an opinion about the Panama treaties, not a fact that can be tested or proved. The word in the passage that signals an opinion is "believed."

16. **D. The mayor has ceremonial duties.** In both the mayor-council and the council-manager forms of city government, at least part of the time, the mayor plays a ceremonial role.

ABOUT THE TEST

Science

The TASC Science Test assesses your ability to understand, interpret, and apply scientific information. You will have 85 minutes to answer approximately 47 multiple-choice questions. Most questions will be multiple-choice, but you may also see multiple-response, drag-and-drop, and constructed-response items. (See the "Question Formats on the TASC" section in the online chapter "About the TASC" for more information about question formats on the TASC test.)

Each question will assess both your familiarity with a content area and your ability to perform a skill related to understanding and interpreting scientific information.

Science Content Areas

Life Science (34%) topics include cell structures and processes, human body systems, health and nutrition, heredity and reproduction, genetics and DNA, evolution and natural selection, and the organization of ecosystems.

Earth and Space Science (33%) topics include the structure of Earth, plate tectonics, geological cycles and processes, renewable and nonrenewable natural resources, weather and climate, the solar system, and the universe.

Physical Science (33%) topics include atoms and molecules, properties and states of matter, chemical reactions, energy and work, motion and forces, waves, electricity, and magnetism.

Science Skills

In addition to testing your understanding of science passages and graphics, the TASC Science Test questions are based on your understanding of skills that are used in scientific study and investigation. After you study these skills, you will reinforce them as you work through the unit. The science skills include:

- **Comprehending scientific presentations** to interpret passages and graphics
- **Using the scientific method** to design investigations, reason from data, and work with findings
- **Reasoning with scientific information** to evaluate conclusions with evidence
- **Applying concepts and formulas** to express scientific information and apply scientific theories
- **Using statistics and probability** in a science context

You will have to perform some calculations on the Science Test. For those questions, you will be able to use a scientific calculator just as you may on the Mathematics Test. See the Mathematics unit on pages 166–167 for more information about using a calculator on the TASC.

See the "TASC Blueprint Alignment: Tables and Notes" section in the online chapter "About the TASC" for more information about how material in this unit aligns to CTB/McGraw-Hill's published TASC test blueprints.

SCIENCE PRETEST
PART I: SCIENCE SKILLS

Directions: You may fill in the circles next to the correct answers or write your answers on a separate piece of paper.

Questions 1 and 2 refer to the following passage.

For many years, scientists believed that all living things depended on sunlight for their energy. For example, human beings derive energy from food. Our food comes either from plants that require sunlight or from animals, which eat plants that require sunlight.

However, in the 1970s scientists discovered hot springs, called *hydrothermal vents*, in the ocean floor. These vents are miles below the surface of the ocean, far beyond the reach of sunlight. Yet these vents are surrounded by fascinating life forms, including giant red tube worms, eyeless shrimp, hairy-looking crabs, and communities of bacteria that grow like carpets on the ocean floor.

Those bacteria feed on minerals, like sulfur, that flow upward through the vents. The bacteria use a process called *chemosynthesis* to turn the minerals into nutrition. The bacteria, in turn, are eaten by many of the animals that live near the vents. Thus, those animals take in a source of energy that does not derive from sunlight.

1. Which of the following would be a good title for this passage?

   ○ A. "The Advantages and Disadvantages of Life Near Hydrothermal Vents"
   ○ B. "Hydrothermal Vents: A Potential Fuel Source for Our Energy-Hungry Economy"
   ○ C. "Hydrothermal Vents Suggest That Not All Life Is Solar-Powered"
   ○ D. "Major 20th-Century Advances in Oceanography"

2. Which of the following is a detail that supports the main idea of the passage?

   ○ A. Many scientists believe that all living creatures depend on sunlight for their energy.
   ○ B. Hydrothermal vents were not discovered until the 1970s.
   ○ C. The hairy-looking crabs are covered in structures that enable them to catch tiny particles of food.
   ○ D. No sunlight penetrates to the world of hydrothermal ocean vents.

Questions 3 and 4 refer to the following passage.

In a *radioactive* element like uranium, atoms give off some of their particles. In the 19th century, chemist Marie Curie discovered that the radioactivity of a compound depends on the amount of a radioactive element it contains.

Then Curie noticed something strange. Pitchblende, a compound that contains radioactive uranium, gives off more radiation than pure uranium. Curie wondered why that would be the case. She guessed that pitchblende might contain another element that was even more radioactive than uranium.

To find out, Curie and her husband isolated the elements that make up pitchblende. After isolating each element, they measured its radioactivity. As a result of this process, the Curies discovered that pitchblende contains a highly radioactive element, which no one had identified before. They named their discovery *polonium*.

3. Which of the following restates Marie Curie's hypothesis about pitchblende?

   ○ A. Pitchblende contains uranium.
   ○ B. Uranium interacts with the nonradioactive elements in pitchblende to increase its radioactivity.
   ○ C. Polonium was discovered by the Curies as a result of their experiment.
   ○ D. Pitchblende contains an element that is more radioactive than uranium.

4. Which of the following is a reasonable conclusion based on Curie's experiment?

   ○ A. Pitchblende is more radioactive than pure uranium because it contains polonium.
   ○ B. Polonium is only one of many reasons why pitchblende is more radioactive than pure uranium.
   ○ C. Marie Curie would become famous.
   ○ D. The Curies were not the first physicists to isolate polonium.

Questions 5 and 6 refer to the following passage.

The **ozone layer** is a part of the upper atmosphere with high concentrations of ozone, a form of oxygen. The ozone layer absorbs between 97 percent and 99 percent of the sun's medium-frequency **ultraviolet light**, which can cause skin damage and even skin cancers. For this reason, depletion of the ozone layer is potentially a global health risk. The ozone layer has been decreasing in thickness for decades due to atmospheric pollution. In particular, **chlorofluorocarbons** (CFCs), used in aerosol sprays and refrigerators, were so harmful to the ozone layer that a global ban was implemented in 1994, and production had almost entirely ceased by 2004. However, this ban was not effective; the hole in the ozone layer that appeared over Antarctica reached its largest recorded size in 2006.

5. Which evidence from the passage supports the conclusion that CFCs remain in the atmosphere for some time after their use?

   A. The ozone layer started thinning decades ago.
   B. The hole in the ozone layer reached its largest size after CFCs were banned from production and use.
   C. CFCs are used both in aerosols and as refrigerants.
   D. CFCs absorb medium-frequency ultraviolet light.

6. Which of the following additional pieces of evidence would best counter the author's opinion that the ban on CFCs was not effective?

   A. The ozone hole is not literally a hole but rather an area in which the ozone layer is depleted by more than 50 percent.
   B. While the ozone layer continues to thin, it is thinning at a rate much lower than it has in the past.
   C. Skin cancer rates near the equator, far from Antarctica, have not changed significantly since 1994.
   D. The CFC ban contains a few extremely narrow exceptions for uses where no suitable replacement exists, such as in fire-suppression systems on airplanes.

Questions 7 and 8 refer to the following text.

Adenosine triphosphate (ATP) is one of the most important chemicals for the function of the cells of all known living organisms. It stores and transports energy within and between cells. When a cell needs to use this energy, a chemical reaction releases it. Adenosine triphosphate and water can combine to remove either a **phosphate** (P_i) or **pyrophosphate** (PP_i) from the ATP, leaving **adenosine diphosphate** (ADP) or **adenosine monophosphate** (AMP) respectively.

Equation	Energy released (in kilocalories per mole)
$ATP + H_2O \rightarrow ADP + P_i$	7.3
$ATP + H_2O \rightarrow AMP + PP_i$	10.9

7. Which answer choice describes the process in the equation $ATP + H_2O \rightarrow AMP + PP_i$?

   A. Adenosine triphosphate is transported from one part of a cell to another.
   B. Adenosine triphosphate is broken down into adenosine monophosphate and a pyrophosphate, releasing energy.
   C. Adenosine monophosphate is broken down into water and a pyrophosphate, releasing energy.
   D. Adenosine monophosphate stores energy, which is transported to another cell.

8. Which of the following chemicals plays a role most similar to that of ATP?

   A. Lactase, which breaks down the lactose sugar found in milk for easier digestion
   B. DNA, which is found in the nucleus of every cell and contains instructions for the cell to manufacture proteins
   C. Hemoglobin, which allows red blood cells to carry oxygen
   D. Glycogen, which stores sugars that can be broken off in differing amounts when the body needs energy

	P	P
w	Pw	Pw
w	Pw	Pw

	P	w
P	PP	Pw
w	Pw	ww

9. An equal number of seeds are produced from each of two pairs of flowers. One pair is a purebred pink plant with dominant pink genes (P) and a purebred white plant with recessive white genes (w). The other pair is made up of two hybrid plants, which are pink. The Punnett squares above show all possible combinations of alleles for the two pairs. If a seed is selected at random from the offspring of those two pairs, what is the probability that the selected seed will grow to be white?

- A. $\frac{1}{8}$

- B. $\frac{1}{4}$

- C. $\frac{3}{4}$

- D. $\frac{7}{8}$

Question 10 refers to the following graph.

Bounce Experiment Results

10. A ball was dropped onto a surface from different heights, and the height of the first bounce of each drop was recorded. The graph above illustrates the initial heights and bounce heights of the six trials in the experiment. What was the average (arithmetic mean) difference between the drop height and the first bounce height, in feet?

○ A. $2\frac{1}{2}$

○ B. $3\frac{1}{2}$

○ C. 8

○ D. 21

SCIENCE PRETEST

PART II: SCIENCE CONTENT

Directions: You may fill in the circles next to the correct answers or write your answers on a separate piece of paper.

Question 1 refers to the following paragraph and diagram.

A neuron is the basic functional unit of the nervous system. Neurons transmit information throughout the body.

A Neuron

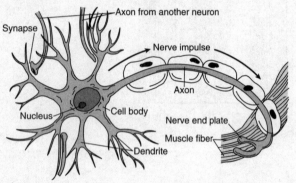

1. Which of the following is implied by the paragraph and the diagram?

   ○ A. Neurons are part of the endocrine system.
   ○ B. Oxygen is carried throughout the body by neurons.
   ○ C. Neurons transmit instructions regarding movement to muscles.
   ○ D. Nerve impulses travel from the axon to the cell body.

2. A comet is a small body made of ice and dust that orbits the sun in an elliptical, or oval, path. As the comet approaches the sun, its core heats up, releasing gas and dust. The gas and dust stream away from the comet in a tail that may be millions of miles long. Some scientists believe that comets formed when the solar system was born.

   Based on the paragraph, which of the following statements is an opinion rather than a fact?

   ○ A. Comets are small bodies of ice and dust.
   ○ B. The orbit of a comet has an elliptical shape.
   ○ C. Comets release gas and dust as they approach the sun.
   ○ D. Comets formed when the solar system was born.

3. In a photochemical reaction, light starts the reaction. Light can start a chemical reaction by exciting atoms and molecules, making them unstable and more likely to react with other atoms and molecules.

   Which of the following is an example of a photochemical reaction?

   ○ A. polymerization, in which long-chain organic compounds are formed from repeating units called monomers
   ○ B. fractional distillation, in which various petroleum products are separated out of crude oil
   ○ C. neutralization, in which an acid and a base react to form a salt and water
   ○ D. photosynthesis, in which green plants use the energy from sunlight to make carbohydrates from water and carbon dioxide

Questions 4 through 6 refer to the following chart.

Some Glands of the Endocrine System

Endocrine Gland	Hormone	Function
Pituitary gland	Growth hormone	Promotes bone and muscle growth
Ovary	Estrogen	Stimulates development of female secondary sexual characteristics
Testis	Testosterone	Stimulates development of male secondary sexual characteristics
Adrenal gland	Adrenaline	Increases heart activity, breathing rate, and blood flow to muscles for "fight or flight"
Thyroid	Thyroxine	Regulates metabolism and growth
Pancreas	Insulin	Regulates blood sugar levels

4. What is the function of the hormone thyroxine?

   ○ A. It controls female secondary sexual characteristics.
   ○ B. It controls male secondary sexual characteristics.
   ○ C. It speeds up the pulse and breathing rate for "fight or flight."
   ○ D. It helps control metabolism and growth.

5. People who have one form of the disease diabetes mellitus do not produce enough insulin. Based on the chart, what is the general effect of this disease?

   ○ A. stunted growth
   ○ B. excess growth
   ○ C. overproduction of estrogen
   ○ D. uncontrolled blood sugar levels

6. Paul, a child who was not growing as rapidly as he should, was given growth hormone to stimulate his growth. Paul anticipated that the hormone would enable him to reach an adult height of over six feet, even though his parents are both below average height. In fact, Paul's adult height was 5 feet 7 inches.

   What was wrong with Paul's thinking?

   ○ A. Growth hormone is only one of several factors that determine a person's adult height.
   ○ B. Growth hormone, when administered as a drug, does not affect a person's height.
   ○ C. In order to grow to over six feet tall, Paul would have had to take insulin, too.
   ○ D. In order to grow to over six feet tall, Paul would have had to take testosterone, too.

7. An emulsion is a mixture of two liquids whose particles are evenly scattered in one another without dissolving. Emulsions are unstable. After a time, the liquids separate.

   Which of the following is an emulsion?

   ○ A. tea with sugar
   ○ B. salt water
   ○ C. oil and vinegar salad dressing
   ○ D. food coloring and water

8. Earth science includes the study of Earth's atmosphere—the layer of gases that surrounds Earth—and Earth's hydrosphere—the oceans, rivers, lakes, and groundwater.

Which of the following scientists would be most likely to apply knowledge from a study of both the atmosphere and hydrosphere to his or her work?

○ A. a geologist who studies volcanoes and mountain formation

○ B. an astronomer who studies the planets of the solar system

○ C. a meteorologist who studies weather patterns and predicts weather

○ D. an ecologist who studies the distribution of populations of organisms

Question 9 refers to the following chart.

Organisms in a Food Chain

Role	Description
Producer	A green plant, which produces its own food using energy from sunlight
Herbivore	An animal that gets nutrients by eating plants
Carnivore	An animal that gets nutrients by eating other animals
Omnivore	An animal that gets nutrients by eating both plants and animals
Decomposer	An organism that gets nutrients from feeding on dead organisms and returns nutrients to the soil in the process

9. Earthworms break down large pieces of dead organic material in the soil. What role do earthworms play in the food chain?

○ A. They are producers.

○ B. They are herbivores.

○ C. They are carnivores.

○ D. They are decomposers.

Question 10 refers to the following graph.

Saturated Fat in Some Common Foods

Food	Grams per Serving
1 oz cheddar	6.0
1 oz low-fat cheddar	1.2
1 c. whole milk	5.1
1 c. 1% milk	1.6
1/2 c. ice cream	4.5
1/2 c. frozen yogurt	2.5
3 oz regular ground beef	7.2
3 oz extra lean ground beef	5.3
croissant	6.6
plain bagel	0.1

10. Suppose a child's diet usually includes two servings of cheese, four servings of milk, one serving of ice cream or frozen yogurt, one serving of ground beef, and a croissant or bagel every day.

If the child's parent wanted to decrease the amount of saturated fat in the child's daily diet, which of the following actions would be most effective?

○ A. switch from regular to low-fat cheddar

○ B. switch from whole milk to 1 percent milk

○ C. switch from frozen yogurt to ice cream

○ D. switch from regular to extra lean ground beef

11. Torque is the ability of a force to produce rotation. The torque of any force is equal to the amount of the force multiplied by the distance from the pivot point to the point where the force is applied. For example, when you go through a revolving door, you are applying force as you push. The torque of your force is equal to the force you apply times the distance between your hand and the axis of the revolving door.

Which of the following actions would decrease torque as you go through a revolving door?

A. moving your hand closer to the center of the revolving door
B. moving your hand closer to the outer edge of the revolving door
C. pushing with two hands rather than one hand
D. leaning toward the door as you push to increase your force

Question 12 refers to the following graph.

U.S. Consumption of Energy by Source, 1997 (in common unit of metric tons oil equivalent [TOE])

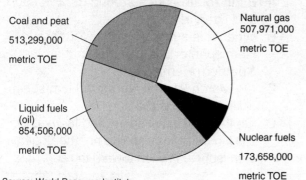

Coal and peat 513,299,000 metric TOE

Natural gas 507,971,000 metric TOE

Liquid fuels (oil) 854,506,000 metric TOE

Nuclear fuels 173,658,000 metric TOE

Source: World Resource Institute

12. Of the four energy sources shown, which two are the most similar in the proportion of energy they supply in the United States?

A. coal/peat and natural gas
B. natural gas and nuclear fuels
C. nuclear fuels and liquid fuels
D. liquid fuels and natural gas

Question 13 refers to the following paragraph and map.

In 1620, the eastern half of the United States was covered by virgin forest—forest that had never been cut down. Many parts of this region today are covered by second-growth forest— the ecosystem that eventually grows back after farmland is abandoned.

Virgin Forest of the United States 1620–1990

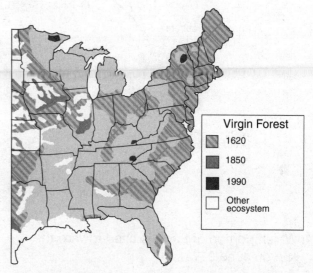

Virgin Forest
1620
1850
1990
Other ecosystem

Source: *National Geographic*

13. Which of the following conclusions is supported by the paragraph and the map?

A. The western half of the United States had far less forest cover in 1620 than did the eastern half.
B. As European Americans moved from the East Coast westward between 1620 and 1850, they cut down forests to build farms.
C. A number of relatively large areas of virgin forest remain in the eastern half of the United States today.
D. Today's second-growth forests in the eastern United States have fewer species of plants and animals than the virgin forest did.

Questions 14 and 15 refer to the following information and diagram.

The seasons occur because the axis of Earth is tilted. At different times of year, different parts of Earth get more hours of higher-intensity sunlight. As the diagram shows, summer begins in the Southern Hemisphere on December 21, when that hemisphere is tilted toward the sun.

Why Earth Has Seasons

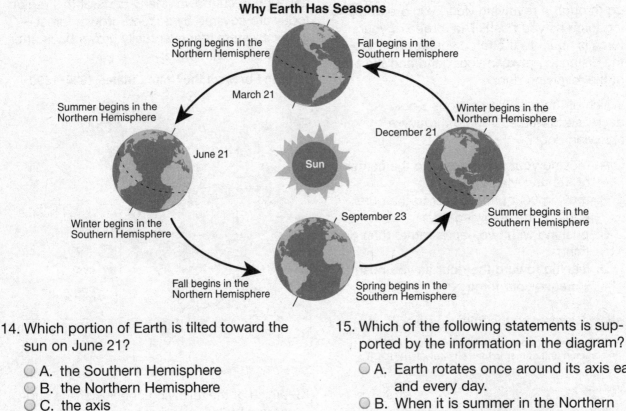

14. Which portion of Earth is tilted toward the sun on June 21?

○ A. the Southern Hemisphere
○ B. the Northern Hemisphere
○ C. the axis
○ D. the equator

15. Which of the following statements is supported by the information in the diagram?

○ A. Earth rotates once around its axis each and every day.
○ B. When it is summer in the Northern Hemisphere, it is summer in the Southern Hemisphere.
○ C. On March 21, the Northern Hemisphere is tilted toward the sun.
○ D. On the first day of spring and fall, neither the Northern Hemisphere nor the Southern Hemisphere is tilted toward the sun.

16. Ecologists use a tool called a quadrat when doing field studies of plant distribution. A quadrat is an open, four-sided structure about a meter square. It is placed on the ground, whether in a meadow, on a hillside, or at the beach. The ecologist then counts the plants of different species inside the quadrat. By using a quadrat, an ecologist can get a more accurate understanding of species distribution than by doing a random count.

Which of the following statements can be inferred from the given facts?

○ A. A quadrat is a tool used by ecologists.
○ B. A quadrat is a frame about a meter square.
○ C. To use a quadrat, the ecologist places it on the ground.
○ D. A quadrat makes plant distribution estimates more reliable.

17. According to Charles's Law, when the pressure of a gas remains constant, the volume of a quantity of gas varies directly with the temperature. In other words, as the temperature of a gas rises, the volume of the gas increases.

Which of the following graphs illustrates Charles's Law?

A.

B.

C.

D.

18. At the beginning of the twentieth century, only three subatomic particles were known: protons, neutrons, and electrons. In the last half of the century, dozens of new particles were discovered using new technology. Machines called particle accelerators push particles to tremendous speeds. When two particles collide at high speed, they annihilate each other and new particles are formed.

Which of the following is not stated in the passage?

A. Protons, neutrons, and electrons are subatomic particles.
B. Atoms are composed of subatomic particles.
C. In particle accelerators, particles are pushed to very high speeds.
D. Particles that collide at high speed annihilate each other, forming new particles.

19. Density is the amount of matter, or mass, in a given volume of a substance. To find the density of an object, you divide its mass by its volume. A student wanted to find the density of a 3-cm cube of lead. First, she used a scale to find the mass of the cube. Next, she calculated the volume by multiplying 3 cm × 3 cm × 3 cm. Finally, she divided the volume by the mass to find the density of the lead cube.

Why was the density the student calculated inaccurate?

A. A scale cannot be used for finding mass.
B. Multiplying three sides of the cube will not give the cube's volume.
C. The student should have found the volume first.
D. The student should have divided the mass by the volume.

Questions 20 and 21 refer to the following information and diagram.

When the U.S. Mint had to design a new dollar coin to replace the old Susan B. Anthony dollar, it faced a problem. It wanted to design an appealing, distinctive golden-color coin that vending machines would recognize as an Anthony dollar, which looks like a quarter. Vending machines identify coins by their weight, size, and electromagnetic signature. They test a coin by passing an electric current through it and measuring the resulting magnetic field. Thus, the new Sacagawea dollar coin had to be similar to the Anthony dollar in size, weight, and electromagnetic signature.

Size and weight were easy to imitate, but the electromagnetic signature was not. The Anthony dollar had a copper core covered by a silver-colored copper-nickel alloy. All the golden alloy sample coins had three times as much electrical conductivity as the Anthony dollar. Vending machines did not recognize them. Finally, metallurgists came up with the idea of adding manganese, which has low conductivity, to zinc and copper. The result was a coin consisting of 77 percent copper, 12 percent zinc, 7 percent manganese, and 4 percent nickel. The pure copper core was covered with a golden alloy of manganese, zinc, copper, and nickel. This golden coin has electromagnetic properties similar to those of the Anthony dollar, so it is recognized by U.S. vending machines.

20. It can be inferred from the passage above that an alloy is

○ A. a magnetic material.
○ B. a material that stops electricity.
○ C. a mixture of metals.
○ D. the core of a coin.

21. The U.S. Mint could have solved its technical problems with the Sacagawea dollar by making it out of the same metals as the Anthony dollar. Why did the people at the Mint decide against this?

○ A. The metals in the Anthony alloy were too rare and expensive to use in the new coin.
○ B. Like nickels, dimes, and quarters, the Anthony dollar was silver-colored and therefore not distinctive.
○ C. The electromagnetic signature of the Anthony coin was not recognized by vending machines.
○ D. The size and weight of the Anthony coin made it impractical for use in vending machines.

Question 22 refers to the following chart.

Types of Plants

Type	Characteristics
Annual	Completes life cycle in one growing season
Biennial	Completes life cycle in two growing seasons; flowers during second year
Perennial	Lives for years and flowers each year
Tender	Sensitive to cold (can be annual, biennial, or perennial)
Hardy	Can withstand frosts (can be annual, biennial, or perennial)

22. Marion has little interest in or time for gardening, yet she would like to have flowers in her front yard. Which of the following types of plants would probably give her the most flowers for the least effort?

○ A. annuals
○ B. biennials
○ C. tender plants
○ D. hardy perennials

Question 23 refers to the following information and diagram.

How a Reflecting Telescope Works

23. If the flat mirror were removed from this telescope, what would happen as a result?

○ A. Light rays would not enter the telescope.

○ B. Light rays would not reflect off the curved mirror.

○ C. A viewer could not see anything through the telescope.

○ D. A viewer could see only objects that were in focus.

24. The discovery of a new drug was once largely the result of trial and error, laboratory experiments, and clinical trials. Although these methods are still used, computer science is being applied to the drug discovery process to refine it and speed it up. For example, computers can analyze genetic material to locate genes that may hold promise in the development of new drugs. Computers can analyze data generated by lab experiments. Computer simulations can even help predict how a particular drug will work under specific circumstances.

What is the main reason that computers are now being used in the drug discovery process?

○ A. They enable scientists to abandon trial-and-error methods.

○ B. They help scientists analyze large amounts of data in a systematic way.

○ C. They have made laboratory experiments unnecessary.

○ D. They have made clinical trials unnecessary.

25. People planning to visit tropical countries may need to be vaccinated against disease. For example, two to four weeks before a trip, travelers should be vaccinated against typhoid fever. The vaccine is 50 to 80 percent effective. Additional precautions against typhoid fever include avoiding food and water that may be dirty.

If a traveler is vaccinated against typhoid fever two to four weeks before a brief trip to the tropics, which of the following best explains why he or she should take extra precautions against contracting the disease?

○ A. The typhoid fever vaccination is effective for only a few months.

○ B. The typhoid fever vaccination is only 50 to 80 percent effective.

○ C. The typhoid fever vaccination can cause soreness, fever, and headache.

○ D. Typhoid fever spreads only through air and water.

STOP. Congratulations! You have completed the Science pretest. Your next step is to check your answers with the Science Pretest Answers and Explanations that begin on the next page and fill in the study planner that appears on page xx.

Science Pretest Answers and Explanations

Part I: Science Skills

1. **C. "Hydrothermal Vents Suggest That Not All Life Is Solar-Powered"** The author's main point is that some of the life forms around hydrothermal vents derive energy from a source other than the sun. Choice (C) captures that idea. Choices (A) and (B) mischaracterize the subject matter of the passage, and choice (D) is far too broad.

2. **D. No sunlight penetrates to the world of hydrothermal ocean vents.** Only choice (D) supports the idea that some life forms derive energy from a source other than the sun. Choice (A) distorts the meaning of the first line of the passage. Choice (B) is true but does not serve to support this idea. Choice (C) is not stated in the passage.

3. **D. Pitchblende contains an element that is more radioactive than uranium.** A hypothesis is a guess made by a scientist before the scientist conducts an experiment. Before Marie Curie and her husband conducted their experiment with pitchblende, she guessed that pitchblende was more radioactive than pure uranium because pitchblende contained a radioactive element other than uranium. Curie already knew choice (A) to be true, so it was not a hypothesis she intended to test. Choice (B) is not stated in the passage. Choice (C) describes the outcome of the Curies' experiment—not their initial hypothesis.

4. **A. Pitchblende is more radioactive than pure uranium because it contains polonium.** As a result of their experiment, the Curies discovered that pitchblende contained polonium, a highly radioactive element. This suggests that Marie Curie's initial hypothesis was correct. Choice (B) is not supported by the passage. Choice (C) is unsupported by the passage.

5. **B. The hole in the ozone reached its largest size after CFCs were banned from production and use.** According to the passage, the hole in the ozone layer reached its largest size after CFCs were discontinued. The presence of CFCs that stayed in the atmosphere for years after use is a likely explanation for this phenomenon.

6. **B. While the ozone layer continues to thin, it is thinning at a rate much lower than it has in the past.** If the rate of ozone depletion has slowed significantly, it is likely that the CFC ban was at least partially effective.

7. **B. Adenosine triphosphate is broken down into adenosine monophosphate and a pyrophosphate, releasing energy.** The text describes this relation between ATP (adenosine triphosphate), AMP (adenosine monophosphate), and PP_i (pyrophosphate).

8. **D. Glycogen, which stores sugars that can be broken off in differing amounts when the body needs energy** Both glycogen and ATP store energy, and both can release different amounts of energy depending on the needs of the cell or organism.

9. **A. $\frac{1}{8}$** Because white is a recessive trait, a plant must have two white genes (ww) in order to be white. Of the 8 possible outcomes illustrated in the Punnett squares, only one has this pair of genes.

10. **B. $3\frac{1}{2}$** The difference between the drop height and the first bounce height for the first drop was 1 foot. For the second, it was also 1 foot, and for the third, 2 feet. Find these differences for all the drops. The average of a set of items is the sum of the items divided by the number of items in the set. Thus, to find the average here, add all the differences and divide by the number of drops:
$$\frac{1+1+2+3+6+8}{6} = \frac{21}{6} = 3\frac{1}{2}.$$

Part II: Science Content

1. **C. Neurons transmit instructions regarding movement to muscles.** Since neurons transmit information and the function of muscles is to move, it follows that neurons transmit instructions regarding movement to muscles. The paragraph and the diagrams show that all the other options contain incorrect information.

2. **D. Comets formed when the solar system was born.** Opinions are usually signaled by words like "believe," "think," or "feel." In this case, the last sentence of the paragraph states that scientists believe that comets formed when the solar system was born, showing that this is an opinion.

3. **D. photosynthesis, in which green plants use the energy from sunlight to make carbohydrates from water and carbon dioxide** The key element in a photochemical reaction is light. Of the options listed, only photosynthesis involves light.

4. **D. It helps control metabolism and growth.** First locate thyroxine in the "Hormone" column, then move along the row to the "Function" column to find the answer.

5. **D. uncontrolled blood sugar levels** The chart shows that insulin regulates blood sugar levels, so problems with insulin production will cause problems with blood sugar levels.

6. **A. Growth hormone is only one of several factors that determine a person's adult height.** Growth hormone alone does not determine height. A person's genetic make-up—the height of his parents and other family members—contributes, as do nutrition and the action of other hormones. Paul's expectations were therefore unrealistic.

7. **C. oil and vinegar salad dressing** This is an example of an emulsion—two liquids mixed together but not dissolving. If you let oil and vinegar dressing stand, the oil will rise to the top. The other options are all solutions, which do not separate over time.

8. **C. a meteorologist who studies weather patterns and predicts weather** Knowledge gained from a study of the atmosphere and hydrosphere is closely related to the study of weather, which is influenced by both.

9. **D. They are decomposers.** Since earthworms are feeding on dead organic matter, which comes from dead organisms, they must be decomposers.

10. **B. switch from whole milk to 1 percent milk** The switch from whole milk to low-fat milk reduces fat intake by 3.5 grams/serving. While the difference in saturated fat per serving is greater in cheddar cheese

than in milk, since the child drinks 4 servings of milk daily, this would be a reduction of 14 grams per day. The reduction from switching cheeses comes to 9.6 grams, since the child eats two servings of cheese per day.

11. **A. moving your hand closer to the center of the revolving door** Moving your hand closer to the center of the door decreases distance to the pivot point. Since the force remains the same in this case, when you multiply distance times force you will come up with a lower number, which indicates decreased torque.

12. **A. coal/peat and natural gas** Look on the circle graph for energy sources occupying wedges of approximately the same size. The only two that are about the same size are coal/peat and natural gas, indicating they provide about the same proportion of energy consumed in the United States.

13. **B. As European Americans moved from the East Coast westward between 1620 and 1850, they cut down forests to build farms.** The map shows and the paragraph implies that the virgin forests of the eastern United States were almost all cut down between 1620 and 1850. The paragraph further implies that the forests were cut down for farmland, which has since been abandoned. Based on this information, choice (B) is the only conclusion that is supported by the map and the paragraph. The map and the paragraph either lack support for or contradict the other options.

14. **B. the Northern Hemisphere** First locate June 21 on the diagram and then examine the tilt of Earth. Note that at that time of year, the Northern Hemisphere tilts toward the sun, and it is summer there.

15. **D. On the first day of spring and fall, neither the Northern Hemisphere nor the Southern Hemisphere is tilted toward the sun.** According to the diagram, on March 21 and September 23 Earth's axis is tilted neither toward nor away from the sun, so neither hemisphere is tilted toward the sun. The remaining choices are not supported by the diagram.

16. **D. A quadrat makes plant distribution estimates more reliable.** This option is a conclusion, or a general statement, that is supported by all the details in the paragraph. The other options are specific details paraphrased from the paragraph.

17. **A.**

Charles's Law involves the relationship of a gas's volume and temperature. Since volume increases with increases in temperature, the first graph must be correct. Note that you can eliminate choice (D) immediately because it involves changes in pressure, and Charles's Law assumes that pressure remains constant.

18. **B. Atoms are composed of subatomic particles.** This is an assumption made by the writer of the paragraph. He or she does not explain this but assumes it is common knowledge. All the other options are statements made or strongly implied in the passage.

19. **D. The student should have divided the mass by the volume.** The paragraph states that density is calculated by dividing mass by volume. The student did the reverse, which is incorrect. All of the other steps the student followed were correct.

20. **C. a mixture of metals.** According to the passage, the Anthony dollar was made of a copper-nickel alloy, and the final Sacagawea dollar, of a manganese, zinc, copper, and nickel alloy. From these examples, you can infer that an alloy is a mixture of metals.

21. **B. Like nickels, dimes, and quarters, the Anthony dollar was silver-colored and therefore not distinctive.** The Mint wanted to replace the Anthony dollar with a distinctive coin—a coin that looked different from the coins already in circulation. Making the new coin out of the same metals as the silver-colored Anthony dollar would not accomplish this.

22. **D. hardy perennials** Hardy plants withstand frost, so they are more likely to survive than tender plants. Perennials come up and flower for many years. Therefore, hardy perennials are likely to provide the most flowers with the least effort on the gardener's part.

23. **C. A viewer could not see anything through the telescope.** The function of the flat mirror is to redirect the light rays toward the eyepiece so the viewer can see the object in the telescope's sights. If the flat mirror were removed, the reflection of the object would no longer be visible through the eyepiece.

24. **B. They help scientists analyze large amounts of data in a systematic way.** The ability of a computer to process lots of data, far more systematically and quickly than a human being can, has helped speed up and refine the drug discovery process although the older methods of running laboratory experiments and clinical trials are still also important.

25. **B. The typhoid fever vaccine is only 50 to 80 percent effective.** Because getting vaccinated against typhoid fever does not completely eliminate the traveler's chance of getting the disease, it makes sense that he or she should take extra precautions against contracting this food and water-borne disease.

Science Skills

Comprehend Scientific Presentations

The TASC Science Test consists of questions based on science passages and graphics. To comprehend science presentations, you need to understand main ideas and their supporting details.

The **main idea** of a science presentation or graphic is its topic or the writer's point. Use this science diagram to practice finding the main idea.

Dry Cell Battery

(−)   (+)

Zinc can (anode)
Carbon rod (cathode)
Porous separator
Ammonium chloride
Manganese dioxide

▶ What is the topic of this diagram?
  (1) the components of a dry cell battery
  (2) how a dry cell battery powers machinery

The correct answer is choice **(1)**. The diagram displays the different components (that is, the parts) of a dry cell battery. It does not show the process by which the battery actually operates or powers machinery, so (2) is incorrect.

Science writers support their main ideas with **details**, **facts**, and **evidence**.

Read the paragraph below and answer the question.

> Earthquakes can be classified as either surface earthquakes or deep-focus earthquakes. Scientists agree that surface earthquakes occur when rock in Earth's crust fractures to relieve stress. Deep-focus earthquakes originate from seismic activity more than 300 kilometers below Earth's surface. The causes of deep-focus earthquakes remain a subject of debate, but scientists believe they may be caused by the pressure of fluids trapped in Earth's tectonic plates.

▶ Which of the following details supports the main point of this paragraph?
  (1) The causes of deep-focus earthquakes remain a subject of debate among scientists.
  (2) Surface earthquakes are caused by stress in Earth's crust, while deep-focus earthquakes may be caused by pressure.

The correct answer is choice **(2)**. The main point of the paragraph is that earthquakes can be classified into two types based on their causes, and **(2)** provides supporting details that illustrate the differences between the two types. While (1) is mentioned in the paragraph, it is not a fact that supports the main point about the classification of earthquakes.

PRACTICE 1

Questions 1 through 3 are based on the passage below.

Despite the prevalence of type 2 diabetes, the causes of the disease remain somewhat uncertain. It is likely that some combination of genetics and lifestyle contributes to the development of type 2 diabetes. However, scientists have not fully determined the roles played by various lifestyle factors (such as diet and exercise).

For Americans, one contributing factor may be high sugar consumption. Sugar from food is broken down and absorbed into the bloodstream, and insulin is required for the body to be able to use that sugar. In a study of individuals 18–25 years old who consumed more than the recommended amount of sugar daily, it was shown that the majority had significantly elevated levels of glucose (that is, sugar) in their blood but normal levels of insulin. In other words, these subjects could not produce enough insulin to allow their bodies to use the amount of sugar they were consuming. Elevated blood glucose levels may put individuals consuming high amounts of sugar at higher risk of developing type 2 diabetes.

1. Which one of the following is the topic of the entire passage?

   A. sources of sugar in Americans' diet
   B. the role of insulin in metabolizing sugar from food
   C. the causes of type 2 diabetes
   D. how to prevent type 2 diabetes

2. Which of the following is the main idea of the first paragraph?

   A. It is likely that sugar consumption contributes to the development of type 2 diabetes.
   B. It is likely that genetics plays a role in the development of type 2 diabetes.
   C. Researchers have discovered the causes of type 2 diabetes.
   D. The causes of type 2 diabetes are not fully understood.

3. The main idea of the second paragraph is that high sugar consumption may put individuals at greater risk of developing type 2 diabetes. Which of the following details supports that main idea?

   A. Sugar from food is absorbed into the bloodstream.
   B. A study of 18- to 25-year-olds showed that a majority did not produce enough insulin to offset the high amounts of sugar they were consuming.
   C. A study of 18- to 25-year-olds showed that high sugar consumption interacted with genetic factors in a majority of those individuals in order to suppress insulin production.
   D. It has not been proven that sugar is a contributing factor to the development of type 2 diabetes.

Question 4 is based on this graphic.

How Topography Contributes to Precipitation

Source: U.S. Geological Survey

4. Which statement correctly describes the process depicted in the graphic above?

   A. As moist, flowing air encounters rising elevations, it cools, which causes condensation, a stage that precedes precipitation and cloud development.
   B. Once above the tree line, flowing air is likely to slow down and stop moving, and then collect in the form of snow.
   C. Clouds dissipate before encountering mountain peaks.
   D. Moist air flows from the west, while drier air usually flows from the east.

LESSON 2

Use the Scientific Method

The **scientific method** is a set of techniques that scientists use to investigate observable facts and occurrences and to acquire new knowledge. Here are the steps in the scientific method:

1. **Observe a phenomenon** and **formulate a question** about it. Formulate the question about something that you can observe and measure.
2. **Collect data** about the phenomenon you are studying. Scientific study is founded on **data**, or observable facts.
3. **Form a hypothesis**. A **hypothesis** is an educated guess about the answer to your question.
4. **Test the hypothesis through an experiment**. Your experiment should be a fair test of the hypothesis. You may need to adjust the experiment. You would do so by changing only one factor at a time while **controlling** other factors. You should also repeat the experiment to make sure the first results are valid.
5. **Draw a conclusion** about the hypothesis based on the experiment. When the experiment is complete, you may conclude that your hypothesis was supported by the data or that it was not, in which case you may formulate a new hypothesis.

KEY IDEAS

- The scientific method is used to investigate events and to acquire knowledge.
- Scientists follow a series of procedures involving observing, collecting information, and forming a hypothesis.
- After the hypothesis has been tested in an experiment or study, scientists draw a conclusion.

Scientists are careful when drawing conclusions. The fact that two events **correlate**, or happen at the same time, does not necessarily mean that one **causes** the other. Remember that causation can never be deduced from correlation alone.

Read about a scientific observation and answer the question below.

> Scientists observed unusual plant and algae growth in a pond. They sampled the water and also discovered very high concentrations of bacteria. The pond was fairly close to neighboring farmland, and two streams carried water from the farm to the pond.

▶ What could be a sound hypothesis about the growth in the pond?
  (1) Runoff from the neighboring farm may be carrying excessive phosphates and nitrates from fertilizers into the pond.
  (2) Proximity to farmland is the cause of plant and algae growth in ponds and other bodies of water.

TASC TEST TIP

The TASC Science Test may present an experiment and ask you to answer multiple-choice questions interpreting it.

Choice **(1)** is correct. That hypothesis is an educated guess about the reason for the unusual plant and algae growth in the pond. It could be tested by an experiment that compares samples from the pond water to samples from streams coming from neighboring fields. Choice (2) is an assertion that is very general and cannot be measured in this specific situation.

The phenomenon you are studying is called the **dependent variable**. A factor that you believe might be affecting that phenomenon is called the **independent variable**. In the example above, the unusual plant and algae growth would be the dependent variable. The runoff from the neighboring farm would be the independent variable.

PRACTICE 2

Questions 1 through 3 are based on this passage.

A majority of teenagers develop acne, but scientists still struggle to explain its cause. It has long been thought that bacteria play a role, although until recently it was assumed that role was purely detrimental—contributing to acne. However, a team of researchers began to wonder whether different strains of bacteria might impact acne in different ways.

The research team studied 49 individuals with acne and 52 individuals without acne, and the researchers collected samples of bacteria from the nasal pores of all those individuals. The researchers found that some combinations of bacterial strains were highly likely to be found in clear-skinned individuals, while other combinations were highly likely to be found in individuals with acne.

After carefully analyzing their data, the scientists concluded that, while some bacterial combinations likely contribute to acne, other bacterial combinations may actually help to ward it off. The researchers suggested that, if further studies confirm these findings, we may want to treat acne by encouraging the growth of helpful bacteria.

1. Use the boxes below to identify the researchers' independent and dependent variables.

Independent variable	Dependent variable

acne symptoms	combinations of bacteria

teenagers	treatments for acne

2. What was the researchers' hypothesis?

A. Combinations of bacteria are a major cause of acne.
B. Different kinds of bacteria may impact acne differently.
C. We may want to change the way we treat acne, treating it by encouraging the growth of beneficial bacteria.
D. Some combinations of bacteria may actually help ward off acne.

3. What conclusion did the researchers reach based on their data?

A. Combinations of bacteria are a major cause of acne.
B. Acne sufferers have more types of bacterial strains in their facial pores than do non-sufferers.
C. The way we currently treat acne is misguided.
D. Some combinations of bacteria may actually help ward off acne.

Question 4 is based on the following information.

Suppose that you notice your right knee hurts every time you play softball. You suspect that one of the movements involved in playing softball is causing your knee to hurt, but you are not sure which movement is the culprit. You decide to do a scientific investigation to find out more.

4. Match each of the following steps of the scientific method with a phase of your investigation (listed below the table).

a) Form a hypothesis.	
b) Design a test for your hypothesis.	
c) Collect data to test your hypothesis.	
d) Form a conclusion based on the data from your test.	

i)   You make a list of each of the movements involved in softball. In the off season (when you are not playing entire games), you plan to perform each movement several times without performing the others.
ii) Based on the data you collected in your experiment, you think it is likely that stopping suddenly after running a short distance is indeed the cause of your knee pain.
iii) Based on your experience, you make a guess about which of the movements involved in playing softball puts the greatest stress on the knees. You suspect that it may be stopping suddenly after running a short distance.
iv) After performing each movement in isolation, record how your knee feels. Let your knee recover between tests of each type of movement.

LESSON 3

Reason with Scientific Information

Some TASC Science questions require recognizing or citing specific evidence to support a conclusion. Another type of question may ask you to judge whether a **conclusion** or a **scientific theory**—a substantiated explanation of the natural world—is challenged by particular data or evidence.

Use the graph below to practice scientific reasoning.

KEY IDEAS

- Reasoning with scientific information requires citing specific evidence to support a conclusion.
- In some cases, an existing theory can be challenged by new data or evidence.
- One of the ways scientists use information is in making predictions.

Rates of Infant Mortality, 1940–2009

Source: CDC/NCHS, National Vital Statistics System, Mortality.

▶ Which conclusion is supported by the data on the graph?
  (1) The rate of infant deaths in the United States experienced its sharpest decline between roughly 1940 and the late 1950s.
  (2) In each year between 1940 and 2009, there were fewer infant deaths than in the year before.

The correct answer is **(1)**. The graph shows that the rate of infant mortality decreased most sharply between the years of 1940 and the late 1950s. After the late 1950s, it continued to decrease, but more gradually. Choice (2) is not a true statement based on the graph: around 1960, there was an uptick in the rate of infant deaths. Moreover, there is a difference between the *rate* of infant deaths (that is, the percent of infants who died) and the *number* of infant deaths. Choice (2) is about the *number* of infant deaths.

Other questions will ask you to make a **prediction** based on evidence or data that the test provides to you. Based on the **trend** observed, scientists use data to predict, or forecast, what they think may happen in the future.

TASC TEST TIP

When you interpret a line graph, carefully follow the direction of each line to see its trend. You can use trends to make predictions.

▶ Which of the following predictions is based on the graph above?
  (1) Since there has not been an increase in infant deaths since 1960, there will likely be such an increase sometime soon.
  (2) The rate of infant deaths is unlikely to experience sharp declines in the near future.

Choice **(2)** is correct: the line on the graph shows the trend in infant mortality has been one of very gradual decrease since the 1950s. A good prediction based on that pattern would be that the trend of gradual decline is likely to continue. The graph shows a downward trend, but gives no information to suggest a future increase, so choice (1) is incorrect.

PRACTICE 3

1. Inertia causes an object to resist changes in its state of motion. In other words, inertia causes an object at rest to resist any attempt to set it in motion. Similarly, inertia causes an object in motion to resist any attempt to stop its motion. Objects with greater mass have greater inertia.

These figures represent the mass of two objects:

Brick: 100 grams
Block of wood: 70 grams

Which of the following is supported by the information above? (Assume there are no other factors, such as friction.)

A. It would require more effort to break the brick than to break the block of wood.
B. If both objects were currently sitting still, it would require more effort to push the block of wood across the floor than it would to push the brick across the floor.
C. If both objects were currently sitting still, it would require more effort to push the brick across the floor than it would to push the block of wood across the floor.
D. The brick would absorb water more readily than would the block of wood.

2. In the last several decades, the spider population has exploded on the island of Guam: parts of the island have as many as 40 times more spiders than nearby islands do. One scientist has concluded that the explosion in the Guam spider population is due to an increase in the population of an invasive species of brown tree snake. The snake was introduced into Guam in the 1940s but was not introduced into the neighboring islands. The brown tree snake preys on birds.

Which one of the following, if true, makes the scientist's conclusion more likely?

A. The birds that the brown tree snake eats are the primary predators of spiders on Guam.
B. The brown tree snake is typically introduced into islands via ships carrying tourists. Guam and the islands nearby have long been popular tourist spots.
C. Brown tree snakes eat spiders as well as birds.
D. In the rainy season, the island of Guam can have more than 40 times as many spiders as it did ten years ago.

Questions 3 and 4 are based on the following passage:

Melting ice sheets in Greenland and Antarctica have the potential to contribute significantly to rising sea levels in the next century. Some ice sheets melt more quickly than others, and scientists have wondered why. A team of researchers recently used data from both satellites and radar to study the composition of many of the ice sheets in Greenland and Antarctica. They found that some of the ice sheets formerly thought to sit on rock actually sit on water. This finding could be significant because it may be the case that ice sheets sitting on water tend to melt more quickly than those sitting on rock.

3. Which of the following is a prediction scientists might make based on the information above?

A. If large areas of ice sheets sit on rock, the rising of sea levels may proceed more quickly than had previously been predicted.
B. If large areas of ice sheets sit on water, the rising of sea levels may proceed more quickly than had previously been predicted.
C. Ice sheets in Greenland will likely melt more quickly than ice sheets in Antarctica.
D. All the ice sheets that are melting more quickly will be found to be sitting on water.

4. A scientist predicts that the ice sheets sitting on water will collectively discharge more water into the ocean than will those sitting on rock. Which of the following facts, if true, might weaken that prediction?

A. Most of the ice sheets sitting on water are covering inland lakes with no access to the ocean.
B. Water sitting under ice sheets flows directly into the ocean.
C. Ice in a glass of water will melt even if the room is very cold.
D. Radar used alone is an unreliable way to assess the composition of ice sheets.

LESSON 4

Express and Apply Scientific Information

Scientific information can be expressed in different forms. On the TASC Test, you may be asked to find relationships among science passages, graphics, formulas, or equations.

Scientific equations for **chemical reactions** often use these symbols:

Symbol	Meaning
+	Positive symbol separates two or more **reactants** or **products** from one another.
→	Yield symbol separates reactants from products and shows the reaction direction.
⇆	Reversible reaction symbol indicates that the reaction can proceed in both directions.

For example, here is the general chemical formula for what happens when carbon (C) is burned:

$$C + O_2 \rightarrow CO_2$$

▶ Which statement describes the process in the formula?

   (1) Carbon combines with oxygen to produce carbon dioxide.

   (2) Carbon creates oxygen, which takes on another oxygen atom in order to produce carbon dioxide.

The correct answer is **(1)**. In this case, carbon and oxygen (O_2) combine without losing any of their components. The result is carbon dioxide, a molecule made up of one carbon atom and two oxygen atoms. (The prefix *di-* means "two," so *carbon dioxide* means "a C and two Os.") The plus sign on the left-hand side of the formula indicates that carbon and oxygen are separate reactants, not that carbon creates oxygen. Thus, statement (2) is incorrect.

Other questions may ask you to understand a science concept and **relate** it to a specific situation.

> The term *desertification* describes a chain of events in which so much soil erodes from land that the land can no longer support plant or animal life. The lack of plant life allows for further soil erosion, making the land even more barren. It is very difficult to reverse desertification.

▶ Which of the following could be an example of the early stages of desertification?

   (1) In a certain valley, overgrazing has nearly eliminated plant life. This lack of vegetation has led to rapid soil erosion.

   (2) In a certain valley, the climate is arid, and soil erosion has occurred when the infrequent rains arrive. Farmers have devised an irrigation system to grow crops and thus reverse the rate of soil erosion.

Choice **(1)** is correct. Soil erosion is the cause of desertification, so the valley may be in the early stages of desertification. In choice (2), farmers have found a way to combat erosion, so this valley does not appear to be undergoing desertification.

KEY IDEAS

- Scientific information can be conveyed in multiple forms: in words, graphics, or formulas.
- Scientific formulas use numbers, letters, and symbols to represent a relationship or process.
- An important science reasoning concept is the ability to apply a scientific concept to a different situation.

ON THE TASC TEST

When you are given a science concept and asked which one of the choices is the best example, carefully eliminate the three that do not have all the same characteristics.

PRACTICE 4

Questions 1 through 4 are based on the information below.

Imagine a substance (such as salt or sugar) dissolved in a liquid (such as water or alcohol). The liquid in which the substance is dissolved is called the *solvent*. *Osmosis* is the diffusion (movement) of a solvent across a semipermeable membrane (a barrier that allows some substances to pass through it). The solvent moves from the side of the membrane with less dissolved material to the side of the membrane with more dissolved material. The result of osmosis is an equilibrium: that is, the rate the solvent flows across the membrane is the same in both directions.

Gillian conducted an experiment to see how quickly various liquids with a specific amount of sugar dissolved in them would undergo osmosis. She used vats of the same size with semipermeable membranes separating one side of the vat from the other, and she put equal quantities of various liquids in both sides:

Container Used for Studying Osmosis

Side A   Side B

Semipermeable
membrane

1. Gillian used one of the vats to test the rate of diffusion of liquid acetone in the process of osmosis. What did she most likely put on the two sides of the semipermeable membrane in that vat?

	Side A	Side B
A.	Pure acetone	Sugar in a glass container, submerged in acetone
B.	A 50 percent solution of sugar in acetone	A 50 percent solution of sugar in acetone
C.	Pure acetone	A solution of sugar in acetone
D.	Pure acetone	Pure acetone

Gillian's experiment yielded the following results.

Solvent	Time Required to Reach Equilibrium
Water	20 minutes
Acetone	25 minutes
Acetic acid	18 minutes
Formic acid	15 minutes

2. Based on the table above, which solvent had the highest rate of diffusion?

   A. water
   B. acetone
   C. acetic acid
   D. formic acid

3. Based on the table, what was the average (mean) time required for the solvents to reach equilibrium?

   Write your answer on the line below.

   _____

4. Osmosis is the reason why it is unhealthy and potentially dangerous to drink seawater. If you drink seawater, which contains a high concentration of salts and other dissolved material, some of the dissolved material will be absorbed into your bloodstream, causing your blood to have a higher-than-normal concentration of dissolved material. As that blood circulates through your body, water will move from your body's tissues into your blood vessels, causing your tissues to lose water and dry out.

   Choose the choice that best completes the sentence: Based on the information given, your tissues would begin to lose water and dry out when your blood has a level of dissolved material _____ that of your body's tissues.

   A. greater than
   B. slightly less than
   C. much less than
   D. equivalent to

LESSON 5

Use Statistics and Probability

Because scientists often need to perform calculations, you will do some math on the TASC Science Test. This math work will include the following:

- Central tendency: average (mean), median, mode, and range
- Independent and dependent probabilities
- Combinations and permutations

You may want to review these topics in the Statistics and Probability chapter of the Mathematics Unit. For some of these questions, you may be able to use your calculator.

Scientists use **measures of central tendency** (mean, median, mode, and range) to summarize many pieces of data with one number.

Use the graph below to answer a question about central tendency.

Annual Tornadoes, 2000–2006, Goodland (Kansas) 19-County Warning Area

Source: National Oceanic and Atmospheric Administration

▶ Calculate the mean (arithmetic average) number of tornadoes that struck the Goodland area per year in the years 2002 through 2005. _____

To find the mean of a set of quantities, sum the quantities and divide by the number of items in the set. The list from 2002 to 2005 is 12, 22, 16, and 18. The sum of those numbers is 68. Divide by the number of items in the list (4), and the result is **17**.

Scientists frequently use data to investigate the **probability** that an event will happen. You may wish to review pages 290–293 to refresh your memory about working with probability.

PRACTICE 5

Questions 1 through 4 are based on the following information.

Metabolism is a set of chemical processes that occur in the tissues of living organisms. One example of a metabolic process in animals is the breaking down of carbohydrates from food into substances the body can store. Another example is the transformation of those same substances into energy that the animal can use. The *rate of metabolism* describes the speed at which these processes take place. Metabolic rate varies among different species. The graph below compares several animal species by both average metabolic rate and average body weight.

Metabolic Rates of Seven Species

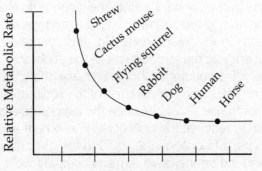

1. Of the species in this graph, which has the median body weight?

   A. shrew
   B. cactus mouse
   C. flying squirrel
   D. rabbit

2. Of the species in this graph, which has the median metabolic rate?

   A. rabbit
   B. dog
   C. human
   D. horse

STUDY ADVICE

When you see a figure, remember to ask:

   What does the figure show?

   What are the units of measurement?

When you see a figure with text, ask yourself how the text and the figure relate to one another.

3. Imagine that you could calculate the average (mean) of metabolic rates of all the animal species in this graph. Now imagine that the shrew were removed from the graph and that you recalculated the average of the remaining species. Without the shrew, the new average metabolic rate would be

   A. higher than the previous average.
   B. lower than the previous average.
   C. the same as the previous average.
   D. equal to the average of the metabolic rates of the horse and cactus mouse.

4. Adult elephants weigh more than adult horses. Based on the graph above, what would you predict would be true of elephants?

   A. Their metabolic rate would resemble that of cactus mice, which, like elephants, live in warm climates.
   B. Their metabolic rate would be equivalent to that of horses.
   C. Their metabolic rate would be slightly lower than that of horses.
   D. Their metabolic rate would be significantly higher than that of horses.

5. Growing the same crop on a field year after year can cause crop yields to decline as the soil becomes depleted and insect populations become firmly established. Crop rotation, or growing different crops in different years, is one way to avoid these problems. However, discovering the most effective rotation of a number of different crops is difficult, because there are so many possible orders in which to grow them and testing any given crop rotation takes several years.

For example, imagine a proposed rotation of corn, peanuts, onions, beets, and carrots, with a different crop grown each year for five years. How many different orderings of these five crops are possible?

   A. 15
   B. 25
   C. 120
   D. 125

SCIENCE SKILLS PRACTICE QUESTIONS

Questions 1 through 3 are based on the following passage.

The 1543 publication of Nicolaus Copernicus's heliocentric, or sun-centered, theory of the universe marked a crucial moment in the history of science. Copernicus's theory that the planets revolve around the sun was controversial: at first, many refused to accept that Earth could be hurtling through space. However, we now know that Copernicus's theory was accurate in many ways.

Despite its importance as a breakthrough, Copernicus's theory contained a number of ideas that today seem primitive. For example, Copernicus maintained that the planets were embedded in crystalline spheres. Additionally, while Copernicus developed the novel, and later widely accepted, idea that Earth rotates on its axis, he also believed that the planets orbit around the sun in perfect circles. We now know that the planets move in elliptical orbits.

1. Which of the following is the main idea of the second paragraph?

   A. Primitive astronomers accepted Copernicus's theory when it was first published.
   B. While Copernicus's theory was an important development, it included elements that are outdated today.
   C. Copernicus believed that Earth moved around the sun, rather than the other way around.
   D. Earth does not hurtle through space.

2. Which of the following would be an appropriate title for this passage?

   A. "Important Landmarks in 16th-Century Science"
   B. "Copernicus: The Life of an Astronomer"
   C. "The Significance and Limitations of the Copernican Theory"
   D. "The Earth-Centered Universe"

3. Which of the following can be inferred from the passage?

   A. Astronomers now believe that the planets are not embedded in crystalline spheres.
   B. Astronomers now know that Earth does not move around the sun in an ellipse.
   C. All aspects of the Copernican theory have now been disproven.
   D. Copernicus took inspiration from the primitive astronomers who came before him.

---

4. Matter is generally found in one of three phases: solid, liquid, and gas. A substance can be converted from a solid to a liquid and then from a liquid to a gas by adding heat. Once the temperature of a solid substance reaches its melting point, any heat added is used to change the solid to the liquid phase. So, while the phase is changing, the temperature of the substance remains constant. Once the phase change is complete, the temperature of the liquid continues to rise. Similarly, once the temperature of a liquid reaches the boiling point, any heat added is used to change the liquid to the gas phase, and the temperature remains constant while the phase is changing.

Temperature and Phase Changes of a Substance

At which points are phase changes occurring in the graph above?

A. A and E
B. A, C, and E
C. B and D
D. C, D, and E

5. While all types of cancer share the common trait of uncontrolled cell growth, the causes of that uncontrolled growth are complex and varied. Nevertheless, a number of specific causes of several types of cancer are known. For example, long-term asbestos exposure can result in mesothelioma (a cancer that can affect multiple organs), while long-term regular inhalation of tobacco smoke can lead to lung cancer. In addition to such chemical causes, viruses are also responsible for a number of types of cancer: human papillomavirus precipitates cervical cancer, while the hepatitis B virus causes liver cancer.

Given the previous information, which of the following medical procedures could potentially prevent a specific type of cancer from forming?

A. surgery to remove a brain tumor
B. chemotherapy to treat lung cancer
C. annual mammography screenings for breast cancer
D. a vaccine to prevent infection with the hepatitis B virus

6. The phalarope, a North American shorebird, feeds on tiny crustaceans. To catch them, the phalarope swims in rapid circles, creating a vortex that raises prey to the surface of shallow water. The bird then opens and shuts its long, narrow beak to draw water droplets containing its prey up to its mouth. Because drawing up the water droplets depends upon the surface tension of water, the phalarope is exceptionally vulnerable to oil spills; the phalarope cannot remove oil from its beak on its own, so once it is exposed to oil-covered water, it cannot feed.

Which of the following must be true based on the passage?

A. The phalarope prefers saltwater to brackish water or freshwater.
B. At least some of the phalarope's prey is smaller than a water droplet.
C. A phalarope whose beak becomes coated in oil will be able to feed if it can find clean water, not coated in oil, that contains tiny crustaceans.
D. In addition to crustaceans, the phalarope feeds on small saltwater fish.

Questions 7 through 9 are based on the following paragraph and graphic.

Record high temperatures were recorded in numerous Australian cities in the summer of 2012. The chart below indicates current and former record temperatures for seven of those cities. For instance, Hobart's previous record was a little below 41°C, and its current record is a little above 41°C.

Record High Temperatures in Australian Cities

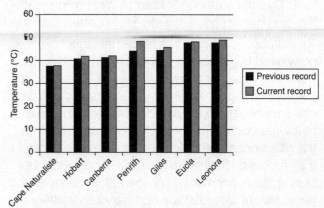

7. According to the chart, which city experienced the largest increase from its previous record to its current record?

A. Hobart
B. Penrith
C. Eucla
D. Leonora

8. Which of the following cities had a previous record equal to the median of all the cities' previous records?

A. Cape Naturaliste
B. Canberra
C. Penrith
D. Eucla

9. According to the chart, which of the following statements is true?

A. Temperatures will likely continue to increase.
B. Temperatures increased 5 degrees or less.
C. Temperatures increased more than 5 degrees.
D. Temperatures usually increase 2–5 degrees in the summer.

Questions 10 through 13 are based on the following passage.

An office manager noticed that each time she touched the metal filing cabinet next to her desk, she experienced an electrostatic shock (commonly known as "static"). Her assistant, however, only rarely experienced such shocks when touching the cabinet. The office manager wondered why this might be.

The office manager developed a hypothesis: perhaps differences in clothing could explain why she was experiencing more shocks than her assistant. The office manager liked to wear nylon clothing, and her assistant usually wore cotton clothing.

To test her hypothesis, the office manager convinced her assistant to wear nylon clothing to work every day for a week, while she herself wore cotton clothing. The next week, they switched: the office manager wore nylon clothing, and the assistant wore cotton. To control for the possibility that the differences in shocks were due to differences in their footwear, they wore identical shoes each day. During the experiment, both the office manager and her assistant recorded the number of times they touched the metal filing cabinet each day, and they also recorded the number of times they experienced electrostatic shocks when doing so.

At the end of the first week, they found that the assistant had experienced 73 electrostatic shocks, while the office manager had experienced 10. During the second week, the office manager experienced 68 shocks, and her assistant 12. The office manager concluded that these results supported her hypothesis, and as a result she decided to switch to wearing mostly cotton clothing.

10. Scientific investigations begin with a question. Which of the following is the question that formed the basis for the office manager's experiment?

   A. Is it better to wear cotton clothing or nylon clothing?
   B. Why does touching the metal filing cabinet produce more electrostatic shocks than touching other office furniture?
   C. Why, when I touch the metal filing cabinet, do I experience more electrostatic shocks than my assistant does when she touches it?
   D. Could my shoes be causing me to experience more electrostatic shocks than my assistant experiences?

11. Which of the following best summarizes how the office manager conducted her experiment?

   A. The office manager suspected that her nylon clothing was causing her to experience electrostatic shocks.
   B. The office manager switched to cotton clothing after seeing that her hypothesis was supported by her data.
   C. The office manager wore shoes of a different material than those of her assistant.
   D. The office manager wore one type of clothing, while her assistant wore another type of clothing, and they recorded the number of shocks they experienced.

12. Why did the office manager and her assistant wear the same type of shoes while conducting the experiment?

   A. They wanted to test the effect of their clothing on the number of shocks they experienced, and wearing different types of shoes might have confused their results.
   B. They wanted to test whether the office manager's shoes were causing the high number of electrostatic shocks she was experiencing.
   C. They believed that wearing cotton might cause the wearer to experience more electrostatic shocks.
   D. They wanted to protect themselves from the effects of electrostatic shock.

13. Imagine that the results of the office manager's experiment had demonstrated that her clothing was not in fact responsible for the large number of electrostatic shocks she was experiencing. After reviewing those findings, the office manager then wondered if her footwear might be responsible, and she decided to conduct a new experiment to test this idea. Before she conducted that experiment, the idea that her shoes might be responsible would be which of the following?

   A. a new conclusion based on findings
   B. a general principle from the study of physics
   C. a new hypothesis
   D. an experiment design

You may use your calculator for questions 14 and 15.

14. Common garden snails are hermaphroditic. That is, each individual snail produces both sperm and eggs. Mating between two garden snails involves the transfer of sperm from each partner to the other. A high school science teacher has created a large terrarium for his classroom that contains 6 adult garden snails. Assuming that all 6 snails are healthy, how many different mating pairs are possible?

   A. 2
   B. 12
   C. 15
   D. 36

15. The sun is a class G star, which is a type of main-sequence star. Approximately 90 percent of all stars in the Milky Way galaxy are main-sequence stars, and approximately 7 percent of all main-sequence stars are class G stars. What is the probability that any given star in the Milky Way galaxy is a class G star?

   Express your answer as a percentage, and write your answer on the line below.

   _____

Questions 16 and 17 refer to the information and table below.

The table below contains data observed in a group of 58-year-old men. The study examined the relationship between tobacco use and formations called plaques that build up on the walls of arteries, which are blood vessels that carry blood from the heart to the body's tissues. The carotid and femoral arteries are two large and very important arteries.

Average Characteristics of 58-Year-Old Men, by Smoking Status

	Never Smokers	Ex-Smokers	Current Smokers
Waist circumference (cm)	93.8	99.1	95.4
Carotid plaques (%)			
None	62	55	53
Small	15	23	16
Large	23	22	31
Femoral plaques (%)			
None	80	54	45
Small	10	13	14
Large	10	33	41

16. In the study described, current smokers showed the highest percentage of which of the following kinds of plaques?

   A. small carotid plaques
   B. large carotid plaques
   C. small femoral plaques
   D. large femoral plaques

17. Why might the ex-smokers have the highest waist circumference of the groups listed in the chart?

   A. People who have never smoked tend to consume more high-calorie foods than do those who smoke currently.
   B. People who have never smoked tend to consume more high-calorie foods than do those who have smoked in the past.
   C. People who quit smoking tend to substitute snacking for smoking.
   D. Ex-smokers tend to exercise more than do current smokers.

SCIENCE ANSWERS AND EXPLANATIONS

Science Skills

Lesson 1: Comprehend Scientific Presentations

Practice 1

1. **C. the causes of type 2 diabetes** The passage as a whole discusses
the causes of type 2 diabetes. Choices (A) and (D) are not discussed in the passage. Choice (B) is mentioned in the second paragraph but is only a supporting detail.

2. **D. The causes of type 2 diabetes are not fully understood.** This question asks for the main point of just the first paragraph, which explains that scientists do not fully understand the role played by various factors in causing diabetes. Choices (A) and (B) both commit the same error: that is, they mention a specific detail from the first paragraph while missing the big picture. Choice (C) contradicts the paragraph.

3. **B. A study of 18- to 25-year-olds showed that a majority did not produce enough insulin to offset the high amounts of sugar they were consuming.** The question asks for a detail that serves to support the idea that high sugar consumption may contribute to the development of type 2 diabetes. Only choice (B) does so. Choice (A) is a detail that is indeed mentioned in the paragraph, but only as background information. It does not serve to support the author's point that sugar consumption may contribute to diabetes. Choice (C) brings in "genetic factors," which are not mentioned in paragraph two. Although choice (D) may be implied by the author's use of hesitant language, such as "one contributing factor *may* be high sugar consumption," this does not support the paragraph's main idea.

4. **A. As moist, flowing air encounters rising elevations, it cools, which causes condensation, a stage that precedes precipitation and cloud development.** In interpreting this diagram, follow the arrows. The diagram depicts air flowing toward hills or mountains. As it does so, the air cools and condensation happens. Based on the arrows, that stage happens before the stages of precipitation and cloud formation. Choice (B) suggests that the air becomes static at the highest elevations, which is not supported by the diagram. Choice (C) contradicts the diagram. Choice (D) is unsupported because the diagram does not have an east-west orientation: just because the air is depicted flowing from the left-hand side of the picture does not mean that it's flowing from the west.

Lesson 2: Use the Scientific Method

Practice 2

1.

Independent variable	Dependent variable
combinations of bacteria	acne symptoms

The researchers were studying the question of how different combinations of bacteria affect acne symptoms. Because the researchers thought acne symptoms might depend on differences in bacteria, acne was the researchers' dependent variable. Combinations of bacteria are not affected by acne symptoms, but the researchers thought bacteria might affect those acne symptoms. Therefore, combinations of bacteria were the researchers' independent variable.

2. **B. Different kinds of bacteria may impact acne differently.** The last sentence of the first paragraph provides this answer as well. The researchers "began to wonder whether different strains of bacteria might impact acne in different ways": that statement represents the idea they sought to test—that is, their hypothesis. Choice (A) describes an assumption that was widely held before the researchers began their study. Choice (C) is a suggestion the researchers made after concluding their study, and choice (D) is their conclusion—not their starting hypothesis.

3. **D. Some combinations of bacteria may actually help ward off acne.** This question asks for the researchers' conclusion—that is, the idea they embraced after concluding their study. That idea is described by choice (D). Choice (A) is an assumption many people held before the research began. Choice (B) is not supported by the passage. Choice (C) is not supported by the passage: after drawing their conclusions, the researchers suggested a way to treat acne in the future, but they did not suggest that current treatments are misguided.

4.

a) Form a hypothesis.	iii. Based on your experience, you make a guess about which of the movements involved in playing softball puts the greatest stress on the knees. You suspect that it may be stopping suddenly after running a short distance.
b) Design a test for your hypothesis.	i. You make a list of each of the movements involved in softball. In the off season (when you are not playing entire games), you plan to perform each movement several times without performing the others.
c) Collect data to test your hypothesis.	iv. After performing each movement in isolation, record how your knee feels. Let your knee recover between tests of each type of movement.
d) Form a conclusion based on the data from your test.	ii. Based on the data you collected in your experiment, you think it is likely that stopping suddenly after running a short distance is indeed the cause of your knee pain.

Lesson 3: Reason with Scientific Information

Practice 3

1. **C. If both objects were currently sitting still, it would require more effort to push the brick across the floor than it would to push the block of wood across the floor.** According to the passage, a heavier object has more inertia, and the brick is heavier than the block. Therefore, you can conclude that it would be harder to move the brick across the floor. Choice

(A), breakage, and choice (D), absorbing water, are not mentioned and are irrelevant to this question. Choice (B) is the opposite of the correct answer.

2. **A. The birds that the brown tree snake eats are the primary predators of spiders on Guam.** The scientist's conclusion is that the brown tree snake is the reason there are so many spiders on Guam. The question asks for a piece of information that makes that conclusion more likely—that is, a choice that makes the scientist's conclusion more reasonable or believable. Choice (A) explains why more brown tree snakes would lead to more spiders. Choices (B) and (D) don't link the spiders and snakes at all. Choice (C) describes a relationship between them, but it suggests that more brown tree snakes would lead to *fewer* spiders.

3. **B. If large areas of ice sheets sit on water, the rising of sea levels may proceed more quickly than had previously been predicted.** The main idea of the passage is that some ice sheets may be sitting on water and that those ice sheets may melt more quickly than ice sheets sitting on rock. The passage also states that melting ice sheets contribute to rising sea levels. Putting those two ideas together, a scientist could predict that ice sheets sitting on water might send more melted water into the oceans than would ice sheets on rock. Choice (A) expresses the opposite of that idea. Choice (C) introduces a comparison that is not supported by the passage. Choice (D) goes too far by insisting that *all* of the quickly melting ice sheets are sitting on water.

4. **A. Most of the ice sheets sitting on water are covering inland lakes with no access to the ocean.** Choice (A) would make the prediction less likely, because if most ice sheets sitting on water have no way to send water into the ocean, then the link between the ice sheets and rising sea levels would be undermined. Choices (B) and (C) actually make the scientist's prediction more likely. Choice (D) may seem to undermine the information in the passage—until you notice that choice (D) criticizes the use of "radar alone" to assess ice sheets. The passage indicates that researchers used both satellite and radar data, which makes choice (D) irrelevant to the prediction.

Lesson 4: Express and Apply Scientific Information

Practice 4

1. **C. pure acetone; a solution of sugar in acetone** The passage states that, during osmosis, a liquid moves from a place where there is a higher concentration of dissolved material to where there is a lower concentration of dissolved material. Thus, to test the rate of osmosis of a liquid, Gillian would want to put that same liquid on two sides of the vat, with more dissolved material on one side than on the other. Only choice (C) describes that arrangement.

2. **D. formic acid** The solvent with the highest rate of diffusion would be the solvent that took the least time to reach equilibrium. Here it took formic acid the least time to do so.

3. **19.5 minutes** To find the average time, add the times of the solvents, then divide by the number of solvents.

$$\frac{20 + 25 + 18 + 15}{4} = \frac{78}{4} = 19.5$$

4. **A. greater than** If your blood has more dissolved material than your tissues, water will move from the tissues into the blood, causing the tissues to dry out.

Lesson 5: Use Statistics and Probability

Practice 5

1. **D. rabbit** The median is the middle number of a set of numbers, and in this graph, the rabbit has a lower body weight than the dog, human, and horse and a higher body weight than the shrew, cactus mouse, and flying squirrel. It isn't necessary to know the animals' actual body weights to determine this.

2. **A. rabbit** Similarly, the graph shows that the rabbit has the middle metabolic rate of the seven species in the graph.

3. **B. lower than the previous average** To find an average, you add up all the numbers in a list and divide by the number of items in the list, like this:

$$\frac{shrew + c.mouse + f.squirrel + rabbit + dog + human + hors}{7}$$

Now, the shrew is the highest of those numbers: it has the highest metabolic rate. Therefore, if you removed it and recalculated the average, the new average would be lower than the previous average.

4. **C. Their metabolic rate would be slightly lower than that of horses.** The question states that elephants weigh more than horses. Thus, elephants would be to the right of horses on the line graph. Based on the curve of the line, you can guess that elephants would have a slightly lower metabolism than that of horses. Because the line continues to decrease slightly, choice (B) is unsupported.

5. **C. 120** The question asks how many different orderings, or sequences, of the five crops are possible. This is a permutations question, because order matters. Thus, multiply to find the number of permutations: $5 \times 4 \times 3 \times 2 \times 1 = 120$

Science Skills Practice Questions

1. **B. While Copernicus's theory was an important development, it included elements that are outdated today.** The first sentence of the second paragraph provides the main idea. The words "[f]or example" help to make clear that the second and third sentences are details supporting that main idea.

2. **C. "The Significance and Limitations of the Copernican Theory"** The title of a passage should reflect its topic or main idea. The topic of this passage is the importance, or significance, of Copernicus's theory, as well as the fact that Copernicus's theory was not completely correct. Choices (A) and (D) are both too broad, while choice (B) is incorrect because the passage is not about Copernicus's life.

3. **A. Astronomers now believe that the planets are not embedded in crystalline spheres.** The question asks

for something that can be inferred, or deduced, from the passage. Choice (A) is supported by the passage. Copernicus's idea that the planets are embedded in crystalline spheres is mentioned in the second paragraph as an example of an idea that is today considered "primitive." This implies that astronomers today no longer believe this to be true. Choices (B) and (C) are contradicted by the passage. Choice (D) is not supported by the passage: primitive astronomers who came before Copernicus are not discussed.

4. **C. B and D** The passage describes what happens when you add heat to a substance: the temperature of the substance increases, up to the point when the substance starts to change from a solid to a liquid or from a liquid to a gas. Then the temperature of the substance holds steady while the substance is undergoing that change. When more heat is added but the temperature of a substance remains constant, it must be undergoing a phase change. The places in the diagram where the temperature is flat—B and D—thus represent the two places where the substance is changing from solid to liquid or from liquid to gas.

5. **D. a vaccine to prevent infection with the hepatitis B virus** According to the passage, hepatitis B virus causes liver cancer. A vaccine that prevents infection with the hepatitis B virus would therefore also prevent liver cancer.

6. **B. At least some of the phalarope's prey is smaller than a water droplet.** If the phalarope feeds on prey that it draws into its beak via water droplets, the prey must be smaller than a water droplet.

7. **B. Penrith** The black bars on the graph represent each city's previous record, and the gray bars represent its current record. Find the city for which the gray bar is furthest above the black bar: Penrith.

8. **C. Penrith** The median number is the middle of a list of numbers. Here, because there are seven cities, the city with the "previous record equal to the median of all the cities' previous records" simply means the city with the middle value (among the previous record values). Fortunately, the cities are represented in the graph in such a way that their previous records are in ascending order, and the median previous record belongs to Penrith.

9. **B. Temperatures increased 5 degrees or less** The largest increase was in the city of Penrith and was approximately 5 degrees.

10. **C. Why, when I touch the metal filing cabinet, do I experience more electrostatic shocks than my assistant does when she touches it?** The first paragraph of the passage explains that the office manager "wondered why" she experienced more static shocks than her assistant. That's the question that prompted her experiment. While it is true that the office manager decided to switch to cotton clothing, she didn't begin by wondering whether it was better, so choice (A) is incorrect. Choice (B) distorts the office manager's thoughts. Choice (D) places too much emphasis on shoes, which were not the subject of the office manager's experiment.

11. **D. The office manager wore one type of clothing, while her assistant wore another type of clothing, and they recorded the number of shocks they experienced.** The office manager wanted to test her hypothesis that her nylon clothing was causing her to experience shocks when touching a metal filing cabinet. To do so, she conducted an experiment in which she wore cotton clothing for a week, while her assistant wore nylon clothing; both wore identical shoes. Then the manager and assistant recorded the number of shocks they each experienced during the course of a week. Choice (D) correctly describes this experiment. Choice (A) describes the office manager's hypothesis. Choice (B) describes the office manager's course of action after she had completed her experiment, while choice (C) is the opposite of what actually occurred during the experiment (both the manager and the assistant wore identical shoes).

12. **A. They wanted to test the effects of their clothing on the number of shocks they were experiencing, and wearing different types of shoes might have confused their results.** In an experiment, it is important to control factors other than the one thing the experimenter wants to study. In this case, the office manager wanted to study the effect of clothing on the number of static shocks she was receiving. Choice (B) wrongly suggests that shoes were the subject of the office manager's experiment. Choices (C) and (D) distort the passage: the two individuals had the opposite hypothesis about cotton clothes, and, during her experiment, the office manager was trying to study static shocks—not avoid them.

13. **C. a new hypothesis** Remember, a hypothesis is a guess that a researcher starts with and then tests through an experiment. If the office manager formed a new guess about what was causing the static shocks, and she intended to study that new guess through an experiment, that would be a new hypothesis. It would not, at that point, be (A), a new conclusion based on findings. While she might, as choice (D) suggests, design an experiment to test this idea, the idea itself is not an experiment design. And the idea is certainly not (B), a general principle from the study of physics; rather, the office manager is making a guess based on observation.

14. **C. 15** This is a combinations question: you are asked for all possible groupings of two out of the six snails, and the order of snails within each group does not matter. Use a table or an organized list to find the number of possible groupings. Name the snails A–F if that makes it easier.

AB				
AC	BC			
AD	BD	CD		
AE	BE	CE	DE	
AF	BF	CF	DF	EF

Count the possible pairs: there are 15.

15. **6.3%** The question asks for the probability that any given star is a class G star, and we have to combine two probabilities to find it. We know that there is a 90 percent chance, or a .9 probability, that a star will be a main sequence star. We also know that, if it is a main sequence star, there is a 7 percent chance, or a .07 probability, that it will be a class G star. Multiply those two probabilities to find the probability of *both* of them happening: $9 \times .07 = .063$ Express your answer as a percentage: 6.3%.

16. **D. large femoral plaques** Forty-one percent of current smokers had large femoral plaques. That is a higher percentage than any other type of plaque listed in the chart.

17. **C. People who quit smoking tend to substitute snacking for smoking.** This is a plausible reason why those who quit smoking tend to gain weight, and why they consequently have a higher waist circumference.

ABOUT THE TEST

Practice Tests

STEP 1: To practice for the actual TASC test, you can take the following five practice tests. When you take the practice tests, follow the same time limits you will face on the actual tests.

Language Arts: Reading, 75 minutes, pages 562–577
 There are 50 questions on the TASC. We are counting two-part questions as being equivalent to two questions. Thus, our practice test has 46 questions, four of which are two part questions.

Language Arts: Writing, 105 minutes, pages 578–595
 Part I: 50 multiple-choice questions, 55 minutes
 Part II: 1 essay, 50 minutes

Mathematics, 105 minutes, pages 596–611
 40 multiple-choice questions and 12 gridded-response questions

Social Studies, 75 minutes, pages 612–627
 47 multiple-choice questions

Science, 85 minutes, pages 628–642
 47 multiple-choice questions

For the multiple-choice questions, you can fill in the circles next to the correct answers in this book, or you can write your answers on a separate piece of paper.

You may use your calculator beginning on page 604 of the Mathematics Test and as needed during the Science Test. You may not use your calculator on the Social Studies Test.

STEP 2: Review your work using the Practice Test Answers and Explanations that begin on page 643, and fill in the Practice Test Evaluation Charts. These charts will allow you to see which study areas may still need work.

STEP 3: Confirm your readiness to take the actual TASC test.

LANGUAGE ARTS: READING PRACTICE TEST

Directions: Use 75 minutes to answer the following 50 questions. (REMINDER: Two-part questions are equivalent to two separate questions. This practice test has 46 distinct questions, four are two-part questions which is equivalent to 50 questions total.)

Questions 1 through 7 refer to the following excerpt from an article.

Excerpted from "Sizing Up the Interviewer"

1   It is intrinsic to human nature to take the measure of the people we meet. We do it all the time, automatically. We develop an instinctive way of reading others that is sometimes the saving of us and at other times can prove to be our undoing. It is this instinct that makes us form instant, lifelong relationships with some people or causes us to give a wide berth to others because we get a "funny" feeling about them. With some careful consideration and planning, though, these "feelings" can be honed into a useful tool for gauging the personality and character of interviewers and, by extension, their expectations of potential employees. Let's examine some clues.

2   **Their e-mail.** You can tell a lot about your interviewer by his or her e-mail messages. Some interviewers are very warm, writing in a conversational style, addressing you by your first name. Others are witty, mixing little jokes and humorous remarks in with job-related questions. Still others get right down to business—no chit-chat or informality. Before you ever meet the interviewer, you begin to form certain "pictures" of the person, based on his or her approach and style. But it still remains for you to check him or her out face-to-face.

3   **Their office.** Let's begin with the physical setting of interviewers' offices. Some put a desk the size of a 747 between themselves and you. This is a clear message to you to keep your distance. A straight-backed, rigid chair for the applicant says, "O.K. Let's get down to business, and then you leave so I can get back to mine." Here, you would be advised to adopt a crisp, businesslike style, with brief, professional answers. And, for heaven's sake, **don't touch that desk!**

4   Then, there is the homey, comfortable environment—kids' pictures on the desk, executive "toys" around, soft chairs, and a sofa. There may not even be a desk between the applicant and the interviewer, but rather two chairs grouped around a coffee table. This environment invites more intimacy. It says, "Be yourself. Tell me about who you are so I can get to know you." Here, your manner, though still professional, should be relaxed and open, more personable. It would be a mistake with this employer to sit ramrod straight and give cool, truncated responses to the questions.

by Fred Jandt and Mary Nemnich, Indianapolis: JIST Works.

1. The purpose of this article is to

   ○ A. raise awareness about incompetent interviewers

   ○ B. describe types of interviewers and how to approach them

   ○ C. guarantee a perfect interview with an employer

   ○ D. explain how to email an interviewer

2. Which of the following is a generalization made in paragraph 1 but NOT supported with evidence in the passage?

   ○ A. Your "feelings" can be honed into a useful tool for gauging the personality and character of interviewers.

   ○ B. An interviewer's office can tell you a great deal about that interviewer.

   ○ C. Our ability to "read" others makes us form instant, lifelong relationships with some people.

   ○ D. There is more than one type of clue you can use to gauge the personality of your interviewer.

3. **Part One:** Which of the following sentences from the text best expresses the author's main point?

○ A. "We develop an instinctive way of reading others that is sometimes the saving of us and at other times can prove to be our undoing."

○ B. "Before you ever meet the interviewer, you begin to form certain 'pictures' of the person, based on his or her approach and style."

○ C. "Then, there is the homey, comfortable environment—kids' pictures on the desk, executive 'toys' around, soft chairs, and a sofa."

○ D. "With some careful consideration and planning, though, these 'feelings' can be honed into a useful tool for gauging the personality and character of interviewers and, by extension, their expectations of potential employees."

Part Two: Which of the following sentences develop(s) the main point you identified in your answer to Part A? Select two.

☐ "Here, you would be advised to adopt a crisp, businesslike style, with brief, professional answers."

☐ "Some interviewers are very warm, writing in a conversational style, addressing you by your first name."

☐ "It is this instinct that makes us form instant, lifelong relationships with some people or causes us to give a wide berth to others because we get a 'funny' feeling about them."

☐ "It would be a mistake with this employer to sit ramrod straight and give cool, truncated responses to the questions."

4. Which of the following best describes the structure of the passage?

○ A. The author makes a generalization about how to read an interviewer and then gives specific suggestions about how to do so.

○ B. The author lists a variety of approaches to email and makes inferences about each one.

○ C. The author presents two sides of a debate about how to read an interviewer.

○ D. The author summarizes other authors' approaches to reading an interviewer.

5. Which of the following is an assumption the author of this passage makes?

○ A. Interviewers have some influence or control over their office arrangements.

○ B. Because email can be impersonal, it is a poor way to communicate with a potential employer.

○ C. Managers who enjoy chatting informally with employees never have large desks in the middle of their offices.

○ D. In preparing for a job interview, it is more important to "read" your interviewer than to research the company where you have applied to work.

6. Which of the following best summarizes the author's main point?

○ A. You should never respond to an interviewer who expects crisp answers with a rambling story about yourself.

○ B. You should focus on details when attempting to understand your interviewer, since details are important.

○ C. You should help your interviewer get to know you during the interview and beforehand.

○ D. You should try to understand your interviewer's personality and tailor your responses to him or her accordingly.

7. What does "truncated" mean in the last sentence?

○ A. short and tense

○ B. angry and complaining

○ C. helpful and informative

○ D. friendly and conversational

Questions 8 through 12 refer to the following excerpt from a short story.

Excerpted from *The Living Is Easy*

1   He gave them each a copper, too, though he could hardly spare it, what with four of them to feed and Mama wanting yard goods and buttons and ribbons to keep herself feeling proud of the way she kept her children. Time was, he gave them kisses for toting his bucket. But the day Cleo brazenly said, I don't want a kiss, I want a copper, the rest of them shamefacedly said it after her. Most times Pa had a struggle to dig down so deep. Four coppers a day, six days a week, was half a day's pay gone up in smoke for candy.

2   Pa couldn't bring himself to tell Mama. She would have wrung out of him that Cleo had been the one started it. And Cleo was his eldest. A man who loved his wife couldn't help loving his first-born best, the child of his fiercest passion. When that first-born was a girl, she could trample on his heart, and he would swear on a stack of Bibles that it didn't hurt.

3   The sisters put their coppers in their pinafore pockets and skipped back through the woods. Midway Cleo stopped and pointed to a towering oak. "You all want to bet me a copper I can't swing by my feet from up in that tree?"

4   Lily clapped her hands to her eyes. "I doesn't want to bet you," she implored. "I ain't fixing to see you fall."

5   Serena said severely, "You bust your neck, you see if Mama don't bust it again."

6   Charity said tremulously, "Cleo, what would us do if our sister was dead?"

7   Cleo saw herself dressed up fine as Josie Beauchamp, stretched out in a coffin with her sisters sobbing beside it, and Pa with his Sunday handkerchief holding his tears, and Mama crying, I loved you best, Cleo. I never said it when you were alive. And I'm sorry, sorry, I waited to say it after you were gone.

8   "You hold my copper, Charity. And if I die, you can have it."

9   Lily opened two of her fingers and peeped through the crack. "Cleo, I'll give you mine if you don't make me see you hanging upside down." It was one thing to hear Cleo tell about herself. It was another thing to see her fixing to kill herself.

10   "Me, too," said Serena, with a little sob, more for the copper than for Cleo, whom she briefly hated for compelling unnecessary sacrifice.

Dorothy West, excerpt from *The Living is Easy*. Copyright 1948, © 1975 by Dorothy West. Reprinted with the permission of The Permissions Company, Inc., on behalf of The Feminist Press at the City University of New York, www.feministpress.org.

8. Whose point of view is explained by this quote from paragraph 2? "A man who loved his wife couldn't help loving his first-born best, the child of his fiercest passion."

    A. Cleo's

    B. Mama's

    C. the narrator's

    D. Pa's

9. Why did Serena offer Cleo her own copper?

    A. Serena wanted Cleo to get in trouble for taking the others' money.

    B. Serena had placed a bet that Cleo could not swing from the oak tree.

    C. Serena felt that she had no choice but to give Cleo her copper to stop Cleo from doing something unsafe.

    D. Serena wanted to show how much she loved her sister.

10. What is meant by the following quote from paragraph 1? "Most times Pa had a struggle to dig down so deep."

    A. It was difficult for Pa to find it within himself to be generous.

    B. Pa had so few coins that they were usually far down in his pockets.

    C. Pa often searched for reasons not to give coppers to Cleo and her sisters.

    D. Pa could not really afford to give Cleo and her sisters money.

11. Which of the following statements best describes the theme of the passage?

    A. Cleo is wrong to take advantage of her sisters and her father.

    B. Cleo's boldness and her family's love for her sometimes make them feel powerless to resist her.

    C. Cleo's longing to be loved makes her vulnerable.

    D. Cleo and her sisters are becoming greedy as they learn how to extract money from each other and from their parents.

12. Which of the following statements best expresses the relationship between Cleo and her sister Serena?

    A. While Cleo wants very much to be loved, Serena withholds love because she is manipulative.

    B. While Serena allows Cleo to manipulate her, she is also angry at what Cleo persuades her to do.

    C. Because Cleo is Pa's favorite, Serena does whatever Cleo asks so that Pa will love her too.

    D. Because Serena is not Pa's favorite, Cleo feels comfortable taking money from Serena.

Questions 13 through 18 refer to the following pair of historical passages.

Passage A

President Andrew Jackson delivered his second Annual Message to Congress on December 6, 1830. In this address, he outlined what he saw as the benefits of the Indian Removal Act, passed by Congress earlier that year. The Act would require Native Americans to move from the southeastern states to territory west of the Mississippi.

It gives me pleasure to announce to Congress that the benevolent policy of the Government, steadily pursued for nearly thirty years . . . is approaching to a happy consummation [that is, completion]. Two important tribes have accepted the provision made for their removal . . . and it is believed that their example will induce the remaining tribes, also, to seek the same obvious advantages.

The consequences of a speedy removal will be important to the United States, to individual States, and to the Indians themselves. . . . It puts an end to all possible danger of collision between the authorities of the General [that is, national] and State governments, on account of the Indians. It will place a dense and civilized population in large tracts of country now occupied by a few savage hunters. By opening the whole territory between Tennessee on the north, and Louisiana on the south, to the settlement of the whites, it will incalculably strengthen the southwestern frontier, and render the adjacent States strong enough to repel future invasion without remote aid. . . . It will separate the Indians from immediate contact with settlements of whites; free them from the power of the States; enable them to pursue happiness in their own way, and under their own rude institutions; will retard the progress of decay, which is lessening their numbers; and perhaps cause them gradually, under the protection of the Government, and through the influence of good counsels, to cast off their savage habits, and become an interesting, civilized, and Christian community. . . .

Toward the aborigines [that is, original residents] of the country no one can indulge a more friendly feeling than myself, or would go further in attempting to reclaim them from their wandering habits, and make them a happy and prosperous people.

Excerpted from President Jackson's Message to Congress "On Indian Removal," December 6, 1830, Records of the United States Senate, 1789–1990, Record Group 46, National Archives, via www.ourdocuments.gov.

Passage 2

Chief Speckled Snake of the Muscogee (later known as the Creeks), a Native American tribe that lived mostly in Alabama, responded to the U.S. federal government's developing Indian removal policy with a speech in 1829.

Brothers! We have heard the talk of our great father; it is very kind, he says he loves his red children.

Brothers! I have listened to many talks from our great father. When he first came over the wide waters . . . he was but a little man. His legs were cramped from sitting long in his big boat, and he begged for a little land to light his fire on. . . .

But when the white man had warmed himself before the Indian's fire, and filled himself with their hominy [a food made from corn], he became very large. With a step he bestrode the mountains, and his feet covered the plains and the valleys. His hands grasped the eastern and western sea, and his head rested on the moon. Then he became our Great Father. He loved his red children, and he said, "Get a little further, lest I tread on thee." With one foot he pushed the red man over the Oconee, and with the other he trampled down the graves of his fathers, and the forests where he had so long hunted the deer.

But our Great Father still loved his red children, and he soon made them another talk. He said "Get a little further; you are too near me." . . . When he found them too slow in moving, he sent his great guns before him to sweep his path.

Brothers! I have listened to a great many talks from our Great Father, but they always began and ended in this—"Get a little further; you are too near me." . . .

Brothers! When our Great Father made us a talk, on a former occasion, and said, "Get a little further; go beyond the Oconee and the Ocmulgee; there is a pleasant country," he also said, "*It shall be yours forever.*" I have listened to his present talk. He says the land where you now live is not yours. Go beyond the Mississippi; there is game; and you may remain while the grain grows or the water runs.

Brothers! Will not our great father come there also? He loves his red children. He speaks with a straight tongue, and will not lie.

Excerpted from Speckled Snake's speech, published June 20, 1829, in *Niles' Weekly Register*. Collected in Vol. 36 (3rd series, Vol. 12) (Baltimore, MD: H. Niles & Son), pp. 274–275.

13. In Passage 1, what is the purpose of the first paragraph?

   ○ A. to argue that Congress should pass further legislation related to the removal of Native Americans from their current location
   ○ B. to outline the history of relations with Native Americans that has led to negotiations for their removal further west
   ○ C. to describe in a positive manner the current status of the effort to move Native Americans further away from white populations
   ○ D. to explain the benefits of removing Native Americans from the southeastern United States

14. In Passage 2, what is the main idea of Chief Speckled Snake's speech?

   ○ A. Due to the generosity of Native Americans, white people have been able to prosper in the United States and expand their population and landholdings.
   ○ B. The U.S. government has been like a father to the Native Americans, treating them kindly and giving them new land.
   ○ C. Native Americans wish white people would treat them as parents treat their children and stop pushing them further away.
   ○ D. The U.S. government has repeatedly asked Native Americans to move and will do so again.

15. When Chief Speckled Snake says, "He loved his red children, and he said, 'Get a little further, lest I tread on thee,'" how does this sentence relate to Speckled Snake's main idea?

   ○ A. The speaker is giving an example to support his mostly positive view of the U.S. government.
   ○ B. The speaker is using irony to contrast the U.S. government's stated views with its actions.
   ○ C. The speaker is expressing regret that the relationship between the U.S. government and Native Americans is not better.
   ○ D. The speaker is stating a conclusion about the status of relations between the U.S. government and Native Americans.

16. Place *one* check mark in each column to indicate that speaker's rhetorical approach to persuading his audience.

Andrew Jackson	Speckled Snake
○ delineates the values and goals he holds in common with Congress	○ uses direct, inflammatory language to criticize his opponents
○ enumerates a number of benefits to all parties who might be affected by the policy under discussion	○ logically outlines a number of adverse effects the policy under discussion will have
○ emphasizes his feelings of friendship toward members of Congress	○ tells a story in which certain plot points are repeated

17. Place *one* check mark in each column to indicate an idea expressed by both speakers and an idea expressed by neither speaker.

Both Jackson and Speckled Snake	Neither Jackson nor Speckled Snake
○ The current U.S. policy of Indian removal will enhance the well-being of Native Americans.	○ Native Americans are nomadic hunters.
○ Some Native Americans helped early European settlers.	○ Whites and Native Americans will be able to coexist in harmony in the western territories.
○ The United States has had a consistent policy of Indian removal.	○ The U.S. government has broken promises to Native Americans.

18. Federalism is the division of power between federal and state governments. In Passage A, what attitude toward federalism does Jackson take?

   ○ A. When conflict arises between the national government and the states, this conflict should be defused.
   ○ B. When states govern themselves, this can result in harm to their populations.
   ○ C. Although the federal government will benefit from the removal of Native Americans, individual states will not.
   ○ D. Tennessee and Louisiana, and the states in between, should be solely responsible for defending themselves from foreign invasion.

Questions 19 through 25 refer to the following passage from a short story.

Excerpted from "The Twins"

1   After a while, there was a ring at the back door. The children scampered in from the garden, while Jennie answered the ring.

2   "Baker," said the man.

3   "Oh, yes," said Jennie: "wait, I'll get my purse."

4   I went on writing my letter, only half hearing the sound of Jennie's small-change as she, presumably, paid the baker's man.

5   In a moment, Marjie was by my side.

6   "Hallo," I said.

7   Marjie did not answer.

8   "Hallo, Marjie," I said. "Have you come to keep me company?"

9   "Listen," said little Marjie in a whisper, looking over her shoulder. "Listen."

10   "Yes," I said.

11   She looked over her shoulder again, as if afraid her mother might come in.

12   "Will you give me half-a-crown?" whispered Marjie, holding out her hand.

13   "Well," I said, "what do you want it for?"

14   "I want it," said Marjie, looking furtively behind her again.

15   "Would your mummy want you to have it?" I said.

16   "Give me half-a-crown," said Marjie.

17   "I'd rather not," I said. "But I'll tell you what, I'll buy you a—"

18   But Marjie had fled, out of the door, into the kitchen. "She'd rather not," I heard her say to someone.

19   Presently, Jennie came in, looking upset.

20   "Oh," she said, "I hope you didn't feel hurt. I only wanted to pay the baker, and I hadn't enough change. He hadn't any either; so just on the spur of the moment I sent Marjie for a loan of half-a-crown till tonight. But I shouldn't have done it. I never borrow anything as a rule."

21   "Well, of course!" I said. "Of course I'll lend you half-a-crown. I've got plenty of change. I didn't understand and I got the message all wrong; I thought she wanted it for herself and that you wouldn't like that."

22   Jennie looked doubtful. I funked explaining the whole of Marjie's act. It isn't easy to give evidence against a child of five.

23   "Oh, they never ask for money," said Jennie. "I would never allow them to ask for anything. They never do that."

24   "I'm sure they don't," I said, floundering a bit.

From "The Twins" by Muriel Spark, from the book *The Go-Away Bird and Other Stories*, J. B. Lippincott Company.

19. What does Marjie's looking over her shoulder suggest to the narrator?

The narrator thinks Marjie

- ○ A. is imagining what she'll do with the money
- ○ B. has forgotten something in the other room
- ○ C. is shy and lacks confidence
- ○ D. is hoping her mother won't hear her asking for money

20. Which of the following becomes evident during the discussion between Jennie and the narrator?

- ○ A. Jennie knows the narrator wanted to lend her the money.
- ○ B. Jennie can't believe that the narrator wouldn't lend her the money.
- ○ C. Jennie is perplexed when the narrator blames Marjie.
- ○ D. The narrator and Jennie eventually forget the misunderstanding.

21. The first-person point of view allows the reader to know

- ○ A. the narrator's thoughts
- ○ B. the thoughts and actions of all characters
- ○ C. only the actions of the narrator
- ○ D. Marjie's opinions about the narrator

22. What kind of relationship do Jennie and the narrator have?

- ○ A. They are cool and indifferent to each other.
- ○ B. They frequently disagree on matters.
- ○ C. They know each other but are not close.
- ○ D. Jennie takes advantage of the narrator.

23. What does "funked" mean in paragraph 22?

- ○ A. had a bad odor
- ○ B. lied about
- ○ C. shied away from
- ○ D. agreed with

24. The author of this passage chose to present the story in first-person perspective, so that we know only the narrator's thoughts. The author also chose not to show us the interactions between Jennie, Marjie, and the baker at the back door. What effect do these choices have on the story?

- ○ A. They make Jennie appear to be shifty and untrustworthy, so the reader trusts the narrator more than Jennie.
- ○ B. They make the baker such a mysterious figure that it is not clear to the reader whether the baker exists or not.
- ○ C. They make the narrator seem like a more intelligent character than Jennie.
- ○ D. They make Marjie's behavior harder to understand, so the reader sympathizes with the narrator's confusion.

25. The short, choppy nature of the dialogue in this excerpt contributes to its mood of

- ○ A. hominess
- ○ B. awkwardness
- ○ C. precision
- ○ D. happiness

Questions 26 through 30 refer to the following passage and graphic.

How Should We Measure the Rate of Poverty?

1   The rate of poverty appears to be increasing. Each year, the U.S. Census Bureau estimates the rate of poverty, or how many people in the U.S. are living in poverty. According to the Census Bureau, about 15.9 percent of the U.S. population was poor in 2011. That was a 15.3 percent increase over 2010. Moreover, the rate of poverty rose each year from 2007 to 2011.

2   It has been argued that the estimated rate of poverty is too low—that, in fact, more Americans are poor. To understand this, it is important first to understand how the Census Bureau determines who is poor. The Bureau surveys people about their income and then compares that income to the official "poverty threshold" (often called the "poverty line"). This poverty threshold varies depending on age, family size, and number of children. For example, in 2011 the poverty threshold for a single individual under 65 was $11,702. For a family of four, it was $23,021.

3   Some researchers have argued that these poverty thresholds do not account for taxes, living expenses, medical costs, or differences in cost of living. For example, in a major city, higher rents may leave individuals with less money for food. If the poverty thresholds were adjusted to account for these considerations, the estimated rate of poverty might be higher.

4   A panel of experts has proposed a different measure of poverty, which they call the Supplemental Poverty Measure, or SPM. The graph below shows what percentage of people are living in poverty as measured by the official poverty threshold and compares it to the percentage of people who would be considered poor by the SPM.

5   Why does it matter how many people are considered poor by the Census Bureau? One answer is that the Bureau's estimate of the rate of poverty is used by the federal government to allot resources to states and local communities. Local governments also use the estimate to figure out how many people are eligible for anti-poverty programs.

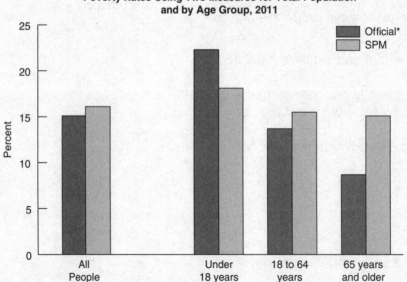

Poverty Rates Using Two Measures for Total Population and by Age Group, 2011

*Includes unrelated individuals under age 15.
Source: U.S. Census Bureau, Current Population Survey, 2012 Annual Social and Economic Supplement.

Adapted information from the U.S. Census Bureau

26. **Part One:** Which of the following best states the main idea of the passage and graph?

    A. The Census Bureau uses a set of poverty thresholds to determine the rate of poverty.

    B. If the Census Bureau adopted the SPM, the estimate of the rate of poverty among seniors would increase.

    C. There may be more people in poverty than the Census Bureau's official estimate suggests.

    D. It is important that the government take action to combat poverty.

Part Two: Which of the following sentences from the text or details from the graph best support your answer to Part One? Select 4.

    ☐ "The rate of poverty appears to be increasing."

    ☐ "Each year, the U.S. Census Bureau estimates the rate of poverty, or how many people in the United States are living in poverty."

    ☐ "It has been argued that the estimated rate of poverty is too low—that, in fact, more Americans are poor."

    ☐ "This poverty threshold varies depending on age, family size, and number of children."

    ☐ "Some researchers have argued that these poverty thresholds do not account for taxes, living expenses, medical costs, or differences in cost of living."

    ☐ "If the poverty thresholds were adjusted to account for these considerations [such as differences in cost of living], the estimated rate of poverty might be higher."

    ☐ The bar graph shows that the number of seniors considered to be living in poverty would be lower under the SPM than under the current thresholds.

    ☐ The bar graph shows that the number of people considered to be living in poverty would be higher for all groups except seniors under the SPM than under the current thresholds.

27. How does the bar graph support the main idea of the passage?

    A. The bar graph supports the claim that some people who do not think they are poor may actually be poor.

    B. The bar graph supports the claim that the government should do more to combat poverty.

    C. The bar graph supports the claim that a different way to measure poverty would produce a different estimate of the rate of poverty.

    D. The bar graph supports the claim that 15.9% of people in the U.S. were poor in 2011.

28. Which of the following describes a cause and effect relationship mentioned in the passage?

    A. The poverty thresholds cause individuals to have lower income.

    B. The Census Bureau's estimated rate of poverty can cause government officials to care about poverty.

    C. Higher rents can cause people to have less money for food.

    D. The SPM would cause more money to be spent on programs for senior citizens.

29. A student reviewed this passage and graph and then said: "It's clear to me that if the Census Bureau adopted the SPM, then local governments would get significantly more federal money to spend on anti-poverty programs." Which of the following best describes the flaw in the student's reasoning?

    A. The student has confused the causes of poverty with the effects of poverty.

    B. The student has overlooked the fact that other factors might impact how much money local governments receive from the federal government.

    C. The student has overlooked the possibility that not all local governments work to combat poverty.

    D. The student has overlooked the fact that other countries have even higher rates of poverty.

30. This piece was most likely written by someone who _____.

    A. worries that the government spends too much money on anti-poverty programs

    B. thinks poverty is too emotional a topic to be discussed publicly

    C. wants governmental actions to be based on an accurate estimate of the rate of poverty

    D. thinks that there is little that government can do about poverty

Questions 31 through 37 refer to the following two passages.

Glenwood Community Improvement Council Member:

As a member of the Glenwood Community Improvement Council, I fully support spending money to beautify our public parks. Over the last few years, several of our community parks have fallen into disrepair. Walking paths through the parks are not clearly marked, graffiti is visible on picnic shelters, and garden areas are overgrown with weeds. My neighbors tell me that they do not visit our parks because of the parks' condition. Some even said that they worry the parks are dangerous! We should spend money to ensure that our parks are good places to spend time with your family.

Improving and maintaining the parks would have a positive effect on crime and vandalism. If the parks are established as a source of pride for all of the community, vandals will be less likely to deface them. Well-maintained basketball and volleyball courts, picnic areas, and special events such as concerts in the parks would provide activities for the whole town and help neighbors spend time together.

Furthermore, beautiful public spaces are essential to community pride. Without community pride, Glenwood residents and others are unlikely to invest in creating and supporting small businesses. And small businesses are the heart of a thriving community. We must present Glenwood as a beautiful place to live in order to attract successful entrepreneurs from the surrounding area. If we do so, our investment in the parks will quickly pay for itself. Thus, we must improve our public parks.

Concerned Local Business Owner:

I think I speak for most of the business owners in Glenwood when I say that spending money to improve parks would be a complete waste of resources. The parks are not popular, and we do not know that they would become popular after being improved.

If we want a shining example of our town's successes to attract businesses, our growing business district is all we need! In the last four years, six new businesses have moved into vacant locations on Main Street. On top of that, several restaurants and shops downtown have survived the recent economic downturn and are now seeing more customers.

The city should do more to support these businesses. We should spend money to improve the infrastructure and appearance of the downtown business district. Improvements could be made to streetlights, signs, and building exteriors along our historic Main Street. We also currently are not able to plant public flower beds or clean and maintain the sidewalks. Investments in these areas would make downtown inviting to both customers and small business owners.

Beautifying our town is important if we want economic growth. But we should make sure that our beautification efforts are in the most important places. Clearly, beautifying downtown would help us build a healthy local economy. And once we have done so, then we can put money toward our parks.

31. The writers of the passages disagree about which of the following claims about Glenwood Public Parks?

○ A. They are in a state of disrepair.
○ B. They are a current source of pride for the community.
○ C. Improving them is a good use of funds right now.
○ D. Park activities can lower the amount of crime.

32. What does "entrepreneurs" mean, in the last paragraph of the first passage?

○ A. residents of the downtown area
○ B. workers who maintain parks
○ C. people who start businesses
○ D. critics who write for newspapers

33. Which of the following is a detail used by the business owner to support her claim that the town's business district will attract new businesses?

○ A. The city's parks are currently unpopular.
○ B. Public flowerbeds have not been maintained.
○ C. Money could be put toward the parks later.
○ D. Several restaurants downtown have survived the bad economy.

34. How does the local business owner feel about projects that improve the appearance of the city?

○ A. They are good when done in the best locations.
○ B. They are always a waste of taxpayer money.
○ C. The city parks are good enough the way they are.
○ D. They have no impact on local business.

35. Which of the following would the two writers most likely agree on?

○ A. Improving Glenwood Public Parks will have an immediate impact on local business.
○ B. Investing in our community is important for the future of Glenwood.
○ C. The parks would be used regularly if they were in better repair.
○ D. Public activities are more important than encouraging new local business.

36. **Part One:** Which of the following best expresses the Glenwood Community Improvement Council member's purpose?

○ A. to advocate for the construction of new parks in Glenwood
○ B. to argue that investing in Glenwood's downtown business district would be unwise
○ C. to argue that Glenwood should improve its public parks
○ D. to explain why reducing crime is more important than attracting new businesses

Part Two: Which of the following techniques does the Glenwood Community Improvement Council member employ in trying to achieve her purpose? Select three.

☐ paraphrasing the concerns of some community members
☐ appealing to well-known authorities in the community
☐ speculating about the probable result of improving the parks
☐ citing examples of other towns that have improved their parks
☐ speculating about the negative consequences of not improving the parks
☐ drawing a comparison between Glenwood's situation and a similar situation elsewhere

37. What relationship does crime reduction have to attracting small businesses, according to the Glenwood Community Improvement Council member?

○ A. Both would result from improvement of Glenwood's parks.
○ B. Crime reduction and park beautification are unrelated but equally important goals.
○ C. Lowering the crime rate would lead the town to invest money in the parks.
○ D. Attracting small businesses would result in reduction in crime.

Excerpted from *The Tale of Genji*

The Tale of Genji is a Japanese novel written around 1000 AD by a woman in the imperial court at the time. The novel is considered a great work of classical Japanese literature. It is about a concubine—that is, a woman who lives in the palace with the Emperor. This excerpt is from the very beginning of the novel.

1   In the reign of a certain Emperor, whose name is unknown to us, there was . . . one who, though she was not of high birth, enjoyed the full tide of Royal favor. Hence her superiors [other concubines], each one of whom had always been thinking—"I shall be the one," gazed upon her disdainfully with malignant eyes, and her equals and inferiors were more indignant still.

2   Such being the state of affairs, the anxiety which she had to endure was great and constant, and this was probably the reason why her health was at last so much affected, that she was often compelled to absent herself from Court, and to retire to the residence of her mother.

3   In due course . . . a jewel of a little prince was born to her. The first prince who had been born to the Emperor was the child of Koki-den-Niogo, the daughter of the Udaijin (a great officer of State). Not only was he first in point of age, but his influence on his mother's side was so great that public opinion had almost unanimously fixed upon him as heir-apparent. Of this the Emperor was fully conscious, and he only regarded the new-born child with that affection which one lavishes on [a favorite servant] . . .

4   When the young Prince [that is, the favored woman's son] was three years old [an important ceremony celebrating the child] took place. It was celebrated with a pomp scarcely inferior to that which adorned the investiture of the first Prince. . . . And again the public [showed its displeasure]. In the summer of the same year the [favored concubine] became ill, and wished to retire from the palace. . . . [H]er illness increased day by day; and she had drooped and pined away until she was now but a shadow of her former self.

5   . . . [One night her death was near.] To the Emperor the night now became black with gloom. He sent messenger after messenger to make inquiries, and could not await their return with patience. Midnight came, and with it the sound of lamentation. The messenger, who could do nothing else, hurried back with the sad tidings of the truth. From that moment the mind of the Emperor was darkened, and he confined himself to his private apartments.

6   He would still have kept with himself the young Prince now motherless, but there was no precedent for this, and it was arranged that he should be sent to his grandmother for the mourning. The child, who understood nothing, looked with amazement at the sad countenances of the Emperor, and of those around him. All separations have their sting, but sharp indeed was the sting in a case like this.

7   Now the funeral took place. During the ceremony, an Imperial messenger came from the Palace, and invested the dead with [a title of honor]. . . . Once more [some people showed their displeasure]. But, in other respects, the beauty of the departed, and her gracious bearing, which had ever commanded admiration, made people begin to think of her with sympathy. It was the excess of the Emperor's favor which had created so many detractors during her lifetime; but now even rivals felt pity for her. . . "When one is no more, the memory becomes so dear," may be [a description] of a case such as this.

Excerpted from *The Tale of Genji* by Murasaki Shikibu, translated into English by Suematsu Kencho.

38. Why does the author include the sentence, "All separations have their sting, but sharp indeed was the sting in a case like this"?

○ A. to show that the young prince understood what was going on
○ B. to illustrate the public's devotion to the young prince
○ C. to underscore the serious consequences his mother's death will have on the young prince's future
○ D. to emphasize the young prince's sadness at losing his mother

39. **Part One:** In paragraph 5, what is the meaning of the phrase, "sad tidings of the truth"?

○ A. a report of the illness of the young prince
○ B. news of the death of the Emperor's favorite concubine
○ C. the unmasking of the young prince's chief rival
○ D. an unfounded report of the young prince's death

Part Two: Which of the following phrases from the text justifies your response to Part One? Select all that apply.

☐ "one who, though she was not of high birth, enjoyed the full tide of Royal favor"
☐ "From that moment the mind of the Emperor was darkened"
☐ "the young prince now motherless"
☐ "All separations have their sting"
☐ "And again the public manifested its disapprobation"
☐ "The child, who understood nothing"

40. What tone is created by the sentence, "When one is no more, the memory becomes so dear"?

○ A. comic
○ B. ominous
○ C. cheerful
○ D. ironic

41. Why does the public resent the son of the favorite concubine?

○ A. The public believes that the emperor's younger son is not yet old enough for the ceremony held in his honor.
○ B. Holding a lavish ceremony is seen as a wasteful expenditure.
○ C. The public believes that the emperor's younger son should be sent to live with his grandmother.
○ D. Public opinion is that the emperor's older son, born to a woman with greater influence than the younger prince's mother, should be the emperor's heir.

Questions 42 through 46 are based on the passage below.

Excerpt from *A Raisin in the Sun*

This play, first performed in 1959, is about a family living on the South Side of Chicago. Walter Younger has died, and his wife, referred to here as "Mama," is expecting a check from his life insurance. Mama and her family have been discussing what she should do with the money.

1   RUTH Well—what are you going to do with it then?

2   MAMA I ain't rightly decided. (*Thinking. She speaks now with emphasis*) Some of it got to be put away for Beneatha and her schoolin'—and ain't nothing going to touch that part of it. Nothing. (*She waits several seconds, trying to make up her mind about something, and looks at RUTH a little tentatively before going on*) Been thinking that we maybe could meet the notes on a little old two-story somewhere, with a yard where Travis could play in the summertime, if we use part of the insurance for a down payment and everybody kind of pitch in. I could maybe take on a little day work again, few days a week—

3   RUTH (*Studying her mother-in-law furtively and concentrating on her ironing, anxious to encourage without seeming to*) Well, Lord knows, we've put enough rent into this here rat trap to pay for four houses by now…

4   MAMA (*Looking up at the words "rat trap" and then looking around and leaning back and sighing in a suddenly reflective mood*—) "Rat trap"—yes, that's all it is. (*Smiling*) I remember just as well the day me and Big Walter moved in here. Hadn't been married but two weeks and wasn't planning on living here no more than a year. (*She shakes her head at the dissolved dream*) We was going to set away, little by little, don't you know, and buy a little place out in Morgan Park. We had even picked out the house. (*Chuckling a little*) Looks right dumpy today. But Lord, child, you should know all the dreams I had 'bout buying that house and fixing it up and making me a little garden in the back—(*She waits and stops smiling*) And didn't none of it happen.

5   (*Dropping her hands in a futile gesture*)

6   RUTH (*Keeps her head down, ironing*) Yes, life can be a barrel of disappointments, sometimes.

7   MAMA Honey, Big Walter would come in here some nights back then and slump down on that couch there and just look at the rug, and look at me and look at the rug and then back at me—and I'd know he was down then . . . really down. (*After a second very long and thoughtful pause; she is seeing back to times that only she can see*) And then, Lord, when I lost that baby—little Claude—I almost thought I was going to lose Big Walter too. Oh, that man grieved hisself! He was one man to love his children.

8   RUTH Ain't nothin' can tear at you like losin' your baby.

9   MAMA I guess that's how come that man finally worked hisself to death like he done. Like he was fighting his own war with this here world that took his baby from him.

10   RUTH He sure was a fine man, all right. I always liked Mr. Younger.

11   MAMA Crazy 'bout his children! God knows there was plenty wrong with Walter Younger—hard-headed, mean, kind of wild with women—plenty wrong with him. But he sure loved his children. Always wanted them to have something—be something. That's where Brother gets all these notions, I reckon. Big Walter used to say, he'd get right wet in the eyes sometimes, lean his head back with the water standing in his eyes and say, "Seem like God didn't see fit to give the black man nothing but dreams—but He did give us children to make them dreams seem worthwhile." (*She smiles*) He could talk like that, don't you know.

42. Which of the following is a central idea of this passage?

   ○ A. The house Mama might buy now would give the family more space.
   ○ B. The grief one experiences over the death of a child is unlike any other grief.
   ○ C. Mr. Younger may have been flawed, but he was a hard-working man and a loving father.
   ○ D. The family has experienced many disappointments and tragedies.

43. Even though Mr. Walter Younger (Mama's late husband) is not present in this scene, the reader learns quite a bit about him. Which of the statements below about Mr. Younger are supported by this passage? Select all that apply.

   ○ He thought the house in Morgan Park was a bad investment.
   ○ He taught his son to dream of one day owning a house.
   ○ He grieved deeply over the baby Claude.
   ○ His love for his children helped keep his dreams alive.
   ○ He finally gave up on his attempts to improve his family's situation.
   ○ He once assumed that the family could improve their situation.
   ○ His moods were unpredictable.
   ○ He may have cheated on Mama.

44. Ruth and Mama both describe their apartment as a "rat trap." Which of the following best describes the impact of that phrase in this passage?

   ○ A. It means that the apartment building is a hangout for criminals.
   ○ B. It suggests that the family see themselves as undesirable, like rats.
   ○ C. It suggests that the apartment is very run-down, and that the family feels trapped there.
   ○ D. It means that the apartment has rats, and the phrase has no other meaning.

45. Mama quotes her late husband as saying, "Seem like God didn't see fit to give the black man nothing but dreams, but He did give us children to make them dreams seem worthwhile." What theme from the passage does this quote summarize?

   ○ A. the contrast between how hard it has been for the family to improve its situation and how much Mama would still like to try
   ○ B. the contrast between the child that survived ("Brother") and the one that died (Claude)
   ○ C. the contrast between the dreams of black people with children and the dreams of other people with children
   ○ D. the contrast between Walter Younger's religious doubts and Mama's unshakeable faith

46. Imagine that you are a director, putting on a performance of this play with a group of actors. The actor playing Mama says to you, "I think I should have my back to Ruth for most of this scene and face outward like I'm talking to thin air." If the actor playing Mama did so, what effect would that have on the scene?

   ○ A. It would suggest that Ruth has to struggle to win Mama's approval.
   ○ B. It would suggest that it's none of Ruth's business what Mama does with the money.
   ○ C. It would suggest that Mama is lost in her own powerful memories.
   ○ D. It would suggest that Ruth is not a strong person and is controlled by Mama.

STOP. You have completed the *Language Arts: Reading Practice Test.*

LANGUAGE ARTS: WRITING PRACTICE TEST
PART I: LANGUAGE SKILLS

Directions: Use 55 minutes to answer the following 50 questions.

<u>**Questions 1 through 5**</u> **refer to the following paragraphs.**

Painting a Room

(A)

(1) Would you like to redecorate a room in your home? (2) Painting is a fast and inexpensive way to give that room a hole new look. (3) First, remove the furniture, or move it to the center of the room and cover it with drop cloths. (4) Prepare the room by stripping paint and extra layers of wallpaper, filling cracks, and add a coat of primer if necessary.

(B)

(5) Now you're ready to paint. (6) Use a brush to paint a clean line along all edges where paint stops, such as where the wall meets the door frame, and in places where the ceiling meet a wall of a different color. (7) This is called "cutting in."

(C)

(8) The next step is to paint the room in the following order ceiling, walls, trim, doors, and windows. (9) Put no more than $\frac{3}{4}$ of an inch of paint in the paint pan. (10) Run your roller through the paint, being careful not to overload the roller. (11) Apply paint to the ceiling and walls in a "W" or "Z" zigzag pattern.

(D)

(12) Spread the paint evenly by rolling either side to side or up and down, using gentle strokes so as not to leave roller marks. (13) After finishing an area, look for spots you missed, go over them with your relatively dry roller.

1. Sentence 2: **Painting is a fast and inexpensive way to give that room a hole new look.**

   Which correction should be made to sentence 2?

   ○ A. change <u>is</u> to <u>are</u>
   ○ B. insert a comma after <u>fast</u>
   ○ C. change <u>to give</u> to <u>giving</u>
   ○ D. replace <u>hole</u> with <u>whole</u>

2. Sentence 4: **Prepare the room by stripping paint and extra layers of wallpaper, filling cracks, and add a coat of primer if necessary.**

   Which correction should be made to sentence 4?

   ○ A. change <u>Prepare</u> to <u>Preparing</u>
   ○ B. insert a comma after <u>paint</u>
   ○ C. remove the comma after <u>wallpaper</u>
   ○ D. change <u>add</u> to <u>adding</u>

3. Sentence 6: **Use a brush to paint a clean line along all edges where paint stops, such as where the wall meets the door frame, and in places where the ceiling meet a wall of a different color.**

   Which correction should be made to sentence 6?

   ○ A. change <u>ceiling meet</u> to <u>ceiling meets</u>
   ○ B. remove the comma after <u>stops</u>
   ○ C. remove the comma after <u>frame</u>
   ○ D. change <u>ceiling meet</u> to <u>ceiling met</u>

4. The next step is to paint the room in the following order ceiling, walls, trim, doors, and windows.

Which of the following should be inserted after the word order to correct this sentence?

- A. a comma
- B. a colon
- C. a semicolon
- D. a hyphen

5. Sentence 13: **After finishing an area, look for spots you missed, go over them with your relatively dry roller.**

Which is the best way to write the underlined portion of this sentence?

- A. missed, and go
- B. missed, and going
- C. missed go
- D. missed, but go

Questions 6 through 7 refer to the following passage.

Technological innovation is especially valuable to society when it promotes freedom. For example, the ability to mass-manufacture automobiles meant that in the 1920s, middle-class Americans could routinely travel hundreds, or even thousands, of miles for work or pleasure. Starting in the mid-20th century, Americans could choose their lifestyle as never before. Working people were freed from having to live within walking distance of their employment, and young people could escape the moral constraints of their community. At the same time, interstate highways meant that traveling by horse and wagon was no longer practical, and the spread of urban areas meant that home and job were often far apart. For this reason, owning a vehicle became almost a necessity, and the technology that freed Americans also trapped them.

6. Which of the following phrases is used to introduce counter examples to the idea that automobiles were especially valuable to society?

- A. For example
- B. Starting in the mid-20th century
- C. Working people were freed
- D. At the same time

7. Which of the following sentences would most effectively provide a conclusion?

- A. Therefore, Americans had to make car payments, keep gas in the tank, and take the car to the shop when it stopped running.
- B. In other words, human geography adapted to the use of motor vehicles, making their ownership that much more convenient.
- C. It was during this time that the "great American road trip" became a prominent plot element in many novels.
- D. Thus, despite its promise, the mass-manufacture of automobiles has not been entirely beneficial to society.

8. Read the sentence below.

Clinical depression is not a state of feeling sad but rather an utter lack of energy or enthusiasm for anything life has to offer, even the most pleasant of experiences.

If the author wishes to illustrate the point of the sentence above, which of the following sentences would be most appropriate to add?

- ○ A. Depression is a cave that no light can penetrate.
- ○ B. Depression is a bird that has flown far away.
- ○ C. Depression is a spider in the center of a web.
- ○ D. Depression is a flaming, punishing hell.

9. Read the short passage below and answer the question that follows.

The author H. P. Lovecraft is most often associated with the horror genre. The majority of his stories feature protagonists who meet a grisly fate or only narrowly avoid such an end. He wrote about the terrifying monster Cthulhu, in whose presence humanity seemed insignificant. Many of his stories set in the "Dreamlands," while disturbing, are more properly considered fantasy than horror. True devotees of Lovecraft acknowledge his contributions to multiple genres.

The passage above lacks transition words that would make it easier to read. Match each transition word below to the sentence it could most appropriately begin.

The majority of his stories feature protagonists who meet a grisly fate . . .	
He wrote about the terrify- ing monster Cthulhu . . .	
Many of his stories set in the "Dreamlands" . . .	
True devotees of Lovecraft acknowledge . . .	

| For example, |
| On the other hand, |
| This is because |
| Therefore, |

10. Read the sentence below.

The wallpaper, whose pattern was a mixture of rose blossoms and bluebell flowers, gave the room a cheerful look.

Which of the following is a correct and effective method of shortening the sentence above?

- ○ A. The wallpaper (rose blossoms and blue- bell flowers were mixed in it) gave the room a cheerful look.
- ○ B. The wallpaper gave the room a cheerful look of roses and bluebells.
- ○ C. The mixed rose blossom and bluebell flower wallpaper gave the room a cheerful look.
- ○ D. The rose-and-bluebell wallpaper gave the room a cheerful look.

11. Read the following short passage and answer the question that follows.

It is sometimes said that Chillyville is a ter- rible place to live, because the winters are harsh. However, Chillyville offers pleasant people, beautiful parks, interesting artistic and cultural events, terrific food, and plenti- ful summertime activities. These advantages more than make up for the winter weather.

The writer of this paragraph used the passive voice in the first sentence: *It is sometimes said that Chillyville is an unpleasant place to live*. What effect does this have on the mean- ing of the passage?

- ○ A. It suggests that the author does not agree that Chillyville is a terrible place to live.
- ○ B. It suggests that large numbers of peo- ple think Chillyville is a terrible place to live.
- ○ C. It suggests that the author is convinced that Chillyville is a terrible place to live.
- ○ D. It suggests that no one has actually said that Chillyville is a terrible place to live.

12. Read the sentence below.

Bryan said to his mom, "If there were school today, the school bus would have already passed."

Assuming that Bryan is being sincere, does he think that there is school today? How do you know?

- A. Bryan thinks there is school today, because it is clear that he saw the bus pass by earlier.
- B. Bryan thinks there is school today, because he is speaking in the present tense.
- C. Bryan does not think there is school today, because he is speaking about a day other than today.
- D. Bryan does not think there is school today, because he is speaking using the subjunctive mood.

13. Read the sentence below.

Being careful, Jamilla never signs her name to any documents until she has read them thoroughly.

What function does the phrase *Being careful* serve in the sentence above?

- A. It modifies the noun *Jamilla*.
- B. It modifies the adverb *thoroughly*.
- C. It modifies the noun *documents*.
- D. It contradicts the adverb *thoroughly*.

14. Review the rules regarding numbers from various style manuals below.

Chicago Manual of Style, 16th edition	Usually write out numbers up to one hundred; use numerals for 101 and up.
AP Stylebook, 2014 edition	Usually write out numbers up to nine; use numerals for 10 and up. Use numerals for ages.
Publication Manual of the APA, 6th edition	Usually write out numbers up to nine; use numerals for 10 and up. Use numerals for quantities of time.

Which of the following conforms to the above guidelines from the *Publication Manual of the APA*?

- A. Our team has 6 tasks to accomplish before ten a.m., and then we'll receive a score between 0 and 100. Three of us competed last year, and we are hoping to beat last year's score, which was seventy-two.
- B. Our team has six tasks to accomplish before 10:00 a.m., and then we'll receive a score between zero and 100. Three of us competed last year, and we are hoping to beat last year's score, which was 72.
- C. Our team has 6 tasks to accomplish before 10:00 a.m., and then we'll receive a score between 0 and 100. 3 of us competed last year, and we are hoping to beat last year's score, which was 72.
- D. Our team has six tasks to accomplish before ten a.m., and then we'll receive a score between zero and one-hundred. Three of us competed last year, and we are hoping to beat last year's score, which was seventy-two.

Questions 15 through 20 refer to the following passage.

Starting a Community Garden

(A)

(1) In many cities, neighborhood groups are forming community gardens in vacant lots, in parks, or on rooftops. (2) These gardens is an ideal way for both children and adults to work with nature while making the neighborhood more beautiful. (3) If you would like to start a community garden, first determine whether people are truly interested in the project. (4) If they are, organize a meeting of interested people, and choose someone to be the garden coordinator. (5) Form committees for tasks like finding money for the garden.

(B)

(6) Once your group is organized, approach a sponsor this could be a group or individual who can support your garden. (7) Keep in mind that contributions of seeds, tools, and land (whether large plots of land or small) are just as important as money. (8) Schools, churches, citizen groups, and private businesses are all potential sponsors.

(C)

(9) Find out how the land has been used in the past to avoid places that may be contaminated. (10) Pick a site that gets at least six hours of direct sunlight a day, and make sure that water is available. (11) Contact the owner of the site try to get a lease that allows you to use the land for at least three years.

(D)

(12) After choosing a site, the group of gardeners needs to decide how to organize the garden. (13) What size should each plot be, and how will plots be assigned? (14) Finally, establish a procedure to follow to maintain tidiness and piece in the garden.

15. Sentence 2: **These gardens is an ideal way for both children and adults to work with nature while making the neighborhood more beautiful.**

Which correction should be made to sentence 2?

- A. change <u>gardens</u> to <u>garden</u>
- B. change <u>is</u> to <u>are</u>
- C. replace <u>way</u> with <u>weigh</u>
- D. insert a comma after <u>children</u>

16. Sentence 6: **Once your group is organized, approach a sponsor this could be a group or individual who can support your garden.**

Which correction should be made to sentence 6?

- A. insert a comma after <u>sponsor</u>
- B. insert a period after <u>sponsor</u> and capitalize <u>this</u>
- C. remove the comma after <u>organized</u>
- D. insert a comma after <u>group</u>

17. Sentence 7: **Keep in mind that contributions of seeds, tools, and land (whether large plots of land or small) are just as important as money.**

A student is writing a paper about community gardens and wishes to quote from this passage. He wants to include sentence 7 in his paper, but he would like to make it shorter by omitting the phrase in parentheses. Which of the following is the correct way to do this?

- A. "Keep in mind that contributions of seeds, tools, and land [material omitted] are just as important as money."
- B. "Keep in mind that contributions of seeds, tools, and land are just as important as money."
- C. "Keep in mind that contributions of seeds, tools, and land _____ are just as important as money."
- D. "Keep in mind that contributions of seeds, tools, and land . . . are just as important as money."

18. Which sentence would be most effective if inserted at the beginning of paragraph C?

- A. Next, choose a site for the garden.
- B. Land use is a very significant factor.
- C. We all know that you are going to need land for your garden.
- D. Learn about the history of your site.

19. Which of the following would improve the effectiveness of paragraph A?

- A. Start a new paragraph before sentence 2.
- B. Start a new paragraph before sentence 3.
- C. Combine sentences 2 and 3 into a compound sentence.
- D. Combine paragraphs A and B.

20. Sentence 14: **Finally, establish a procedure to follow to maintain tidiness and piece in the garden.**

Which correction should be made to sentence 6?

- A. change <u>to follow</u> to <u>to be following</u>
- B. change <u>piece</u> to <u>peace</u>
- C. change <u>tidiness</u> to <u>tidyness</u>
- D. change <u>establish</u> to <u>establishing</u>

Sick Building Syndrome

(A)

(1) Do you often feel sick when at you're workplace? (2) Do you experience symptoms such as coughing, sneezing, nausea, headaches, and difficulty breathing? (3) Do these symptoms seem to disappear once you leave work magically? (4) If so, you may be working in a sick building.

(B)

(5) "Sick building syndrome" is a term that refers to working in a building that makes you sick. (6) The syndrome may be caused by improper building design. (7) Over the past 20 years, architects have designed office buildings with an eye to saving energy. (8) The buildings are tightly sealed so that little heat escapes, and the air inside the buildings is recirculated to avoid the cost of heating fresh air. (9) Although this design reduces energy costs, the lack of ventilation causes a buildup of toxins in the air. (10) On the other hand, an older isn't necessarily immune to the syndrome. (11) Even if the windows originally opened to let in fresh air, adding insulation, caulking, and weather stripping at a later date may have made the windows airtight.

(C)

(12) Toxins in the air come from a variety of sources. (13) Biological agents, including bacteria, viruses, fungi, and pollen, may be found in poorly maintained air circulation systems and dirty washrooms. (14) Fungi can also be found in damp places like woodlands and bogs. (15) The deadly gas carbon monoxide can seep into a building's air through an improperly ventilated garage or a leaky duct. (16) Formaldehyde is frequently found in furniture, paneling, glues, and upholstery, even in draperies!

21. Sentence 1: **Do you often feel sick when at you're workplace?**

Which correction should be made to sentence 1?

○ A. insert a comma after <u>sick</u>
○ B. change <u>sick</u> to <u>sickly</u>
○ C. replace <u>you're</u> with <u>your</u>
○ D. change <u>Do</u> to <u>Are</u>

22. Sentence 3: **Do these symptoms seem to disappear once you leave work magically?**

The most effective revision of sentence 3 would include which group of words?

○ A. disappear magically once you leave
○ B. once you disappear magically
○ C. upon leaving work magically
○ D. seem to disappear, once you leave

23. Sentence 16: **Formaldehyde is frequently found in furniture, paneling, glues, and upholstery, even in draperies!**

Which of the following would be the best way to rewrite the last part of sentence 16?

○ A. furniture, paneling, glues, and upholstery—even in draperies!
○ B. furniture, paneling, glues, and upholstery: even in draperies!
○ C. furniture, paneling, glues, and upholstery. Even in draperies!
○ D. furniture, paneling, glues, and upholstery-even in draperies!

24. Which of the following sentences from the passage should be deleted because it is irrelevant to the author's main point?

○ A. (2) Do you experience symptoms such as coughing, sneezing, nausea, headaches, and difficulty breathing?
○ B. (6) The syndrome may be caused by improper building design.
○ C. (13) Biological agents, including bacteria, viruses, fungi, and pollen, may be found in poorly maintained air circulation systems and dirty washrooms.
○ D. (14) Fungi can also be found in damp places like woodlands and bogs.

Questions 25 and 26 are based on the following short passage.

Writers vary their syntax in order to convey effects. The excerpt below is from an Edgar Allen Poe story, in which the narrator describes committing a murder.

Now this is the point. You fancy me mad. Madmen know nothing. But you should have seen me. You should have seen how wisely I proceeded—with what caution—with what foresight—with what dissimulation I went to work! I was never kinder to the old man than during the whole week before I killed him. And every night, about midnight, I turned the latch of his door and opened it—oh so gently! And then, when I had made an opening sufficient for my head, I put in a dark lantern, all closed, closed, that no light shone out, and then I thrust in my head. Oh, you would have laughed to see how cunningly I thrust it in! I moved it slowly—very, very slowly, so that I might not disturb the old man's sleep. It took me an hour to place my whole head within the opening so far that I could see him as he lay upon his bed. Ha! would a madman have been so wise as this?

Excerpted from Edgar Allen Poe, *The Tell-Tale Heart*, 1843.

25. The fifth sentence reads, "You should have seen how wisely I proceeded—with what caution—with what foresight—with what dissimulation I went to work!" Poe could have shortened this sentence like this: "You should have seen how I proceeded with wisdom, caution, foresight, and dissimulation!" Rather, he chose to use several repetitive phrases separated with dashes. Which of the following are effects achieved by this choice? Select all that apply.

☐ emphasizing how enthusiastically the narrator is praising himself

☐ increasing the mood of suspense in the story

☐ emphasizing the patience and stealth used by the narrator

☐ preparing the reader to learn that the narrator takes an hour to put his head inside a door

26. The excerpt ends with a rhetorical question: "Ha! would a madman have been so wise as this?" Which of the following does Poe emphasize by using a rhetorical question?

○ A. the narrator's desire to persuade the reader of his sanity

○ B. the narrator's ability to represent himself well in writing

○ C. the fact that madmen are generally not wise

○ D. the narrator's accusation that the old man was mad

27. Read the following short sentences.

Viktoriya sat down on the couch and thought with dismay about the week ahead. She was going to have to work double shifts at her job almost every day, run some errands that were already overdue, see her doctor, and somehow manage to get a plumber to come and fix the boiler. If only she was a comic book heroine, it would all be easier!

Which of the following represents a correction that should be made to the sentences above?

- A. Viktoriya sat down on the couch, and she thought with dismay about the week ahead.
- B. She was going to have almost every day to work double shifts at her job,
- C. and somehow manage to get a plumber to come because the boiler was broken.
- D. If only she were a comic book heroine, it would all be easier!

28. Which of the following sentences contains a verb in the imperative mood?

- A. Malik voted by mail in the last general election.
- B. Malik would vote if he could find his voter registration card.
- C. Please vote for the candidate of your choice by filling in the corresponding bubble.
- D. Why would anyone vote for a candidate she disagreed with?

29. In 1819, the poet Percy Bysshe Shelley wrote a letter that included the following sentence:

"Every body here is talking of a Steam Ship which is building at Leghorn."

In Shelley's day, the sentence might have been considered error-free. Today, an editor would probably ask the writer to correct, among other things, the verb *building*. Why is that?

- A. People's opinions about the correct use of the verb have changed over time.
- B. The verb is now more ambiguous than it once was.
- C. The verb is now considered too casual to be used in formal writing.
- D. Editors now want writers to use more colorful language than was used in the past.

30. Read the following short passage and answer the question that follows.

Van Anh wanted to make sure she put the shelves together properly. She read in the instructions that she should start by laying all the parts out on the floor. She counted the pieces to make sure nothing was missing. Then, the instructions explained, the two long side pieces should be joined to the base of the shelving unit. After that, you should fit the top of the shelving unit to the two long side pieces; be sure that the front of the top piece is facing the front of the unit. Finally, attach the back of the shelving unit with the nails provided.

Which of the following describes an error in the sentences above?

- A. It contains an inappropriate shift from the declaratory mood to the subjunctive mood.
- B. It uses the words *shelves* and *shelving unit* in an ambiguous way.
- C. It contains an inappropriate shift from the third person to the second person.
- D. It misuses the connecting words *Then*, *After that*, and *Finally*.

Questions 31 through 34 refer to the following flyer.

Save Compton Point!

(A)

(1) Compton Point, home to many, animal species that are threatened with extinction, now faces a threat of its own. (2) Developers are attempting to change the zoning in order to build a hotel, a tourist center, and an observation tower. (3) If they succeed in getting the rights to build, construction will begin next August.

(B)

(4) Sam Wanamaker, director of the Society for the Protection of Nature, warns that construction of the development is likely to drive out more than 30 animal species that live on the point. (5) Air pollution from tourist traffic will further reduce the animals' chances for survival, not to mention litter left behind by floods of tourists wandering through the area.

(C)

(6) The Compton Point area is zoned as natural parkland. (7) There are several other areas in the county that are zoned as natural parkland. (8) However, because this project is potentially so lucrative for the city, the zoning board seems to be bending to the will of the developers.

(D)

(9) Register your opposition to the development of Compton Point! (10) Come to a demonstration at 10 A.M. on Saturday, May 7, in front of the mayor's office, 34 Wilton Road. (11) Bring signs with slogans that tell how you feel. (12) A strong turnout at this demonstration did send a message to developers.

31. Sentence 1: **Compton Point, home to many, animal species that are threatened with extinction, now faces a threat of its own.**

Which of the following represents the best correction to sentence 1?

- A. Compton point, home to many, animal species that are threatened with extinction, now faces a threat of its own.
- B. Compton Point, home too many, animal species that are threatened with extinction, now faces a threat of its own.
- C. Compton Point, home to many animal species that are threatened with extinction, now faces a threat of its own.
- D. Compton Point, home to many, animal species who are threatened with extinction, now faces a threat of its own.

32. Sentence 5: **Air pollution from tourist traffic will further reduce the animals' chances for survival, not to mention litter left behind by floods of tourists wandering through the area.**

The most effective revision of sentence 5 includes which group of words?

- A. Tourism increases both air pollution and litter, which will
- B. Litter, which tourists leave behind, and besides
- C. Animals will have less chance for survival when air pollution
- D. Air pollution and litter, having been caused by tourists,

33. Which revision would improve the effectiveness of paragraph C?

- A. remove sentence 6
- B. move sentence 6 to follow sentence 7
- C. remove sentence 7
- D. move sentence 7 to follow sentence 8

34. Sentence 12: **A strong turnout at this demonstration did send a message to developers.**

Which correction should be made to sentence 12?

- A. change <u>did</u> to <u>will</u>
- B. change <u>did</u> to <u>have</u>
- C. change <u>did</u> to <u>has</u>
- D. no change necessary

35. Which one of the following sentences contains an infinitive phrase used as the object of a verb?

A. To swim in the lake early in the morning is delightful.

B. Swimming in the lake early in the morning is delightful.

C. I love to swim in the lake early in the morning.

D. I love swimming in the lake early in the morning.

36. Which of the sentences below makes correct use of the phrase *is said to be*?

A. Gloria was unhappy with what her test results is said to be.

B. Saul is said to be that he is going to the store tomorrow.

C. Philippa is said to be an excellent instructor.

D. Nabil heard the rumor that is said to be by his friends.

Question 37 is based on the following passage.

(A)

Business continuity is the ability of a company to recovery quickly from a disaster. The success of a business continuity plan is measured in various ways, including how long service to customers is interrupted and how the public views the company after a disaster. Disasters come in many forms: natural disasters, criminal activity, and accidents.

(B)

The giant energy company Exxon saw its reputation plummet due to its seemingly uncaring response to the *Exxon-Valdez* oil spill, which wreaked havoc on Alaskan wildlife. Likewise, BP, another energy company, earned the wrath of the American public when it failed to stop the Deepwater Horizon oil spill in the Gulf of Mexico for several weeks. Johnson & Johnson, on the other hand, earned praise for its swift and compassionate response to the murder of several people by way of poison introduced to the company's Tylenol capsules.

37. Which of the following sentences could best be added to the beginning of paragraph B to increase the cohesion of the passage?

A. Because business continuity means coordinating the separate disciplines of risk management, disaster planning, and information technology data recovery, it is a significant undertaking.

B. Investing in business continuity is crucial: mishandling a disaster can hurt the company's reputation with a generation of consumers, while efficiently limiting the damage can earn public trust.

C. The field of business continuity has been evolving, shifting its focus from managing the response to a disruptive event after it occurs to building in organizational resilience, a capacity to avoid service interruptions even when disaster strikes.

D. Business continuity management has become more important as the global economy has become more interdependent, because companies are exposed to the risk of disruption from more sources.

Questions 38 through 45 refer to the following paragraphs.

Kites and Science

(A)

(1) Who doesn't enjoy flying a kite? (2) When you seen people in your community flying kites on a windy day, you might think that kites are just for fun. (3) Kites have been flown in countries around the world and for centuries, by young and old alike. (4) However, kite flying, it may surprise you to know, have been responsible for a number of scientific discoveries.

(B)

(5) In 1752, Benjamin Franklin used a kite to prove the presence of electricity in storm clouds. (6) He did it by flying a kite during a thunderstorm with a brass key attached to the end. (7) The story goes that, when lightning struck the kite line and traveled down to the key, there was a spark of electricity.

(C)

(8) Kites also played a role in learning about the weather. (9) In 1749, Alexander Wilson of Scotland became the first scientist to send a thermometer aloft in a kite. (10) Starting in the 1890s, kites held meteorological instruments that also measured humidity and wind speed. (11) They measured barometric pressure too.

(D)

(12) Kites were an early form of aircraft kites and airplanes employ some of the same principles of physics. (13) The Wright Brothers, inventors of the first plane, experimented with kites. (14) Alexander Graham Bell, the physicist and inventor, used kites to learn about problems of airplane construction.

(E)

(15) So the next time you see some neighborhood children flying kites, just think. (16) You may be watching budding young scientists.

38. Sentence 2: **When you <u>seen</u> people flying kites in your community on a windy day, you might think that kites are just for fun.**

Which is the best way to write the underlined portion of the sentence?

○ A. might see
○ B. saw
○ C. see
○ D. have seen

39. Sentence 3: **Kites have been flown in countries around the world and for centuries, by young and old alike.**

Which revision should be made to the placement of sentence 3?

○ A. move sentence 3 to the beginning of paragraph A
○ B. move sentence 3 to follow sentence 1
○ C. remove sentence 3
○ D. no revision is necessary

40. Sentence 6: **He did it by flying a kite during a thunderstorm with a brass key attached to the end.**

The most effective revision of sentence 6 would begin with which group of words?

○ A. By flying a kite with a brass key
○ B. The kite was flown during a thunderstorm
○ C. A brass key was attached to the end
○ D. During a thunderstorm, he flew a kite with

41. Sentences 10 and 11: **Starting in the 1890s, kites held meteorological instruments that measured humidity and wind speed. They measured barometric pressure too.**

The most effective combination of sentences 10 and 11 would include which group of words?

○ A. one of the purposes was measuring wind
○ B. humidity, wind speed, and barometric pressure
○ C. barometric pressure was measured along with
○ D. the measurement of barometric pressure

42. Sentence 12: **Kites were an early form of aircraft kites and airplanes employ some of the same principles of physics.**

Which of the following punctuation marks could be inserted after the word <u>aircraft</u> in order to correct this sentence?

○ A. a comma
○ B. a semicolon
○ C. an ellipsis
○ D. a hyphen

43. Sentence 14: **Alexander Graham <u>Bell the physicist and inventor used</u> kites to learn about problems of airplane construction.**

Which is the best way to write the underlined portion of the sentence?

○ A. Bell, the physicist and inventor, used
○ B. Bell the physicist and inventor, used
○ C. Bell, the physicist and inventor used
○ D. Bell, the physicist and inventor, he used

Questions 44 through 47 are based on the following passage.

What Is a Hybrid Car?

(A)

(1) A hybrid vehicle uses at least two different sources of power, you have probably seen examples of hybrid vehicles without realizing it. (2) Some types of trucks or buses, and some trains use a combination of diesel fuel and electric power. (3) The most common hybrid cars in use today combine gasoline and electric power.

(B)

(4) There are two primary types of hybrid engine designs: the parallel hybrid and the series hybrid. (5) Both kinds have electric motors and gasoline-powered engines. (6) In the parallel-hybrid design, the electric motor and the gasoline engine can power the car together or independently. (7) In the series-hybrid design, the gasoline engine does not power the car directly. (8) Instead, it run a machine called a generator that charges the batteries or powers the electric motor. (9) The electric motor actually powers the car. (10) However, the car cannot move unless the gasoline engine is on. (11) One of the benefits of hybrid cars is their fuel efficiency.

(C)

(12) In some hybrid models, the gasoline engine is used only when the car would move faster than 15 miles per hour. (13) That reduces fuel consumption in heavy traffic. (14) The designers who have created the hybrid car have tried to increase its efficiency in every way they can think of. (15) Hybrids are made from lightweight materials. (16) They are designed to drive smoothly, without being slowed down by things like wind, and even the tires on hybrid cars are designed to make the car run as efficiently as possible.

44. Sentence 1: **A hybrid vehicle uses at least two different sources of power, you have probably seen examples of hybrid vehicles without realizing it.**

Which correction should be made to Sentence 1?

- A. change <u>uses</u> to <u>will use</u>
- B. change <u>two different</u> to <u>two and different</u>
- C. change <u>power, you</u> to <u>power. You</u>
- D. change <u>realizing it</u> to <u>realizes it</u>

45. Sentence 2: <u>**Some types of trucks or buses, and some trains**</u> **use a combination of diesel fuel and electric power.**

What is the best way to revise the underlined portion of the sentence?

- A. Some types of trucks, buses, some trains
- B. Some types of trucks or buses or trains
- C. Some types of trucks, buses, and trains
- D. Some types of trucks, buses, or trains

46. Sentence 12: **In some hybrid models, the gasoline engine is used only when the car would move faster than 15 miles per hour.**

Which correction should be made to sentence 12?

- A. remove the comma
- B. change <u>is used</u> to <u>is being used</u>
- C. change <u>would move</u> to <u>moves</u>
- D. change <u>faster</u> to <u>more</u>

Questions 47 through 49 are based on the short passage below.

Learning how to ride a skateboard or inline skates is similar to how you learn to ride a bicycle. In the beginning, it can mean repeated stumbles and falls. While knees and elbows are usually the first to get scraped up, they typically heal quickly. _____, head injuries are more severe—they can even prove deadly. Even a low-speed fall can do considerable damage, and the head has to be protected, and the right helmet—which you can purchase from a store that sells quality sporting goods—can do just that if worn properly.

47. Which of the following is a grammatical error in the first sentence?

  ○ A. It should employ the imperative mood.
  ○ B. It does not display parallel structure.
  ○ C. It should contain a semicolon.
  ○ D. It does not employ the correct tense.

48. Which of the following would be the best word to fill in the blank above?

  ○ A. Additionally
  ○ B. Similarly
  ○ C. However
  ○ D. Nonetheless

49. Which of the following would be the best way to revise the last sentence of the passage?

  ○ A. change the dashes to commas
  ○ B. split it into two sentences
  ○ C. change the commas to semicolons
  ○ D. remove the first clause

50. Susan is writing a short essay about a miserable trip she made to the hospital. She starts out by writing this paragraph:

As soon as I arrived at the emergency room, I was dazzled by the glittering lights and cream-colored walls. My heart was racing with anticipation. I was taken to a room and immediately given a drink that helped me sleep soundly.

When Susan rereads the paragraph she just wrote, she thinks it sounds a great deal happier than she meant it to. Which of the following changes could Susan make to her paragraph in order to convey the feeling that her trip to the hospital was a bad experience? Select all that apply.

  ☐ Change *was dazzled by* to *was overwhelmed by*.
  ☐ Change *was dazzled by* to *noticed*.
  ☐ Change *glittering* to *sparkling*.
  ☐ Change *glittering* to *glaring*.
  ☐ Change *cream-colored* to *drab*.
  ☐ Change *racing with anticipation* to *speeding with anticipation*.
  ☐ Change *racing with anticipation* to *racing with anxiety*.
  ☐ Change *taken to a room* to *shown into a room*.
  ☐ Change *taken to a room* to *shoved into a room*.
  ☐ Change *given a drink* to *provided with a drink*.
  ☐ Change *helped me sleep soundly* to *made me unaware of what was happening*.

STOP. You have completed Part I of the *Language Arts: Writing Practice Test.* You may take a 15-minute break before beginning Part II.

PART II: ESSAY

Directions: Based on both passages on pages 594 and 595, write a response to the prompt below. This task may take up to 50 minutes to complete.

The following two passages give the two sides of a debate about whether schools in a certain community should continue to require physical education. Read the two passages and weigh the claims on both sides. Then write an argumentative essay in which you argue for or against requiring students to complete physical education courses in order to graduate.

Before you begin planning your essay, read the two passages:

(1) Passage A: Why Physical Education Should No Longer Be a Requirement for Graduation
(2) Passage B: Physical Education Is an Important Requirement for Students

As you read the passages, think about what details you might use to support your argument. Take notes or highlight portions of the passages as you read. In your essay, be sure to:

- Introduce your thesis statement.
- Support your thesis statement with evidence from the passages and logical reasoning.
- Argue against the opposing claim.
- Organize your essay logically.
- Use connecting words and phrases to show the relationships between ideas.
- Use a businesslike style.
- Provide a concluding statement or paragraph that summarizes your argument.

Passage A: Why Physical Education Should No Longer Be a Requirement for Graduation

This is the text of Councilwoman Juanita Sanchez's speech at last week's school board meeting.

The job market is increasingly competitive. Because of this, we must ensure that our students' education fully prepares them to succeed in the future. A limited budget and limited time during the school day force us to make difficult decisions concerning what we teach. We must be willing to make these decisions with the best interests of our students at heart. With these goals in mind, I support the proposal to eliminate physical education as a core requirement for high school graduation in our district.

Time spent completing physical education requirements is time away from more productive educational pursuits. While our state's standardized test scores have continued to rise in past years, we are still seeing results that are below average in both mathematics and reading. Added instructional time is necessary to see our test scores meet the standards set for us. This additional time spent on core subjects will also better prepare students for a pursuit of higher education after high school graduation.

No one is suggesting that physical education and fitness classes be completely eliminated from our curriculum. Physical education is a worthwhile pursuit and should be provided for those students who are interested. But it should be an elective, or optional, course in the same way that music, art, and theater classes are offered as electives. Thus, this outdated requirement will no longer get in the way of more academically important pursuits.

Passage B: Physical Education Is an Important Requirement for Students

Letter from concerned parent published in the City *Journal newspaper*

No one would disagree that preparing our students for a successful future is essential. Changes need to be made in order to help our children compete for college scholarships and career advancement. But as we make these changes, we have to be careful not to cause more harm than good. The current proposal places us in danger of damaging successful programs in our efforts to make improvements.

Having a healthy lifestyle is at least as important to a happy and successful future as mathematics and reading skills are. We currently are in the middle of an epidemic of health problems caused by lack of physical fitness among the children in our community. In our state, almost 20% of children between the ages of 12 and 18 are classified as obese. And obesity is linked to a number of life-threatening health problems including diabetes and heart disease. Thus, this is a trend that we must make every effort to reverse.

Programs to offer healthier lunch choices for students have already been introduced. It would be ridiculous to now eliminate requirements that teach our children about other aspects of healthy living. What good is longer time spent in so-called core classes if students aren't healthy enough to fully participate?

I understand that the School Board members have students' best interests at heart. And I agree that it is important to find ways to improve the math and reading scores of our students. Unfortunately, the current plan to eliminate physical education will do much more harm than good. There is a reason P.E. has been a part of our school curriculum for so many years!

STOP. You have completed the *Language Arts: Writing Practice Test*.

MATHEMATICS PRACTICE TEST

MATHEMATICS REFERENCE SHEET

The next two pages display formulas that you will be given when you take the TASC. You can refer to these pages as you work through the *Mathematics Test.*

Volume

Cylinder: $V = \pi r^2 h$

Pyramid: $V = \frac{1}{3} Bh$

Cone: $V = \frac{1}{3} \pi r^2 h$

Sphere: $V = \frac{4}{3} \pi r^3$

Coordinate Geometry

Midpoint formula:

$$\left(\frac{x_1 + x_2}{2}, \frac{y_1 - y_2}{2} \right)$$

Distance formula:

$$d = \sqrt{(x_2 - x_1)^2 + (y_2 - y_1)^2}$$

Slope: $m = \frac{y_2 - y_1}{x_2 - x_1}, x_2 \neq x_1$

Special Factoring

$a^2 - b^2 = (a - b)(a + b)$

$a^2 + 2ab + b^2 = (a + b)^2$

$a^2 - 2ab + b^2 = (a - b)^2$

$a^3 + b^3 = (a + b)(a^2 - ab + b^2)$

$a^3 - b^3 = (a - b)(a^2 + ab + b^2)$

Quadratic Formula

For $ax^2 + bx + c = 0$

$$x = \frac{-b \pm \sqrt{b^2 - 4ac}}{2a}$$

Interest

Simple interest Formula:
$I = prt$

Interest Formula (compounded n times per year):

$$A = p \left(1 + \frac{r}{n} \right)^{nt}$$

$A =$ Amount after t years

$p =$ principal

$r =$ annual interest rate

$t =$ time in years

$i =$ Interest

Trigonometric Identities

Pythagorean Theorem: $a^2 + b^2 = c^2$

$\sin \theta = \dfrac{opp}{hyp}$

$\cos \theta = \dfrac{adj}{hyp}$

$\tan \theta = \dfrac{opp}{adj}$

$\sin^2 \theta + \cos^2 \theta = 1$

$\text{Density} = \dfrac{Mass}{Volume}$

Central Angle

$$m\angle AOB = m\overset{\frown}{AB}$$

Inscribed Angle

$$m\angle ABC = \frac{1}{2}m\overset{\frown}{AC}$$

Intersecting Chords Theorem

$$A \bullet B = C \bullet D$$

Probability

Permutations: $\quad {}_nP_r = \dfrac{n!}{(n-r)!}$

Combinations: $\quad {}_nC_r = \dfrac{n!}{(n-r)!\,r!}$

Multiplication rule (independent events): $P(A \text{ and } B) = P(A) \cdot P(B)$

Multiplication rule (general): $P(A \text{ and } B) = P(A) \cdot P(B|A)$

Addition rule: $P(A \text{ or } B) = P(A) + P(B) - P(A \text{ and } B)$

Conditional Probability: $P(B|A) = \dfrac{p(A \text{ and } B)}{p(A)}$

Arithmetic Sequence: $a_n = a_1 + (n-1)d$ where a_n is the nth term, a_1 is the first term, and d is the common difference.

Geometric Sequence: $a_n = a_1\, r^{(n-1)}$ where a_n is the nth term, a_1 is the first term, and r is the common ratio.

PART I: NO CALCULATOR ALLOWED

Directions: Use 55 or fewer minutes to answer the following 23 questions. Refer to the formula sheet on pages 596–597 as needed. YOU MAY NOT USE YOUR CALCULATOR ON THIS SECTION.

1. Brad's average golf score after six rounds was 81. For the first five rounds his scores were 78, 86, 82, 81, and 82. What was his score on the sixth round?

   Mark your answer in the grid below.

2. Simplify the following expression:
   $2x^2 - 2xy + 4xy$

   ○ A. $x(x + y)$
   ○ B. $x(x - y)$
   ○ C. $2x(x - y)$
   ○ D. $2x(x + y)$

3. A pole is supported by a cable as shown. The cable is attached to the ground 9 feet from the base of the pole, and it is attached to the pole 12 feet above the ground.

   Which of the following expressions could be used to find the length of the cable?

   ○ A. $9^2 + 12^2$
   ○ B. $12^2 - 9^2$
   ○ C. $\sqrt{9^2 + 12^2}$
   ○ D. $\sqrt{12^2 - 9^2}$

4. $\dfrac{2x^2 - 6x - 36}{2x - 12} =$

   ○ A. $x - 6$
   ○ B. $x - 3$
   ○ C. $x + 3$
   ○ D. $x^2 + 3x + 18$

5. One number is 12 more than 3 times another number. The sum of the two numbers is –20. What are the numbers?

   ○ A. 8 and 12
   ○ B. 8 and –12
   ○ C. –2 and –18
   ○ D. –8 and –12

6. Evening tickets to a play are $24.50 each. Tickets for the afternoon show are $19 each. Janice wants to buy 6 tickets. Arrange terms from the options below to construct the expression Janice would use to determine how much less she would spend if she chooses an afternoon show instead of an evening show. (You do not need to use all of the terms offered as options. Use any term only once.)

+		$19

(		÷

)		$24.50

6		$\frac{1}{2}$

–

7. What is the area of the following triangle, in units squared?

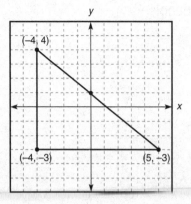

Mark your answer in the grid below.

```
      ⊘ ⊘ ⊘
   ⊙ ⊙ ⊙ ⊙ ⊙
   ⓪ ⓪ ⓪ ⓪ ⓪
   ① ① ① ① ①
   ② ② ② ② ②
   ③ ③ ③ ③ ③
   ④ ④ ④ ④ ④
   ⑤ ⑤ ⑤ ⑤ ⑤
   ⑥ ⑥ ⑥ ⑥ ⑥
   ⑦ ⑦ ⑦ ⑦ ⑦
   ⑧ ⑧ ⑧ ⑧ ⑧
   ⑨ ⑨ ⑨ ⑨ ⑨
```

8. The CEO of company Z has promised his employees that he will never make more than 20 times the amount his lowest-salaried employee makes. If the CEO's salary is represented with c and the lowest-salaried employee with e, which inequality below correctly expresses the CEO's salary limit?

   ○ A. $c < 20e$
   ○ B. $c \leq 20e$
   ○ C. $e \geq 20c$
   ○ D. $e > 20c$

9. Which of the following triangles are congruent with each other?

Triangle *P*

Triangle *Q*

Triangle *R*

○ A. *P* and *Q* only
○ B. *P* and *R* only
○ C. *Q* and *R* only
○ D. *P*, *Q*, and *R*

10. Identify the equation that expresses the following arithmetic sequence if n_x represents the number in position x in the sequence: 2, 6, 14, 30, 62, 126

○ A. $n_x = 2(n_{x-1}) + 2$
○ B. $n_x = 2(n_{x+1}) + 2$
○ C. $n_{x-1} = 2(n_x) + 2$
○ D. $n_{x+1} = 2(n_{x-1}) + 2$

11. Which of the following equations defines the line that connects the two points (2,7) and (5,13)?

○ A. $y = 3x + 2$
○ B. $y = 2x + 3$
○ C. $x = 3y + 2$
○ D. $x = 2y + 3$

12. What is the only positive solution of the equation $x^2 - 4x - 21 = 0$?

13. Which of the following is a graph of the inequality $-2 \le x < 4$?

○ A. ![number line from -5 to 5, filled circle at -2, open circle at 4]
   -5 -4 -3 -2 -1 0 1 2 3 4 5

○ B. ![number line from -5 to 5, open circle at -2, filled circle at 4]
   -5 -4 -3 -2 -1 0 1 2 3 4 5

○ C. ![number line from -5 to 5, filled circles at -2 and 4]
   -5 -4 -3 -2 -1 0 1 2 3 4 5

○ D. ![number line from -5 to 5, filled circle at -2, open circle at 4]
   -5 -4 -3 -2 -1 0 1 2 3 4 5

14. Ten artists have entered an art show. There are three prizes to be awarded in the art show: first prize, second prize, and third prize. How many possible ways could those prizes be awarded among the ten artists?

Mark your answer in the grid below.

15. In the diagram below, Circle Q has a radius measuring 10 cm. What is the length of arc AB?

![Circle Q with radius 10 cm, angle of 90° at center Q, points A and B on circle]

○ A. 2.5π
○ B. $\ \ 5\pi$
○ C. 20π
○ D. 25π

16. If the area of circle *O* is 36π, what is its diameter?

  ○ A. 6
  ○ B. 6π
  ○ C. 12
  ○ D. 18

17. Which of the following equations correctly describes the line on the graph?

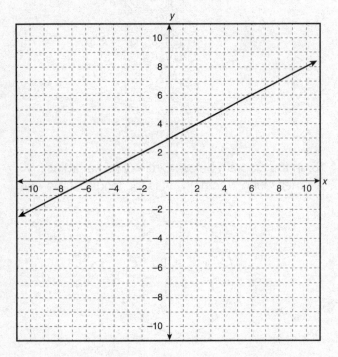

  ○ A. $y = -\frac{1}{2}x - 6$
  ○ B. $y = 2x + 3$
  ○ C. $y = \frac{1}{2}x - 6$
  ○ D. $y = \frac{1}{2}x + 3$

18. What is the slope of the function presented in this table? Mark your answer in the grid below.

x	y
−1	4
0	2
1	0
2	−2
3	−4

19. The sum of the values of all the interior angles of a polygon is equal to 180° times a number that is two less than the number of sides in the polygon. For example, a triangle has three sides, and all its interior angles add up to 180°. Which of the following formulas could be used to find the measurement of any interior angle in a <u>regular</u> polygon that has *S* sides?

  ○ A. 90*S*°
  ○ B. 180(*S*−2)°
  ○ C. $\dfrac{180(S-2)°}{S-2}$
  ○ D. $\dfrac{180(S-2)°}{S}$

20. Simplify the expression:
$(6x^4 + 7x + 5x^3) - (4x^4 - 2x^3 + 3x)$

○ A. $10x^4 + 7x^3 + 18x$
○ B. $2x^4 + 7x^3 + 4x$
○ C. $2x^4 + 7x^3 + 18x$
○ D. $10x^4 + 3x^3 + 12x$

21. $3^3 + 4^2 - (2^2)^2 = ?$

Mark your answer in the grid below.

22. Which of the following is a simplified version of the expression $\sqrt{225} + \sqrt[3]{81}$?

○ A. $25 + 3\sqrt[3]{3}$
○ B. $25 + \sqrt[3]{3}$
○ C. $15 + 3\sqrt[3]{3}$
○ D. $15 + \sqrt[3]{3}$

23. On hot days, Tina loves to mix a pitcher of lemonade with plenty of ice. The pitcher Tina uses holds several servings of lemonade. Tina will use two more ice cubes than the square of the number of servings of lemonade she makes in the pitcher. If x represents the number of servings of lemonade and y represents the number of ice cubes, which of the following graphs accurately displays this relationship?

PART II: CALCULATOR ALLOWED

Directions: Use a maximum of 50 minutes to answer 38 questions. Refer to the formula sheet on pages 596–597 as needed. YOU MAY USE YOUR CALCULATOR ON THIS SECTION.

24. Which of the following is the graph of the function $f(x) = x^3 + 1$?

A.

B.

C.

D.

25. The Whitmans are trying to pay off their credit card debt, so they developed the following budget based on their monthly take-home pay.

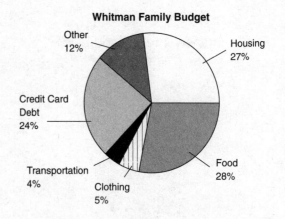

Whitman Family Budget

Other 12%
Housing 27%
Credit Card Debt 24%
Food 28%
Transportation 4%
Clothing 5%

If the Whitmans' monthly take-home pay is $2,500, about how much do they plan to pay each month on their credit card debt?

- A. $600
- B. $450
- C. $300
- D. $240

26. The table below presents some values for the linear function, $f(x)$.

x	f(x)
1	1
2	4
3	7
4	10

Which of the following functions has the same y-intercept as $f(x)$?

- A. $g(x) = 6x - 4$
- B. $h(x) = \frac{x}{3} - 1$
- C. $r(x) = x - 3$
- D. $j(x) = x^2 - 3x - 2$

27. If the following triangles are similar, what is the value of x? Mark your answer in the grid below.

28. At the end of baseball season, 5% of the children enrolled in a local youth baseball program will be chosen to play in the state tournament. If 12 children will be chosen to play in the tournament, how many children are enrolled in the program? Mark your answer in the grid below.

29. Risa wants to order business cards. A printing company determines the cost (C) to the customer using the following function, where b = the number of boxes of cards and n = the number of ink colors.

$$C = \$25.60b + \$14.00b(n - 1)$$

If Risa orders 4 boxes of cards printed in 3 colors, how much will the cards cost?

- A. $214.40
- B. $168.00
- C. $144.40
- D. $102.40

30. The right cone shown below has a base with a radius of 6.4 cm.

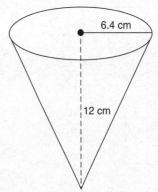

What is the volume of the cone, in cubic centimeters? Use 3.14 for pi. Round your answer to the nearest ones digit and mark your answer in the grid below.

31. Identify the zeroes of the function
$y = x^2 - x - 6$ in order to determine which of
the graphs below correctly depicts the function.

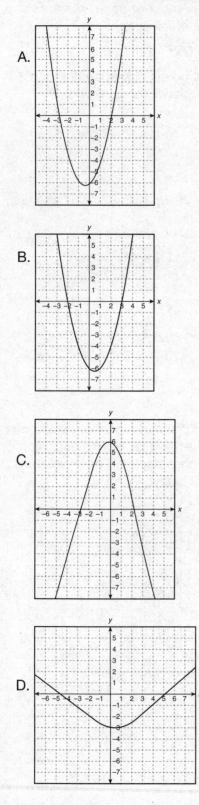

32. Consider this set of numbers: {−4, −2, −1,
3, 4, 8} and the function $y = x^2 - 5x + 2$.
Three of the numbers in that set can be in-
putted into the function in order to produce
three other numbers in that set. In other
words, three numbers in the set are x-values
that will produce y-values equal to the other
three numbers in the set. Fill in the chart
below accordingly.

Domain (x-values)	Resulting range (y-values)

33. A certain data set fits the normal distribution
shown below.

The mean of this data _____ the median of
the data.

○ A. is greater than
○ B. is less than
○ C. is equal to
○ D. has no relation to

34. In the triangle below, what are the approximate values of sides a and c? Round your answers to the nearest tenth.

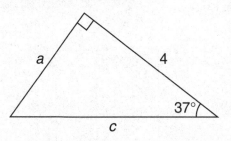

- A. $a = 0.6$; $c = 0.8$
- B. $a = 3$; $c = 5$
- C. $a = 3$; $c = 6.7$
- D. $a = 3.75$; $c = 5$

35. What is the minimum of the function $y = 2x^2 + 4$, shown graphically below?

- A. -8
- B. 0
- C. 4
- D. 8

36. Solve for x and round to the nearest tenth. Mark your answer in the grid below.

$$x + 8 - 4(x - 1) = 2x + 3$$

37. For the function $y = x^4 - 5x^2 + 3$, fill in the counts of each listed characteristic in the chart below. (*Hint*: Drawing a rough graph will help.)

Parameter	# of occurrences
Global Minimums	
Global Maximums	
Inflection Points	
x-intercepts	
y-intercepts	

38. A bag contains 12 red, 3 blue, 6 green, and 4 yellow marbles. If a marble is drawn from the bag at random, what is the probability that the marble will be either blue or yellow?

○ A. 7%
○ B. 12%
○ C. 25%
○ D. 28%

39. If the shape below were in three-dimensional space and were rotated 360 degrees around the line shown, which of the following shapes would be produced?

A. 　B.

C. 　D.

40. What is the volume of the following cylinder, in units squared? Round your answer to the nearest unit, and mark your answer in the grid below.

41. A perfectly spherical balloon is filled with helium. The balloon has a radius of 10 centimeters. Helium has a density of approximately 0.0002 g/cm^3. Approximately how many grams of helium are in the balloon? Use 3.14 for pi.

○ A. 0.0008 g
○ B. 0.008 g
○ C. 0.002 g
○ D.　 0.8 g

42. A researcher wants to learn more about the connection between household income and television viewing choices—that is, do people at a certain income level tend to prefer different television programs than people at other income levels? The researcher has limited resources, so she cannot use workers or equipment to directly monitor the television viewing habits of her study participants.

Which of the following types of studies would be most appropriate for the researcher to use?

○ A. survey
○ B. experiment
○ C. theoretical modeling
○ D. observational study

43. In the graph below, the boundaries of the inequalities $2x + y \leq 6$ and $3y - 9 \geq x$ have been graphed, which means that some portion of the graph represents the solution set to *both* inequalities. However, the half-planes have not been shaded. Identify the area of the graph that should be shaded to represent the solution set to *both* inequalities.

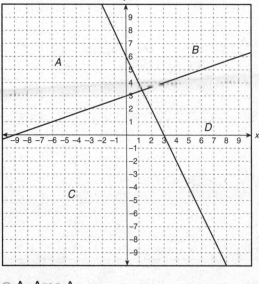

○ A. Area A
○ B. Area B
○ C. Area C
○ D. Area D

44. In a certain state, the legislature has 100 seats. In 2010, Party X held 54 seats. In the 2012 election, the party gained two seats. If, in the 2014 election, Party X loses 6 seats, but then gains 2 seats in the 2016 election, what will the absolute change in the number of seats held by Party X from 2010 to 2016 be?

Mark your answer in the grid below.

45. Place a dot on the coordinate plane below to represent the solution to the following system of equations:

$y = x + 4$

$2y + 4x = 44$

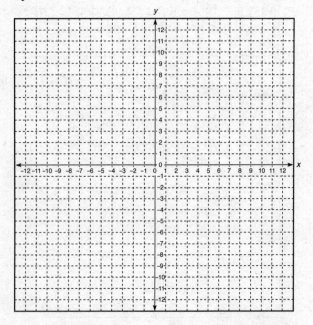

46. The sine of a certain angle in a right triangle is approximately 0.19 and the cosine of the same angle is approximately 0.98. What is the approximate value of the cotangent of that angle? Round your answer to the nearest hundredth.

○ A. 0.19

○ B. 1.02

○ C. 2.57

○ D. 5.16

47. Imtaez works as a server in a restaurant. On a certain night, he collected $157 in tips and paid y dollars to the food runner who helped him. The amount Imtaez had remaining after paying the runner was equal to ($101 + y).

Arrange terms from the options below to construct the equation you would use to determine how much Imtaez paid to the food runner. (You may not need to use all of the terms offered as options. Use any term only once.)

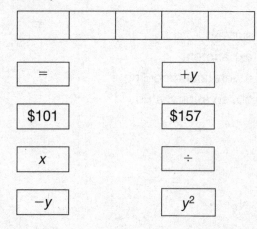

48. If $\dfrac{ab}{a-b} = 1$, what is the value of a in terms of b?

○ A. $a = b + 1$

○ B. $b = \dfrac{a}{a+1}$

○ C. $a = \dfrac{-b}{b-1}$

○ D. $a = b - 1$

49. The graph below describes a worker's progress painting a wall. For a portion of time the worker was distracted. During which period of time did the distraction most likely occur?

Square feet

Time (min)

○ A. 0−3 minutes

○ B. 3−6 minutes

○ C. 6−9 minutes

○ D. 12−15 minutes

50. The number pi (π) is *irrational*. That means that it cannot be expressed as a fraction with integers on the top and bottom of the fraction. It also means that the digits of pi continue infinitely without any pattern emerging in the digits, like this:

3.14159265358979323846264338327950288
41971693993751058209749445923078164062862089986280348253421170679821480865132823066470938446095505822317253594081284811745 . . . and on and on and on forever.

Which of the following expressions would also be irrational?

○ A. 0π

○ B. π + 4

○ C. 1 ÷ 9

○ D. $\dfrac{2\pi}{\pi}$

51. The diagram below represents a three-dimensional figure. If you were to remove the top portion of the figure by cutting along the dotted line, what would the remaining shape (that is, the bottom part) look like when viewed from above?

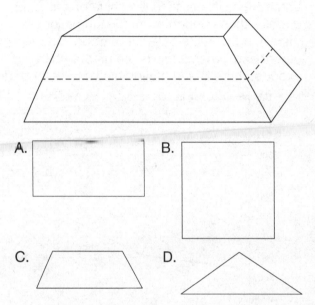

A.

B.

C.

D.

52. The total resistance of a circuit (R) consisting of two resistors (R_1 and R_2) in parallel can be found using the formula $\dfrac{1}{R} = \dfrac{1}{R_1} + \dfrac{1}{R_2}$. Based on that formula, which of the equations below could be used be used to find R_2 if you knew the values for R and R_1?

○ A. $R_2 = R - R_1$

○ B. $R_2 = \dfrac{R \times R_1}{R_1 - R}$

○ C. $R_2 = \dfrac{R \times R_1}{R_1 + R}$

○ D. $R_2 = \dfrac{R}{R_1 - R}$

STOP. You have completed the *Mathematics Practice Test.*

SOCIAL STUDIES PRACTICE TEST

Directions: Use 75 minutes to answer the following 47 questions.

Question 1 is based on the following paragraph and graph.

When the value of exported goods—those sold abroad—is greater than the value of imported goods—those bought from foreign nations—there is a favorable balance of trade. On the other hand, when imports are greater than exports, there is an unfavorable balance of trade.

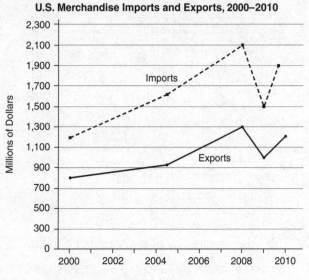

U.S. Merchandise Imports and Exports, 2000–2010

Source: *Statistical Abstract of the United States*

1. Which of the following statements is supported by the paragraph and the graph?

   ○ A. Exports equaled imports at the start of the 2000s.
   ○ B. Exports exceeded imports throughout the 2000s.
   ○ C. The United States had a favorable balance of trade in merchandise during the 2000s.
   ○ D. The United States had an unfavorable balance of trade in merchandise during the 2000s.

2. Which of the following IS typically a function of local government and IS NOT typically a function of state or federal governments?

   ○ A. imposing income tax
   ○ B. providing relief after a disaster
   ○ C. funding the creation of highways
   ○ D. maintaining the condition of streets

Question 3 is based on the following table.

In an opinion poll, people were asked, "In politics, as of today, do you consider yourself a Republican, a Democrat, or an independent?" The chart below represents the results, by month, for the first six months of 2013.

	Republicans %	Independents %	Democrats %
Jan 2013	27	38	33
Feb 2013	28	38	32
Mar 2013	27	36	35
Apr 2013	26	40	33
May 2013	28	39	32
Jun 2013	26	41	31

Source: Gallup

3. Which of the following statements about the first six months of 2013 is supported by the table?

   ○ A. Independents outnumbered Republicans in the ratio of 2:1.
   ○ B. There were roughly 10 percent more independents than Republicans.
   ○ C. Two percent of Americans surveyed belonged to a third party such as the Green Party.
   ○ D. More people identified as independents than as Democrats, and more identified as Democrats than as Republicans.

Questions 4 through 6 are about New Deal programs.

The *New Deal* is the name given to a set of laws and presidential orders enacted over a period of several years beginning in 1933. The New Deal was designed to combat the Great Depression—that is, to help the country recover from years of deflation, poverty, unemployment, drought, and human displacement.

4. Before Congress passed the Social Security Act of 1935, the Social Security Administration (SSA) and its programs of old-age insurance and disability insurance did not exist. While these programs are largely accepted today, they were wildly controversial at the time. Some people believed that Social Security was not economically sustainable. Others objected on ideological grounds, claiming that the programs were socialist in nature. Some objectors made a legal argument—namely that, because the Constitution does not explicitly give the federal government the power to institute an old-age or disability insurance program, the federal government has no such power.

That last claim was brought before the Supreme Court in 1937. The Supreme Court approved the SSA programs. The Constitution gives the federal government the power to impose taxes. The Court said that this taxing power could be broadly interpreted to allow the federal government to create and run the SSA.

Which of the following phrases describe the Court's decision and its consequences? Select three.

☐ a strict construction of the Constitution
☐ a loose construction of the Constitution
☐ a limiting of the federal government's power
☐ an expansion of the federal government's power
☐ an expansion of government bureaucracy
☐ increased variation among the states in welfare and unemployment programs

5. Another New Deal program was the establishment of the Securities and Exchange Commission (SEC), whose job it is to regulate the stock market. A large stock market crash had helped to bring about the Great Depression in 1929, so part of the SEC's mission is to protect individual investors. The SEC does this by making companies disclose certain information publicly, by prohibiting insider trading (that is, making use of secret knowledge to make money on the stock market), and by trying to prevent fraud.

Which of the following is NOT a likely outcome of stock market fraud?

○ A. If people stopped trusting the stock market, trading would slow, which would harm the economy.
○ B. People who have lost their money due to fraud contribute less to the economy.
○ C. Large-scale fraud eventually results in lowered tax revenue for the federal government.
○ D. More legitimate companies would allow their shares to be traded on the stock market.

6. The Civilian Conservation Corps was a popular New Deal program that put unemployed young men to work on public land. CCC workers improved and beautified parks, built infrastructure (such as fire towers and service roads) in wildlife areas, planted trees, maintained waterways, and worked to control flooding, among other things. Service in the CCC was voluntary, but the young men who signed up had to send a certain amount of their pay home to their families, most of whom were impoverished.

Which of the following are potential consequences of widespread unemployment, which the CCC was intended to alleviate? Select all that apply.

☐ lower income tax and sales tax revenue for federal, state, and local governments
☐ budget cuts to government programs because of decreased tax revenue
☐ rising crime rates in areas of high unemployment
☐ economic slowdown as people purchase fewer goods and services
☐ lost opportunity as the unemployed spend time not building skills as part of a job

Question 7 refers to the following information and chart.

The Consumer Price Index (CPI) is a measure of the average prices paid by consumers for a typical assortment of goods and services, including housing, food, clothing, transportation, recreation, and medical care. A higher CPI indicates that prices have risen. The table below shows the CPI for several years, as well as the percent change in CPI over the previous year.

Year	CPI	Percent Change in CPI over Previous Year
2008	215.3	3.8
2009	214.5	–0.4
2010	218.1	1.7
2011	224.9	3.1
2012	229.6	2.1

Source: Bureau of Labor Statistics

7. Which one of the following statements is supported by the table?

   A. The CPI increased in exactly three of the five years represented in the table.

   B. The economic downturn in 2008 caused a subsequent decrease in the CPI.

   C. The CPI almost doubled between 2010 and 2011.

   D. The CPI grew in all but one of the years represented in the table.

8. The period from the mid-1700s to the mid-1800s, during which manufacturers adopted new technologies such as steam engines and machine tools, is referred to as the "Industrial Revolution." During this time, many people who were previously farmers began to work in factories.

Which of the following was most likely a result of the Industrial Revolution?

   A. Fewer children had to leave school to work.

   B. Many lower-class individuals were able to purchase machinery.

   C. Many people moved to cities to be near factory jobs.

   D. There were shortages of food due to a drop in farm production.

9. Like the ancient Chinese, the ancient Greeks thought that a sound political system and well-established social relationships were necessary for a stable society. Greek rule was decentralized, and as a result, many political structures coexisted. In contrast, Chinese rule was largely centralized, and a single political system prevailed. The Greeks placed more value on councils, participation, and law; the Chinese, on bureaucracy, hierarchy, and rules.

Based on the paragraph, what did the ancient Greeks and the ancient Chinese have in common in regard to politics and government?

   A. Both governed through a hierarchical bureaucracy.

   B. Both valued a stable political framework for society.

   C. Both had centralized councils.

   D. Both had decentralized political systems.

Question 10 refers to the following chart.

The Effect of World War II on Industry

Measure	1939	1940	1941
Index of manufacturing output (1939 = 100)	100	116	154
Corporate profits before taxes	$6.4 billion	$9.3 billion	$17 billion
Corporate profits after taxes	$5 billion	$6.5 billion	$9.4 billion

Source: Fute, Gilbert C., and Reese, Jim E. *An Economic History of the United States*

10. Which of the following best explains why the war had the effect on industry indicated by the chart?

   ◯ A. Even before the United States entered the war, corporate profits had increased sharply.
   ◯ B. Manufacturing output increased by over 50 percent in two years.
   ◯ C. The war created a huge demand for military equipment and supplies.
   ◯ D. With men gone to serve as soldiers, more women were employed in factories.

11. Read the list below and choose the option that best fills in the list title.

Important Events Leading to, During, and Resulting from the _____

   • Austrian Archduke Franz Ferdinand was assassinated.
   • The Austro-Hungarian Empire invaded Serbia.
   • Russia supported Serbia despite popular opposition within Russia.
   • Britain, alarmed by German aggression, declared war on Germany.
   • The Ottoman Empire was dissolved.
   • The Treaty of Versailles forced Germany to pay reparations to the Allies.
   • The League of Nations was formed.

   ◯ A. Crimean War
   ◯ B. First World War
   ◯ C. Second World War
   ◯ D. Croatian War of Independence

12. To combat the anticompetitive nature of monopolies or "trusts" such as US Steel, Standard Oil, and the American Tobacco Company, the US Congress passed the Sherman Antitrust Act in 1890. That act made it illegal for an individual to monopolize or conspire to monopolize an industry or to act with others to restrain trade or commerce among the States or abroad. While the Sherman Antitrust Act was, and remains, very influential, it was not sufficient to solve all of the problems raised by monopolies. Because of its broad language and its focus on the intent to create monopolies, courts interpreted the Sherman Antitrust Act differently and inconsistently in the many cases to which it was applied. As a result, Congress passed the Clayton Antitrust Act in 1914, which targeted specific actions—such as favorable price discrimination and exclusive dealings contracts—that were used to create monopolies.

In the passage above, the writer's main point is that

   ◯ A. courts struck down the Sherman Antitrust Act because its broad language made it unconstitutional.
   ◯ B. problems with consistently enforcing the Sherman Antitrust Act led to further legislation to prevent monopolies.
   ◯ C. monopolies like US Steel, Standard Oil, and the American Tobacco Company successfully avoided prosecution under the Sherman Antitrust Act.
   ◯ D. the Sherman Antitrust Act ended monopolies like US Steel, Standard Oil, and the American Tobacco Company, but did not prevent new monopolies from arising.

Questions 13 and 14 are based on the following passage.

Environmental scientists have long been warning about the impact of unchecked carbon emissions into the atmosphere, a threat that many researchers conclude has already led to climate change. Of the many dangers of climate change, some of the most destructive involve lengthy droughts, diminishing fresh water supplies, and decreased world food production. Although some point to the potential benefits of the temperature changes, such as longer growing seasons and more temperate climates in some places, the hazards far outweigh any potential advantages. Since the United States has the second highest rate of carbon emissions per person, it must lead the way by dramatically cutting industrial emissions and finding alternate sources of fuel that do not release carbon dioxide as a byproduct. Positive efforts are underway, particularly through the Environmental Protection Agency, which has fostered several international partnerships to limit the production of carbon dioxide.

13. With which one of the following would the author agree?

    A. The United States has failed to take any action against carbon emissions.

    B. The dangers of climate change are more significant than the possible benefits.

    C. Wind energy is preferable to solar energy.

    D. Climate change will not impact the world food supply.

14. Some people think that switching from gasoline to biofuels made from corn, soybeans, or other crops would produce fewer carbon dioxide emissions. Others object that switching to these *biofuels* would drive up food prices (thus contributing to world hunger) and encourage people to cut down more forests to plant biofuel crops. Some proponents of biofuels contend that there are ways to avoid these consequences, but the topic is still controversial.

Which of the following titles would best introduce an article describing both sides of the controversy surrounding biofuels?

    A. "From white lightning to white lightening: The evolution of corn-based combustibles"

    B. "Let them maybe not eat cake: Is our love of grain-based foods good for the planet?"

    C. "The land of milk and honey (and chicken-apple sausage): Will increasing non-grain-based foods help the planet?"

    D. "Soylent green or not so green: Are biofuels good or bad for us and the planet?"

15. One assumption economists have often made is the idea that consumers and producers act rationally and in their own best economic interests. Which of the following statements describes a situation in which that assumption is true?

    A. A consumer has shopped at the same hardware store for years because he knows the owner personally.

    B. A manufacturer believes that it has higher costs to produce a certain product than its competitors do, so it charges more for the product.

    C. A consumer buys a certain brand of product because his favorite football player is featured in that product's advertisements.

    D. A consumer obtains prices from several dealers and researches specifications, features, and consumer reviews before buying a new automobile.

16. Most elections in the United States are dominated by the two major parties—Democratic and Republican. However, candidates from third parties (such as the Libertarian Party or Green Party) do sometimes run for office.

An election is coming up, and Joe really likes a third-party candidate on the ballot. Joe is debating whether or not to vote for this candidate. Match the considerations below to the two sides of Joe's debate with himself. Use all the considerations below; you will fill up both columns of the table.

Reasons why Joe might *WANT* to vote for the third-party candidate	Reasons why Joe might *NOT WANT* to vote for the third-party candidate

If many people support a third-party candidate, that can influence what issues the major parties support, because the major parties will want to win over those voters.

By supporting a third-party candidate, Joe can voice his true opinion, and he may find this satisfying regardless of the outcome.

By supporting a third-party candidate, Joe may miss an opportunity to vote for the major-party candidate he likes best. Then the major-party candidate he most dislikes will be more likely to win.

The direction of national policy is often shaped by which of the major parties took the most seats in an election. By voting for a third-party candidate, Joe will have no influence on this dynamic.

Questions 17 and 18 refer to the following chart.

Acts of Parliament Directed at the American Colonies

Act	Description
Revenue Act of 1764 (Sugar Act)	Imposed duties (tariffs) on foreign sugar and luxuries to raise money for Great Britain
Quartering Act of 1765	Required colonists to provide food and shelter for British soldiers
Stamp Act of 1765	Required colonists to purchase revenue stamps for all important documents, including legal documents, newspapers, and ads
Declaratory Act of 1766	Asserted the right of Parliament to make laws for the colonies
Townshend Acts of 1767	Imposed new duties on the import of tea, glass, and paper

17. The information in this chart would have been most useful for the writing of which of the following documents?

○ A. The Declaration of Independence, which explained why the colonies broke away from Great Britain
○ B. The Articles of Confederation, which established a central government consisting of a congress
○ C. The U.S. Constitution, which established the structure of government for the newly independent nation
○ D. Washington's Farewell Address, in which he warned the new nation of policies and practices he thought unwise

18. Years later, when leaders from the various states gathered to write the U.S. Constitution, they kept their previous experiences in mind. The framers of the Constitution debated for a very long time about how to describe the powers of the central government and whether or not to include a list of individual rights that should be respected. Which of the following best describes why the Constitution's framers believed that specific wording was extremely important?

○ A. They believed that the Constitution could be changed in the future by an act of Congress.
○ B. They intended the new government to be defined and limited by the Constitution.
○ C. They wanted the new Constitution to closely mimic aspects of the English constitution.
○ D. They wanted the wording to be ambiguous so that it could be interpreted in various ways.

Questions 19 and 20 are based on the passage below.

Europe after World War II was a bleak picture. As many as 60 million people died in World War II, including the 6 million Jews murdered by the Nazi regime in what has come to be known as the Holocaust. All over Europe, great cities had been destroyed, millions of people were displaced or starving or both, and factories and farms had been so thoroughly ruined that they could not produce. The once-great imperial powers of Great Britain and France had been impoverished by the war effort, and their empires began to collapse. Germany was cleaved into two nations: democratic, capitalist West Germany was dominated by American influence, while communist East Germany was under the thumb of the Soviet Union. Germany became one of the points of tension between communist and democratic world powers. National borders all over Eastern Europe were redrawn by these victors in the global conflict.

19. Which one of the following events stemmed, at least in part, from the consequences of World War II as described above?

○ A. British traders gained greater and greater influence in the Indian subcontinent.

○ B. The Indian subcontinent fell entirely under British rule.

○ C. Mahatma Gandhi began to organize civil disobedience against British rule in India.

○ D. The British withdrew from the Indian subcontinent, which was then divided into India and Pakistan.

20. United States involvement in the Vietnam War lasted from 1959 to 1974, but the roots of the conflict go back much farther. Which of the following factors are mentioned in the passage above and also describe aspects of the Vietnam War? Select three.

☐ the reduction of French imperialism

☐ the destruction of Kiev

☐ the splitting of one nation into two

☐ tension between communist and democratic powers

☐ the migration of displaced persons from Eastern Europe

21. In the late 1800s, industrialization caused a large-scale migration from rural to urban areas in the United States. Parents who moved to cities with their children left behind the social support of their extended families. In addition, city families found that children, who were an asset on the farm because they could work at an early age, were more of an economic drawback in the city. As a consequence, the birthrate dropped during this period and average family size shrank.

Which of the following is the best summary of this passage?

○ A. Industrialization led to increased urbanization in the late 1800s.

○ B. City families lost the social support of their extended families back on the farm.

○ C. Industrialization and urbanization caused many changes in family life in the late 1800s.

○ D. In the late 1800s, average family size shrank due to the fall in the birthrate.

Forced Resettlement of American Indians, 1830s

22. Which of the following is the most likely reason that American Indians were forcibly relocated in the 1830s?

○ A. Whites wanted lands in the Kansas and Nebraska territory for settlement.

○ B. Whites wanted to take over Indian lands in the eastern states.

○ C. Indians of different tribes wanted to settle in a single Indian territory.

○ D. Indians in the eastern states wanted to look for gold in the West.

Important Political Documents Preceding the Declaration of Independence and the U.S. Constitution

Year	Document	Description
1215	Magna Carta	Limited the power of the English king and granted rights to the nobles
1620	Mayflower Compact	Set rules by which the Pilgrims would govern themselves in Plymouth colony
1628	Petition of Right	Limited the English king's powers further
1636	Great Fundamentals	Established the first basic system of laws in the English colonies, in Massachusetts Bay Colony
1688	English Bill of Rights	Declared that the king rules with the consent of the people's representatives in Parliament; granted ordinary people certain rights

23. The documents in this chart represent a slow evolution from unlimited government to limited government. Which of the following is a characteristic of limited government, as suggested by the chart above?

   ○ A. the supremacy of a monarch over the legislature
   ○ B. the idea that judges elected by the people can invalidate unfair laws
   ○ C. the upholding of individual rights that government cannot violate
   ○ D. the importance of geographic expansion and exploration

24. One of the major grievances the American colonists had against the British was that the British taxed the colonists without granting them representation in the British Parliament. Part of the Declaration of Independence is a list of political and economic rights that American colonists complained that the British king had deprived them of.

   By which of the following documents were the writers of the Declaration probably most influenced as they drafted their list?

   ○ A. the Mayflower Compact
   ○ B. the Petition of Right
   ○ C. the Great Fundamentals
   ○ D. the English Bill of Rights

25. The civil rights movement of the 1950s and 1960s inspired historians to reinterpret slavery's impact on U.S. society in general and on African Americans in particular. One interpretation that emerged was that slaves and owners were always in conflict and that slavery was destructive. The extent of slavery's destructiveness was debated. Some historians argued that slavery destroyed the culture and self-respect of the slaves and their descendants. Others thought that slaves overcame hardship by developing a unique African American culture that included, among many different things, strong religious and musical traditions.

Based on the paragraph, which of the following statements is an opinion rather than a fact?

   ○ A. The civil rights movement took place during the middle of the twentieth century.
   ○ B. The civil rights movement caused historians to take another look at slavery.
   ○ C. Historians debated slavery's negative effects on slaves and their descendants.
   ○ D. Slavery destroyed the culture of the slaves, diminishing their self-respect.

Question 26 refers to the following paragraph and graph.

The market price of a product tends to change in a way that brings supply and demand into balance, a condition called equilibrium. This is illustrated in the graph below, which shows supply and demand for apples.

Supply and Demand for Apples

26. Which of the following would result if part of the apple crop were destroyed but demand remained the same?

○ A. Supply would increase.
○ B. The market price would remain the same.
○ C. The market price would go down.
○ D. The market price would go up.

Question 27 refers to the following paragraph and map.

The Battle of Fort Sumter was the first battle of the American Civil War. South Carolina had seceded from the Union and insisted that Union troops in South Carolina leave. A small band of Union soldiers was finally forced to evacuate Fort Sumter, on the South Carolina coast. After that, President Lincoln called for 75,000 volunteers to help put down the rebellion in the south. Following his call, four additional states seceded from the Union and joined the Confederacy. The progress of secession is shown here.

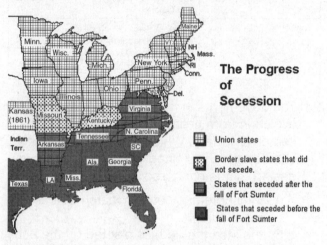

The Progress of Secession

Union states

Border slave states that did not secede.

States that seceded after the fall of Fort Sumter

States that seceded before the fall of Fort Sumter

Reprinted from "The South Secedes," U.S. History Online Textbook, ushistory.org.

27. Which of the following states belonged to the Confederacy both before the battle of Fort Sumter and after the battle of Fort Sumter?

○ A. Iowa
○ B. North Carolina
○ C. Delaware
○ D. Alabama

Questions 28 and 29 refer to the following paragraph and diagram.

Most cases that arise under federal law are tried in the federal court system. The federal court system has several levels of courts and several routes by which cases may be appealed to a higher court.

Routing Cases Through the Federal Court System

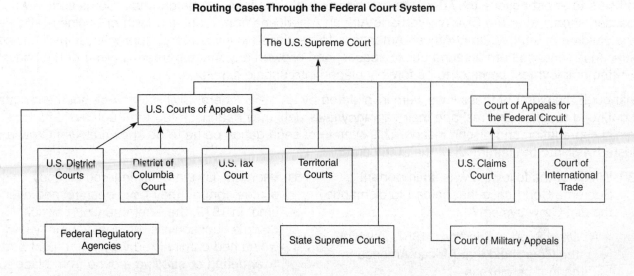

28. The U.S. Constitution established only the Supreme Court, but it gave Congress the power to create inferior (lower) federal courts.

   Which of the following is the most likely reason that Congress established other federal courts?

   ○ A. The justices of the U.S. Supreme Court were not well versed enough in the law to handle all federal cases.
   ○ B. The volume and variety of federal cases were too great for a single court to handle.
   ○ C. A system of inferior federal courts gave the United States prestige in the eyes of the rest of the world.
   ○ D. The Supreme Court's power to interpret the Constitution was established in *Marbury v. Madison*.

29. If cases are not resolved in any of the lower federal courts, to which court may they eventually, finally be appealed?

   ○ A. the Supreme Court of the United States
   ○ B. the United States Courts of Appeals
   ○ C. the Court of Appeals for the Federal Circuit
   ○ D. the Court of Military Appeals

Questions 30 and 31 are based on the passage below.

The Thirteenth Amendment to the Constitution abolished slavery, and the Fourteenth Amendment extended all the rights of citizenship to former slaves. However, many southern states and some northern states responded to these amendments by expanding their *vagrancy laws*. In general, vagrancy laws criminalize homelessness and unemployment. In practice, they allow law enforcement officers to arrest anyone they deem to be undesirable using fairly vague grounds. Some state laws passed shortly after the Civil War forbade African Americans from running a farm or business, allowed the children of impoverished African Americans to be placed in involuntary "apprenticeships," forbade African Americans from entering public spaces, and allowed any African American who did not have a written employment contract to be forcibly placed into unpaid servitude.

Although the worst of these laws were invalidated by an 1866 federal Civil Rights Act, southern states continued to refine and reshape their vagrancy laws until they had instituted thorough systems of racial segregation and discrimination. This system of segregation came to be known as *Jim Crow* and lasted well into the latter half of the 20th century.

30. Which of the following was an important Supreme Court case that helped to dismantle the Jim Crow system?

   ○ A. *Dred Scott v. Sandford*, 1857, in which the Court held that African Americans cannot be citizens
   ○ B. *Plessy v. Ferguson*, 1896, in which the Court approved of a system of "separate but equal" facilities for African Americans
   ○ C. *Brown v. Board of Education*, 1954, in which the Court outlawed segregation in schools
   ○ D. *Bowers v. Hardwick*, 1986, in which the Court upheld Georgia's ban on "sodomy"

31. Vagrancy laws are still in force in many places, though they have been refined over time. In 1972, the Supreme Court struck down a Jacksonville, Florida, vagrancy law, which had criminalized walking at night and "wandering or strolling around from place to place without any lawful purpose or object," among other things. The Supreme Court said that the law failed to explain what conduct was and was not illegal, and the law was therefore invalid. The Court also said that the law encouraged "arbitrary and erratic arrests and convictions . . . and place[d] almost unfettered discretion in the hands of the police."

Which two important societal values were in tension and at stake in this Supreme Court case? Select two from the list below.

   ☐ the right of citizens to move about freely
   ☐ the right of prostitutes to walk the streets at night
   ☐ a city's desire to enable police to maintain order
   ☐ the right of well-to-do people to be unemployed
   ☐ a city's desire to change their laws frequently

32. Not all democratic systems are organized exactly like the United States'. For example, parliamentary systems, such as that used in the United Kingdom, display several differences. Match each of the characteristics below the table to the appropriate column in the table. Use all of the characteristics. You may or may not fill up each of the columns in the table.

Parliamentary System (such as the United Kingdom)	Presidential System (such as the United States)

The head of government is elected by the people and responsible to them.

The majority party in the legislature chooses the leaders of the new government after each election.

The executive and legislative branches are separately elected and have separate powers.

The head of government is chosen by the legislature and is responsible to it.

The executive branch is overseen by the legislature.

33. Which of the following federal government bodies can strike down state laws if it decides that those laws violate people's constitutional rights?

○ A. the president
○ B. the Administrative Conference of the United States
○ C. Congress
○ D. federal courts

34. The government of country X is concerned that its farms don't produce enough wheat, so the legislature is considering paying farmers a subsidy of $1 for every bushel of wheat they produce and sell. The subsidy will be paid by taxpayers rather than by wheat buyers. Which of the scenarios described below is most likely to be the result of implementing such a subsidy program?

○ A. Farmers will produce less wheat because they make more money per bushel than they did previously. The price of wheat will increase as a result of the reduced supply. Farmers will leave some of their arable land idle.
○ B. Farmers will shift some of their arable land from growing other crops to growing wheat. The increased wheat crop will reduce the market price of wheat. The reduced production of other crops will result in an increased price for those goods.
○ C. Farmers will not make any changes in the allocation of their land to various crops, but the market price of wheat will increase because of the government's subsidy.
○ D. Farmers will not make any changes in the allocation of their land to various crops, but the market price of wheat will decrease because of the government's subsidy.

35. Haiti, which became a republic in 1804, is the second-oldest republic in the Western Hemisphere. Previously, it had been controlled by France and was important in the slave trade. Slaves in Haiti fought for independence for almost 10 years before finally breaking away from France. When the Republic of Haiti was established, it was the first independent nation in the Caribbean or Latin America. It would be several decades before another Caribbean nation would gain independence. Haiti was also the first democratic republic in the world to be led by African Americans. It is the only country in the Western Hemisphere where the dominant language is French.

Which of the following is the best summary of this passage?

○ A. Several factors make Haiti unique among Caribbean nations.
○ B. Haiti became a republic in 1804, long before any other Caribbean nation.
○ C. Haiti has long been led by African Americans.
○ D. Haiti is a French-speaking republic in the Caribbean.

36. Which of the following were characteristics of the states that seceded from the Union before and during the United States Civil War? Select three.

☐ less manufacturing industry than in many northern states
☐ unitary state governments with no state legislatures
☐ legal tolerance of slavery
☐ widespread sympathy with the Republican Party
☐ an agrarian economy
☐ widespread support for abolition

37. Review the table and answer the following question.

Differences Between _____

• Citizens vote on each issue or governmental action • The system of ancient Athens	• Citizens elect representatives who vote on issues or actions • The system of the United States national government

Which of the following best completes the title of the table?

○ A. Democracy and Aristocracy
○ B. Democracy and Oligarchy
○ C. Direct Democracy and Referendum
○ D. Direct Democracy and Representative Democracy

38. In the United States, the _____ establishes the branches of the federal government, lists specific powers that each branch has, limits those powers, protects some individual rights of citizens, and is still in effect today.

○ A. Declaration of Independence
○ B. Articles of Confederation
○ C. Constitution
○ D. Magna Carta

Question 39 is based on the following passage.

In 1096 C.E., peasants and soldiers from Europe invaded Jerusalem in the first of a long series of conflicts in the Middle East. The soldiers and their leaders were motivated by several factors. Some, who were influenced by the Pope at the time, wanted to regain control of Christian holy sites. Some wanted to unite the Eastern and Western branches of the Christian church. Some were likely motivated by religious prejudice against Islam or Judaism. It is probable that some wanted to rob Middle Eastern cities of gold and other resources. Some may have been adventurers hoping to achieve personal glory. Regardless of why they happened, the resulting wars killed hundreds of thousands over a period of two centuries.

39. What historical event does the preceding passage describe?

   A. the Crusades
   B. the Wars of the Roses
   C. the Palestinian Conflict
   D. World War I

40. Read the list contained in the box and answer the question.

   - Rising unemployment
   - Slowdown in consumer spending
   - Slowdown in business expansion
   - Businesses and consumers avoiding risk

Which of the following does the preceding box describe?

   A. inflation
   B. recovery
   C. saturation
   D. recession

41. The Amazon rainforest, which covers 5.5 million square miles of South America, has been described as "the lungs of the world," for the role it plays or could play in absorbing carbon dioxide, producing oxygen, and regulating humidity. However, the rainforest is being destroyed at a pace that alarms many. There are several reasons for the deforestation: logging companies cut down trees in order to sell the wood; farmers clear the land to raise soybeans or beef, both of which are lucrative exports for the region; and in some places the forest is leveled to make room for towns and roads. Clearing the rainforest in order to farm it is, for many residents, a way out of poverty. However, the easiest way to clear the rainforest is to burn it, and a blanket of air pollution now haunts the rainforest as a result. In some parts of the former rainforest, desertification has set in. This means that, even if all the people left the land, the rainforest would not grow back on its own.

In the scenario described above, which two basic human needs are in conflict with each other?

   A. the need for clean air and the need to preserve natural beauty
   B. the need for food and shelter and the need to avoid being crowded
   C. the need for clean air and the need to earn an independent living
   D. the need for food and shelter and the need to build roads for transport

42. James Madison, who helped draft the Constitution, wrote about it: "The powers delegated by the proposed Constitution to the federal government are few and defined. Those which are to remain in the State governments are numerous and indefinite. The former will be exercised principally on external objects, as war, peace, negotiation, and foreign commerce . . . The powers reserved to the several states will extend to all the objects which, in the ordinary course of affairs, concern the lives, liberties, and properties of the people, and the internal order, improvement and prosperity of the State."

What aspect of the United States' government's structure was Madison describing?

○ A. democracy
○ B. federalism
○ C. the Commerce Clause
○ D. representation

43. The first three Articles of the Constitution of the United States define the powers of the legislative, executive, and judicial branches of the government. The following table gives brief summaries of the duties of those three branches:

Legislative	Executive	Judicial
• Makes laws • Declares war and raises armies • Establishes tariffs • Regulates commerce between the states	• Executes the laws • Establishes executive agencies to help execute laws	• Decides disputes between individuals or between branches of government and individuals

Which of the following functions is NOT performed by the Supreme Court of the United States?

○ A. deciding whether state laws violate the Constitution
○ B. deciding whether federal laws violate the Constitution
○ C. hearing the final appeal in criminal cases
○ D. outlawing behavior such as drug use or robbery

44. Much of the money spent on political campaigns is spent by individuals or companies who are not officially part of the campaign. For example, XYZ Corporation might pay for an expensive television ad supporting Candidate Smith for election. Because some feel that this gives wealthy people or companies too much influence, the federal government restricted this type of spending in 2002. However, in 2010, the U.S. Supreme Court ruled that part of the 2002 law was unconstitutional because the law restricted the expression of political ideas.

Which of the following parts of the Constitution did the Supreme Court most likely base its decision on?

○ A. the First Amendment, which protects the right of free speech
○ B. the Commerce Clause, which gives Congress the power to regulate trade
○ C. the Fifth Amendment, which prohibits government from taking property without legal process
○ D. the Necessary and Proper Clause, which gives Congress the power to make laws

45. Place the statements below into the correct column of the table based upon whether they are generally true or generally not true regarding entrepreneurship. Use all the statements. You may or may not fill up the columns.

Generally true of entrepreneurship	Generally not true of entrepreneurship

Excess cash is generated during the growth phase of a new business.

Marketing is key to the success of a new business.

Entrepreneurs must understand computer programming.

Government regulations do not affect small businesses.

Many new businesses fail within a few years.

New businesses account for a significant number of new hires.

46. The National Labor Relations Act, passed by Congress in 1935, guarantees the right of workers to organize into unions, engage in collective bargaining, and strike if collective bargaining fails.

Which one of the following activities is most likely NOT protected by the National Labor Relations Act?

- A. George is offended by a joke made by a co-worker and complains to his manager about it.
- B. Lupe tells her co-worker that she thinks they should join a union and gives him a union pamphlet.
- C. Workers at the XYZ Company hold a vote about whether they want to be represented by a union.
- D. A union decides that negotiations with a company have failed and calls for a strike.

47. For many centuries, a set of important international trade routes, called the "Silk Road," brought traders from Europe into Asia and vice versa. Silk from China was being sold in Europe and Africa by the first century B.C.E. (if not before), and gold and other valuables from Europe and Africa flowed into the Far East in exchange. Over time, not only silk but also spices, minerals, and many other types of goods were carried along the Silk Road. As a by-product of this trade, ideas, religions, and even diseases were also carried back and forth between East and West.

The city of Damascus was on one of the Silk Road routes. Which of the following was most likely true of Damascus?

- A. Even its poorer citizens possessed silk clothing.
- B. People in Damascus were aware of religions practiced elsewhere.
- C. Some of the gold flowing into China was mined in Damascus.
- D. People in Damascus never died from foreign diseases.

STOP. You have completed the *Social Studies Practice Test.*

SCIENCE PRACTICE TEST

Directions: Use 85 minutes to answer the following 47 questions.

Question 1 refers to the following paragraph and diagram.

Newton's third law of motion states that when one object exerts a force upon another object, the second object exerts an equal force on the first, in the opposite direction. An airplane in motion changes the speed and direction of the air, exerting a force on it. The opposing force of the air keeps the airplane aloft.

How an Airplane Flies

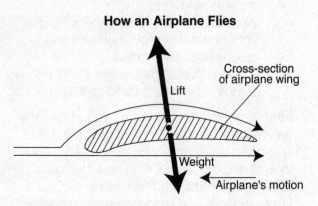

1. What vertical force holds the airplane up?

   ○ A. lift
   ○ B. Newton's third law
   ○ C. weight
   ○ D. air resistance

2. Deoxyribonucleic acid (DNA) is found in every animal and plant cell. It is composed of strands of nucleotides that twist around each other in a double helix. The order of nucleotides within a gene specifies the order and types of amino acids that must be put together to make a protein. Which of the following statements best describes how DNA is used to produce proteins in the body?

   ○ A. RNA polymerase unwinds the strands of DNA, starting at the beginning of a gene, and uses one strand of the DNA as a template to create a complementary copy of the gene, called messenger RNA. Then this mRNA is translated into proteins.

   ○ B. DNA reads the nucleotide code on a strand of RNA, starting at the beginning of a gene, and uses the RNA as a template to create a complementary copy of the gene, called messenger DNA. Then this mDNA is translated into proteins.

   ○ C. Messenger RNA locates two strands of DNA and brings them together. Then, starting at the beginning of a gene, the RNA polymerase twists the two strands together to form a protein.

   ○ D. DNA spins off genes from its double-helix structure, and messenger RNA carries these genes away to the appropriate part of the body. There it uses them as a template to create complementary copies, which are the proteins.

3. You **MAY** use your calculator on this question.

   A scientist shines a laser through six beakers, each containing a different liquid substance, and measures the laser beam's angle of refraction. The scientist records her measurements for liquids A–E in the table below; her measurement for liquid F is lost.

Liquid	Angle of Refraction (degrees)
A	15
B	32
C	12
D	47
E	15
F	?

   However, the scientist recalls that the mean of all six angle measurements was 23 degrees. What must the laser beam's angle of refraction through liquid F have been?

   ○ A. 15
   ○ B. 17
   ○ C. 23
   ○ D. 32

Questions 4 and 5 are based on the following information and graphic.

The processes that circulate nitrogen between the atmosphere, land, and organisms are called the nitrogen cycle.

The Nitrogen Cycle

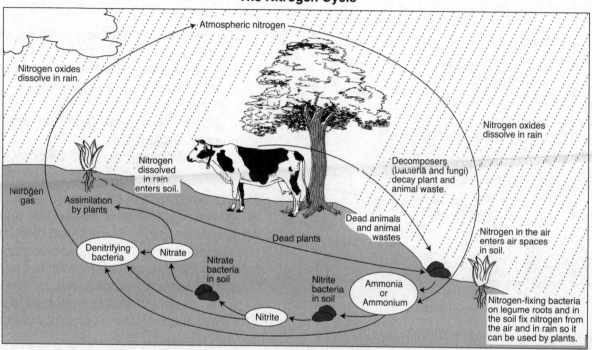

4. Nitrogen-fixing bacteria are found both in the soil and on the roots of legumes like peas and beans. From where do these bacteria get nitrogen?

   ○ A. ammonia and ammonium
   ○ B. the air and rainwater in the soil
   ○ C. animals and animal wastes
   ○ D. animal wastes and decaying plants

5. To increase the nitrogen content of the soil, many farmers spread synthetic fertilizers containing nitrogen compounds. What might an organic farmer, who does not use synthetic fertilizers, do to improve the fertility of the soil?

   ○ A. switch to crops requiring more potassium
   ○ B. compost with plant and animal wastes
   ○ C. plant more nonleguminous plants
   ○ D. switch to crops requiring more nitrogen

Question 6 refers to the following graph.

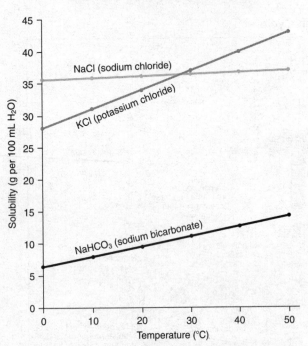

Solubility of Common Compounds
in Grams of Solute per 100 mL of Water

6. Which of the following statements is supported by the information in the graph?

  A. About 15 grams of sodium bicarbonate will dissolve in 100 mL of water at 10°C.

  B. About 30 grams of potassium chloride will dissolve in 100 mL of water at 30°C.

  C. Sodium chloride shows the greatest increase in solubility with increase in temperature.

  D. For the three compounds shown, solubility increases as temperature increases.

7. Mitosis is a type of cell division in which two daughter cells are formed that have the same genetic material as the parent cell. A scientist is observing mitosis in the human body. For which of the following purposes is this observation best suited?

  A. understanding how eggs and sperm achieve genetic variation

  B. understanding how old red blood cells are broken down and recycled or eliminated

  C. understanding how dead skin is continuously replaced

  D. understanding how feedback mechanisms regulate the release of hormones

8. Cellular respiration is the process by which molecules of food are converted into energy the body can use. In the "Inputs?" column, place a check mark next to each component that is an input to cellular respiration. In the "Outputs?" column, place a check mark next to each component that is an output of cellular respiration. Note that a component may be both an input and an output.

Inputs?	Outputs?
○ glucose	○ glucose
○ carbon dioxide	○ carbon dioxide
○ water	○ water
○ oxygen	○ oxygen

9. Weathering is the breaking down of rock by rain, frost, wind, and other elements. No transport is involved in weathering. The weathered rock remains in place. Weathering can be physical, involving abrasion—the wearing away of a surface—or changes in temperature; it can be chemical, involving chemical reactions; or it can be organic, involving the action of living things.

Which of the following is an example of physical weathering?

○ A. the cracking of granite from the expansion of freezing water
○ B. the breakdown of calcite by reaction with acids in fertilizer
○ C. the transport of sand by the wind
○ D. the breakdown of crumbling rock in the soil by burrowing worms

10. When removed from the body, large organs live only a few hours or days under cold conditions. Therefore, organ transplants must be performed quickly. Many organs go to waste because the organ cannot be transported to an appropriate patient in the short time available. Unfortunately, it is not yet possible to freeze large organs to preserve them for a longer period. That's because they contain many different types of cells, all of which react differently to freezing. Some cells are even destroyed by the ice crystals that form during freezing.

Which of the following studies is most likely to yield information that might help solve the specific problem of freezing whole organs for transplant?

○ A. how the time it takes to locate patients who need organs can be decreased
○ B. how the time it takes to transport organs to their destinations can be decreased
○ C. how special fluids keep insects alive during subfreezing weather
○ D. how radioactive isotopes can be used to diagnose the condition of donated organs

11. Which of the following predictions of the Big Bang theory has NOT been supported by astronomical observations?

○ A. The Big Bang would have created microwave radiation throughout the universe.
○ B. The Big Bang would have resulted in all galaxies moving away from each other, as though they had begun their movement at a central point.
○ C. The Big Bang would have created mass that would exert gravity, eventually slowing the expansion of the universe.
○ D. The Big Bang would have caused a red shift in the observed wavelengths of light from other galaxies.

12. Hydrogen peroxide molecules are composed of two hydrogen atoms and two oxygen atoms. Water is also composed of hydrogen and oxygen, but water has one fewer oxygen atom than hydrogen peroxide does. Which of the following statements best describes the chemical reaction shown in the equation below?

$$2H_2O_2 \rightarrow 2H_2O + O_2$$

○ A. Hydrogen peroxide is being made out of water and air.
○ B. Hydrogen peroxide is decomposing into pure water.
○ C. Hydrogen peroxide is decomposing into water and oxygen.
○ D. Water and oxygen are combining to make hydrogen peroxide.

Melting and Boiling Points

Element	Melting Point, °F	Boiling Point, °F
Mercury	−38	675
Bromine	19	138
Iron	2,795	5,184
Carbon	6,420	8,720
Gold	1,945	5,379

13. Which of the following statements is supported by the information in the chart?

   ○ A. Mercury and bromine are liquids at room temperature.
   ○ B. Iron has a higher melting point than carbon.
   ○ C. Iron has a higher boiling point than gold.
   ○ D. Mercury, bromine, iron, carbon, and gold are all metals.

14. A 1 kg mass moving with a velocity of 5 m/s collides with a 500 g mass that is initially at rest. The velocity of the larger mass after the collision is 1 m/s. Assuming that the two masses are hard enough that the momentum lost in the collision is negligible, what is the velocity of the smaller mass immediately after the collision?

   ○ A. 1 m/s
   ○ B. 2 m/s
   ○ C. 4 m/s
   ○ D. 8 m/s

15. A student did an experiment to see how far a ball would roll on different surfaces. He made five different ramps, each with a different surface: a plain pine board, a painted board, a board covered with sandpaper, a board covered with artificial turf, and a board covered with shag carpet. He set up his experiment on a smooth, level floor. To make the ramps, he raised one end of each board with a book. He collected four copies of the science textbook his class was using and set up four of the ramps with these books. He couldn't find a fifth copy of the book, so he used a thinner science study guide to set up the fifth ramp. He rolled a tennis ball down each ramp and measured how far the ball traveled each time. Then he compiled his data and drew conclusions.

Why was the student's experiment flawed?

   ○ A. The student should have used a ball with a smooth surface rather than a tennis ball.
   ○ B. The student should have used books of the same height for all of the ramps.
   ○ C. The student should not have used sandpaper as one of the surfaces.
   ○ D. For a control, the student should have rolled the ball across a piece of wood that was level.

Question 16 refers to the following paragraph and diagram.

Herbivores are animals that eat only plants; carnivores are animals that eat animals. Typical herbivore and carnivore teeth patterns are shown below.

Typical Teeth Patterns in Carnivores and Herbivores

Carnivore (dog)

Incisors

Canines

Premolars

Molars

Herbivore (sheep)

Incisors

Premolars

Molars

16. What is the most notable difference between the dog's teeth and the sheep's teeth?

○ A. The dog has fewer teeth than the sheep does.

○ B. The dog has molars and the sheep does not.

○ C. The dog has incisors and the sheep does not.

○ D. The dog has canines and the sheep does not.

Question 17 refers to the following chart.

The Five Largest Asteroids

Name	Average distance from sun (Earth = 1)	Time to orbit sun
Ceres	2.77	4.6 years
Pallas	2.77	4.6 years
Vesta	2.36	3.6 years
Hygeia	3.13	5.5 years
Interamnia	3.06	5.4 years

17. Which of the following statements is supported by the information in the chart?

○ A. Pallas is further away from the sun than Hygeia is.

○ B. Of the five largest asteroids, Vesta has the longest orbital period.

○ C. The five largest asteroids are all farther from the sun than Earth is.

○ D. Of the five largest asteroids, only Interamnia takes more than five years to orbit the sun.

18. The American lobster, *Homerus americanus,* is typically bluish-green to brown in coloration. However, a rare genetic mutation, estimated to occur in 1 in 2 million lobsters, can result in a bright blue-colored shell. In 2011, 220 million pounds of lobsters, typically weighing 1–9 pounds each, were caught, of which two were blue.

In 2011, the experimental probability of catching a blue lobster was _____ the estimated probability of a lobster having the blue mutation.

○ A. greater than

○ B. approximately the same as

○ C. less than

○ D. dependent upon

Structure of a Volcano

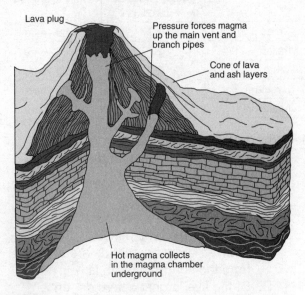

19. Based on the diagram, what causes a volcano to erupt?

    A. Pressure builds up inside the magma chamber and vent.

    B. Magma flows down toward the underground chamber.

    C. The lava plug at the top of the main vent wears away.

    D. The lava plug at the top of the main vent collapses inward.

20. In a chemical reaction, the atoms of the reactants are rearranged to form products with different chemical and physical properties. A catalyst is a substance that speeds the rate at which a chemical reaction takes place. The catalyst itself is unchanged at the end of the reaction. In which of the following reactions is a catalyst at work?

    A. when an acid is neutralized, as when hydrochloric acid is added to sodium hydroxide yielding sodium chloride and water

    B. when food is digested, as when an enzyme in saliva called ptyalin breaks down starch into sugars without itself changing

    C. when copper is oxidized by combining with nitric acid to yield copper nitrate, nitrogen dioxide, and water

    D. when baking soda is heated, causing the sodium bicarbonate to break down, yielding carbon dioxide gas as a byproduct

21. An automobile's engine creates a constant forward force of 7,500 N. The automobile has a mass of 1,500 kg. If the vehicle is initially stopped and reaches a velocity of 20 m/s 5 seconds after the engine's force is applied, what is the average resisting force acting on the vehicle? (*Hint:* Use the formula for Newton's second law of motion, which is $F = ma$, but keep in mind that you're looking for the force that is acting *against* the automobile's progress.)

    A. 1,500 N

    B. 3,000 N

    C. 5,000 N

    D. 9,000 N

Question 22 and 23 are based on the information and table below.

In 2010, cats were introduced to an island eco-system. Scientists took an annual census of the cat, fox, mosquito, and swift populations in the five years that followed. The scientists' data appear in the table below.

	2011	2012	2013	2014	2015
Cats	10	25	35	40	40
Foxes	100	95	90	85	85
Mosquitoes	50,000	55,000	65,000	80,000	100,000
Swifts	500	425	350	300	275

22. Based on the data, which are the native spe-cies most affected by the introduction of cats to the ecosystem?

○ A. foxes
○ B. mosquitoes
○ C. swifts
○ D. No species were affected.

23. Which of the following is the most likely explanation for the trend identified in your answer to question 22?

○ A. Predators of the most affected species are also predators of cats.
○ B. Predators of the most affected species are a prey species for cats.
○ C. The prey of the most affected species are also prey for cats.
○ D. The prey of the most affected species are predators of cats.

Question 24 refers to the following diagrams.

24. What do the wheel and axle and the screw have in common?

○ A. Both increase the effort needed to move a load.
○ B. Both involve effort applied with circular motion.
○ C. Both involve effort applied with horizon-tal motion.
○ D. Both involve effort applied with vertical motion.

25. During various periods in Earth's history, average global temperatures have dropped, resulting in ice ages. During an ice age, gla-ciers cover large regions of Earth. Scientists disagree about what causes ice ages. One hypothesis suggests that there have been long term changes in Earth's orbit, causing the planet to periodically move farther from the sun. Another view proposes that a peri-odic increase in volcanic activity increases the dust in the atmosphere, blocking the sun's rays. Still another hypothesis suggests that changes in Earth's own radiant energy cause ice ages. And finally, other scientists propose that changes in the direction of ocean currents cause ice ages.

Which of the following statements is a fact and NOT an opinion or hypothesis?

○ A. During an ice age, temperatures drop and ice covers vast areas of Earth.
○ B. Changes in Earth's orbit cause temper-ature fluctuations and ice ages.
○ C. Large amounts of volcanic dust block-ing the sun's energy cause ice ages.
○ D. Changes in the Earth's own radiant en-ergy cause ice ages.

Question 26 refers to the following diagram.

26. What is the main difference between the hydrocarbons ether and ethanol?

   ○ A. Ether has carbon, hydrogen, and oxygen atoms, and ethanol has only carbon and hydrogen atoms.
   ○ B. Ether has three carbon atoms and ethanol has two carbon atoms.
   ○ C. Ether has one oxygen atom and ethanol has two oxygen atoms.
   ○ D. The arrangement of the carbon, hydrogen, and oxygen atoms in the two hydrocarbons is different.

27. Earth's atmosphere has several distinct layers. The layer closest to Earth's surface, called the troposphere, is the densest. Most familiar weather phenomena, such as rain clouds and thunderstorms, occur exclusively in the troposphere. The layer above the troposphere is called the stratosphere. Blue jets, a type of upper-atmosphere lightning not typically seen from Earth's surface, occur in the stratosphere, generally several miles directly above a thunderstorm discharging ordinary lightning. However, phenomena occurring far above the stratosphere, such as meteor showers and auroras, may be visible from Earth's surface without a telescope.

Which of the following phenomena can occur in either the troposphere or the stratosphere?

   ○ A. lightning
   ○ B. meteor showers
   ○ C. rain clouds
   ○ D. blue jets

28. The four types of processes that create minerals in Earth's crust are called *magmatic*, *hydrothermal*, *metamorphic*, and *surficial*. Magmatic processes involve the heating and cooling of magma deep inside the Earth's mantle to form crystals. Hydrothermal processes are caused by the movement of water within Earth's crust. Metamorphic processes involve combinations of heat, pressure, time, water, and various solutions to change existing mineral deposits and form new ones. Surficial processes are physical processes that affect rock at Earth's surface or in the loose material—soil and dust—that covers Earth's crust.

Fill in the blanks. Wind eroding away the softer components of sandstone is an example of a _____ process, while the movement of seawater through fractured rock underground is an example of a _____ process.

   ○ A. magmatic; surficial
   ○ B. hydrothermal; metamorphic
   ○ C. surficial; hydrothermal
   ○ D. metamorphic; hydrothermal

1 IA																	18 VIIIA
1 **H** 1.0	2 IIA											13 IIIA	14 IVA	15 VA	16 VIA	17 VIIA	2 **He** 4.0
3 **Li** 6.9	4 **Be** 9.0											5 **B** 10.8	6 **C** 12.0	7 **N** 14.0	8 **O** 16.0	9 **F** 19.0	10 **Ne** 20.2
11 **Na** 23.0	12 **Mg** 24.3	3 IIIB	4 IVB	5 VB	6 VIB	7 VIIB	8	9 VIIIB	10	11 IB	12 IIB	13 **Al** 27.0	14 **Si** 28.1	15 **P** 31.0	16 **S** 32.1	17 **Cl** 35.5	18 **Ar** 39.9
19 **K** 39.1	20 **Ca** 40.1	21 **Sc** 45.0	22 **Ti** 47.9	23 **V** 50.9	24 **Cr** 52.0	25 **Mn** 54.9	26 **Fe** 55.8	27 **Co** 58.9	28 **Ni** 58.7	29 **Cu** 63.5	30 **Zn** 65.4	31 **Ga** 69.7	32 **Ge** 72.6	33 **As** 74.9	34 **Se** 79.0	35 **Br** 79.9	36 **Kr** 83.8
37 **Rb** 85.5	38 **Sr** 87.6	39 **Y** 88.9	40 **Zr** 91.2	41 **Nb** 92.9	42 **Mo** 96.0	43 **Tc** (98)	44 **Ru** 101.0	45 **Rh** 102.9	46 **Pd** 106.4	47 **Ag** 107.9	48 **Cd** 112.4	49 **In** 114.8	50 **Sn** 118.7	51 **Sb** 121.8	52 **Te** 127.6	53 **I** 126.9	54 **Xe** 131.3
55 **Cs** 132.9	56 **Ba** 137.3	*	72 **Hf** 178.5	73 **Ta** 180.9	74 **W** 183.8	75 **Re** 186.2	76 **Os** 190.2	77 **Ir** 192.3	78 **Pt** 195.1	79 **Au** 197.0	80 **Hg** 200.6	81 **Tl** 204.4	82 **Pb** 207.2	83 **Bi** 209.0	84 **Po** (209)	85 **At** (210)	86 **Rn** (222)
87 **Fr** (223)	88 **Ra** (226)	†	104 **Rf** (267)	105 **Db** (268)	106 **Sg** (269)	107 **Bh** (270)	108 **Hs** (269)	109 **Mt** (278)	110 **Ds** (281)	111 **Rg** (281)	112 **Cn** (285)	113 **Uut** (286)	114 **Fl** (289)	115 **Uup** (288)	116 **Lv** (293)	117 **Uus** (294)	118 **Uuo** (294)

	57 **La** 138.9	58 **Ce** 140.1	59 **Pr** 140.9	60 **Nd** 144.2	61 **Pm** (145)	62 **Sm** 150.4	63 **Eu** 152.0	64 **Gd** 157.3	65 **Tb** 158.9	66 **Dy** 162.5	67 **Ho** 164.9	68 **Er** 167.3	69 **Tm** 168.9	70 **Yb** 173.1	71 **Lu** 175.0
†	89 **Ac** (227)	90 **Th** 232.0	91 **Pa** 231.0	92 **U** 238.0	93 **Np** (237)	94 **Pu** (244)	95 **Am** (243)	96 **Cm** (247)	97 **Bk** (247)	98 **Cf** (251)	99 **Es** (252)	100 **Fm** (257)	101 **Md** (258)	102 **No** (259)	103 **Lr** (262)

The periodic table of the elements displays multiple pieces of information. The number above each element's symbol is its atomic number, or number of protons. Each row, called a period, contains elements with the same number of shells (the orbits through which electrons move). The first row has one shell, the second row has two shells, etc. Elements are organized vertically into groups; a group contains elements with the same number of electrons in their outermost shells. Elements in Group I have one electron in their outer shells; elements in Group II have two electrons in their outermost shells; etc.

29. Which of the following pairs of elements would create a covalent bond when combined with each other?

○ A. Ne and Al
○ B. S and O
○ C. K and Cl
○ D. Na and F

30. Nitrogen and hydrogen react to form ammonia. Use the properties of the outermost electron states of these elements to determine the correct formula for ammonia.

○ A. NH
○ B. NH_2
○ C. NH_3
○ D. N_2H_3

31. In a laboratory experiment, two identical beakers containing 100 ml each of two different liquids were left open in the same conditions for two days. The remaining volumes were then measured. Beaker A had 70 ml remaining, and beaker B had 80 ml remaining. What conclusion can be properly drawn from the results of this experiment?

○ A. Because of the slow rate of evaporation, both solutions had molecules with ionic bonds.
○ B. Because of the rapid rate of evaporation, both solutions had molecules with covalent bonds.
○ C. Solution A had stronger intermolecular forces.
○ D. Solution B had stronger intermolecular forces.

32. "Dead zones," so-called because of their very low levels of oxygen, exist in a number of bodies of water on Earth. One of the largest is in the northern Gulf of Mexico. Nitrogen- and phosphorous-containing fertilizer from farmland runs off into the Mississippi River, and this in turn empties into the Gulf. Algae that feed on these nutrients grow in very large numbers and then die, promoting a surge in the population of the bacteria that feed on dead algae. These bacteria consume most of the oxygen in the water.

Which of the following is a likely eventual outcome if conditions in the northern Gulf of Mexico do not change?

- ○ A. Fish populations will decline for some time but then stabilize at lower levels.
- ○ B. Species of algae that consume nitrogen and phosphorous will die out.
- ○ C. Bacteria that produce oxygen as part of their respiration cycle will evolve.
- ○ D. Jellyfish, which tolerate low-oxygen conditions, will increase in number.

33. The following table lists actions that are part of the carbon cycle on Earth. Match the activity to the sphere from which it removes carbon.

Fossil fuels are burned to power automobiles.	
A saltwater crab molts, shedding its shell.	
A tree uses photosynthesis to produce energy.	
A volcano erupts.	

- ○ A. atmosphere
- ○ B. biosphere
- ○ C. geosphere
- ○ D. hydrosphere

34. Light waves travel in a straight line, but when they strike most surfaces, they bounce off; this is known as reflection. When light is reflected off a smooth surface like a mirror, the incoming rays, called the incident rays, hit the surface at the same angle as the reflected rays bounce off it.

The Reflection of Light

In the preceding diagram, all of the reflected light rays are parallel. Under which of the following circumstances would the reflected light rays travel in many different directions?

- ○ A. if the source of light were distant
- ○ B. if the surface were irregular or rough
- ○ C. if the surface were perfectly flat
- ○ D. if the incident rays were parallel

35. Photosynthesis is the process by which living plants take in carbon dioxide and water and turn those into nutrients and energy that the plant can use. The chemical equation for photosynthesis is:

$$6CO_2 + 6H_2O \rightarrow C_6H_{12}O_6 + 6O_2$$

Based on this equation, which of the following must be true?

- ○ A. Plants do not need oxygen to survive.
- ○ B. Oxygen is one of the products of photosynthesis.
- ○ C. Plants produce oxygen out of pure energy.
- ○ D. Photosynthesis destroys energy.

36. Air enters the human lungs through the left and right *bronchi*, which divide into smaller airways called *bronchioles*. The bronchioles end in sacs called *alveoli*, which are surrounded by tiny blood vessels called *capillaries*. Deoxygenated blood is pumped by the heart from the various parts of the body to the lungs. In the lungs, the blood takes on oxygen. This happens when oxygen moves from air in the alveoli to the blood in the surrounding capillaries. Oxygenated blood then leaves the lungs through the pulmonary veins and flows back to the heart, which pumps it to the various body parts.

The movement of oxygen from the alveoli into the surrounding capillaries is called *diffusion*. Which two bodily systems are involved in diffusion?

- A. urinary and respiratory
- B. circulatory and endocrine
- C. circulatory and respiratory
- D. respiratory and nervous

37. Sixty-five million years ago, many plant and animal species died out all at once, but scientists are not sure what caused this mass extinction. One theory states that a gigantic asteroid struck the Earth, kicking up a tremendous dust cloud. The dust in the atmosphere prevented the sun's energy from reaching plants growing on Earth. The plants could not photosynthesize and died. The effect of the dying vegetation was devastating all the way up the food chain, with the result that many plant and animal species went extinct.

If the mass extinction 65 million years ago was caused by a dust cloud, but that dust cloud was not in fact caused by an asteroid, which of the following events might have led to the mass extinction?

- A. a solar eclipse
- B. a series of massive volcanic eruptions lasting many years
- C. a massive flood
- D. a solar flare

38. Brock's physics teacher has assigned everyone in his class the task of conducting an experiment. To write up their experiments, everyone must use the outline provided below.

Match each summary of the steps in Brock's experiment to the appropriate category in the experiment outline.

Experiment outline	Brock's steps
Step 1. Formulate a question about a phenomenon	
Step 2. Collect data	
Step 3. Form a hypothesis	
Step 4. Test the hypothesis through an experiment	
Step 5. Draw a conclusion	

a. Brock placed wooden cubes that were 1 cc, 10 cc, and 100 cc in water. He observed their buoyancy. Then he placed iron cubes of 1 cc, 10 cc, and 100 cc in water and observed their buoyancy.
b. Brock noted that ice floats in water, whether it is a small ice cube or a huge iceberg.
c. Brock said: "Since all wooden cubes float and all iron cubes sink, size does not affect the buoyancy of an object in water."
d. Brock asked, "Does size affect the buoyancy of an object in water?"
e. Brock thought: "For an object made of a given material, increasing the size of the object won't affect its buoyancy in water."

39. Hurricanes are circular storms with high wind speeds. These storms tend to form near the equator. The *Coriolis effect* causes hurricanes to rotate counterclockwise in the northern hemisphere and clockwise in the southern hemisphere. Initially, east-to-west trade winds tend to blow hurricanes westward. The Coriolis effect also causes hurricanes to move north or south toward one of the poles. When a hurricane moving toward one of the poles encounters the mid-latitude westerly winds, a hurricane turns eastward.

Global Wind Patterns

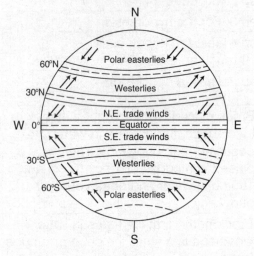

Which of the following most accurately describes the probable rotation and path of a hurricane in the northern hemisphere?

A. It would rotate counterclockwise and move westward, then southward, and finally eastward.

B. It would rotate clockwise and move eastward, then northward, and finally westward.

C. It would rotate counterclockwise and move eastward, then northward, and finally westward.

D. It would rotate counterclockwise and move westward, then northward, and finally eastward.

40. Newton's Law of Gravitation states that the force (represented by *F*) of gravitation (or attraction) between two objects is represented by the following equation.

$$F_g = \frac{Gm_1m_2}{r^2}$$

The equation shows that the force of gravitation is directly proportional to the product of the objects' masses (where each mass is represented by *m*) but inversely proportional to the square of the distance between them (where the distance between them is represented by *r*).

Consider two objects that both have the same mass. If the distance between these objects is increased, what will happen to the force of gravitation between them?

A. The force will be increased.

B. The force will be reduced.

C. The force will not change.

D. The force will change, but in a way that cannot be predicted.

41. Frogs living in temperate climates reproduce in the spring and summer months, when food is plentiful. They are often exposed to freezing temperatures during the winter. Frogs are amphibians—that is, creatures that live part of their lives on land and part of their lives in water.

Given this information, which of the following must be true?

A. Frogs maintain a stable body temperature year-round, even in the winter.

B. Frogs exposed to freezing temperatures during the winter invariably die.

C. Frogs' bodies have a way to prevent their cells from freezing in cold temperatures.

D. Frogs can find sufficient food in the winter to reproduce even in freezing temperatures.

42. In a healthy person, blood sugar levels in the bloodstream do not exceed a tightly controlled range. This metabolic control is called *homeostasis*. In a person with diabetes mellitus, homeostasis is interrupted, and blood sugar levels are higher than in a healthy individual. Diabetes mellitus can have a number of different causes. However, the most direct reason for high blood sugar is either the inability of the pancreas to produce sufficient insulin, or the inability of cells in the body tissues to respond to whatever insulin is produced.

Which of the following might be an appropriate treatment for a person with diabetes mellitus?

- A. bed rest
- B. blood transfusions
- C. insulin injections
- D. medication to restore calcium homeostasis

43. Merle, or dappled, coat coloring is valued in several dog breeds. A breeder mates a male and female dog with merle coloring, and they produce a litter of four puppies as follows:

merle deaf	merle not deaf	merle not deaf	solid color not deaf

Then the breeder mates the same male dog with another female dog with merle coloring. Another litter of four puppies is produced:

merle deaf	merle deaf	merle not deaf	merle not deaf

Which of the following conclusions about the gene for coat pattern (merle or solid) is supported by the results of these breedings?

- A. The gene for deafness is linked with the gene for the merle trait, but deafness is recessive.
- B. The gene for deafness is linked with the gene for the merle trait, and deafness is also dominant.
- C. The gene for deafness is linked with the gene for the merle trait, but the merle trait is recessive.
- D. The merle trait is dominant, and deafness is determined by another gene.

44. An old growth forest is a climax community and tends to be a fairly stable ecosystem. When the trees in an old growth forest burn or are cut down, they are replaced by a succession of other species, and the food web changes dramatically. Eventually, the forest returns to its climax state, but this process can take hundreds of years.

Imagine a mature Adirondack hemlock forest in New York State shortly after all the trees were cut down sometime in the 19th century. Which of the following changes probably took place?

- A. Shade-loving animal species, such as the red-backed salamander, were replaced by sun-loving species such as the northern black racer.
- B. Sun-loving species, such as the northern black racer, were replaced by shade-loving species, such as the red-backed salamander.
- C. The forest regenerated within a decade, and the climax community present before the forest was cut down became re-established.
- D. The forest was permanently replaced by grasslands.

45. The following variations are observed in the marsh marigolds inhabiting a particular wetland. Although this species typically produces a bright yellow flower, the marigolds in this wetland have long produced a pale yellow flower with white spots. Match each variation with the most likely explanation.

A marigold plant develops female flowers with a non-sticky stigma (a plant part that receives pollen from a source such as bees) to which pollen cannot attach.	
Some marigolds produce flowers that are bright yellow with white spots.	
A marigold plant develops bright orange flowers, which attract more pollinating bees.	

a. an unhelpful mutation caused by an environmental factor
b. a non-harmful error occurring in the genome during replication
c. a new combination of genes occurring through interbreeding

46. All the planets of the solar system, including Earth, revolve counterclockwise around the sun, and their paths are on a plane. This distribution of their orbits is evidence that the planets were created

- A. at different times and outside the solar system
- B. at the same time and before the sun formed
- C. at the same time and within the solar system
- D. at different times, both before and after the sun was formed

Question 47 refers to the following information.

Aestivation is a state of dormancy similar to hibernation. (While *hibernation* comes from the Latin word for winter and describes a dormant winter state, *aestivation* derives from the Latin word for summer and describes a similar state occurring during summer.) Scientists studying a species of frogs observe that during a drought, these frogs dig underground burrows and aestivate. As a drought's duration increases, the proportion of frogs that survive decreases. Following are data documenting the survival rate of frogs during droughts of various durations in 1990.

Year: 1990				
Drought duration	1 month	3 months	9 months	2 years
Rate of frog survival	99%	90%	30%	5%

Some of these frogs have a gene (called *FRMD*) that allows them to depress their metabolism by 85%, while frogs that lack this gene can depress their metabolism by only 75%. Following are data documenting the incidence of the *FRMD* gene in this frog population over time.

1990	1995	2000	2005	2010	2015
15%	18%	25%	35%	55%	80%

47. Based on the above information, which of the following is the most reasonable inference about environmental conditions in the frogs' habitat?

- A. Because genes are distributed randomly in a population, the increase in the proportion of frogs with *FRMD* is due to coincidence, and no conclusions about environmental conditions can be drawn.
- B. Droughts have increased in frequency but not necessarily in duration, and the *FRMD* gene helps frogs survive short dry periods.
- C. Droughts have increased in duration but not necessarily in frequency, and the *FRMD* gene helps frogs survive long dry periods.
- D. The environment has become less hospitable for frogs, but which environmental conditions have changed cannot be determined.

STOP. You have completed the *Science Practice Test.*

LANGUAGE ARTS: READING
PRACTICE TEST ANSWERS AND EXPLANATIONS

1. **B. describe types of interviewers and how to approach them** The author is chiefly concerned with explaining that different interviewers have different personalities and that you should approach those interviewers differently.

2. **C. Our ability to "read" others makes us form instant, lifelong relationships with some people.** The author makes this general claim in the first paragraph but does not support it with evidence. Choices (A) and (D) are stated or implied in the first paragraph and then supported with evidence in paragraphs 2–4. Choice (B) is a generalization made in paragraph 3, not paragraph 1.

3. **Part One: D. "With some careful consideration and planning, though, these "feelings" can be honed into a useful tool for gauging the personality and character of interviewers and, by extension, their expectations of potential employees."** The sentence that expresses the author's main idea is the sentence from paragraph 1 that speaks specifically to understanding what interviewers are looking for in a potential employee (choice (D)). Choice (A) is also from paragraph 1, but it provides background information to support the main idea, which is specifically about interviewing for a job. Choices (B) and (C) are details.
Part Two: "Here, you would be advised to adopt a crisp, businesslike style, with brief, professional answers." "It would be a mistake with this employer to sit ramrod straight and give cool, truncated responses to the questions." In Part Two of this question, correct answers are details that develop the idea that one can conform to an interviewer's expectations by "reading" that person correctly. The first and fourth answer choices provide such details. The second answer choice describes some interviewers but does not tell how you can use this information. The third answer choice is a general observation that functions as background for the main point; it is not a detail that develops the main point.
Only count this question correct if you answered all parts correctly.

4. **A. The author makes a generalization about how to read an interviewer and then gives specific suggestions about how to do so.** The author begins by introducing the idea that a job applicant can read an interviewer and then discusses the specifics of interpreting an interviewer's email and office arrangements.

5. **A. Interviewers have some influence or control over their office arrangements.** In paragraphs 3 and 4, the author explains that you can learn a great deal about an interviewer's personality from the type and arrangements of furniture in the interviewer's office. However, in order for this to make sense, the author must be assuming that interviewers have some say about their office arrangements. If an interviewer had no influence over her office, then the office would not provide reliable information about the interviewer's personality. The passage does not discuss the virtues of email (as

in choice (B)) or the relative importance of different aspects of preparing for an interview (as in choice (D)). Choice (C) is out of scope. This passage is about prospective hires, not employees.

6. **D. You should try to understand your interviewer's personality and tailor your responses to him or her accordingly.** Only choice (D) summarizes the author's overall argument. The other choices are either details (such as choice (A)) or not mentioned in the passage (such as choice (C)).

7. **A. short and tense** You can infer the meaning of this word from the context. In this paragraph, you are told that in a homey, comfortable environment, your responses to interview questions should be friendly, open, and relaxed. It makes sense that "truncated" would mean the opposite of open and relaxed.

8. **D. Pa's** In this paragraph, the author describes Pa's love for Cleo and why she has so much influence over him.

9. **C. Serena felt that she had no choice but to give Cleo her copper to stop Cleo from doing something unsafe.** Serena does not want to give Cleo her copper; rather, Cleo is "compelling unnecessary sacrifice." Cleo does so by threatening to do something dangerous.

10. **D. Pa could not really afford to give Cleo and her sisters money.** The quote explains that Pa did not really have enough money to give some to Cleo and her sisters for doing chores. The phrase "dig deep" suggests that it was a sacrifice for him to do without that money, although he wanted to be generous. The language in the quote is figurative rather than literal, so choice (B) is incorrect.

11. **B. Cleo's boldness and her family's love for her sometimes make them feel powerless to resist her.** This passage is chiefly concerned with Cleo's character, which is bold and daring, and with the fact that her family members clearly love her. Both in the case of Pa giving the girls coppers and in the case of the sisters giving theirs to Cleo, Cleo's family members sometimes feel that they cannot refuse her.

12. **B. While Serena allows Cleo to manipulate her, she is also angry at what Cleo persuades her to do.** In the first paragraph, you are told that Cleo "brazenly" asks Pa for money instead of a kiss, and in the second paragraph, you are told she can "trample" on Pa's heart and he doesn't mind. Then in the seventh paragraph, Cleo enjoys the fantasy of being dead while her family grieves. These details establish that Cleo is manipulative. She ultimately manipulates her sisters into giving her money, for which Serena "briefly hate[s]" her.

13. **C. to describe in a positive manner the current status of the effort to move Native Americans further away from white populations** Jackson says that a 30-year policy is coming to a "happy consummation [completion]." Choice (D) represents the purpose of the second paragraph.

14. **D. The U.S. government has repeatedly asked Native Americans to move and will do so again.** The speech follows a pattern of describing apparently friendly relations between the United States and Native American tribes, followed by the U.S. government's insistence that Native Americans move away. The sentence, "I have listened to a great many talks from our Great Father, and they always began and ended in this," refers to this repeating pattern.

15. **B. The speaker is using irony to contrast the U.S. government's stated views with its actions.** In this paragraph, Speckled Snake says that the U.S. government "loved" Native Americans but "pushed" them away and "trampled" their graves. Pushing and trampling are not loving actions, so you can infer that Speckled Snake does not really mean it when he says that the government "loved" Native Americans. *Only count this question correct if you answered all parts correctly.*

16.

Andrew Jackson	Speckled Snake
☐ delineates the values and goals he holds in common with Congress	☐ uses direct, inflammatory language to criticize his opponents
☑ enumerates a number of benefits to all parties who might be affected by the policy under discussion	☐ logically outlines a number of adverse effects the policy under discussion will have
☐ emphasizes his feelings of friendship toward members of Congress	☑ tells a story in which certain plot points are repeated

Jackson seeks to reassure Congress that the legislation it passed is helping the federal and state governments, white Americans, and Native Americans by listing the benefits the law will have for these groups. Speckled Snake seeks to persuade other members of his tribe of a pessimistic forecast for the outcome of the current policy by narrating how a series of similar policies has affected Native Americans.

17.

Both Andrew Jackson and Speckled Snake	Neither Andrew Jackson nor Speckled Snake
☐ The current U.S. policy of Indian removal will enhance the well-being of Native Americans.	☐ Native Americans are nomadic hunters.
☐ Some Native Americans helped early European settlers.	☑ Whites and Native Americans will be able to coexist in harmony in the western territories.
☑ The United States has had a consistent policy of Indian removal.	☐ The U.S. government has broken promises to Native Americans.

Both speakers refer to a longstanding practice of making Native Americans move from their land. Jackson does so when he refers to "the benevolent policy of the Government, steadily pursued for nearly thirty years." Speckled Snake does so when he describes the U.S. government as repeatedly saying "Get a little further; you are too near me." Only Jackson says this policy will help Native Americans (the first choice in column one), and only Speckled Snake mentions that Native Americans helped early white settlers (the second choice in column one). As for column two, neither speaker says the two populations will coexist on better terms: Jackson speaks of separating Native Americans from whites, and Speckled Snake believes future conflict is inevitable. The first choice in column two is incorrect because Jackson describes Native Americans as being "a few savage hunters" and as having "wandering habits." The third choice in column two is incorrect because Speckled Snake states that the U.S. government promised their land "shall be yours forever" but now has said "the land where you now live is not yours."

18. **A. When conflict arises between the national government and the states, such conflict should be defused.** In the second paragraph, where he lists the benefits of his policy, Jackson says, "It puts an end to all possible danger of collision between the authorities of the General [that is, national] and State governments." That tells you that he believes that conflict between federal and state governments should be reduced. Choice (B) is incorrect because Jackson says that Native Americans are suffering these negative effects due to contact with whites. He never says that populations can be harmed due to the states having power. Choice (C) is incorrect because Jackson says that opening up land currently occupied by Native Americans will allow some states to become more populous and to better defend themselves. Choice (D) is incorrect because, although Jackson says these states will be able to defend themselves without outside help, he does not say doing so is solely their responsibility.

19. **D. is hoping her mother won't hear her asking for money** The narrator misinterprets Marjie's actions. She thinks Marjie is asking for money for herself, not her mother. She therefore interprets Marjie's actions as trying to hide her request from her mother.

20. **C. Jennie is perplexed when the narrator blames Marjie.** When the narrator explains that she thought Marjie wanted the money for herself, "Jennie looked doubtful."

21. **A. the narrator's thoughts** The passage is written with a first person point of view from the narrator's perspective. This allows the reader access to the thoughts of the narrator as well as a description of the action that the narrator sees.

22. **C. They know each other but are not close.** The narrator is staying with Jennie and her family and obviously knows them, yet there is a formal tone to Jennie's explanation about borrowing money, and the narrator is unable to explain how she misunderstood Marjie and is left "floundering." Those aspects of their relationship help you infer they are not on close, intimate terms.

23. **C. shied away from** The narrator decides not to explain why she thought Marjie wanted the money

for herself. That's because, as she says, "It isn't easy to give evidence against a child of five." Tattling on Marjie was something she shied away from, or "funked."

24. **D. They make Marjie's behavior harder to understand, so the reader sympathizes with the narrator's confusion.** By the end of this except, the narrator is feeling awkward and embarrassed. She had misinterpreted Marjie's behavior, and as a result she and Jennie are now having a misunderstanding. The fact that we only see Marjie's behavior as the narrator sees it helps us to understand why the narrator made this mistake. The narrator's focus is on Marjie's actions. There is no evidence in the text to support the ideas that (A) Jennie is untrustworthy, that (B) the baker does not exist, or that (C) the narrator is smarter than Jennie.

25. **B. awkwardness** The situation depicted is an awkward one, full of misunderstandings. The author of this passage has made a number of choices that contribute to that feeling of awkwardness, and the choppy dialogue she uses is one of those choices.

26. **Part One: C. There may be more people in poverty than the Census Bureau's official estimate suggests.** Overall, the passage conveys this main point. Choices (A) and (B) are details rather than main ideas, and choice (D) is not supported by the passage.
Part Two: "It has been argued that the estimated rate of poverty is too low—that, in fact, more Americans are poor."
"Some researchers have argued that these poverty thresholds do not account for taxes, living expenses, medical costs, or differences in cost of living."
"If the poverty thresholds were adjusted to account for these considerations [such as differences in cost of living], the estimated rate of poverty might be higher."
The bar graph shows that the number of people considered to be living in poverty would be higher for all groups except seniors under the SPM than under the current thresholds.
Other details listed are either background information, which is useful to help you understand the passage but not directly supportive of the author's claim, or facts that do not support the author's claim at all.

27. **C. The bar graph supports the claim that a different way to measure poverty would produce a different estimate of the rate of poverty.** The bar graph shows that the SPM would produce different estimates of how many people are poor, a claim that the author makes in paragraph 4.

28. **C. Higher rents can cause people to have less money for food.** Paragraph 3 explains that "higher rents may leave individuals with less money for food." Higher rents are the cause, and less money for food is the effect. Choices (B) and (D) are too extreme. Choice (A) distorts the passage: the poverty thresholds measure who is poor—they don't cause people to be poor.

29. **B. The student has overlooked the fact that other factors might impact how much money local governments receive from the federal government.** The student has read in the passage that government spending on poverty is affected by the estimated rate of poverty. But even if the estimated rate of poverty were higher, that does not necessarily mean that government (at any level) would automatically spend more on poverty. After all, many factors go into governmental decision-making.

30. **C. wants governmental actions to be based on an accurate estimate of the rate of poverty** The author's chief concern is with the estimated rate of poverty and whether or not it is accurate. Moreover, the author states in paragraph 5 that this matters because government spending is involved. None of the other choices here are supported by the passage.

31. **C. Improving them is a good use of funds right now.** While both writers agree that the parks are not in good repair, they disagree over whether improving them is the best way to use resources at the present time.

32. **C. people who start businesses** The author's emphasis in the last paragraph of the first passage is on small businesses. He believes Glenwood needs more of them. Thus, you can infer that "entrepreneurs" are people who might start small businesses.

33. **D. Several restaurants downtown have survived the bad economy.** The business owner introduces her claim that the business district can attract new businesses in the second paragraph of the second passage. Choice (D) is one of the details used in that paragraph to support her claim.

34. **A. They are good when done in the best locations.** The local business owner doesn't feel that improving the public parks is the best use of funds right now, but she does feel that using those resources to improve the appearance of the business district would contribute to economic growth.

35. **B. Investing in our community is important for the future of Glenwood.** Both writers are arguing that public resources should be invested in improving the community to help ensure its prosperity in the long term.

36. **Part One: C. to argue that Glenwood should improve its public parks** The Glenwood Community Improvement Council member states her purpose in the first sentence: "I fully support spending money to beautify our public parks." The rest of the passage supports that idea.
Part Two: paraphrasing the concerns of some community members; speculating about the probable result of improving the parks; speculating about the negative consequences of not improving the parks To achieve that purpose, the Improvement Council member paraphrases the concerns of some community members when she says in paragraph 1 that her neighbors worry that the parks are dangerous. In paragraph two, the Improvement Council member speculates about the probable result of improving the parks—for example: "Improving and maintaining the parks would have a positive effect on crime and vandalism." In paragraph 3,

the Improvement Council member speculates about what might happen if the town does not improve the parks: "Furthermore, beautiful public spaces are essential to community pride. Without community pride, Glenwood residents and others are unlikely to invest in creating and supporting small businesses." She does not employ authorities, examples involving other towns, or comparisons.

37. **A. Both would result from the improvement of Glenwood's parks.** In the second paragraph, the Improvement Council member says: "Improving and maintaining the parks would have a positive effect on crime and vandalism." In the third paragraph, she says that "We must present Glenwood as a beautiful place to live in order to attract successful entrepreneurs from the surrounding area. If we do so, our investment in the parks will quickly pay for itself." Thus, she believes that improving the parks would lead to a reduction in crime and the attraction of small businesses. Choices (C) and (D) both have the council member's thinking backwards.

38. **C. to underscore the serious consequences his mother's death will have on the young prince's future** The emperor's younger son must be sent away from the palace. Now that his mother is no longer alive, the child's ties to the imperial court will weaken, and he will lose the emperor's protection.

39. **Part One: B. news of the death of the Emperor's favorite concubine** The phrase "sad tidings" indicates that emperor has received a report from his messenger that his favorite concubine has died. **Part Two: "one who, though she was not of high birth, enjoyed the full tide of Royal favor"; "From that moment the mind of the Emperor was darkened"; "the young prince now motherless"** The "Royal favor" conferred on the woman explains why the news is described as "sad." The Emperor's mind was "darkened" because of this sadness. The phrase "now motherless" indicates that the young prince's mother has died.

40. **D. ironic** Irony is the name given to a state of affairs that is contrary to what one would expect. The meaning of the quoted proverb is that once someone has died (as the young prince's mother has just done), that person is remembered with more affection than she received during her lifetime. The last paragraph explains that the people who disliked and resented the concubine during her lifetime began to like her after her death, and that is contrary to what one would expect.

41. **D. Public opinion is that the emperor's older son, born to a woman with greater influence than the younger prince's mother, should be the emperor's heir.** The first paragraph of the passage states that the older son's grandfather has strong political influence, and that the public believes that the emperor's older son should therefore be the heir. Therefore, they disapprove of the attention paid to the younger prince—the one born to the favorite concubine.

42. **D. The family has experienced many disappointments and tragedies.** While all of the other answer choices are supported by pieces of text, none of them is a central idea of the passage. Choice (D) is supported by Mama's discussion of the house she once wanted in Morgan Park, the loss of the baby Claude, the frustration and disappointment experienced by Mr. Younger, and the refrain of the word "dreams" throughout the passage.

43. **He grieved deeply over the baby Claude. His love for his children helped keep his dreams alive. He once assumed that the family could improve their situation. He may have cheated on Mama.** All of these statements are supported by the text. Mama describes how Mr. Younger grieved over the baby when she says, "Lord, when I lost that baby little Claude I almost thought I was going to lose Big Walter too. Oh, that man grieved hisself!" Mr. Younger's words explain that his love for his children helped him keep dreaming of a better life: "Seem like God didn't see fit to give the black man nothing but dreams, but He did give us children to make them dreams seem worthwhile." When Mama explains that she and Mr. Younger originally thought that they would only live in the apartment for a year, she is explaining that they thought they could improve their situation. Finally, Mama describes Mr. Younger's flaws briefly in her last speech. The phrase "wild with women" suggests that he may have been unfaithful. None of the other choices are supported by specific pieces of text.

44. **C. It suggests that the apartment is very run-down, and that the family feels trapped there.** While the family's apartment might actually have rats, the phrase "rat trap" implies more than just that literal meaning (so choice (D) is incorrect). It suggests that the apartment is run-down and probably not worth the money the family spends on rent. The word "trap" also suggests that the family members themselves feel trapped. Choice (A) is incorrect because nothing suggests that the building attracts criminals. Choice (B) is unsupported by the passage because Ruth and Mama do not insult themselves in this way.

45. **A. the contrast between how hard it has been for the family to improve its situation and how much Mama would still like to try** Mr. Younger never gave up trying to improve his family's situation despite the fact that he got very discouraged about it from time to time. Mama still clings to the dream she and her husband once had of providing their family with a house. The quote ties together Walter Younger's experiences and Mama's current aspirations.

46. **C. It would suggest that Mama is lost in her own powerful memories.** If Mama turned away from Ruth, this scene would seem less like an ordinary conversation between the two women. It would suggest that Mama was so wrapped up in her own memories that she had almost forgotten that she was talking to Ruth.

Language Arts: Reading Practice Test Evaluation Charts

Questions 1–46

Circle the numbers of the questions that you got correct and then total them in the last column of each row.

Column A	Column B	Column C
Content area	Question numbers	Count up the number of questions from column B you got correct, and enter that total for each row in this column
Interpreting Informational Text	4, 6, 7, 14, 17, 18, 28, 30, 32, 34, 37	___ out of 11
Two-part questions: for each of these you got correct, enter a "2" in the last column.	3, 26	___ out of 4
Analyzing Informational Text	1, 2, 5, 13, 15, 16, 27, 29, 31, 33, 35	___ out of 11
Two-part questions: for each of these you got correct, enter a "2" in the last column.	36	___ out of 2
Reading Literature	8, 9, 10, 11, 12, 19, 20, 21, 22, 23, 24, 25, 38, 40, 41, 42, 43, 44, 45, 46	___ out of 20
Two-part questions: for each of these you got correct, enter a "2" in the last column.	39	___ out of 2
Total points		_____ out of 50

If you do not have time to review the entire *Reading* unit, you may want to review the sections that need the most work.

Using the points total from the bottom right hand corner of the table above, use the information below to assess your readiness to take the TASC test.

If your points total was . . .	then you are . . .	Kaplan recommends
26–50	very likely to pass the TASC Reading test.	that you do a relatively brief, high-level review of all reading concepts, especially ones you've struggled with, before test day.
23–25	fairly likely to pass the TASC Reading test.	that you give yourself a few more days or weeks to do a final comprehensive review of reading material before testing.
20–22	somewhat likely to pass the TASC Reading test.	that you set a goal date by which you would like to complete a final review of the material. As you do that review, focus on the material you have struggled with the most.
0–19	unlikely to pass the TASC Reading test.	that you do an in-depth review of the subject matter. Be sure to look for patterns among the questions you got wrong, and study those topics in greater depth.

LANGUAGE ARTS: WRITING PRACTICE TEST ANSWERS AND EXPLANATIONS

Part I: Language Skills

1. **D. replace hole with whole** A hole is a place that is dug out of the ground; whole means "entire."

2. **D. change add to adding** The verb "add" should end with *-ing* to match "stripping" and "filling." All the verbs in a series should be in the same form.

3. **A. change ceiling meet to ceiling meets** "The ceiling" is a singular subject and requires a singular verb.

4. **B. a colon** A colon should be used to introduce a list.

5. **A. missed, and go** Choice (A) corrects the comma splice with a logical conjunction.

6. **D. At the same time** The author says that technology is especially valuable to society when it promotes freedom and gives examples of how automobiles gave people more freedom. "At the same time" introduces a sentence containing the counterexamples that support the idea that automobiles also "trapped" people, depriving them of some freedom and, by implication, making automobiles less valuable.

7. **D. Thus, despite its promise, the mass-manufacture of automobiles has not been entirely beneficial to society.** The author begins by showing how automobiles made a positive contribution to society by promoting freedom. Then the author shows, with counterexamples, that automobiles also "trapped" people. Therefore, a logical conclusion to this passage states that cars have had a negative effect on society as well.

8. **A. Depression is a cave that no light can penetrate.** The answer choices are all metaphors. The idea needing illustration is that the person with depression cannot respond to the positive aspects of life. The image of a lightless cave matches this idea. The given sentence does not speak to a distance between the person and life experiences, so neither the far-away bird nor the spider in the web is an accurate metaphor. The "flaming, punishing hell" is appropriately negative, but nothing in the given sentence suggests this much pain.

9.

The majority of his stories feature protagonists who meet a grisly fate . . .	This is because
He wrote about the terrifying monster Cthulhu . . .	For example,
Many of his stories set in the "Dreamlands" . . .	On the other hand,
True devotees of Lovecraft acknowledge . . .	Therefore,

The first sentence of the passage states a fact. The second sentence, "The majority of his stories . . . ," gives a reason for this fact, making the connector "because" appropriate. The third sentence, "He wrote about . . . ," gives an example illustrating the previous sentence. In the fourth sentence, "Many of his stories . . . ," the words "while disturbing" signal a contrast with the previous idea. You learn that not all of Lovecraft's stories were horror, so a contrasting introduction such as "On the other hand" is fitting. The last sentence expresses the author's conclusion, and "Therefore" is a conclusion keyword.

10. **D. The rose-and-bluebell wallpaper gave the room a cheerful look.** There are potentially many correct ways to shorten this sentence, but of the given answer choices, only choice (D) does so. Choice (A) fails to shorten the sentence. Choice (B) introduces a misplaced modifier, by suggesting that the "look" was "of roses and bluebells." Choice (C) includes a too-long modifying phrase before "wallpaper."

11. **A. It suggests that the author does not think that Chillyville is a terrible place to live.** If the author thought that Chillyville was a terrible place to live, she would simply say outright: "Chillyville is a terrible place to live." Instead, she distances herself from the idea by using the passive voice. This is a common technique authors use to introduce an idea that they intend to disagree with. The rest of this paragraph makes it clear that the author does not think Chillyville is a terrible place to live.

12. **D. Bryan does not think there is school today, because he is speaking using the subjunctive mood.** The subjunctive mood is indicated by the verbs "were" and "would have." That mood tells you that the school bus has not passed (or at least Bryan thinks it has not passed). The subjunctive mood is used to describe a situation that's contrary to fact. Thus, you can infer that Bryan does not think that there is school today. Choice (C) is incorrect because Bryan is talking about today. You might have been tempted by choice (C) if you misread these verbs as indicating the past tense rather than the subjunctive mood.

13. **A. It modifies the noun *Jamilla*.** The introductory phrase is a modifier that tells the reader more about Jamilla.

14. **B. Our team has six tasks to accomplish before 10:00 a.m., and then we'll receive a score between zero and 100. Three of us competed last year, and we are hoping to beat last year's score, which was 72.** The table gives the following guidelines for the *Publication Manual of the APA*: "Usually write out numbers up to nine; use numerals for 10 and up. Use numerals for quantities of time." To follow these guidelines, the words "six," "zero," and "Three" should be written out, and all other quantities should be given using numerals.

15. **B. change is to are** The verb "are" agrees with the plural subject "gardens."

16. **B. insert a period after sponsor and capitalize this** Separating this sentence into two corrects the run-on.

17. **D. "Keep in mind that contributions of seeds, tools, and land . . . are just as important as money."** An ellipsis (three periods with spaces in between) should be used to indicate that material has been omitted from the middle of a quote.

18. **A. Next, choose a site for the garden.** Choice (A) is specific enough to be clear and general enough to cover all the details in the paragraph. It also includes a transition from the preceding paragraph.

19. **B. Start a new paragraph before sentence 3.** The

first two sentences are about the benefits of community gardens. Sentence 3 begins a discussion of the steps involved in forming a community garden. Thus, a new paragraph is warranted.

20. **B. change piece to peace** A piece is a part of something;
peace is a sense of calm and absence of conflict.

21. **C. replace you're with your** Because the workplace belongs to you, the possessive pronoun "your" is correct.

22. **A. disappear magically once you leave** What happens magically is that the symptoms disappear, not that you leave work. "Magically" should be placed closer to the part of the sentence that it modifies—symptoms disappearing.

23. **A. furniture, paneling, glues, and upholstery—even in draperies!** — The phrase "even in draperies!" is not just another item in the list of things that can contain formaldehyde. The adverb "even" and the repetition of the preposition "in" make this phrase different in structure from the rest of the list. One way to fix the original sentence would be to give it the same structure as the rest of the list: "furniture, paneling, glues, upholstery, and draperies." However, the author seems to intend the phrase "even in draperies!" to sound a dramatic note by standing alone. Thus, it should be separated from the list with a dash.

24. **D. (14) Fungi can also be found in damp places like woodlands and bogs.** The passage is about sick building syndrome, and paragraph (C) in particular is about sources of airborne toxins in buildings. The subject of airborne toxins in outside areas like woodlands and bogs is irrelevant to the passage.

25. **emphasizing how enthusiastically the narrator is praising himself; increasing the mood of suspense in the story; emphasizing the patience and stealth used by the narrator; preparing the reader to learn that the narrator takes an hour to put his head inside a door** All of these things are achieved by Poe's choice of syntax. The repetition of the preposition "with" serves to emphasize each word and also intensifies the narrator's style, which is suspenseful, persuasive, and self-congratulatory. Moreover, Poe's emphasizing each of the adjectives makes the reader curious about exactly how the narrator was wise and cautious. That makes the story more suspenseful and paves the way for narrator's description of how he took an entire hour to put his head inside the old man's door.

26. **A. the narrator's desire to persuade the reader of his sanity** Sometimes speakers or writers use questions to which they do not actually expect answers. These are referred to as rhetorical questions, and they are frequently intended to persuade others.

27. **D. If only she were a comic book heroine, it would all be easier!** The last sentence describes something that isn't actually the case: Viktoriya is not actually a comic book heroine. When an author makes a hypothetical or wishful statement, the verb should be in the subjunctive mood. The correct form of the

subjunctive mood here is "if she were a comic book heroine," not "if she was a comic book heroine."

28. **C. Please vote for the candidate of your choice by filling in the corresponding bubble.** The imperative mood is the verb form used for commands or requests. Only choice (C) expresses a command or request. Choice (A) is in the declarative mood: it states a fact. Choice (B) is in the subjunctive mood: it describes a statement that is contrary to fact. Choice (D) is in the interrogative mood: it asks a question.

29. **A. People's opinions about the correct use of the verb have changed over time.** What counts as correct grammar and usage is a matter of social consensus, and that consensus sometimes changes over time. Today, a writer would not say that a ship is *building* when what he means is that the ship *is being built.*

30. **C. It contains an inappropriate shift from the third person to the second person.** The passage begins by describing what Van Anh does or reads that she should do. Then the passage shifts to telling "you" what to do. However, you are not assembling the shelves—Van Anh is—and the passage should reflect that.

31. **C. Compton Point, home to many animal species that are threatened with extinction, now faces a threat of its own.** No comma is needed between "many" and "animal." Now, it is true that, in general, you should put a comma between two adjectives that both modify a noun. However, you should make an exception when the adjective closest to the noun helps to *define* the person or thing being described rather than *modify* the person or thing being described. Here, "animal" defines the species being discussed. "Many," in turn, modifies the entire phrase "animal species." Each of the other answer choices introduces another error.

32. **A. Tourism increases both air pollution and litter, which will** Choice (A) makes clear that tourists cause both pollution and litter.

33. **C. remove sentence 7** The flyer focuses on the land on Compton Point. This sentence about other areas in the county is irrelevant and should be deleted.

34. **A. change did to will** The demonstration is in the future, so the message will be sent to developers in the future.

35. **C. I love to swim in the lake early in the morning.** An infinitive is a verb form that begins with *to.* Choices (A) and (C) both contain an infinitive phrase, *to swim.* However, in choice (A), the infinitive is the subject of the sentence: "To swim . . . is a delight." In choice (C), *to swim* is the object of the verb *love.*

36. **C. Philippa is said to be an excellent instructor.** The phrase *is said to be* is an example of a verb in the passive voice. That means that the subject of the sentence is receiving the action of the verb rather than performing the action. In choice (C), the passive voice means that other people are saying that Philippa is an excellent instructor. None of the other choices use this verb phrase correctly.

37. **B. Investing in business continuity is crucial: mishandling a disaster can hurt the company's reputation with a generation of consumers, while efficiently limiting the damage can earn public trust.** The first paragraph describes what business continuity is and some types of disasters that companies must consider. The second paragraph gives specific examples of companies that did or did not handle disaster well and how their response impacted their reputation. Choice (B) effectively links the two paragraphs, introducing the idea that the examples in the second paragraph will support.

38. **C. see** The verb form "see" is required with the subject "you." "Seen" requires the helping verb "have," but the present perfect tense "have seen" is not needed in the sentence, just the simple present.

39. **B. move sentence 3 to follow sentence 1** With sentence 1, sentence 3 catches the reader's attention and gives background information about the topic of the whole article. Sentences 2 and 4 introduce the main idea of the article.

40. **D. During a thunderstorm, he flew a kite with** In the original sentence, it sounds as if the thunderstorm had a key attached to it.

41. **B. humidity, wind speed, and barometric pressure** Choice (B) combines two sentences that have related details.

42. **B. a semicolon** As written, sentence 12 has two independent clauses with nothing separating them. This could be fixed by adding a comma and a conjunction after "aircraft." However, the question asks you to identify a single punctuation mark that could join the two independent clauses. A semicolon can be used to join two independent clauses. None of the other marks of punctuation listed can be used in this way.

43. **A. Bell, the physicist and inventor, used** The phrase "the physicist and inventor" is an appositive describing Bell, so that phrase should be set off with commas.

44. **C. change <u>power, you</u> to <u>power. You</u>** The sentence as written contains a comma splice. Answer choice (C) corrects the comma splice.

45. **C. Some types of trucks, buses, and trains** In the original, there are three items in a series: trucks, buses, and some train engines. So the three things should be separated with commas. But the three things should also display parallel construction: the phrase "some types of" should apply to all three of them.

46. **C. change <u>would move</u> to <u>moves</u>** The clause containing the verb "would move" modifies the main clause, which is in the present tense and the declarative mood ("is used"). Therefore, the modifying phrase should have the present tense as well. The word "would," by contrast, indicates the subjunctive mood and is not appropriate here.

47. **B. It does not display parallel structure.** The phrases "Learning how to ride" and "how to learn to ride" should employ parallel structure. The most natural way to correct this error would be to write the sentence: "Learning how to ride a skateboard or inline skates is similar to learning how to ride a bicycle."

48. **C. However** The author contrasts head injuries, which do not heal easily, with the knee and elbow injuries mentioned in the sentence before. Therefore, a contrast word such as *however* is needed.

49. **B. split it into two sentences** The sentence as written is long and unwieldy. It would be more effective if it were split into two sentences.

50. Change *was dazzled by* to *was overwhelmed by*. Change *glittering* to *glaring*. Change *cream-colored* to *drab*. Change *racing with anticipation* to *racing with anxiety*. Change *taken to a room* to *shoved into a room*. Change *helped me sleep soundly* to *made me unaware of what was happening*. All of these changes would allow Susan's writing to convey unhappiness, fear, and discomfort. The other changes listed are either neutral (such as "Change *taken to a room* to *shown into a room*.") or would substitute positive-sounding language (such as "Change *glittering* to *sparkling*.").

Part II: Essay

Use the **Essay Evaluation Guide for Argument/Opinion Essays** on page 651 to evaluate your work.

Essay Evaluation Guide for Argument/Opinion Essays*

Assign your essay a score of 0–4 based on which of the following descriptions best fits your essay. Then double that score to obtain a score of 0–8.

4 My response is well developed. It effectively develops and supports an argument.

- My thesis statement is stated in the first paragraph. It is clear and confident in tone.
- I supported my thesis statement with several pieces of logical reasoning and relevant evidence.
- My essay is organized into paragraphs, each of which introduces and supports one idea.
- The words I chose clearly convey my meaning while maintaining a businesslike tone.
- I frequently used connective phrases to show the relationships between ideas (for example, such as, because, however, therefore, etc.).
- I acknowledged and argued against the opposing view.
- I used grammar and writing mechanics correctly. Any grammatical errors do not interfere with my meaning.
- I concluded my essay by summarizing my argument.

3 My response is a complete essay. It develops and supports an argument.

- My thesis statement is clearly stated.
- I used reasons and evidence to support my thesis statement, but some of them could have been developed more effectively.
- My essay is organized into paragraphs, most of which develop one idea.
- My word choice does not interfere with my meaning, and I maintained a businesslike tone.
- I often used connective phrases to show the relationships between ideas (for example, such as, because, however, therefore, etc.).
- I tried to argue against the opposing view, but I could have done so more effectively.
- My essay has only a few errors in grammar and writing mechanics that interfere with my meaning.
- I concluded my essay by summarizing my argument.

2 My response develops an argument, but it is not complete, or it is oversimplified.

- My thesis statement is unclear or is buried in the middle of my essay.
- I used evidence and reasons to support my thesis statement, but some of those ideas seem incomplete or not as effective as they could be.
- My essay has paragraphs, but some paragraphs have more than one topic sentence or no topic sentence at all.
- My word choice could have been improved to make my meaning clear.
- I mentioned the opposing side, but I didn't argue against it effectively.
- My essay has some errors in grammar and writing mechanics, some of which make my meaning unclear.
- I included a concluding sentence or paragraph, but it doesn't effectively summarize my argument.

1 My response was an attempt to develop an argument, but it was not effective or clear.

- My thesis statement is missing, weakly stated, or only implied.
- I didn't include enough reasons or evidence to support my claim.
- My essay is very short or is not divided into paragraphs.
- I neglected to mention or argue against the opposing side.
- My word choice frequently interferes with my meaning.
- My essay has several errors in grammar or writing mechanics, and these interfere with my meaning.
- I did not include a concluding statement or paragraph.

0 My response is completely irrelevant, only a sentence or two, or makes no sense.

*NOTE: This evaluation rubric was adapted by Kaplan for student use. The rubric is based on criteria provided by CTB/McGraw-Hill. CTB/McGraw-Hill may have made changes to the TASC essay evaluation rubric since the time of this printing. Visit www.tasctest.com for more information.

Essay Evaluation Guide for Informative/Explanatory Essays*

Assign your essay a score of 0–4 based on which of the following descriptions best fits your essay. Then double that score to obtain a score of 0–8.

4 My response thoroughly and clearly discusses or explains the topic and presents information relevant to that topic.

- I clearly introduce the topic of my essay in the first couple of sentences.
- I explain the topic using several relevant and specific facts, details, and examples.
- My essay is organized into paragraphs, each of which develops one idea.
- The words I chose clearly convey my meaning while maintaining a businesslike tone.
- I frequently used connective phrases to show the relationships between ideas (for example, such as, because, however, therefore, etc.).
- I used grammar and writing mechanics correctly. Any grammatical errors do not interfere with my meaning.
- I concluded my essay by summarizing my explanation of the topic.

3 My response discusses or explains the topic and gives relevant information but could have been more developed.

- The topic of my essay is introduced in the first paragraph.
- I used relevant facts, details, and examples to explain my topic, but some of them could have been developed more effectively.
- My essay is organized into paragraphs, most of which develop one idea.
- My word choice does not interfere with my meaning, and I maintained a businesslike tone.
- I often used connective phrases to show the relationships between ideas (for example, such as, because, however, therefore, etc.).
- My essay has only a few errors in grammar and writing mechanics that interfere with my meaning.
- I concluded my essay by summarizing my explanation of the topic.

2 My response discusses the topic, but it is not complete, or it is oversimplified.

- My introduction of my topic is unclear or not included in the first paragraph.
- I used facts, details, and examples to explain my topic, but some of them are irrelevant or incomplete.
- My essay has paragraphs, but some paragraphs have more than one topic sentence or no topic sentence at all.
- My word choice could have been improved to make my meaning clear.
- My essay has some errors in grammar and writing mechanics, some of which make my meaning unclear.
- I included a concluding sentence or paragraph, but it doesn't effectively summarize my explanation of the topic.

1 My response was an attempt to discuss the topic, but it was not effective or clear.

- My introduction of my topic is missing, weakly stated, or only implied.
- I included very little information to develop my topic.
- My essay is very short or is not divided into paragraphs.
- My word choice frequently interferes with my meaning.
- My essay has several errors in grammar or writing mechanics, and these interfere with my meaning.
- I did not include a concluding statement or paragraph.

0 My response is completely irrelevant, only a sentence or two, or makes no sense.

*NOTE: This evaluation rubric was adapted by Kaplan for student use. The rubric is based on criteria provided by CTB/McGraw-Hill. CTB/McGraw-Hill may have made changes to the TASC essay evaluation rubric since the time of this printing. Visit www.tasctest.com for more information.

Language Arts: Writing Practice Test Evaluation Charts

Questions 1–50

Circle the numbers of the questions that you got correct and then total them in the last column of each row.

Content Area	Question Numbers	Number Correct/Total
Writing Effective Sentences Pages 90–107	2, 5, 13, 16, 22, 41, 44, 45, 47	_____ out of 9
Connecting Ideas Pages 108–119	6, 7, 8, 9, 18, 19, 24, 37, 48	_____ out of 9
Using Grammar Correctly Pages 120–139	3, 11, 12, 15, 27, 28, 30, 34, 35, 36, 38, 46	_____ out of 12
Using Writing Mechanics Pages 140–157	1, 4, 17, 20, 21, 23, 31, 42, 43	_____ out of 9
Polishing Your Writing Pages 28–41 in the online chapter "Extended Response"	10, 14, 25, 26, 29, 32, 33, 39, 40, 49, 50	_____ out of 11
Points subtotal		_____ **out of 50**

My essay score, based on the **Essay Evaluation Guide for Argument/Opinion Essays** on page 651, is _____.

If you do not have time to review the entire Writing unit, you may want to review the sections that need the most work.

Add your essay score to the points subtotal from the bottom right cell of the table. Use that sum and the information below to assess your readiness to take the TASC test.

If your points total was . . .	then you are . . .	Kaplan recommends
30–58	very likely to pass the TASC Writing test.	that you do a relatively brief, high-level review of all writing concepts, especially ones you've struggled with, before test day.
27–29	fairly likely to pass the TASC Writing test.	that you give yourself a few more days or weeks to do a final comprehensive review of writing material before testing.
23–27	somewhat likely to pass the TASC Writing test.	that you set a goal date by which you would like to complete a final review of the material. As you do that review, focus on the material you have struggled with the most.
0–22	unlikely to pass the TASC Writing test.	that you do an in-depth review of the subject matter. Be sure to look for patterns among the questions you got wrong, and study those topics in greater depth.

MATHEMATICS PRACTICE TEST ANSWERS AND EXPLANATIONS

Part I: No Calculator Allowed

1. **77** Brad's average golf score would be found like this:
$$\frac{sum\ of\ scores}{number\ of\ scores} = average\ score$$
Plug the information you are given in the question into the formula and solve for the unknown:
$$\frac{78 + 86 + 82 + 81 + 82 + x}{6} = 81$$
$$78 + 86 + 82 + 81 + 82 + x = 486$$
$$409 + x = 486$$
$$x = 77$$

2. **D. $2x(x + y)$** To begin adding the polynomials together, factor out any like terms: $2x(x - y + 2y)$. Then combine any like terms together: $2x(x + y)$

3. **C. $\sqrt{9^2 + 12^2}$** The cable forms the hypotenuse of a triangle with side lengths of 9 feet and 12 feet. Use the Pythagorean theorem ($9^2 + 12^2 = c^2$) to determine the length of the hypotenuse c: $c = \sqrt{9^2 + 12^2}$.

4. **C. $x + 3$** Every term in the expression is divisible by two, so begin by simplifying: $\frac{2x^2 - 6x - 36}{2x - 12} = \frac{x^2 - 3x - 18}{x - 6}$.
Next, factor the numerator of the fraction and cancel:
$\frac{x^2 - 3x - 18}{x - 6} = \frac{(x - 6)(x + 3)}{x - 6} = x + 3$

5. **D. −8 and −12** To solve this system of linear equations, first write two equations with the information given. Call the numbers x and y. The first sentence tells you that $x = 12 + 3y$, and the second sentence tells you that $x + y = -20$.
Rewrite the second equation so that x is isolated on one side of the equal sign: $x = -20 - y$. Now that each equation is written in terms of x, set the two expressions for x equal to each other: $12 + 3y = -20 - y$.
Simplify this equation: $4y = -32$, so $y = -8$. Substitute this value for y back into the second equation: $x + -8 = -20$, so x must equal −12.

6.

| 6 | (| \$24.50 | − | \$19 |) |

To determine how much Janice will save, she needs to determine the price difference between one evening and one afternoon ticket (\$24.50 − \$19) and then multiply that number by 6, the total number of tickets she intends to purchase. Thus, the equation that will supply her total savings is 6(\$24.50 − \$19).

7. **31.5** To find the area of a right triangle, first find the base and the height. In this triangle, the base is the length along the x-axis: $5 - (-4) = 9$. The height is the length along the y-axis: $4 - (-3) = 7$. Plugging these into the area formula for a triangle is: $A = \frac{1}{2} \times b \times h = \frac{1}{2} \times 9 \times 7 = 31.5$.

8. **B. $c \blacklozenge 20e$** The CEO's limit is 20 times the lowest-paid employee's salary, which is represented by $20e$. The CEO will never make more than that, but he could make exactly that amount, so the equation should set c less than or equal to $20e$, $c \blacklozenge 20e$.

9. **B. P and R only** Two shapes are congruent if they are exactly the same shape and size. In the case of a triangle, that means that all three angle measures would have to be the same, and corresponding legs would have to be the same length. Begin by filling in missing information for Triangle P:

Triangle P

The three angles of any triangle add up to 180 degrees, so here you can calculate:
$55 + 55 + missing\ angle\ measure = 180$
$missing\ angle\ measure = 70$ degrees Thus, Triangle P has angle measures of 55°, 55°, and 70°.
Also remember that if a triangle has two angles with the same measures, the sides opposite those angles will be the same length. So the missing side length for Triangle P is x. Triangle P has sides of length x, x, and y.
Now you know that Triangles P and Q are not congruent, since Q has an angle measure of 80°.
To determine whether Triangles P and R are congruent, find the missing angle measure for Triangle R:
$55 + 70 + missing\ angle\ measure = 180$
$missing\ angle\ measure = 55$ degrees
Thus, Triangle R has angle measures of 55°, 55°, and 70°. Moreover, the two legs of Triangle R that are opposite its 55° angles will be the same length. Now you know that Triangle R has legs of length x, x, and y. Triangles P and R have the same angle measures and the same leg lengths. Choice (B) is correct.

10. **A. $n_x = 2(n_{x-1}) + 2$** First, determine the relationship between the subsequent numbers in the sequence. Each number is twice the number before it plus 2: $2(2) + 2 = 6$, $2(6) + 2 = 14$, $2(14) + 2 = 30$. The question tells you to use n_x to represent the item in position x in the sequence, so n_{x-1} represents the number prior to the number in position x. Thus, the equation to represent this arithmetic sequence is $n_x = 2(n_{x-1}) + 2$.

11. **B. $y = 2x + 3$** The linear equation that connects two points can be represented with the slope-intercept formula $y = mx + b$. First, calculate the slope (m) by calculating the change in y over the change in x:
$m = \frac{(13 - 7)}{(5 - 2)} = \frac{6}{3} = 2$. Then determine the y-intercept (b) by plugging one of the points into the slope-intercept formula and solving: $13 = 2(5) + b$; $13 = 10 + b$; $b = 3$. The linear equation that connects the two points is $y = 2x + 3$.

12. **7** First, factor to find the solutions to this quadratic equation: $x^2 - 4x - 21 = (x + 3)(x - 7)$. Then, set those factors equal to 0 to find the solutions to the quadratic equation: $x + 3 = 0$, $x = -3$ and $x - 7 = 0$, $x = 7$. The two solutions to the equation are −3 and 7. The

question asks for the only positive solution, so the answer is 7.

13. D. The ≤ symbol indicates "greater than or equal to," which is indicated with a filled-in dot. The symbol < indicates "less than" (but not equal to), which is indicated with an open dot.

14. 720 This question asks how many orderings, or permutations, of three out of ten are possible. Multiply: $10 \times 9 \times 8 = 720$.

15. B. 5π To determine the length of an arc, first calculate the circle's circumference, and then determine what fraction of that circumference is contained in the arc. This circle has a radius of 10 cm. Plugging that into the formula for circumference:

$C = 2\pi r$

$C = 20\pi$

The circle's entire circumference is 20π.

Now determine what portion of the circumference is contained in that arc. The length of an arc has the same proportional relationship to the circumference that its angle does to 360:

$$\frac{length\ of\ arc\ AB}{circumference} = \frac{m\angle AQB}{360}$$

Now plug in the values you know:

$$\frac{length\ of\ arc\ AB}{20\pi} = \frac{90}{360}$$

Simplify the proportion. You can cross-multiply, but it will be easier to simplify $\frac{90}{360}$ before you do so. 90 goes into 360 four times, so:

$$\frac{length\ of\ arc\ AB}{20\pi} = \frac{1}{4}$$

The length of arc AB is 5π.

16. C. 12 The formula for the area of a circle is $A = \pi r^2$ where r refers to the radius of the circle. The diameter of a circle (a straight line segment that goes from one edge of the circle to the other and passes through the center of the circle) is $2r$, or two times the length of the radius. The circle shown in this problem has an area of 36π. Plug that into the area formula and find the length of the circle's radius:

$36\pi = \pi r^2$

$\dfrac{36\pi}{\pi} = \dfrac{\pi r^2}{\pi}$

$36 = r^2$

$\sqrt{36} = \sqrt{r^2}$

$6 = r$

Now that you know the radius has a length of 6, multiply that length by 2 to get the diameter:

$6 \times 2 = 12$

17. D. $y = \frac{1}{2}x + 3$ You can use the point-slope form to figure out the slope of the line first. Use (–6, 0) and (0, 3) as two points:

$0 - 3 = m(-6 - 0)$

$-3 = m(-6)$

$-3 = -6m$

$m = \frac{-3}{-6} = \frac{1}{2}$

Now that you have the slope of the line, use either of the points to plug into the equation for a line, $y = mx + b$. Using (0, 3),

$3 = \frac{1}{2}(0) + b$

$3 = 0 + b$

$b = 3$

The equation of the line is $y = \frac{1}{2}x + 3$

18. –2 The slope is rise over run. In this table, each time x is increased by 1, y is decreased by 2. That produces a slope of $-\frac{2}{1} = -2$.

19. D. $\frac{180(S - 2)°}{S}$ The question tells you that "the sum of the values of all the interior angles of a polygon is equal to 180° times a number that is two less than the number of sides in the polygon." In other words, you would take the number of sides and subtract two, giving you $(S - 2)$. Now multiply that number by 180 to get the sum of the measures of all angles of any polygon: $180(S - 2)$. However, there's one more step: the question asks you to identify a formula that could be used to calculate the value of *one* angle of a regular polygon. The key here is to realize that in a regular polygon, all angles have the same measure. So if you could divide that sum (that is, $180(S - 2)$) by the number of angles, then you would have the value of one of those angles. But the question only gives you the variable S to work with. That's fine, though, because any polygon has as many sides as it has angles. So you can divide the sum of the angles by the number of sides and achieve the same result. Thus, $\frac{180(S - 2)°}{S}$ allows you to find the value of any one angle of a regular polygon with S sides.

20. B. $2x^4 + 7x^3 + 4x$ Combine like terms from the exponent with the largest degree, which is 4: $6x^4 - 4x^4 = 2x^4$. Combine like terms from the exponent with the next largest degree, which is 3: $5x^3 + 2x^3 = 7x^3$. Finally, combine the terms from the exponent with the smallest degree: $7x - 3x = 4x$. The simplified polynomial is $2x^4 + 7x^3 + 4x$

21. 27 Use the rules of exponents to solve each term of the equation: $3^3 = 27$, $4^2 = 16$, and $(2^2)^2 = (4)^2 = 16$. The equation then becomes $27 + 16 - 16 = 27$.

22. C. $15 + 3\sqrt[3]{3}$ The square root of 225 is 15. To take the cube root, you need to find a number that multiplies by itself 3 times. Rewrite the second term with 81 broken down into its prime factorization:

$\sqrt[3]{3 \times 3 \times 3 \times 3}$. Since the number 3 multiplies by itself 3 times, you can pull those three out of the radical and you are left with $\sqrt[3]{3}$, which makes the entire equation simplify to $15 + 3\sqrt[3]{3}$.

23. D.

First, formulate an equation with x representing the number of glasses and y representing the number of ice cubes. Because Tina is going to square the number of servings, that produces x^2. Then Tina is going to add two more ice cubes. Thus, the equation is $y = x^2 + 2$. Making a table with a few coordinates will help you identify the correct graph. There is no need to calculate outputs for negative values of x, since there is no such thing as a negative number of servings of lemonade.

x	y
0	2
1	3
2	6
3	11

Since the y-intercept is 2, that allows you to eliminate answer choices (B) and (C). Because the y-values grow exponentially, the graph will be a curve rather than a straight line. Eliminate choice (A). Choice (D) is correct.

Part II: Calculator Allowed

24. A.

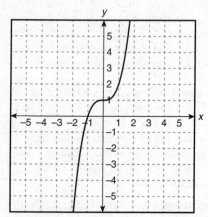

Calculate a couple of points for positive x-values to get coordinate pairs: (1,2), (2,9), (3, 28), (4,65). Then do the same for some negative x-values (−1,0), (−2,−7), (−3,−26), (−4,−63). Graph those points and connect them.

25. A. $600 Find 24% of $2500. $2500 × 0.24 = $600. You could estimate this answer by thinking 24% is

roughly $\frac{1}{4}$, and choice (A) is closest to one-fourth of the Whitman's budget.

26. D. $j(x) = x^2 − 3x − 2$ The interval between values of x in the table is 1 and the interval between values of $f(x)$ is 3, so the slope of $f(x)$, which is also the coefficient of x in $f(x)$, is 3. Substitute known values for $f(x)$ and x to find the missing value which, for a linear equation, will be the y-intercept.
$4 = 3(2) + b$
$4 = 6 + b$
$b = −2$
You can find the y-intercept of any of the answer choices by setting $x = 0$. Only choice (D) results in an intercept of −2.

27. 39 The two given legs of triangle A are 3 times the length of the two legs in triangle B. Because the triangles are similar, the hypotenuse of triangle A will be three times the length of the hypotenuse of triangle B:
$3 × 13 = 39$.

28. 240 Use the percent formula, $\% = \frac{\text{part}}{\text{whole}} × 100\%$. You are given the part and the percent, and are solving for the whole.

$$5\% = \frac{12}{x} × 100\%$$

$$x = \frac{12 × 100\%}{5\%}$$

$$x = 12 × 20 = 240$$

29. A. $214.40 Substitute 4 for b and 3 for n into the function. Then solve the equation.
$C = \$25.60(4) + \$14(4)(3 − 1)$
$= \$102.40 + \$112.00$
$= \$214.40$

30. 514 To find the volume of a cone, use the formula from the formula sheet: $V = \frac{1}{3}\pi r^2 h$. Plug in values from the question stem and the approximate value of pi:
$V = \frac{1}{3}\pi(6.4)^2(12)$
$V = \frac{1}{3}(3.14)(40.96)(12) \approx 514$.

31. B.

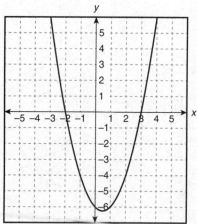

If $x = 0$, then $y = -6$. This fact alone allows you to eliminate answer choices (C) and (D). In order to find the values of x when $y = 0$, set up the quadratic equation $x^2 - x - 6 = 0$. This factors to $(x - 3)(x + 2) = 0$, so when $y = 0$, x is either 3 or –2. Only the graph in answer choice (B) has these intercepts.

32.

Domain (x-values)	Range (y-values)
–1	8
3	–4
4	–2

A certain amount of trial and error is needed to complete this task. Choose a number as a possible domain (x) value and calculate the range (y). If there is a matching range value in the set, then enter the range and domain in the table. If there is no match, continue the trial and error process.

For instance, you could start by choosing –4 as a possible value for the domain:

$y = (-4)^2 - 5(-4) + 2$

$y = 16 + 20 + 2 = 38$

However, 38 is not a value contained in the set, so (–4) must be not a number in the domain.

Since –4 produced a number that's so much larger than anything in the set, pick a number with a much smaller absolute value to try next. A good candidate is –1.

$y = (-1)^2 - 5(-1) + 2 = 8$

Perform similar calculations with the other values in the set until you've filled in the table.

33. C. **is equal to** When data falls into a normal distribution, the mean and median of that data are the same value.

34. B. $a = 3; c = 5$ Since this is a right triangle, start by using trigonometry to find the length of side a or side c (you can start with either one). To start by finding c (the hypotenuse), use the cosine function:

$\cos 37 = \dfrac{4}{c}$.

Use your calculator to find the value of cos 37, which is approximately 0.8. (It's fine to round because the question says "approximately.")

$0.8 = \dfrac{4}{c}$

$0.8c = 4$

$c = 5$

Now, at this point, you *could* use more trigonometric relationships to find the length of side a. For example, $\tan 37 = \frac{a}{4}$. However, this step is not necessary. As soon as you know that one leg of the triangle has length 4 and that the hypotenuse has length approximately 5, you know that the triangle roughly displays the ratio

3:4:5 (a ratio sometimes displayed by right triangles; see page 382). So the length of side a is approximately 3, and no further calculations are required.

35. 4 The minimum of this function occurs at $x = 0$. Plugging that into the equation gives $2(0)^2 + 4 = 2(0) + 4 = 0 + 4 = 4$.

36. $x = 1.8$ Use the correct order of operations. Multiply to eliminate parentheses:

$x + 8 - 4x + 4 = 2x + 3$

Combine like terms:

$-3x + 12 = 2x + 3$

Add $3x$ to both sides:

$12 = 5x + 3$

Subtract 3 from both sides:

$9 = 5x$

Divide both sides by 5:

$x = \frac{9}{5} = 1.8$

37.

Parameter	# of occurrences
Global Minimums	2
Global Maximums	0
Inflection Points	3
x-intercepts	4
y-intercepts	1

To answer this question, set up a table of values to roughly determine the graph's behavior. Use a calculator to save time.

For the equation $y = x^4 - 5x^2 + 3$:

x	y
–3	–33
–2	
–1	
0	
1	
2	
3	

Here's an example of how you would use the TI-30XS MultiView™ calculator to find one of those values. To find the value of y when $x = 2$:

② △ ④ ▶ ⊖ ⑤ ⊗ ② x^2 ⊕ ③

Press *enter* to see the answer, –1. Keep in mind that if you are inputting a negative value for x, you must use parentheses in order to raise it to an exponent. To calculate the value of y when $x = -3$:

((⊖ ③) △ ④ ▶ ⊖ ⑤ ⊗ ((⊖ ③) x^2 ⊕ ③

Press *enter* to see the answer, 39. You could also calculate each term separately and then add them, if you prefer.

A graph of the function is below (note the difference in scale on the x- and y-axes):

Your graph did not need to be this polished in order to be helpful. A rough sketch is enough to tell you that the value of y increases without limit whenever $|x|$ is greater than or equal to roughly 1.5 (the exact value doesn't matter for this question). The value of y decreased in value when $0 \le |x| \le$ roughly 1.5. Thus, there is no global maximum, since both "arms" travel upward indefinitely. There are two global minimums: at roughly -1.5 and $+1.5$. The graph has three inflection points—that is, points where the slope goes from negative to positive or vice versa. These points come at roughly -1.5, 0, and roughly $+1.5$. The graph crosses the x-axis four times and the y-axis once.

38. D. 28% Probability is the ratio of the number of favorable outcomes to the number of possible outcomes. Add up the numbers of marbles to find out how many marbles are in the bag. $12 + 3 + 6 + 4 = 25$. Therefore, 25 is the number of possible outcomes. 7 marbles are either blue or yellow. 7 is the number of favorable outcomes. $\frac{7}{25} \times \frac{4}{4} = \frac{28}{100}$, or 28%.

39. C.

Rotating the shape around the y-axis will create a uniform solid in the shape of a cone.

40. 628 To find the volume of a cylinder, use the formula $V = \pi r^2 h$. In this case, the radius is 5 and the height is 8. Plugging the equation into a calculator yields $V = \pi \times 5^2 \times 8 \approx 628.3$. Round to the nearest unit. If you use 3.14 for pi, the answer to this problem will be the same: $3.14 \times 5^2 \times 8 = 628$.

41. D. 0.8 g This question gives you the density of helium in grams per cubic centimeter and asks you

to calculate the quantity of helium within a specific balloon. To do this, first calculate how big the balloon is—that is, the balloon's volume. Use the formula for the volume of a sphere:

$$V = \frac{4}{3}\pi r^3$$

$$V = \frac{4}{3}\pi (10)^3$$

$$V = \frac{4}{3}\pi (1,000)$$

Since the question tells you to use 3.14 for pi, plug in that value and calculate:

$$V = \frac{4}{3}(3.14)(1,000) \approx 4,187$$ (Since the question stems says "approximately," you can round to save time.) The balloon has a volume of 4,187 cm³. Now multiply that by the given density of helium:
$4,187$ cm³ $\times$ 0.0002 g/cm³ $= 0.8374$ g
Rounding that result to the nearest tenth produces answer choice (D).

42. A. survey A survey is a relatively low-cost way to research the correlation between two factors. An experiment (choice (B)) would not be appropriate here: In an experiment, a researcher controls the independent variable. In this case, that would mean the researcher would be assigning income levels to households, but that isn't practical or realistic. Theoretical modeling (choice (C)) is not a statistical technique at all. Now, it would be possible for a researcher to monitor television viewing habits through some type of technological device or by having research workers actually observe what viewers do. This would be an observational study (choice (D)). However, the question stem tells you that the researcher does not have the resources to do this.

43.

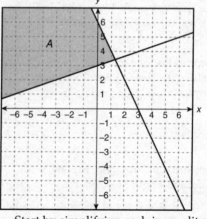

Start by simplifying each inequality in turn:
$2x + y \le 6$
$y \le 6 - 2x$
Or, in point-slope form:
$y \le -2x + 6$

If that were an equation $(y = -2x + 6)$, it would be the line that slopes from the top middle to the lower right-hand corner of the graph. Because y is less than or equal to the values along that line, the area to the left of it would be shaded:

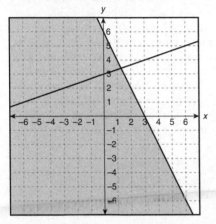

Now simplify the second inequality:
$3y - 9 \geq x$
$3y \geq x + 9$
$y \geq (\frac{x}{3}) + 3$

If that were the equation $y = (\frac{x}{3}) + 3$, the line that travels from the left-hand edge of the graph to the upper right-hand corner would represent it. Because the value of y is greater than or equal to the values along that line, the area above it should be shaded:

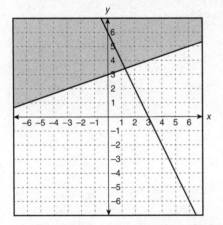

The area that represents the solution set to both inequalities is the area where those half-planes overlap—that is, the upper left-hand portion.

44. 2 Absolute change refers to the difference, either positive or negative, between two numbers. Over the three elections listed, party x gained 2 seats, lost 6 seats, and then regained 2 seats. That's a net loss of 2.

45. Place a dot on the graph as shown:

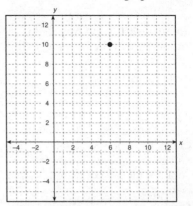

You can solve either by graphing the lines or by substitution. To solve by substitution, use the first equation to substitute the value of y in the second equation:
$2(x + 4) + 4x = 44$
$2x + 8 + 4x = 44$
$6x + 8 = 44$
$6x = 36$
$x = 6$

Now use that value of x to find the value of y using the first equation:
$y = 6 + 4$
$y = 10$

46. D. 5.16 The tangent of an angle can be found by determining the value of $\frac{\text{sine}}{\text{cosine}}$. This question asks you to find the cotangent, which is the reciprocal of the tangent: $\frac{\text{cosine}}{\text{sine}}$. Set up the fraction and then divide: $\frac{0.98}{0.19} = 5.16$.

47.

$157	$- y$	=	$101	$+ y$

Imtaez had $101 + y$ remaining after paying y to the runner. The equation would be $157 - y = 101 + y$.

48. C. $a = \frac{-b}{b - 1}$ Algebraic equations are solved by manipulating the equations so that the desired term is isolated on one side of the equation. Often you will need to take several steps to do this; each step involves starting with the results of the prior step and then performing the same operation on both sides of the equation.
$(a - b) \times (\frac{ab}{a - b}) = 1(a - b)$
$ab = a - b$
Since you are told to solve for a, move all terms involving a to one side of the equation by subtracting a from both sides.

$ab - a = a - b - a$

$ab - a = -b$

Now look for a way to isolate a. A good way to do this would be to factor the a out of the left-hand side of the equation.

$a(b - 1) = -b$

$a = \dfrac{-b}{b - 1}$

49. C. 6–9 minutes You would expect the worker's rate of progress to slow somewhat when he is distracted. Since the slope of the graph represents square feet painted per minute, look for the area of the graph that has the least steep slope.

50. B. $\pi + 4$ Adding 4 to the number pi would not change the infinite digits that extend to the right of the decimal place in pi. Choice (A) is equal to 0, which is not irrational (that is, zero is *rational*). Choice (C) produces a decimal that continues indefinitely (0.1111111 . . .) but those digits display a pattern. Choice (C) can also be expressed as a fraction with integers on top and bottom: $\frac{1}{9}$. Thus, it does not fit the definition of *irrational* given in the question. Choice (D) is equal to 2, which is a rational number.

51. A.

Rotating the shape to view the top, you would see a rectangle. If a cross section is cut and the top half removed, the new top would be a slightly larger rectangle.

52. B. $R_2 = \dfrac{R \times R_1}{R_1 - R}$ Translate the original expression so that R_2 is isolated on one side of the equation.

Start by getting rid of the fractions. The shortest way to do this is to multiply each term by $(R_1)(R_2)(R)$ so that the fractions are eliminated. If you aren't sure why that works, think about it this way: The right-hand side of the formula needs to become one fraction with a common denominator. Since you don't know the values of any of the variables, you'll have to simply use R_1R_2 as the common denominator. Multiply both fractions by R_1R_2—but you can't perform an operation to just one side of an equation. You'll have to multiply both sides by R_1R_2:

$$(R_1R_2)\frac{1}{R} = (R_1R_2)(\frac{1}{R_1} + \frac{1}{R_2})$$

$$\frac{R_1R_2}{R} = \frac{R_1R_2}{R_1} + \frac{R_1R_2}{R_2}$$

$$\frac{R_1R_2}{R} = R_2 + R_1$$

Now, in order to get rid of the fraction on the left-hand side, you'll have to multiply both sides by R.

$R_1R_2 = RR_2 + RR_1$

Subtract RR_2 from both sides to get all terms with R_2 on one side.

$R_1R_2 - RR_2 = RR_1$

Factor out R_2 on the left side of the equation.

$R_2(R_1 - R) = RR_1$

Divide both sides by $(R_1 - R)$.

$$R_2 = \frac{R \times R_1}{R_1 - R}$$

Mathematics Practice Test Evaluation Charts

Circle the numbers of the questions that you answered correctly and then total them in the last column of each row.

Content Area	Question Numbers	Number Correct/Total
Number and Quantity: Problem Solving; Decimals and Fractions; Ratio, Proportion, and Percent Pages 184–265	21, 22, 28, 44, 50	____ out of 5
Statistics and Probability Pages 266–305	1, 14, 25, 33, 38, 42	____ out of 6
Algebraic Expressions Pages 306–327	2, 4, 5, 6, 20, 48	____ out of 6
Functions Pages 328–373	8, 10, 11, 12, 13, 17, 18, 23, 24, 26, 29, 31, 32, 35, 36, 37, 43, 45, 47, 49	____ out of 20
Geometry Pages 374–417	3, 7, 9, 15, 16, 19, 27, 30, 34, 39, 40, 41, 46, 51, 52	____ out of 15
Total points		____ **out of 52**

If you do not have time to review the entire *Mathematics* unit, you may want to review the sections that need the most work.

Using the points total from the bottom right hand corner of the table above, use the information below to assess your readiness to take the TASC test.

If your points total was . . .	then you are . . .	Kaplan recommends
21–52	very likely to pass the TASC Mathematics test	that you do a relatively brief, high-level review of all math concepts, especially ones you've struggled with, before test day.
19–20	fairly likely to pass the TASC Mathematics test	that you give yourself a few more days or weeks to do a final comprehensive review of math material before testing.
16–18	somewhat likely to pass the TASC Mathematics test	that you set a goal date by which you would like to complete a final review of the material. As you do that review, focus on the material you have struggled with the most.
0–15	unlikely to pass the TASC Mathematics test	that you do an in-depth review of the subject matter. Be sure to look for patterns among the questions you got wrong, and study those topics in greater depth.

SOCIAL STUDIES PRACTICE TEST ANSWERS AND EXPLANATIONS

1. **D. The United States had an unfavorable balance of trade in merchandise during the 2000s.** According to the passage, the balance of trade is the difference between exports and imports. When imports are greater than exports, the balance of trade is unfavorable. Since the graph shows that imports consistently exceeded exports during the 2000s, you can conclude that the balance of trade in merchandise was unfavorable during the decade.

2. **D. maintaining the condition of streets** You might have found process of elimination to be a helpful strategy on this question. The federal government and some states impose income tax on individuals. The federal government frequently provides money to state and local governments to aid in disaster relief, highway creation, and other projects. Only choice (D), maintaining the condition of streets, is a responsibility solely of local government.

3. **D. More people identified as independents than as Democrats, and more identified as Democrats than as Republicans.** This statement was true for all months represented in the chart. Choice (A) overstates the numerical gap between independents and Republicans. Choice (B) might have looked tempting if you misread "10 percent more" as "10 percentage points more." Choice (C) is unsupported as well. While it's true that the three columns total to 98 percent for most months, you cannot draw an inference about the remaining 2 percent.

4. **a loose construction of the Constitution; an expansion of the federal government's power; an expansion of government bureaucracy** The Court interpreted Congress's constitutional taxing power very broadly, and in doing so it employed a "loose construction" of the Constitution. A "strict construction" would usually result in limiting the federal government's power. The federal government's influence expanded greatly in the New Deal era, including through the SSA. Finally, because Social Security programs require a large organization to run them, the federal government's so-called "fourth branch," or bureaucratic arm, expanded as a result of the SSA surviving.

5. **D. More legitimate companies would allow their shares to be traded on the stock market.** Large-scale fraud in the stock market would not benefit the companies whose shares are bought and sold on the stock market. Just the opposite: large-scale fraud would cause people to stop trusting the stock market and stop trading (as choice (A) reflects), and that means companies would also lose money on the stock market.

6. **lower income tax and sales tax revenue for federal, state, and local governments; budget cuts to government programs because of decreased tax revenue; rising crime rates in areas of high unemployment; economic slowdown as people purchase fewer goods and services; lost opportunity as the unemployed spend time not building skills as part of a job** All of the factors listed are consequences of unemployment, which negatively impacts individuals, government services, and communities.

7. **D. The CPI grew in all but one of the years represented in the table.** Look at the second column, which lists the actual CPI. In each year except for 2009, the CPI was higher than the year before. Choice (A) is unsupported because the CPI grew in four of the five years (not three of them). Choice (B) is incorrect because the table contains no information about what caused changes in the CPI. Choice (C) might have looked tempting if you were looking at the third column of the table, but that third column represents not the CPI itself but the percent of change over the previous year.

8. **C. Many people moved to cities to be near factory jobs.** The passage states that many people left farms to work in factories. You can infer that many of them moved from rural areas, where farms are located, to urban areas, where factories are often located. The other choices are not supported by the facts given.

9. **B. Both valued a stable political framework for society.** The paragraph indicates that this was one thing the ancient Chinese and the ancient Greeks had in common.

10. **C. The war created a huge demand for military equipment and supplies.** The chart shows that there was a substantial increase in manufacturing output between 1939 (when World War II began in Europe) and 1941. Even though the United States did not enter the war until late 1941, industry had already geared up to sell equipment and supplies to the Allies in Europe.

11. **B. First World War** The events listed include some factors that led up to the first world-wide war (that is, World War I) and some of the consequences of that war.

12. **B. problems with consistently enforcing the Sherman Antitrust Act led to further legislation to prevent monopolies** In the passage, the author explains the intention behind the Sherman Antitrust Act: to make monopolies illegal. He goes on to outline the limitations of the act, arguing that its broad language rendered it insufficient to solve the problems created by monopolies. He concludes the paragraph by telling how Congress responded to the problems in the Sherman Antitrust Act by passing additional laws to control monopolistic practices.

13. **B. The dangers of climate change are more significant than the possible benefits.** The author states that climate change may lead to benefits such as longer growing seasons but that "the hazards far outweigh any potential advantages." Choices (A) and (D) are contradicted by the passage. The author does not address choice (C).

14. **D. Soylent green or not so green: Are biofuels good or bad for us and the planet?** The question explains that proponents of biofuels believe they would be good for the planet, and by extension, humans. Opponents of biofuels believe they would be bad for humans and for the planet. Thus, the central question in the debate over biofuels is whether they are good for humans and for the environment.

15. D. A consumer obtains prices from several dealers and researches specifications, features, and consumer reviews before buying a new automobile. By obtaining prices from multiple dealers and thoroughly understanding the features and value of the automobile, the consumer is clearly acting rationally to optimize her own economic interest. Shopping at the same store out of loyalty to a friend (choice (A)) may be praiseworthy, but the consumer does not know that she is receiving the best prices available in the marketplace. The manufacturer that charges higher prices (choice (B)) is not acting rationally. Its sales will suffer when consumers pay a lower price to get the same product from a competitor. Consumers who act rationally disregard celebrity endorsements (choice (C)) and buy products based on price and quality.

16.

Reasons why Joe might WANT to vote for the third-party candidate	Reasons why Joe might NOT WANT to vote for the third-party candidate
If many people support a third-party candidate, that can influence what issues the major parties support, because the major parties will want to win over those voters.	By supporting a third-party candidate, Joe may miss an opportunity to vote for the major-party candidate he likes best. Then the major-party candidate he most dislikes will be more likely to win.
By supporting a third-party candidate, Joe can voice his true opinion, and he may find this satisfying regardless of the outcome.	The direction of national policy is often shaped by which of the major parties took the most seats in an election. By voting for a third-party candidate, Joe will have no influence on this dynamic.

There are benefits and drawbacks to voting for a third-party candidate. Because third-party candidates are unlikely to win, some people think that voting for a third-party candidate is unwise. For example, Joe may think one of the major-party candidates is preferable to the other and that one of the major parties has a platform that's better than the other major party. But by voting for a third-party candidate, Joe would not immediately affect which of the major-party candidates wins or which of the major parties gains power. However, some people would say that Joe should still vote for his preferred third-party candidate. For one thing, if a third-party candidate generates enough support, this will gain the attention of the major parties. One or more of the major parties may decide that they would like to gain those votes, and they may adjust their platforms to try to appeal to the people who voted for the third-party candidate. Also, some would say that voting your true opinions is always valuable, either for the sake of personal satisfaction or for the sake of registering an objection to the major parties' platforms.

17. A. The Declaration of Independence, which explained why the colonies broke away from Great Britain The acts of Parliament listed in the chart were grievances used to justify declaring independence.

18. B. They intended the new government to be defined and limited by the Constitution. The colonists' experience with English rule had left a bad taste in their mouths. The English constitution is not a single document but rather a collection of documents and traditions, and it can be changed by an act of Parliament. The framers of the U.S. Constitution intended for it to be more rigid—that is, they intended for it to definitively outline the limits of government and to be very difficult to change.

19. D. The British withdrew from the Indian subcontinent, which was then divided into India and Pakistan. A quick look at the answer choices for this question show that they all mention Britain, so look back to the passage for clues about Britain. The passage mentions that World War II left Great Britain impoverished, so you can assume that it was weaker after the war. Now look at the answer choices for something that would seem to follow from this fact. Answer choice (D) is the only fit. While there were many factors, evolving over many years, that led to British withdrawal from India, the condition of Britain after World War II was one of those factors. All of the other answer choices suggest British strength; in fact, they all happened prior to World War II.

20. the reduction of French imperialism; the splitting of one nation into two; tension between communist and democratic powers The French occupied Vietnam from the 19th century until they were eventually driven out as part of the Vietnam War. For a time during the Vietnam War, the nation was split into two: the communist North and the capitalist South. The United States became involved in the war in an effort to drive back the expansion of communism.

21. C. Industrialization and urbanization caused many changes in family life in the late 1800s. This covers the main points of the passage, which discusses the impact of industrialization and urbanization on the American family. The other choices are all supporting details.

22. B. Whites wanted to take over Indian lands in the eastern states. The graphic shows the Indians being moved away from eastern states to Kansas and Oklahoma. The question asks about "forcible" relocation, so the correct answer can't be about what Indians wanted.

23. C. the upholding of individual rights that government cannot violate The chart suggests that, to begin with, the English king had unlimited power. The Magna Carta began the process of limiting the king's power and granting some power to other components of society. By the time the English Bill of Rights was enacted in 1688, the idea had evolved that the king served at the pleasure of the people and could not violate the people's rights. Consent of the governed and individual rights are important ideas in systems of limited government, including ours.

24. D. the English Bill of Rights The English Bill of Rights tied the king's right to rule to the consent of the people's representatives, and the colonists' major grievance was taxation without representation.

The colonists felt they should be granted the same representation and rights as other British citizens, which were listed in the English Bill of Rights.

25. **D. Slavery destroyed the culture of the slaves, diminishing their self-respect.** According to the paragraph, this is an opinion, or belief, held by some historians. The other choices are all facts stated in the paragraph.

26. **D. The market price would go up.** When the supply decreases and demand stays the same, the market price increases. The same number of people want to buy fewer apples, so the people will generally be willing to pay more for the apples.

27. **D. Alabama** Iowa and Delaware never seceded, so they never belonged to the Confederacy. Alabama seceded before the Battle of Fort Sumter, so it belonged to the Confederacy both before and after the Battle of Fort Sumter. North Carolina also belonged to the Confederacy, but it didn't secede until after the Battle of Fort Sumter.

28. **B. The volume and variety of federal cases were too great for a single court to handle.** It would be impractical to have just one court handling all cases; the workload would be too great.

29. **A. the Supreme Court of the United States** According to the passage, cases are appealed to higher level courts; according to the diagram, the Supreme Court is the highest court of appeal.

30. **C. *Brown v. Board of Education*, 1954, which outlawed segregation in schools** Segregation of public schools was a key feature of the Jim Crow system. In 1954, the Supreme Court ruled that this system was illegal. In *Plessy v. Ferguson* (the case mentioned in choice (B)), the Court ruled that "separate but equal" facilities satisfied the Fourteenth Amendment. The Court in 1954 reversed itself. The 1954 decision said that the *Plessy* decision was illogical and that "separate educational facilities are inherently unequal."

31. **the right of citizens to move about freely; a city's desire to enable police to maintain order** Vaguely worded vagrancy laws are usually intended to allow police to maintain order and prevent undesirable activities. However, the enforcement of these laws is sometimes arbitrary and sometimes driven by prejudice. The Supreme Court in this case weighed this desire for public order against the right of citizens to move about freely.

32.

Parliamentary System (such as the United Kingdom)	Presidential System (such as the United States)
The majority party in the legislature chooses the leaders of the new government after each election.	The head of government is elected by the people and is responsible to them.
The head of government is chosen by the legislature and is responsible to it.	The executive and legislative branches are separately elected and have separate powers.
The executive branch is overseen by the legislature.	

In a parliamentary system, the people elect legislators. Then, whatever party controls the legislature chooses the chief executive, who is also known as the head of government. (In many parliamentary systems, including the United Kingdom, that executive is called the *prime minister*.) Because that executive is chosen by the legislature, she is also responsible to it. By contrast, in a presidential system such as ours, the head of government (that is, the chief executive) is elected by the people and is usually called the *president*. The president is accountable chiefly to the people who elected him. This arrangement also means that the executive and legislative branches are separate: they must choose to work together since neither one is subordinate to the other. In our system, the executive and legislative branches have separate powers defined by the Constitution.

33. **D. federal courts** Early in our country's history, the Constitution was interpreted as giving federal courts enforcement power—that is, federal courts can strike down (that is, invalidate) laws that they interpret as violating people's constitutional rights. Federal courts can strike down both federal and state laws, as well as presidential orders and bureaucratic actions and rules.

34. **B. Farmers will shift some of their arable land from growing other crops to growing wheat. The increased wheat crop will reduce the market price of wheat. The reduced production of other crops will result in an increased price for those goods.** Arable land is a limited resource, so farmers will allocate that resource in a manner that will maximize their profits. Since the subsidy will increase the profit they receive for wheat, farmers will allocate more land to growing wheat. As a result, less land will be available for other crops, and their production will decrease. This shift in the supply curve will increase the market-clearing price of these other crops.

35. **A. Several factors make Haiti unique among Caribbean nations.** Most of the facts cited in the passage explain how Haiti differs from other nations. Choice (A) summarizes these facts. The other choices are details and fail to summarize the gist of the passage.

36. **less manufacturing industry than in many northern states; legal tolerance of slavery; an agrarian economy** The southern states that seceded tended to have economies built largely on agriculture, with a workforce composed of African slaves. The northern states had developed more manufacturing than had southern states. It is not true to say that southern states had no legislatures. The Republican Party was the party of Lincoln, and those who pushed for secession tended to be hostile to it. The "abolition" referred to in the final wrong answer choice means abolition of slavery, and southern lawmakers were largely opposed to abolition.

37. **D. Direct Democracy and Representative Democracy** The table's left column describes direct democracy, and

its right column describes representative democracy. Thus, choice (D) is the best title for the table.

38. **C. Constitution** The sentence describes the U.S. Constitution. The Declaration of Independence (A) claimed that the colonies were no longer under English rule but did not establish the structure of government. The Articles of Confederation (B) established an older system of government and are no longer in effect. The Magna Carta (D) is an English document.

39. **A. the Crusades** The Crusades were a series of Medieval conflicts in which Europeans invaded Middle Eastern cities.

40. **D. recession** A recession is a general slowdown in economic activity; the list in the box describes the various facets of a recession.

41. **C. the need for clean air and the need to earn an independent living** The passage describes a situation in which the very reasonable need of some people to make money and gain independence contributes to deforestation. The passage also describes how this deforestation lowers air quality.

42. **B. federalism** Madison's quote describes a division of powers between the national (or federal) government and the state governments. That division of powers is federalism.

43. **D. outlawing behavior such as drug use or robbery** Legislatures (such as Congress or state legislatures) write laws. Courts, such as the Supreme Court, may sometimes pass judgment about whether or not those laws are Constitutional, but courts do not write laws.

44. **A. the First Amendment, which protects the right of free speech** The last sentence of the passage states that the Court decided that the law restricted the expression of political ideas—in other words, that it restricted speech.

45.

Generally true of entrepreneurship	Generally not true of entrepreneurship
Marketing is key to the success of a new business.	Excess cash is generated during the growth phase of a new business.
Many new businesses fail within a few years.	Entrepreneurs must understand computer programming.
New businesses account for a significant number of new hires.	Government regulations do not affect small businesses.

Marketing is very important to a new business. Customers must be aware of the products or services offered by a new business and must believe that purchasing from the entrepreneur's company offers them value. According to the U.S. Bureau of Labor Statistics, just over half of new businesses fail within six years. Some estimates state that small businesses are responsible for up to 65 percent of net new jobs in the United States.

The growth phase is often when businesses need the greatest cash inflow in order to finance additional capital investments, new hires, and inventories of both raw materials and finished goods. Most start-up businesses can choose from a variety of "off the shelf" applications to help manage the various facets of their companies. While businesses with just a few employees are exempt from some federal and state workplace regulations, there are myriad regulations regarding taxes, safety, employment practices, environmental protection, and other practices that apply to all businesses. Such regulations not only compel compliance, but also may have stringent reporting requirements as well.

46. **A. George is offended by a joke made by a co-worker and complains to his manager about it.** While many employers have policies prohibiting offensive jokes, the National Labor Relations Act does not cover that activity. It does cover employees discussing unions (B), joining unions (C), and striking (D).

47. **B. People in Damascus were aware of religions practiced elsewhere.** If Damascus was on the Silk Road, and traders from Europe, Africa, China, and other parts of the world passed through Damascus, then it is highly likely that the citizens of Damascus learned a little about those traders' cultures and religions. None of the other choices are supported by the facts given.

Social Studies Practice Test Evaluation Charts

Questions 1–34

Circle the numbers of the questions that you got correct and then total them in the last column of each row.

Content Area	Question Numbers	Number Correct/Total
U.S. History Pages 486–499	10, 12, 17, 18, 21, 22, 24, 25, 27, 30, 36	____ out of 11
Civics and Government Pages 500–517	2, 3, 4, 16, 23, 28, 29, 31, 32, 33, 37, 38, 42, 43, 44	____ out of 15
World History Online Chapter	8, 9, 11, 19, 20, 35, 39, 47	____ out of 8
Economics Online Chapter	1, 5, 6, 7, 15, 26, 34, 40, 45, 46	____ out of 10
Geography Online chapter	13, 14, 41	____ out of 3
Total points		**____ out of 47**

Most of the social studies questions in this practice test also test one of the Social Studies skills discussed on pages 468–485. For the sake of simplicity and readability, those skills have been omitted from this chart. However, if you missed several questions on the Social Studies Practice Test, be sure to review not only the relevant content area but also the chapter on Social Studies Skills.

If you do not have time to review the entire *Social Studies* unit, you may want to review the sections that need the most work.

Using the points total from the bottom right hand corner of the table above, use the information below to assess your readiness to take the TASC test.

If your points total was . . .	then you are . . .	Kaplan recommends
21–47	very likely to pass the TASC Social Studies test	that you do a relatively brief, high-level review of all social studies concepts, especially ones you've struggled with, before test day.
19–20	fairly likely to pass the TASC Social Studies test	that you give yourself a few more days or weeks to do a final comprehensive review of social studies material before testing.
15–18	somewhat likely to pass the TASC Social Studies test	that you set a goal date by which you would like to complete a final review of the material. As you do that review, focus on the material you have struggled with the most.
0–14	unlikely to pass the TASC Social Studies test	that you do an in-depth review of the subject matter. Be sure to look for patterns among the questions you got wrong, and study those topics in greater depth.

SCIENCE PRACTICE TEST ANSWERS AND EXPLANATIONS

1. **A. lift** As the diagram shows and the paragraph implies, the wing's weight and the opposing force of the air under it result in an upward force called *lift*.

2. **A. RNA polymerase unwinds the strands of DNA, starting at the beginning of a gene, and uses one strand of the DNA as a template to create a complementary copy of the gene, called messenger RNA. Then this mRNA is translated into proteins.** You may not have been familiar with all the details of how RNA works, but as long as you know the basics, this question is conquerable. Something called *messenger RNA* gets information from DNA, records that information on bits called *codons*, and uses it to create amino acids (the building blocks of proteins). With that in mind, look at the answer choices. Choice (A) goes into greater detail, but its broad strokes are a match. Choice (A) is therefore correct. If you weren't sure, you could have used some process of elimination on the other choices. Choice (B) suggests that there's something called *messenger DNA* that does the building of proteins—that's backwards. Choice (C) suggests that messenger RNA makes proteins by twisting DNA together. That is incorrect: DNA contains instructions for building proteins but isn't itself twisted together to form them. Choice (D) seems to take the idea of "messenger" too literally, by suggesting that RNA goes running around all over the body. Choice (D) is also wrong because it suggests that "copies" of the DNA themselves become proteins. Again, DNA doesn't make protein; rather, it contains instructions for doing so.

3. **B. 17** If the mean is 23 degrees, then the sum of all six angle measurements must be $23 \times 6 = 138$ degrees. Since the five given angles add up to 121 degrees, the sixth angle must make up the difference, or $138 - 121 = 17$ degrees.

4. **B. the air and rainwater in the soil** According to the diagram, nitrogen-fixing bacteria take nitrogen from both the air and rain found in soil.

5. **B. compost with plant and animal wastes** According to the diagram, plant and animal waste contains nitrogen compounds that decomposers, including nitrite bacteria and nitrate bacteria, break down. In this way, composting with plant and animal wastes results in the addition of usable forms of nitrogen to the soil. So composting with organic waste (plant and animal materials) would be an alternative to synthetic fertilizers.

6. **D. For the three compounds shown, solubility increases as temperature increases.** The graph shows all three substances having increased solubility as the temperature rises from 0°C to 50°C. None of the other statements is supported by information in the graph.

7. **C. understanding how dead skin is continuously replaced** The question stem tells you that mitosis is the process by which cells divide, creating identical daughter cells. That tells you to look for an answer choice in which cells are replaced by identical cells. Answer choice (C) describes just that kind of situation.

8. The equation that represents cellular respiration is as follows:
   [food molecule, such as glucose] $C_6H_{12}O_6 + 6O_2$ →
   $6H_2O + 6CO_2 + ATP$
   (ATP (adenosine triphosphate) is a nucleotide that the body uses to store energy for use in cells.)

Inputs?	Outputs?
☑ glucose	☐ glucose
☐ carbon dioxide	☑ carbon dioxide
☐ water	☑ water
☑ oxygen	☐ oxygen

9. **A. the cracking of granite from the expansion of freezing water** This is an example of physical weathering because it involves changes of temperature causing physical effects on rock. Choice (C) is not an example of weathering because transport is involved.

10. **C. how special fluids keep insects alive during subfreezing weather** Understanding how insects can survive freezing may be a key to finding a way to freeze organs without destroying them.

11. **C. The Big Bang would have created mass that would exert gravity, eventually slowing the expansion of the universe.** The Big Bang theory states that at the beginning of the universe, all matter and energy was compressed in an extremely small space and expanded explosively outward. Evidence that corresponds to this theory includes the fact that galaxies are moving away from each other (shown by a shift in the wavelength of their emitted light toward the red end of the spectrum, or red shift); galaxies do all move away from each other; and microwave radiation permeates the cosmic background. Unanswered questions include why the expansion of the universe is *speeding up* (whereas the Big Bang theory would have predicted that the expansion of the universe would slow) and what caused the Big Bang to occur in the first place.

12. **C. Hydrogen peroxide is decomposing into water and oxygen.** The chemical reaction begins on the left hand side of the equation, which represents two hydrogen peroxide molecules. Thus, it is incorrect to say that hydrogen peroxide is being made (as in choices (A) or (D)). Rather, hydrogen peroxide is decomposing, or breaking up, into two substances. What remains after the chemical reaction is written on the right hand side of the equation. The question stem explains that water is composed of two hydrogen atoms and an oxygen atom, so the results of the reaction are water and O_2, which you can infer represents oxygen. Choice (B) is incomplete and (C) is correct.

13. **A. Mercury and bromine are liquids at room temperature.** Room temperature is about 70°F. The chart indicates that both mercury and bromine are liquids at that temperature: each has a melting point—the

temperature at which it becomes a liquid—well below room temperature. Also, each has a boiling point—the temperature at which it goes from liquid to gas—well above room temperature.

14. **D. 8 m/s** When no external force acts upon a system, the momentum of objects in that system is conserved. Just prior to the collision, the total momentum is that of the larger mass. The formula for momentum is $p = mv$, so the initial momentum is $1 \times 5 = 5$ kg m/s. After the collision, the momentum of the larger mass is $1 \times 1 = 1$ kg m/s. Since momentum is conserved, the momentum of the smaller object must be $5 - 1 = 4$ kg m/s. Rearrange the formula so that $v = \dfrac{p}{m} = \dfrac{4}{0.5} = 8$ m/s.

15. **B. The student should have used books of the same height for all of the ramps.** The height of the ramp affects how far the ball rolls. So the height of the ramp should be a controlled variable in this experiment. By using one ramp that is not as high as the others, the student is introducing a second variable into the experiment, which makes his data invalid for the ramp that is lower than the others.

16. **D. The dog has canines and the sheep does not.** If you compare the two diagrams, you will see that the sheep does not have any canines; instead the sheep has a large gap where the canines would be.

17. **C. The five largest asteroids are all farther from the sun than Earth is.** According to the chart, Earth's distance from the sun is set at 1, so any value greater than 1 indicates that the asteroid is farther from the sun than Earth is. All the asteroids have distance values of 2 or greater, so they are all farther from the sun than Earth is.

18. **C. less than** If all the lobsters weighed the maximum of 9 lbs, the 220 million pounds of lobster would still account for more than 20 million individual animals. Two blue lobsters out of 20 million lobsters is substantially less likely than the estimated 1 in 2 million occurrence of the blue mutation.

19. **A. Pressure builds up inside the magma chamber and vent.** If you examine the diagram, you will see that hot magma wells up into the volcano's cone. You need to infer that when the pressure builds up sufficiently, the volcano explodes, or erupts. None of the other events described would cause a violent explosion from the inside of the volcano.

20. **B. when food is digested, as when an enzyme in saliva called ptyalin breaks down starch into sugars without itself changing** The catalyst is the enzyme ptyalin; you can identify ptyalin as the catalyst, because it aids the chemical reaction of digestion but itself remains unchanged after the reaction. None of the other reactions include a substance that remains unchanged.

21. **A. 1,500 N** Newton's second law states that $F = ma$, or force equals mass multiplied by acceleration. If the velocity increases by 20 m/s in 5 seconds, then you can write that as a rate of acceleration: $\dfrac{20\,\frac{m}{s}}{(5\ s)} = 4$ m/s^2. Therefore,

the total force acting on the automobile is 4 m/s$^2 \times$ 1,500 kg = 6,000 N. However, the question tells you that the engine is exerting 7,500 N of force to move the car forward. That's more than 6,000 N, so there must be some force or forces acting against the car's forward motion. (Examples might be friction or air resistance, but what those forces are don't matter for this question.) The resisting force acts in the opposite direction to reduce the 7,500 N applied by the engine to a net of 6,000 N, and 7,500 N – 6,000 N = 1,500 N.

22. **B. mosquitoes** The mosquito population increases by 100% over the 5-year observation period. The fox population declines by 15%, and the swift population declines by 45%.

23. **B. Predators of the most affected species are a prey species for cats.** The mosquito population is most likely increasing because a species that eats mosquitoes is being eaten by the cats. Specifically, one can hypothesize that the reduction in the number of swifts, which are insect-eating birds, is allowing the mosquito population to burgeon.

24. **B. Both involve effort applied with circular motion.** The diagrams show that the effort applied to each of these machines is circular.

25. **A. During an ice age, temperatures drop and ice covers vast areas of Earth.** According to the passage, scientists aren't sure what causes ice ages. Choices (B), (C), and (D) each offer a different hypothesis for what causes an ice age. By contrast, choice (A) is an objective fact.

26. **D. The arrangement of the carbon, hydrogen, and oxygen atoms in the two hydrocarbons is different.** Although ether and ethanol both have the same number of carbon, hydrogen, and oxygen atoms, the different arrangements of atoms in each compound results in two substances with different properties.

27. **A. lightning** The passage states that thunderstorms, which often generate lightning, occur in the troposphere, and that blue jets, a special kind of lightning, occur in the stratosphere.

28. **C. surficial; hydrothermal** The passage explains that surficial processes happen at the Earth's surface, so the action of wind would be one such process. Hydrothermal processes involve the movement of water underground, so the movement of seawater underground would be an example of a hydrothermal process.

29. **B. S and O** Elements on the left side of the periodic table generally have electrons in their outermost shell that are relatively easily released; those on the right have a strong attraction for electrons to complete their outer shell. Therefore, if an element from the left side combined with one from the right as in choices (C) and (D), the bond would be ionic rather than covalent. Ne is a noble gas with a complete outer shell; it would therefore not bond with Al (or any other element).

30. **C. NH$_3$** N is in group 15 and is 3 electrons short of a full outer shell; hydrogen has one electron. Therefore, they combine in a ratio of 1:3.

31. **D. Solution B had stronger intermolecular forces.** The rate at which a liquid evaporates relates to the forces between molecules, not to the forces holding atoms together within molecules. Therefore, answer choices (A) and (B) cannot be concluded from the results of the experiment. Weaker intermolecular forces make a liquid more susceptible to evaporation. Since more of the liquid in Beaker A evaporated, the liquid in Beaker B had stronger intermolecular forces.

32. **D. Jellyfish, which tolerate low-oxygen conditions, will increase in number.** The environmental conditions described will favor species that do not require much oxygen. While a lack of oxygen would likely hurt fish, there is no reason to think that fish populations would eventually stabilize (as choice (A) suggests). Choice (B) may be tempting because it refers to the death of algae, but the question doesn't suggest that algae would die out entirely. Thus, choice (B) is too extreme. Choice (C) is not supported because the question doesn't mention anything about bacteria that *produce* oxygen.

33.

Fossil fuels are burned to power automobiles.	b. biosphere
A saltwater crab molts, shedding its shell.	d. hydrosphere
A tree uses photosynthesis to produce energy.	a. atmosphere
A volcano erupts.	c. geosphere

Plants remove carbon, in the form of carbon dioxide, from the atmosphere during photosynthesis. Another way carbon leaves the atmosphere is by dissolving in water, creating acid rain. Carbon in the biosphere includes carbon in living and dead organisms; combustion, as when fossil fuels are burned for power or when a forest fire breaks out, releases this carbon into the atmosphere. Carbon in the geosphere is stored in Earth's lithosphere (crust and upper mantle). The geosphere releases carbon very slowly, but one way carbon leaves the geosphere is when a volcano erupts. The oceans are constantly exchanging carbon with the atmosphere.

34. **B. if the surface were irregular or rough** If a surface is rough, each light ray will hit the surface at a different angle. Therefore, light rays reflecting off of a rough surface travel in all different directions.

35. **B. Oxygen is one of the products of photosynthesis.** The products of the chemical reaction appear on the right hand side of the arrow. One of those products is six atoms of O_2, which is oxygen.

36. **C. circulatory and respiratory** The passage describes how the heart and blood vessels, which are part of the circulatory system, work with the lungs, which are part of the respiratory system, to infuse blood with oxygen and carry it throughout the body.

37. **B. A series of massive volcanic eruptions lasting many years** The dust from a series of major volcanic eruptions might block out sunlight, just as an asteroid impact could do.

38.

Experiment outline	Brock's steps
Step 1. Formulate a question about a phenomenon	d. Brock asked, "Does size affect the buoyancy of an object in water?"
Step 2. Collect data	b. Brock noted that ice floats in water, whether it is a small ice-cube or a huge iceberg.
Step 3. Form a hypothesis	e. Brock thought: "For an object made of a given material, increasing the size of the object won't affect its buoyancy in water."
Step 4. Test the hypothesis through an experiment	a. Brock placed wooden cubes that were 1 cc, 10 cc and 100 cc in water. He observed their buoyancy. Then he placed iron cubes of 1 cc, 10 cc and 100 cc in water and observed their buoyancy.
Step 5. Draw a conclusion	c. Brock said: "Since all wooden cubes float and all iron cubes sink, size does not affect the buoyancy of an object in water."

39. **D. It would rotate counterclockwise and move westward, then northward, and finally eastward.** The passage states that hurricanes tend to rotate counterclockwise in the Northern Hemisphere, and that hurricanes initially move westward, then toward the poles (which would be northward in the Northern Hemisphere), and finally eastward after encountering the mid-latitude westerly winds.

40. **B. The force will be reduced.** If the distance between the two objects were increased, the denominator of the fraction shown in the equation would become bigger. Increasing the denominator of a fraction makes the value of the fraction smaller. So the force would be reduced.

41. **C. Frogs' bodies have a way to prevent their cells from freezing in cold temperatures.** All amphibians, frogs included, are ectothermic, or cold-blooded. Given the fact that frogs reproduce in the spring, if all the frogs of a given species died in the winter, the species would go extinct. So it must be that frogs have some physiological mechanism that prevents their cells from freezing when a frog's body temperature drops during the winter.

42. **C. insulin injections** Some cases of diabetes mellitus are caused by the inability of the pancreas to produce insulin. Individuals with this form of the disease can keep their blood sugar levels stable only by regular use of insulin.

43. **A. The gene for deafness is linked with the gene for the merle trait, but deafness is recessive.** The fact that the first pairing of merle dogs produces one solid-color puppy is evidence that the merle trait is dominant. If the dominant allele is M and the recessive allele (for a solid color) is m, then both these parents likely have a genotype of Mm. This is why when mated, they produce puppies of genotypes MM, Mm, Mm, and mm. The next pairing is of the Mm father with a different mother. All these puppies have merle coloring and therefore must have at least

one M. This would only happen if the mom is MM, so two of the puppies are Mm and two are MM. In the first litter, the sole MM puppy is deaf, and in the second litter, the two MM puppies are deaf. Thus, it can be inferred that the genes for the merle trait and the gene for deafness are linked, but deafness is recessive.

44. **A. Shade-loving animal species, such as the red-backed salamander, were replaced by sun-loving species such as the northern black racer.** The immediate impact of cutting down an old growth forest is that species that favor a shaded forest habitat will be replaced by species favoring sunny, open spaces.

45.

A marigold plant develops female flowers with a non-sticky stigma (a plant part that receives pollen from a source such as bees) to which pollen cannot attach.	a. an unhelpful mutation caused by an environmental factor
Some marigolds produce flowers that are bright yellow with white spots.	c. a new combination of genes occurring through interbreeding
A marigold plant develops bright orange flowers, which attract more pollinating bees.	b. a non-harmful error occurring in the genome during replication

If pollen cannot attach to the female flower, this plant will not be able to reproduce. Thus, this is a harmful change in the genome and is likely the result of an environmental factor, such as radiation. The flowers that are bright yellow with white spots are probably the result of pollen from bright yellow flowers fertilizing local marigolds with pale flowers with white spots. The bright orange flowers are a new trait and so probably arose spontaneously, and they will aid the plant's reproductive success.

46. **C. at the same time and within the solar system** The fact that all the planets revolve around the sun on the same plane and in the same direction suggests that they were created as part of the same process. Specifically, they formed about 4.6 billion years ago from the gravitational pull and collisions between particles that were thrown off from the formation of the sun.

47. **D. The environment has become less hospitable for frogs, but which environmental conditions have changed cannot be determined.** While it can be inferred that something is causing the species to naturally select for the FRMD gene, there isn't enough data provided to support the conclusion that longer droughts are the cause or correlated in any way. Additional data that could provide that support includes the duration of droughts in 1995, 2000, 2005, 2010, and 2015 and the survival rate tables for those years. This data would be an essential part of supporting a specific conclusion about which environmental conditions are causing the increased presence of the FRMD gene.

Science Practice Test Evaluation Charts

	Life Science Online chapter	Earth and Space Science Online chapter	Physical Science Online chapter	Number Correct Out of Total
Science Skills				
Comprehend Scientific Presentations Pages 542–543	2, 4, 16, 22, 36, 41	19, 27, 28, 39	1, 24, 26	____ out of 13
Use the Scientific Method Pages 544–545	10		15, 31, 38	____ out of 4
Reason with Scientific Information Pages 546–547	5, 7, 8, 23, 32, 42, 44, 45	9, 11, 17, 25, 33, 37, 46	14, 21, 29, 30, 34, 40	____ out of 21
Express and Apply Scientific Information Pages 548–549	35, 43		6, 12, 13, 20	____ out of 6
Use Statistics and Probability Pages 550–551	18, 47		3	____ out of 3
Total points	____ out of 19	____ out of 11	____ out of 17	____ **out of 47**

If you do not have time to review the entire *Science* unit, you may want to review the sections that need the most work.

Using the points total from the bottom right hand corner of the table above, use the information below to assess your readiness to take the TASC test.

If your points total was . . .	then you are . . .	Kaplan recommends
20–47	very likely to pass the TASC Science test	that you do a relatively brief, high-level review of all science concepts, especially ones you've struggled with, before test day.
17–19	fairly likely to pass the TASC Science test	that you give yourself a few more days or weeks to do a final comprehensive review of science material before testing.
14–16	somewhat likely to pass the TASC Science test	that you set a goal date by which you would like to complete a final review of the material. As you do that review, focus on the material you have struggled with the most.
0–13	unlikely to pass the TASC Science test	that you do an in-depth review of the subject matter. Be sure to look for patterns among the questions you got wrong, and study those topics in greater depth.